NATIONAL SECURITY LAW

ERIC P. MERRIAM
ASSOCIATE PROFESSOR
UNIVERSITY OF CENTRAL FLORIDA

DOUGLAS B. MCKECHNIE
PROFESSOR OF LAW
UNITED STATES AIR FORCE ACADEMY

WEST ACADEMIC PUBLISHING

444 Cedar Street, Suite 700
St. Paul, MN 55101
1-877-888-1330

Printed in the United States of America

ISBN: 978-1-68328-912-8

To those whose security and liberty we hold most dear:

Erica, Marissa, Mackenzie, and Matthew

-EM

Kristin, Mairin, Orla, and Carys

-DBM

Acknowledgments

I would know very little about national security law without the profound influence of the teachers from whom I have been fortunate to learn. In particular, Professors John Norton Moore and Robert F. Turner, both of whom recently retired from the University of Virginia School of Law where they founded and directed the Center for National Security Law, were the first to introduce me to the subject. Professor Moore literally "invented the field" by offering the first national security law course in the nation, and Professor Moore's and Professor Turner's multiple courses on the topic piqued an interest that launched my military and academic careers. More recently, Professor Peter Raven-Hansen of The George Washington University School of Law strengthened my understanding; his teaching framed the way I now comprehend national security law. The textbooks and other writings Professors Moore, Turner, and Raven-Hansen authored and co-authored have similarly played an important role in forming the foundation of my understanding, and remain a constant reference, many years after I first encountered them as a student. Thank you.

The opportunity to study and teach national security law was first afforded to me by the United States Air Force Academy and then the University of Central Florida, and I am very grateful to both. Cadets at the former, and undergraduate and graduate students at the latter, have inspired this effort. I am forever grateful to students who entrust a piece of their education to me. A special thanks to some of the specific students who have not only inspired, but directly assisted this endeavor: Wil Pinkley, Julieta Bautista, and Dana Barbos. My colleagues at both institutions have been very supportive, and especially regarding this textbook, Professors Alisa Smith and Kerstin Hamann have patiently encouraged my work. Thank you.

Speaking of colleagues, this book simply would not have happened without the efforts of my co-author, Professor Douglas McKechnie. Doug is a career-long champion of individual liberty and social justice, a first-rate First Amendment scholar, and an exceptional teacher. His willingness to wade into the national security swamp with me and bring his unique expertise to this project provided balance and richness this text otherwise would have lacked. Doug is far more than a colleague; he is a wonderful human being whose close friendship through thick and thin has enriched my life and means more to me than he knows. Thank you.

And on the point of friendship, ultimate thanks to my best friend and the love of my life, Dr. Erica (Mailler) Merriam. Her support, both moral and practical, as I completed my portions of this text went beyond what I deserve. Despite her own demanding professional obligations, and extra stresses at home while this text was finished during the initial height of the COVID-19 pandemic, Erica repeatedly provided direct assistance in the form of proofreading and editing (remaining errors are mine) and indirect, though no less valuable, assistance in the form of picking up my slack while I worked seven days a week to finish this manuscript. Her superhuman endurance and strength were, as usual, greater than mine, and an inspiration to me. Thank you, Love.

-EM

When one thinks about whom to thank in the acknowledgment section of a book, the experience can quickly become overwhelming. I realize I will inevitably, but unintentionally, omit people. To those I overlook, I apologize. First, I would like to recognize my colleagues, both former and current. I would likely not be in a position to work on this project and write this acknowledgment without them. I will always be grateful to Mike Healey and Jay Hornack, my former colleagues with whom I practiced law in my hometown, Pittsburgh. They provided me with the opportunity to litigate free speech issues and put my passion for civil liberties and civil rights into practice. I likewise owe a debt of gratitude to my former colleagues at the Appalachian School of Law, specifically Professors Patrick Baker, Stewart Harris, and Maryann Herman. They provided me with the opportunity to begin, and encouraged me to develop, my academic career. Finally, I must thank my colleagues at the United States Air Force Academy. Special thanks go to Professors Chad Austin, Dave Fitzkee, John Hertel, and Lt Col Shawn McKelvy for taking a chance on hiring someone like me, and to Brigadier General Linell Letendre for encouraging me to take on this project. I must also recognize and thank all of my students, at both the Appalachian School of Law and the United States Air Force Academy, for inspiring and challenging me. It has been my great honor to be in the classroom alongside each one of you.

I write separately about a colleague to whom I owe my deepest gratitude. Professor Eric Merriam has shepherded this project from the beginning, and I can never thank him enough for including me, encouraging me, and tolerating me throughout. Readers, students, faculty, and I have him to thank for this book. Eric's knowledge of national security law is intimidatingly deep and his passion for it is infectious. His students are extremely fortunate because in addition to his national security law expertise, Eric's talents and joy for teaching are unmatched.

Eric, however, is not just my colleague. I cannot begin to express how fortunate I am to count Eric as one of my closest friends. Eric's intellect, compassion, and willingness to laugh at my jokes never cease to amaze me. Above all else, I thank him for his wonderful friendship.

Any acknowledgment I am ever fortunate enough to write will end with this: my most profound appreciation for the sacrifices and support I have received from my best friend and the love of my life, my wife Kristin McKechnie. I was fortunate to marry someone who is smarter, stronger, and more patient than I am. I have leaned on her, relied on her, and received more encouragement from her than I can ever repay. Since I wrote my first academic manuscript, Kristin has proofread almost every word. The portions of this book that I have written are no exception. To the reader and my coauthor, my apologies for any remaining mistakes; they are mine alone. What I can never repay Kristin for is her patience and support while I worked in the early morning hours, late into the evenings, and over the weekends to complete this project. For these and the other sacrifices you have made for me and for our family, I can never thank you enough. I hope I am half the spouse and parent you are. I love you.

-DBM

Together, we appreciate our editors at West Academic who first extended the invitation to write this text, and then extended their patience to await its completion.

-EM and DBM

All views expressed herein are the authors' alone and do not necessarily reflect the official policy or position of their employers, including the United States Air Force Academy, the United States Air Force, the United States Government, or the University of Central Florida.

Introduction

Unlike many fields of legal study, national security law is an amalgamation of several diverse areas of law. Tort law addresses torts. Criminal law addresses crime. Constitutional law addresses the Constitution. But national security law encompasses *all* law that directly or tangentially relates to furthering the security of the nation and its people. This includes many common topics traditionally taught in separate courses, such as constitutional law, criminal law, criminal procedure, evidence, torts, international law, and administrative law, to name a few. While this broad collection of subjects may seem daunting, we believe it also makes the study of national security law a complex, challenging, and fascinating adventure.

National security law addresses the central questions of whether, despite all its threats, the nation continues to exist and what values can be preserved while protecting that existence. National security law thus seeks to balance two sides of an equation: security and liberty.

The *security* aspect of *national security* focuses on the government's ability to exert power to keep the nation and its people secure. Topics include authorizing and using force to defeat enemies who threaten the nation, interrogating terrorists, or eavesdropping on a suspect's telephone call. The use of force may be massive, like full-scale military combat operations, or small, such as a covert operation executed by a lone intelligence agent. The target of these uses of force may be an enemy state, a terrorist, or even a United States citizen.

Thinking of national security law only from the perspective of security ignores half of the equation. While national security law certainly focuses on the protection of the nation, it also considers the costs of that protection. That is, national security law addresses what the People may be called upon to sacrifice in order to achieve security: their lives, liberty, and property. This unique area of legal study is fundamentally about how to balance competing values. As the United States Supreme Court observed in *United States v. Robel*:

> [the] concept of "national defense" cannot be deemed an end in itself, justifying any exercise of legislative power designed to promote such a goal. Implicit in the term "national defense" is the notion of defending those values and ideals which set this Nation apart. . . . [O]ur country has taken singular pride in the democratic ideals enshrined in its Constitution . . . . It would indeed be ironic if, in the name of national

> defense, we would sanction the subversion of one of those liberties . . . which makes the defense of the Nation worthwhile.

Similarly, and perhaps more succinctly, President Barack Obama once noted, "it's important to recognize you can't have 100 percent security and also 100 percent privacy, and also zero inconvenience. We're going to have to make some choices as a society." This book focuses on such choices.

This book also highlights law's role as a policy constraint and a policy tool. The rule of law must not be blindly sacrificed at the mere invocation of national security. However, in studying national security law we are often forced to confront the extent to which law actually constrains a political actor's behavior, or whether law is simply another tool to achieve political ends. While it is naïve to assume policy actors are driven only—or even primarily—by the rule of law, it is similarly unwise to believe policy actors are completely unmindful of law's effects on policy choices.

The first part of this book focuses on the United States Constitution, an instrument concerned with constructing and preserving the countervailing tensions that support democratic government and individual freedom. Chapter 1 addresses the overall constitutional design and explores the dichotomy between the original design and the realities of the nation's history and the world in which we live. Chapters 2 through 5 address the tension between the national security powers of the three branches of the federal government. In exploring this tension, readers will learn about the branches' shared and overlapping responsibilities for national security that is a predominant theme of this text. Chapters 6 through 8 highlight key conflicts between individual liberties and the power government claims in order to achieve and preserve security.

Having examined the Constitution, the supreme domestic law, the book then addresses the fight to ensure national security on a global stage, complete with new legal questions that arise. While this book focuses on United States national security law, it acknowledges that international law plays an important role in enabling and constraining the United States' national security efforts. Chapter 9 examines the extent to which international law affects United States' security actions and how United States law affects national security activities beyond the United States' borders. Chapter 10 presents the international law governing the use of military force. And Chapter 11 examines international law of war relating specifically to the cyber domain.

For the United States, the defining national security issue of the first two decades of the twenty-first century has been its counter-terrorism efforts in the wake of the 9/11 terror attacks. Chapters 12–16 address the many vexing legal questions posed by counter-terrorism operations, which seem to fall in the space between the distinct legal paradigms of war and law enforcement. In addressing the interrogation, detention, rendition, prosecution, and targeted killing of suspected terrorists, we engage in a practical application of the central question of whether *who* we are must be sacrificed to ensure *if* we are.

Chapters 17 and 18 recognize the important contributions and constraints of gathering intelligence and conducting covert actions to support national security. The chapters not only describe the governing laws and agencies that participate in these national security missions, they illustrate the need for shared legal responsibility between the Legislative and Executive Branches, as these missions are typically hidden from public view. Finally, Chapter 19 details the primary laws and federal agencies that play a role in ensuring homeland security.

Given the immense breadth of law that relates in some way to national security, most national security law texts exclude some topics. This book is no different, excluding discussion of security-related economic powers, military law, international weapons control treaties, immigration law, foreign domestic law, and environmental law (sometimes referred to as "natural security law"), and only skimming the surface of international humanitarian law (*jus in bello*).

This book is intended for readers who do not (yet) have a technical background in the law and perhaps have not studied foundational areas of law such as constitutional law, international law, criminal law, and administrative law. Many typical law school casebooks present the primary source material, posing numerous questions while providing little explanation. We have decided to take the opposite approach: presenting our distillation of those primary sources to explain what the law is. By explaining the basic material rather than leaving that to the reader untrained in reading statutes and judicial decisions, we hope readers will spend their mental energy asking not "what is the law?" but rather the more profitable—and perhaps enjoyable—task of asking "what should the law be, and what role should it play in achieving national security and liberty?"

More than just a list of statutes, cases, legally relevant orders, and policies, this book is intended to contextualize the law and help readers understand that law does not exist in a legal, political, historical, or social vacuum. To accomplish this aim, some chapters employ a topical approach, some include a historical review to place the law in context, and some include an examination of institutions and organizations that make up the United States' national security apparatus. In the historical approach, we attempt to explain the development of the law over time to demonstrate how the rule of law, democracy, transparency, and individual liberty have developed into our current national security efforts. Some chapters present the legally mandated structures and authorities of relevant agencies that are responsible for effectuating national security laws and policies within their legal purview. We believe this straightforward approach to presenting national security law will appeal to readers who wish to not only understand the law, but also to appreciate how it evolves and is implemented.

At its core, national security law is about keeping the nation and its people safe and free. We hope the readers of this book endeavor to understand and do both.

Table of Contents

Table of Cases

NATIONAL SECURITY LAW

CHAPTER 1

The Constitutional Design

Howard Chandler Christy's Painting of the Constitutional Convention, Philadelphia, 1787

Learning Objectives

1. Know some of the legal theorists' ideas that influenced the Framers' approach to foreign affairs and national security in the Constitution.

2. Understand how American colonial and pre-constitutional experience affected how national security issues were addressed in the Constitution.

3. Know the key national security powers explicitly given to Congress and the President in Articles I and II of the Constitution.

4. Understand how various provisions of the Constitution relate to national security.

5. Understand and be able to apply the Founders' ideas about these central national security questions:

(a) How should powers be shared between the Legislative and Executive branches?

(b) What is the extent of the President's power over foreign affairs?

(c) What role does the Commander in Chief power play in preserving peace (avoiding war) and starting war?

1.1. INTRODUCTION

The United States Constitution, the self-proclaimed "Supreme Law of the Land," is the first source to consider for every question involving national security law. The Constitution established a system of **limited government**, meaning the government has only those powers given to it by the people. Of the limited powers the Constitution bestowed on the new federal government, security of the nation is a primary responsibility. Despite that importance, the **Framers'** vision for exactly *who* would have authority to do *what* is sometimes murky. Scholars today dispute the extent to which the Framers allocated responsibility and authority for national security and foreign affairs to Congress or to the President. Additionally, debate rages regarding whether the Framers established a system of *separation* of powers or a system of *shared* powers.

Among other evidence, each camp points to various writers, jurists, and theorists known to have influenced the Framers. A basic understanding of these early "influencers" can assist in developing a more informed view of what the Framers created, or at least, what they thought they were creating.

1.2. THE FRAMERS' INTELLECTUAL INFLUENCES

As they constructed the Constitution, the Framers were heavily influenced by three important legal theorists who had published works on government and law during the preceding century: the Baron de Montesquieu, John Locke, and William Blackstone. The work of these three appears repeatedly in the ultimate design of the Constitution. Here, we will identify a few ways in which these theorists' ideas became manifest in the Framers' conception of foreign affairs and national security.

1.2.1. The Oracle: Baron de Montesquieu

Published in 1787 and 1788, the **Federalist Papers** were a series of 85 essays written by James Madison, Alexander Hamilton, and John Jay, attempting to convince the American public to ratify the newly drafted Constitution. The Federalist Papers thus serve as a window into the minds of some of the key Framers. When discussing the concept of separation of powers in Federalist 47, James Madison wrote that "[t]he oracle who is always consulted and cited on this subject is the celebrated Montesquieu." Indeed, the Framers borrowed heavily from the theories of separation of powers Baron de Montesquieu articulated in The Spirit of Laws, first published in 1748. Montesquieu wrote:

> In every government there are three sorts of power: the legislative; the executive in respect to things dependent on the law of nations; and the executive in regard to matters that depend on the civil law.

Referring to the second sort of power, Montesquieu asserted that the Executive "makes peace or war, sends or receives embassies, establishes the public security, and provides against invasions." He also labeled the "executive in regard to matters that depend on the civil law" as the *judicial* power. It is easy to see Montesquieu's influence in the Constitution, which clearly established those three types of power, and conferred those powers on three separate branches.

Regarding the executive power, Montesquieu asserted it "ought to be in the hands of a monarch, because this branch of government, having need of dispatch, is better administered by one than by many. . . ." Montesquieu also asserted that "once an army is established, it ought not to depend immediately on the legislative, but on the executive power; and this from the very nature of the thing, its business consisting more in action than in deliberation." While the Framers rejected the idea that the Executive must be a monarch, they clearly understood Montesquieu's concern that efficiency requires that the executive power to conduct war is better controlled by one than by many. Indeed, the colonies' experience during the Revolutionary War would later demonstrate that running a military campaign by committee is unworkable.

1.2.2. John Locke

Among the many influential ideas John Locke presented in his *Two Treatises of Government*, first published in 1690, was the suggestion that there are two types of executive power, which he labeled "executive" and "federative." The executive power focuses on execution of the "municipal laws of the society," meaning domestic law, and the federative power involves the "management of the security and interest of the publick without," meaning representing the national interest internationally. Locke asserted that the executive power could be directed by the legislative power with "antecedent, standing, positive laws." However, he claimed:

> what is to be done in reference to Foreigners, depending much upon [the foreigners'] actions, and the variation of designs and interest, must be left in great part to the Prudence of those who have this Power committed to them, to be managed by the best of their Skill, for the advantage of the Commonwealth.

In other words, Locke believed it would be impractical for a legislature to attempt to pass laws in advance of foreign affairs situations, because unlike domestic law, foreign affairs require interactivity with foreign entities for which the more deliberative legislative power would be ill-suited. Locke argued both the executive and federative power should be placed in the same hands, which is ostensibly what the Framers did in Article II of the Constitution.

What is less clear is the extent to which Locke's theory of the Executive's "prerogative power" was included by the Framers in the Constitution. Under Locke's view, the Executive has complete discretion to act for the good of the people when laws passed by the legislature are unclear, or even when the legislature's laws prohibit an act the Executive believes is for the good of the people. Locke argued that in such circumstances, a prudent Executive would act in the public interest with the expectation that the people would eventually ratify (approve) the Executive's decision. Certainly, the Constitution does not explicitly authorize the President to flout Congress just because the President believes doing so would be more prudent. Nevertheless, may Presidents do precisely that?

1.2.3. Blackstone

Like John Locke before him, William Blackstone recognized executive authority in its two spheres, domestic and foreign. Referring to foreign affairs, Blackstone asserted "the king is the delegate or representative of his people. It is impossible that the individuals of a state, in their collective capacity can transact the affairs of that state with another community equally numerous as themselves." Blackstone thus asserted the same practical problem with conducting foreign affairs by legislature, specifically, that when transacting the affairs of state, a nation must speak with one voice, not many. He added another practical problem with too much legislative influence on foreign affairs when he queried "who would scruple to enter into any engagements, that must afterwards be revised and ratified by a popular assembly." In other words, Blackstone wondered whether foreign states would be willing to engage in agreements when such accords would subsequently be subject to legislative debate. The Framers ultimately seemed less concerned with this issue, as it gave the Senate an effective legislative veto over treaties the President has entered into on behalf of the nation.

1.2.4. International Law Theorists Regarding Perfect and Imperfect War

Though Montesquieu, Locke, and Blackstone were probably the three political thinkers most broadly influential on the Framers, other theorists were important to one of the central questions of national security law: the authority to initiate and control war. As we will explore, this understanding of different types of war may shed some light on what the Framers' meant when they gave to Congress the authority to "declare war."

Hugo Grotius was a Dutch jurist whose work influenced John Locke, among others. Grotius argued that under international law there is a difference between "**perfect war**" and "**imperfect war**" or "informal war." Perfect wars involve opposing nations, formally "denouncing" (declaring) war, and complying with the "usual formalities of the law of nations." By contrast, imperfect or informal wars involved "certain violent Prosecution of our Right," but without formal declaration or otherwise being "conformable" to the law of nations. To Grotius, both types of wars were potentially lawful and just.

Jean-Jacques Burlamaqui, a Genevan legal theorist, distinguished between perfect and imperfect war based less on the legal formalities and more on the characteristics and effects of the conflict. For Burlamaqui, perfect war interrupts the "tranquility" of the entire state, meaning the whole nation is affected. By contrast, imperfect war "does not entirely interrupt the peace, but only in certain particulars, the public tranquillity [sic] being in other respects undisturbed."

1.3. PRE-CONSTITUTIONAL EXPERIENCE

As students of the creation of the Constitution know, the Revolutionary War and subsequent Constitution were, in significant part, a reaction to the pre-Revolutionary War American colonial experience. In some instances, the Framers rejected the British system under which they had suffered, while in other areas, they adopted a system similar to that from which they had just rebelled. Here we consider just a sampling of the areas where pre-Constitutional experience influenced the Constitution's treatment of national security.

1.3.1. Executive vs. Legislative Power to Declare and Make War

Most colonial governments placed important powers in the hands of the governors who were British agents and were ultimately disliked and distrusted by the colonists. These powers included command of the military and the ability to veto and delay implementation of legislation. On the other hand, colonial legislatures had significant fiscal control, which included some exercise of foreign affairs powers. After the Revolution, most of the first newly formed states continued to subordinate the Executive to the legislature, though eventually a few, including populous New York and Massachusetts, gave some increased authority to governors.

Imparting executive power to a strong legislature was an experiment conducted not only at the state level, but also at the national level. Under the Continental Congress, the national legislature was used by the states to manage the Revolutionary War, with disastrous results. Though subordination of the military to civilian control was deemed important, managing a cohesive war effort soon posed an existential threat to the rebellion. Ultimately, the legislature, with its factions and time-consuming bureaucracy, delegated significant powers to General George Washington as a matter of practical necessity. Beyond tactical management of military efforts, the First Continental Congress's largely failed attempt to fulfill both legislative and executive roles, including its significant difficulty in funding the national government, ultimately led Washington and Hamilton to urge a stronger national Executive when it came time to draft the Constitution.

1.3.2. National vs. State Power

The constitutional rivalry between the national and state governments is due not only to brilliant experimental political design, but also to the political realities of the time in which the Constitution was crafted, when many favored the continuation of state primacy, while others saw a need for a national government for fiscal and security purposes. The tension intentionally created between federal and state government is, in part, the product of some compromise.

State legislatures were perceived as responsive to popular local concerns. But while this populism might suggest a responsive democratic system, the parochial focus of individual states eventually led to some chaos. States' unilateral attempts to control interstate and international commerce and foreign affairs, which were often at counterproductive cross-purposes with other states, prompted calls for a national government.

1.3.3. Standing Armies

Americans were suspicious of standing armies, in large part because they had rebelled against one. The face of the protracted control of daily colonial life by Britain was the British Army. This recent experience caused the Framers to attempt to limit the ability to have a standing army, both by placing control for funding the military in the hands of the legislature and in limiting the legislature's ability to fund the army to two-year increments. The distaste for an overly intrusive military would also be addressed in the Third Amendment to the Constitution, which prohibited quartering troops in people's homes during peacetime.

1.4. CONSTITUTIONAL DESIGN AND NATIONAL SECURITY

At fewer than 8,000 words (including the Amendments), the United States Constitution is not as long as one might expect for a document many credit as the foundational text of western democracy. And yet, it contains many references to national security. Arguably, the entire Constitution is about "national security," in that it outlines the existence of the nation and defines anything that threatens that existence as a threat to national security. Further, it is the core document federal officers swear to "support and defend." However, looking at specific portions of the text that directly relate to national security can reveal how prominent national security was in the minds of the Framers, and demonstrates how the text raises as many questions as it answers.

Excerpted here are some provisions from the United States Constitution, with some observations and questions those provisions raise, identified in italics.

The Constitution of the United States

Preamble

We the People of the United States, in Order to form a more perfect Union, establish Justice, insure domestic Tranquility, provide for the common defence, promote the general Welfare, and secure the Blessings of Liberty to ourselves and our Posterity, do ordain and establish this Constitution for the United States of America.

- *If one of the primary purposes for establishing the Constitution was to "provide for the common defense," what does that suggest about how ambiguities or contradictions in the Constitution should be interpreted? How does that purpose interact with, coincide with, or conflict with the other purposes the Framers claimed?*

Article I

Section 1

All legislative Powers herein granted shall be vested in a Congress of the United States, which shall consist of a Senate and House of Representatives.

- *Does "herein" mean in Article I? In the whole Constitution? Does it matter?*

Section 4

Clause 2: The Congress shall assemble at least once in every Year, and such Meeting shall be on the first Monday in December, unless they shall by Law appoint a different Day.

- *What does the fact that the Framers anticipated Congress might meet only annually suggest about their view of the various branches' power to keep the nation secure?*

Section 8

Clause 1: The Congress shall have Power To lay and collect Taxes, Duties, Imposts and Excises, to pay the Debts and provide for the common Defence and general Welfare of the United States; but all Duties, Imposts and Excises shall be uniform throughout the United States;

- *How broad is the power given to Congress to "provide for the common Defence?" Does this authorize Congress to do whatever it pleases, so long as it is spending money for defense?*

Clause 3: To regulate Commerce with foreign Nations, and among the several States, and with the Indian Tribes;

- *As we will see in this text, presidents have often claimed they are "sole organ of foreign affairs." What does Congress's power to regulate commerce with foreign nations suggest about that claim?*

Clause 10: To define and punish Piracies and Felonies committed on the high Seas, and Offences against the Law of Nations;

- *Does the power to define and punish offenses against the Law of Nations mean that Congress may decide what international law is?*

Clause 11: To declare War, grant Letters of Marque and Reprisal, and make Rules concerning Captures on Land and Water;

- *What does "declare war" mean? Can the President engage in war if Congress has not declared it?*
- *What are letters of marque and reprisal and how do they relate to the other powers granted in Clause 11?*
- *Does the authority to make rules concerning captures on land and water give Congress the authority to do whatever it likes regarding detention of enemies?*

Clause 12: To raise and support Armies, but no Appropriation of Money to that Use shall be for a longer Term than two Years;

- *If Congress is granted the authority to provide for the common defense in Clause 1, why is this provision necessary?*
- *Why did the Framers limit appropriations for the army to no more than two years?*

Clause 13: To provide and maintain a Navy;

- *Why does Clause 12 limit appropriations for the army to two years, but Clause 13 does not similarly impose a time limit on the length of appropriations for a navy?*
- *Neither Clause 12 nor Clause 13 provide for an Air Force or a Space Force. Does Congress have constitutional authority to raise, provide, maintain, or support such forces?*

Clause 14: To make Rules for the Government and Regulation of the land and naval Forces;

- *Does authority to make rules for government and regulation include authority to make rules for when and how the military will be used?*

Clause 15: To provide for calling forth the Militia to execute the Laws of the Union, suppress Insurrections and repel Invasions;

- *Does "provide for calling forth" mean Congress has the authority to make the rules for how to call forth the militia, or also to actually call forth the militia?*
- *What is meant by the term militia?*
- *In Article II, the President is given authority to ensure that all laws be faithfully executed. What does this suggest about control over the militia?*

Clause 16: To provide for organizing, arming, and disciplining, the Militia, and for governing such Part of them as may be employed in the Service of the United States, reserving to the States respectively, the Appointment of the Officers, and the Authority of training the Militia according to the discipline prescribed by Congress;

- *This suggests there will be times when the militia will serve the United States. Can you tell from this text when that might be?*
- *Why are states given sole authority to train and appoint officers in the militia when the militia might sometimes be used by the United States?*

Clause 18: To make all Laws which shall be necessary and proper for carrying into Execution the foregoing Powers, and all other Powers vested by this Constitution in the Government of the United States, or in any Department or Officer thereof.

- *"[A]ll laws . . . necessary and proper" seems to be a massive grant of authority. What limitations do you see on this power?*

Section 9

Clause 2: The Privilege of the Writ of Habeas Corpus shall not be suspended, unless when in Cases of Rebellion or Invasion the public Safety may require it.

- *Why might rebellion or invasion require the suspension of the **writ of habeas corpus**?*
- *This language prohibits suspending the writ, but from where does the privilege of the writ of habeas corpus come?*
- *Who may suspend the privilege?*

Clause 7: No Money shall be drawn from the Treasury, but in Consequence of Appropriations made by Law; and a regular Statement and Account of the Receipts and Expenditures of all public Money shall be published from time to time.

- *At first glance, this Clause may not seem like it relates directly to national security. But in fact, it represents one of the most important national security powers Congress enjoys. Can you articulate why?*

Section 10

Clause 1: No State shall enter into any Treaty, Alliance, or Confederation; grant Letters of Marque and Reprisal; coin Money; emit Bills of Credit; make any Thing but gold and silver Coin a Tender in Payment of Debts; pass any Bill of Attainder, ex post facto Law, or Law impairing the Obligation of Contracts, or grant any Title of Nobility.

- *While the prohibitions in this Clause may seem obvious today, they were not at the time the Constitution was created. Why was it important to national security that no state be permitted to enter into a treaty, alliance, or confederation?*

Clause 3: No State shall, without the Consent of Congress, lay any Duty of Tonnage, keep Troops, or Ships of War in time of Peace, enter into any Agreement or Compact with another State, or with a foreign Power, or engage in War, unless actually invaded, or in such imminent Danger as will not admit of delay.

- *How can a state be ready to defend against invasion if it is not permitted to keep troops in peacetime?*
- *Must state militias be separately authorized by Congress in order to not violate this Clause?*

Article II

Section 1

The executive Power shall be vested in a President of the United States of America. . . .

- *How is this "vestiture clause" different from the Article I vestiture clause granting power to Congress? Is that difference legally significant?*
- *Where might you look to determine what "the executive power" is?*

Section 2

Clause 1: The President shall be Commander in Chief of the Army and Navy of the United States, and of the Militia of the several States, when called into the actual Service of the United States. . . .

- *Like the "Declare War" clause in Article I, this is the most often-cited source of the President's national security authority. Of course, this Clause presumes the President has an army or navy to command. Does "Commander in Chief" mean the President may use the military whenever and however he determines is in the national interest?*

Clause 2: [The President] shall have Power, by and with the Advice and Consent of the Senate, to make Treaties, provided two thirds of the Senators present concur; and he shall nominate, and by and with the Advice and Consent of the Senate, shall appoint Ambassadors, other public Ministers and Consuls. . . .

- *Does the power to make treaties mean the President alone may initiate agreements with foreign nations? May the President make agreements with foreign nations other than treaties?*
- *Does the power to appoint Ambassadors imply broader control over foreign affairs than just the power to make those appointments?*

Section 3

[The President] shall receive Ambassadors and other public Ministers; he shall take Care that the Laws be faithfully executed, and shall Commission all the Officers of the United States.

- *Does the authority to receive ambassadors imply broader control over foreign affairs, such as whether to recognize foreign nations?*
- *Does the "Take Care Clause" vest power in the President that is not explicitly identified elsewhere in the Constitution?*
- *If the President is responsible for taking care that the laws be faithfully executed, does that come with authority to do whatever he deems necessary to accomplish that mission?*
- *If laws conflict, does this clause vest the President with discretion to determine which to faithfully execute?*

Article III

Section 2

Clause 1: The judicial Power shall extend to all Cases, in Law and Equity, arising under this Constitution, the Laws of the United States, and Treaties made, or which shall be made, under their Authority;—to all Cases affecting Ambassadors, other public Ministers and Consuls;—to all Cases of admiralty and maritime Jurisdiction;—to Controversies to which the United States shall be a Party;—to Controversies between two or more States;—between a State and Citizens of another State;—between Citizens of different States,—between Citizens of the same State claiming Lands under Grants of different States, and between a State, or the Citizens thereof, and foreign States, Citizens or Subjects.

- *Does this Clause suggest the courts have a broad or narrow national security role?*

Section 3

Treason against the United States, shall consist only in levying War against them, or in adhering to their Enemies, giving them Aid and Comfort. No Person shall be convicted of Treason unless on the Testimony of two Witnesses to the same overt Act, or on Confession in open Court.

- *Treason is the only crime that is defined in the Constitution. What does that suggest about the priority of national security in the minds of the Framers? About the concern about the charge of treason itself?*

Article IV

Section 4

The United States shall guarantee to every State in this Union a Republican Form of Government, and shall protect each of them against Invasion; and on Application of the Legislature, or of the Executive (when the Legislature cannot be convened) against domestic Violence.

- *How does this section enhance the national security powers of the federal government? Of the President? Of state legislatures? Of state governors?*

Article VI

Clause 2: This Constitution, and the Laws of the United States which shall be made in Pursuance thereof; and all Treaties made, or which shall be made, under the Authority of the United States, shall be the supreme Law of the Land; and the Judges in every State shall be bound thereby, any Thing in the Constitution or Laws of any State to the Contrary notwithstanding.

- *What does this "Supremacy Clause" suggest about the importance of treaties?*
- *If the Constitution, and laws made in pursuance of the Constitution, and treaties, are all "supreme," which prevails when there is a conflict between them?*

Amendment I

Congress shall make no law respecting an establishment of religion, or prohibiting the free exercise thereof; or abridging the freedom of speech, or of the press; or the right of the people peaceably to assemble, and to petition the Government for a redress of grievances.

- *How does the freedom of speech affect the government's ability to protect classified information or prosecute those who share it unlawfully?*
- *How does the right of the people to assemble peaceably impact that government's power to ensure security by ordering people* not *to assemble?*

Amendment II

A well regulated Militia, being necessary to the security of a free State, the right of the people to keep and bear Arms, shall not be infringed.

- *Though this amendment usually is referenced in discussion of the right to bear arms, what does it reveal about the Framers' fear of tyranny? About the best way to protect against tyranny?*

Amendment III

No Soldier shall, in time of peace be quartered in any house, without the consent of the Owner, nor in time of war, but in a manner to be prescribed by law.

- *Involuntary quartering of troops in houses was of such concern to the Framers that its prohibition was included in the Bill of Rights. What does this suggest about the Framers' concern regarding federal military power?*
- *Does this amendment have any practical relevance today?*

Amendment IV

The right of the people to be secure in their persons, houses, papers, and effects, against unreasonable searches and seizures, shall not be violated, and no Warrants shall issue, but upon probable cause, supported by Oath or affirmation, and particularly describing the place to be searched, and the persons or things to be seized.

- *Does the prohibition on unreasonable searches and seizures apply when national security is at risk? Or does the meaning of "unreasonable" change when national security is at risk? Who should decide?*

Amendment V

No person shall be held to answer for a capital, or otherwise infamous crime, unless on a presentment or indictment of a Grand Jury, except in cases arising in the land or naval forces, or in the Militia, when in actual service in time of War or public danger; nor shall any person be subject for the same offence to be twice put in jeopardy of life or limb; nor shall be compelled in any criminal case to be a witness against himself, nor be deprived of life, liberty, or property, without due process of law; nor shall private property be taken for public use, without just compensation.

- *Based on this text, are you clear when a grand jury is or is not required for persons who are associated with the armed forces?*
- *When the United States government seeks to kill its enemies, what "due process of law" must they be afforded? Does it matter whether the enemies are, or are not, United States citizens?*
- *This amendment suggests that some rules may not apply when emergencies (time of War or public danger) arise. Does that imply that other constitutional rights are also flexible or expendable in cases of emergency? Which?*

Amendment X

The powers not delegated to the United States by the Constitution, nor prohibited by it to the States, are reserved to the States respectively, or to the people.

- *This provision is often pointed to when making an argument that the federal government is exceeding its authority. Does this mean some national security powers are reserved to the states, or to the people, because they are not explicitly identified in the Constitution?*

1.5. IN THEIR OWN WORDS: THE FOUNDERS EXPLAIN THEIR CREATION

As is apparent from the selected constitutional provisions above, there are many national security questions the text of the Constitution does not answer. First, the text is not precise and rarely defines its terms. Second, the text fails to address some issues altogether. Third, while the Constitution clearly values separation of power, Articles I and II also seem to assign some overlapping responsibilities to the Congress and the President, with little guidance regarding how those overlapping responsibilities should be shared. According to James Madison, principal author of much of the Constitution, this was by design, to help the government "control itself."

The extent of constitutional authority—including the authority of one branch of government versus another or the authority of government over individual liberties—is a continuing source of academic, legal, and political disputes. Sometimes, the views of those who created the Constitution are available and may shed some light on its original meaning, while other times the evidence is muddy or even contradictory. Of course, whether the original meaning is of great significance to answering constitutional questions today is itself a subject of debate.

Throughout this text we will explore the Framers' views regarding the Constitution's treatment of various national security matters. To appreciate the nature of some of the arguments and the conflicting evidence regarding the original understanding of the Constitution's attempts to address national security, consider the following excerpts of opinions some **Founders** of the United States expressed in the time surrounding debate and ratification of the Constitution. The selected comments are just a sampling of the many observations the Founders made regarding the best way to ensure national security. We have arranged the commentary topically. As you read the observations, consider whether you agree with the positions asserted.

In developing your own views of the issues discussed, do not forget the audiences to whom the observations were being made, and what that might suggest about the speaker's or writer's intentions in making the statements. For example, some commentaries below were made during debate at the Constitutional Convention, when delegates were trying to convince one another other what the draft Constitution should say. By contrast, the Federalist Papers were a series of published essays in which the authors were attempting to convince the American people to ratify the Constitution that the Constitutional Convention had created, and their authors are engaged in salesmanship.

1.5.1. Legislative vs. Executive Powers

A constant question in national security law is which branch of the federal government has authority to take which actions in the interest of national security. Some argue the Constitution creates a government of separate powers, while others contend it created a government of shared powers. As the following statements demonstrate, this debate is not new.

James Madison, Remarks to the Constitutional Convention, 1787

> Experience has proved a tendency in our governments to throw all power into the Legislative vortex. The Executives of the States are in general little more than Cyphers; the legislatures omnipotent. If no effectual check be devised for restraining the instability & encroachments of the latter, a revolution of some kind or other would be inevitable.

James Madison, Federalist No. 51, 1788

> The provision for defense must in this, as in all other cases, be made commensurate to the danger of attack. Ambition must be made to counteract ambition. The interest of the man must be connected with the constitutional rights of the place. It may be a reflection on human nature, that such devices should be necessary to control the abuses of government. But what is government itself, but the greatest of all reflections on human nature? If men were angels, no government would be necessary. If angels were to govern men, neither external nor internal controls on government would be necessary. In framing a government which is to be administered by men over men, the great difficulty lies in this: you must first enable the government to control the governed; and in the next place oblige it to control itself. A dependence on the

> people is, no doubt, the primary control on the government; but experience has taught mankind the necessity of auxiliary precautions. This policy of supplying, by opposite and rival interests, the defect of better motives, might be traced through the whole system of human affairs, private as well as public. We see it particularly displayed in all the subordinate distributions of power, where the constant aim is to divide and arrange the several offices in such a manner as that each may be a check on the other that the private interest of every individual may be a sentinel over the public rights.

Alexander Hamilton, Federalist No. 70, 1788

> Energy in the executive is a leading character in the definition of good government. It is essential to the protection of the community against foreign attacks. . . .
>
> In the legislature, promptitude of decision is oftener an evil than a benefit. The differences of opinion, and the jarrings of parties in that department of the government, though they may sometimes obstruct salutary plans, yet often promote deliberation and circumspection: and serve to check excesses in the majority. . . . But no favourable circumstances palliate or atone for the disadvantages of dissention in the executive department. Here they are pure and unmixed. There is no point at which they cease to operate. They serve to embarrass and weaken the execution of the plan or measure, to which they relate, from the first stop to the final conclusion of it. They constantly counteract those qualities in the executive, which are the most necessary ingredients in its composition, vigour and expedition, and this without any counterbalancing good. In the conduct of war, in which the energy of the executive is the bulwark of the national security, every thing would be to be apprehended from its plurality. . . .

Madison, Remarks During Debate on Establishing Department of Foreign Affairs, 1789

> When we review the several parts of this constitution, when it says that the Legislative powers shall be vested in a Congress of the United States, under certain exceptions, and the executive power vested in the President with certain exceptions, we must suppose they were intended to be kept separate in all cases in which they are

> not blended, and ought, consequently, to expound the Constitution so as to blend them as little as possible.

1.5.2. President's Power over Foreign Affairs

Another consistent subject of debate is whether the President's authority over foreign affairs is plenary, or shared in some significant way with Congress.

Act Creating Department of Foreign Affairs, 1789

The first Congress created the Department of Foreign Affairs, later to become the Department of State. The text of the act sheds some light on the first Congress's view regarding the President's authority over foreign affairs:

> BE it enacted by the Senate and House of Representatives of the United States of America in Congress assembled, That there shall be an executive department, to be denominated the department of foreign affairs, and that there shall be a principal officer therein, to be called the Secretary for the department of foreign affairs, who shall perform and execute such duties as shall, from time to time, be enjoined on or entrusted to him by the President of the United States, agreeable to the Constitution, relative to correspondences, commissions or instructions, to or with public ministers or consuls, from the United States, or to negotiations with public ministers from foreign States or princes, or to memorials or other applications from foreign public ministers, or other foreigners, or to such other matters respecting foreign affairs, as the President of the United States shall assign to the said department: And furthermore, that the said principal officer shall conduct the business of the said department in such manner as the President of the United States shall, from time to time, order or instruct.

Thomas Jefferson to George Washington, Opinion on the Powers of the Senate Respecting Diplomatic Appointments, 1790

President Washington asked the first Secretary of Foreign Affairs (later known as the Secretary of State) for his opinion regarding whether the Constitution had vested all foreign affairs power in the President. Here is part of Jefferson's reply:

> The transaction of business with foreign nations is Executive altogether. It belongs, then, to the head of that department, except as to such portions of it as are specially submitted to the Senate. Exceptions are to be construed strictly.

President George Washington, Papers of George Washington, 1790

Within a few days of receiving Jefferson's letter, President Washington made the following entry in his diary:

> Had some conversation with Mr. Madison on the propriety of consulting the Senate on the places to which it would be necessary to send persons in the Diplomatic line, and Consuls; and with respect to the grade of the first—His opinion coincides with Mr. Jay's and Mr. Jefferson's—to wit—that they have no Constitutional right to interfere with either, and . . . their powers extending no further than to an approbation or disapprobation of the person nominated by the President, all the rest being Executive and vested in the President by the Constitution.

Hamilton, Pacificus No. I, 1793

During a protracted and public debate regarding President Washington's authority to declare the nation at peace with France and England, Alexander Hamilton wrote the following, under the pseudonym Pacificus:

> It will not be disputed that the management of the affairs of this country with foreign nations is confided to the Government of the UStates.
>
> . . .
>
> The inquiry then is—what department of the Government of the UStates is the prop(er) one to make a declaration of Neutrality. . . .
>
> . . .
>
> The Legislative Department is not the *organ* of intercourse between the UStates and foreign Nations. It is charged neither with *making* nor *interpreting* Treaties. It is therefore not naturally that Organ of the Government which is to pronounce the existing condition of the Nation, with regard to foreign Powers, or to admonish the Citizens of their obligations and duties as founded upon that condition of things.
>
> . . .
>
> The second Article of the Constitution of the UStates, section 1st, establishes this general Proposition, That "The Executive Power shall be vested in a President of the United States of America."

The same article in a succeeding Section proceeds to designate particular cases of Executive Power. It declares among other things that the President shall be Commander in Cheif [sic] of the army and navy of the UStates and of the Militia of the several states when called into the actual service of the UStates, that he shall have power by and with the advice of the senate to make treaties; that it shall be his duty to receive ambassadors and other public Ministers and to take care that the laws be faithfully executed.

It would not consist with the rules of sound construction to consider this enumeration of particular authorities as derogating from the more comprehensive grant contained in the general clause, further than as it may be coupled with express restrictions or qualifications; as in regard to the cooperation of the Senate in the appointment of Officers and the making of treaties; which are qualifications of the general executive powers of appointing officers and making treaties: Because the difficulty of a complete and perfect specification of all the cases of Executive authority would naturally dictate the use of general terms—and would render it improbable that a specification of certain particulars was designd [sic] as a substitute for those terms, when antecedently used. The different mode of expression employed in the constitution in regard to the two powers the Legislative and the Executive serves to confirm this inference. In the article which grants the legislative powers of the Govern[men]t. the expressions are—"All Legislative powers herein granted shall be vested in a Congress of the UStates"; in that which grants the Executive Power the expressions are, as already quoted "The Executive Po[wer] shall be vested in a President of the UStates of America."

The enumeration ought rather therefore to be considered as intended by way of greater caution, to specify and regulate the principal articles implied in the definition of Executive Power; leaving the rest to flow from the general grant of that power, interpreted in conformity to other parts [of] the constitution and to the principles of free government.

The general doctrine then of our constitution is, that the Executive Power of the Nation is vested in the President; subject only to the exceptions and qu[a]lifications which are expressed in the instrument.

> Two of these have been already noticed—the participation of the Senate in the appointment of Officers and the making of Treaties. A third remains to be mentioned the right of the Legislature "to declare war and grant letters of marque and reprisal." With these exceptions the Executive Power of the Union is completely lodged in the President. This mode of construing the Constitution has indeed been recognized by Congress in formal acts, upon full consideration and debate. The power of removal from office is an important instance.
>
> . . .
>
> It deserves to be remarked, that as the participation of the senate in the making of Treaties and the power of the Legislature to declare war are exceptions out of the general "Executive Power" vested in the President, they are to be construed strictly—and ought to be extended no further than is essential to their execution.
>
> While therefore the Legislature can alone declare war, can alone actually transfer the nation from a state of Peace to a state of War—it belongs to the "Executive Power," to do whatever else the laws of Nations cooperating with the Treaties of the Country enjoin, in the intercourse of the UStates with foreign Powers.
>
> In this distribution of powers the wisdom of our constitution is manifested. It is the province and duty of the Executive to preserve to the Nation the blessings of peace. The Legislature alone can interrupt those blessings, by placing the Nation in a state of War.

James Madison, Helvidius No. I, 1793

Though they had earlier enjoyed a cordial and productive partnership, by the time of the Pacificus-Helvidius debate, Alexander Hamilton and James Madison found themselves on opposite sides of many issues. In response to Hamilton's view in Pacificus I that the President had authority to unilaterally declare peace, James Madison argued the following in Helvidius, No. I:

> Several pieces with the signature of Pacificus were lately published, which have been read with singular pleasure and applause, by the foreigners and degenerate citizens among us, who hate our republican government, and the French revolution; whilst the publication seems to have been too little regarded, or too much despised by the steady friends to both.

. . .

If we consult for a moment, the nature and operation of the two powers to declare war and make treaties, it will be impossible not to see that they can never fall within a proper definition of executive powers. The natural province of the executive magistrate is to execute laws, as that of the legislature is to make laws. All his acts therefore, properly executive, must pre-suppose the existence of the laws to be executed. A treaty is not an execution of laws: it does not pre-suppose the existence of laws. It is, on the contrary, to have itself the force of a law, and to be carried into execution, like all other laws, by the executive magistrate. To say then that the power of making treaties which are confessedly laws, belongs naturally to the department which is to execute laws, is to say, that the executive department naturally includes a legislative power. In theory, this is an absurdity—in practice a tyranny.

The power to declare war is subject to similar reasoning. A declaration that there shall be war, is not an execution of laws: it does not suppose pre-existing laws to be executed: it is not in any respect, an act merely executive. It is, on the contrary, one of the most deliberative acts that can be performed; and when performed, has the effect of repealing all the laws operating in a state of peace, so far as they are inconsistent with a state of war: and of enacting as a rule for the executive, a new code adapted to the relation between the society and its foreign enemy. In like manner a conclusion of peace annuls all the laws peculiar to a state of war, and revives the general laws incident to a state of peace.

These remarks will be strengthened by adding that treaties, particularly treaties of peace, have sometimes the effect of changing not only the external laws of the society, but operate also on the internal code, which is purely municipal, and to which the legislative authority of the country is of itself competent and compleat.

From this view of the subject it must be evident, that although the executive may be a convenient organ of preliminary communications with foreign governments, on the subjects of treaty or war; and the proper agent for carrying into execution the final determinations of the competent authority; yet it can have no pretensions from the nature of the powers in question compared with the nature of the executive trust, to that essential agency which gives validity to such determinations.

It must be further evident that, if these powers be not in their nature purely legislative, they partake so much more of that, than of any other quality, that under a constitution leaving them to result to their most natural department, the legislature would be without a rival in its claim.

. . .

It remains to be enquired whether there be any thing in the constitution itself which shews that the powers of making war and peace are considered as of an executive nature, and as comprehended within a general grant of executive power.

It will not be pretended that this appears from any direct position to be found in the instrument. If it were deducible from any particular expressions it may be presumed that the publication would have saved us the trouble of the research.

Does the doctrine then result from the actual distribution of powers among the several branches of the government? Or from any fair analogy between the powers of war and treaty and the enumerated powers vested in the executive alone?

Let us examine. In the general distribution of powers, we find that of declaring war expressly vested in the Congress, where every other legislative power is declared to be vested, and without any other qualification than what is common to every other legislative act. The constitutional idea of this power would seem then clearly to be, that it is of a legislative and not an executive nature.

This conclusion becomes irresistible, when it is recollected, that the constitution cannot be supposed to have placed either any power legislative in its nature, entirely among executive powers, or any power executive in its nature, entirely among legislative powers, without charging the constitution, with that kind of intermixture and consolidation of different powers, which would violate a fundamental principle in the organization of free governments. If it were not unnecessary to enlarge on this topic here, it could be shewn, that the constitution was originally vindicated, and has been constantly expounded, with a disavowal of any such intermixture.

The power of treaties is vested jointly in the President and in the Senate, which is a branch of the legislature. From this arrangement merely, there can be no inference that would necessarily exclude the power from the executive class: since the senate is joined with the President in another power, that of appointing to offices, which as far as relate to executive offices at least, is considered as of an executive nature. Yet on the other hand, there are sufficient indications that the power of treaties is regarded by the constitution as materially different from mere executive power, and as having more affinity to the legislative than to the executive character.

One circumstance indicating this, is the constitutional regulation under which the senate give their consent in the case of treaties. In all other cases the consent of the body is expressed by a majority of voices. In this particular case, a concurrence of two thirds at least is made necessary, as a substitute or compensation for the other branch of the legislature, which on certain occasions, could not be conveniently a party to the transaction.

But the conclusive circumstance is, that treaties when formed according to the constitutional mode, are confessedly to have the force and operation of laws, and are to be a rule for the courts in controversies between man and man, as much as any other laws. They are even emphatically declared by the constitution to be "the supreme law of the land."

So far the argument from the constitution is precisely in opposition to the doctrine. As little will be gained in its favour from a comparison of the two powers, with those particularly vested in the President alone.

As there are but few it will be most satisfactory to review them one by one.

"The President shall be commander in chief of the army and navy of the United States, and of the militia when called into the actual service of the United States." There can be no relation worth examining between this power and the general power of making treaties. And instead of being analogous to the power of declaring war, it affords a striking illustration of the incompatibility of the two powers in the same hands. Those who are to conduct a war cannot in the nature of things, be proper or safe judges, whether a war ought to be commenced, continued, or concluded. They are barred from the latter functions by a great principle in free government, analogous to that which separates the sword from the purse, or the power of executing from the power of enacting laws.

. . .

"He shall take care that the laws shall be faithfully executed and shall commission all officers of the United States." To see the laws faithfully executed constitutes the essence of the executive authority. But what relation has it to the power of making treaties and war, that is, of determining what the laws shall be with regard to other nations? No other certainly than what subsists between the powers of executing and enacting laws; no other consequently, than what forbids a coalition of the powers in the same department.

I pass over the few other specified functions assigned to the President, such as that of convening of the legislature, [etc.] which cannot be drawn into the present question.

. . .

Thus it appears that by whatever standard we try this doctrine, it must be condemned as no less vicious in theory than it would be dangerous in practice. It is countenanced neither by the writers on law; nor by the nature of the powers themselves; nor by any general arrangements or particular expressions, or plausible analogies, to be found in the constitution.

Whence then can the writer have borrowed it? There is but one answer to this question. The power of making treaties and the power of declaring war, are *royal prerogatives* in the *British government*, and are accordingly treated as Executive prerogatives by *British commentators*.

Representative John Marshall, Speech to Congress, 1793

John Marshall, who would later become the most influential Chief Justice of the Supreme Court, was first a Congressman from Virginia. In closing a debate regarding whether President Adams should have surrendered a British military deserter to Great Britain, Marshall uttered the following, which would be quoted by the Supreme Court over one hundred years later in the famed Curtis-Wright case, and repeated enthusiastically by presidents and their supporters since:

> The President is the sole organ of the nation in its external relations, and its sole representative with foreign nations. Of consequence, the demand of a foreign nation can only be made on him.
>
> He possesses the whole Executive power. He holds and directs the force of the nation. Of consequence, any act to be performed by the force of the nation is to be performed though him.

1.5.3. Commander in Chief Power

Alexander Hamilton, Federalist No. 69, 1788

Comparing the Commander in Chief power under the Constitution to that of the British Crown, Hamilton argued the President's Commander in Chief power was far less, because:

> It would amount to nothing more than the supreme command and direction of the military . . . while that of the British King extends to the declaring of war, and to the raising and regulating of fleets and armies—all which by the Constitution under consideration, would appertain to the legislature.

1.5.4. Avoiding War

John Jay, Federalist No. 4, 1787

> It is too true, however disgraceful it may be to human nature, that nations in general will make war whenever they have a prospect of getting anything by it; nay, absolute monarchs will often make war when their nations are to get nothing by it, but for the purposes and objects merely personal, such as thirst for military glory, revenge for personal affronts, ambition, or private compacts to aggrandize or support their particular families or partisans. These and a variety of other motives, which affect only the mind of the sovereign, often lead him to engage in wars not sanctified by justice or the voice and interests of his people.

James Madison, Essay "Political Observations," 1795

> Of all the enemies to public liberty war is, perhaps, the most to be dreaded, because it comprises and develops the germ of every other. War is the parent of armies; from these proceed debts and taxes; and armies, and debts, and taxes are the known instruments for bringing the many under the domination of the few. In war,

> too, the discretionary power of the Executive is extended; its influence in dealing out offices, honors, and emoluments is multiplied; and all the means of seducing the minds, are added to those of subduing the force, of the people. The same malignant aspect in republicanism may be traced in the inequality of fortunes, and the opportunities of fraud, growing out of a state of war, and in the degeneracy of manners and of morals engendered by both. No nation could preserve its freedom in the midst of continual warfare.

1.5.5. Declaration of War

Probably no more significant national security law question exists than the respective authorities of Congress and the President to initiate and direct the use of military force. Much of this debate focuses on the meaning of the "Declare War Clause" in Article I, Section 8, Clause 11 of the Constitution.

James Madison's Notes in Max Farrand, The Records of the Federal Convention of 1787, (rev. ed. 1911)

The 1787 Constitutional Convention took place in secret and few notes of the discussions exist. James Madison's personal notes are one of a few sources detailing the debates. At one point, the delegates debated whether to change the original text of the Constitution, which stated Congress had the power "to make war." Here are Madison's notes of that debate:

> "To make war"
>
> Mr Pinkney opposed the vesting this power in the Legislature. Its proceedings were too slow. It wd. meet but once a year. The Hs. of Reps. would be too numerous for such deliberations. The Senate would be the best depositary, being more acquainted with foreign affairs, and most capable of proper resolutions. If the States are equally represented in Senate, so as to give no advantage to large States, the power will notwithstanding be safe, as the small have their all at stake in such cases as well as the large States. It would be singular for one authority to make war, and another peace.
>
> Mr Butler. The Objections agst the Legislature lie in a great degree agst the Senate. He was for vesting the power in the President, who will have all the requisite qualities, and will not make war but when the Nation will support it.

> Mr. M[adison] and Mr Gerry moved to insert "declare," striking out "make" war; leaving to the Executive the power to repel sudden attacks.
>
> Mr Sharman thought it stood very well. The Executive shd. be able to repel and not to commence war. "Make" better than "declare" the latter narrowing the power too much.
>
> Mr Gerry never expected to hear in a republic a motion to empower the Executive alone to declare war.
>
> Mr. Elseworth. There is a material difference between the cases of making war, and making peace. It shd. be more easy to get out of war, than into it. War also is a simple and overt declaration. peace attended with intricate & secret negociations.
>
> Mr. Mason was agst giving the power of war to the Executive, because not [safely] to be trusted with it; or to the Senate, because not so constructed as to be entitled to it. He was for clogging rather than facilitating war; but for facilitating peace. He preferred "declare" to "make."

The state delegate representatives voted seven to two (with one abstention) in favor of replacing "make" with "declare." Interestingly, an unidentified representative made an additional motion to add "and peace" after "war," but that motion was rejected ten to zero. Madison provided no notes regarding that discussion.

James Wilson, Debates at the Pennsylvania Convention, 1787

At the Pennsylvania constitutional ratification convention, James Wilson, who had been a delegate to the Constitutional Convention, assured Pennsylvanians that the Constitution:

> will not hurry us into war . . . . It will not be in the power of a single man, or a single body of men, to involve us in such distress; fort the important power of declaring war is vested in the legislature at large.

Thomas Jefferson, Letter to James Madison, 1789

Similarly, in a letter written to his friend and political ally, Thomas Jefferson noted how the Framers had attempted to control the use of military force:

> We have already given in example one effectual check to the Dog of War by transferring the power of letting him loose from the

> Executive to the Legislative body, from those who are to spend to those who are to pay.

1.5.6. Standing Army vs. Part-Time Militia

A more specific, yet significant concern, of the Framers and early United States was the existence of standing armies, which they viewed as a primary instrument of British tyranny.

James Madison, Remarks to the Constitutional Convention, 1787

> A standing military force, with an overgrown Executive will not long be safe companions to liberty. The means of defence agst. foreign danger, have been always the instruments of tyranny at home. Among the Romans it was a standing maxim to excite a war, whenever a revolt was apprehended. Throughout all Europe, the armies kept up under the pretext of defending, have enslaved the people.

Alexander Hamilton, Federalist No. 24, 1787

Initially, Alexander Hamilton argued that the Constitution should not prohibit standing armies:

> Previous to the Revolution, and ever since the peace, there has been a constant necessity for keeping small garrisons on our Western frontier. No person can doubt that these will continue to be indispensable, if it should only be against the ravages and depredations of the Indians. These garrisons must either be furnished by occasional detachments from the militia, or by permanent corps in the pay of the government. The first is impracticable; and if practicable, would be pernicious. The militia would not long, if at all, submit to be dragged from their occupations and families to perform that most disagreeable duty in times of profound peace. And if they could be prevailed upon or compelled to do it, the increased expense of a frequent rotation of service, and the loss of labor and disconcertion of the industrious pursuits of individuals, would form conclusive objections to the scheme. It would be as burdensome and injurious to the public as ruinous to private citizens. The latter resource of permanent corps in the pay of the government amounts to a standing army in time of peace; a small one, indeed, but not the less real for being small. Here is a simple view of the subject, that shows us at once the

> impropriety of a constitutional interdiction of such establishments, and the necessity of leaving the matter to the discretion and prudence of the legislature.

Alexander Hamilton, Federalist No. 29, 1787

Curiously, Hamilton later argued that the existence of a militia could obviate the need for a standing army:

> If a well-regulated militia be the most natural defense of a free country, it ought certainly to be under the regulation and at the disposal of that body which is constituted the guardian of the national security. If standing armies are dangerous to liberty, an efficacious power over the militia, in the body to whose care the protection of the State is committed, ought, as far as possible, to take away the inducement and the pretext to such unfriendly institutions. If the federal government can command the aid of the militia in those emergencies which call for the military arm in support of the civil magistrate, it can the better dispense with the employment of a different kind of force. If it cannot avail itself of the former, it will be obliged to recur to the latter. To render an army unnecessary, will be a more certain method of preventing its existence than a thousand prohibitions upon paper.

President James Madison, Address to Congress, 1815

The practical realities of being President often alter the political, ideological, and constitutional theories the person espoused before becoming President. Though he was a principle author of the Constitution, James Madison was no different. His suspicion of a standing army, and his theory about how best to prevent the tyranny he believed came along with standing armies, was altered by his experience as a wartime president during the War of 1812. After reflecting on lessons learned in that conflict, Madison observed:

> Experience has taught us that neither the pacific dispositions of the American people nor the pacific character of their political institutions can altogether exempt them from that strife which appears beyond the ordinary lot of nations to be incident to the actual period of the world, and the same faithful monitor demonstrates that a certain degree of preparation for war is not only indispensable to avert disasters in the onset, but affords also the best security for the continuance of peace. The wisdom of Congress will therefore, I am confident, provide for the

> maintenance of an adequate regular force; for the gradual advancement of the naval establishment; for improving all the means of harbor defense; for adding discipline to the distinguished bravery of the militia, and for cultivating the military art in its essential branches, under the liberal patronage of Government.

1.6. CONCLUSION

The text of the Constitution is the appropriate starting place for any understanding of national security law. And yet, the text of the Constitution raises more questions than it answers. The Constitution divides the power to secure the nation, including to use military force, between Congress and the President, but the text is ambiguous. Though quantitatively more national security powers are granted to the Legislative Branch, in practice the Executive Branch has exercised seemingly greater control over national security. Moreover, the Constitution altogether omits some national security powers, such as the authority to repel an attack in an undeclared war, or to engage in covert intelligence gathering.

The Constitution was a novel experiment in self-governance, based largely on the theories of a few legal thinkers and in reaction to the experience of abuses at the hands of a too-powerful executive and his standing army. The Framers also experienced the challenges associated with a legislative control of a military campaign. When it came time to draft the Constitution, the Framers gave the executive control over the military, but gave the Legislative Branch the authority to declare war and exclusive authority to fund and "raise" the military the President may control.

Much of the study of constitutional law is the study of the deliberately created friction between competing interests. Three branches of the national government are deliberately placed somewhat odds with each other, and so too the national government and states are deliberately established in tension with each other, competing for power and responsibility. Following the inclusion of the Bill of Rights in the Constitution, the power of government is in tension with individual liberties. These structural tensions are as critical to understanding national security law as any other area of constitutional law, as they serve simultaneously as the strengths and weaknesses of the constitutional national security arrangement. As we explore national security law questions and reflect on the Constitution's guidance, consider not only what the Framers intended, but *why*.

REVIEW QUESTIONS

1. Who were the three primary political theorists who influenced the Framers?

2. According to Grotius and Burlamaqui, what are the differences between "perfect" and "imperfect" wars? What relevance do those differences have to the question of what "declare war" means?

3. What pre-constitutional experiences influenced the Constitution?

4. What key national security powers does the Constitution give Congress? The President? The Judiciary?

CRITICAL THINKING QUESTIONS

1. Did the Constitution create a government of separate powers or shared powers? Explain, citing examples from the text of the Constitution and comments from the Founders.

2. In what ways did Montesquieu's, Locke's, and Blackstone's theories identified in this chapter appear in the Constitution?

3. Consider the Founders' views on how the national government could best protect national security, as expressed in the Constitution and in other commentary. In light of the nation's experience since the late 1700s, in what ways have their ideas turned out to be correct and incorrect?

4. Based on the discussion at the Constitutional Convention and what you know about Grotius's and Burlamaqui's theories, what do you think "declare war" means in the Constitution?

5. Based on the Founders' statements excerpted above, who has the authority to determine whether the United States will use military force? Cite examples.

CHAPTER 2

The President's National Security Powers

Portrait of *General* George Washington, Commander in Chief, Charles Willson Peale

Portrait of *President* George Washington, Commander in Chief, Gilbert Stuart

Learning Objectives

1. Understand the spectrum of the President's national security powers granted by the Constitution.

2. Understand the range of views regarding the extent of the President's "Commander in Chief power."

3. Appreciate the various theories of presidential power expressed by the Supreme Court Justices in the *Youngstown* case.

2.1. INTRODUCTION

Perhaps because the first President had previously been the military Commander in Chief of a rebellion, the Executive Branch has been the most active and visible of the branches in the national security arena. It is the President, not the Congress or the Judiciary, who gives the final order for military action, covert operations, and other activities he deems necessary to ensure national security. So, our examination of the branches' constitutional national security powers begins with the Executive.

The President's authority derives from the Constitution, but the extent of the Executive's powers is far from clear. Indeed, competing theories have been offered regarding the scope of the Executive's authority and function. For example, President Theodore Roosevelt asserted that "The President is a steward of the people bound actively and affirmatively to do all he could for the people. It is not only his right but his duty to do anything that the needs of the Nation demand, unless such action [is] forbidden by law." In other words, as steward of the nation, the President's authority and duty are constrained only by explicit law. The default presumption under this theory is that the President has *all* power he deems necessary to protect the nation, and that presumption is only overcome when there is an explicit legal limitation on that authority. President Harry Truman echoed this sentiment, noting:

> We live in an age when hostilities begin without polite exchanges of diplomatic notes. . . . The President, who is Commander in Chief and who represents the interest of all the people, must [be] able to act at all times to meet any sudden threat to the nation's security. A wise President will always work with Congress, but when Congress fails to act or is unable to act in a crisis, the President, under the Constitution, must use his powers to safeguard the nation.

A competing view was asserted by President William Taft, who said "the President can exercise no power which cannot be fairly and reasonably traced to some specific grant of power or justly implied and included within such express grant as proper and necessary to its exercise." Under this theory, the default presumption is that the President has *no* power, except that which can be clearly identified from an explicit grant of power in the law. Taft's theory seems more consistent with the underlying constitutional theory of **limited government**, which is that the federal government has no power except that which has been given to it by the People through the Constitution.

Alexander Hamilton, a prominent proponent of federal power generally, suggested that on the issue of limited government, there was a difference between the Legislative and the Executive Branches. He noted that the opening sentence of Article I gives Congress "all legislative Powers *herein granted*," expressly limiting Congress's authority to only those powers identified and specifically provided in the Constitution. By contrast, Hamilton observed that Article II gives the President "[t]he Executive Power," without any "herein granted" limitation, suggesting the Executive power is broader.

Regardless of one's view regarding the total or limited power of the Executive, the variety of presidential authorities in the national security arena that have been suggested by Presidents, Justices, and scholars tend to lie along a spectrum. At one end of the spectrum are **explicit powers**, or authorities that are specifically identified in the Constitution. At the other end of the spectrum lie **inherent powers**, or authorities that are neither explicitly nor implicitly provided by the Constitution, but rather are simply inherent in the nature of the office of "Executive." Lying somewhere between the two are **implicit powers**, or authorities that are *suggested* by the constitutional text, but not explicitly.

This chapter organizes the potential national security powers of the President along this spectrum. Though there is some legitimate dispute regarding how to categorize a particular type of presidential national security power (for example, whether the President's "emergency" and "take care" powers are implied or inherent), we will proceed from most explicit to least: the Commander in Chief power, foreign affairs power, emergency power, aggregate vestiture/take care power, and finally, the "customary power."

2.2. COMMANDER IN CHIEF POWER

The constitutional provision most often cited by the President for authority to engage in national security activities is Article II, Section 2's "Commander in Chief Clause," which states that "[t]he President shall be Commander in Chief of the Army and Navy of the United States, and of the Militia of the several States, when called into the actual Service of the United States." This clause clearly gives the President the right to command the United States military. What is less clear is the extent of that command authority, including whether it suggests the President can do whatever he pleases with the military he is given. Several types of power arising from the Commander in Chief Clause have been articulated, including: 1) the "core" Commander in Chief authority; 2) a defensive Commander in Chief authority; and 3) an offensive Commander in Chief authority.

2.2.1. Core Command Authority

The idea of military command is the authority to compel subordinates to act in conformity with one's orders. At a minimum, the Commander in Chief Clause means there is no higher commander for the United States military. But the real debate exists not where the minimum authority begins—the floor—but rather the extent of the President's Commander in Chief authority—the ceiling.

Most would agree that the Commander in Chief power gives the President the authority to oversee tactical decisions of a particular mission. So, if invasion of a foreign country is the mission, the Commander in Chief has authority to dictate how the invasion will occur militarily. This might include decisions regarding what types of forces may be employed or when the invasion will begin. This view suggests the Commander in Chief clause gives the President a "core" of command authority that cannot be limited by Congress. Thus, even if the President must obtain permission from Congress to use the military to accomplish a particular objective, Congress cannot direct *how* the mission will be accomplished within that permission.

Those favoring the most limited scope of the President's Commander in Chief authority argue that this tactical command authority is *all* the Commander in Chief Clause confers on the President. Under this view, the President is only the "first commander" or "first general," meaning everyone in the military must obey him, but suggesting his authority is only over military actions, not over whether and when the military may be used. In fact, some suggest even tactical decisions can be limited by Congress. For example, under this view, Congress does not encroach on the President's powers when it authorizes use of military force to accomplish an objective—for example, permitting use of air power but prohibiting "boots on the ground."

The extent of Congress's control over the military's tactical decisions was first addressed early in the nation's history. In 1804, in a case captioned *Little v. Barreme*, the Supreme Court examined a case involving hostilities between the United States and France. During this undeclared war, Congress passed the 1799 Intercourse Act, which very specifically authorized the President to seize United States vessels headed to French ports that were suspected of illegally carrying cargo to France. President John Adams ordered the Navy to execute the law, but his order did not limit the seizure only to ships going *to* French territory, as Congress had explicitly said in the statute; he also authorized seizure of United States ships coming *from* French territory. When United States Navy Captain George Little intercepted a ship coming *from* a French port rather than *to* a French port, the owner of the seized ship sued, arguing Captain Little (and by extension, the President), did not have authority. The Court determined the President only had the authority to carry out the existing law. So, the President's discretion as Commander in Chief was not entirely unfettered. Even though an order to seize ships going in both directions might seem like an entirely tactical decision over which the Commander in Chief would have absolute authority, the Court held the President could not contravene Congress's specific statute. This suggests that even the President's core command authority as Commander in Chief can be limited by Congress. In other words, when Congress clearly occupies the field by authorizing "war" with limitations, the President and those acting under his orders are required to adhere to those limitations.

2.2.2. Defensive Commander in Chief Authority

The Commander in Chief power is generally believed to include the ability to employ United States military forces in a defensive context, even without prior authorization from Congress. The most often cited Supreme Court opinion for this idea came in *The Prize Cases* during the early Civil War. Shortly after the rebellion began, and while Congress was in recess, President Lincoln proclaimed a blockade of southern ports, allowing in certain circumstances for vessels to be seized for prize. Owners of subsequently seized southern vessels sued, arguing President Lincoln had no authority to issue such a proclamation in an undeclared war. In a closely divided (5–4) opinion, the Supreme Court ruled the Civil War was an actual war, even though Lincoln acted before any formal **declaration of war** from Congress. The Court held that the President has the power and responsibility to meet and respond to an attack by whatever means he deems necessary, and that he need not wait until Congress authorizes military action to defend the nation. The Court found that this authority to respond was implied by the Commander in Chief Clause, could possibly be implied by the Oath Clause, and was inherent in the President's position. The dissent adopted a more literal approach, asserting that the President could only have legal authority to wage war if Congress declared war.

2.2.3. Offensive Commander in Chief Authority?

Though the President's Commander in Chief authority to use the military to defend against attack without first obtaining congressional authorization is now well-settled, his authority to use the military *offensively* without congressional authorization is subject to significant dispute. Presidents have routinely cited their Commander in Chief authority when engaging in offensive military operations that have not yet been authorized by Congress. For example, President George H.W. Bush cited his position as Commander in Chief as authority to attack Iraq following Iraq's invasion of Kuwait in 1990. Similarly, in 2014, President Barack Obama cited his authority as Commander in Chief to order air strikes against ISIS (the so-called "Islamic State") forces in Syria when Congress had not yet authorized such military operations.

The Supreme Court has never held that the President has an offensive Commander in Chief power to engage in military operations that Congress has not authorized. In fact, the Court has rarely come close to entertaining the question. In one instance where the Court approached the issue, it suggested the Commander in Chief power is insufficient to permit the President to engage in offensive military operations without congressional authorization. In *The Prize Cases* (discussed above), in which the Court held the President did have a *defensive* Commander in Chief power to repel invasion without congressional authorization, the Court suggested the President did not have a corresponding offensive Commander in Chief power. In the sentence immediately following the Court's explicit recognition that the President is Commander in Chief, the Court stated: "[The President] has no power to initiate or declare a war either against a foreign nation or a domestic State."

Similarly, recall the facts of *Little v. Barreme*. An argument could be made that though Congress had authorized seizing ships heading to France, it had not *prohibited* seizing ships coming from France. And yet, the Court found the seizure of a ship coming from France exceeded the President's authority. If the Commander in Chief authority allows the President to use the military as he sees fit even in an offensive capacity, should not the Court have recognized this independent Commander in Chief authority?

2.3. FOREIGN AFFAIRS POWER

As noted in Chapter 1, the Constitution contains several provisions regarding the President's authority to engage in matters relating to foreign affairs. In Article II, Section 2, in addition to being identified as Commander in Chief, the President is given the power to make treaties and appoint ambassadors and consuls. These provisions *imply* the President is the nation's primary representative in foreign affairs. In *United States v. Curtiss-Wright*, the Supreme Court seemed to agree with this idea. The Court's broad pronouncement of a foreign affairs power has since been cited numerous times by presidents asserting broad and primary authority in the area of foreign affairs.

To address armed conflict in the Chaco region of South America, Congress passed a statute that said if the President determines "prohibition of sales of arms will contribute to peace between countries and makes a proclamation to that effect, then it will be unlawful to sell, except under such limitations and exceptions as the President prescribes any arms and munitions. . . ." President Roosevelt made such a proclamation on the same day the statute became law, and the Curtiss-Wright Corporation was subsequently criminally **indicted** for selling arms—fighter and bomber planes—to Bolivia, in violation of the law. At the district court, the Curtiss-Wright Corporation argued the **Joint Resolution** constituted an unlawful delegation by Congress of its lawmaking power to the President. The trial court ruled in favor of Curtiss-Wright and the United States appealed. In upholding the President's order as constitutional, the 1936 Supreme Court determined the President had multiple bases of authority for issuing the order—he was acting pursuant to a lawful **delegation of authority** by Congress and his presidential authority in matters of foreign affairs did not depend on the Constitution. The Supreme Court sided with the President, holding that the delegation by Congress to the President to have discretion in a specific foreign affairs matter (in this case, deciding that prohibition of arms sales would lead to peace) was constitutional. The Court noted that if the joint resolution had related solely to domestic affairs, it might have been an unconstitutional delegation of legislative power to the Executive.

Even though the case clearly involved delegation of authority by Congress to the President, some language in the Court's opinion *suggests* the President enjoys broad foreign affairs power aside from congressional delegation. Selectively quoting former Chief Justice John Marshall, the majority observed that "the President is sole organ of the nation in its external relations, and its sole representative with foreign nations" and that given the "delicacy of foreign relations and of the power peculiar to the President in this regard," the President must enjoy greater discretion and freedom in international relations than in domestic affairs. John Marshall had uttered the famous "sole organ" words while he was a Congressman, and the context of the speech clearly indicated Marshall saw a significant role for Congress in foreign affairs. Nevertheless, the Court articulated the idea that the President has foreign affairs authority beyond that which is delegated by Congress, and perhaps even beyond what the Constitution specifically provides:

> It is important to bear in mind that we are here dealing not alone with an authority vested in the President by an exertion of legislative power, but with such an authority plus the very delicate, plenary and exclusive

> power of the President as the sole organ of the federal government in the field of international relations—a power which does not require as a basis for its exercise an act of Congress. . . .

Additional portions of the majority opinion suggest the presidential foreign affairs power is not just implied by the powers granted in the Constitution, but is *inherent* in the nature of the presidency. First, Justice Sutherland explained that the nation's ability to act on the international stage—its sovereignty—came not from the People through the Constitution, but rather inherently and immediately passed from Great Britain to the Union. Thus, as the head of the nation and sole representative of the sovereign United States, the President enjoys great authority that did not come from Congress or from the Constitution or even from the People. Moreover, the Court noted several practical reasons why the President should have greater discretion and authority in the area of foreign affairs, including: 1) the need for a single voice when interacting with foreign countries; 2) the greater access the President has to information than Congress; and 3) the special need for flexibility and speed in the area of foreign affairs that prevents a deliberative body from being effective.

Whether the power articulated in *Curtiss-Wright* is best described as implied or inherent, Presidents routinely cite this language from *Curtiss-Wright* for plenary foreign affairs power. Indeed, Presidents' (and their lawyers') overuse of this portion of the *Curtiss-Wright* opinion led scholar and former Legal Advisor to the United States State Department, Harold Koh, to facetiously refer to the case as "*Curtiss-Wright*, so I'm right."

Those countering broad claims of presidential foreign affairs power based on *Curtiss-Wright* point to the "sole organ" language as ***dicta***, meaning it was not essential to the holding of the case, and therefore does not have precedential value. Moreover, the "sole organ" quote came from a longer quote of Congressman (later Chief Justice) John Marshall, implying that it is the President's role to execute Congress' foreign policy. They argue the holding of the *Curtiss-Wright* case does not stand for the proposition that the President has unlimited foreign affairs authority, but rather only that Congress is permitted to delegate significant authority to the President in the area of foreign affairs.

Though as early as 1953 Justice Jackson had observed that much of *Curtiss-Wright* opinion was dicta, after nearly 80 years of presidential reliance on *Curtiss-Wright*, in 2015 the Supreme Court explicitly rejected the idea that *Curtiss-Wright* stands for unlimited presidential power in the area of foreign affairs. In *Zivotofsky v. Kerry*, the Court held that the Executive has exclusive authority to *recognize* foreign nations, based on the Article II authority to receive ambassadors and engage in other international relations such as **treaty** negotiation, and based on the practical reality that nations must speak with one voice on questions of recognizing foreign nations. However, the Court went further and specifically addressed the Obama Administration's argument that the President enjoys broad, undefined powers over foreign affairs, relying on *Curtiss-Wright.* The Court opined that *Curtiss-Wright* did not extend as far as the Obama Administration claimed. Specifically, the Court noted that though the *Curtiss-Wright* majority opinion contained a broad description of the President's exclusive power, it was not necessary to the decision. This was, because *Curtiss-Wright* dealt with congressionally authorized action, not a unilateral presidential determination based solely on his plenary foreign affairs power. In other words, the *Zivotofsky* Court concluded the broad language Presidents liked to cite as evidence of expansive powers was non-binding dicta.

Further, the *Zivotofsky* Court observed that though the President has a unique role in communicating with foreign governments, Presidents do not make law, whether in the domestic or foreign realm: "The Executive is not free from the ordinary controls and checks of Congress merely because foreign affairs are at issue. It is not for the President alone to determine the whole content of the Nation's foreign policy."

In conclusion, though the President's foreign affairs power exists, and we know it is not unlimited, its boundaries are still undefined.

2.4. EMERGENCY POWERS

In the national security context, emergencies are situations where the government is faced with new circumstances that must be dealt with expeditiously because the potential consequences of delay are severe. The idea of "emergency" can be colloquially summarized as "someone has to do something, and quick!" Usually, the emergency involves a potential physical or digital threat to the nation. There are two positive sources of presidential emergency powers: the Constitution and federal statutes.

2.4.1. Constitutional Presidential Emergency Powers

The existence and extent of *constitutional* emergency powers are unclear, and thus subject to disagreement. Some have argued that a variety of constitutional provisions imply the existence of emergency powers. For example, Article I, Section 8, Clause 15 implies there are circumstances in which the militia may be necessary to "execute the law and repel invasions and insurrections." Article I, Section 9, Clause 2, demonstrates there can be circumstances in which the "public safety" might require suspending the important right to the **writ of habeas corpus**. Article I, Section 10, Clause 3 acknowledges there may be circumstances in which states can act unilaterally because "imminent Danger . . . will not admit of delay." Article II, Section 2, envisions circumstances under which the President may convene both Houses of Congress on "extraordinary Occasions." For some, the provisions just identified demonstrate a recognition by the **Framers** that emergencies will exist and imply a power to deal with them.

The idea that the President enjoys *inherent* emergency powers stems from the notion that when "someone has to do something," expediency nearly always demands that that "someone" be the President or other Executive official. Deliberative legislative bodies such as Congress are inherently ill-suited to acting in an emergency. And the Judiciary, though capable of acting more quickly, usually has no authority to meet the emergency. Imagine the Chief Justice of the Supreme Court ordering the First Infantry Division to mobilize against an invasion! Thus, an inherent emergency power is "part of the job" of the Executive, in part because the Executive is the only Branch that can act in emergencies. But these theories of constitutional emergency powers do little to explain the extent of the power or its limits, and courts have done little to identify boundaries.

2.4.2. Statutory Presidential Emergency Powers

In hundreds of statutes, Congress has explicitly delegated to the President the authority to take certain actions when he determines a national emergency exists. These so-called "**standby statutes**" contain little guidance regarding what constitutes a national emergency, and thus these laws confer significant flexibility and power upon the President. The actions the President is authorized to take often are not *military* action, but are the kinds of measures that can respond to or precipitate military action. Moreover, once emergency power has been conferred in this way, withdrawing it requires an act of Congress that would be subject to a presidential veto, producing a **ratcheting effect** that results in ever-increasing presidential emergency power. Some have argued these emergency authorities provide the President too much power, but courts have done little to limit Congress's ability to delegate its authority in this way, subject to general constitutional limitations on delegation of authority.

2.4.3. Managing Executive Emergency Power

If one accepts that emergencies will occur and that a deliberative legislative body may not be able to respond quickly enough to meet emergencies, *some* sort of executive emergency power seems inevitable. Two general theories have arisen regarding how to limit or manage this power. One approach is *not* to authorize emergency actions by Executive Branch actors in advance, but rather to rely on government officials to "do the right thing." Under this approach, the government officials will act cautiously and do the right thing because they know they will be subject to the mercy of juries, judges, or voters to excuse unauthorized behavior after the fact. For example, if the President were to act unconstitutionally in an emergency, Congress would have the sanction of impeachment. Some have suggested this approach results in limiting executive emergency power, while critics suggest it allows political calculation to play too important a role in emergency response. The alternative approach is to establish very clear standards by which government officials can act in an emergency, in effect authorizing actions in advance. Standby statutes are an example of this approach. Proponents of this approach suggest it provides clear guidance to officials regarding acceptable actions, but some critics have argued this approach leads to expansion of emergency power over time, and incentivizes using emergency powers more liberally.

2.5. "AGGREGATE" POWERS

Alexander Hamilton thought it significant that Article II of the Constitution begins "the Executive power shall be vested in a President of the United States of America," without the limiting language with which Article I begins ("all legislative Powers *herein granted* shall be vested in a Congress of the United States"). Article II's so-called "Vestiture Clause" has been cited for the idea that there are executive powers not enumerated in the Constitution, but with which the President has nevertheless been vested. This idea is that the Constitution gives the President all powers an Executive *should* have, whether or not they are specifically listed in the Constitution.

In addition, some Presidents, Justices, and scholars have asserted the "Take Care Clause" also suggests inherent powers that are not specifically identified in the Constitution. This clause charges the President to "take care that the laws be faithfully executed."

Taken together, the Vestiture Clause and Take Care Clause can be referred to as "aggregate powers," meaning the amassed powers an Executive who is responsible for ensuring execution of all law must inherently have.

The Supreme Court has acknowledged that the President enjoys some aggregate authority by virtue of his role as Executive and his responsibility to ensure execution of all law. The best-known case in which the Court accepted this theory of power is *In re Neagle*, decided in 1890. Without any specific statutory basis, the President assigned United States Marshals to protect Supreme Court Justices. Deputy United States Marshal Neagle was assigned to protect Supreme Court Justice Field while he was traveling on the West Coast. Neagle killed someone attacking Justice Field and was jailed in California. Neagle sought release from California state prison on the basis that he had killed Field's assailant in the discharge of his official (federal) duties. The ability to use this avenue for being released from a state facility relied on the point that the person to be released must have been imprisoned for actions they took in the course of their official duties. Because there was no federal statute authorizing United States Marshals to protect United States Supreme Court Justices, the only way it was Neagle's "duty" to kill in defense of Justice Field was if the President's assignment of Marshals to protect Justices was valid. If so, Neagle was acting within his duties, and he could be released; if not, Neagle was not acting within his official duties, and he could not be released based on this theory. Thus, the President's authority to assign United States Marshals to protect Supreme Court Justices was challenged.

In deciding the President *did* have the authority to assign United States Marshals to protect Justices, the Court noted that the President is enabled by the Constitution to fulfill his duty to "take care the laws be faithfully executed." Rhetorically, the Court asked:

> Is this duty limited to the enforcement of acts of Congress or of treaties of the United States according to their express terms, or does it include the rights, duties and obligations growing out of the Constitution itself, our international relations, and all the protection implied by the nature of the government under the Constitution?

The Court held that the Take Care Clause implies presidential powers to act even without explicit constitutional or statutory authority. In this case, taking care that the laws be faithfully executed included the power to protect someone (Justice Field) doing government business. In other words, the Court found the President has the authority to protect the operations of the general government, even the operations of another branch.

The dissent disagreed with the notion of implied or inherent powers to protect the nation, arguing that by appointing United States Marshals to protect Supreme Court Justices, the President was invading Congress's authority to make law. The dissent observed that though "it is the President's duty to take care that the laws be faithfully executed, it is not his duty to make laws or a law of the United States. The laws he is to see executed are manifestly those contained in the Constitution and those enacted by Congress . . . ." This is a good articulation of the view that there are no "aggregate powers" for the President in the Constitution.

The other case most frequently cited for the President's power to use military force to protect or rescue United States persons is *Durand v. Hollins*, in which a circuit court judge held that the duty to protect the lives or property of United States citizens abroad "must, of necessity, rest in the discretion of the President." Ultimately, however, the case was dismissed because of the **political question doctrine**, rendering the judge's pronouncements on the power of the President to use force to protect United States citizens dicta with little precedential value.

The Constitution is silent regarding the rescue of United States citizens abroad, so it is perhaps somewhat surprising that no judicial case has squarely addressed the power of the President to rescue Americans. Apparently concerned that the use of force to rescue citizens abroad could lead to broader war, in 1868, Congress passed the Hostage Act. The Hostage Act states that when a United States citizen has been "unjustly deprived of his liberty by or under the authority of any foreign government," it is the duty of the President to demand reasons for the imprisonment, and if it appears wrongful, the President must attempt to secure release of the citizen, and may "use such means, not amounting to acts of war and not otherwise prohibited by law, as he may think necessary and proper to obtain or effectuate the release." The Hostage Act thus again raises issues of the fight between the President and Congress for control of foreign affairs and war powers.

The President can point to the Hostage Act as support for actions short of acts of war, as he did in defending his decision to strike a deal that was upheld by the Supreme Court in *Dames & Moore,* discussed in further detail in Chapter 5. On the other hand, the Hostage Act appears to be a significant limitation on the President's authority to use military force to rescue, raising the question of whether Congress may limit the President's authority to rescue American hostages. The Hostage Act defeats the argument of **acquiescence** and thus a customary authority for the President to use military force for rescue (discussed in the next section), but whether Congress can limit the President's authority in this area in the first place is uncertain.

2.6. CUSTOMARY POWER

The least defined and most controversial presidential national security power is a "customary war power." The idea is this: the Executive has created a power that did not previously exist by exercising that power and not having that exercise subsequently restricted by Congress. In other words, by using the military in a variety of contexts without prior authorization from Congress, a succession of Presidents have created *through practice* a power that did initially not exist *in law*.

President George H.W. Bush's assertion that he had the authority to attack Iraq following Saddam Hussein's invasion of Kuwait in 1990 was noted above in the context of the President's offensive Commander in Chief authority, but it is also a helpful example of the articulation of customary war power. In arguing that he did not need congressional authorization to invade Iraq, President Bush cited 200 prior unilateral uses of force by Presidents without congressional authorization.

President Bush was at least factually correct. Though as of 2020 the United States has formally declared war only 11 times, the armed forces have been used hundreds of times, and usually without prior explicit congressional approval. The "it's legal because lots of people have done it repeatedly" argument strikes most students of the law as flawed. Nevertheless, there is some legal argument for a customary war power. Most notably, in his concurrence in *Youngstown,* Justice Frankfurter suggested the President may act unilaterally, and beyond the power explicitly granted in the Constitution, when such actions are part of a "systematic, unbroken, Executive practice, long pursued to the knowledge of Congress and never before questioned, and engaged in by Presidents sworn to uphold the Constitution." Though Justice Frankfurter described this customary authority as a "gloss on Executive power," and thus derived from the Executive power vested in the President by Article II, Section 1, it really is a separate idea: the Executive gains power by exercising power.

Even assuming the President has a customary war power, its extent is far from clear. Some scholars and presidential administrations have urged a very broad understanding of the power, arguing the many prior congressionally unauthorized uses of force added up to the authority to "deploy American forces abroad and commit them to military operations when . . . necessary to maintain the security and defense of the United States." Leonard Meeker, Legal Advisor to the State Department, *The Legality of United States Participation in the Defense of Viet-Nam*, 75 YALE L.J. 1085 (1966). Under this theory, the longstanding practice of the political branches has distributed political power between the Legislative and Executive Branches in a way that settles the question in favor of the President having the power to commit armed forces to hostilities. Of course, many scholars have made the countervailing claim: that even if there is some type of customary war power, it is far more limited, perhaps only to "protective intervention," or some subset of the use of force.

Whatever the nature of a customary power, it relies on the notion of congressional acquiescence, which suggests both that the President does not enjoy this authority unchecked and that Congress could withdraw the power. We will return to this separation and distribution of powers concept in Chapter 5, but for now, note that some accept the idea that the presidency has legal power because Presidents have exercised power.

2.7. *YOUNGSTOWN SHEET AND TUBE CO. V. SAWYER*—AN ENCYCLOPEDIA OF PRESIDENTIAL AUTHORITY THEORIES

In 1952, in the face of an impending labor strike at privately owned steel mills in the United States, President Truman issued **Executive Order** 10340 directing the Secretary of Commerce (Sawyer) to take control of the mills to keep them operating. Truman cited multiple national security reasons for the seizure, including: 1) the need to produce weapons for the ongoing Korean war; 2) the need to carry out the programs of the Atomic Energy Commission in the early days of the Cold War; 3) the general economic damage a strike would do to the United States economy; and 4) the impact of that economic damage on the military strength of the United States. President Truman notified Congress of the Executive Order, inviting it to address the problem, but in response to the order, Congress did nothing.

Congress had not declared war on Korea and had not authorized President Truman's seizure of private industry. In fact, in 1947, Congress had passed the Taft-Hartley Act, a statute regarding labor stoppages, that required the President to report to Congress if he determined seizure of industry was necessary to address labor issues. At the time, Congress had explicitly considered giving the President the authority to seize industries beset by labor stoppages, but had decided not to include that power in the Act. Truman had vetoed the bill, but Congress overrode the veto, and Truman would go on to invoke powers under the bill several times during his presidency.

After the seizure order, the steel mill owners sued, arguing President Truman lacked authority to order their mills be seized by the government. The case proceeded at an unusually fast pace. On April 29, 1952, the district court sided with the mill owners and issued an **injunction** against Truman's seizure. The government immediately appealed, and on the very next day the Court of Appeals heard oral arguments and issued its ruling staying the district court's injunction awaiting decision by the Supreme Court regarding whether it would hear the case. On May 2, the Supreme Court agreed to hear the case. Oral arguments took place on May 12, and the Supreme Court issued its ruling on June 6. Justices' case files indicate they began drafting their opinions even before oral arguments occurred.

Six Justices agreed that Truman did not have authority to seize the mills and ruled the steel mill owners should win. But none of the Justices in the "majority" fully agreed with any other Justice in the majority regarding the legal basis for the judgment. In all, the nine Justices issued seven different opinions. Justice Black issued the "opinion of the Court" and the three Justices siding with Truman issued a joint dissent.

Youngstown Sheet & Tube Company v. Sawyer, also known as *The Steel Seizure Case*, is the most widely analyzed and discussed Supreme Court opinion regarding presidential authority in the national security context. Though they carry limited precedential value, the seven different opinions serve as an encyclopedia of constitutional presidential authority theories. Here we will explore how the Justices' opinions illustrate the various presidential powers discussed above. Additionally, in Chapter 5 we will return to Justice Jackson's well-known concurring opinion in *Youngstown* to discuss the Court's approach to the balance of powers.

Presidential Power and the Consequences of Bad Lawyering?

The Department of Justice representing the Truman Administration made strategic errors in the case, the most significant of which was its argument at the District Court level that the President's power was unlimited in the face of an emergency. At the District Court hearing in the case, DOJ attorney Holmes Baldridge asserted:

> We say that Article II of the Constitution provides that the Executive power of the Government shall reside in the President, that he shall faithfully execute the laws of the office and he shall be Commander-in-Chief of the Army and of the Navy and that he shall take care that the laws be faithfully executed, are sufficient to permit him to meet any national emergency that might arise, be it peace time, technical war time, or actual war time.

When the district court judge challenged Mr. Baldridge on this assertion, Mr. Baldridge doubled down:

> **The Court**: So you contend the Executive has unlimited power in time of an emergency?
>
> **Mr. Baldridge**: He has the power to take such action as is necessary to meet the emergency.
>
> **The Court**: If the emergency is great, it is unlimited, is it?
>
> **Mr. Baldridge**: I suppose if you carry it to its logical conclusion, that is true. But I do want to point out that there are two limitations on the Executive power. One is the ballot box and the other is impeachment.
>
> . . .

> **The Court**: [T]he Executive determines the emergencies and the Courts cannot even review whether it is an emergency?
>
> **Mr. Baldridge**: That is correct.
>
> Mr. Baldridge continued pressing his case, asserting that the Constitution distinguishes between the Legislative and Executive Branches by enumerating specific powers to Congress, but vesting *all* executive power in the President (a position not dissimilar to Alexander Hamilton's, noted at the beginning of this chapter). The judge was not persuaded:
>
> **The Court**: So, when the sovereign people adopted the Constitution, it enumerated the powers set up in the Constitution [and] limited the powers of the Congress and limited the powers of the Judiciary, but it did not limit the powers of the Executive. Is that what you say?
>
> **Mr. Baldridge**: That is the way we read Article II of the Constitution.
>
> In later filings and argument, the government tried to walk back from this extreme position, but the damage had been done, in both the court and the court of public opinion. The American public, which was closely following this case, was aghast. In reacting to Truman's order, the *New York Daily News* had proclaimed "Truman Does a Hitler," and Baldridge's argument seemed to confirm the President's perceived omnipotence. The District Court plainly rejected Baldridge's assertion, as did the Court of Appeals, ultimately setting the stage for Supreme Court opinions seeking to reign in the notion of unchecked presidential power, rather than simply addressing use of power in the specific case.

2.7.1. *Youngstown* and the Commander in Chief Power

For a variety of reasons, the Commander in Chief power was not central to the Justices' opinions in *Youngstown*. Four Justices explicitly opined that the Commander in Chief power did not provide the President authority to seize private industry under the circumstances. Justice Black opined that the President cannot invoke Commander in Chief when the nation is not at war (note: the Korean War was a "police action," not a declared war), and when the actions he is taking are not in the theater of war (the seizure occurred in the United States, far from the military operations on the Korean Peninsula). Black acknowledged that the Commander in Chief Clause may give the President military powers, but military powers do not apply to taking private property domestically. Justice Jackson was similarly concerned that the President not be able to declare his own war, then justify any action he sought to take based on the existence of the war. He continued:

> I should indulge the widest latitude of interpretation to sustain his exclusive function to command the instruments of national force, at least when turned against the outside world for the security of our society. But, when it is turned inward, not because of rebellion but

> because of a lawful economic struggle between industry and labor, it should have no such indulgence.

Justice Frankfurter echoed Justices Black's and Jacksons' concern that the Korean conflict was not a declared war, noting that a declaration of war might make a difference in conferring Commander in Chief authority on the President. Likewise, Justice Burton recognized the Commander in Chief power might support the seizure if there was a threat of "total war" and the entire nation was mobilized, but not in the limited police action in Korea.

Even the dissent, which one might expect would be looking anywhere for sources of presidential authority, did not clearly rest its conclusion that Truman should be able to seize the mills on his authority as Commander in Chief. In fact, the closest the dissent came to relying on the Commander in Chief power was quoting an argument their colleague Justice Robert Jackson had made in support of President Franklin Roosevelt's seizure of industry during WWII, when Jackson was Roosevelt's attorney general:

> The Constitution also places on the President the responsibility and vests in him the powers of Commander in Chief of the Army and of the Navy. These weapons for the protection of the continued existence of the Nation are placed in his sole command and the implication is clear that he should not allow them to become paralyzed by failure to obtain supplies for which Congress has appropriated the money and which it has directed the President to obtain.

2.7.2. *Youngstown* and Emergency Powers

Six Justices suggested the possible existence of some kind of presidential emergency power, though only the three dissenters actually found it applied to the circumstances and the President's action. The dissent opined that Executive inaction in such a situation, courting national disaster, is foreign to the concept of the "energy and initiative in the Executive" created by the Founders. The dissenters argued the Constitution itself was "adopted in a period of grave emergency. . . . While emergency does not create power, emergency may furnish the occasion for the exercise of power." Even the dissenters acknowledged, however, that there is a limit to emergency power, suggesting the President can operate unilaterally in emergencies only until Congress can act.

Of the six Justices siding with the steel mill owners, Justice Clark was most accepting of an inherent or implied constitutional presidential emergency power. He noted the President must have inherent emergency powers in times of "grave and imperative national emergency," but opining the President must follow congressional dictates in meeting such emergencies, which President Truman had not. Justice Burton believed the President would have such power in "catastrophic" situations, but not under the *Youngstown* circumstances, where there was no imminent invasion or attack. Justice Jackson approved of emergency powers if they came in the form of delegations from Congress in standby statutes, but he was skeptical that the President had any emergency powers beyond those explicitly delegated by Congress.

He famously noted that the Framers omitted emergency powers from the Constitution, perhaps because they knew "emergency powers tend to kindle emergencies." Justice Frankfurter observed that the question of whether the President could have seized the mills "only for a short, explicitly temporary period, to be terminated automatically unless Congressional approval were given" was a different question not before the Court, suggesting more limited action by President Truman might have been appropriate under some kind of emergency. Finally, Justice Black, the ultimate **textualist** and author of the "Opinion of the Court," did not dismiss the idea of emergency powers, which are of course not explicitly mentioned in the text of the Constitution, though he perhaps implicitly foreclosed the possibility of an emergency power when he noted "The Founders of this Nation entrusted the lawmaking power to the Congress alone in both good and bad times."

2.7.3. *Youngstown* and Aggregate Powers (Vestiture and Take Care Clauses)

In all, five Justices suggested there could be some kind of aggregate power, though only the three dissenters found it supported President Truman's actions in this case. The dissent urged that the President clearly has "take care authority", as he has the unique responsibility to execute the "entire mass of legislation," and must do the best he can with inconsistencies. They argued President Truman was ensuring execution of the overall economic scheme established by other statutes, such as Congress's price stabilization programs and programs for procurement of military equipment.

Justice Black vehemently opposed the notion that some kind of aggregate power exists. Invoking the dissent in *In re Neagle*, Black observed the President is to *execute* laws, not make them. Justice Frankfurter noted there could be an "Executive Power" that would give Presidents the ability to take actions beyond those specifically identified in Article II, but described that power more as a customary authority (see below). Justice Jackson agreed an Executive/Vestiture power does exist, but not as President Truman had asserted it: "all the executive powers of which the Government is capable." Rather, Jackson asserted it is "an allocation to the presidential office of the generic powers thereafter stated." In other words, the Vestiture Clause does not provide more powers to the Executive than are stated in Article II. Justice Douglas similarly concluded that Article II does not give the President power to make laws, and a taking must be authorized by lawmakers.

2.7.4. *Youngstown* and Customary Powers

As discussed above, in his concurrence, Justice Frankfurter advanced the idea there could be a customary authority. Under his formulation of the idea, customary authority could be established when "Presidents sworn to uphold the Constitution engage in systematic, unbroken executive practice, long pursued to the knowledge of Congress, and never before questioned." Frankfurter found that the record of presidential seizures of industrial facilities did not add up "in number, scope, duration or contemporaneous legal justification" to broad Executive powers, and thus Truman could not rely on customary authority to seize the mills.

Justice Jackson's approach to categorizing overlapping legislative and executive powers, which we will discuss in detail in Chapter 5, allows that the President has greater authority when Congress acquiesces to his exercise of that power. However, Jackson firmly rejected the notion that the presidency should have powers beyond those given it by the Constitution and Congress. Jackson argued the presidency should not be given additional power because it was already too strong, due to the nature of executive power, the "vast accretions" of federal power that used to be state power, and the reality of the President's political power ("he often may win, as a political leader, what he cannot command under the Constitution.") Jackson lamented "Men have discovered no technique for long preserving free government except that the Executive be under the law, and that the law be made by parliamentary deliberations. Such institutions may be destined to pass away. But it is the duty of the Court to be last, not first, to give them up."

REVIEW QUESTIONS

1. Explain the difference between explicit, implied, and inherent powers.

2. What is the "core" Commander in Chief authority?

3. How do proponents and opponents of plenary presidential foreign affairs power interpret the *Curtiss-Wright* case to support their arguments? What is the current legal

status of the idea, expressed in *Curtiss-Wright*, that the President is the "sole organ of foreign affairs?"

4. What are the primary theories of presidential power discussed by the various justices in *Youngstown*?

CRITICAL THINKING QUESTIONS

1. Was constitutional designation of the President as Commander in Chief just a designation with no substantive power conferred? Was it just a method for the Framers to ensure civilian control of the military and to avoid the problems of decentralized war management the colonies had experienced during the Revolutionary War?

2. Did the congressional authority in *Little v. Barreme* not intrude upon the President's Commander in Chief authority?

3. Do you agree with the idea expressed in *Curtiss-Wright* that the President might have inherent authority that comes from the nature of the position, not from a grant of authority by the Constitution or the People? What are the dangers of such a view? The advantages?

4. If you accept Justice Sutherland's assertion in *Curtiss-Wright* that sovereignty came from Britain, not the People, does that necessarily prove the point that the *President* has primacy in the area of foreign affairs? Does the sovereignty argument just mean the entire national government has sovereignty?

5. Should delegations of authority by Congress to the President be judged differently when they relate to foreign affairs policymaking rather than domestic policymaking?

6. Did the President possess independent constitutional power to do what he did in *Curtiss-Wright*? In other words, did the President need Congress's delegation?

7. Is the President more capable of handling foreign relations than Congress?

8. Do you agree President Lincoln had the legal authority to order the blockade discussed in *The Prize Cases*? Based on what law? If you believe the President did not have the authority to order the blockade, why, and what are the practical implications of that legal opinion?

9. Did the 9/11 attacks provide President Bush the same type of authority Lincoln had to order the blockade?

10. Does a foreign nation's attack increase the President's *legal* authority or just the *political* authority? How might a foreign nation use that reality to its advantage?

11. Why is the *Youngstown* case so important in the area of presidential national security powers?

CHAPTER 3

Congress's National Security Powers

The United States Capitol Building, Architect of Congress

Learning Objectives

1. Understand Congress's sources of authority, and methods of exercising that authority, in the national security area, especially in authorizing use of military force.

2. Understand how Congress's responsibility to appropriate funds serves as a source of national security authority.

3. Understand how Congress can delegate its authority in the national security context.

3.1. INTRODUCTION

Over 200 years after ratification of the Constitution, the extent of Congress's national security powers is still unclear. Though the Constitution explicitly grants Congress authority to declare war, raise and support an army and a navy, and appropriate funds for various Executive Branch activities, Congress's ability to control the application of United States' military power is just as uncertain today as it was at the nation's founding.

Among the many powers granted to Congress in the Constitution that relate to national security, the most obvious is the power to declare war, a power Congress has not used since World War II. And yet, since Congress's last **declaration of war**, the United States has engaged in numerous large scale national security operations, including wars in Korea, Vietnam, Iraq (twice), and Afghanistan, and the Cold War, which was accompanied by the creation of the most destructive military arsenal ever assembled by mankind. In addition to these large-scale military operations, numerous smaller military operations have been conducted since Congress last used its declaration of war power. And many non-military national security activities have been conducted, especially including intelligence collection, covert actions, and the expenditure of money and diplomatic activities aimed at protecting the nation's security.

If Congress no longer uses its power to declare war, what is the primary source of Congress's national security power? Courts have accepted substitute methods of approving the President's use of military force, most often in the form of an "**authorization for the use of military force**" **(AUMF)**. Congress's absolute power to appropriate funds allows it to control the size, nature, scope, and possibly the actions of the national security apparatus, including the military, diplomatic, and intelligence-gathering functions. Additionally, Congress can delegate some of its authority to the Executive Branch, authorizing specific actions with immediate effect or contingent upon some future circumstance, usually involving an emergency. Finally, Congress may implicitly authorize Executive Branch action through acquiescing (not objecting). Each of these sources of authority, and methods of exercising that authority, is discussed below.

3.2. CONGRESSIONAL AUTHORIZATIONS FOR MILITARY ACTION

3.2.1. Congress's Declaration of War Power

Article I, Section 8, of the United States Constitution grants Congress the authority to "declare war," a power Congress has invoked only eleven times in the nation's history. The first declaration of war occurred when the United States declared war on Great Britain in what would become known as the War of 1812, and the last when it declared war on various nations during World War II. A declaration of war can signal the beginning of an offensive armed conflict or be the response to an attack, as was the case with the United States' declaration of war after Japan attacked Pearl Harbor in 1941. Typically, declarations of war have authorized the "perfect" or "total" wars discussed in Chapter 1.

United States' Declaration of War on Japan

JOINT RESOLUTION Declaring that a state of war exists between the Imperial Government of Japan and the Government and the people of the United States and making provisions to prosecute the same.

Whereas the Imperial Government of Japan has committed unprovoked acts of war against the Government and the people of the United States of America: Therefore be it

Resolved by the Senate and House of Representatives of the United States of America in Congress assembled, That the state of war between the United States and the Imperial Government of Japan which has thus been thrust upon the United States is hereby formally declared; and the President is hereby authorized and directed to employ the entire naval and military forces of the United States and the resources of the Government to carry on was against the Imperial Government of Japan; and, to bring the conflict to a successful termination, all of the resources of the country are hereby pledged by the Congress of the United States.

Approved, December 8, 1941

As discussed in Chapter 1, it is uncertain what the **Founders** meant by the power to "declare War." In its historical context, it meant at least the ability to announce publicly to enemies and the world that a state of war or hostility existed between countries. In fact, some modern scholars assert that declaring the legal status of war is *all* the declaration power was meant to confer on Congress. Under this view, the Constitution confers upon the President the ability to use military force unilaterally, with Congress' role essentially limited to providing the force to be used and providing a reactive check on the President through its appropriations and impeachment powers. The more mainstream understanding is that, in addition to announcing that a state of war exists, the declaration of war power provides Congress with one mechanism for authorizing military action against foreign states. This view is consistent with the early Supreme Court position that "[t]he whole powers of war [are], by the constitution of the United States, vested in congress." *Talbot v. Seeman.*

By the time the power was included in the Constitution in 1789, declarations of war were already falling into disuse. Alexander Hamilton wrote in Federalist No. 25 that "the ceremony of formal denunciation of war has of late fallen into disuse." This raises the question of why the **Framers** would have included the Declaration of War Clause in the Constitution if all a declaration of war signified was a formal announcement of war. That is, if the Declaration of War Clause was intended to mean only that Congress has the authority to announce that a state of war exists, and if such formal denunciations were no longer necessary, the Declaration of War Clause would have little meaning.

Whatever its status in 1789, formally "declaring war" has fallen out of favor, not just in the United States, but internationally. In fact, since 1950, only four nations have formally declared war on another state. This may be due to the proliferation of peace treaties, under which a declaration of war would serve as unambiguous evidence of a violation of the **treaty's** prohibition on non-defensive military action. The most obvious example of such a treaty is the United Nations' Charter, which permits self-defense, but not offensive military action against another state that is not authorized by the United Nations Security Council. Practically, formally declaring war in advance of attack is likely to disadvantage the attacking nation's military action by eliminating surprise. Whatever the reason, formal declarations of war are more a vestige of prior state practice than a modern source of national security authority.

3.2.2. Congressional Authorizations for the Use of Military Force

The declaration of war power is not the *only* mechanism by which Congress can authorize the President to engage in the use of military force. Despite the possible extinction of formal declarations of war, Congress clearly retains the ability to authorize military action against a foreign state. In fact, nearly from the beginning of the nation, courts have recognized that Congress may authorize military action using mechanisms *other* than a formal declaration of war. Indeed, Congress authorized the use of military force years before it ever declared war on another nation.

Early in the history of the Republic, the Supreme Court acknowledged that war might exist despite the lack of a formal declaration of war. In 1800 in *Bas v. Tingy*, the Court assessed whether a war existed with France. In that case, whether a captain who recaptured a vessel from France was entitled to a reward from the ship's owner of either one half or one eighth of the vessel's value hinged on whether France was legally considered an "enemy" of the United States. Bas, the ship's owner, argued France was not an enemy because Congress had not declared war. But the Court sided with the captain who had recovered the vessel, noting that there are multiple types of "wars" and that France could be an "enemy" of the United States absent a formal declaration of war, especially in light of Congress's specific authorization of the use of military force against France and French interests on the high seas. The Court was not troubled by the existence of military hostilities with a foreign nation, despite the absence of declaration of war, because of Congress's explicit authorization of those hostilities by a different mechanism.

Most commonly, Congress has authorized military hostilities by passing an **authorization for the use of military force**. An AUMF is an act of Congress passed by both houses specifically authorizing the President to engage in hostilities. No special language is required for an AUMF. Such resolutions typically say something like "the President is authorized to use the United States Armed Forces against Country X," though sometimes the military is referred to more euphemistically, such as when Congress authorizes the President to "use all necessary and appropriate force" to address a situation. AUMFs have usually named specific enemies and have sometimes included expiration dates. AUMFs have traditionally been used to authorize the "imperfect" or "limited" wars discussed in Chapter 1.

Text of Authorization for Use of Military Force Against Iraq Resolution of 2002

. . .

SEC. 2. SUPPORT FOR UNITED STATES DIPLOMATIC EFFORTS.

The Congress of the United States supports the efforts by the President to—

(1) strictly enforce through the United Nations Security Council all relevant Security Council resolutions regarding Iraq and encourages him in those efforts; and

(2) obtain prompt and decisive action by the Security Council to ensure that Iraq abandons its strategy of delay, evasion and noncompliance and promptly and strictly complies with all relevant Security Council resolutions regarding Iraq.

SEC. 3. AUTHORIZATION FOR USE OF UNITED STATES ARMED FORCES.

(a) Authorization.—The President is authorized to use the Armed Forces of the United States as he determines to be necessary and appropriate in order to—

(1) defend the national security of the United States against the continuing threat posed by Iraq; and

(2) enforce all relevant United Nations Security Council resolutions regarding Iraq.

(b) Presidential Determination.—In connection with the exercise of the authority granted in subsection (a) to use force the President shall, prior to such exercise or as soon thereafter as may be feasible, but no later than 48 hours after exercising such authority, make available to the Speaker of the House of Representatives and the President pro tempore of the Senate his determination that—

(1) reliance by the United States on further diplomatic or other peaceful means alone either (A) will not adequately protect the national security of the United States against the continuing threat posed by Iraq or (B) is not likely to lead to enforcement of all relevant United Nations Security Council resolutions regarding Iraq; and

(2) acting pursuant to this joint resolution is consistent with the United States and other countries continuing to take the necessary actions against international terrorist and terrorist organizations, including those nations, organizations, or persons who planned, authorized, committed or aided the terrorist attacks that occurred on September 11, 2001.

The AUMF Congress passed following the 9/11 attacks on the United States contained neither a specifically identified enemy, nor an expiration date. Successive Presidents have relied on this AUMF for authority for many years, including as authority for military operations against the so-called Islamic State (ISIS), an enemy that did not yet exist when the AUMF was originally passed. In failing to name a specific enemy or even limit the AUMF to a specific geographic region, the 2001 AUMF was unique in United States history. In 2002, Congress returned to a more traditional AUMF when it identified a specific enemy in authorizing military force against Iraq.

Text of Authorization to Use Military Force Following 9/11/2001 Terror Attacks

Public Law 107–40

107th Congress

Joint Resolution

To authorize the use of United States Armed Forces against those responsible for the recent attacks launched against the United States.

Whereas, on September 11, 2001, acts of treacherous violence were committed against the United States and its citizens; and

Whereas, such acts render it both necessary and appropriate that the United States exercise its rights to self-defense and to protect United States citizens both at home and abroad; and

Whereas, in light of the threat to the national security and foreign policy of the United States posed by these grave acts of violence;

and

Whereas, such acts continue to pose an unusual and extraordinary threat to the national security and foreign policy of the United States; and

Whereas, the President has authority under the Constitution to take action to deter and prevent acts of international terrorism against the United States: Now, therefore, be it Resolved by the Senate and House of Representatives of the United States of America in Congress assembled,

SECTION 1. SHORT TITLE.

This joint resolution may be cited as the "Authorization for Use of Military Force".

SEC. 2. AUTHORIZATION FOR USE OF UNITED STATES ARMED FORCES.

(a) IN GENERAL.—That the President is authorized to use all necessary and appropriate force against those nations, organizations, or persons he determines planned, authorized, committed, or aided the terrorist attacks that occurred on September 11, 2001, or harbored such organizations or persons, in order to prevent any future acts of international terrorism against the United States by such nations, organizations or persons.

(b) WAR POWERS RESOLUTION REQUIREMENTS.—

(1) SPECIFIC STATUTORY AUTHORIZATION.—Consistent with section 8(a)(1) of the War Powers Resolution, the Congress declares that this section is intended to constitute specific statutory authorization within the meaning of section 5(b) of the War Powers Resolution.

(2) APPLICABILITY OF OTHER REQUIREMENTS.—Nothing in this resolution supersedes any requirement of the War Powers Resolution.

Approved September 18, 2001.

3.2.2.1. Limitations Within an AUMF

Some have suggested that once the use of military force has been authorized by Congress, the President has *carte blanche* to pursue the objectives of that military force and how military operations will be conducted, based on his Commander in Chief powers. But what if the AUMF contains explicit limitations on that authority? Early in the nation's history, the Supreme Court held that when congressional authorization of hostilities is limited, such limitations must be obeyed by the Executive Branch. *Little v. Barreme* addressed whether a United States Navy captain improperly captured a French vessel. By statute, Congress had authorized the President (through the Navy) to seize vessels sailing *to* any French port, but had not stated that seizure of vessels coming *from* French ports was similarly authorized. Because Captain Little's vessel seized a ship coming *from* a French port, the Court found that he was personally liable, as his actions had exceeded the authority given by Congress, even though the President authorized the captain's actions. The Court reasoned that in a "perfect" or "total" war, there are no limitations on the President's actions, whether the war is authorized by a declaration of war or some other method. By contrast, in an "imperfect" or "limited" war, whatever limitations are imposed by Congress must be obeyed.

3.3. CONGRESSIONAL APPROPRIATIONS POWER

3.3.1. General Appropriations Power

As noted previously, the Constitution grants to Congress a variety of specific authorities related to national security, including the authority to declare war, make rules concerning captures, raise and support the armed forces, regulate commerce with foreign nations, and call forth the militia to suppress insurrections and repel invasions. Importantly, the Constitution also grants to Congress the **appropriations power**, sometimes referred to as the "power of the purse," which is the authority to decide how much money will be collected by the federal government and on what activities that money will be spent. This ability to control how money is spent is perhaps the greatest authority Congress has to direct national security.

Congress's "power of the purse" comes primarily from Article I, Section 9, which states "No money shall be drawn from the treasury, but in consequence of appropriations made by law." As it has been interpreted, the Appropriations Clause means no branch of the government can do anything that costs money unless Congress has appropriated money for that activity. In 1884, in response to massive spending abuses by the Executive Branch, especially spending on the armed forces, Congress passed the Anti-Deficiency Act (ADA), which clarified that the government may not incur debts that exceed the money appropriated for a particular activity. The combined effect of the Appropriations Clause and the Anti-Deficiency Act is profound: if Congress does not fund a government activity, and the government may not incur unapproved debts for activities, the activity cannot lawfully occur.

Congress has historically treated authorizations and appropriations separately. That is, Congress often authorizes a particular activity in one piece of legislation and appropriates money for that activity in another. Arguably, an activity or program that has been authorized, but for which funds are not appropriated, cannot actually do anything. On the other hand, sometimes Congress appropriates money for an activity without a corresponding authorization. Though some have argued that appropriations without authorizations are insufficient for the activity to occur, most courts and scholars agree that appropriations have equivalent legal effect to other kinds of legislation and can implicitly "authorize" the funded activity.

3.3.2. Authorization by Appropriation

Whether Congress can authorize military action by appropriation alone is not entirely clear. The question is this: when Congress provides funding for a military entity, activity, or program, can the context surrounding that appropriation implicitly authorize or condone the *use* of that entity, activity, or program in a military conflict that has not otherwise been specifically authorized?

The idea that appropriation constitutes authorization makes intuitive sense. If Congress is willing to pay for an activity, does that not imply that Congress approves of that activity? More specifically, if Congress funds an activity it knows will be used in the application of military force, its approval of that use of force seems clear. For example, in 2003, in a supplemental defense appropriations bill, Congress appropriated an additional $15 million "to be used primarily in Iraq and Afghanistan." In light of the well-publicized ongoing military operations in those countries at the time, such an appropriation would have been a clear authorization of those operations, even if Congress had not previously authorized the use of military force in those countries (in this case, it had). If, as courts have suggested, there is no specific required language regarding how Congress indicates its approval for the use of force, providing funds seems like yet another way for Congress to indicate its approval of military action.

Less clear is whether a defense appropriation can *implicitly* authorize military operations that the appropriation does not specifically reference. For example, if the President initiates a bombing campaign in a foreign nation without congressional approval, do subsequent congressional appropriations to the military to purchase airplanes, bombs, and jet fuel constitute approval of the ongoing bombing operations? In 1994 in *Ex parte Endo*, the Supreme Court held that an "appropriation must plainly show a purpose to bestow the precise authority which is claimed." In that case, the Court rejected the government's argument that Congress's general appropriation of money for World War II detention operations demonstrated authorization for detaining American citizens of Japanese ancestry specifically. The Court found that it could "hardly deduce such a purpose here where a lump appropriation was made for the overall detention program . . . and no sums were earmarked for [the detention of Japanese American citizens.] The idea that an appropriation must "plainly show a purpose to bestow the precise authority which is claimed" in order to ratify executive action has been called by some the "Clear Statement Rule."

The Supreme Court seemed to reiterate this requirement in *Greene v. McElroy*, another case where it found that Congress's funding of the national security apparatus did not mean it authorized the detailed security clearance program procedures the Department of Defense created as part of that apparatus. The government argued that Congress had authorized security clearance revocation hearings that lacked normal due process because Congress had appropriated money to a program under which reimbursement for lost wages would be made to employees of government contractors who were temporarily denied, but later granted, security clearances. The Court rejected this interpretation, noting that the hearing procedures at issue were not part of the reimbursement program. The Court repeated its earlier admonition in *Endo* that for an appropriation to constitute an authorization, it must "plainly show a purpose to bestow the precise authority which is claimed."

You Be the Judge: Authorization by Appropriation

Suppose the President, claiming he is acting in self-defense, and without any specific authority from Congress, orders the land invasion and occupation of a portion of the fictional country of Mexada. After initially using the United States Air Force to eliminate Mexadan air defense and soften Mexadan ground forces, the vast majority of the effort to seize and hold ground in Mexada has been undertaken by United States Army armored divisions, using a large number of M1A2 battle tanks and M2 Bradley Fighting Vehicles. In its latest budget request, the Army asked for "$2 billion to purchase 500 additional M1A2 tanks and $1 billion to purchase 330 additional M2 vehicles." These numbers are far higher than the usual 50 new tanks and 50 new M2 vehicles the Army usually requests Congress to fund. If, in its next regularly scheduled National Defense Authorization Act (NDAA) and appropriation, Congress appropriates funds for all the M1A2s and M2s the Army requested, has it implicitly authorized the President's ongoing use of force in Mexada? Is your answer different if Congress provides the money for these requests in some sort of special authorization that is separate from a routine NDAA? What if the Army's request specifically says the extra vehicles are to "support ongoing operations in Mexada?"

Whatever the extent of Congress's ability to authorize by appropriation, there is a clear limit on this authority: Congress cannot use its appropriations power in a manner that violates direct constitutional commands. This principle was demonstrated in *Lovett v. United States*. In *Lovett*, Congress had enacted a rider to a bill forbidding the Executive Branch from distributing salaries to certain named "subversive" employees. The President signed the bill, while asserting the rider was unconstitutional. The Court held that the rider violated the Bill of Attainder Clause of the Constitution by inflicting punishment without a judicial trial. The Court noted that even an exercise of Congress's appropriation power is "subject to the limitation that it must not be exercised in a way that would nullify another provision of the Constitution." *Lovett* has been cited for the idea that Congress cannot intrude on the President's constitutional authority. Thus, for example, though only Congress can provide the President with an army and navy to command, it cannot deprive the President of the command of the Army and Navy.

3.3.3. Limitation by Appropriation or Non-Appropriation

In addition to *authorizing* military action by appropriation, Congress can *limit* or even *deauthorize* military action by appropriation or non-appropriation. The Appropriations Clause of the Constitution ("No money shall be drawn from the Treasury, but in Consequence of Appropriations made by Law"), in combination with the Anti-Deficiency Act, limits federal agencies, including the military, to activities for which Congress has decided it will pay. This is one of Congress's greatest tools in directing Executive Branch action. Indeed, since World War II, appropriations limitations and riders (the "strings attached" to appropriations) have been the primary way Congress has directed national security policy. As will be discussed in further detail in Chapter 5, the appropriations power was key to ending the war in Vietnam.

An appropriations limitation or rider can operate very simply. For example, Congress can say in appropriations legislation that "$1 trillion is appropriated to the Department of Defense for operations during the next two years, except that no money here appropriated shall be used for military activities in Country X." Unless money for military activities in Country X are appropriated elsewhere, such a limitation would effectively prohibit any United States military operations in Country X. Whether such a limitation could terminate an already-existing military operation there is the subject of some debate. Presidents would likely argue that limiting an already-ongoing operation would intrude on the President's constitutional authority as Commander in Chief.

3.4. CONGRESSIONAL DELEGATIONS OF AUTHORITY

Throughout the nation's history, Congress has repeatedly delegated some of its authority to the Executive Branch. Courts have permitted this **delegation of authority** subject to three limitations. First, the delegation cannot violate the "**nondelegation doctrine**." Second, the delegation must include "intelligible principles," that is standards by which the executive discretion can be channeled and measured. Third, the delegation cannot violate constitutional process or another substantive constitutional provision.

The nondelegation doctrine means that Congress cannot delegate its core legislative powers—its "lawmaking function"—to Executive agencies. However, recognizing that Congress is unable to envision and author every specific rule executing its legislation, courts have permitted delegation as long as Congress provides the Executive agency with an "intelligible principle" upon which to base its regulations and activities. *Whitman v. American Trucking Associations, Inc.* In other words, *Congress* must make any fundamental legislative judgments—the underlying policy—and those legislative judgments must be included in any statutory delegation, both so that Executive Branch discretion is channeled and so Executive Branch action can be reviewed by the Judicial Branch. The Supreme Court has only twice used the nondelegation doctrine to strike down a congressional delegation of power to the Executive, with the most recent occurrence in 1935. *Schechter Poultry Corp. v. United States*; *Panama Refining Co. v. Ryan*. The Supreme Court has ruled that congressional delegations of authority must contain "intelligible principles" by which execution of the delegated authority can be assessed. In other words, when Congress delegates authority, it must include standards or boundaries for the President to follow, and those principles must be sufficiently clear for courts to assess whether the President has stayed within Congress's intended delegation.

Delegations of authority to the Executive Branch must also comply with constitutional procedural limitations. In the seminal case in this area, *Immigration & Naturalization Service v. Chadha*, the Supreme Court examined a law in which Congress had delegated some of its authority to the Executive Branch. Specifically, Congress had delegated to the Attorney General the authority to change the legal status of aliens, effectively allowing the Attorney General to determine if an "illegal" alien should become a "legal" alien. Along with this delegation, however, Congress retained the right to a "one-house veto," under which either house of Congress could overturn an Attorney General's decision regarding particular aliens. By 1983 when *Chadha* was decided, Congress had included similar "legislative vetoes" in nearly 200 statutes delegating its authority to the Executive. In *Chadha*, the Supreme Court struck down this scheme, demanding that if "legislative action," which the Court defined as "action that had the purpose and effect of altering the legal rights, duties, and relations of persons outside the legislative branch," is to occur, Congress must follow the Constitution's explicit procedures for legislative action: passage by a majority of both houses of Congress and presentment of the legislation to the President.

Finally, in addition to complying with constitutional processes, delegations from Congress to the Executive cannot otherwise violate substantive constitutional provisions. In other words, Congress cannot authorize the President to violate the Constitution just by delegating its authority. A delegation is not an opportunity for the government to collectively evade constitutional limitations. For example, if the First Amendment prevents Congress from restricting free speech in a particular way, Congress cannot get around that restriction by authorizing the President to restrict speech in that way.

3.4.1. Delegation for National Security Matters

Though the Supreme Court has never held that constitutional limitations do not apply in the context of delegations of national security authority, the Court has *suggested* the requirements for delegation may be relaxed, or at least the courts may exercise greater deference to the Executive, in the national security context.

The *Curtiss-Wright* case, discussed in Chapter 2 in the context of the President's power, is also important to the question of Congress's ability to delegate its national security powers. Recall that in *Curtiss-Wright*, Congress had given the President the power to determine whether prohibiting weapons sales would be beneficial to peace between warring nations and, if so, such sales would become unlawful, subject to limitations and exceptions imposed by the President.

Ordinarily, deciding what is unlawful is a legislative function, the delegation of which to the Executive Branch might run afoul of the nondelegation doctrine. In *Curtiss-Wright*, the Supreme Court specifically recognized that if Congress's delegation had related solely to domestic affairs, it likely would have been unconstitutional. But, because the purpose of the delegation in this case was related to *foreign* affairs, the Court found the delegation constitutional. As noted in Chapter 2, to support this assertion, the Court offered theoretical and practical differences between domestic and foreign powers. First was the source of the power to engage in international relations. The Court contended that this power did not come from the states through the Constitution, but rather directly from the English Crown. The Court reasoned the President's authority to act internationally came not from the Constitution, but from the direct passage of sovereignty from England to the Union at the moment the Union's existence became separate from England. Thus, the President, as head of the nation, did not need foreign affairs power delegated to him, because he had it as an inherent feature of his position as head of the nation. The Court further explained that even if Congress had the power it purportedly delegated to the President, the practical realities of foreign affairs activities also favored loose application of the non-delegation doctrine. First, the Court recognized that it is important for the nation to speak with one voice on the international stage, and that the President was the obvious figurehead to do so. Additionally, the Court noted that the President often has access to foreign affairs information Congress does not have, rendering Congress incapable of providing informed direction like it can in domestic matters. Finally, the Court asserted that speed and flexibility are especially important in the area of public affairs, and the deliberative legislative process was ill-suited to predicting international developments or responding quickly. Thus, as a matter of necessity, Congress could delegate to the President great discretion to act.

The Supreme Court again affirmed a broad understanding of Congress's ability to delegate national security authority to the President a few years later in *Lichter v. United States*. *Lichter* addressed whether the Renegotiation Act of 1942 authorized the Executive Branch to determine if private government contractors were enjoying "excessive profits" due to wartime contracts and, if so, to recapture those profits. The Court held that Congress could delegate this authority to the Executive Branch, reasoning that a constitutional power also implies the power to delegate authority sufficient to accomplish its purposes. In *Lichter*, Congress's constitutional war powers implied the ability to do whatever necessary—including delegate authority—to *win* the war. The Court held that because the definition of "excessive profits" in the delegation was adequate, the Executive's ability to take back what it deemed to be excessive profits was not an unconstitutional exercise of legislative power by an administrative official. In other words, the Executive Branch did not have the sole authority to determine what was "excessive." The Court also noted the importance of the specific legislative powers being employed: national security powers. In other words, the Court again decided that delegation to the Executive was different when in the context of foreign affairs.

Unlike with *appropriations*, the Supreme Court appears not to have imposed a "Clear Statement Rule" for Congressional *delegations*. In *Greene v. McElroy*, mentioned above, the government also argued that Congress had delegated authority to the Department of Defense to create the contested security clearance hearing procedures through "acquiescence or implied ratification." The Court acknowledged that under some circumstances, delegation could be inferred this way, but that delegation could not be inferred in this case, where the procedure at issue was so contrary to due process. Thus, the Court has suggested that delegation may be inferred even when not explicit.

Another form of Congressional delegation of authority is in the form of **emergency statutes**, also known as **standby statutes**. Under these laws, Congress provides authorizations to, and sometimes imposes restrictions on, the President when a "national emergency" exists. The President is given the authority to determine whether a "national emergency" exists, meaning she decides for herself whether to assume additional authority. There are hundreds of emergency statutes, potentially granting the Executive Branch massive power that it can yield very quickly and entirely at its own discretion by simply declaring an emergency. Withdrawing that authority would require Congress to pass a new law and present it to the President, who would presumably veto the reducing of her power. Thus, providing the President with "emergency authority" in this way has a **ratcheting effect**: with each new emergency statute, the President's authority grows, while reducing that power involves a politically difficult and unlikely process of overcoming a veto. Additionally, courts have given broad deference to Presidents' determinations that a national emergency existed, often finding it to be a non-justiciable political question, as will be discussed in Chapter 4. The National Emergencies Act, passed in 1976, attempted to provide some structure to presidential emergency declarations, at least by imposing a requirement to identify a clear beginning and end to emergency powers, and articulate the process by which an emergency must be declared. Even the National Emergencies Act, however, was unable to include a definition of "emergency."

3.5. CONGRESSIONAL AUTHORIZATION THROUGH ACQUIESCENCE

Supreme Court Justices and scholars have occasionally entertained the counterintuitive idea that Congress can give, or allow, the President authority for a particular action simply by failing to object to it. Known as "**acquiescence**," this theory suggests that the absence of objection implies authorization. In other words, when Congress knows of an executive decision or action and does not object, that failure to object confers *implied* authority to the Executive. This idea is strongest when the Executive has engaged in a long, unbroken, and well-known (to Congress) practice or interpretation of the law, and Congress has done something affirmative that indicates its agreement. That said, there are two variants of the acquiescence theory. In one, affirmative acquiescence, Congress's acquiescence is manifested by an affirmative act that demonstrates it has not disapproved of a presidential action. For example, Congress may legislate in a specific area in which the President has acted and not refer to the President's action or limit the President's authority in any way. Congress's action therefore serves as affirmative evidence of its approval—had it wanted to disapprove, it could have. In the second variation of the theory, silent acquiescence, Congress can approve presidential action by doing nothing at all. In other words, congressional silence regarding a President's action serves as evidence of its approval.

The idea of acquiescence as a basis of congressional authorization has been explored in several key national security cases. The most significant of these, *Youngstown Sheet and Tube Co. v. Sawyer*, is discussed at length in Chapters 2 and 5. In that case, Justice Jackson's concurrence articulated three categories for assessing the President's power. The second category, sometimes called the "zone of twilight," includes an uncertain distribution of powers between Congress and the President. Justice Jackson noted that in such circumstances, congressional "inertia, indifference or quiescence may sometimes. . .enable. . .measures on independent presidential responsibility." In the same case, Justice Felix Frankfurter, also writing a concurring opinion, supported the theory of silent acquiescence. Though he found acquiescence did not apply in the case the Court was deciding, he allowed for the idea that a President's "executive power" under Article II, Section 1 of the Constitution could include "a systematic, unbroken, executive practice, long pursued to the knowledge of the Congress and never before questioned. . . ." Scholar Michael Glennon later expanded on Frankfurter's factors by suggesting that when determining whether presidential authority by congressional acquiescence exists, courts should consider the consistency, frequency, duration, density, continuity, and normalcy of the executive practice, whether Congress had notice of the practice, and the extent to which Congress's objection would be meaningful—in other words, if congressional objection would be useless, its absence carries less weight.

In *Dames & Moore v. Regan*, the Supreme Court agreed that congressional acquiescence might serve to confirm the President's authority. In that case, President Jimmy Carter had declared a national emergency and blocked removal of Iranian assets from the United States. Subsequently, as part of negotiations to secure release of United States citizens held hostage by Iran, President Carter agreed with Iran that all legal proceedings in United States courts involving claims against Iran would be terminated. When a United States company with claims against Iran challenged the President's authority to do this, the Court held that because Congress had acquiesced in the President's actions, the Court was "not prepared to say that the President lacks the power to settle such claims." The Court agreed that Congress's acquiescence may be enough to give the President authority for certain actions in the spheres of foreign affairs and national security, even if no statute explicitly gives the President that authority. Acquiescence is a potent avenue for presidential assertions of authority, especially if acquiescence can be silent, or through inaction.

REVIEW QUESTIONS

1. When was the last time the United States formally declared war?

2. What is the method by which Congress has most frequently explicitly approved military action?

3. What significance does *Little v. Barreme* have regarding Congress's control over the President's use of the military?

4. Why might the "power of the purse" be Congress's most influential source of authority to direct national security policy?

5. Explain the two theories of congressional acquiescence.

CRITICAL THINKING QUESTIONS

1. Is Congress' overall national security power today greater than, less than, or roughly the same as the Framers envisioned it should be when drafting the Constitution?

2. Why has Congress not declared war since World War II?

3. Should all Authorizations for Uses of Military Force have clearly identified enemies and expiration dates?

4. Does the Supreme Court's holding in *Ex parte Endo* eliminate the "implied authorization through appropriation" argument?

5. What motivation might Congress have to authorize military operations by appropriation rather than explicitly?

6. In *Lovett*, the Court noted that even an exercise of Congress's appropriation power is "subject to the limitation that it must not be exercised in a way that would nullify another provision of the Constitution." Can you think of examples of how that limitation mighty apply in appropriations for national security?

7. What objections can you think of to the notion of approval through acquiescence?

8. What do you think best explains congressional acquiescence? Laziness? Gridlock? Or is it a wise approach because Congress can withdraw acquiescence more easily than delegated power?

CHAPTER 4

The Courts' National Security Authority

Chief Justice John Marshall, by Henry Inman

"It is emphatically the province and duty of the judicial department to say what the law is." Marbury v. Madison

Learning Objectives

1. Be able to explain the federal judiciary's cautious approach to involvement in national security matters.

2. Understand the justiciability doctrines of standing, ripeness, state secrets, and the political question doctrine and how they have been used in national security cases.

4.1. INTRODUCTION

Article III of the Constitution established the Supreme Court, provided lifetime tenure for federal judges, and asserted that federal courts' authority reaches to "all Cases . . . arising under this Constitution." In the well-known case of *Marbury v. Madison*, the Supreme Court also assumed for the federal judiciary the power of **judicial review**, which is the power to review the actions of government, determine if they are constitutional or lawful, and strike down those it determines are not. In *Marbury*, Chief Justice Marshall asserted that it is "the province and duty of the judicial department to say what the law is," thus ensuring "a government of laws, and not of men." The judiciary has played an important national security role in refereeing the struggle between government power to ensure collective security and individual rights, and in maintaining the system of separation of powers the Constitution establishes. Many of the cases in this book demonstrate the judiciary's involvement in national security matters. However, the judiciary has often played a less significant role in deciding national security matters than it has in other areas, sometimes demonstrating repeated reluctance to decide national security issues.

Though Articles I and II of the Constitution explicitly grant national security powers to the Legislative and Executive Branches, the Constitution makes no such mention of a national security role for the Judicial Branch. Courts have frequently deferred to the political branches—especially the Executive—in national security matters. This chapter explains some of the methods courts have used to avoid deciding national security cases and concludes by discussing *why* courts have been so reluctant to adjudicate these cases.

As has been demonstrated in previous chapters, national security legal questions are generally one of two types: questions regarding *authority*—who has the power to do what—and questions regarding *policy*—what *should* be done. As we will discover in this chapter, the judiciary is occasionally willing to dabble in questions of authority and rarely willing to decide cases that would dictate national security policy.

4.2. JURISDICTION

Article III grants federal courts the power to hear cases:

> arising under this Constitution, the Laws of the United States, and Treaties arising under this Constitution, the laws of the United States, and treaties made, or which shall be made, under their authority . . . to all cases affecting ambassadors, other public ministers and consuls . . . to all cases of admiralty and maritime jurisdiction [and] to controversies to which the United States shall be a party. . . ."

The majority of questions related to national security address the constitutional or statutory *authority* of an actor in the national security arena to take a particular action. So, the federal judiciary has **jurisdiction**—the authority of a court to hear and render judgment in a particular case against a particular defendant or defendants—to decide the vast majority of national security questions. Perhaps unsurprisingly then, lack of jurisdiction has infrequently been the legal basis for courts to decline to hear cases.

4.3. JUSTICIABILITY DOCTRINES

The fact that the federal judiciary has jurisdiction to hear a case does not necessarily mean that it *should*. Even though courts usually do have jurisdiction to hear national security cases, they often find such cases "nonjusticiable" for one reason or another. **Justiciability** addresses whether a particular legal question or case is capable of being decided by a court. This concept includes mandatory constitutional limitations on the ability of a court to hear a case, but it also includes prudential reasons for not hearing a particular case. That is, reasons why it may not be wise for a court to decide a case, even if it has the authority to do so. Unlike mandatory constitutional limitations, prudential reasons are solely within the discretion of the courts to determine.

The federal judiciary decides national security cases very selectively and forgoes the opportunity to play a more significant role. This frequent abstention is not accidental. Indeed, the Supreme Court has said that "[m]atters intimately related to foreign policy and national security are rarely proper subjects for judicial intervention." *Haig v. Agee*. Courts have drawn an important distinction between cases they *can* decide—cases over which the federal judiciary has *jurisdiction* and which meet the Constitution's justiciability requirements—and those they believe they *should* decide.

When courts have declined to hear or decide national security cases or issues on their substantive merits, they have usually done so by asserting that the case is non-justiciable based on one or more of the following justiciability doctrines: **standing**; **ripeness**; the **political question doctrine**; or because the case involves "state secrets."

4.3.1. Standing

One of the primary limitations on the courts' involvement in national security cases is Article III's requirement that for a court to have authority, there must be a "case or controversy." This requirement prevents federal courts from providing advisory opinions or issuing opinions on whatever subjects suit them. Judges and Justices cannot simply decide to issue opinions by virtue of their positions; rather, they can issue opinions only when an actual case has been brought before them to decide. In this sense, the judiciary is passive or reactive, without any power until someone else has acted by initiating a criminal complaint or lawsuit or other request for adjudication.

Dear Mr. President, The Supreme Court Is Not Your Lawyer

One of the first Supreme Court "opinions" addressing the case or controversy requirement arose in the national security context, and came not in the usual form of a published opinion in a case, but rather in a letter. In 1793, President George Washington requested an advisory opinion from the Supreme Court through his Secretary of State, Thomas Jefferson. President Washington wanted to know whether the United States' **treaty** obligations required it to allow French citizens to sail from United States ports in armed vessels. Chief Justice John Jay responded by letter, telling President Washington that he could not answer his question because doing so would improperly blur the separation of powers and that the Constitution provided the President the ability to seek the advice of Heads of Departments. Note that even this letter was, perhaps ironically, a legal opinion. By issuing the responsive letter, the Court implicitly decided a legal question: that it would not issue advisory opinions. In any event, this situation was one of the earliest examples of the Supreme Court abstaining from participation in national security matters.

The Supreme Court has interpreted Article III's conferring of jurisdiction over "cases and controversies" to require that a plaintiff have standing to sue, and mandated that three requirements must be met for standing to exist. First, the plaintiff must have suffered an "injury in fact," defined as an invasion of a legally protected interest that is: (a) concrete and particularized; and (b) actual or imminent, not conjectural or hypothetical. Second, there must be a causal connection between the defendant's conduct and the plaintiff's injury. Third, it must be likely, not just speculative, that the injury would be redressed if the court reached a decision favorable to the plaintiff. In short, the plaintiff must have been (or are about to be) harmed by the conduct of the defendant in the case, and winning the case must be able to prevent or remedy, at least partially, the damage caused by that injury.

In national security matters where standing is an issue, the primary question is usually whether the plaintiff has been "injured in fact." This requirement most often limits national security cases brought by two types of plaintiffs: "concerned citizens" and members of the government.

Some citizens (sometimes called "concerned citizens") wish to challenge a particular action by Congress or the President as unconstitutional simply because they think the action is wrong or illegal. However, for a court to hear such a case, it must find that the action being challenged has or will cause the *actual plaintiff* to suffer some sort of actual harm. Federal courts have repeatedly held that a citizen's mere interest that the government "follow the law" or "act constitutionally" is not a sufficient harm. Instead, the plaintiff must be hurt by the government's alleged failure to follow the law or act constitutionally. For example, before the start of the Persian Gulf War in 1991, a citizen who objected to the impending military action sued, claiming that as a citizen of the United States, he was being made an "accessory to murder against his will." The court held this was too abstract an injury to meet the standing requirement. *Pietsch v. Bush.* Additionally, standing cannot be based on a generalized interest that affects all citizens, even one as seemingly important as wanting the government to obey the law. By contrast, when an individual military servicemember challenged the legality of the same conflict, a court found he did have standing to sue, based on the very real possibility of physical injury or death caused by the allegedly unconstitutional or illegal order to participate in the military conflict. *Ange v. Bush.* Thus, whereas an otherwise uninvolved citizen might not have standing to sue the President for failing to obtain a **declaration of war** or **authorization for the use of military force** from Congress, a servicemember who could suffer literal injury from the President's decision clearly would have standing.

You Be the Judge: The Terrorist Surveillance Program and Standing

The Terrorist Surveillance Program (TSP) conducted by the National Security Agency raised important new questions regarding standing. Journalists and lawyers have sued the government, claiming their ability to perform their jobs was hampered by the fear that their communications with persons overseas—for example, journalists' sources and lawyers' clients—might be monitored by the NSA. In 2007, a federal circuit court of appeal found that these professionals did not have standing because they could not demonstrate they *actually* had been the targets of surveillance, and thus their injuries were too speculative. *American Civil Liberties Union v. National Security Agency.* Given that subjects of surveillance are intentionally kept in the dark about the surveillance, it might seem they would never be able to demonstrate their injuries. However, in 2011, a different federal circuit court of appeals found that such professionals could have standing. *Amnesty International USA v. Clapper*. In that case, the court held that the public interest organizations and lawyers involved were injured by the warrantless surveillance program because of their reasonable fear of future harm and the costs they incurred in order to protect their communications with overseas persons from surveillance.

Is worrying that one's communications might be surveilled by itself a sufficient injury to confer standing?

In addition to "ordinary citizens," sometimes Congresspeople have attempted to use the court system to challenge executive actions related to national security. In these kinds of cases the legislators typically do not sue as individual citizens: instead, they sue on behalf of Congress or a part of Congress, alleging their branch of government has been wronged. The ability of Congresspeople to sue in this capacity has been severely curtailed by the Supreme Court, which has ruled that for legislators suing in their institutional capacity to have standing, they must prove their votes have been "completely nullified" by the action they are complaining about. *Raines v. Byrd*. While it is not entirely clear what "completely nullified" means, the Supreme Court has exhorted that simply being on the losing side of a legislative vote does *not* mean a legislator's vote has been nullified. For discussion of what "completely nullified" might mean, see No Standing: *Campbell v. Clinton*. This "completely nullified" standard seems unlikely to be met except in rare cases, possibly requiring that Congress properly enact a law, including presidential signature or overriding a presidential veto, and then the President clearly violating that law, thus nullifying Congress' constitutional right to enact law. The "completely nullified" standard is in part intended to prevent courts from becoming ensnared in political battles between the branches, especially before it is clear that the political differences have produced an actual legal controversy.

No Standing: *Campbell v. Clinton*

In 1999, approximately 30 members of the House of Representatives sued President Clinton for his use of United States military forces in the former Yugoslavia. Congress' actions regarding the authorization for the use of force in the conflict were confusing. On one hand, the House had voted against a declaration of war and against an authorization of air strikes. On the other hand, the House had also voted against a resolution ordering an immediate end to the United States contribution to NATO activities in the region and had approved a prohibition on using appropriated funds for deployment of United States *ground* troops unless a specific appropriation was made. Both houses of Congress approved an appropriations bill for the conflict in Yugoslavia.

> When President Clinton subsequently authorized continued air strikes in Yugoslavia, the Representatives sued to block the military action. When challenged on standing, they argued that their votes had been completely nullified by President Clinton's actions. Both the federal district court and circuit court of appeals disagreed. The district judge noted that Congress (as a whole) had not specifically prohibited (or required) the President from doing anything that he had done (or not done) and thus there was no actual "confrontation or impasse between the branches." Extending this logic further, the circuit court of appeals noted that the "complete nullification" standard is not met when the government simply did something that part of Congress voted against. Rather, the court held that for standing to exist, the legislator plaintiffs would have to have "no legislative remedy" for their alleged injury. In other words, unless the Legislative Branch has no ability to restrict the President's action by using its legislative power (for example, when Congress has acted unambiguously and the President has acted contrary to that unambiguous action), legislators suing will not be considered to have been sufficiently "injured" to have standing.

4.3.2. Ripeness

In contrast to standing, which focuses on *who* can bring a claim, three other doctrines—ripeness, the political question doctrine, and the **state secrets privilege**—focus on the claim itself. The Supreme Court has created the rule that before a court can adjudicate a case it must be "ripe." Ripeness relates primarily to the *timing* of a case. A court might dismiss a case because the facts are not yet sufficiently developed. A case that is not ripe is simply not yet ready for adjudication because it is contingent on future events that might not occur as anticipated, or might not occur at all.

The requirement that a case be "ripe" is based on constitutional and prudential concerns. Courts have decided that they should not entangle themselves in abstract disagreements. Waiting until the facts of a case are fully developed allows the court's opinion to benefit from a focus sharpened by clearly knowable, actual facts. Additionally, waiting until the facts are clear enough to present an actual controversy, rather than a hypothetical one, allows courts to avoid unnecessary constitutional decisions. This is consistent with the doctrine of **constitutional avoidance**, which holds that courts should decide cases without resorting to interpreting the Constitution if at all possible.

As with the issue of standing, courts have been especially reluctant to decide cases brought by members of Congress, or Congress itself, against the President until the political branches have reached a "constitutional loggerhead." This likely requires an affirmative vote by Congress and a contrary action by the President.

In *Doe v. Bush*, the judiciary used the ripeness doctrine to avoid deciding a case regarding the President's and Congress's national security powers prior to the 2003 invasion of Iraq by the United States A group of plaintiffs that included servicemembers, their families, Congresspeople, and others, sued to prevent President George W. Bush from beginning a war with Iraq. The plaintiffs argued that the military action would be unconstitutional because the President would be violating the terms of the Authorization for the Use of Military Force that Congress had passed in October of 2002 (2002 AUMF). They contended the 2002 AUMF required that the United Nations Security Council also authorize the use of military force, which had not occurred. The federal district and appellate courts determined that the case was not yet ripe. On March 13, 2003, the First Circuit Court of Appeals found that "[m]any important questions remain unanswered." According to the court, one of those questions was whether there would be a war at all, given that diplomatic negotiations were ongoing. The court pointed to the President's repeated emphasis that hostilities could be avoided if Iraq took certain actions, actions that Iraq still had the opportunity to take. Additionally, the court noted that the Security Council was still debating the possibility of passing a new resolution. The court found that to decide the plaintiffs' claim would require the court to "pile one hypothesis on top of another. [The court] would need to assume that the Security Council will not authorize war, and that the President will proceed nonetheless." Noting that the "the circumstances call for judicial restraint," the court dismissed the case. On March 19, 2003, less than one week after the court's ruling that the case was not yet ripe, the United States invaded Iraq.

4.3.3. Political Question Doctrine

The **political question doctrine** is the idea that courts should not answer questions that are properly the province of the political—Legislative and Executive—Branches. At its core, the political question doctrine is concerned with the judiciary's proper role in our system of government, a concern that involves both judicial competence—the *ability* of the courts to comprehend and decide such questions—and constitutional function. Unfortunately, the political question doctrine is famously complex and unclear, making it difficult to predict accurately whether the courts will apply the political question doctrine in a particular case. Indeed, some argue this lack of predictability provides courts the flexibility to use the political question doctrine to avoid deciding cases they do not want to decide.

The political question doctrine was first articulated by the Supreme Court in *Baker v. Carr*, which was a voting apportionment case, not a national security case. In *Baker*, the Court noted that there are some questions courts should not answer and identified a variety of factors courts should consider when deciding whether a case poses a "political question"—rather than a legal question—that is inappropriate for judicial determination:

> (1) whether there is a textually demonstrable constitutional commitment of the issue to a coordinate political department;
>
> (2) a lack of judicially discoverable and manageable standards for resolving it;
>
> (3) the impossibility of deciding without an initial policy determination of a kind clearly for non-judicial discretion;
>
> (4) the impossibility of a court's undertaking independent resolution without expressing lack of the respect due coordinate branches of government;
>
> (5) an unusual need for unquestioning adherence to a political decision already made;
>
> (6) the potentiality of embarrassment from multifarious pronouncements by various departments on one question; or
>
> (7) other prudential considerations.

The difficulty in predicting the applicability of the political question doctrine starts from the ambiguous meaning of most of the factors in the above list. For example, what does "textual commitment to a coordinate political branch" mean? Most basically, it means that Courts cannot do things the Constitution says other branches do. However, while it is perfectly clear that, for example, the Court cannot appoint ambassadors—the President is given that power in Article II—does that mean the Court cannot decide cases related to the President's appointment of ambassadors? Additionally, the judiciary's power of judicial review allows it to strike down entire acts passed by Congress and signed by the President, even though the responsibility to create law is "textually committed" to the other branches. Moreover, what if the case involves "explicit textual commitment" to multiple branches? Indeed, as discussed elsewhere in this book, the Constitution does not grant the war power exclusively to either the Legislative or the Executive Branch. Typically, this factor presents itself in the form of courts demanding that where the Constitution seems to confer on both political branches some authority, some level of participation by both branches is required.

However, once such participation is demonstrated, courts often defer to the branches regarding the manner of mutual participation, deciding that such questions are political.

Another factor, the "impossibility of deciding an issue without an initial policy determination," suggests some reluctance on the part of courts to decide issues that will have an impact on public policy. However, it also recognizes the real limitation that sometimes a case cannot be decided until one of the other branches acts first. For example, a court cannot decide whether a particular foreign official has immunity, unless and until the President formally recognizes that foreign government.

Perhaps the most significant factor is the third in the *Baker v. Carr* list: lack of criteria or standards by which court can make a decision. Courts apply law to facts to make decisions. Stated differently, the law constitutes a "standard" against which the court can measure facts to determine whether the standard has been met or violated. When no legal standard is available, the court simply cannot decide whether it has been met. *El-Shifa Pharmaceutical Company* is an example of such a case. In response to Al Qaeda bombings of United States embassies in Kenya and Tanzania, President William Clinton ordered missile strikes against various locations, including the Shifa pharmaceutical factory in Sudan. The factory was thought to be funded by Osama Bin Laden and producing an essential ingredient for nerve gas. After the bombing, the Shifa plant owners, who argued they had no part in production of nerve gas, sued the United States in United States federal court. They argued the CIA acted negligently in investigating the plant's alleged ties to chemical weapons production.

The First Circuit Court of Appeals held that the case presented a non-justiciable political question because the decision to launch the military attack on the Shifa plant was constitutionally committed to the political branches (Art I, Section 8, Clause 11; and Art II, Section 2, Clause 1) and because the court was "neither an effective nor appropriate forum" for reexamining the merits of the attack. The court noted that some questions in their nature are political and beyond the power of the courts to resolve. The court observed that the United States' response to alleged terrorist activities of foreign organizations present nonjusticiable political questions because the judiciary has neither the aptitude nor the responsibility to address the appropriateness of a response.

Courts lack the competence to assess strategic decisions of military matters such as the sufficiency of intelligence. Moreover, regardless of the sufficiency of intelligence, *whether* to conduct a military strike is a policy decision with political consequences, the merits of which courts should not address. In addition to the competence of the court, the lack of judicially discoverable standards was clear in this case. Though the suit was a tort claim that the government acted negligently, and courts routinely examine tort claims applying the standards of tort law, the *real* question presented by the case was whether the United States "did the wrong thing" in choosing to attack the pharmaceutical plant. When viewed that way, it was a political question.

Federal courts commonly use the political question doctrine to avoid deciding cases that relate to foreign relations. But, as demonstrated throughout this book, courts have occasionally decided such cases. In fact, as recently as 2012, the Supreme Court heard a case involving the recognition of Jerusalem as part of Israel and explicitly declared that it did *not* present a political question. *Zivotofsky v. Clinton*. The 8–1 opinion suggested most Justices did not accept the idea that "foreign affairs" automatically equals "political question."

Predicting whether a court might dismiss an action due to the political question doctrine seems to be extraordinarily difficult. Indeed, as one former Acting Legal Adviser for the United States Department of State once opined, there is "no generally applicable principle that helps us determine in advance whether a court will determine that a particular matter is a political question." Nevertheless, in assessing whether a case might present a political question, it is important to identify clearly what specific question the case poses. Then, if answering that question would require the court to make a policy determination, or if the law does not provide a standard for answering the question, the case might pose a political question. For example, in *El-Shifa Pharmaceutical*, though the case presented a question of whether a tort had been committed, answering that question necessarily required the court to answer this question: *should* the United States have bombed the plant under the circumstances? Because that question is a policy question for which there was no legal standard for the court to apply, it declined to adjudicate the case.

4.4. STATE SECRETS

4.4.1. State Secrets Privilege

The inadmissibility at trial of critical evidence can significantly affect, or even terminate, a court's ability to resolve a case. Federal courts have decided that some evidence is "**privileged**," and therefore protected from disclosure during litigation and from admission at trial. Privileged communications can occur in a variety of contexts, such as between spouses, between a patient and his doctor, or between an attorney and her client. The purpose of a privilege is to encourage and protect full and honest communications by removing the fear that the statement may later be used against the person making it.

In the national security context, there is an evidentiary privilege protecting "state secrets," which under certain circumstances, can be excluded altogether from the case. When the government decides that certain evidence in a case is a "state secret," it must assert the privilege. Though courts have not provided a concrete definition of "state secrets," former United States Attorney General Eric Holder once identified those circumstances in which information would constitute a state secret: "information the unauthorized disclosure of which reasonably could be expected to cause significant harm to the national defense or foreign relations." The information need not be "classified" to be considered a "state secret," though in practice, it usually is. Importantly, the government can assert that certain communications are state secrets even when the government is not a party to the case. If the state secrets privilege is applied by the court, the privileged evidence cannot be used in the litigation. The case can move on to trial, unless state secrets are so interconnected with the case that the case cannot proceed without the information. In this situation, dismissal of the entire case is required.

The process of applying the state secret privilege involves multiple steps. First, the government must assert the privilege; no other party can claim or waive the privilege. Then, the court must make an independent determination of whether "from all the circumstances of the case . . . there is a reasonable danger that compulsion of the evidence will expose . . . matters which, in the interest of national security, should not be divulged." *United States v. Reynolds*. This places on the court a special burden to strike an appropriate balance between protecting national security matters and preserving an open court system. If the privileged evidence can be disentangled from the non-privileged evidence, the case can proceed with the non-privileged evidence. However, there are three circumstances in which the court may have to dismiss the entire case: 1) if the plaintiff cannot prove the required elements of the claim without the privileged evidence; 2) if the privilege deprives the defendant of the information that would otherwise give the defendant a valid defense to the claim; or 3) if the excluded evidence is so inseparable from non-privileged evidence that litigating the case would present an unacceptable risk of disclosing state secrets.

State Secrets and *United States v. Reynolds*

The case in which the Supreme Court first announced the state secrets privilege was *United States v. Reynolds,* which involved the crash of a United States Air Force B-29 aircraft containing secret electronic surveillance equipment. The spouses of three deceased passengers on the flight sued the Air Force for wrongful death, and in the course of the litigation requested a copy of the Air Force's accident investigation report. The United States asserted that an evidentiary privilege should apply to the accident investigation report because it referenced secret electronic equipment that should not be disclosed. The government further argued that because the existence of the electronic equipment on the flight was a state secret, and the crash of the flight was central to the plaintiff's claim, the entire case should be dismissed. In 1953, the Supreme Court ruled that certain evidence was a state secret, but allowed the case to proceed without the privileged evidence. The government subsequently settled the case with the plaintiffs for $300,000. In 2000, the accident investigation report the plaintiffs had requested, but had been denied, was declassified and made available to the public. The report showed the cause of the crash to be a fire. Though the report mentioned that secret electronic equipment was on board, it provided no details about the equipment beyond what had been reported in the press at the time of the crash, suggesting to some that the government's assertion of the privilege had been fraudulent.

4.4.2. The *Totten* Bar

State secrets' impact on the judicial process has arguably expanded an evidentiary privilege to a justiciability issue because some state secrets evidence can be so integral to the case that its exclusion has the practical effect of ending the case. Related to the idea that some secrets are privileged and cannot be disclosed during litigation is the idea that in rare instances the very subject matter of the litigation itself is a state secret. The Supreme Court has said courts should dismiss such cases entirely. The Court first announced this rule in *Totten v. United States*, a case in which the estate of a Civil War spy sued the federal government for breaching an alleged contract for espionage under which the United States owed compensation to the spy. The Supreme Court held that the entire litigation was barred because the "existence of a contract for secret services with the government" could itself not be disclosed.

Later national security-related cases affirmed this principle. In one case, plaintiffs sued the United States Navy, complaining that an environmental impact study should be conducted for a facility in Hawaii where the Navy was suspected of storing nuclear weapons. The Supreme Court again held that even the allegations themselves were "beyond judicial scrutiny" because, for national security reasons, the Navy could "neither admit nor deny that it proposes to store nuclear weapons" at the site. *Weinberger v. Catholic Action of Hawaii*. In a more recent spy-related case reminiscent of *Totten*, the Supreme Court again held that a suit in which two Cold War-era spies alleged the CIA breached its contract for espionage services could not be adjudicated because the very existence of such an agreement would be a state secret. *Tenet v. Doe.*

Distinguishing between the ***Totten* bar** and the state secrets *privilege* can be difficult, especially because the result of either can be the non-adjudication of a case due to a required dismissal. The key difference is that the state secrets privilege means that specific evidence cannot be disclosed or admitted, whereas a *Totten* bar means that the case itself is about a state secret.

Perhaps because of the draconian result of applying the *Totten* bar (the litigation is ended), it has been applied by the Supreme Court in only the three cases mentioned above. The Court offered little guidance in those three cases regarding how and when the *Totten* bar should be applied, and courts prefer to address these issues by applying the somewhat clearer state secrets privilege. Regardless of the method by which courts limit such cases, however, the result is reduced judicial participation in matters of national security.

4.5. COURTS' LIMITED INVOLVEMENT IN NATIONAL SECURITY CASES

Though the above discussion explains some common ways courts have avoided deciding national security cases, the question remains: why do courts seem to be more deferential to the other branches in this area than in other legal areas? Why, as the Supreme Court noted, are "matters intimately related to foreign policy and national security . . . rarely proper subjects for judicial intervention?" *Haig v. Agee.* The Supreme Court occasionally hears national security cases, but agrees to consider very few, and ultimately chooses not to actually decide some of the few it considers.

One explanation for the judiciary's irregular and hesitant participation in national security matters is the lack of authority granted to the judiciary in the constitutional text. In contrast to the explicitly articulated national security powers for Congress and the President in Articles I and II of the Constitution discussed in previous chapters, Article III of the Constitution is relatively silent regarding the courts' powers in the national security context. Indeed, courts have expressed their awareness of this difference. For instance, in a case assessing the indefinite military detention of a detainee that the military had labeled an "enemy combatant," one federal appeals court noted "Article III contains nothing analogous to the specific powers of war carefully enumerated in Articles I and II." *Hamdi v. Rumsfeld.* But that is true of many areas not mentioned in Article III, where courts nevertheless regularly exert immense influence. Most significantly, the power of judicial review was not explicitly given to the courts by the Constitution, but nevertheless the Supreme Court assumed it in *Marbury v. Madison.* Additionally, records of the Constitutional Convention tell us little about the **Framers'** original intent regarding federal courts' responsibility in general, and virtually nothing about their intent regarding judicial participation in national security matters.

A more cynical explanation of courts' behavior in this area might be concerns for their own institutional legitimacy. One important check on judicial overreach is the reality that courts have no way to enforce their decisions, so they rely on adherence to, and enforcement of, those decisions by the other branches. Perhaps in this area more than any other, courts may be worried their pronouncements would go unheeded in the face of a security crisis. It is not difficult to imagine a President, firmly convinced that military action was necessary to protect the nation, electing to ignore a judicial decision that the military action was unconstitutional or illegal. Indeed, the only known example of a President explicitly announcing he would ignore a Supreme Court decision occurred in the context of treaties with Native American tribes. After the Supreme Court struck down a Georgia law regulating white citizens' abilities to come and go from Indian Territory, President Jackson famously quipped "John Marshall has made his decision; now let him enforce it." But, not all national security cases from which courts seem to shy away relate to clear existential threats to the nation, suggesting something other than concern that their edicts might be ignored may be involved.

A practical explanation may simply be that courts are aware of their relative lack of competence to decide national security cases. Most judges lack the training and experience to assess the sufficiency of intelligence, the reality of threats, the costs and benefits of various military responses, and other factors that might impact whether a particular national security action should, or should not, be taken.

Beyond competence, however, is the idea that in the realm of national security, courts have recognized that it is not their role to decide matters potentially affecting the continued security—or existence—of the Nation. Unlike most other areas of law, where judicial decisions affect *how* government works, in the national security arena, judicial decisions, if obeyed, could affect *if* government works—or exists—at all. Perhaps Justices and judges realize such portentous policy questions are usually best left to democratically elected officials, as the political question doctrine suggests.

And yet, courts do participate from time to time. As Justice Jackson asserted in *Youngstown*, a case in which the Supreme Court powerfully participated to strike down President Truman's action, courts are responsible to preserve the "equilibrium established by our constitutional system." Courts' vital role requires "just enough" participation to ensure balance in the national security system, and courts largely determine for themselves what is "just enough."

REVIEW QUESTIONS

1. What three elements must a plaintiff show to demonstrate standing?

2. Explain ripeness and how it relates to justiciability.

3. What factors does a court consider when deciding whether a case poses a "political question?"

4. What is required for the state secrets privilege to apply? What are the two principal ways in which a successful assertion of the state secrets privilege might affect a case?

5. What are some explanations for why courts seem to participate less in national security matters than in other areas of legal dispute?

CRITICAL THINKING QUESTIONS

1. Given that courts decide whether a case or controversy exists, how significant a limitation on the federal courts' authority to hear national security cases is the Constitution's "case and controversy" requirement?

2. Which of the various reasons why courts might not want to decide national security cases is most persuasive to you? Can you think of a better reason?

3. Considering the state secrets privilege, is it fair to a plaintiff that an otherwise valid case may be dismissed simply because proving the case or defending against it would risk exposing a national security secret? Should such plaintiffs be compensated in some other way? Is there a better way to balance the federal government's need for secrecy in some matters with injured parties' need for compensation?

4. Are the state secrets privilege and so-called *Totten* bar examples of the national security power of courts or the Executive? Both?

5. If courts create and interpret their own rules governing when they will hear cases, are the justiciability doctrines and privileges discussed in this chapter *actual limitations* on judicial involvement in national security matters?

6. Some scholars have labeled the courts' role in national security matters as "self-defining." Do you agree with that label?

CHAPTER 5

Separate and Overlapping Constitutional Powers

Vietnam War Memorial at night, Washington, D.C.

Learning Objectives

1. Understand how courts analyze national security questions where the authority of multiple branches is at issue and develop a personal methodology for how such questions should be decided.

2. Know the legal authorities applicable during various points during the Vietnam War.

3. Analyze provisions of the War Powers Resolution in light of the Constitution and each branch of government's national security responsibilities.

5.1. INTRODUCTION

In the three previous chapters, we examined the legal authority of each of the branches somewhat independently. We now turn to a more thorough discussion of how the authority of each branch may relate and overlap with each other. First, we will briefly identify the most significant structural change Congress implemented in the government's national security apparatus in the Twentieth Century: the 1947 National Security Act. Then we will consider two judicial articulations of the relationship between the political branches: Justice Jackson's approach in *Youngstown Sheet and Tube Co. v. Sawyer* and the Supreme Court's modern adaptation of that understanding in *Dames & Moore v. Regan*. Then we will analyze the interplay between the three branches in the context of a real and controversial national security situation: the Vietnam War. Next, we will examine Congress's attempt to "prevent another Vietnam" through enactment of the War Powers Resolution, a statute still in effect today, but which has been challenged as unconstitutional by Presidents. Finally, we will examine modern uses of force to assess the efficacy of the War Powers Resolution.

5.2. THE NATIONAL SECURITY ACT OF 1947

In the wake of World War II, the National Security Act of 1947 (NSA) constituted a massive reorganization of the military and intelligence functions of the United States government. The NSA created a unified national security system, and placed it entirely under the President's control.

Militarily, the NSA created what is now called the Department of Defense (DOD), and placed within it the Army, Navy, and newly-formed Air Force. Importantly, the NSA reaffirmed civilian control of the military by placing the integrated military services under the Secretary of Defense, who answers directly to the President. Congress later ensured civilian control of the military in subsequent statutes requiring that the Secretary of Defense and principal deputies be "appointed from civilian life."

In the NSA, Congress gave formal, explicit authority to the President for intelligence gathering by creating the Central Intelligence Agency (CIA). This was the first peacetime authorization of an intelligence agency. Some argue that in the NSA, Congress for the first time implicitly gave authority for covert actions by an intelligence agency, when it authorized "such other functions and duties related to intelligence affecting the national security as the National Security Council may from time to time direct."

Finally, the NSA created the National Security Council (NSC) to advise the President regarding military and intelligence activities, and directed the President to coordinate national security policy through the NSC.

Critically, what Congress did *not* do in the NSA was mention or defend its role or the courts' role in foreign policy decision making. After the controversial and protracted Vietnam War, Congress appeared to recognize this omission, enacting numerous foreign policy-related statutes that asserted a congressional role in foreign policy. Most significant of these was the War Powers Resolution (WPR), which we will analyze at the end of this chapter.

5.3. *YOUNGSTOWN SHEET AND TUBE CO. V. SAWYER*: AN ANALYTICAL FRAMEWORK FOR SEPARATION OF POWERS

In Chapter 2 we examined one of the most important cases the Supreme Court has decided regarding the national security powers of the President and Congress: *Youngstown Sheet & Tube Co. v. Sawyer*. The significance of the case was highlighted by the five different opinions the Justices filed regarding various theories of presidential power. Recall that President Truman's seizure of the steel mills to support the Korean War effort was ultimately overturned by the Supreme Court, which rejected a variety of arguments for a presidential power to seize domestic steel mills, including the President's Commander in Chief power, emergency power, take care power, and customary power.

The *Youngstown* opinion that has withstood the test of time as most important among those offered by the Justices is not Justice Black's "opinion of the Court," but rather Justice Jackson's concurrence. In fact, 30 years later, Justice Jackson's concurrence would become precedent, when adopted by a majority of the Supreme Court in *Dames & Moore v. Regan*, discussed below. Justice Jackson understood the complexity of questions regarding which branch has authority to do what under the Constitution. At the beginning of his concurrence, he lamented:

> A judge, like an executive adviser, may be surprised at the poverty of really useful and unambiguous authority applicable to concrete problems of executive power as they actually present themselves. Just what our forefathers did envision, or would have envisioned had they foreseen modern conditions, must be divined from materials almost as enigmatic as the dreams Joseph was called upon to interpret for Pharaoh. A century and a half of partisan debate and scholarly speculation yields no net result but only supplies more or less apt

quotations from respected sources on each side of any question. They largely cancel each other.

With that awareness, Justice Jackson then attempted to make sense of the question of each branch's national security power. Regarding Congress's role in national security, Justice Jackson suggested Congress should have an opportunity to participate in setting foreign policy, and that the President should not act without Congress's participation except in a few narrow areas in which the President has "conclusive and preclusive" authority. And Justice Jackson charged courts with preserving the "equilibrium established by our constitutional system." Justice Jackson asserted a vital role in maintaining *balance* in the national security system, imploring courts not to simply defer to the political branches in matters of national security and allow imbalance.

The primary focus of Justice Jackson's concurrence was on describing this balance between the President's and Congress's national security power. In constructing this equilibrium, Jackson suggested three categories of situations where the executive and legislative authority interact: 1) when the President acts consistently with authority delegated or approved by Congress; 2) when the President acts with Congress's **acquiescence**; and 3) when the President acts inconsistently with Congress's will.

Table 5.1

Category 1

Category 2

Category 3

5.3.1. When the President Acts Pursuant to *Delegated Authority* ("Category One")

Citing the *Curtiss-Wright* and *Lichter* cases we discussed in Chapter 2, Justice Jackson noted that the President's authority is at its maximum when the President acts pursuant to congressionally delegated authority. Stated "mathematically," in this situation, the President's authority equals all the powers the President has under the Constitution *plus* all of Congress' powers that it has lawfully delegated. Thus, the President's action can only be unconstitutional if the federal government *as a whole* lacks the authority for that action. As Justice Jackson asserted, a President's action taken pursuant to specific congressional authorization is "supported by the strongest of presumptions and the widest latitude of judicial interpretation, and the burden of persuasion would rest heavily upon any who might attack it."

5.3.2. When President Acts with Congressional *Acquiescence* ("Category Two")

Justice Jackson described Category Two cases as when the President acts in the absence of an explicit congressional grant of authority or disapproval—in other words, with Congress's acquiescence. Referring to this category as the "zone of twilight," Jackson noted that in these cases, the President and Congress have uncertain—and perhaps shared—authority. The idea is that when the President's actions are not clearly within his constitutional power, but also do not clearly violate Congress's will, it is difficult to say whether the President is acting outside his authority. Acquiescence, discussed in detail in Chapters 2 and 3, is the idea that when Congress knows about a practice of the Executive and fails to object or interfere, it is accepting that the President has the authority he is exercising. In these situations, Congress's view is unknown. To the Supreme Court, an important element of determining which branch has which powers relies on the branches themselves to exert their power. Congressional silence creates a vacuum the President's actions may fill.

5.3.3. When the President Takes Measures Incompatible with the Will of Congress ("Category Three")

According to Justice Jackson, Category Three cases are those where the President acts in a way that is incompatible with the will of Congress. Thus, the sum of the President's power is his constitutional power, *minus* Congress's asserted constitutional power. In these cases, courts must choose which branch has the contested power. The court first decides whether a branch has "acted outside the constitutionally prescribed means of conduct," or aggrandized itself by using power that is demonstrably and uniquely committed to the other branch. If so, then that branch's action is unconstitutional. If not, the court must consider whether the acting branch has exercised power in such a way that it disrupts the functioning of one or both of the other branches, and weigh that disruption against the asserted need for the exercise of power.

In 1989, Justice Kennedy elaborated on the Court's approach to "Category Three" cases. *Public Citizen v. DOJ*. He suggested there are two types of Category Three cases: those where the Constitution expressly confers power on one branch and those where the Constitution is silent. In the former types of cases, the Constitution has already struck a balance between branches and assigned the power to one branch. An example of this would be Justice Black's approach to *Youngstown*, in which he noted that the Constitution gave Congress the specific applicable authorities and did not give such authority to the President. An example in the other direction might be if Congress attempted to pardon someone; Congress does not share any part of the power that the Constitution expressly grants to the President to confer pardons, so Congress would not have that authority.

In cases where the Constitution is silent, Justice Kennedy opined that a court should strike down attempts by one branch to usurp the other's power. Courts use a balancing approach to determine whether the congressional action prevents the President from accomplishing his constitutionally assigned functions and whether the extent of the intrusion on the President's powers is "justified by an overriding need to promote objectives within the constitutional authority of Congress." For example, in the investigation into President Nixon's involvement in the Watergate scandal, the Supreme Court allowed potentially incriminatory tape recordings to be turned over to the independent counsel. This took away prosecutorial decision-making from the branch under investigation, but when Congress requested the same recordings, the Supreme Court said no, because of its concern about one branch exerting too much power over the other.

As Justice Kennedy noted, national security cases are usually "Category Two" cases, because either (a) the Constitution is silent or (b) authority over the action at issue is assigned to both branches. National security cases rarely fall into Jackson's "Category Three."

Justice Jackson's approach has since been adopted as binding precedent, but it is difficult to say how useful it is. Though the tripartite approach might help us *categorize* cases, his approach is more descriptive than prescriptive. That is, Justice Jackson's approach might explain which "category" of case is presented by a particular set of facts, but it does not always instruct courts what to *do* with a case in that category, especially when Congress's **delegation of authority** is unclear, its acquiescence uncertain, or its authority to express a contrary will indeterminate. When confronted with a difficult question, as category two and three cases often present, Justice Jackson's approach describes the question, but does not provide the *answer* to the question. And of course, it is not always entirely clear in which category a particular case should be placed. For example, Justice Jackson opined that *Youngstown* was a Category Three case. Buy why was it not a Category Two case? Congress had not specifically barred what President Truman did. And in fact, Congress did nothing when President Truman notified Congress that he had acted until Congress legislated. Though an earlier Congress had considered a similar law, it did not pass it. But it is unclear whether that inaction meant it was implicitly disapproving the President's authority to seize an industry under the circumstances or just not expressing an opinion at all.

5.3.4. *Dames & Moore*: Jackson's View of *Youngstown* Made Law

The more recent case of *Dames & Moore v. Regan* builds upon *Youngstown*, establishing two important precedents. First, the Court explicitly canonized the idea that congressional acquiescence can serve as a basis for presidential authority. Second, the majority opinion accepted Justice Jackson's approach to classifying executive action in three categories, while recognizing its limitations.

After 52 American hostages were captured in Iran in 1979, President Carter declared a national emergency under the International Emergency Economic Powers Act (IEEPA), and blocked removal or transfer of Iranian assets. Eventually, the hostages were released pursuant to an agreement between Iran and the United States under which the United States was required to: 1) terminate all legal proceedings in United States courts involving claims by United States nationals against Iran; 2) nullify all attachments of assets and judgments in those cases; and 3) transfer United States-held Iranian assets to foreign banks for satisfaction of any arbitration awards that might arise. President Carter issued an order consistent with the United States obligations under the agreement, and *Dames & Moore*, a company that lost its significant financial claims against Iran because of President Carter's orders, filed an action to prevent enforcement of the orders.

In response to the plaintiffs' assertion that President Carter did not have authority to suspend claims pending in American courts, the government claimed that both the IEEPA and the Hostage Act provided statutory authority for the President to suspend claims. The Supreme Court held those *statutes* did not themselves provide authority, but the Court was unwilling to say the President lacked the power to settle the claims under the circumstances because Congress had acquiesced in the President's actions. Specifically, the Court noted that though the statutes themselves did not provide authority, "enactment of legislation closely related to the question of the President's authority in a particular case which evinces legislative intent to accord the President broad discretion may be considered to 'invite measures on independent presidential responsibility.' " (quoting Justice Jackson's *Youngstown* concurrence). The Court agreed that Congress's acquiescence may be enough to give the President authority for certain actions, even when there is no statute or constitutional provision explicitly granting that authority. Quoting Justice Frankfurter's *Youngstown* concurrence, the Court articulated the requirements for such Congressional acquiescence: "a systematic, unbroken, executive practice, long pursued to the knowledge of the Congress and never before questioned . . . may be treated as a gloss on 'Executive Power' vested in the President by [Article II, Section 1]" Importantly, the Court did not fully explain what acquiescence must involve. Specifically, the Court did not answer whether acquiescence required actual action by Congress, like IEEPA and the Hostage Act represented in the case, or if Congress's acquiescence could come in the form of mere silence. The Court distinguished the facts in *Dames & Moore* from those in *Youngstown* by noting that President Truman's actions in *Youngstown* involved not the " 'plenary and exclusive power of the President,' but rather . . . a claim of virtually unlimited powers for the Executive."

In addition to firmly establishing precedent that acquiescence is a viable constitutional theory of presidential authority, the *Dames & Moore* opinion clarified the significance of Justice Jackson's tripartite classification of executive actions. The Court agreed that Jackson's approach was "analytically useful," but cautioned against deducing that questions of executive authority could be neatly divided. Noting that Justice Jackson himself understood his categories represented "a somewhat over-simplified grouping," the Court issued the modern understanding of the relationship between executive action and congressional authority: "it is doubtless the case that executive action in any particular instance falls not neatly in one of three pigeonholes, but rather at some point along a spectrum running from explicit congressional authorization to explicit congressional prohibition." Nevertheless, the Court's decision in *Dames & Moore* can be viewed as preserving the "equilibrium established by our constitutional system" in upholding a presidential action to which there had been no congressional objection.

5.4. SEPARATION OF POWERS CASE STUDY: VIETNAM

With this background of the Supreme Court's understanding of shared national security authority, we now turn to an in-depth examination of the legality of the conflict in Vietnam. This study is a helpful way to review what we understand about each branch's national security authorities and how they work together in the context of real military hostilities. Examining a war that concluded nearly a half century ago is worthwhile for several reasons. First, it is perhaps the most controversial external war the United States has undertaken, meaning there were numerous legal and political challenges to the claimed authority for the war. Second, the conflict presents an outstanding example of the tension between Congress and the President that demonstrates how the Constitution, treaties, and statutes interrelate to affect policy decisions. Additionally, the Vietnam conflict highlights questions of whether law can control policy or political branches. Third, the war presents a practical example of the various theories of executive power discussed in previous chapters. Fourth, the various judicial opinions regarding the legality of the conflict suggest the limited extent to which courts will opine on the legality of military action. Finally, investigating the legal authorities for the conflict sheds light on the view that the Vietnam conflict was illegal because Congress did not declare war or authorize the conflict. After our exploration, you will have a more informed view of the conflict, and of how national security law applies in practice.

5.4.1. Vietnam: The War

Vietnam was a French colony occupied by the Japanese during WWII. In the power vacuum that followed the Japanese withdrawal after WWII, France asserted that Vietnam was still its colony. But, an indigenous government led by Ho Chi Minh declared an independent state: the Democratic Republic of Vietnam. France and the Viet Minh (Ho Chi Minh's followers) subsequently engaged in a guerrilla-style war. Ho Chi Minh requested assistance in this war from the United States, which refused. Beginning in 1950, Ho Chi Minh's independence movement began to receive assistance from communist China.

Following an embarrassing military defeat at the hands of the Viet Minh in 1954, the French agreed to withdraw from Vietnam and a conference involving numerous nations produced an agreement (the **Geneva Accord**) to divide the country into North Vietnam, controlled by the Viet Minh, and South Vietnam, eventually governed by elected President Ngo Dinh Diem. The agreement also provided for an election in 1956 to create a government for a unified Vietnamese state. Concerned that the communist-backed Viet Minh might win the election, thereby creating a communist reunified Vietnam, the United States began engaging in paramilitary operations against North Vietnam and militarily supporting South Vietnam. The 1956 election would never occur.

Despite, or perhaps in part because of, United States assistance to South Vietnam, a communist-based rebel insurgency began in the South, run by the Viet Cong. Eventually, the Viet Cong became controlled by Ho Chi Minh, who began sending North Vietnamese military forces into South Vietnam to support the Viet Cong insurgency.

In 1954, the United States entered into the **Southeast Asia Collective Defense Treaty (SEATO Treaty)**, which provided for the collective defense of all member nations. The United States successfully added South Vietnam to the list of states that would be defended, despite South Vietnam not being a member of the treaty or an independent state recognized by most nations. The United States' motivation for this **collective self-defense** was primarily to address the "**domino theory**," which imagined that the spread of communism to one country would lead to many other Asian nations adopting communism. In 1961, President Kennedy sent over 400 special forces troops to South Vietnam and the United States engaged in covert attacks against North Vietnam and North Vietnamese forces in neighboring Laos. United States military involvement in Vietnam grew steadily, and by the time President Johnson replaced the assassinated President Kennedy in November 1963, over 16,000 United States troops were in South Vietnam.

Though accounts differ, the United States' military buildup and activity in Vietnam and Laos was largely hidden from Congress until some North Vietnamese boats attacked a United States Navy vessel in the Tonkin Gulf. Though significant factual dispute remains over whether the attacks on the United States Navy were the result of United States provocation, the United States responded to the North Vietnamese attacks militarily. The Johnson

Administration then sought approval of military action in Vietnam from Congress, which gave its approval in the form of the Tonkin Gulf Resolution.

5.4.2. Tonkin Gulf Resolution

In August 1964, Congress enacted, and the President signed into law, the **Gulf of Tonkin Resolution** (also known as the Tonkin Gulf Resolution or TGR), which provided the President with congressional authority to take military action in Vietnam. Specifically, it said:

> The Congress approves and supports the determination of the President, as Commander in Chief, to take all necessary measures to repel any armed attack against the forces of the United States and to prevent further aggression.
>
> . . .
>
> [T]he United States is . . . prepared, as the President determines, to take all necessary steps, including the use of armed force, to assist any member or protocol state of the Southeast Asia Collective Defense Treaty requesting assistance in defense of its freedom.

Following passage of the Tonkin Gulf Resolution, President Johnson escalated the scope of United States military involvement in Vietnam. In May, 1965, Congress approved a $700 million appropriation specifically for the military effort, including increasing troop levels. By the end of 1965, over 184,000 United States troops were in Vietnam, a number that grew to over 530,000 at its peak in 1968.

After suffering military and political setbacks, and amid a growing public opposition to the war effort, in 1968 President Johnson began to reduce troop levels in Vietnam. Eventually, Congress repealed the Tonkin Gulf Resolution in 1971. But Congress continued appropriating funds and renewing the selective service law that enabled **conscription** (the draft). In fact, Congress did not unambiguously end appropriations for combat operations in Vietnam, Laos, or Cambodia until August 15, 1973, at which point President Nixon ordered a halt to United States military action.

5.4.3. Legal Authorities for the Vietnam War

Congress never formally "declared war" in the Vietnam conflict, leading some to claim there was no legal basis for the United States military action there. That is both an oversimplification of the legal question, and the wrong conclusion.

In 1966, the Legal Adviser to the State Department, Leonard Meeker, issued a written defense of the legality of the United States' participation in the military conflict in Vietnam. His memorandum serves as the foundation for the following discussion of various arguments for the legality of the conflict and is a helpful starting point for debates regarding national security authority and the legality of United States participation in any military conflict. The arguments regarding legal authority are divided into three parts: 1) constitutional; 2) statutory, including appropriations; and 3) treaty-based. For this analysis we will consider the various legal arguments for the President's authority as of 1966, the year in which Legal Adviser Meeker issued his memorandum. As you consider each of the asserted bases for the President's authority to use military force in Vietnam, attempt to consider them in isolation from the other theories. Though legal arguments rarely apply only in isolation, and they certainly did not do so in the Vietnam context, understanding the sufficiency of each basis for authority alone will help you more fully understand that basis and determine its applicability to other national security law questions.

5.4.3.1. Constitutional Arguments for the Legality of the Vietnam Conflict

Several constitutional bases for the executive power apply to the President's power to engage the United States military in Vietnam, including the Commander in Chief Power, the implied power to repel attack, and the customary authority theory. Here we will explore these arguments and potential counterarguments.

Commander in Chief Power

Legal Adviser Meeker's memorandum came close to saying that the Commander in Chief power alone gave the President authority to engage in the military conflict in Vietnam. The argument distills to this: the President controls the military and is thus permitted to use it how he sees fit in the nation's interest. Citing *Curtiss-Wright*'s language that the President is the "sole organ" of foreign affairs, the most robust version of the Commander in Chief argument sets this standard: the President can use military force any time he deems it necessary to maintain the security and defense of the United States.

Several counterarguments to Mr. Meeker's analysis have been raised, including two discussed here. First, as the Supreme Court has made clear, the President is not permitted to respond to foreign affairs matters in any way he chooses. For example, recall that in *Little v. Barreme*, the Supreme Court required the President to follow Congress's dictates in using military force (in that case, Congress the destination of the ships that could be seized). Second, even if the

President has some authority under the Commander in Chief Clause, that clause cannot be interpreted in a vacuum. For example, it must be read in conjunction with the Constitution's Declaration Clause, which strongly suggests the **Framers** intended Congress to have some role in the decision to go to war.

Repel Attack/Defensive Power

Legal Adviser Meeker's memorandum also defended the Presidents' actions under the theory that the Constitution "leaves to the President the judgment to determine whether the circumstances of a particular **armed attack** are so urgent and the potential consequences so threatening to the security of the United States that he should act without formally consulting Congress." This is an articulation of the "repel attack" or "defensive" power. Arguably, this assertion was in response to the attacks on United States naval vessels in the Tonkin Gulf. *The Prize Cases* are authority for the idea that the President must determine the appropriate level of response to an attack on the United States and need not wait for Congress to convene in order to defend the nation. Thus, defending ships in the Gulf of Tonkin was within the President's sole authority. More broadly than the Gulf of Tonkin attacks, this theory could be extended to a defense against the general "communist threat," which arguably could include the threat of *eventual* attack on the United States homeland that the domino theory suggested.

Multiple concerns regarding the "repel attack" theory for the President's military use of force in Vietnam exist. Several of these relate to the nature of the alleged "attack." First, North Vietnam's attack against the United States ship in the Tonkin Gulf was not really against the United States itself, as was the case in the early days of the Civil War and *The Prize Cases*—it occurred halfway around the world. Nevertheless, it *was* against United States personnel and property. Second, the attack was arguably a *defensive* action by the North Vietnamese in response to provocative covert United States military actions. A theory of presidential authority that would allow the President to covertly provoke "attacks" that then become the basis for the use of military force would leave the President wholly unconstrained. Additionally, the so-called "defensive action" of invading North Vietnam with a massive ground troop and air assault campaign for the purpose of defending a few ships in the Gulf of Tonkin seems dubious. And if the "attack" being defended against was not the attack against United States ships, but rather the attack against a United States ally (South Vietnam), that would involve the notion of a defensive war power for collective defense.

The idea that the President's defensive (repel attack) war power extends to defending other nations without approval from Congress has never been endorsed by the Supreme Court. Moreover, South Vietnam was arguably not an independent sovereign state under international law, and the United States never sought UN Security Council approval of collective self-defense under Article 51, suggesting the United States did not genuinely view its actions as collective self defense. Perhaps most importantly, the defensive war power the Supreme Court endorsed in *The Prize Cases* depends on an emergency in which there is no time to assemble Congress. Under this theory, the President can repel the attack as it occurs, but then must turn to Congress for authorization for continued military activity. Thus, though military action to defend against attacks on United States ships and prevent subsequent attacks might have been authorized initially under the defensive war power theory, the continuing full-scale military assault two years later could not.

Customary Authority

In his memorandum, Legal Advisor Meeker cited "at least 125 instances in which the President has ordered the armed forces to take action or maintain positions abroad without prior congressional authorization, starting with the 'undeclared war' with France." In referencing these instances, Mr. Meeker was asserting the President's customary authority to take military action without congressional approval. This draws on the theory articulated by Justice Jackson's and Justice Frankfurter's *Youngstown* concurrences, in which they suggested the President might gain or lawfully exercise power through congressional acquiescence. Recall that in Justice Frankfurter's view, such authority arose from "a systematic, unbroken, executive practice, long pursued to the knowledge of the Congress and never before questioned. . . ."

One of the significant challenges to the general theory of customary authority is that it is difficult to determine how similar the facts of the current crisis must be to the prior acts to which Congress previously acquiesced—in other words, how analogous the situation in question is to the executive practice purportedly serving as its customary basis. For example, though Mr. Meeker was correct that Presidents had used military force many times before without explicit congressional authorization, most of those actions were quite dissimilar from the Vietnam conflict. Mr. Meeker's 125 instances included many attacks on pirates in defense of United States merchant shipping. In fact, of the 125 instances, only *one* was a military conflict of the same magnitude as Vietnam: the Korean War the decade prior. Though the Korean conflict may be sufficiently similar to be analogous to the Vietnam conflict, one instance hardly establishes a "systematic, unbroken practice." Mr. Meeker's historically misleading statement that the United States engaged in an "undeclared war with France" without congressional authorization demonstrates another issue with customary authority: that prior instances of supposed acquiescence can be misrepresented. Mr. Meeker cited the war with France, claiming it was without congressional approval, but Congress *did* authorize that military action, which was the subject of *Bas v. Tingy*, discussed in Chapter 3. Another problem with the idea that the President had customary authority to engage in the Vietnam conflict was the question of whether Congress's acquiescence was with full knowledge. Significant evidence suggests Congress was not fully aware of, and indeed was deliberately misled about, the extent of the military buildup and the nature of United States activities that some might have considered to be provocations of the Tonkin Gulf incident. Whether by its own ignorance and negligence or through deliberate deception, Congress could not be said to have "full knowledge" of the President's actions, and thus its "acquiescence" was arguably invalid.

5.4.3.2. Statutory Basis for Authority, Including Appropriations

The strongest argument for the President's authority to conduct military operations in Vietnam as of 1966 is the statutory authorization provided by Congress in the form of the Tonkin Gulf Resolution and, to a somewhat lesser degree, subsequent appropriations for the action.

Tonkin Gulf Resolution

The Tonkin Gulf Resolution (TGR) was a **joint resolution** of Congress signed into law by the President. By its plain terms, it was an **authorization for the use of military force (AUMF)**, making the Vietnam conflict a Congressionally authorized war. The TGR gave the President broad discretion to take necessary measures to "prevent further aggression" in Southeast Asia. The TGR could be interpreted as a delegation of Congress's war-making authority. Under cases like *Lichter*, such a delegation should be interpreted broadly (recall that *Lichter* was the World War II excessive profits case in which the Court observed that the power to wage war is the power to wage war successfully).

Perhaps the strongest counterargument to the President's authority coming from the TGR is that Congress was misinformed, or at least underinformed, about what was really occurring in Vietnam, including the United States military's actions leading up to the Tonkin Gulf Incident. Absent adequate information, can there be adequate delegation? Stated differently, this argument suggests Congress did not really know what it was doing, and just as a contract procured by fraud is void, a delegation founded on presidential misrepresentation should be void. However, though Congress might not have had all the information, that is often true in the national security arena, where Congress is asked to act with incomplete understanding. Congress could have acted more carefully, sought more information, or even rescinded the TGR after it learned more about the facts. But in the end, "the statute says what it says." Whether Congress was or was not fully and accurately informed does not matter, or if it does, it was Congress's fault because it is Congress's responsibility to be informed prior to granting great authority.

The idea that "the statute says what it says" raises another counterargument: the TGR is rather vague and ambiguous and Congress may not have intended to give the President broad war-making powers or expect him to use them. In fact, the sponsor of the TGR, Senator J. William Fulbright, recalled many years later that the intent of the TGR was to express "unity and support for the President in a moment of national crisis." Fulbright suggested that as far as military action was concerned, the TGR was intended allow the President to respond to an attack on United States Navy ships, but Congress did not mean to give the President the power to conduct a full-scale, eight year war.

Senator Fulbright's recollection does not square with the actual language of the statute, which was broad and open-ended. Indeed, Congresspeople who have suggested the TGR was not intended to confer significant war-making authority on the President seem to want to have their cake and eat it, too. As Professor John Hart Ely has noted, Congress's actions with respect to the TGR exemplify "Congress [lacking] the will and/or courage to stop the President from involving us in military ventures, but at the same time [having] no wish to be held accountable for the wars he gets us into."

Appropriations and Conscription

The Tonkin Gulf Resolution was far from the only congressional action that appeared to authorize the President's military use of force in Vietnam. In 1974, Congress appropriated $700 million for troops and material for Vietnam. The appropriations were accompanied by a congressional statement of intent: "[T]hese appropriations show our firm intent to provide all necessary support for members of the Armed Forces of the United States fighting in Vietnam." The President contended that the appropriations were the equivalent of an AUMF. Indeed, Congress's appropriations continued even after it rescinded the TGR, a fact courts later found significant (discussed below). Had Congress wished for the appropriations not to be considered authorization for military action in Vietnam, it could have placed limits on the purpose and use of the appropriations. But it did not.

Recall that in *Greene v. McElroy*, the Supreme Court had said that to authorize or ratify an Executive Branch action, an appropriation must "plainly show a purpose to bestow the precise authority which is claimed." The *Greene* Court had said that general appropriations cannot be viewed as an affirmation of the act or program. In this view, Congress was trying to "support the troops," not "support the war." Indeed, it may have been political suicide for Congresspeople not to fund the war, given the casualties that were accumulating. But how could a special appropriation for a specific purpose not "plainly show" Congress approved of what the President was doing in Vietnam?

In addition to appropriations, Congress renewed the Military Selective Service Act multiple times during the Vietnam War. In 1967, Congress renewed the draft through 1971, and in 1971, renewed it through 1973. This reauthorization of conscription during the Vietnam War, when it was well-known that thousands of draftees were being sent to Vietnam, has been viewed as another demonstration of Congress's tacit approval for the war.

5.4.3.3. Treaty Basis of Authority

SEATO was a treaty that was approved by the Senate and ratified, making it, according to the Supremacy Clause of the Constitution, part of the "Supreme Law of the land," on par with federal statutes. The President asserted the following language from SEATO imposed not only the legal *authority*, but the legal *obligation* to defend South Vietnam:

> Each Party recognizes that aggression by means of armed attack in the treaty area against any of the Parties or against any State or territory which the parties by unanimous agreement may hereafter designate, would endanger its own peace and safety, and agrees that it will in that event act to meet the common danger in accordance with its constitutional processes.

The administration argued that because the President is charged to "take care the law be faithfully executed," he was legally obliged to comply with the treaty and defend South Vietnam.

The primary thrust of counterarguments to the idea that SEATO alone provided the President with authority for military activity in Vietnam is that the treaty did not, in fact, impose a legal obligation on the United States. First, though the treaty was legally effective, it was non-self-executing, meaning further action by Congress was required to implement the treaty. (For more on non-self-executing treaties, see Chapter 9.) Thus, the treaty was a valid international obligation, but the obligation was not for the United States to use military force to defend treaty partners, but rather the obligation was for Congress to authorize war to fulfill treaty commitments.

Another counterargument noted the "in accordance with its constitutional processes" language of the SEATO provision. Some argued that the United States' constitutional process, as it relates to the use of military force, is for the House and Senate to authorize such force. Thus, absent such an authorization, the treaty obligation and authorization did not exist. On the other hand, could the required "constitutional process" simply be the approval by two thirds of the senate that treaties require?

A related counterargument relies on the generally held belief that treaties cannot conflict with the Constitution, an idea the Supreme Court has only ever articulated in a plurality, non-binding opinion. If true, SEATO could not be interpreted in a way that was at odds with the constitutional design. In this case, that means the President and two thirds of the Senate cannot decide to go to war; such a decision requires approval by *both* houses of Congress.

5.4.4. The Judiciary's Limited Role in the Vietnam War

Remarkably, despite many legal challenges to the protracted conflict, the Supreme Court never opined on the legality of the Vietnam War. Several explanations have been offered as to why. One primary theory is institutional self-preservation. That is, the Court was concerned about its legitimacy and perceptions of its authority in the event it issued an opinion that the President ignored or that otherwise put the judiciary in conflict with the political branches. Moreover, the Court may have been concerned about public perception if it explicitly approved a war that was increasingly unpopular with the American public. It is also possible the Court saw danger in applying the facts of Vietnam to create precedent for legal authority for future wars. Though the Supreme Court did not opine on the legality of the Vietnam conflict, several lower federal courts of appeal did. Possibly, the Supreme Court simply always agreed with those courts' decisions. In any event, the courts of appeals opinions cast light on the authority for the conflict amidst shifting legal and factual scenarios and suggest how future uses of military force might be evaluated.

5.4.4.1. Orlando v. Laird

The most significant of the cases decided by federal appellate courts was *Orlando v. Laird*, decided in 1971 by the Second Circuit Court of Appeals. *Orlando* is a great example of the competing interests of all three branches of federal government colliding in one case. In *Orlando*, two enlistees sought to prevent enforcement of the deployment orders issued by the Secretary of Defense, the Secretary of the Army, and commanding officers. The plaintiffs contended that the defendants exceeded their constitutional authority by ordering them to participate in a war that was not properly authorized by Congress.

Though the substantive issue for the court to decide was whether Congress had acted sufficiently to authorize or ratify the war, the court was first concerned with whether the case was justiciable. Specifically, the court addressed standing and the **political question doctrine**.

The court determined the plaintiffs had standing because they were soldiers in danger of being physically harmed or killed. Thus, the plaintiffs had a particularized and discrete injury, and although the danger had not yet occurred, it was imminent upon their deployment.

In answering the next **justiciability** question—whether the case presented a political question—the court also addressed the substantive issue the case posed. Citing an earlier appeals court decision, *Berk v. Laird*, the court held that the case did not present a non-justiciable political question because "the war declaring power of Congress, enumerated in Article I, section 8, of the Constitution contains a 'discoverable standard calling for *some mutual participation by Congress*.' " This seems like a reasonable interpretation of the various applicable constitutional provisions in Articles I and II, and a reasonable attempt to preserve balance between the branches, but what is the legal basis for that understanding? Where did the "some mutual participation standard" come from? The *Orlando* court copied that standard from *Berk v. Laird*, and the court in that case had found the standard in law review articles, not from any prior precedent. In addition to the concern that the most significant precedent regarding how Congress must authorize a war comes from an appellate court opinion that did not cite Supreme Court precedent, the standard itself may be problematic because it seems so broad almost anything could satisfy it.

For a moment, consider the counterargument to the *Orlando v. Laird* court's holding that whether the Constitution required a **declaration of war** was not entirely a political question. Does Article I, Section 8's Declare War Clause sound like a "discoverable standard" that courts can interpret and apply? Asked differently, can a court read the language of the Clause and know in a particular case whether Congress and the President have complied? Article I, Section 8, does not prescribe a precise way in which Congress must "declare war." Recall that as early as *Bas v. Tingy*, the Supreme Court determined that Congress did not need to issue a formal Declaration of War to approve of military use of force. Indeed, one could argue that *Orlando v. Laird* presented the quintessential political question: the Constitution envisions the branches participating in the decision to wage war, but because the Constitution does not explain *how much* working together is required, the political branches should decide. In fact, that is what the court ultimately concluded, ruling that:

> Beyond determining that there has been some mutual participation between the Congress and the President, which unquestionably exists here, with action by the Congress sufficient to authorize or ratify the military activity at issue, it is clear that the constitutional propriety of the means by which Congress has chosen to ratify and approve the protracted military operations in Southeast Asia is a political question.

The court reached this conclusion because "The form which congressional authorization should take is one of policy, committed to the discretion of the Congress and outside the power and competency of the judiciary, because there are no intelligible and objectively manageable standards by which to judge such actions."

The court also noted a variety of practical reasons why the method by which Congress authorizes military conflict is a political question. For example, a decision to authorize war without "declaring" it may have been in the best interest of the United States, so as to not telegraph the United States' position to adversaries, allies, or neutrals, or Congress may not have wanted to trigger numerous statutory provisions that activate special presidential powers automatically upon a formal declaration of war. As the court noted, "decisions regarding the form and substance of congressional enactments authorizing hostilities are determined by highly complex considerations of diplomacy, foreign policy and military strategy inappropriate to judicial inquiry."

When examining whether Congress had engaged in "some mutual participation" in authorizing the Vietnam War, the court opined that originally Congress's participation came in the form of the Tonkin Gulf Resolution. However, because that had been repealed by Congress in December 1970, some other congressional participation was required. The court found this in Congress's continued appropriations to carry out military operations and its extension of the Military Selective Service Act with knowledge that draftees would be deployed to Vietnam.

The Supreme Court did not grant certiorari in *Orlando v. Laird*, leaving in place the appeals court's holding that the Constitution requires "some mutual participation," a holding that has not been subsequently overturned. Thus, the "some mutual participation" standard remains the clearest articulation of the federal judiciary's approach to the Constitution's requirements for the legality of authorization for the use of military force.

5.4.5. Congress's Attempts to Limit the Scope and End the Vietnam War

The Vietnam War presents a useful practical example of the legal questions involved when Congress wants to *limit* the scope of a military conflict. Assuming Congress has initially authorized a military conflict, and given that the President is the Commander in Chief of the military, *can* Congress limit where and how the military is used in the conflict it has authorized?

The nations of Cambodia and Laos, which border Vietnam to the west, were militarily significant in the Vietnam conflict. Northern Vietnam used locations in Cambodia and Laos as bases from which to attack the South Vietnamese and United States forces. Additionally, the famed Ho Chi Minh trail, a critical resupply route for Northern Vietnamese forces fighting in South Vietnam, transited Laos. This presents a practical problem faced in real military conflict: an enemy often uses territory outside its own geographic boundaries for military advantage, an advantage that must either be accepted or thwarted. In this case, North Vietnam's use of Cambodia and Laos presented the United States with a dilemma: the United States military strategically needed to eliminate threats arising from North Vietnam's activities in Cambodia and Laos, but that also would constitute a geographic expansion of an already unpopular war into new territory. President Nixon determined that bombing the bases and supply routes in Cambodia and Laos was critical to ending the war, and began a large-scale carpet-bombing operation, which the administration largely kept hidden from Congress. When the bombing campaign failed to achieve its intended effects, President Nixon authorized a ground offensive into Cambodia, a decision that was unpopular with much of the American public. Reaction to the invasion of Cambodia by the United States included the protests at Kent State University that led to the notorious killing of four students by National Guard troops.

The President had strong legal arguments for authority to use military force in Cambodia and Laos. First, until it was repealed, the Tonkin Gulf Resolution's broad language to "assist any member or protocol state of SEATO requesting assistance" allowed use of force necessary to defend South Vietnam. Indeed, the TGR was written so broadly it arguably authorized nuclear conflict with China, North Vietnam's principle ally, so long as doing so would "prevent further aggression." Even once the TGR was rescinded, and thus removed as legal authority, the President arguably retained his authority as Commander in Chief to make strategic decisions regarding how the ongoing military conflict would be waged. Then-Assistant Attorney General William Rehnquist (later Chief Justice) made that exact assertion in defense of the United States' activities in Cambodia. Rehnquist argued President Nixon had not only the authority, but the constitutional obligation as Commander in Chief, to take whatever steps he deemed necessary to assure the military's safety and success.

As the Vietnam War became less popular among United States citizens, some members of Congress sought to prevent the conflict from expanding. Congress first attempted to limit United States military activities in Laos by passing an amendment to the DOD Appropriation Act of 1970 that said no funds appropriated "by this Act" shall be used to finance the introduction of "American ground combat troops into Laos or Thailand." This language had several large loopholes. First, specific prohibition of ground troops implicitly permitted a continued air campaign over Laos, which could include both bombing and air support of South Vietnamese ground troops. Additionally, reference to "this Act" meant that though funds in the 1970 Appropriations Act could not be used, the Nixon Administration might look for funds elsewhere.

Congress's first attempt to limit the United States' activities in Cambodia came a year later in the form of a rider to a defense appropriations bill in 1971, which prohibited use of funds in "this or any other act" to finance *introduction* of United States ground troops into Cambodia. In response, President Nixon's legal team engaged in some creative legal reasoning and notoriously relied on the obscure Feed and Forage Act of 1861 to provide money to "care for troops" who were already in Cambodia, but for whom the Administration had no appropriated funds. The Feed and Forage Act said that the general ban on expenditures for which there was no congressional appropriation "does not apply to a contract or purchase made by a defined Secretary for clothing, subsistence, forage, fuel, quarters, transportation, or medical and hospital supplies." Designed to ensure Union troops and their horses did not starve during the Civil War, the Act's applicability to combat operations in Cambodia, was, to put it mildly, a stretch.

These only partially successful attempts to limit the scope of the United States military activities in certain geographic areas highlight the larger questions of how and when Congress can limit war it has already authorized. In general, it seems easier for Congress to limit an **imperfect war** at the beginning, rather than attempt to impose new limitations after it has begun. For example, Congress might in its original authorization for the use of military force allow air combat, but no "boots on the ground." In fact, the Supreme Court has upheld such congressional restrictions on the President's use of the military. Recall the early case of *Little v. Barreme*, in which the Supreme Court explicitly required the President to stay within the limits of Congress's authorization to use force against ships headed *to*, but not *from*, French ports. Similarly, *Bas v. Tingy* involved a congressional authorization for the use of force against France, but only using naval forces, which the Supreme Court upheld.

The President's Commander in Chief power necessarily allows the President to make military operational decisions that affect the methods by which the military engages in the conflict. Limiting a conflict after it has begun is more complicated. A restriction on methods or location of military activities instituted after the conflict has begun inevitably involves tying the President's hands in a way that could have more harmful effects on the success of the operation than if the limitations had been in place from the beginning, during the planning stages of the operation. On the other hand, at what point does the President's authority to determine a strategy for winning constitute starting a new conflict? For example, even for those who believe the United States military's activities in Cambodia and Laos were both militarily necessary and authorized by the TGR, it is not clear whether attacking China to discourage its financial support of North Vietnam would have been within the scope of the TGR or would have constituted a "new war."

5.4.6. Congress's Attempts to End the Vietnam War

Eventually, Congress did not want simply to limit the scope of the Vietnam War, it wanted to *end* it. But how can Congress end wars it has authorized? The Constitution gives Congress the Declare War power, but no "Declare the End of War" power, raising the question of whether the ability to end a war is implicit in the power to authorize it. As one delegate observed at the Constitutional Convention, it should be "more easy to get out of war than into it." And as another delegate, George Mason, advocated, it is better to clog than facilitate war. This suggests at least one Framer believed Congress should have the ability to end the war. But by itself this comment does not provide clear authority. Can the President end a war unilaterally? Can Congress?

It is both practically and politically difficult for Congress to end a military conflict once the President has committed troops. Congressional "deauthorization" could have the effect of leaving troops without money or supplies. Even giving a deadline for withdrawal can have the effect of telegraphing to the enemy when United States forces will stop fighting. This can encourage the enemy to simply outlast the deadline and signals to the enemy when United States troops might withdraw, jeopardizing the safety of that movement. Moreover, deauthorizing a conflict runs into the President's Commander in Chief power to take actions to protect the safety of deployed military forces. Practically, the form and speed of an end to military conflict needs to be within the control of the person(s) best able to determine the military's needs and abilities. Additionally, Congress would face political risk in deauthorizing a war, both because of the political risk of taking actions perceived to be not "supporting the troops," and because of possible blame if withdrawal goes poorly.

Congress's first official action—beyond the numerous individual pronouncements by Congresspeople "on the Capitol steps" and in the media—to end the Vietnam War came in 1971 with the repeal of the Tonkin Gulf Resolution. Significant debate has addressed whether Congress's repeal of the TGR alone ended legal authorization for the war. Those who argue the repeal did end authorization point to the fact that the TGR was the most obvious authorization for the war and its repeal was a clear way for Congress to demonstrate the war was no longer sanctioned. This argument is premised on the idea that if Congress gives authority, it can take it back, and is consistent with the idea that it should be easier to get out of war then to get into one.

However, the repeal of the TGR alone still left the President with the other bases of legal authority identified earlier in this chapter. And courts rejected the idea that repeal of the TGR alone ended the authorization for the war. In *Orlando v. Laird* and *DaCosta v. Laird*, federal courts pointed to appropriation statutes and selective service statutes that were enacted or survived *after* the TGR repeal. For those courts, the other types of statutes represented the continued *mutual participation by Congress and the President*, which was all that was necessary. This interpretation was supported by the fact that the TGR repeal was accomplished by a single sentence in an unrelated statute, which included no explanation, allowing the courts to interpret the TGR repeal as Congress's decision that the TGR was superfluous. The *Orlando* and *DaCosta* courts essentially viewed the continuing appropriations as functional AUMFs. Importantly, those courts determined that *how* a war can be ended is a political question.

Whatever Congress's intent, repeal of the TGR did not end the United States' military action in Southeast Asia. By spring 1973, though the United States and North Vietnam had signed an agreement to end the war, President Nixon ordered the Air Force to continue bombing Cambodia. Congress's next efforts at limiting the conflict were a similarly ineffective model for how *not* to end a war.

Several months after repealing the TGR, Congress attached the so-called "Mansfield Amendment" to a defense appropriations measure. The Mansfield

Amendment, which President Nixon signed into law, declared the "policy of the United States" to "terminate *at the earliest possible date* all military operations of the United States in Indochina." The ambiguity of its terms rendered the Mansfield Amendment ineffective in stopping the war. What is the "earliest possible date?" Who decides? Is a "policy" a legal requirement? Ultimately, though it may at first sound firm, the Mansfield Amendment's vague language rendered the law aspirational rather than obligatory.

In May of 1973, Senator Thomas Eagleton introduced an amendment to a bill that declared that "none of the funds herein appropriated under this Act or heretofore appropriated under any other Act may be expended to support directly or indirectly combat activities in, over or from off the shores of Cambodia or in or over Laos by United States forces." In contrast to the earlier efforts to limit the scope of the war in Cambodia and Laos discussed above, this might have been an effective mechanism by which to end the war in Cambodia and Laos. But President Nixon successfully opposed the measure, leading to a compromise between the President and Congress that some argued was a capitulation to the President's intrusion on Congress's constitutional role of deciding when the United States would be engaged in war. Recognizing Congress would not have the necessary votes to override a presidential veto, the Eagleton Amendment failed.

Congress passed a new joint resolution regarding the Vietnam conflict, which the President signed into law on July 1, 1973. It stated:

> On or after August 15, 1973, no funds herein or heretofore appropriated may be obligated or expended to finance directly or indirectly combat activities by United States military forces in or over or from off the shores of North Vietnam, South Vietnam, Laos or Cambodia.

With this action, Congress unambiguously ended appropriations for combat operations related to Vietnam. Nevertheless, combat operations continued through July. In *Holtzman v. Schlessinger*, a federal appeals court considered a challenge to those operations. The plaintiffs, a group of Air Force pilots and Representative Elizabeth Holtzman, argued Congress had never authorized military combat in Cambodia. Additionally, the plaintiffs contended the Mansfield Amendment had called for earliest possible termination of conflict, the Eagleton Amendment had indicated Congress' disapproval of the conflict, and the July 1st, 1973 Joint Resolution had called for an end to the war on August 15th, 1973, further indicating Congress' disapproval.

The District Court agreed with the plaintiffs and issued an **injunction** prohibiting the Department of Defense from "participating in any way in military activities in or over Cambodia or releasing any bombs which may fall in Cambodia." However, the government appealed and the Second Circuit Court of Appeals stayed the District Court's injunction, holding that the case presented a political question, and that even if it were to decide the issue, it could not determine whether the Cambodian bombing was *furthering* or *hindering* the goal of the Mansfield Amendment to bring an end to the war. The Second Circuit also observed that the Joint Resolution explicitly *allowed* the conflict to continue until August 15th, contradicting the argument that Congress was opposed to the bombing in Cambodia. The court rejected the plaintiffs' assertion that President Nixon's veto threat had "coerced" Congress into authorizing an additional 45 days of bombing, noting that the Constitution does not prohibit the President from exercising his veto power, even with respect to matters vested to Congress.

Congress's experience in attempting to end the Vietnam War demonstrates the difficulty in doing so. Ground forces had already been withdrawn from Vietnam, weakening the argument that the bombing in Cambodia was merely protective in nature. The bombing of Cambodia had never been explicitly authorized. Large majorities of Congress opposed the bombing. And still, Congress lacked the political will and veto-proof votes to end the conflict when it wanted to. Ultimately, President Nixon ended United States military operations in Vietnam on August 14th, 1973, the day before appropriations ended.

5.5. CONGRESS'S RESPONSE TO VIETNAM: THE WAR POWERS RESOLUTION

In response to what it viewed as abuses by successive Presidents in expanding the Vietnam War beyond congressional authorization, and in an attempt to prevent future Presidents from forcing Congress to capitulate to the President's will, Congress attempted to control the President's use of force through statute. Congress was attempting to limit the President's ability to entangle the nation in military conflict that Congress would have little political choice but to support once troops were in harm's way, as had occurred in Vietnam. This "response" relied in part on Congress's somewhat revisionist history of the problems of Vietnam. Congress wanted to lay the blame for the failures on the Executive Branch, despite the fact that it had repeatedly approved the war.

The War Powers Resolution (WPR) has struggled to gain acceptance outside of Congress. In 1973, Congress enacted the WPR over President Nixon's veto. Successive Presidents have often debated its constitutionality, while simultaneously claiming to comply with it. The Supreme Court has never opined on the WPR's constitutionality. Despite a continuing debate regarding the WPR's constitutionality and effectiveness, the WPR is important because it is Congress's clearest articulation of *its* understanding of the relative authorities and responsibilities of the Legislative and Executive Branches in approving the use of military force by the United States.

5.5.1. The Text of the War Powers Resolution

Read the War Powers Resolution carefully. As you read, consider the following:

1. Where is the language of the WPR ambiguous enough to allow multiple plausible interpretations?

2. What practical problems with complying with the WPR might be presented?

3. Where is the WPR consistent or inconsistent with your understanding of the constitutional balance of national security authority?

Section 1

This joint resolution may be cited as the "War Powers Resolution."

Section 2

(a) Congressional declaration

It is the purpose of this chapter to fulfill the intent of the framers of the Constitution of the United States and insure that the collective judgment of both the Congress and the President will apply to the introduction of United States Armed Forces into hostilities, or into situations where imminent involvement in hostilities is clearly indicated by the circumstances, and to the continued use of such forces in hostilities or in such situations.

(b) Congressional legislative power under necessary and proper clause

Under article I, section 8, of the Constitution, it is specifically provided that the Congress shall have the power to make all laws necessary and proper for carrying into execution, not only its own powers but also all other powers vested by the Constitution in the Government of the United States, or in any department or officer thereof.

(c) Presidential executive power as Commander-in-Chief; limitation

The constitutional powers of the President as Commander-in-Chief to introduce United States Armed Forces into hostilities, or into situations where imminent involvement in hostilities is clearly indicated by the circumstances, are exercised only pursuant to (1) a declaration of war, (2) specific statutory authorization, or (3) a national emergency created by attack upon the United States, its territories or possessions, or its armed forces.

Section 3

The President in every possible instance shall consult with Congress before introducing United States Armed Forces into hostilities or into situations where imminent involvement in hostilities is clearly indicated by the circumstances, and after every such introduction shall consult regularly with the Congress until United States Armed Forces are no longer engaged in hostilities or have been removed from such situations.

Section 4

(a) Written report; time of submission; circumstances necessitating submission; information reported

In the absence of a declaration of war, in any case in which United States Armed Forces are introduced—

(1) into hostilities or into situations where imminent involvement in hostilities is clearly indicated by the circumstances;

(2) into the territory, airspace or waters of a foreign nation, while equipped for combat, except for deployments which relate solely to supply, replacement, repair, or training of such forces; or

(3) in numbers which substantially enlarge United States Armed Forces equipped for combat already located in a foreign nation;

the President shall submit within 48 hours to the Speaker of the House of Representatives and to the President pro tempore of the Senate a report, in writing, setting forth—

(A) the circumstances necessitating the introduction of United States Armed Forces;

(B) the constitutional and legislative authority under which such introduction took place; and

(C) the estimated scope and duration of the hostilities or involvement.

(b) Other information reported

The President shall provide such other information as the Congress may request in the fulfillment of its constitutional responsibilities with respect to committing the Nation to war and to the use of United States Armed Forces abroad.

(c) Periodic reports; semiannual requirement

Whenever United States Armed Forces are introduced into hostilities or into any situation described in subsection (a) of this section, the President shall, so long as such armed forces continue to be engaged in such hostilities or situation, report to the Congress periodically on the status of such hostilities or situation as well as on the scope and duration of such hostilities or situation, but in no event shall he report to the Congress less often than once every six months.

Section 5

(a) Transmittal of report and referral to Congressional committees; joint request for convening Congress

Each report submitted pursuant to section 1543(a)(1) of this title shall be transmitted to the Speaker of the House of Representatives and to the President pro tempore of the Senate on the same calendar day. Each report so transmitted shall be referred to the Committee on Foreign Affairs of the House of Representatives and to the Committee on Foreign Relations of the Senate for appropriate action. If, when the report is transmitted, the Congress has adjourned sine die or has adjourned for any period in excess of three calendar days, the Speaker of the House of Representatives and the President pro tempore of the Senate, if they deem it advisable (or if petitioned by at least 30 percent of the membership of their respective Houses) shall jointly request the President to convene Congress in order that it may consider the report and take appropriate action pursuant to this section.

(b) Termination of use of United States Armed Forces; exceptions; extension period

Within sixty calendar days after a report is submitted or is required to be submitted pursuant to section 1543(a)(1) of this title, whichever is earlier, the President shall terminate any use of United States Armed Forces with respect to which such report was submitted (or required to be submitted), unless the Congress (1) has declared war or has enacted a specific authorization for such use of United States Armed Forces, (2) has extended by law such sixty-day period, or (3) is physically unable to meet as a result of an armed attack upon the United States. Such sixty-day period shall be extended for not more than an additional thirty days if the President determines and certifies to the Congress in writing that unavoidable military necessity respecting the safety of United States Armed Forces requires the continued use of such armed forces in the course of bringing about a prompt removal of such forces.

(c) Concurrent resolution for removal by President of United States Armed Forces

Notwithstanding subsection (b), at any time that United States Armed Forces are engaged in hostilities outside the territory of the United States, its possessions and territories without a declaration of war or specific statutory authorization, such forces shall be removed by the President if the Congress so directs by concurrent resolution.

[Omitted *Sections 6 and 7 discuss congressional procedures for passing a joint or* ***concurrent resolution***.]

Section 8

(a) Inferences from any law or treaty

Authority to introduce United States Armed Forces into hostilities or into situations wherein involvement in hostilities is clearly indicated by the circumstances shall not be inferred—

(1) from any provision of law (whether or not in effect before November 7, 1973), including any provision contained in any appropriation Act, unless such provision specifically authorizes the introduction of United States Armed Forces into hostilities or into such situations and states that it is intended to constitute specific statutory authorization within the meaning of this chapter; or

(2) from any treaty heretofore or hereafter ratified unless such treaty is implemented by legislation specifically authorizing the introduction of United States Armed Forces into hostilities or into such situations and stating that it is intended to constitute specific statutory authorization within the meaning of this chapter.

(b) Joint headquarters operations of high-level military commands

Nothing in this chapter shall be construed to require any further specific statutory authorization to permit members of United States Armed Forces to participate jointly with members of the armed forces of one or more foreign countries in the headquarters operations of high-level military commands which were established prior to November 7, 1973, and pursuant to the United Nations Charter or any treaty ratified by the United States prior to such date.

(c) Introduction of United States Armed Forces

For purposes of this chapter, the term "introduction of United States Armed Forces" includes the assignment of members of such armed forces to command, coordinate, participate in the movement of, or accompany the regular or irregular military forces of any foreign country or government when such military forces are engaged, or there exists an imminent threat that such forces will become engaged, in hostilities.

(d) Constitutional authorities or existing treaties unaffected; construction against grant of Presidential authority respecting use of United States Armed Forces

Nothing in this chapter—

(1) is intended to alter the constitutional authority of the Congress or of the President, or the provisions of existing treaties; or

(2) shall be construed as granting any authority to the President with respect to the introduction of United States Armed Forces into hostilities or into situations wherein involvement in hostilities is clearly indicated by the circumstances which authority he would not have had in the absence of this chapter.

5.5.2. Analyzing the War Powers Resolution

Now that you have read the WPR, we will examine sections in detail.

Section 2

Section 2 provides Congress's rationale and perceived authority for the WPR. Section 2(a) claims to fulfill the intent of the Framers of the Constitution. Section 2(b) provides clear authority for Congress's role in decisions to use military force: Article I, Section 8, of the United States Constitution. Note that Congress cites the broad "necessary and proper" authority for carrying into execution not only its own powers, but also all other powers vested in the federal government. Congress's claimed authority could not be broader.

Section 2(c) may be the most controversial part of Section 2, as it claims to define the boundaries of the constitutional powers of the President as Commander in Chief. Congress asserts the President can only commit armed forces in three situations: 1) a declaration of war; 2) specific statutory authorization (AUMF); or 3) national emergency created by attack. This list is an important acknowledgment by Congress that a "declaration of war" is not the only circumstance in which the President is constitutionally authorized to use military force. In conjunction with Section 8, this provision demonstrates Congress's position that authorization through implication or acquiescence is insufficient for presidential war-making.

Section 2 is controversial because it purports to establish an exclusive list for when the President may use military force. Critics have suggested the list is too short, noting it does not include the President's ability to use force to rescue Americans, engage in **peacekeeping**, ensure freedom of navigation, provide military advisers, protect American embassies, and other common uses of the military abroad. More generally, critics also contend the list does not comport with historical reality, as hundreds of actual uses of the military by Presidents throughout history are not included in the listed situations.

In Section 2, Congress recognizes only the President's Commander in Chief authority, and not other theories of presidential authority. For example, the President's inherent authority as Chief Executive is unlisted. It is unclear whether this was an omission or intended exclusion, and if intentional, whether it reflects a decision not to try to limit the other bases for authority or simply to not recognize other bases for authority as legitimate.

Section 2(c) also raises questions about the President's emergency power. The text does not clarify what a "national emergency" is or which types of "attacks" qualify. Nor does it explain what the "United States" means, including whether that term refers only to geographic territory or includes United States citizens or interests.

Section 3

Section 3's purpose was to increase communication between the Legislative and Executive Branches, perhaps fulfilling the intent of the Framers that the branches jointly make war decisions. As its subheading suggests, Section 3 addresses consultation. So, it is somewhat surprising that the WPR does not specifically state what "consult" means. Does it mean the President is required only to inform Congress? To request advice? To consider advice? To follow advice? The House Report on the WPR explicitly envisioned more than simply being informed. It said consultation meant "Members of Congress are being asked by the President for their advice and opinions. . . ." House Reports may be evidence of intent, but they are not themselves law. Similarly, the Senate Committee on Foreign Relations has interpreted the consultation requirement as "permitting Congress to participate in the decision-making." Yet Congress did not state in the WPR that consultation means an opportunity to provide advice or participate in decision-making, as it easily could have. Not surprisingly, Presidents generally have not interpreted the consultation provision to require seeking Congress's advice before deciding to introduce troops.

The WPR requires the President consult with Congress if he introduces United States armed forces into hostilities or situations where hostilities are imminent. And this consultation must occur *before* introduction of armed forces "in every possible instance." Note this exception gives the President latitude to determine when it is "possible" to consult in advance. In practice, Presidents have usually informed Congress of military activities just *after* they have begun. This practice is at least in part because of real military concerns regarding losing the element of surprise. As noted in our discussion of the Vietnam War above, it is harder for Congress to limit or end a military conflict after it has begun than before. Given this difficulty, the "in every possible instance" exception swallows the rule, with significant effects.

The WPR also does not specify who "Congress" is for purposes of consultation. A joint session with every member of Congress seems impractical for numerous reasons. At the other end of the spectrum, picking a single congressperson to consult seems to defeat the purpose of the provision. Some commentators have suggested consulting the leadership of each House of Congress is sufficient. This idea seems consistent with WPR Section 5, which requires reporting in certain circumstances and specifies to whom the reports must be made: the Committee on Foreign Affairs of the House of Representatives, the Committee on Foreign Relations of the Senate, the Speaker of House, and President Pro Tempore of the Senate. Congressional attempts to revise the WPR to specifically identify who "Congress" is for the purposes of this provision have failed.

Section 3 does not include exceptions to the consultation provision based on the size of the military intervention, meaning any military action involving hostilities or imminent hostilities requires congressional consultation. Additionally, Section 3 does not include everything the President might do with the military, or even every activity mentioned by other sections of the WPR (for example, see Section 4(a)(2–3)). Things potentially not covered by Section 3's reporting requirement include:

- Low-level deployments for regional peacekeeping;
- Naval actions in defense of free transit;
- Humanitarian interventions;
- Non-combat deployments of military advisers;
- Rescue missions of United States citizens;
- Protection of non-Americans in association with protecting Americans;
- Protection of United States embassies and consulates; and
- Suppression of civil insurrection in the United States.

Note that military actions like those in this list can escalate into full-scale military conflict. In fact, the non-combat deployment of military advisers was how the

United States' involvement in the conflict that would become the Vietnam War began.

The consultation requirement raises another question about the practical effectiveness of consultation with Congress. Many congresspeople have limited foreign policy experience. And the more people who are "consulted" about a potential use of military force, the greater the chance for leaks that could doom a military operation before it begins. If the Executive Branch has better information and more expertise than Congress regarding the diplomatic, political, and military reality and consequences of a proposed action, what value does consultation with Congress add?

Section 4

As noted in our discussion of the Vietnam War, even once congressional and public support have waned, it can be legally and politically difficult to extricate the United States from conflict. Recognizing that it is more difficult to terminate hostilities than to prevent them from beginning, the purpose of Section 4 is to require that Congress be informed as soon as possible of all movements of United States forces that might lead to military conflict, thus giving Congress an opportunity to object. If the President "introduces" troops into imminent hostilities without a declaration of war, he must report to Congress within 48 hours, explaining: why introduction of United States forces is necessary; the legal authority for introducing forces; and the estimated scope and duration of United States involvement. At its core, Section 4 is a mandate that the President inform Congress in certain circumstances. As straightforward as that may seem, Section 4 raises a host of questions.

First, Congress did not define "hostilities." Again, a House Report included some evidence of the House's intent: "In addition to a situation in which fighting actually has begun, "hostilities" also encompasses a state of confrontation in which no shots have been fired but where there is a clear and present danger of armed conflict." Failure to include a definition of "hostilities" in the statute, however, has given Presidents great flexibility in determining the applicability of Section 4(a). Presidents have used this flexibility to conclude that activities such as the 1988 deployment of 31 United States Navy ships to patrol the Persian Gulf to defend against Iranian attacks on oil tankers and the 2011 participation in military attacks on Libya were "limited in mission and exposure to United States troops" and therefore not "hostilities." Whether this flexibility was intended by Congress's omission of a definition of "hostilities" is a matter for debate.

Note that other significant phrases and terms are not explained, and thus provide the President with significant flexibility. For example, Congress does not specify what "equipped for combat" means. Are troops armed only with defensive weapons "equipped for combat"? Might a President deliberately under-equip troops to avoid triggering Section 4? Does that fact that nearly all troop movements around the world include arming the military for force protection mean that all such deployments require notification? Additionally, the WPR does not explain what "substantially enlarge" means. Lack of specificity arguably leaves to the President the ability to determine when reporting is required. In any event, legal challenges based on congressional or presidential interpretations of these provisions are likely to fail. Given the ambiguity of the terms, it is unsurprising that federal district courts have determined that whether a report is required is a non-justiciable political question.

Congress did choose to define one phrase—"introduction of United States Armed Forces"—to include "the assignment of members of such armed forces to command, coordinate, participate in the movement of, or accompany the regular or irregular military forces of any foreign country or government when such military forces are engaged, or there exists an imminent threat that such forces will become engaged, in hostilities." However, Congress's focus on the President's "introduction" of troops also potentially excludes use of troops already in place to engage in hostilities. For example, the United States has stationed tens of thousands of troops in South Korea for decades. Would using those troops in hostilities against North Korea not trigger reporting under Section 4 because the troops are already in place and thus not being "introduced"?

Importantly, certain requirements in Section 5 of the WPR are only triggered when the President reports activities under Section 4(a)(1). These requirements do *not* apply, for example, if the President introduces forces "into the territory, airspace or waters of a foreign nation, while equipped for combat, except for deployments which relate solely to supply, replacement, repair, or training of such forces" or "in numbers which substantially enlarge United States Armed Forces equipped for combat already located in a foreign nation."

Finally, note that Congress excluded from Section 4 situations where it has already declared war. This makes sense, as one would assume Congress is aware of a situation before it declares war. But note that, unlike Section 2, Congress does not exclude situations where it has authorized military force without a formal declaration of war. This means Presidents are required to submit a report in situations covered in Section 4(a) where Congress has already issued an authorization for the use of military force. It is unclear whether Congress's omission was intentional or an oversight.

To Report or Not to Report: the United States Deployment to Panama

In an effort to protect United States interests in keeping the Panama Canal open for United States shipping and to pressure General Manuel Noriega to abandon his dictatorship, in 1988 and 1989 President George H.W. Bush ordered a significant buildup of troop levels in Panama. Included in this troop buildup were troops assigned to conduct combat training in Panama. Within months of their arrival, in December 1989, the United States military attacked Panamanian military forces loyal to General Noriega, leading to his capture by the United States. President Bush did not notify Congress of the troop deployment.

Section 5

Section 5 is the operational portion of the WPR designed to "prevent another Vietnam." Section 5(b) mandates that when the President submits a report under Section 4(a)(1), meaning United States forces have been introduced into hostilities or into situations where imminent involvement in hostilities is clearly indicated, the President must terminate the use of troops within 60 days unless Congress (1) has declared war or given specific authorization; (2) has extended by law the 60 days; or (3) is physically unable to meet as a result of an armed attack on the United States. If 60 days pass without congressional action, the President would have to withdraw, or at least stop using, United States forces. In other words, Congress must "ratify" the President's Section 4(a)(1) actions in order for the use of force to continue lawfully.

Section 5(b) seems to reverse the default presumption. Previously, congressional inaction could be considered acquiescence to the President's actions. After the WPR, congressional inaction requires the President to stop using military force. The title of Section 5—"Congressional Action"—seems ironic, given that Section 5 empowers Congress through *inaction*. Through the WPR, Congress is attempting to *increase* (or at least protect) its role in national security policy decisions through a provision that requires it to take no action at all. While this may seem counterintuitive, some have suggested this is the central idea the Framers were trying to accomplish. By requiring both the Legislative and the Executive to actively participate in the authorization for war, we might be less likely to go to war.

Section 5(b) also raises the perplexing issue of what congressional inaction actually indicates. At least one federal court ruled that it is uncertain whether inaction by Congress in the face of the President's use of force constitutes acquiescence to the President's action or constitutes congressional intent to require the President to stop using military force. *Crocket v. Reagan*. The court reached the perhaps counterintuitive conclusion that "it is consistent with the purposes and structure of the WPR to require further congressional action before the automatic termination provision operates." Note that this is the *opposite* of what the text of Section 5 says. Responding to that idea, one commentator argued "Congress should not have to pass a new law in order to enforce a law already on the books." Steven V. Roberts, *War Powers? What War Powers?*, N.Y. Times, Oct. 6, 1987.

Contrary to popular misperception, advanced in part by successive Presidents' effective use of the media, Section 5(b) was not intended to provide Presidents a 60-day "blank check" to use military force in situations where they did not already have legal authority. In fact, Section 8 explicitly says the WPR is not intended to confer rights on the President that he did not have absent the WPR.

Note that the situations in sections 4(a)(2) and 4(a)(3) do not trigger the 60-day clock. Thus, reports under those sections do not create a time limit for operations. The fact that only 4(a)(1) reports trigger the 60-day clock has tempted Presidents to misreport, either by choosing to report uses of military forces under Section 4(a)(2) or 4(a)(3), or by reporting action "consistent with Section 4," without specifying which subsection applies. In fact, between enactment of the WPR in 1973 and March 2017, Presidents submitted 168 reports under the War Powers Resolution, but only *one*—the 1975 military rescue of a United States ship's crew taken hostage in Cambodia—cited Section 4(a)(1). And in that one case, the military action was completed, and United States armed forces had departed, before President Ford made the Section 4(a)(1) report to Congress.

Aside from constitutional questions, the 60-day clock poses practical concerns. Assuming the 60-day clock is enforceable, or at least followed, it could significantly alter the mission or methods of military activities by imposing an artificial timeline for their conclusion. Or it could require a President to end a military conflict before the objective had been met, with potentially disastrous military consequences. Additionally, it might encourage enemies to "wait out the clock," focus military efforts on the expected United States withdrawal after two months, and attempt to engage politically in the United States to ensure Congress does not act within 60 days.

In contrast to Section 5(b), which requires termination of the use of military force if Congress does not act, Section 5(c) provides Congress with an affirmative opportunity to act. Specifically, Section 5(c) says Congress can, by concurrent resolution, order the President to remove troops, even before the 60-day clock has run out. However, Section 5(c) is clearly unconstitutional after *INS v. Chadha*. In *Chadha*, the Supreme Court required that for a congressional action to have the force of law, it must follow the constitutional requirements of passage by both houses of Congress and presentment to the President. Unlike joint resolutions, which are sent to the President, concurrent resolutions are not. Thus, a concurrent resolution has no direct legal effect.

Section 8

Section 8 has prompted plenty of scholarly debate, but so far no known reported federal court opinions. Section 8 purports to provide a **rule of construction** for how the WPR is to be interpreted. In response to the legal arguments offered by Presidents throughout the Vietnam War, Section 8(a) attempts to limit the ways in which Presidents can creatively "find" legal authority to use military force. Specifically, Section 8(a) says authority to use military force cannot be inferred from other statutes (such as the Military Selective Service Act), appropriations, or treaties, unless those statutes specifically authorize the use of force in question and explicitly state they are intended to constitute statutory authorization. An example of this is the post-9/11 2001 AUMF, which stated "Consistent with section 8(a)(1) of the WPR, the Congress's declares that this section is intended to constitute specific statutory authority within the meaning of section 5(b) of the WPR." Section 8's explicit reference to selective service statutes and appropriations statutes was clearly a response to courts' interpretation of those types of statutes as continuing authorization for the use of force in Vietnam after repeal of the Tonkin Gulf Resolution.

Similarly, in response to presidential administrations' use of the SEATO Treaty as a basis for military action in Vietnam, Section 8(a) says authority to use force cannot be inferred from any treaty. This raises some interesting legal questions. First, is it constitutional to limit the effect of a treaty through a statute? Does the **last in time rule** mean that the United States' mutual defense treaties, nearly all of which *predate* the WPR, can no longer be interpreted as obligating United States participation in the defense of its allies? Section 8(c) says "Nothing in this chapter is intended to alter. . . the provisions of existing treaties," but does Section 8(a) not effectively attempt do just that?

Section 8(d) claims that the WPR is not intended to alter the constitutional authority of Congress or the President, or grant the President powers he does not otherwise have. Section 8(d)(1) and (2) clearly defeat the "60 day blank check" interpretation of Section 5 popularized by Presidents and the media.

5.5.3. Presidents' Options Under WPR

Presidents have a few options regarding compliance with the War Powers Resolution. First, they can claim, as President Nixon did in his initial veto of the bill, that the WPR is unconstitutional. And in fact, every President since President Nixon has publicly or privately voiced skepticism about the WPR's constitutionality. On the other hand, if attempting to comply with the WPR, Presidents could frontload operations so that they take fewer than 60 days. Or, as noted above, Presidents can misreport under Section 4, to avoid triggering the Section 5 60-day clock. The approach most favored by Presidents has been to report military activities "*consistent* with WPR," rather than "in *compliance* with the WPR," but then not act as though their actions are limited by a 60-day clock. Presidents' behavior demonstrates the WPR does not work as intended. The WPR has resulted in numerous reports to Congress, but has not stopped Presidents from using United States armed forces without specific congressional authorization. And courts refuse to rule on these political questions.

5.5.4. War in the Twilight Zone?

Section 8 attempts to eliminate arguments of presidential authority resulting from congressional acquiescence or implied support, removing one of Justice Jackson's three tiers. Whether the War Powers Resolution legally or effectively addresses such actions, Presidents have increasingly relied on the "implied support" or "lack of express prohibition" theory to justify their military actions. The WPR is viewed by some as an attempt by Congress to limit the President's ability to engage in military hostilities in a context like that described by Justice Jackson's Category Two, where the President initiates military action neither authorized nor prohibited by Congress. If the President complies with the WPR, the military conflict is a "Category One" situation; if he engages in military conflict not authorized by Congress, the conflict is a "Category Three" situation. The Twilight Zone (Category Two) is arguably eliminated.

Before the Vietnam conflict detailed above, President Truman conducted a non-defensive conflict in Korea, a war that cost roughly 36,000 American lives and $70 billion. President Truman relied in part on a complicated international law justification for the hostilities, but also relied on Congress' implicit authorization of the war in the form of authorizing conscription, activating military reserve forces, and appropriating funds for the war. What Congress did *not* do is provide an authorization for the use of military force or declaration of war.

Other examples of the "implied support and no express prohibition" context for presidential use of the military, where hostilities were likely or actually occurred include President Reagan's deployment of the military to Lebanon in 1983, President George H.W. Bush's military intervention in Somalia in 1992, and President Clinton's use of the military in Bosnia in 1995, and Kosovo in 1999. Presidents have also used force in similar contexts in the conflicts detailed below.

United States Airstrikes in Serbia, 1999

When Serbian President Slobodan Milosevic initiated a military campaign of "ethnic cleansing" of Muslims from Kosovo, the United States and its **North Atlantic Treaty Organization (NATO)** allies engaged in an Air Campaign against Serbia. Hoping to prevent another genocide as had previously occurred when Serbia supported ethnic cleansing of Muslims in Bosnia, President Clinton ordered sustained airstrikes against Serbia. President Clinton did not seek explicit authorization from Congress, and claimed he did not need such authorization, citing his inherent power as Commander in Chief, foreign affairs power, the need to support the NATO alliance, and claimed permission from the WPR to use force for up to 60 days without congressional authorization. In a collage of measures reminiscent of its actions during the Vietnam conflict, Congress's response to President Clinton's use of military force in Serbia was mixed. The House of Representatives voted against a declaration of war, against a resolution to authorize continued military force in Kosovo, but also against a resolution directing the President to remove United States armed forces from Serbia. On top of this group of mixed messages, Congress used its **appropriations power**, prohibiting the use of appropriated funds for ground troops in Kosovo, implicitly approving the air campaign, and later appropriating funds to continue the air campaign against Serbia. Thus, President Clinton could argue that continuing the air campaign in Serbia was consistent with the implied will of Congress.

United States Military Campaign Against the Islamic State, 2014

In August 2014, President Barack Obama ordered airstrikes against a terrorist group known as the Islamic State (ISIS). The airstrikes included targets in Iraq and Syria. On August 8, 2014, President Obama reported these military operations to Congress "consistent with the War Powers Resolution." The Obama Administration initially argued that the airstrikes against the Islamic State were within the President's Article II authority. About one month later, the Administration added to its rationale that the strikes were legally justified by the 2001 and 2002 AUMFs. The 2001 AUMF had authorized use of force against nations and organizations who "planned, authorized, committed, or aided the terrorist attacks that occurred on September 11, 2001." And the 2002 AUMF authorized the use of force to "defend the national security of the United States against the continuing threat posed by Iraq." The Islamic State did not exist in 2001, and though it was operating in the territory of Iraq, it was not "Iraq." On the other hand, the Islamic State induced the collapse of portions of Iraq, and the resulting destabilization arguably was a "threat posed by Iraq." Though Congress subsequently entertained various authorizations for the use of military force against the Islamic State, it did not enact any legislation. Airstrikes against ISIS continued for years without congressional authorization.

United States Missile Attacks on Syria, 2017

In April 2017, President Donald Trump ordered the United States military to carry out missile attacks on Syrian forces and chemical facilities in response to the Syrian government's use of chemical weapons against civilians. President Trump notified Congress of the attacks "consistent with the War Powers Resolution." The missile attacks lasted only hours. Congress did not authorize the attacks.

REVIEW QUESTIONS

1. What are Justice Jackson's three categories and what do they signify? Explain why Justice Jackson's "three categories" approach can be both helpful and unhelpful in answering separation of powers questions.

2. What are the various ways through which Congress authorized the use of military force in Vietnam?

3. Could Congress have limited the United States military's actions to Vietnam, excluding Cambodia and Laos, in the original Tonkin Gulf Resolution? What precedent would support that?

4. How does the War Powers Resolution address the various theories of presidential national security power?

CRITICAL THINKING QUESTIONS

1. In *Youngstown*, Justice Jackson warned: "The opinions of judges, no less than executives and publicists, often suffer the infirmity of confusing the issue of a power's validity with the cause it is invoked to promote. . . ." How is that point demonstrated or refuted by the various struggles for national security power discussed in this chapter?

2. Was any of the following theories of presidential power *alone* (by itself) a sufficient basis for the President's military activities in Vietnam?

- Commander in Chief power
- "Defensive" or "repel attack" power
- Customary authority
- SEATO and President's treaty authority

3. Were Congress's special appropriations for the Vietnam War by themselves a sufficient legal basis for the President's military activities in Vietnam?

4. What is the best explanation for why the Supreme Court decided no cases assessing the legality of the military conflict in Vietnam? Explain.

5. If Congress authorizes use of force against a particular terrorist organization, is it a "new war" when the President orders military attacks against a terrorist group that has splintered off from the original terrorist group? Can Congress limit the President's authority to do so?

6. Professor John Hart Ely suggested that Congress's decision to repeal the TGR, without doing more, was "just more of Congress's playing Pontius Pilate," meaning Congress was trying to wash its hands of the conflict without having to take any real position. Is that a fair assessment?

7. Can anything less than a veto-proof majority in both houses of Congress legally end a war? Is the July 1, 1973 joint resolution the best blueprint for how Congress can try to end a war? As a practical matter, can Congress or the courts end a war when the President wishes it to continue?

8. Does the use of drones or cyber warfare, neither of which technically involved the introduction of United States *troops* into hostilities, not require consultation under Section 3 of the WPR? What about the use of government civilians and contractors, who arguably are also not "United States armed forces?"

9. Applying what you know of the political question doctrine from Chapter 4, do you agree that whether a report is required under the WPR is a political question?

10. Do you agree that interpreting the WPR to require further congressional action before the President must terminate a conflict is consistent with the purposes of the WPR? With the constitutional design?

11. In Sections 2 and 8 of the WPR, Congress seems to have eliminated all methods of conveying support or cooperation with a President's use of force other than explicit authorization. And, under the WPR, congressional failure to explicitly take a position must be interpreted as opposition to the President's use of force. Should the Congress in 1973 be able to dictate to subsequent Congresses how their support or opposition to military action must be expressed?

12. Did the troop deployments to Panama ordered by President Bush leading to General Noriega's arrest fall within Section 4(a)(2)'s exception for deployments related to training deployments? What other basis was there for President Bush to not notify Congress of a deployment that ultimately led to combat?

13. Does the fact that President Clinton had already begun the air campaign in Serbia diminish the argument that Congress's decision to appropriate funding constituted authorization for the conflict?

14. Why might the War Powers Resolution have caused the Obama Administration to switch its rationale for continuing airstrikes from the President's Article II authority to the 2001 and 2002 AUMFs? Did the Obama Administration violate the WPR by continuing the airstrikes beyond October 8, 2014?

15. Did the limited duration missile attacks on Syria—a sovereign nation—in 2017 violate the War Powers Resolution? The Constitution?

16. The airstrikes on Serbia in 1999, the Islamic state in 2014, and Syria in 2017, involved the United States' use of air power—attacks by plane and missile—against an enemy. Does the lack of "boots on the ground," and corresponding reduction in the likelihood of American casualties, in these situations alter the legal analysis of the President's authority?

17. Can you devise a better standard than "some mutual participation by Congress" for a court to employ when determining the sufficiency of Congress's involvement in authorizing the use of military force?

18. In Section 2(a), Congress claims the WPR fulfills the intent of the Framers of the Constitution. Does it?

CHAPTER 6

The Fourth Amendment and National Security

The National Security Operations Center Floor, National Security Agency

Learning Objectives

1. Understand why the Fourth Amendment of the United States Constitution requires the government to obtain a warrant before it conducts a search for evidence of criminal activity and how the government can obtain a warrant to conduct a search.

2. Understand and identify the facts and circumstances that create national security-related exceptions to the Fourth Amendment warrant requirement.

3. Understand the common techniques the government uses to search for evidence of threats to national security.

6.1. INTRODUCTION

Perhaps no other topic more clearly demonstrates the difficult and constant balance between national security and liberty than the Fourth Amendment. Unlike many other Constitutional rights, the language of the Fourth Amendment specifically recognizes both the government's interests and the individual's interests. On one hand, the Fourth Amendment recognizes the government's interest in seeking evidence of criminal activity and detaining those suspected of a crime. On the other hand, the same Amendment tempers the government's powers and protects against "unreasonable" searches and seizures. John Adams, the first Vice President and second President of the United States, once remarked that the English abuses that led to the adoption of the Fourth Amendment were the same abuses that inspired the American Colonies' push for independence.

Many years before the adoption of the Fourth Amendment, the King of England, royal officials, and English courts issued documents called **general warrants**. These documents gave law enforcements officers extremely broad powers and discretion; they were often issued without limitations. With a general warrant in hand, a law enforcement officer could search virtually any person or place and take hold of anything the officer believed to be related to criminal wrongdoing. Additionally, law enforcement officers did not need to provide a reason for needing a general warrant. For example, there was no requirement that law enforcement officers present evidence of potential criminal activity before a general warrant was issued. Equally troubling, general warrants in England were often used not to search for evidence of traditional criminal activity, but instead to find and destroy writings critical of the government. General warrants were not necessarily an accepted part of crime fighting in England. In fact, many in England criticized the use of general warrants and claimed they were a violation of English **common law**.

Writs of assistance, a specific kind of general warrant, were often used by the King's colonial administration in the American Colonies. They provided British officials unlimited power to search and seize the colonists' property in an effort to enforce trade laws that prohibited smuggling in the colonies. While the colonists objected to the Crown's use of writs of assistance, their complaints were rejected by the British government. In fact, despite the colonists' grievances, the British Parliament passed a law reaffirming the right of colonial officials to use writs of assistance. After the American Revolution, motivated by the misuses and mistrust of general warrants, states prohibited them in their constitutions. Finally, in 1792, the Fourth Amendment was ratified as part of the Bill of Rights. When reading the Fourth Amendment, one can see in its language the colonists' experiences and distrust of general warrants. One can also see their desire to place limitations on government power. Of course, some of these colonists would go on to become **Framers** of the Constitution.

James Otis, the Fourth Amendment, and the Birth of Independence

Many historians credit a colonial lawyer and American Revolutionary from Massachusetts, James Otis, as one of the earliest and most inspiring advocates against British abuses in the American Colonies. Much of his advocacy for revolution centered on the use of writs of assistance by the British. As a successful and well-connected lawyer in Boston, Otis made a name for himself as a rising star in his profession. In 1756, at the young age of 31, he was appointed to the position of Advocate General, or prosecutor, in a colonial Vice Admiralty Court. These courts were responsible for enforcing British maritime law in the colonies and often used evidence collected with the help of writs of assistance. Though troubled by writs of assistance and their potential for abuse, it was a personal conflict that finally drove Otis into the hands of the revolutionary cause. In 1761, the British Crown chose a new Governor for the Massachusetts colony. At the same time, the Chief Justice position on the colony's highest court was vacant. While many expected Otis's father to be appointed to the position, the Governor instead chose his father's political opponent. Otis was so infuriated by the decision that he resigned his position as Advocate General and soon agreed to represent a group of merchants challenging the use of writs of assistance. In a five-hour speech, Otis railed against writs of assistance as a violation of the colonists' natural, fundamental rights and argued that any law passed by the British Parliament authorizing them was void. He argued:

> *A man's house is his castle; and whilst he is quiet, he is as well guarded as a prince in his castle. This writ, if it should be declared legal, would totally annihilate this privilege. Custom-house officers may enter our houses when they please; we are commanded to permit their entry. Their menial servants may enter, may break locks, bars, and everything in their way; and whether they break through malice or revenge, no man, no court can inquire. Bare suspicion without oath is sufficient.* James Otis, *Argument at Trial Against Writs of Assistance*, 1761.

While Otis lost his challenge to the use of writs of assistance, John Adams credited Otis's speech with being the moment that American independence was born.

6.2. THE FOURTH AMENDMENT—THE BASICS

While it is comprised of a single sentence, the Fourth Amendment is often thought of as having two distinct, but related, components—searches and **warrants**. In the first instance, the Fourth Amendment prohibits unreasonable government searches of "persons, houses, papers and effects . . . ." While seemingly straightforward, the Amendment lacks any definition of what constitutes a search or what makes a search unreasonable. The second part of the Amendment requires that, in order to obtain a warrant to search for evidence of criminal activity, the government must demonstrate it has **probable cause** to believe it will find the evidence. Moreover, the government must describe, with particularity, where it wants to search and what it wants to seize.

6.2.1. Fourth Amendment Searches and Warrants

Fourth Amendment Searches

The understanding of what constitutes a search for Fourth Amendment purposes has changed over time. Initially, in a case from 1928 called *Olmstead v. United States*, the Supreme Court interpreted the term "search" to only include situations where the government trespassed into constitutionally protected areas. In *Olmstead*, the government wiretapped the telephone calls of a suspected bootlegger. At his criminal trial, the bootlegger claimed that the wiretap amounted to a search for evidence of criminal activity. The Court disagreed and determined that a Fourth Amendment search only occurs when the government physically invades a person's home in an effort to search for and seize evidence.

Thirty-nine years later, in *Katz v. United States*, the Court's interpretation of the Fourth Amendment changed drastically. In *Katz*, police attached a listening device to the outside wall of a telephone booth in an effort to listen to a suspect's telephone conversation. The Court specifically rejected the physical trespass concept it had announced in *Olmstead* and expanded the idea of what constituted a search. The Court held that the Fourth Amendment protects not just physical places, but people. As a result, in order to determine whether a search occurred, the Court would ask whether a person had a **reasonable expectation of privacy**. This question requires courts to determine whether 1) the subject of the search had exhibited a subjective expectation of privacy and 2) society would recognize that subjective expectation as reasonable. If both of these elements exist, the Fourth Amendment requires the government to obtain a warrant. In fact, when the government fails to obtain a warrant, the law presumes the search is unreasonable and the evidence obtained is inadmissible in court.

Warrants and Probable Cause

If law enforcement officers plan to conduct a search for evidence of criminal activity, the Fourth Amendment suggests the Judicial Branch has a role to play. Before conducting the search, law enforcement must obtain a warrant from a judge and the Fourth Amendment specifically sets forth the legal burden to obtain that warrant. In addition to specifically describing the places they intend to search and the things they are looking for, law enforcement officers must prove that they have probable cause to believe they will find the evidence they seek. There is no single definition of probable cause. However, a common definition courts apply requires a judge to review the facts and information provided by law enforcement officers and to use practical, common sense to determine whether there is a fair probability that evidence of a crime will be found.

6.2.2. The National Security Exception to the Warrant Requirement

In the *Katz* case discussed above, the Supreme Court noted that the Fourth Amendment's warrant requirement is not absolute. In fact, the Fourth Amendment's first clause only prohibits unreasonable searches. Does this imply that warrantless searches can, under some circumstances, be "reasonable" and therefore permissible? One could imagine situations where law enforcement officers may want to search for evidence of criminal activity and obtaining a warrant is impractical or the search is, in some other way, "reasonable" and therefore a warrant is unnecessary. Based on these realities, the Supreme Court has, over time, determined that there are exceptions to the Fourth Amendment's warrant requirement. Should one of those exceptions be "national security"? In other words, should the government be able to forgo obtaining a warrant and search whomever and wherever it wants simply by claiming the search is related to national security? That question has been a subject of debate throughout much of America's history. However, in the mid-Twentieth Century, at the beginning of the Cold War, the Executive Branch began earnestly laying the groundwork for a judicially recognized national security exception to the Fourth Amendment.

After World War II, as the Cold War got underway, there was great concern in the United States that agents of the Soviet Union and communist sympathizers were engaged in espionage, or even plotting to overthrow the United States government. In response to these concerns, United States intelligence agencies began to investigate people suspected of being involved in such efforts. Inevitably, these investigations required the government to search the suspects' homes and businesses and eavesdrop on their correspondences and conversations. However, many of these searches occurred without a warrant. In an effort to balance Fourth Amendment concerns against the need to ensure national security, the Executive Branch's federal prosecutors allowed the warrantless searches, but would not use the discovered evidence at trial. So long as an intelligence agency was only engaging in an intelligence gathering operation, and not engaging in law enforcement in an effort to catch and jail criminals, Executive Branch lawyers tolerated the warrantless searches.

In the 1960s, the Judicial Branch began to contemplate the effect of the Fourth Amendment on national security investigations. One of the first Supreme Court cases to mention the possibility of a national security exception to the Fourth Amendment warrant requirement was the *Katz* case, discussed above. In *Katz*, the government was trying to collect evidence of illegal gambling; national security was not an issue in the case. However, in a footnote, the Court specifically stated that it was leaving open the question of whether the government would need to obtain a warrant for national security related searches even where the suspect had a reasonable expectation of privacy. The Court pondered, though did not answer, whether other safeguards might satisfy the Fourth Amendment in those situations. The Executive Branch's intelligence agencies and federal prosecutors took this as a green light from the Court that warrantless searches for national security purposes did not violate the Fourth Amendment. This was the position the government would take five years after *Katz* in a case that constituted a turning point in Fourth Amendment-related national security questions—*United States v. United States District Court*, also known as the *Keith* case.

In 1968, the CIA office in Ann Arbor, Michigan was bombed. Three defendants were charged with conspiring to bomb the office and one of the defendants, Lawrence Plamondon, was charged with carrying out the bombing. The government had obtained evidence against Plamondon by wiretapping his telephone. However, the government had not requested a warrant from a judge before conducting the wiretap. The defendants argued that the government's wiretap and eavesdropping on Plamondon's conversations violated the Fourth Amendment and were therefore unlawful. The government responded by arguing that there is a national security exception to the Fourth Amendment's warrant requirement. The government argued that under this exception, the President, and those he designates, has the power to conduct warrantless searches in order to protect national security. The government posited that if the Court required prior **judicial review** of national security related searches, it would impede the President's authority and responsibility to protect the nation's security.

The government further argued that national security-related investigations are extremely complex and secretive and the court system is ill equipped to understand and keep pre-surveillance warrant requests secret. Moreover, national security-related searches are often an attempt to collect intelligence, not evidence of criminal activity for the purposes of arresting a suspect. The Fourth

Amendment, the government argued, was not intended to apply to these sorts of searches. Finally, the government suggested that if a court must review a national security-related search, the review should happen after the search has occurred and courts should only find a search unlawful if the government unreasonably relied on the national security exception without any justification.

The Supreme Court recognized the President's inherent constitutional authority to protect the United States from those who would harm it and to use technology, like surveillance and wiretapping, to collect evidence to thwart attacks. However, the Court also recognized an equally important right to privacy found in the Fourth Amendment and noted that this right protects private conversations. In fact, the Court also noted, the government often violates the right to privacy when, in an effort to maintain security, it collects evidence on those who express unorthodox political beliefs or opposition to government policies. As a result, there are not only important Fourth Amendment interests implicated in national security-related surveillance, but also interests that revolve around the right to free speech and dissent, which are protected by the First Amendment.

Responding to the government's suggestion that requiring a warrant impedes national security-related searches, the Court determined that the Fourth Amendment's reasonableness requirement must be read in conjunction with the warrant requirement. The Fourth Amendment's requirement that law enforcement obtain a warrant before conducting a search serves an important function in a free society. It ensures that a judge, a neutral person not involved in the Executive Branch's law enforcement goals, plays a role in determining when the government is justified in invading its citizens' privacy. Otherwise, the Executive Branch's law enforcement efforts might become overzealous and unrestrained. Moreover, a review of the reasonableness of a search after it happens would not suffice. The Constitution contemplates a separation of powers among the branches of government in an effort to preserve fundamental civil liberties. To that end, the Court found, the Fourth Amendment specially requires the Judicial Branch to play a role before the government sets out to search for evidence of criminal activity. If the Judicial Branch only played a role in approving a search after it happened, searches that do not turn up evidence of criminal activity or do not end in a prosecution would never be reviewed to determine if they were reasonable.

The Court also held that the Fourth Amendment's warrant requirement applies equally to criminal investigations and intelligence gathering, as both risk infringing constitutionally protected liberties. To only require a warrant for criminal investigations would exempt a significant number of government surveillance efforts that, because of the nature of intelligence gathering, are often sustained, extensive, and focused on political dissent. Finally, the Court was not persuaded by the government's argument about the risks to secrecy associated with having to disclose information to a court in order to obtain a warrant. The Court found that the judicial system was well equipped to deal with sensitive, national security-related warrant requests. The government's requests for warrants occur ***ex parte***, which means the target of the search is not informed that the government is requesting a warrant. In addition, if the government is concerned about the potential for security leaks from administrative staff, it could provide its own secretarial personnel. Though this may add additional burdens to the process, the Court determined those burdens are justified in light of the liberties the Fourth Amendment was intended to protect.

Importantly, the group that was charged with conspiring to bomb the CIA office in *Keith* was made up of United States citizens and was a domestic organization. As a result, the government was conducting electronic surveillance of internal threats to national security. The Court in *Keith* specifically noted that its decision only analyzed whether a warrant was required in domestic national security cases. The Court recognized that some national security-related searches are focused on foreign security threats and it did not address whether a warrant would be required if the subject of a search or surveillance was a foreign power or its agents. Moreover, the Court did not wholly reject the distinction between typical criminal investigations and domestic national security surveillance. It recognized that domestic national security investigations and intelligence gathering are often focused on preventing future threats, which can cause it to be imprecise and complex. As a result, while prior judicial approval would be required for domestic national security-related surveillance, the Court left open the possibility that Congress could establish reasonable standards for the issuance of those warrants.

6.2.3. The Warrant Requirement and Threats to Public Safety

Typically, when thinking about national security in the context of the Fourth Amendment, the government is searching for evidence that will protect the nation from hostile acts or threats to the structure or existence of the United States government. In the *Keith* case, the Supreme Court considered whether there was an exception to the Fourth Amendment's warrant requirement when the government is collecting information about domestic threats to national security. Certainly, however, there are situations where the government may be searching for evidence of activity that poses less catastrophic security threats. The presumption is that the government must obtain a warrant before conducting these searches. However, the Supreme Court has determined that, in some circumstances, there is an exception to the warrant requirement when a warrant would be impractical. In yet other situations, even though the government may be searching for evidence, the Fourth Amendment is not implicated by the search and thus a warrant is not required.

When the government is running a typical investigation into criminal activity it must obtain a warrant before conducting a search. However, in a limited number of situations, where the government has special needs, apart from a typical criminal investigation, the Supreme Court has permitted warrantless searches. These "special needs" exceptions are often related to immediate threats to public safety and focused on gathering information to combat the threat, not to further the criminal prosecution of a suspect. While the government's warrantless search may intrude upon a person's reasonable expectation of privacy, it is nonetheless permissible because requiring the government to obtain a warrant for each search would be unworkable.

For example, courts have determined that warrantless searches are permissible before a passenger can board an airplane or subway. These courts have found that pre-boarding, warrantless searches are designed to prevent passengers from carrying on dangerous items, like weapons or explosives, and to prevent hijacking and terrorist attacks. The courts reasoned that these searches are not particularized attempts to find evidence of criminal activity and enforce criminal laws. Instead, the goal is public safety generally and if a passenger did not want to be searched, he could choose a different form of travel.

Though generally citizens retain a reasonable expectation of privacy in the contents of their automobiles, the Supreme Court has recognized an exception to the warrant requirement for some traffic roadblocks and checkpoints. For instance, in *Illinois v. Lidster*, the Supreme Court determined that the government was not required to obtain a warrant where it set up a roadblock to stop and ask motorists whether they had any information about a recent crime that occurred in the area. In *Michigan Dept. of State Police v. Sitz*, where the government set up sobriety checkpoints to deter drunk driving, the Court found that the government's important goal outweighed any brief, minimal intrusion into the motorists' privacy. Similarly, in *United States v. Martinez-Fuerte*, the government used a checkpoint to stop and search for undocumented immigrants on a highway leading out of Mexico. The Court determined that the government's interest in deterring human trafficking and illegal immigration outweighed the brief imposition on the motorists' privacy.

Finally, the Supreme Court has recognized the need to waive the warrant requirement when **exigent circumstances** exist. Exigent circumstances are those situations where a law enforcement officer has probable cause to search and reasonably believes waiting for a search warrant would result in harm to the officer or public, escape of a suspect, or destruction of evidence. The Court has also recognized the exigent circumstances exception in situations where law enforcement has entered a home to provide emergency assistance to an occupant or when law enforcement is in "hot pursuit" of a fleeing suspect. There is no specific rule to determine whether exigent circumstances exist; courts will consider all of the evidence and information available to the law enforcement officer when she determined exigent circumstances existed and there was no time to obtain a warrant. However, the negative outcome of waiting for a warrant cannot merely be a possibility. The law enforcement officer must have truly been presented with a compelling "now or never" situation.

6.2.4. Searches That Do Not Require a Warrant

The conditions described above constitute exceptions to the rule that warrants are required before conducting a search. In other words, a warrant would have been required but, for public policy reasons, the circumstances surrounding the search make obtaining a warrant impractical. Still, there are other situations where the government is searching for evidence and a warrant is not necessary in the first place. Therefore, while these may be warrantless searches, they are not necessarily exceptions to the warrant requirement because warrants are not required to conduct these searches. Courts sometimes refer to these activities as "non-searches," even though the government is actually looking for evidence.

For example, law enforcement officers do not need a warrant to conduct a search if they gain **consent** from the target of the search. An officer simply needs to ask if he can conduct a search and, if the target of the search agrees, the search can proceed without a warrant. The officer does not even need probable cause to believe he will find evidence of criminal activity. Interestingly, this is one of the most common ways searches are conducted. The only burden on the government is to prove that the consent was voluntary. Courts will consider all the facts and circumstances surrounding the interaction between the officer and the target of the search to determine whether consent was given freely or coerced. Once given, consent can be revoked, at which time the search cannot continue without a warrant or an exception to the warrant requirement.

Law enforcement officers do not need a search warrant if they find an item in **plain view**. So long as a law enforcement officer has a legal right to be in a particular location, she need not avert her eyes if she sees something she reasonably believes to be contraband or other evidence of a crime. For example, if a law enforcement officer has a warrant to enter a home in search of stolen money and sees illegal drugs in plain view while searching for the money, the officer can confiscate the illegal drugs without a warrant. The officer can confiscate the illegal drugs even if she thought she might find them while searching for the stolen money, but did not have a specific warrant authorizing her to look for illegal drugs. In this example, however, the illegal nature of the drugs must be readily apparent to the officer. In relying on the plain view doctrine to confiscate an item without a search warrant, an officer may not move or manipulate the item to determine if it is contraband or evidence of a crime—the nature of the item must be clear just by looking at it.

The Plain View Doctrine and the Contents of Your Cell Phone

In 2009, David Leon Riley was arrested, during a traffic stop, for possessing concealed handguns. After Riley's arrest, police officers conducted a search of his person pursuant to the "search incident to arrest" exception. This exception allows, for safety reasons, arresting officers to conduct a warrantless search of an arrestee's person at the time of his arrest. Upon conducting their search, the officers discovered Riley's cell phone. The officers accessed Riley's cell phone and looked through his photographs, videos, and contacts. They also read his text messages and saw information that suggested Riley was a gang member. At trial, Riley argued that the police officers conducted a warrantless search of his cell phone. The government argued that, because Riley's cell phone was legally discovered during a search incident to arrest, the search of his cell phone was permissible and the information was discovered under the plain view doctrine.

Riley's case ultimately made its way to the Supreme Court. In *Riley v. California*, the Court rejected the government's argument and held that the search of Riley's cell phone violated the Fourth Amendment. The Court found that information on a cell phone, like pictures and text messages, do not pose an immediate safety risk to police officers and cannot be used to help an arrestee escape. As a result, the search incident to arrest exception would not permit the police officer to access the phone's data after an arrest. The police would, of course, be free to inspect the cell phone itself for razor blades or other physical items that might harm them. However, because the police officers did not have a legal right to access the information on the phone, the Court found they were not able to rely on the plain view exception to collect whatever information they inadvertently found while they scrolled through the phone's data.

The Supreme Court has also determined that law enforcement need not obtain a warrant to search something when it has been turned over to a third-party. By giving something to a third-party, one no longer has a reasonable expectation of privacy in that thing and thus can no longer claim Fourth Amendment protection. This **third-party doctrine** arises most often in the context of information intentionally and voluntarily given to a third-party. For example, in *United States v. Miller*, the Supreme Court determined that bank records, such as deposits and withdrawals, were not the bank account owner's private records but were instead the bank's business records. Because the information contained in the banking transactions had been voluntarily conveyed to the bank by the account owner, the owner had no reasonable expectation of privacy in the information. Therefore, the government did not need a warrant to search the information contained in the account. The third-party doctrine has wide-ranging implications in light of today's technology and the **metadata** we share with private companies.

Consider the information turned over to a cell phone company when one places a telephone call—the phone numbers on both ends of the call, the time and place of the call, and the duration of the call. In 1979, in *Smith v. Maryland*, the Supreme Court determined that this sort of information is not subject to the Fourth Amendment's warrant requirement due to the third-party doctrine. Now consider companies that provide internet access to their customers, known as internet service providers, and the information stored by those companies—the search terms customers use as well as the websites viewed and the duration of viewing. If the third-party doctrine applies to this information because it has been voluntarily turned over to the cell phone company or internet service provider, then the government can search the information without a warrant. In 2018, the Supreme Court considered a similar scenario in *Carpenter v. United States*. In *Carpenter*, the Court held that cell phone users voluntarily turn over their location data to cell phone companies simply by using their cell phones. Nevertheless, the Court refused to apply the third-party doctrine. It reasoned that a warrant was required because of the "seismic shifts in digital technology" and the detailed and vast amount of information the government could effortlessly collect.

Finally, the Supreme Court has long recognized that searches at the border, before a person or property enters the country, are inherently reasonable and do not require a warrant. These searches are reasonable based on a nation's right to protect itself by controlling who and what enters the country. In fact, the same Congress that proposed the Fourth Amendment also passed a statute, before the Fourth Amendment was adopted, that permitted customs officials to enter a ship or vessel without a warrant if they reasonably believed it to contain contraband. As a result, in *United States v. Ramsey*, where customs officials had reason to believe that international mail, bound for an address in the United States, contained narcotics, the government was free to open the mail without a warrant. In *United States v. Villamonte-Marquez*, a customs officer boarded a vessel in waters that provided ready access to the open sea. When the customs official smelled marijuana, he searched the vessel and discovered large amounts of the drug intended for sale. The Court determined that boarding and searching the vessel without a warrant, or even a suspicion that criminal activity was afoot, did not violate the Fourth Amendment.

6.3. COMMON TECHNIQUES THE GOVERNMENT USES TO SEARCH FOR EVIDENCE OF THREATS TO NATIONAL SECURITY

The government uses a variety of methods to search for evidence of domestic and international threats to national security. It is important to understand the capabilities, limitations, and legal implications of some of the most important means by which the government collects this evidence. Electronic surveillance, **National Security Letters**, and **mail cover**—the three techniques discussed below—each have the potential to reveal a wealth of information. Because the government is using these techniques to conduct a search for information, each technique also has Fourth Amendment implications. As you read about each technique, consider why an intelligence agency may choose one method over another to collect information.

6.3.1. Electronic Surveillance

One of the most powerful and revealing means by which the government collects information about threats to national security is electronic surveillance. Electronic surveillance is the collection of information about a target through using electronic devices and technology. Electronic surveillance has become the subject of much debate since the 9/11 terrorist attacks on the United States and the government's subsequent electronic surveillance programs. Yet the government has engaged in electronic surveillance since the invention of the telegraph. Still, as modern life so heavily relies on electronic technology and communication, the government has the ability to gather much more information about a surveillance target than was possible 150 years ago.

The laws that govern electronic surveillance vary depending on the target of the surveillance. If the government is surveilling a domestic threat to national security, the **Electronic Communications Privacy Act (ECPA)** and its amending legislation, controls the government's surveillance. If the government is surveilling a foreign threat to national security, the **Foreign Intelligence Surveillance Act (FISA)**, and its amending legislation, controls the government's surveillance.

6.3.1.1. The Electronic Communications Privacy Act

The ECPA governs law enforcement's use of three distinct surveillance tools: 1) intercepting wire, oral, or electronic communication—often referred to as wiretapping; 2) accessing the content of electronically stored files; and 3) the use of **pen registers** and **trap and trace devices**. Each of these surveillance tools, and the information they reveal, implicate the privacy interests of Americans in different ways. As a result, the ECPA provides different legal protections depending on the surveillance tool the government is using and the corresponding information the tool can reveal.

If the government wants to intercept and listen to or read electronic communication in an attempt to collect evidence of certain enumerated crimes, Title I of the ECPA, sometimes referred to as the Wiretap Act, requires law enforcement agents to seek permission from a court. When applying for judicial permission to intercept electronic communication, law enforcement must prove there is probable cause to believe that the target of the wiretap is committing or will commit a crime and communication about the crime will be collected by wiretapping the target. Law enforcement must also prove there is probable cause to believe that the communication device the government wants to wiretap, or the place the communication is to be intercepted, is being used in connection with the suspected crime. In addition, unlike a traditional Fourth Amendment warrant, under the ECPA law enforcement agents must also prove they have tried normal investigative procedures, normal investigative procedures would be unlikely to succeed, or normal investigative procedures would be too dangerous.

If a judge is convinced the government has met its burden, the judge's order must specify 1) the person whose communication will be intercepted, 2) the place where the government can perform the intercept, 3) the type of communication that may be intercepted, 4) the crime to which the communication relates, 5) the agency authorized to intercept the communication, and 6) how long the government may intercept the target's communication. A judge's intercept order under the ECPA cannot permit the government to conduct a wiretap for longer than 30 days. However, the government can request an unlimited number of extensions, but must provide all the same information required for an initial request.

While the government is intercepting electronic communication pursuant to a judge's order, it must have procedures in place to minimize the collection of information that is not covered by the judge's order. This can be accomplished by, for example, turning off the equipment the government is using to listen to oral communication or delete the irrelevant portion of an email once a law enforcement agent determines the communication is not covered by the judge's order. In emergency situations, the government can intercept electric communication without a court order if there is a reasonable likelihood that the communication will provide evidence of immediate danger of death or serious physical injury to any person, threats to national security interest, or organized crime. The government must seek judicial approval within 48 hours of beginning to intercept the communication. If a judge does not issue an interception order, the information collected will be treated as if it was obtained illegally.

Title II of the ECPA, the Stored Communications Act (SCA), contains procedures the government must follow if it wants to access the files stored by electronic communication service providers or a customer's information, such as names, billing records, and the unique set of numbers that identify computers on the internet—IP addresses. If the government seeks to obtain the informational content of files stored by service providers it must obtain a traditional Fourth Amendment search warrant. However, if the file has been held by the service provider for longer than 180 days, the government can forgo a formal warrant. In that case, the government must provide notice to the customer and issue an administrative subpoena to the service provider, or prove to a court that the information is reasonably likely to be relevant to an ongoing criminal investigation. If the government is seeking to obtain basic information about a service provider's customer, such as a customer's name, address, telephone numbers dialed, duration of telephone calls, or how a customer pays for the service, the government need not obtain a warrant from a court. As reflected in the third-party doctrine discussed above, the customer's privacy interest in this sort of information is arguably lower than the informational content of an electronic file. Therefore, pursuant to the SCA, the government need only issue an administrative subpoena demanding the information from the service provider.

Title III of the ECPA governs the government's use of pen registers and trap and trace devices. These surveillance tools do not record the content of communication but instead record the information associated with the process of communicating through electronic means. The information includes, for example, the outgoing (pen register) and incoming (trap and trace) phone numbers dialed and the duration of a phone call or the outgoing or incoming email addresses contacted by a surveillance target. In *Smith v. Maryland*, the Supreme Court determined that the government's use of these sorts of devices does not constitute a search under the Fourth Amendment. Therefore, pursuant to the ECPA, the government need only certify to a judge that "the information likely to be obtained by such installation and use is relevant to an ongoing criminal investigation."

6.3.1.2. Foreign Intelligence Surveillance Act

While the ECPA governs the government's electronic surveillance of domestic threats to national security, FISA governs the government's surveillance, both traditional and electronic, of foreign threats to national security. FISA authorizes the government's intelligence agencies to use four tools to investigate foreign threats to national security: 1) electronic surveillance that intercepts the content of communication; 2) physical searches; 3) the use of pen registers and trap and trace devices; and 4) court orders requiring the production of tangible things. The government's surveillance of foreign threats is coordinated through a special, secret court created by FISA. This secret court, the Foreign Intelligence Surveillance Court (FISC), is responsible for reviewing, approving, or rejecting the government's surveillance requests. The discussion below is intended to provide a basic introduction to FISA. FISA's origins, development, and investigative tools are more fully discussed in Chapter 7.

Electronic Surveillance and Physical Searches

If the government seeks to wiretap the electronic communication or conduct a physical search of a foreign threat to national security, whether a foreign power or its agent, it must first obtain permission to do so from the FISC. The government must provide the following information to the FISC: 1) the identity, or a description, of the person to be electronically surveilled or physically searched—also known as the target; 2) the facts that demonstrate there is probable cause to believe the target is a foreign power or the agent of a foreign power; 3) the connection between the places to be surveilled or physically searched and the foreign power or agent of a foreign power; 4) the type of communication activities that will be surveilled or a description of the physical premises or property to be searched; 5) the nature of the information sought; 6) the **minimization procedures** the government will use to reduce the collection of unrelated information; 7) a description of how the electronic surveillance or physical search will be conducted; and 8) a description of any previous FISA applications regarding the target of the surveillance.

If the FISC judge is convinced the government has met its burdens, particularly regarding probable cause and minimization requirements, she may issue an order—the functional equivalent of a search warrant—that closely tracks the information required in the government's request. The order must memorialize who will be surveilled or searched, the kind of communications to be surveilled or the type and location of property to be searched, the type of information sought, the minimization procedures the government must use, how the surveillance or search will be carried out, and the duration of the government's surveillance or search authority. The government may seek unlimited renewals of the court's surveillance or search orders, so long as it meets the requirements of an original order request. Though a FISC order is usually required to conduct surveillance or a search, the government has the authority in emergency situations to conduct unauthorized surveillance or a search without a court order. In those cases, the Attorney General of the United States must reasonably determine an emergency exists and there are facts to support the issuance of an order if there was time to seek one from the FISC. The Attorney General may then authorize the surveillance or search without a FISC order and has seven days to apply for one. If an order is ultimately issued, the surveillance or searches proceed. If the FISC does not issue an order, the government must cease its surveillance or searches.

Pen Registers and Trap and Trace Devices

Like the ECPA, FISA authorizes the government to use pen registers and trap and trace devices to collect the dialing, routing, and transmittal information of a target's electronic communication. The government must seek permission from the FISC to use these devices and must certify that the collection of the information is part of either 1) an effort to collect **foreign intelligence** not concerning a United States person or 2) an investigation into international terrorism or clandestine intelligence activities. The FISC is not required to determine the truth of information contained in the government's certification. Instead, it simply determines whether the government made the required certifications. The FISC must then issue an order specifying the person who is the subject of the investigation, the means of communication that will be subjected to investigation, the geographic limitations of the order, and the duration of the government's authority. The duration of the government's authority may not exceed 60 days if the subject of the investigation is a United States person or a year for non-United States persons. The order may be renewed prior to expiring, so long as the government meets the certification requirements of an original order.

Production of Tangible Things

The final investigative tool available to the government through FISA is the ability to compel the production of tangible things. The term "tangible things" seems to be extraordinarily broad and at the same time narrow. It is broad in the sense that it could include any physical item imaginable and narrow in that intangible items are not covered. In practice, the government most often uses this FISA tool to collect documents, records, and files, whether physical or electronic, from the entity, whether an individual or business, that possesses them. To collect these items from the entity that possesses them, the government must first obtain an order from the FISC.

The government must prove there are reasonable grounds to believe the things sought are relevant to an investigation to obtain foreign intelligence information not concerning a United States person, to protect against international terrorism, or clandestine intelligence activities. Unlike pen registers and trap and trace devices, the FISC judge must be convinced that the government's assertions are true, otherwise the judge must deny the order. The government must also inform the FISC how it will minimize the retention and dissemination of information not relevant to the investigation. The FISC order to produce tangible things must describe, with particularity, the things to be turned over to the government so the recipient of an order can fairly identify them. In addition, it must provide a date by which the things must be provided to the government and a notice that the recipient may not tell anyone about the order, accept an attorney and those who are needed to help comply with the order.

6.3.2. National Security Letters

A National Security Letter (NSL) is yet another tool the government can use to collect evidence of threats to national security. NSLs enable the government to collect transactional non-content records, documents, and files. Because of the third-party doctrine, courts have determined that the government need not get permission from a court to issue a NSL and require the recipient to turn over the requested documents. The only limitation is that the request for records must be related to a national security investigation and not an investigation into traditional criminal activity. Additionally, unlike FISA being the exclusive statute that authorizes a "production of tangible things" order, there are multiple statutes that authorize the government to use NSLs to collect records—the Right to Financial Privacy Act; the Fair Credit Reporting Act; the Electronic Privacy Act (discussed above); and the National Security Act.

Each statute authorizes the government to issue NSLs to statutorily specified entities for statutorily specified information. The Right to Financial Privacy Act authorizes the government to issue NSLs to financial institutions, like banks or credit unions, directing them to turn over financial records to investigators. The Fair Credit Reporting Act authorizes the government to issue NSLs to consumer reporting agencies to obtain a list of financial accounts and other identifying information about the target of an investigation, such as current and former home addresses and employment history. The ECPA authorizes the government to issue NSLs to companies that provide communication services, like telephone companies or internet service providers. NSLs issued pursuant to the ECPA can be used to collect information in possession of these sorts of companies such as billing information and how long someone has been a customer. Finally, under the National Security Act, the government can issue NSLs as part of an investigation of government employees suspected of leaking classified information. These NSLs can be issued to financial companies, consumer reporting agencies, and companies that possess information about a government employee's travel history.

The statutes that authorize NSLs also prohibit those who receive an NSL from disclosing their existence if a government official certifies that disclosure would endanger national security, interfere with an investigation, or endanger someone. NSLs can be disclosed to those within a company or organization who are needed to assist in complying with the NSL. Additionally, an NSL recipient can inform an attorney in order to get legal advice. Unauthorized disclosure is a felony and punishable by five years in prison.

6.3.3. Mail Covers

The investigative technique known as mail cover is the collection of the information on the outside of a letter or package sent through the mail. It can also include measuring and recording the physical attributes of the item such as its size, shape, and weight. Like a pen register or trap and trace device, mail covers are used to collect information like the address to which an item is sent, the location from which the item is sent, and the return address on the item, which may indicate who sent it. The government is authorized to conduct a mail cover for national security reasons when there is an actual or potential threat that a foreign power or its agents will engage in 1) an attack or other hostile act; 2) sabotage or international terrorism; or 3) clandestine intelligence activities. Pursuant to United States Postal Service Regulations, only law enforcement agencies and agencies whose function is to protect national security may request a mail cover; most often it is the FBI. The request must specify reasonable grounds to demonstrate the mail cover is necessary to protect national security or pursue other law enforcement goals and must be approved by the Chief Postal Inspector.

The mail cover technique of collecting evidence does not include the collection and recording of the *contents* of an item sent through the mail. In other words, conducting a mail cover does not include the government opening a sealed letter. The informational contents of a domestic, sealed letter are protected by the Fourth Amendment. Therefore, the government must obtain a warrant to open a domestic letter or package. International mail, however, is not protected by the Fourth Amendment. Pursuant to the government's authority to control who and what enters the country, letters and packages sent internationally, whether to or from the United States, are subject to having their contents inspected without notification or a warrant.

6.4. CONCLUSION

For over 200 years in the United States, there has been a constant struggle to accommodate the government's obligation to protect national security and the Fourth Amendment's protections. The Fourth Amendment was intended to protect both the fundamental rights of privacy and freedom from arbitrary intrusions into our personal lives. However, as the threats to national security become more complex, more technological, and more difficult to combat, the government is constantly pursuing new ways to gather evidence and combat these threats. As a result, new challenges to national security bring with them a renewed need to understand the Fourth Amendment and its importance in our lives.

REVIEW QUESTIONS

1. Why did the drafters of the Constitution include the language of the Fourth Amendment and its requirement that the government obtain a warrant before it searches for evidence of criminal activity? What had been the colonists' experience that motivated the desire for this sort of protection from the government?

2. In what way do the concepts of "reasonable expectation of privacy" and "probable cause" effect the warrant process?

3. If the government is searching for evidence that is related to a national security threat, must the government obtain a warrant or is there a national security exception to the Fourth Amendment?

4. Why are there exceptions to the Fourth Amendment's warrant requirement? What are some of those exceptions?

5. What are the common techniques used by the government to collect evidence of threats to national security and what are the Fourth Amendment implications of those techniques?

CRITICAL THINKING QUESTIONS

1. Is the Fourth Amendment's warrant requirement really necessary? If the target of a government investigation has nothing to hide, why be concerned about the government conducting a search?

2. What are the tradeoffs between security and freedom associated with requiring the government to obtain a warrant?

3. Consider the various statutory burdens placed on the government to collect evidence under the ECPA and FISA. What are those burdens and why are they different based on the information the government is trying to collect? Do these statutes strike the right balance between privacy and the government's need for the specific information it seeks to collect?

4. This chapter discusses various exceptions to the Fourth Amendment's warrant requirement. Should there be a "terrorism" exception that allows the government to forgo the warrant requirement in terrorism investigations? Why might the government need the ability to forgo a warrant in a terrorism investigation? How might the government abuse the exception if it existed?

CHAPTER 7

Foreign Intelligence Surveillance

The Elijah Barrett Prettyman United State Courthouse, Washington, D.C., location of the Foreign Intelligence Surveillance Court

Learning Objectives

1. Understand how the United States' historical experience with intelligence gathering has driven the enactment of laws that regulate the government's surveillance authority.

2. Understand the events that led to Congress enacting the Foreign Intelligence Surveillance Act.

3. Understand the changes to the Foreign Intelligence Surveillance Act after the 9/11 terrorist attacks, the Bush Administration's surveillance programs, and the ensuing controversies.

4. Understand the Foreign Intelligence Surveillance Act's processes and the surveillance tools available to the government.

7.1. INTRODUCTION

The **Foreign Intelligence Surveillance Act (FISA)** is the primary statutory authority for the United States government to collect intelligence on foreign adversaries. Initially, FISA was focused on regulating electronic surveillance alone. However, intelligence surveillance, electronic or otherwise, did not begin with the enactment of FISA. Intelligence gathering has always been an important tool used to protect national security. Because of its predominantly clandestine nature, the temptation to abuse intelligence surveillance is ever-present. As a result, the need for, and benefit of, gathering intelligence is often balanced against a fundamental American value—the right to privacy. This tension has only increased in the digital age with the government's ability to collect vast amounts of electronic data. As you will see below, this tension is precisely what motivated Congress to enact FISA. While surveillance laws will undoubtedly continue to be updated and changed, the tension will inevitably endure. This tension embodies the struggle between the government's duty to ensure national security while at the same time respecting privacy and the rule of law.

7.2. THE HISTORY OF ELECTRONIC SURVEILLANCE AUTHORITY IN THE UNITED STATES BEFORE FISA

7.2.1. The Early Days of Wiretapping

The government has long used surveillance to collect communications, also known as signals intelligence, for national security purposes. As long ago as the Civil War, the Union Army collected intelligence through intercepted telegraph messages. In fact, the term "wiretapping," which has become synonymous with government surveillance of electronic communication, originated in the late Nineteenth and early Twentieth Centuries. It consisted of physically cutting a telegraph or telephone wire and attaching a listening or recording device to the exposed line. Under **common law**, eavesdropping, though not often prosecuted, was a criminal offense and many states enacted legislation in the late Nineteenth Century to outlaw wiretapping. It was not until the beginning of the Twentieth

Century that the federal government officially, though temporarily, outlawed wiretapping to prevent the disclosure of government secrets during World War I. At the same time, the government was engaging in wiretapping of its own. It was intercepting otherwise private, domestic communication to combat subversion by those in the United States who were suspected of being sympathetic to Germany, the country's World War I enemy.

After the war, the prohibition on wiretapping ended. Nevertheless, while the government did not reauthorize the law, it did continue to recognize the privacy concerns associated with the surreptitious interception of electronic communication. These concerns led to the Radio Act of 1927, which prohibited intercepting and divulging private radio communication. Moreover, by 1928, virtually every state in the country outlawed wiretapping or revealing information conveyed via telegraph or telephone communication. Meanwhile, after World War I, the federal government continued its surveillance of electronic communication through the Cypher Bureau, the first peacetime governmental organization created with the sole purpose of collecting national security-related communication intelligence. While it was disbanded in 1929, the Cypher Bureau's role in communications surveillance would ultimately pave the way for the **National Security Agency (NSA)**.

Perhaps the most consequential legal impact on the collection of communications intelligence in the early Twentieth Century did not arise from congressional legislation or Executive Branch action. Instead, it came from the Supreme Court's 1928 decision in *Olmstead v. United States*, where the Court was asked to review the federal government's warrantless wiretapping of a criminal suspect's phone calls. The Court determined that because the government had not physically intruded into the suspect's physical property, the government had not violated the Constitution. Based on the *Olmstead* decision, the government was legally permitted to wiretap conversations without judicial approval. Congress reacted to the *Olmstead* decision by passing the Communications Act of 1934, which specifically outlawed the interception and disclosure of information obtained through wiretapping. While the Act did not address government wiretapping, in *Nardone v. United States* the Supreme Court later interpreted the Act to prohibit the government's use of evidence in criminal trials when the government obtained the evidence through a wiretap.

7.2.2. World War II, the Cold War, and Public Outrage

In spite of the public's unhappiness with the *Olmstead* decision and Congress's enactment of the Communications Act, government agencies' use of wiretaps to collect intelligence only increased in the mid-Twentieth Century. After World War II, the fear of communism gripped the country. The Federal Bureau of Investigation (FBI) used wiretaps not only to collect intelligence on suspected communist spies, but others accused of subversive activity, such as civil rights activists. During this same time, President Harry S. Truman became increasingly unhappy with the Department of Defense's (DOD) inability to consolidate its collection of national security intelligence and its lack of coordination with civilian agencies. In 1952, President Truman secretly ordered the reorganization of the DOD's then-existing signals intelligence agency, which resulted in the establishment of the NSA.

The NSA continued the Executive Branch's collection of national security-related communication intelligence and oversaw two infamous, warrantless wiretapping operations—Projects SHAMROCK and MINARET. Project SHAMROCK, initiated to catch communist spies, was a mass collection of telegraph communication. With the help of telegraph companies, the NSA copied and analyzed all communication entering and exiting the country, and referred noteworthy intelligence to other federal law enforcement, military, and intelligence agencies. Project MINARET, a similar operation that started in the late 1960s, facilitated the collection of electronic communication between United States citizens and persons overseas. In particular, the NSA collected the international communications of prominent Americans who were thought to oppose the Vietnam War, including journalists, United States Senators, and civil rights activists Martin Luther King and Muhamad Ali.

As the media began to expose these and other intelligence operations in the early 1970s, the public was outraged by the warrantless, unbridled collection of communication and the lack of judicial oversight. This outrage, on the heels of the Watergate scandal, culminated in the Senate's creation of the bipartisan United States Senate Select Committee to Study Governmental Operations with Respect to Intelligence Activities, also known as the Church Committee. The Church Committee, named for Senator Frank Church who chaired the Committee, spent more than a year investigating and holding hearings on the allegations of alleged abuses by the intelligence community, including NSA warrantless wiretapping.

The Church Committee

In January, 1975 the Senate approved a resolution, by a vote of 82–4, to form a special committee to investigate the reported improper domestic and international surveillance activities of the federal government's intelligence agencies. The 11-member Church Committee, as it came to be known, investigated intelligence gathering abuses, as well as other alleged illegal activities, by a variety of government agencies including the CIA, FBI, and NSA. The Committee held a handful of publicly televised, and at times sensational, hearings. For example, one public hearing explored the CIA's rogue assassination activities and, remarkably, included the displaying of a CIA poison dart gun. However, because of the sensitive nature of the information discussed, most of the Committee's work was done behind closed doors.

Over the course of 16 months, the Committee held over 160 hearings, interviewed approximately 800 witnesses, and reviewed over 100,000 documents. The Committee's investigation revealed numerous illegal surveillance activities by the Executive Branch, beginning in the early 1930s, and perpetrated by both Democratic and Republican administrations. The Committee determined that these abuses occurred primarily because of the breakdown of the checks and balances between the three branches of government and that the unlawful surveillance undermined the constitutional rights of United States citizens. In April, 1976, the Committee issued its final report. The report detailed extensive misuse of the intelligence agencies' powers. The report recommended more involvement by the Legislative, Executive, and Judicial Branches in setting intelligence policies so that intelligence practices would no longer diverge from constitutional constraints. This recommendation, and others, ultimately led to the passage of laws that would become the framework that governs **foreign intelligence** surveillance today.

The investigations revealed that since the early Twentieth Century, the Executive Branch had routinely authorized, and abused, warrantless electronic surveillance for national security purposes. Troubled by the previously unchecked actions of the Executive Branch's intelligence agencies, the Committee's recommendations included the creation of congressional oversight committees in both the House of Representatives and the Senate. In addition, the Committee's findings resulted in the passage of the Foreign Intelligence Surveillance Act (FISA) in 1978. This new Act constituted a turning point in United States foreign intelligence surveillance.

7.3. FISA

7.3.1. FISA's Early Days

FISA sought to balance the Executive Branch's desire for secrecy in foreign intelligence surveillance with the need for oversight and restraint brought by Congress and the Judiciary. In fact, FISA was specifically intended to "curb the practice by which the Executive Branch may conduct warrantless electronic surveillance on its own unilateral determination that national security justifies it, while permitting the legitimate use of electronic surveillance to obtain foreign intelligence information." Senate Judiciary Committee Report, *Background*, S. Rep. No. 95-604(I), 1978. Functionally, FISA outlined procedures for foreign intelligence gathering through electronic surveillance. It instituted a requirement that federal intelligence agencies obtain permission before conducting surveillance of foreign powers and agents of foreign powers, including United States citizens suspected of working in concert with them. FISA also created a new court, called the Foreign Intelligence Surveillance Court (FISC). The FISC would be the court from which intelligence agencies were required to obtain authorization to engage in surveillance. Because of the sensitive, national security-related issues with which the court would deal, its hearings and decisions would be secret and non-adversarial. As a result, the public would generally not have access to FISC decisions and the government would be the only party presenting arguments to the court.

There were two noteworthy amendments to the law in the late Twentieth Century, both of which expanded the types of foreign intelligence gathering the government could conduct. The Intelligence Authorization Act of 1995 provided a process for authorizing physical searches and the Intelligence Authorization Act of 1999 provided a process for authorizing access to business records and the use of **pen registers** and **trap and trace devices**. While a handful of court cases challenged the constitutionality of FISA in the 1980s and 1990s, FISA remained relatively unquestioned and unchanged. It was not until the 9/11 terrorist attacks against the United States that the most significant challenges and changes were made to FISA.

A "Wall" Between Intelligence Gathering and Law Enforcement

While there were a few significant statutory changes to FISA in the late Twentieth Century, perhaps some of the most important changes to intelligence gathering were a product of the internal operating policies of the intelligence agencies. For example, during the 1980s the FBI had a set of informal, unwritten rules that limited the types of information domestic law enforcement agents could share with agents responsible for collecting foreign intelligence. These institutional customs were an attempt to avoid the potential constitutional problems created by sharing FISA-acquired foreign intelligence with law enforcement agents who were focused on domestic criminal law. In the mid-1990s, the FBI imposed upon itself formal, written procedures that created a "wall" separating its intelligence gathering mission from its law enforcement mission. This "wall" went beyond what was required by law. The perception within the FBI was that if an agent wrongly breached the "wall" and shared information, it would have a detrimental impact on his career. Some suggest that this "wall" between foreign intelligence and law enforcement was an important, contributing factor in the United States' failure to thwart the 9/11 terrorist attacks.

7.3.2. The 9/11 Terrorist Attacks, the Bush Administration's Secret Surveillance Programs, and a New FISA

Within a month of the 9/11 terrorist attacks, President George W. Bush signed the Uniting and Strengthening America by Providing Appropriate Tools Required to Intercept and Obstruct Terrorism Act of 2001 (**Patriot Act**). The Patriot Act contained changes to various federal statutes and had a significant impact on FISA. For example, the Patriot Act expanded the use of FISA surveillance authorization from situations where the "primary" purpose was obtaining foreign intelligence to situations where a "significant" purpose of the authorization was to obtain foreign intelligence. Additionally, the Patriot Act expanded FISA's initial focus on electronic surveillance by permitting searches of "tangible things" including books and paper documents.

The Patriot Act also changed the legal burdens the government would have to meet when invoking many of FISA's surveillance powers. For instance, in order to obtain FISC surveillance authorization, the law originally required the Executive Branch to provide "specific and articulable facts" that the target of surveillance was an agent of a foreign power. The Patriot Act, however, reduced that burden and simply required a statement by a government official that the information sought was part of an investigation into terrorism or clandestine intelligence activities. The Patriot Act also enabled intelligence agencies to conduct "roving wiretaps." Before this change, FISA required a new FISC authorization for each tapped communication device. With the change, the FISC could authorize the wiretapping of all of a person's communication, regardless of the device he used. These changes are more fully discussed below.

Around the same time the Patriot Act was passed, President Bush secretly authorized the NSA to intercept international communications into and out of the United States, in an effort to thwart future attacks. The surveillance focused on people suspected to be linked to the terrorist organization that had coordinated the 9/11 attacks, Al Qaeda, and other terrorist organizations. These wiretaps were authorized by the Executive Branch alone, without **warrants** and without FISC authorization. Approximately four years after warrantless wiretapping began, the *New York Times* newspaper uncovered the program. The Bush Administration, however, was able to convince the newspaper to delay publishing a story about the program for over a year. There was a public uproar when, in late 2005, the *New York Times* ultimately published the story revealing the NSA's warrantless surveillance program.

Months after the story's publication, the Bush Administration, through the Department of Justice (DOJ), articulated its legal justification of the warrantless surveillance program. By way of letters to Congress, the Administration made three arguments regarding the President's legal authority to initiate and conduct the wiretapping. The Administration argued that the President has inherent, virtually unrestricted, authority to conduct warrantless surveillance in the foreign intelligence context. Because the NSA's surveillance focused on foreign threats, the Administration asserted the surveillance did not implicate the Fourth Amendment's prohibition on warrantless searches of domestic threats. The Administration also argued that as Commander in Chief, the President has the inherent constitutional responsibility and authority to protect the United States from attack. The Administration posited that the NSA's surveillance was simply a tool the President used to achieve that goal.

Finally, the Administration posited that the **Authorization for Use of Military Force (AUMF)** Congress passed after the Al Qaeda terrorist attack in 2001 gave the President the power to "use all necessary and appropriate force against those nations, organizations, or persons he determines planned, authorized, committed, or aided the terrorist attacks" to thwart "any future acts of international terrorism against the United States." As a result, the Administration argued, Congress authorized the President to use all tools available, including the use of electronic surveillance of the enemy, to respond to and prevent future attacks. With regard to the AUMF's relationship to FISA's authorization requirements, the Administration noted that FISA prohibited electronic surveillance "except as authorized by statute." The Administration argued that the AUMF's statutorily broad grant of power to the President, discussed above, was the type of statutory exception envisioned by FISA.

In a response to the Bush Administration's arguments defending the use of warrantless surveillance, a group of constitutional scholars and former government officials wrote their own letters to Congress rebutting the Bush Administration's arguments. The group argued that although the President may have the unfettered authority to collect signals intelligence, that authority only extends to wiretapping enemies outside of the United States. However, when the surveillance is conducted within the United States or directed at United States citizens, the Executive Branch's authority to collect signals intelligence both implicates the Fourth Amendment's warrant protections and was curtailed by FISA. Regarding the Bush Administration's Commander in Chief argument, the group suggested that the President's role as Commander in Chief could be limited by Congressional and Judicial oversight. While there have been few successful challenges to presidential power during wartime, the group posited that where the President's unilateral actions have conflicted with implicit or explicit congressional intent, the Supreme Court has invalidated those Executive Branch policies.

As for the President's position that the AUMF authorized the Administration's surveillance, the group argued that the AUMF's language authorizing "all necessary and appropriate force" was simply a general, notional authorization. This vague permission, however, was curtailed by FISA's express, specific language limiting the Executive Branch's ability to engage in electronic surveillance both in times of peace and war. If the AUMF authorized the Executive Branch's wiretapping activities, it would mean that the Congress implicitly intended that the AUMF repeal FISA's role as the exclusive statute governing electronic intelligence surveillance. In fact, the Bush Administration admitted that it believed Congress would be reluctant to amend FISA. Finally, the group also argued that warrantless domestic wiretapping was simply not reasonably related to "waging war," particularly since Congress stated in FISA itself that FISA would be the exclusive means to conduct such surveillance.

In addition to the Bush Administration's warrantless wiretapping, FISC-approved surveillance dramatically increased. In the year preceding the 9/11 attacks, law enforcement and surveillance agencies filed 1,012 warrant applications through FISA. By 2005, the year the *New York Times* revealed the warrantless wiretapping program, FISA warrant requests doubled to 2,074. While the FISC exercised its authority to modify, or bring into legal compliance, 61 of those requests, it denied none. This would lead some to criticize the FISC as a rubber stamp for the Bush Administration's FISA requests.

7.3.3. Continued Changes to FISA

While the *New York Times* was investigating and exposing the Bush Administration's warrantless wiretapping program, Congress continued to make changes in an attempt to modernize and expand FISA surveillance powers. In the Intelligence Reform and Terrorism Prevention Act of 2004 (IRTPA), Congress expanded permissible targets of FISA-sanctioned surveillance. FISA had previously required that a target of surveillance have a direct connection to a foreign power or entity. The "lone wolf" amendment in IRTPA authorized surveillance of a non-U.S. person who is engaging in, or preparing to engage in, international terrorism even if he has no direct connection to a foreign power. IRTPA also created the position of Civil Liberties Protection Officer. Residing in the Office of the Director of National Intelligence (DNI), the Civil Liberties

Protection Officer is responsible for advocating for civil liberties and privacy in the programs and policies implemented by United States intelligence agencies.

The public revelation of the warrantless wiretapping program, and the outcry that followed, led Congress to amend FISA within two years of the *New York Times'* exposé, though perhaps not in ways that critics of the Bush Administration had hoped. The Protect America Act, submitted to Congress by President Bush and passed in 2007, sought to remove some of the perceived barriers to conducting electronic surveillance and modernize FISA. Most notably, the Act removed the requirement that surveillance agencies obtain authorization from the FISC before wiretapping persons who were reasonably believed to be outside the United States. Pursuant to this change, so long as the target of the surveillance was outside the United States, the target's communication with someone inside the United States could be wiretapped without FISC authorization. The Attorney General of the United States was required to submit a description of the procedures the government would use to determine a target was outside the United States. Civil liberties advocates criticized this change. They argued, among other things, that this would enable "reverse targeting." Surveillance agencies could evade the Fourth Amendment protections of persons in the United States that they wanted to wiretap by targeting a person overseas who communicates with the government's real target in the United States.

The Protect America Act also provided the Attorney General and the DNI the authority to order third-parties, including telecommunication companies, to assist in wiretapping targets outside the United States without the need for FISC authorization. Finally, the Act provided legal immunity for third-parties that cooperate with these wiretapping orders. This immunity was expanded and became retroactive with the FISA Amendments Act of 2008, which ended lawsuits against telecommunication companies that assisted the Bush Administration with its warrantless wiretapping. Notably, the FISA Amendments Act of 2008 also attempted to foreclose future arguments by the Executive Branch that it could rely on a "war powers" argument to avoid complying with FISA. The FISA Amendments Act of 2008 asserted that following FISA's procedures would be the exclusive means to conduct electronic surveillance.

In 2013, Edward Snowden changed the country's discussion regarding national security-related electronic surveillance. Snowden, a former NSA subcontractor, disclosed the existence of the NSA's secret, bulk surveillance programs that indiscriminately collected and reviewed global electronic data and communication. The government defended its bulk collection of electronic data by arguing that the post-9/11 FISA amendments expanded the type of electronic data the government could collect. The government further argued that the amendments reduced the legal burden by requiring the information collected to be merely "relevant" to a FISC approved investigation. Moreover, the government asserted that FISA permitted the bulk collection of the content of communication, so long as the surveillance was directed at foreign citizens. Critics suggested that communication among United States citizens could be swept up in this bulk surveillance and the NSA reserved the right to review and analyze that communication.

In what many argue was a response to the Snowden revelations, Congress passed the USA Freedom Act in 2015. The Act prohibited the government's bulk collection of United States citizen's data. Instead, the government would need to seek an order from the FISC authorizing the collection of data from telecommunications companies. The Act also limited the government's ability to collect information by requiring that surveillance requests be tied to a **specific selection term**. That is to say, when applying for a surveillance order from the FISC, the government would have to identify, as precisely as possible, the target of the surveillance. As a result, the government would be unable to obtain a surveillance order authorizing, for example, the collection of all the data flowing through a particular geographic area or internet service provider. The Act also permitted the government to collect intelligence from targets that are "two hops," or two degrees of separation, away from the original target of the surveillance. In other words, the government could access the date, time, duration, phone numbers called and any other electronically identifiable information of a target, his contacts, and those with whom his contacts are in contact.

The USA Freedom Act contained additional changes that were geared toward providing more transparency and preventing abuses of the government's intelligence surveillance power. It required the government to report the number of warrants requested and issued by the FISC and permitted businesses to reveal whether they had received orders to provide surveillance-related data to the government. The Act also required the DNI to declassify, to the extent possible, FISC opinions that contain significant interpretations of the law. The Act also permitted the FISC to appoint a **public interest advocate** to provide counter-arguments to the government's interpretations of FISA. However, the FISC retained the authority to decide whether a public interest advocate would be appointed.

7.4. THE FISC AND FISA OPERATIONS

FISA was created to authorize and govern the United States government's foreign intelligence surveillance, as well as the court system that would be responsible for reviewing the government's compliance with the laws. While the original name and purpose of the law essentially remain intact, the numerous changes discussed above have affected how FISA functions in practice. Below is a discussion of how the law and court system operate today.

7.4.1. The FISC, Its Jurisdiction, and Its Procedures

FISA governs the government's collection of information to protect the national security of the United States. More specifically, FISA governs surveillance intended to protect against the hostile acts of a foreign power, international terrorism, sabotage, and spying. FISA's **jurisdiction** is limited to surveillance of a specific group of people, sometimes referred to as the "targets" of surveillance. First, the targets of FISA surveillance may be "foreign powers," which includes foreign governments, entities and organizations based in or controlled by foreign governments, and groups engaged in international terrorism or the proliferation of weapons of mass destruction. FISA also governs the surveillance of "agents of foreign powers," which includes "non-U.S. persons" that are employees or spies collecting intelligence on behalf of foreign powers. It also includes non-U.S. persons engaging in international terrorism. Finally, FISA permits the surveillance of "U.S. persons"—United States citizens, permanent residents, and corporations—who act as spies on behalf of a foreign power, engage in sabotage or international terrorism, or adopt a false identity on behalf of a foreign power.

If the government wants to conduct foreign intelligence surveillance, it must first obtain permission from a special court—the FISC. This unique court, with limited purview, was created by Congress. The FISC is comprised of eleven federal district court judges, each of whom is appointed by the Chief Justice of the Supreme Court of the United States to serve seven-year terms on the FISC. Each week, one of the eleven judges is responsible for acting as the FISC judge. The acting FISC judge, referred to as the "duty judge," occupies a secure courtroom in Washington, D.C. At least three of the FISC judges must live within 20 miles of Washington, D.C. The FISC has the authority to grant, deny, or modify the government's applications for permission to conduct surveillance.

The government's applications for FISC orders—similar to warrants—authorizing surveillance are presented to the duty judge. The applications are considered by the FISC judge ***ex parte***, or one-sided. As a result, unlike other federal courts, the FISC is non-adversarial and the FISC judge will only hear arguments from the government in favor of approving the application for an order authorizing surveillance. If the FISC judge believes that the government's application for an order raises a novel or significant interpretation of the law, the judge may appoint an attorney to submit arguments discussing the privacy and civil liberty implications of the government's request. These *amici curiae*, or "friends of the court" are attorneys selected from a group appointed by the FISC and who have security clearance.

All arguments in favor of and opposed to the government's application for a surveillance order are classified. The FISC's decisions whether to grant a request and issue an order are also classified. However, the DNI must perform a declassification review of decisions that contain significant legal interpretations. If there are national security problems presented by the declassification of a legally significant FISC decision, a summary of the decision must be produced. This required declassification review and publication of important decisions, or summaries of those decisions, is an attempt to ensure some transparency of the FISC.

If the FISC judge denies the government's application for an order, the government can appeal the decision. It can request the FISC hear the appeal *en banc*, which means all the judges of the FISC would act as the appellate court. This *en banc* collection of FISC judges can either affirm, modify, or overrule the duty judge's original decision. In the alternative, the government can appeal the FISC judge's decision to the FISA Court of Review (FISCR). The FISCR has the authority to review the FISC's denial of applications for permission to conduct electronic surveillance, physical searches, and demands for production of tangible things. If the FISC authorizes the government to require the production of tangible things, the FISCR may also hear appeals from those compelled to produce the tangible things. Ultimately, the Supreme Court has the authority to review decisions of both the FISC and the FISCR.

7.4.2. FISA Authorized Methods of Collecting Foreign Intelligence

FISA authorizes and regulates the government's use of four investigative techniques for the collection of foreign intelligence: 1) electronic surveillance; 2) physical searches; 3) pen register and trap and trace devices; and 4) orders compelling the production of tangible things. Originally, Congress's passages of FISA was a reaction to the Executive Branch's misuse of electronic surveillance. As a result, the earliest version of FISA only regulated electronic surveillance. In the 1990s, however, Congress expanded FISA's regulatory authority to include physical searches, the use of pen register and trap and trace devices, and requests for business records. Following the 9/11 terrorist attacks, Congress amended FISA to authorize FISC orders requiring the production of tangible things. Each of these methods is discussed in greater detail below.

7.4.2.1. Electronic Surveillance

FISA defines electronic surveillance as the acquisition of the contents of wire communication to or from a person in the United States by way of an electronic, mechanical, or other surveillance device. When engaging in electronic surveillance, FISA permits the government to collect information about the identity of the people communicating with each other as well as the substance and meaning of the communication. FISA requires that, when conducting foreign intelligence surveillance, the government use **minimization procedures** to curtail the collection, retention, and dissemination of private information about U.S. persons. The minimization procedures must be designed to avoid and reduce the amount of information collected that is unrelated to foreign intelligence.

To obtain an order authorizing electronic surveillance, a government agent must describe, in writing: 1) the identity or a description of the target of the electronic surveillance; 2) the facts that justify the belief that the target is a foreign power or agent of a foreign power and the place to be surveilled is used by a foreign power or agent of a foreign power; 3) the government's minimization procedures; and 4) the information sought and the type of communications or activities to be surveilled. A designee of the President must also certify that the information being sought is foreign intelligence and cannot reasonably be obtained by normal investigative techniques. The government must describe the techniques it will use to collect the information, including whether it will have to physically enter a building or other location to accomplish the surveillance. The government must also detail previous surveillance of the intended target. Finally, the government must describe the length of time the surveillance will last.

If the FISC judge is convinced that the government's assertions in its application are true, the judge must issue an *ex parte* order that authorizes the surveillance. Because it is *ex parte*, the target of the surveillance does not receive notice of the order. FISC judges use a **probable cause** standard to determine whether to issue an order authorizing electronic surveillance. Probable cause is a common legal standard that requires a judge to be convinced that, based on a common-sense review of the facts presented, it is likely that the government's assertions are true. When determining whether there is probable cause, the FISC may consider the target's history, as well as current and alleged future activities.

If the judge chooses, he may request additional information from the government in order to make a decision. In addition, the judge, or the government, can request a hearing to discuss the application. In the end, the judge has the authority to grant, deny, or require modifications to the government's surveillance plans. The judge's order must identify the target, the places the surveillance will take place, the type of information the government is seeking, the surveillance technique the government will use, and how long the surveillance is authorized. While the surveillance is being conducted during the time authorized by the judge's order, the judge retains the authority to ensure compliance with the minimization procedures.

In the event of an emergency, the Attorney General of the United States has the authority to use electronic surveillance without FISC permission. To use these emergency powers, the Attorney General must reasonably believe there is an emergency situation that requires the use of electronic surveillance, that a FISC order would likely be issued if there was time to apply for one, and there is no time to obtain one. The Attorney General must then inform the FISC that he has made the decision to deploy emergency electronic surveillance and must also apply for authorization from the FISC within seven days of authorizing the surveillance.

Emergency electronic surveillance may only be conducted for seven days, until the information being sought is obtained, or until the FISC approves or denies the government's request to continue the surveillance. If the FISC denies the government's request to approve the emergency electronic surveillance after it is deployed, the information collected must remain secret and may only be disclosed if the Attorney General determines it is evidence of a threat of death or serious injury. The government may also conduct electronic surveillance without the FISC's permission for up to fifteen days following a Congressional **declaration of war**. Finally, FISA authorizes the Attorney General to use electronic surveillance for up to a year without seeking FISC permission if the targets are not U.S. persons and it is unlikely the surveillance will intercept communication to or from a U.S. person.

7.4.2.2. Physical Searches

FISA authorizes the government to collect foreign intelligence by physically intruding into and searching property located within the United States. The government must seek permission from the FISC for these physical searches if the owner of the property has a **reasonable expectation of privacy** in the property and a warrant would be required if the government was seeking information for law enforcement purposes. The government's application for FISC authorization to conduct a physical search must contain essentially all of the same information as an application to conduct electronic surveillance, including minimization procedures, the target of the search, and the information sought. Moreover, the FISC's issuance of an order granting the government the authority to conduct a physical search is subject to the same burdens, including a FISC finding of probable cause. Finally, like electronic surveillance, the Attorney General may authorize, for limited periods of time and absent FISC approval, physical searches in emergency situations, physical searches following a declaration of war, and physical searches of non-U.S. citizens.

7.4.2.3. Pen Registers and Trap and Trace Devices

FISA also authorizes and regulates the government's use of pen registers and trap and trace devices for the purposes of foreign intelligence surveillance. Pen registers are devices that can identify the dialing or routing information transmitted by wire or electronic communication, including telephones and internet platforms. In other words, for example, pen registers record the telephone numbers called by a surveillance target or the email addresses to which a surveillance target sends messages. Trap and trace devices, on the other hand, record the incoming electronic markers that identify the source of wire or electronic communication. These devices can detect and record the phone number or email address that is calling or sending messages to a surveillance target. While FISA refers to pen registers and trap and trace devices as separate surveillance techniques, most modern equipment can accomplish both incoming and outgoing identification and recording. Neither technique, however, includes the recording of actual conversations or other content.

Pen registers and trap and trace devices record information that is often referred to as **metadata**—data that identifies, describes, and defines other data. This sort of information is useful in identifying, among other things, a target's associates and tracking his communication habits. The NSA's indiscriminate, bulk collection of metadata was one of the revelations made by Edward Snowden in 2013. After the Snowden revelations, the NSA argued that it only reviewed a small amount of the data it collected and, as discussed above, could not listen to or read the content of the communication pursuant to this section of FISA. Civil liberties advocates argued that the bulk collection of metadata is still an invasion of privacy because a comprehensive picture of an individual can be generated by metadata. The 2015 USA Freedom Act prohibited the government from collecting and preserving bulk metadata. Instead, the Act required the government to apply for permission from the FISC to access the metadata stored by telecommunication companies. The Federal Communications Commission, which regulates national and international communications, requires all telecommunications companies to retain their customers' metadata for at least 18 months.

Due to the Supreme Court's **third-party doctrine**, the government need not meet the probable cause standard when requesting an order authorizing the application of a pen register or trap and trace device. In *Smith v. Maryland*, police officers asked a telephone company to install a pen register and record the outgoing telephone numbers dialed from a particular home. The target of the investigation challenged the warrantless collection of information by police and argued it violated his Fourth Amendment rights. The Supreme Court determined that telephone users voluntarily convey information, like the numbers they dial, to the telephone company. As a result, the Court held that because a telephone user knows the telephone company retains that information, the telephone user has no reasonable expectation of privacy in the numbers he dials. As a result of *Smith v. Maryland*, the government is free to collect pen register and trap and trace information without a warrant.

In light of *Smith v. Maryland*, the Attorney General, or some other designated government attorney, need only certify that the metadata likely to be collected is related to one of two goals: obtaining foreign intelligence information, so long as it is not concerning a U.S. person, or as part of an investigation intended to protect the United States against international terrorism or covert intelligence activities. If the investigation is directed at combating terrorism or spying, and includes the investigation of a U.S. person, the investigation cannot be based on the target's activities that are protected by the First Amendment. In other words, the government cannot base its request for permission to collect a person's metadata solely on the ideas he expresses. In an effort to discourage bulk data collection, the government must provide the FISC with a "**specific selection term**." The specific selection term identifies a person, account, address, personal device, or some other precise target that will be the focus of the pen register or trap and trace device. These terms must then be used to limit the scope of information sought and collected with the pen register or trap and trace device.

The FISC can require that telecommunications companies cooperate with the government, and provide information about their customers whose accounts are being monitored. This information includes things like the customer's name, address, and how long the target has been the company's customer. Telecommunication companies that are required to cooperate with the government may not disclose that an investigation is ongoing. FISA also provides immunity for telecommunication companies that cooperate with the government. As a result, a surveillance target cannot file a lawsuit against a telecommunication company where it has installed a pen register or trap and trace device in compliance with a FISC order. Like electronic surveillance and physical searches, the government is authorized to install pen register or trap and trace devices without FISC authorization, for limited periods of time, on an emergency basis, or after a declaration of war. However, unlike electronic surveillance and physical searches, the FISA does provide an exception for the use of pen registers or trap and trace devices directed solely at non-United States citizens or foreign powers.

7.4.2.4. Access to Business Records and Tangible Things

FISA allows the FBI to seek a FISC order requiring records, papers, documents, books, and other tangible things be turned over to the government. Some examples of the sorts of records that could be sought by the government include library records, book sales records, firearms sales records, and educational records. Like the use of pen register and trap and trace devices, an order authorizing the production of tangible things cannot be based on a U.S. person's activities that are protected by the First Amendment. The recipient of a FISC order to turn over records may not disclose the government's attempt to obtain the information, except to an attorney for the purposes of legal advice or help with collecting and producing the information. The recipient may challenge the order and the nondisclosure requirement in the FISC.

The government's request for an order compelling the production of tangible things must contain the government's minimization procedures, the target of the search, and the information sought. In addition, like a request to use pen register or trap and trace devices, a tangible things request must include a specific selection term. The government must establish that there are reasonable grounds to believe that the information sought is relevant to collecting foreign intelligence information not concerning a U.S. person, or to protect against international terrorism or spying. If the government is seeking records of call details from a telecommunications company, it can obtain the call records of individuals that are "two hops" or two steps removed from the original target. That is to say, the government can collect the call records of every target, the call records of every phone number the target contacts, and the call records of the second number's contacts. (See Table 7.1.) Like with the FISC's review of government requests to conduct electronic surveillance and physical searches, the FISC can approve, deny, or modify the request. Under emergency situations, the government, through the

Attorney General, may require the production of tangible things, for up to seven days, without an order from the FISC.

7.4.3. Targeting Non-U.S. Persons Outside of the United States

FISA permits the Attorney General, in coordination with the DNI, to authorize the surveillance of non-U.S. persons located outside the United States without a FISC order. This surveillance authority cannot be relied on to intentionally target a United States citizen abroad, a person known to be in the United States, or a person outside the United States if the actual purpose is to acquire information regarding a person inside the United States. These limitations attempt to ensure that foreign intelligence surveillance conducted within the United States or foreign intelligence surveillance where the target is a United States citizen anywhere in the world will be conducted only pursuant to the traditional FISC orders discussed above. Nevertheless, a United States citizen's communication can be collected under this authority if he is communicating with the targeted non-U.S. person.

When targeting and acquiring foreign intelligence from foreigners abroad, FISA does not require the government to obtain a specific order from the FISC authorizing the surveillance of an explicitly named target. Instead, the Attorney General and DNI must file a certification that a surveillance program is focused on targeting foreigners reasonably believed to be located outside the United States. The certification must also describe the targeting and minimization procedures the government will employ to ensure the surveillance is limited to collecting information from foreigners outside the United States. These certifications are subject to annual FISC review and authorization. However, the FISC need not make a finding of probable cause to believe the government's assertions and may take them at face value.

Government Secrecy and the FISA Debate

FISA requires the Attorney General to submit a report to Congress, twice a year, regarding the government's foreign intelligence surveillance activities. The report must include the aggregate number of people targeted by each of the surveillance techniques authorized by FISA and a breakdown of those targeted. The report must also include the number of times the Attorney General has authorized the use of information obtained to be used in a criminal proceeding. Finally, the report must include important legal interpretations of FISA, whether contained in the government's filings with the FISC or the FISC's orders and decisions, along with a summary of those filings and interpretations. These reports are submitted to the Permanent Select Committee on Intelligence of the House of Representatives, the

Select Committee on Intelligence of the Senate, and the Committees on the Judiciary of the House of Representatives and the Senate.

The Committees above are responsible for overseeing the United States intelligence agencies and the federal court system. Each Committee, both in the House and Senate, is entitled to hold hearings, either classified or unclassified, regarding foreign intelligence surveillance or the FISA. When the hearings are classified, members of Congress are prohibited from discussing the information shared by the intelligence agencies about their surveillance activities. As a result, even if a member of Congress disagrees with a particular surveillance technique or believes it violates the law, he is unable to speak publicly about the specifics of his reservations and concerns. Moreover, because the FISC's decisions are classified, it is difficult for the public to access and understand the inner workings of the intelligence agencies and their surveillance.

For example, during the 2011 debate to reauthorize the Patriot Act, Senator Ron Wyden of Oregon, a member of the Senate's Intelligence Committee, warned that American people would be shocked when they learned about the government's abuses of FISA. Senator Wyden, however, was unable to reveal the specific government surveillance he was concerned about because of the secrecy surrounding FISA, the FISC, and his classified briefings. He believed government officials from the Executive Branch were providing misleading information to the public, while at the same time he was prohibited from correcting what he believed to be misinformation. It was not until Edward Snowden's revelations, at which time many of the government's surveillance programs became public knowledge, that Senator Wyden was able to speak publicly about his specific concerns.

This particular surveillance authority has been the subject of much debate and criticism. The government uses this authority to gather a significant amount of communication content through accessing the major computer networks and routers on the Internet—also known as upstream collection. The government also relies on this authority to pursue and collect data and communication content stored by Internet companies that provide communication platforms, like email and text messaging. In addition to the significant amount of information that can be collected, the government can search the information collected for evidence of criminal activity by a U.S. person, even if it is targeting a non-U.S. person. Because the government would otherwise have to obtain a FISC order and prove it had probable cause to surveil a U.S. person, many people criticize the government's ability to search this information for crimes by a U.S. person and refer to it as the "backdoor search loophole."

REVIEW QUESTIONS

1. What events led Congress to enact FISA? Why did Congress enact FISA?
2. What were two changes Congress made to FISA when it enacted the Patriot Act?

3. What were the Bush Administration's three arguments in defense of its secret, warrantless surveillance after the 9/11 terrorist attacks? What were the counterarguments by those who opposed the program?

4. How does the government obtain a FISA order from the FISC?

5. What are the four investigative techniques authorized by FISA for collecting of foreign intelligence? What kinds of intelligence data is collected using each of the techniques?

6. What are the different legal burdens FISA places on the government when it seeks to conduct electronic surveillance as opposed to using a trap and trace device?

CRITICAL THINKING QUESTIONS

1. Did FISA accomplish Congress's goal of reestablishing parity between the branches of government when it comes to foreign intelligence surveillance?

2. How much deference should the Legislative and Judicial Branches give to the Executive Branch when it decides on the most effective ways to collect foreign intelligence for national security purposes?

3. Does FISA place too much of a burden on the Executive Branch? If law enforcement or intelligence agencies are collecting information about foreign adversaries and threats to national security, should they be able to do so without obtaining permission from a court?

4. Consider the Bush Administration's arguments in defense of its secret, warrantless surveillance programs and the counterarguments. Which side's arguments were more persuasive?

5. What are the potential benefits and problems with the FISC reviewing government requests for surveillance authorization *ex parte*?

6. Does FISA provide sufficient protections to the civil liberty interests of United States citizens when government surveillance is targeting non-U.S. persons outside of the United States? How would you accommodate the concerns of some civil liberty advocates regarding the collection, storage, and review of communication between a United States citizen and a targeted non-U.S. person?

Table 7.1.

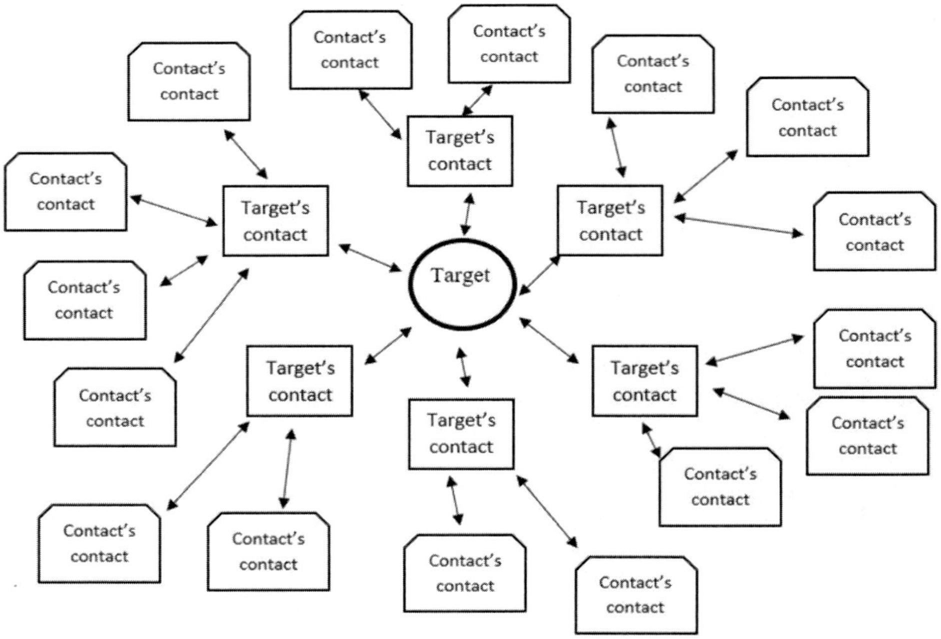
Target
Target's contact
Target's contact
Target's contact
Target's contact
Target's contact
Target's contact
Contact's contact

CHAPTER 8

Free Speech and National Security

Congress shall make no law . . . abridging the freedom of speech, or of the press . . . .
United States Constitution, Amendment 1

Learning Objectives

1. Appreciate how the United States balances the right to free speech and national security.

2. Understand how the interpretation of the First Amendment and its relationship to national security has developed throughout the United States' history.

3. Understand the Freedom of Information Act, what role it plays in ensuring an informed public and transparent government, and how it protects the disclosure of information that threatens public safety and national security.

8.1. INTRODUCTION

The modern understanding of the right to free speech in the United States was shaped, in no small part, by national security concerns. Whether it was the Federalists' concerns about French sympathizers in the Eighteenth Century, President Lincoln's concerns about those who opposed the Civil War in the Nineteenth Century, or the Red Scare in the Twentieth Century, the government has routinely sought to regulate speech it perceived to be a threat to national security. Laws regulating speech that challenge the government are often supported by many in society at the time they are enacted. Yet speech that supports the government and its policies is rarely in need of protection. It is speech that objects to the government's policies or seeks to disrupt its efforts that is most often in need of protection.

In the United States, it is the Supreme Court's responsibility to interpret the First Amendment and determine whether a law regulating speech is constitutionally permissible. In making those determinations throughout its history, the Court has had to balance two competing values that are, at times, in competition: citizens' freedom to engage in an uninhibited and critical debate about government policies and the government's desire to protect national security. As you will see below, many of the Court's broadest, most speech-protective interpretations of the First Amendment have arisen out of laws that sought to regulate speech that undermined respect for the government or subverted its national security efforts. Yet the Court has not always been a champion of free speech. Instead, it has developed its modern, speech-protective interpretation of the First Amendment over time. In addition to the Supreme Court, Congress has also played a role in promoting a vigorous and informed public debate through the Freedom of Information Act (FOIA). By ensuring citizens can access information about how their government functions, Congress joins the Supreme Court in playing a vital role in facilitating the freedom of speech and a more informed public debate.

8.2. THE RIGHT TO CRITICIZE THE GOVERNMENT

The modern interpretation of the Constitution's Free Speech Clause reflects the most expansive and protective commitment to freedom of expression in the world. It is very difficult for governments in the United States—whether federal, state, or local—to regulate speech simply because they disapprove of the content of the speech or the ideas being conveyed. However, this understanding of the freedom of speech has not always been the norm in the United States. One has to remember that in the early part of its history, the United States was a much less stable government than what we see today. After drafting and helping to ratify the Constitution, **Framers** like James Madison and Alexander Hamilton would spend the rest of their lives concerned about the stability and viability of the new Republic they helped create. In fact, only seven years after the First Amendment was adopted, some of the very people who drafted the Constitution enacted national security laws that, by today's standards, restricted speech in unthinkable ways.

8.2.1. The Founding Generation

Soon after Americans ratified their Constitution in 1789, another revolution was taking shape in Europe—the French Revolution. Initially, many in the United States were supportive of the French Revolution. They saw the French rejection of their monarchy and the attempts to build a republic as similar to what Americans had sought in the American Revolution. However, as the French Revolution became more violent and called for more radical change, some Americans became concerned about its influences in the United States. These differing views of the French Revolution were reflected in the two political parties that had emerged in late Eighteenth Century United States politics. The Federalist Party, led by Alexander Hamilton, supported a strong federal government and a representative democracy that could curb the desires of commoners. The Democratic-Republicans, led by Thomas Jefferson, wanted a less powerful federal government, held more egalitarian views, and believed that the Federalists harbored aristocratic attitudes. As France began to wage war with Great Britain and several other European monarchies in 1792, the United States formally remained neutral. Nevertheless, the new American political parties had their own views of these conflicts. The Federalists advocated for stronger ties with Great Britain while the Democratic-Republicans advocated for stronger ties with France.

In 1794, with France and Great Britain still at war, the United States entered into a **treaty** with Great Britain known as the Jay Treaty. The Jay Treaty recognized certain commercial rights and geographical boundaries between the countries. Two years later, in response to the Jay Treaty and a feeling of being betrayed by the United States, French **privateers** began seizing United States merchant ships. Accusations began to surface that French spies and provocateurs had infiltrated the United States and the prospect of war with France threatened the young nation's security. President John Adams, a Federalist elected in 1797, and his allies in Congress, advocated for war. The Democratic-Republicans were suspicious of the Federalists' goals and, in light of their affinity for the French revolutionary cause, opposed the Federalists' calls for a conflict with France. With partisan politics in mind, the Federalists in Congress passed the Alien and Sedition Acts of 1798 to fight the perceived threat posed by immigrants and prevent public opposition to the United States government.

John Adams: Founding Father and President

John Adams, Vice President under George Washington and the second President of the United States, was a Framer and played an integral role in the American Revolution. President Adams was born in Massachusetts and spent the early part of his professional career as a lawyer. As opposition to Great Britain and its taxation policies grew among American colonists, Adams was one of four delegates sent to represent Massachusetts at the First Continental Congress and subsequently led the Massachusetts delegation at the Second Continental Congress. It was his nomination of George Washington, at the Second Continental Congress, that resulted in Washington being appointed Commander of the Continental Army. A year later, Adams worked with four other members of the Second Continental Congress, including Thomas Jefferson and Benjamin Franklin, to draft the Declaration of Independence. After the Declaration of Independence was signed, Adams took up a post as an American envoy to France. While in France, he helped negotiate the Treaty of Paris, ending hostilities between the American Colonies and Great Britain. He then served as the United States' first ambassador to Great Britain and participated in the Constitutional Convention. Following the Constitutional Convention, Adams was elected Vice President of the United States and, after serving eight years, won the first contested election for President.

The Alien and Sedition Acts were a group of four laws regulating United States immigration policy as well as speech critical of the government. The Naturalization Act increased the residency requirements for becoming a United States citizen from five years to 14 years. The **Alien Enemy Act** permitted the government to imprison or deport any male, 14 years or older, who was a citizen of a country with which the United States was at war. The Alien Friends Act empowered the President to imprison or deport non-citizens who were found to be a danger to the United States. However, the most controversial law, from the perspective of the freedom of speech, was the Sedition Act. The first draft of the Sedition Act that the Senate considered declared that France was the United States' enemy and any aid provided to France amounted to treason, which was punishable by death. The draft also punished any speech that supported what some in America believed was France's contemptuous treatment of the United States. These specific references to France were ultimately stricken from the final law passed by Congress. Nevertheless, for the reasons discussed below, the

Sedition Act is still regarded as one of the most significant affronts to free speech in United States history.

Licensing Laws and Seditious Libel in England

From the moment Johannes Gutenberg introduced Europe to the printing press in 1439, European governments sought to regulate speech. While many countries enacted laws to punish speech, England's licensing laws and seditious libel prosecutions had the most significant and direct impact on the First Amendment. As early as the Sixteenth Century, the English Monarchy and its government officials sought to suppress what they perceived to be dangerous and offensive speech in order to preserve public peace and government stability. English government officials controlled speech primarily through enforcing licensing laws and prosecuting seditious libel. Licensing laws were used to censor printed materials to ensure they did not contain treasonous or inflammatory content. Pursuant to the licensing laws, books, pamphlets, and other written works intended for publication were submitted to government licensing authorities for review and approval before distribution. Failure to submit material prior to publishing was a punishable offense. Like licensing laws, the criminalization of seditious libel was intended to regulate speech. However, unlike the licensing laws which were statutory in nature, seditious libel was a crime first recognized by judges under English **common law**. Seditious libel prohibited the dissemination of ideas that were critical of the King or the government, or tended to place them in a negative light. Courts construed this definition broadly to include pure political advocacy such as arguments for universal suffrage. Moreover, prosecutions for seditious libel were difficult to defend against in court. Even if a defendant could prove a statement was true, it was not a defense to the crime and, in fact, could increase the punishment.

The intent and effect of the Sedition Act was to prohibit **seditious libel** or any form of expression, whether spoken or published, that was critical of the government. The Sedition Act authorized fines and imprisonment for those who

> "write, print, utter or publish . . . any false, scandalous and malicious writing or writings against the government of the United States, or either house of the Congress of the United States, or the President of the United States, with intent to defame the said government . . . or to bring them . . . into contempt or disrepute; or to excite against them . . . the hatred of the good people of the United States, or to stir up sedition within the United States. . . ."

Notably, the Vice President, who at the time was Thomas Jefferson, a Democratic-Republican, was not included in the list of federal government officials protected under the Sedition Act. Soon after President Adams signed the Act into law, the government began to fine and imprison its critics.

Perhaps the most infamous prosecution was one of the first. Matthew Lyon, a Vermont Congressman who had served under President George Washington in the Continental Army, opposed the Federalists, and accused them of being elitist and pro-British. He directed much of his opposition, published as open letters to his constituents, at President Adams. In October 1798, Lyon was accused of depravity, wickedness, and sedition. He was arrested and charged with violating the Sedition Act. At trial, one of Lyon's many arguments was that the Sedition Act violated the First Amendment. Even so, the jury found him guilty. He was sentenced to a fine and four months in jail. Undeterred, Lyon ran for reelection and won by a landslide, all while serving his prison sentence. The enforcement of the Sedition Act, however, did not end with Lyon. Newspapers that published pro-Democratic-Republican or anti-Federalist views were shuttered. Newspaper editors and reporters were imprisoned and fined. Even average Americans, some of whom had fought in the Revolutionary War, were imprisoned for speaking out.

The Sedition Act itself, along with the prosecutions, brought fierce resistance. Vice President Jefferson called the Act "an experiment on the American mind to see how far it will bear an avowed violation of the Constitution." Thomas Jefferson, *Letter to Stevens Thomson Mason*, October 11, 1798. Jefferson joined forces with James Madison, who had been a fervent supporter of the new federal government, to oppose the Sedition Act. They successfully worked to encourage the Kentucky and Virginia legislatures to pass **nullification** resolutions rejecting the Sedition Act as unconstitutional. These and other political statements, however, were the extent of the opposition to the Sedition Act. The Supreme Court never reviewed the Sedition Act's constitutionality. The Court had not yet decided *Marbury v. Madison* where it established the doctrine of **judicial review**. Even if it had, it is likely the Court would have found the Sedition Act to be constitutional as the then-serving Justices were all Federalists who supported President Adams. It was not until Thomas Jefferson defeated President Adams in the election of 1800, that the silencing of government critics ended. After his inauguration, President Jefferson pardoned all those who had been convicted under the Sedition Act, and in 1801 Congress refused to renew the Act after it expired. These, however, were political decisions. It took more than 150 years for the Supreme Court to review the government's legal authority to punish seditious libel.

8.2.2. The "Actual Malice" Standard

In the early 1900s the question of whether the First Amendment protected seditious libel was hotly debated by legal scholars. Zechariah Chafee, a Harvard law professor, argued that the **Founders** had rebelled against a monarchical system that routinely punished seditious libel. In the United States, unlike in a monarchy, the people possess absolute sovereignty and thus must be free to criticize their government. Therefore, Chafee reasoned, the First Amendment was intended to prohibit the government from punishing that criticism. On the other side of the debate was Leonard W. Levy, a historian and professor at Claremont Graduate School in California. He argued that American revolutionaries routinely silenced and censured newspapers that opposed the revolution. Only publishers who supported the revolution were free to express their opinions. Moreover, the Continental Congress celebrated state laws that punished criticism of the revolution or even the Continental Currency. As a result, Levy argued that the Framers did not intend for the First Amendment to strip the government of its power to punish seditious libel. This debate was settled by the Supreme Court in its landmark 1964 decision in *NY Times v. Sullivan.*

The *NY Times v. Sullivan* decision arose out of an advertisement placed in the *New York Times* by African American clergymen who were involved in the Civil Rights movement. The advertisement accused the police in Montgomery, Alabama, of harassing and terrorizing civil rights demonstrators. It also accused them of attempting to starve activists and intimidate them with shotguns and teargas. The advertisement contained some inaccuracies. For example, it stated that civil rights demonstrators sang "My Country, 'Tis of Thee" when, in reality, they sang the National Anthem. It also alleged that police had ringed the campus of Alabama State College while student protesters were demonstrating on the State Capitol steps. In reality, the police never surrounded the campus, but they had been deployed near the campus in large numbers on three occasions. L. B. Sullivan, the Commissioner of Public Affairs for Montgomery, Alabama, who supervised the police, sued the authors of the advertisement and the *New York Times* for libel.

After Sullivan won a $500,000 jury verdict, the *New York Times* and civil rights leaders lost their appeals in the Alabama state court system. Ultimately, the Supreme Court agreed to review the case. In a unanimous decision, the Court held that the First Amendment places an extraordinarily high burden on public officials when they file libel and defamation lawsuits. The Court found that public officials would have to prove the speaker or author had "actual malice" when they made the defamatory statement. This "actual malice" standard required public officials to prove that the defendant knew the statement was false or that the defendant made the statement with a **reckless disregard** for whether it was true or false. Proving a speaker's state of mind when he makes a statement, especially such a specific state of mind, is extremely difficult, which is precisely why the Court announced the "actual malice" standard.

The Court reasoned that the First Amendment was intended to protect a robust, uninhibited, and open exchange of ideas, particularly regarding the government and government officials. The Court recognized that by interpreting the First Amendment in a way that makes it very difficult for government officials to sue for defamation or libel, some false statements would go unchallenged in the court system. However, the tradeoff was worth it in the Court's view because without the "actual malice" requirement, citizens might self-censor out of fear of being sued. The Court was so adamant about its decision, that it revisited the Sedition Act from 1798. Although the Court could not specifically rule on the constitutionality of the 166 year-old law, it did not hide its scorn for it. Finding that "the attack upon [the Sedition Act's] validity has carried the day in the court of history," the Court determined that "the restraint [the Sedition Act] imposed upon criticism of government and public officials, was inconsistent with the First Amendment." The Court's decision in *NY Times v. Sullivan* finally cemented, in the Constitution, both the right to criticize the government and the United States' commitment to a vibrant, participatory democracy.

8.3. SUBVERSION AND INCITEMENT TO IMMINENT LAWLESS

The First Amendment and freedom of speech may not be the first things that come to mind when one thinks about national security law. However, the modern understanding of freedom of speech in the United States developed within the context of national security concerns. The famous "marketplace of ideas" metaphor in First Amendment law grew out of the United States' involvement in World War I and the government's attempt to regulate speech through the Espionage Act of 1917 and the Sedition Act of 1918. These laws were Congress's attempt to protect the nation from spoken and written words that might pose a threat to national security. The Espionage Act targeted **subversive speech** that incited the listener to commit crimes that Congress determined threatened national security whereas the Sedition Act, like its counterpart from 1789, punished seditious libel. The laws, however, were enacted well after World War I had begun.

8.3.1. The "Clear and Present Danger" Test

Although World War I began in 1914, the United States was initially a neutral country and did not officially enter the war until 1917. The repeated German U-boat attacks on United States commercial and passenger vessels turned American opinion against Germany and eventually led to a **declaration of war** against Germany in April 1917. There is no doubt that some in the United States, including President Woodrow Wilson, were concerned about the loyalties of certain United States citizens. In his address to a joint session of Congress requesting the declaration of war against Germany, President Wilson referred to the "millions of men and women of German birth and native sympathy who live amongst us." While he believed "most of them [were] loyal Americans," he warned that "[i]f there should be disloyalty, it will be dealt with a firm hand of repression." Woodrow Wilson, *War Message*, 65th Congress, April 2, 1917. Two months later in June 1917, at the urging of President Wilson, Congress passed the Espionage Act. The following year, Congress amended the Espionage Act to include the Sedition Act.

The goal of the Espionage Act was to punish interference with the United States war effort. Among many other things, it criminalized: 1) willfully making or conveying false reports or false statements with intent to interfere with the operation or success of the military or naval forces of the United States; 2) promoting the success of the United States' enemies; 3) causing or attempting to cause insubordination, disloyalty, mutiny, refusal of duty, in the military; and 4) willfully obstructing the recruiting or enlistment service of the United States. Violators of the Act were subject to up to $10,000 in fines or imprisonment for up to 20 years, or both. The Sedition Act, when Congress added it to the Espionage Act, broadened the scope of speech that could be punished. The Sedition Act made it a crime to, among other things, "utter, print, write or publish any disloyal, profane, scurrilous, or abusive language about the form of government of the United States or the Constitution of the United States, or the military or naval forces of the United States, or the flag of the United States . . . ." It also forbade urging, inciting, or advocating curtailment of the production of the things "necessary or essential to the prosecution of the war." While many Americans supported the United States war effort, there were also those who opposed the war. Much of the opposition in the United States came from socialists and the Socialist Party of America. This opposition to the War gave rise to enforcement of the Espionage and Seditions Acts and the Supreme Court's first substantive examination of the rights protected by the First Amendment's Free Speech Clause.

In 1917, soon after the United States entered World War I, Charles Schenck, the General Secretary of the Socialist Party, and Elizabeth Baer, a member of the Executive Committee, authorized the distribution of 15,000 leaflets to men in

Philadelphia who were slated to be conscripted into military service. The leaflets encouraged the men to assert their rights, oppose the draft, "not submit to intimidation," and referred to the draft as "involuntary servitude." Schenck and Baer were arrested and convicted of violating the Espionage Act for causing insubordination in the military and obstructing the recruiting and enlistment services of the United States. Around this same time, the publisher of a newspaper in Missouri, Jacob Frohwerk, was arrested for publishing a newspaper that opposed the draft, claimed it was a mistake to send United States soldiers to Europe, and praised the German nation. Frohwerk was likewise convicted of interfering with the draft and thus violating the Espionage Act. About a year later, Eugene Debs, a socialist and labor activist, was arrested for a speech in Ohio. During the speech, Debs celebrated people who had been jailed for obstructing the draft. He also criticized the war effort. He too was convicted and sentenced to prison for violating the Espionage Act.

The defendants appealed their respective convictions and argued that the Espionage Act violated the First Amendment. In a trio of unanimous decisions, all authored by Justice Oliver Wendell Holmes, the Supreme Court held that the First Amendment did not protect the defendants' speech. First, in *Schenck v. United States*, the Court found that Schenck's words created a "clear and present danger" that his readers might resist the draft. The First Amendment, the Court reasoned, protected Schenk's words no more than it would "protect a man [] falsely shouting fire in a crowded theater, and causing a panic." The Court suggested that if words create a public harm, they are not protected by the First Amendment, even if the harm does not occur. Next, in *Frohwerk v. United States*, the Court found that although Frohwerk did not make "any special effort to reach men who were subject to the draft," his paper was circulated in a community that was open to his ideas. Because "a little breath would be enough to kindle a flame" of opposition to military recruitment, his speech was not protected. Finally, in *Debs v. United States*, the Court found that Debs's words had the tendency and likely effect of obstructing the United States military's recruiting service. As a result, his speech was not protected by the First Amendment.

These three unanimous decisions reflected an attitude toward the freedom of speech that is rarely found among modern Supreme Court Justices. Instead, the modern understanding of the First Amendment was, notably, introduced by the very Justice that authored the three decisions above—Justice Holmes. Only eight months after the *Debs* decision, the Supreme Court announced another Espionage Act decision in *Abrams v. United States*. In *Abrams*, the defendant was convicted of violating the Espionage Act for distributing leaflets that praised the Bolshevik

Revolution in Russia and encouraged labor strikes to cease production at munitions plants. The Court, citing its decisions in *Schenk* and *Frohwerk*, upheld the conviction and found the First Amendment did not protect the language in the leaflets because their purpose was to defeat the United States' military plans. The Court's decision, however, was not unanimous. Justice Holmes authored a dissenting opinion and found that the First Amendment did protect the language in the leaflet. Justice Holmes argued that the First Amendment protected speech unless it so "imminently threaten[ed] immediate interference with the lawful and pressing purposes of the law that an immediate check is required to save the country." Although the government was ostensibly punishing obstruction of the war effort, Justice Holmes seemed to be concerned that what was really being punished was anti-American sentiments. He warned that "we should be eternally vigilant against attempts to check the expression of opinions that we loathe and believe to be fraught with death . . . ." Finally, he articulated what became a famous metaphor to explain the value of protecting the freedom of speech—the best test of truth is to compete with opposing views and be accepted in the marketplace of ideas.

8.3.2. The Supreme Court's Abandonment of the "Clear and Present Danger" Test

While Justice Holmes's dissent planted the seed for what would become a First Amendment maxim, 50 years passed until the Supreme Court essentially rejected the "clear and present danger" standard and adopted a legal test much more protective of subversive speech and speech advocating illegal conduct. Throughout the early and mid-Twentieth Century, the Cold War between the United States and the Soviet Union began to develop along with the concern, in the United States, that communists were infiltrating society. As a result, many United States citizens were fired from jobs and blacklisted because of their suspected communist sympathies. These concerns were reflected in the Supreme Court's decisions, particularly from 1920–1950, as it continued to reject claims that the First Amendment protected speech advocating subversive conduct like overthrowing the government. In the late 1950s, however, the Court began to shift its thinking. As the Red Scare and McCarthyism abated, the Court began to become more protective of subversive speech, even as it continued to apply the same "clear and present danger" test. It decided that while exhortation to immediate illegal action could be criminalized, vague abstract advocacy was protected by the First Amendment. Finally, in 1969, in *Brandenburg v. Ohio,* the Supreme Court replaced 50 years of decisions with its current interpretation of the First Amendment—one that is decidedly more protective of speech.

In *Brandenburg*, a Ku Klux Klan leader in Ohio gave a speech at a rally. In addition to racist comments about Jews and African Americans, he threatened "some revengeance" for the United States government's perceived mistreatment of the "Caucasian race." The Klan leader was convicted and sentenced to jail for violating Ohio's Criminal Syndicalism statute. The statute forbade "advocat[ing] . . . the duty, necessity, or propriety of crime, sabotage, violence, or unlawful methods of terrorism as a means of accomplishing industrial or political reform." After his conviction, the Klan leader appealed to the Supreme Court and argued the Ohio law violated the First Amendment. The Court agreed.

In its decision, the Court did two noteworthy things. First, although it had spent 50 years applying the "clear and present danger" test to determine whether advocacy of illegal conduct was protected speech, the Court wholly omitted the test from its decision. Second, it announced a new analytical framework, which consisted of two parts. Speech advocating illegal conduct would be protected by the First Amendment unless: 1) the speech was directed at inciting imminent lawlessness and 2) the lawless conduct was likely to result imminently. Thus, the First Amendment protects a speaker from criminal prosecution for advocating sedition or other illegal conduct unless the government can prove a speaker's intent, the imminence of the crime, and the likelihood the crime will occur. This interpretation of the First Amendment provides an extraordinary amount of leeway for speakers to advocate for unlawful conduct, even conduct that threatens national security.

8.4. THE FIRST AMENDMENT AND GOVERNMENT SECRETS

Throughout history, governments have zealously guarded their secrets and enacted laws to prohibit them from being revealed. The United States is no different. In the United States, the government's desire to keep secrets can be in tension with both the public interest in access to information so people can make informed political decisions and the First Amendment rights of those who possess the information and wish to share it. The United States has primarily relied on the Espionage Act of 1918 to punish those who are privy to government secrets and reveal them to unauthorized sources. The Espionage Act was primarily used throughout the Twentieth Century to prosecute spies. However, the United States government's more recent use of the Espionage Act has caused concerns for First Amendment advocates where it has been used to prosecute self-described whistleblowers who leak classified information.

8.4.1. Whistleblower Leaks

In relevant part, the Espionage Act prohibits willfully transmitting or communicating information that relates to the national defense when the person in possession of the information has reason to believe it could be used to the advantage of a foreign nation or to injure the United States. During the Cold War, the Espionage Act was used to jail, and even execute, spies for passing secrets to the Soviet Union. As early as the late 1930s, the government prosecuted spies like Mihail Gorin for selling classified information to Soviet agents. In 1941, in *Gorin v. United States*, the Supreme Court considered Gorin's challenge to the Espionage Act's prohibition on sharing national security secrets. The Court rejected Gorin's arguments that terms like "national defense" and "intent to give advantage to a foreign nation" were too vague to give a person fair notice as to what was prohibited. As the Cold War continued, the Federal Bureau of Investigation and other United States law enforcement agencies continued to rely on the Espionage Act to prosecute both foreign nationals and United States citizens for passing classified information to the Soviets.

While the United States routinely relied on the Espionage Act to prosecute spies throughout the Twentieth Century, it rarely prosecuted self-described whistleblowers who leaked government secrets to draw attention to government misdeeds. That changed under President Barack Obama's presidency. With new technology that enabled the release of huge amounts of data, the United States government became increasingly concerned about leaks of classified information. The conviction of Chelsea Manning for leaking classified information to WikiLeaks and the **indictment** of Edward Snowden for releasing classified information to *The Guardian* newspaper certainly took center stage. Yet these are only a few examples where the United States government, during the Obama Administration, turned to the Espionage Act in an effort to punish self-identified whistleblowers. This application of the Espionage Act continued into President Donald Trump's Administration with prosecutions of leakers like Reality Winner who shared classified National Security Agency documents with *The Intercept* newspaper. In addition to prosecuting leakers, the Trump Administration has taken the unprecedented step of indicting the publisher of classified information, WikiLeaks founder Julian Assange. Based on the United States' accusations, Assange allegedly conspired with Chelsea Manning to obtain and publish classified information.

First Amendment advocates have raised concerns about the United States government's increased reliance on the Espionage Act to prosecute leakers and those who publish leaks. Yet the Supreme Court has never considered a First

Amendment challenge to the Espionage Act's prohibition on communicating classified information. The Fourth Circuit Court of Appeals, however, rejected such a challenge in 1988. It found a civilian Navy intelligence analyst was not protected by the First Amendment when he leaked classified photos of a Soviet submarine to a magazine. The Court rejected the analysist's argument that the Espionage Act was only intended to prevent "classic spying." Even though the analyst's intent was to inform the public through the release of the information, the court found the First Amendment did not protect him simply because the recipient of the information was a media outlet. *United States v. Morison.*

8.4.2. Publishing State Secrets

One of the most fundamental First Amendment concepts is that, from a legal perspective, it should be more difficult for the government to stop speakers before they express themselves than it is to punish them after they have already spoken. This legal doctrine—**prior restraint**—applies not only to the average citizen, but also to newspapers that want to publish government secrets and classified information. The difficulty posed by the prior restraint doctrine is one that is virtually impossible to overcome. While the government may be able to punish a newspaper after it publishes classified information, the government cannot return to the **status quo *ante***, or the state of affairs before the information was released. This may seem like a difficult situation for the government when it discovers secret national security information has been leaked to the media. However, in the Vietnam War Era case discussed below, the Supreme Court suggested that barring the most extreme threats to national security, the prior restraint doctrine prohibits the government from stopping a news outlet from publishing government secrets.

In the 1950s, the United States began sending military aid to Vietnam to assist French forces in their operations against communist insurgents. Over the course of the next two decades, the United States would increase its military involvement in fighting the communist North Vietnamese government. This military conflict would become known in the United States as the Vietnam War. In 1967, Secretary of Defense Robert S. McNamara commissioned a secret report detailing the political and military history of the United States involvement in Vietnam. The report became known as the *Pentagon Papers*. The report was leaked to the *New York Times* and the newspaper began to publish excerpts. After failing to persuade the newspaper to stop publishing the report, the United States government filed a lawsuit in federal court asking for an **injunction** that would force the newspaper to stop any further publications. Once the case made its way through the federal court system, the Supreme Court applied the prior restraint doctrine and decided the government was not entitled to an injunction prohibiting the publication of the *Pentagon Papers*.

The Court began its short decision in *NY Times v. United States* by describing the burden the government faced in light of the First Amendment. The First Amendment, the Court held, places "a heavy burden" on the government to justify a prior restraint and the government would have to overcome a "heavy presumption against its constitutional validity." Then, with virtually no analysis, the Court declared the government failed to meet its burden and thus could not stop the publication of the *Pentagon Papers*. While the precedential portion of the decision failed to describe fully the "heavy burden" the government faces, various Justices wrote concurring opinions to illustrate their view of the government's burden. While these opinions are not binding, they are nevertheless instructive and provide a sense of how difficult it would be, in the future, for the government to obtain an injunction like the one it sought in *NY Times v. United States*.

In Justice Brennan's concurrence, he noted that the government had argued the publication of the *Pentagon Papers* "could" or "might" prejudice the national interest. However, in Justice Brenan's view, this possible injury to national security was not enough to prohibit the newspaper from publishing the information. Instead, the government would have to prove the publication would "inevitably, directly, and immediately cause the occurrence of an event kindred to imperiling the safety of a transport already at sea . . . ." Justice Stewart announced a similar burden where he posited the government would only be able to prohibit the *New York Times*' publication if it would "surely result in direct, immediate, and irreparable damage to our Nation or its people." Finally, Justice Black, who had an absolutist view of the First Amendment, did not describe the sort of national security threat that would need to exist for the government to succeed. Instead, he proposed that the First Amendment was enacted to abolish the government's authority to censor the press. In his view, neither the Judicial Branch, nor the Executive Branch, nor the Legislative Branch had the authority to prohibit the publication of news or abridge the freedom of the press in the name of national security.

8.5. SYMBOLIC SPEECH

When people think about the First Amendment and its guarantee of freedom of speech, the first thought that often comes to mind is the freedom to communicate through words, either spoken or written. However, human beings have many ways to communicate. People often communicate ideas through actions, art, or symbols. As a result, the Supreme Court has recognized that the freedom of "speech" guaranteed in the First Amendment is really a freedom to express oneself. Expressing oneself through symbolic action, however, may conflict with laws that were legitimately intended to regulate the underlying action and not the message conveyed by the action. As an example, consider someone who disagrees with the erection of a new traffic light signal near her house. One way to protest the new traffic signal would be to refuse to stop at the red light. Can the scofflaw rely on the First Amendment to defend her actions? Though this may seem like a farfetched example, legitimate attempts at symbolic speech can have real world consequences. In fact, the Supreme Court's most famous symbolic speech cases have grown out of what the government identified as national security concerns.

8.5.1. Regulating Conduct That Has Both Speech and Non-Speech Elements

Under current United States law, all male citizens between the ages of 18–25 are required to register with the Selective Service and provide their full name, home address, Social Security Number, and email. The Selective Service is then responsible for retaining that information in the event the United States enters a war and institutes a military draft. While one can now register with the Selective Service online, since 1917, when the first national **conscription** system was enacted, the government historically retained Selective Service registration information in hard copy form. In addition to the government retaining the information, at one time, each man who registered with the Selective Service was mandated, by law, to carry his Selective Service registration certificate with him at all times. The certificate—also known as a draft card—contained various information including the registrant's name, his date and place of birth, and his address. It also contained the registrant's Selective Service number, which identified his fitness for military service and when the registrant would be drafted. The certificate also contained the address of the registrant's local draft board, which was responsible for administering conscription into the military. Finally, the certificate contained a notice reminding the registrant he must notify his local draft board when he changed his address, physical condition, occupation, or marital status.

In the 1960s, as public support for the Vietnam War waned in the United States, unrest and protests erupted throughout the Nation. It became increasingly common for men to burn their draft cards as a form of protesting the war. While the Universal Military Training and Service Act had already outlawed altering draft cards, in 1965 Congress amended the Act to prohibit knowingly destroying, mutilating, or changing them in any way. A year later, David O'Brien burned his draft card in front of the South Boston Courthouse. A crowd had gathered and witnessed O'Brien's actions. Presumably, the crowd was unhappy about witnessing this form of protest and they attacked O'Brien. FBI agents who were in the crowd escorted O'Brien into the Courthouse in an effort to protect him from the crowd. Once inside, O'Brien told the FBI agents he knew he was violating the law by burning his draft card but was motivated to do it because of his beliefs. At his criminal trial, O'Brien told the jury he burned his draft card with the intent to influence others to adopt his anti-war beliefs. He also argued that the First Amendment protected this symbolic form of speech. The judge rejected O'Brien's First Amendment argument and the jury found him guilty.

Once the case made its way to the Supreme Court, O'Brien argued his conduct was symbolic speech protected by the First Amendment. He further argued that because he burned his draft card with the intent to communicate an idea—his opposition to the war and the draft—punishing him for his symbolic speech was unconstitutional. While the Supreme Court recognized that some conduct can be expressive, it rejected O'Brien's argument that if conduct is intended to express an idea, it is necessarily protected by the First Amendment. The Court was concerned that this interpretation of the First Amendment could lead to a "limitless variety of conduct" being labeled "speech." Instead, the Court created a test to determine whether a law is permissible under the First Amendment when it regulates conduct that can be undertaken for the purposes of expressing an idea. The law will not violate the First Amendment: 1) "if it is within the constitutional power of the Government;" 2) "if it furthers an important or substantial governmental interest;" 3) "if the governmental interest is unrelated to the suppression of free expression;" and 4) "if the incidental restriction on alleged First Amendment freedoms is no greater than is essential to the furtherance of that interest." *United States v. O'Brien.*

As for the first part of the test, the Court held that the law regulating the issuance of draft cards was well within Congress's constitutional power, in Article I, Section 8, to raise and support armies. It further held, pursuant to the second part of the test, that Congress had a substantial interest in requiring the continued availability of draft cards. Punishing the destruction of draft cards ensured that they would be intact and available for inspection. Intact draft cards provided proof that the holder had registered and complied with the Selective Service law, facilitated any necessary communication between the board and the registrant, ensured the card would act as a continued reminder of the holder's legal obligations, and prevented misuse of the card. These interests, the Court held, were unrelated to the suppression of free expression. Instead, they were focused on assuring the smooth and effective function of the draft and the entire Selective service system. Thus, the third prong of the test was satisfied in the government's favor as well. Finally, the Court found that unlike, for example, waiving a flag, the prohibition on destroying the draft card punished non-communicative actions. Thus, while the law may have inhibited O'Brien's expressive activity, it was no more than was necessary to ensure the Selective Service program functioned properly. As a result, the fourth prong was also satisfied in the government's favor and the Court held the law did not violate the First Amendment.

8.5.2. Burning the Flag of the United States

Symbolic speech can take many forms, including desecrating revered objects. A person who intentionally defaces a revered object to express himself is likely to have chosen the object for its symbolic meaning. For those who respect the object, witnessing its defilement can invoke a significant emotional response. Moreover, some argue that allowing a revered object to be defiled erodes respect for the object and the ideas it symbolizes. For these reasons, many countries throughout the world, both authoritarian and democratic, prohibit the desecration of their flag. Some countries go further and prohibit the desecration of any official government emblem. From the early Twentieth Century until 1989, the United States government and every state except Alaska and Wyoming had laws prohibiting the burning of the United States flag. A common example of the statutory language read: "No person shall publicly mutilate, deface, defile, defy, trample upon, or by word or act cast contempt upon any such flag, standard, color, ensign or shield." South Dakota Code Section 65.0603. These laws, however, became unconstitutional violations of the First Amendment in the landmark case *Texas v. Johnson.*

In 1984, Gregory Johnson, along with approximately 100 other demonstrators, attended a protest march in Dallas, Texas. The Republican National Convention was taking place in Dallas and the demonstrators were there to protest President Ronald Reagan's Administration along with various corporations. While the protesters marched through the Dallas streets, some of them engaged in vandalism like spray painting buildings and overturning potted plants. Johnson did not participate in these activities, yet at some point during the march he took possession of a United States flag a fellow protester stole from a flagpole outside a Dallas building. Once the march ended in front of the Dallas City Hall, Johnson doused the flag with kerosene and set it on fire. Protestors chanted "America, the red, white, and blue, we spit on you," while the flag burned.

No one was hurt during the protest. The flag burning, however, seriously offended several witnesses. Johnson alone was arrested. He was charged with violating Texas's law that prohibited desecrating a venerated object—the National flag—and was convicted by a jury.

Upon review by the Supreme Court, Johnson's case posed two fundamental questions: 1) whether Johnson's burning of the flag constituted expressive conduct; and if so 2) whether Texas's flag desecration statute was related to the suppression of free expression. If Johnson's actions were not expressive conduct, then the First Amendment would not apply and Johnson's conviction would stand. However, if his conduct was expressive, then the Court would need to determine whether the Texas's flag desecration statute was intended to regulate expression. If it was not intended to regulate expression, the Court would apply the test it articulated in *United States v. O'Brien*. If the law was intended to regulate expression, the Court would apply "a more demanding standard."

Was burning the flag expressive conduct?

As for the first fundamental question, the Court noted that flags themselves, as well as conduct connected to flags, are often communicative. Moreover, when considering the context of Johnson's actions, the flag burning took place during a political protest that was planned around the Republican National Convention and its nomination of Ronald Reagan for President. At his trial, when asked why he burned the flag, Johnson testified that the flag "was burned as Ronald Reagan was being renominated as President. . . . We had new patriotism and no patriotism." Finally, Texas itself conceded at oral argument in front of the Supreme Court that Johnson's conduct was expressive conduct. For these reasons, the Court found that the First Amendment applied to Johnson's case.

Was Texas's flag burning law related to the suppression of free expression?

With regard to the second fundamental question, as discussed above, the Court laid out two possible analytical paths. If Texas's flag desecration statute was simply an attempt to regulate conduct, unrelated to the expression of an idea, it would apply the test from *United States v. O'Brien*. The Court described the *O'Brien* test as a "lenient standard." If, however, the Court determined the law was intended to regulate flag burning because of its expressive elements, the law would be subjected to "the most exacting scrutiny."

Texas first argued that it prosecuted Johnson because he breached the peace by burning the flag. Yet, though Johnson and his fellow demonstrators may have engaged in disruptive behavior during the march, there were no disruptions when he burned the flag. The only response to Johnson burning the flag was the emotional response and offense taken by some who witnessed it. The Court reasoned that because the First Amendment specifically protects communication that insults and offends people, those negative emotional responses alone cannot constitutionally be the basis for a breach of the peace arrest. Texas also argued that its flag desecration statute was necessary to ensure the flag is preserved as a symbol of nationhood and national unity. The Court interpreted this argument as a concern that desecration of the flag will convince people that the flag represents less positive ideas. This concern, however, would only be warranted if desecrating the flag communicated an idea. Moreover, if Johnson had burned the flag for a different reason, such as disposing of it because it was dirty, he would not have been convicted. Therefore, the Court found the Texas law was "related to the suppression of free expression," and thus the more lenient standard from *United States v. O'Brien* did not apply. Because the *O'Brien* standard did not apply, the Court reviewed Texas's reasons for the flag desecration statute with exacting scrutiny.

Does Texas's flag burning law survive exacting scrutiny?

Texas argued both that it should be able to prohibit flag desecration as a form of expression and that its reasons for the law survived an exacting First Amendment scrutiny. Texas posited that, because of the flag's historic and symbolic role in American society, allowing the desecration of the flag casts doubt on the idea that the nation is united. This message is so harmful to society, Texas argued, the government should be permitted to punish it. The Court rejected these arguments and began its exacting scrutiny analysis by stating a fundamental First Amendment premise: "the government may not prohibit the expression of an idea simply because society finds the idea itself offensive or disagreeable." What Texas's law would permit is a person burning the flag in a way that showed respect and reverence such as when a person properly disposes of a flag; that person would not fear punishment. Another person who destroys the flag to send a different message, however, would face punishment. These opposite outcomes demonstrate that the flag desecration law was Texas's attempt to foster its own view of the flag by prohibiting expressive conduct that contradicts its view. The Court found that this is precisely the sort of government-imposed orthodoxy the First Amendment was intended to prevent. As a result, the Court held that Johnson's conviction for engaging in expressive conduct by burning the United States flag was a violation of his First Amendment rights.

8.6. MATERIAL SUPPORT FOR TERRORISM

One of the bedrock principles of the First Amendment is that, with very few exceptions, the government cannot punish a speaker for the content of her message. Moreover, the Supreme Court has routinely pronounced that "expression on public issues has always rested on the highest rung of the hierarchy of First Amendment values." *Federal Communications Commission v. League of Women Voters of California.* Even those who have a narrower, less protective view of the First Amendment believe that it was intended to protect political speech, if nothing else. Nevertheless, national security concerns pose a unique test of these values. Whether it was jailing opposition newspaper editors during the Civil War, jailing anti-war protestors during World War I, or jailing communists during the Red Scare, the commitment to a robust protection of speech on matters of public concern has been tested throughout United States history. The most recent example of the clash between national security and the First Amendment grew out of the 9/11 terrorist attacks and one of Congress's many legislative responses.

Just over a month after the 9/11 terrorist attacks, Congress enacted the Uniting and Strengthening America by Providing Appropriate Tools Required to Intercept and Obstruct Terrorism Act of 2001 (**Patriot Act**). The Patriot Act provided the government with a number of new avenues to fight terrorism including increased surveillance powers, increased sharing of intelligence, and increased immigration authority. In addition to these new powers, the Patriot Act enacted new criminal laws to combat terrorism. Included in the new list of crimes was providing **material support** or resources to organizations designated as foreign terrorist organizations by the Secretary of State. The law was amended twice. First, Congress added the requirement that a defendant must have knowingly provided material support to a foreign terrorist organization. Later, Congress amended the law to define "material support" and included examples like service, training, advice, or other specialized knowledge.

A group of organizations and individuals based in the United States that advocated for human rights filed a lawsuit challenging the material support law. They claimed they wanted to provide non-violent assistance to the humanitarian and political activities of two organizations the Secretary of State had designated "terrorist organizations." In particular, the advocates wanted to provide monetary contributions as well as training in law and political advocacy. The training would take the form of teaching the organizations to use international law to peacefully resolve disputes, engage in political activity, and petition international relief agencies. The advocates were concerned, however, that these forms of assistance would run afoul of the "material support" provision of the Patriot Act. Because the assistance would necessarily include speaking with the terrorist organizations, the advocates filed a lawsuit and claimed the material support law violated their constitutional rights, including their right to freedom of speech. The advocates' case ultimately made its way to the Supreme Court in a case called *Holder v. Humanitarian Law Project.*

In *Holder v. Humanitarian Law Project*, the government disagreed with the advocates' argument that the material support law violated their First Amendment rights. Instead, the government asserted that the law regulated conduct, not speech. More specifically, the government argued the material support crime regulated the advocates' interaction with the terrorist organizations. Any burden the law placed on their expression was, the government posited, incidental. As a result, the government urged the Court to apply the more lenient standard in *O'Brien v. United States*. The advocates, however, argued they needed to speak to the organizations in order to work with them. As a result, they argued the law did not regulate conduct, it regulated pure political speech. The Court rejected both the advocates' and the government's arguments.

First, the Court determined that the material support law regulated more than just conduct. The Court reasoned that if the advocates wanted to speak to the terrorist organizations, depending on what they said, they might violate the material support law. If their speech imparted specialized knowledge, they could be prosecuted. If their speech only imparted general knowledge, they could not be prosecuted. Therefore, contrary to the government's argument, the material support law regulated speech based on its content. On the other hand, the Court also found that the law did not ban pure political speech. The Court found the law only prohibited a narrow category of speech. The advocates were free to speak with anyone about the terrorist organizations, human rights, or international law. Additionally, they could speak with international aid agencies and the United Nations, and could even join the terrorist organizations. The only thing they could not do is speak with the terrorist organizations themselves in a way that constituted providing "material support."

Once the Court determined the material support law prohibited some speech based on its content, it analyzed the law under the most demanding and rigorous First Amendment judicial scrutiny available. The Court often refers to this analytical framework as "strict scrutiny." Under the strict scrutiny judicial review framework, the government must prove that 1) the government has a compelling interest in enacting the challenged law and 2) the law is necessary to further that interest. All the litigants agreed that the government's interest in impeding and combating terrorism was a compelling government interest. As a result, the Court focused its analysis on the second step in the strict scrutiny framework—whether the law was necessary to further the government's interest in combating terrorism.

The advocates argued the law was unnecessary and should not be applied to them based on what they wanted to talk about. The advocates posited that their speech would only be focused on supporting the non-violent activities of the terrorist organizations and thus the enforcement of the law was unwarranted and inessential. The Court, however, rejected this argument. The Court reasoned that any support provided to a terrorist organization ultimately furthers its illegitimate goals. While the advocates might speak about non-violent or legitimate tactics, obtaining this information from the advocates frees up the terrorist organizations' resources to pursue their illegitimate goals. Moreover, the Court suggested, the information the advocates impart to the terrorist organizations could tend to lend some appearance of legitimacy to the terrorist organizations, thus allowing them to raise more funds and recruit more members. Finally, the Court deferred to the Legislative and Executive Branches' determinations and held that the material support law advanced the United States government's international relationships and cooperation with other nations to combat terrorism.

Three Justices dissented and disagreed with the outcome of the case. They argued the First Amendment has long protected the right to speak to organizations thought to be a threat to national security. In this case, the dissenting Justices argued, the advocates were not proposing to solicit criminal activity like fraud or murder. Moreover, even if they were proposing to advocate unlawful conduct, that speech would be protected by the First Amendment unless it met the *Brandenburg v. Ohio* standard, discussed above. The dissenters suggested the Court was allowing the government to use the threat of international terrorism to abrogate First Amendment rights when, even in times of war, Americans retain their fundamental liberties. This prohibition on material support was not unlike laws in the mid Twentieth Century that prohibited membership in the Communist Party. The dissenters reasoned that just as the First Amendment protects an American's right to belong to the Communist Party as long as he did not share its unlawful purposes, it protects an American's right to speak to a terrorist organization as long as he does not share its unlawful purposes. Thus, the dissenters believed the material support law violated the advocates' First Amendment rights.

8.7. FOIA AND ACCESS TO GOVERNMENT INFORMATION

A fundamental tenet of the First Amendment is that the discussion of matters of public concern must be uninhibited, robust, and wide-open. This is particularly so when the issues discussed are those that are relevant to self-governance. Many legal scholars suggest that in order to have a well-functioning democracy, the freedom of speech must be guaranteed. This enables citizens to exchange ideas about who should govern them and how they should be governed. Every government, however, has an interest in withholding some information from its citizens for national security reasons. Still, every piece of information withheld from the electorate is, arguably, one less data point upon which it can make informed decisions. In the United States, the Freedom of Information Act (FOIA) is the statutory attempt to strike a balance between government transparency and the government's right to withhold information.

FOIA has periodically been amended since its inception, but the law's fundamental commitment to making government information available and accessible has remained the same. To that end, FOIA is organized into a three-part system for releasing, disclosing, and withholding information. The first two parts of the FOIA system mandate the publication of information, while the third part provides a disclosure process for those documents and information not already affirmatively published. It is the third part of the system, the "disclosure" process, that often gets the most attention because of the sensitivity of documents and information sought by citizens and the media through requests for information. However, the first two affirmative disclosure provisions of the system are equally as important as they ensure an ongoing, presumptive public sharing of routine government information.

FOIA's publication requirements and disclosure process apply to all federal agencies. The term "agency," for the purposes of FOIA requirements, is defined broadly. It "includes any executive department, military department, Government corporation, Government controlled corporation, or other establishment in the executive branch of the Government (including the Executive Office of the President), or any independent regulatory agency." Section 552(f)(1). Notably absent from the definition is Congress and the Judicial Branch. Additionally, in *Kissinger v. Reporters Committee for Freedom of the Press*, the Supreme Court held that the term "agency" does not include "the President's immediate personal staff or units in the Executive Office whose sole function is to advise and assist the President."

8.7.1. FOIA's Affirmative Disclosure Requirements

FOIA contains two requirements for the publication of basic information about federal agencies, their organization, and their functioning. Sections 552(a)(1) and (2) of FOIA list the information that must be disseminated and the means by which the information must be shared with the public. First, Section 552(a)(1) mandates that each federal agency must affirmatively file certain information in the federal government's official publication source for public notices and information—the **Federal Register**. Section 552(a)(1) requires federal agencies to publish:

1) A description of their organization and information regarding how the public may obtain information, make submissions or requests, or obtain decisions;
2) An explanation of how agency functions are directed and determined, including the nature and requirements of all available procedures;
3) A list of procedural rules, descriptions of agency forms or the places where forms may be obtained, and instructions as to the scope and contents of all papers, reports, or examinations;
4) A list of substantive rules of general applicability adopted as authorized by law, as well as agency statements of general policy or interpretations; and
5) Any amendment, revision, or repeal of the information listed above.

The requirement to publish this information is intended to ensure that members of the public have sufficient information to effectively interact with federal agencies. If an agency fails to publish the required information listed above, it may not use the undisclosed information to the disadvantage of an individual who deals with the agency. This statutory penalty for noncompliant agencies ensures they are unable to use secret rules or processes.

Section 552(a)(2) also requires the affirmative disclosure of certain federal agency information. Instead of the Federal Register, however, Section 552(a)(2) mandates that agencies must make the information available for inspection and copying. While this section of the law was at once referred to as the "reading-room" provision because agencies often had a physical room dedicated for inspection and review by the public, most agencies now publish the materials online on their websites. Pursuant to Section 552(a)(2), agencies must make available:

1) Final opinions and orders, made in the adjudication of cases that come before the agency;
2) Policy statements and interpretations that have not appeared in the Federal Register;
3) Administrative staff manuals and instructions that affect the public;
4) Copies of records that had been released in response to a FOIA request and that (a) the agency determines have become or are likely to become the subject of subsequent requests for substantially the same records due to their nature or (b) have been requested 3 or more times; and
5) Indexes of previously released records.

Congress's intent in requiring these disclosures was to avoid the creation of secret or difficult to obtain agency-created rules and orders that can become the equivalent of bureaucratic law. Similar to the statutory penalty in Section 552(a)(1), Section 552(a)(2) provides that an agency may not make a decision in reliance on the information listed above if the agency has not made it available for inspection.

8.7.2. Disclosures in Response to Requests

Perhaps the most well-known provision of FOIA is Section 552(a)(3) which permits the public to make requests for records directly to government agencies. More specifically, this provision permits the public to request records and information not "made available under" under Sections 552(a)(1) or (2). FOIA's Section 552(a)(3) also lays out a specific process by which someone seeking information can make a formal request for information, thus triggering a variety of potential responses by the agency. Finally, Section 552(a)(3) provides an administrative review process by which a requester can appeal an agency's decision to withhold requested information before challenging it in court.

First, Section 552(a)(3) requires an agency to make any records available to a requesting person who reasonably describes the records in a way that would enable the agency's personnel to locate them. However, a reasonable description of the records sought is not sufficient to trigger a mandatory search for the records under Section 552(a)(3). Each agency publishes rules describing the procedures that must be followed to file a formal request. In addition to the reasonable description, a requester must comply with an agency's published rules stating the procedures to be followed. These procedures typically require a requester to submit his name and address and file the request with designated FOIA personnel in the agency.

Once an agency receives a properly submitted request, it must conduct a reasonably adequate search that would be likely to locate the information requested. While the search need not be exhaustive, agencies cannot simply conduct a cursory review. Agencies that receive a properly submitted request must make a determination regarding the request within 20 days. The agency can either provide the information sought or it can notify the requester that the information sought is exempted from FOIA's requirements. If the agency invokes an exception to providing the requested information, it must provide the requester an explanation of the reasons it has invoked an exception. The agency must also notify the requester how he can appeal the determination within the agency and to whom the appeal must be directed. If the decision is upheld within the agency's administrative appeal process, the requester can seek review of the agency's decision in court. When courts review an agency's decision to withhold information, they conduct the review **de novo** without deference to the agency's decision.

8.7.3. Exemptions to FOIA's Publication, Disclosure, and Production Requirements

While Congress's goal in enacting FOIA was to create an open and transparent government, Congress also recognized that some information retained by government agencies must remain undisclosed. As a result, FOIA exempts from disclosure nine categories of information for various policy and privacy reasons. As discussed above, if an agency determines requested information falls within an exemption category, it may not act as if the information does not exist. Instead, it must disclose the fact that the requested information exists and identify the reasons for withholding it. There are nine categories of information exempt from FOIA's disclosure requirements, some of which are less relevant to national security. Those that are less relevant are internal personnel rules and practices; matters exempted by other statutes; trade secrets and commercial or financial information; personnel and medical files; financial institution reports; and geological and geophysical information and data concerning wells. The three categories of information that are more often relevant to national security are national defense or foreign policy; inter-agency or intra-agency memoranda or letters; and law enforcement records. Each of these is discussed more fully below.

National Defense or Foreign Policy—Exemption 1

An agency may withhold requested information under FOIA if it concerns "national defense or foreign policy." Section 552(b)(1). This exemption is often referred to as Exemption 1 as it is the first exemption listed in FOIA. Under Exemption 1, an agency may not simply invoke national defense or foreign policy concerns and withhold information from a requester. Instead, Exemption 1 is limited to information that meets two criteria: 1) it is specifically authorized, under criteria established by an **Executive Order**, to be kept secret in the interest of national defense or foreign policy and 2) it is properly classified pursuant to the order. Both criteria must be met. Thus, simply because information is sensitive or otherwise should be classified, if it has not been properly classified pursuant to the procedures listed in an applicable Executive Order, Exemption 1 does not apply.

Exemption 1 is a reflection of Congress's recognition that some information must remain secret and the President bears the primary responsibility for ensuring national security. Beginning with President Harry S. Truman, Executive Orders have described the Executive Branch's policy regarding national security information and have described both the substantive and procedural requirements to classify information. Under Executive Order 13,526, the currently operative Executive Order for classifying information, information may only be classified if "the unauthorized disclosure of the information reasonably could be expected to result in damage to the national security, which includes defense against transnational terrorism." While courts conduct a de novo review of an agency's decision to invoke an exemption, courts routinely defer to the Executive Branch's expertise in applying the national security designation to information.

Inter-Agency or Intra-Agency Memoranda or Letters—Exemption 5

The inter- or intra-agency memoranda or letters exemption, also known as Exemption 5, permits agencies to withhold from disclosure information that "would not be available by law to a party other than an agency in litigation with the agency." Section 552(b)(5). In civil litigation, lawyers have procedural tools they can utilize to compel opposing parties to share documents and information before trial. The requesting lawyers then use these documents and information to build and strengthen their case. Exemption 5 statutorily ensures that agencies cannot be compelled, through a FOIA request, to produce **privileged** information that would not even be produced in a civil lawsuit. These privileges, like the attorney-client privilege, are found in both statutory and common law. In *United States v. Weber Aircraft Corp.*, the Supreme Court determined that Exemption 5 encompasses both sets of privileges.

Numerous privileges can be invoked to prevent the disclosure of information during a civil lawsuit. However, agencies primarily rely on three privileges when they invoke Exemption 5. These privileges are the deliberative process privilege, or executive privilege; the attorney work-product privilege; and the attorney-client privilege. The deliberative process privilege is arguably the most often relied upon. This privilege protects information produced as part of the discussions and considerations that occur while agencies make decisions and formulate policy. It encourages and protects, from public disclosure, open and frank conversations and debates. It also protects the public from confusion between pre-decisional rationales and options that were debated before, and may be different from, the particular policy ultimately settled upon by an agency. Perhaps more important, from a national security perspective, is the protection this privilege affords to Presidential communication. In *Nixon v. Administrator of General Services*, the Supreme Court held Exemption 5 protected from disclosure all the President's communications in performance of his official responsibilities and those "made in the process of shaping policies and making decisions." Courts interpret this privilege broadly and have found it also applies to communications by the President's staff as well as post-decisional material.

Exemption 5 also protects attorney work-product and attorney-client communication. Agencies routinely rely on advice and assistance from government lawyers while making decisions and crafting policy. In doing so, government lawyers produce materials in anticipation of litigation and communicate with agency personnel and leaders. Exemption 5 protects these materials and communications. It is important to note, however, that the attorney work-product privilege does not automatically protect every document produced by a lawyer. Those materials produced in an agency's normal course of business, even if produced by a lawyer, are not included in Exemption 5. However, if a lawyer produces materials in anticipation of litigation, the attorney-work product privilege will apply. The attorney-client privilege is more expansive. It applies to any confidential communication between a lawyer and her client whenever the client has sought legal advice, not only when the communication relates to litigation.

Law Enforcement Records or Information—Exemption 7

The third national security related exemption under FOIA is the Law Enforcement Records or Information exemption. As this is the seventh exemption found in FOIA, it is also known as Exemption 7. Exemption 7 allows agencies to withhold from dissemination any "records or information compiled for law enforcement purposes . . . ." Section 552(b)(7). This exemption ensures that sensitive law enforcement materials remain undisclosed while investigations proceed toward thwarting dangers and apprehending suspects. Courts have interpreted the term "law enforcement" broadly. It encompasses agencies' enforcement of federal civil, criminal, and administrative laws. It also covers the enforcement of state and foreign laws, such as when federal agencies assist and cooperate with their state and foreign counterparts. It has also been interpreted by courts to not only include traditional domestic law enforcement materials, but also materials produced as part of investigating international and terrorist threats to national security.

Exemption 7 may appear to be a broad exemption that could relieve multiple federal agencies from FOIA's responsibilities because their sole or primary function is law enforcement. However, Exemption 7 only applies where information has been "complied" for law enforcement purposes and where releasing the information will result in one of six harms specifically enumerated in FOIA. For the purposes of the compilation requirement, the Supreme Court in *FBI v. Abramson* determined that information originally compiled for law enforcement purposes does not lose that designation when it is summarized or incorporated into a new document unrelated to law enforcement. Relatedly, in *John Doe Agency v. John Doe Corp.*, the Court held that information that was not originally compiled for law enforcement purposes can be designated as such if it is later compiled for law enforcement purposes prior to the government invoking Exemption 7.

As mentioned above, in addition to the compilation requirement, an agency must also demonstrate that one or more of six harms listed in FOIA will occur as a result of disclosing the information. Exemption 7(A) permits an agency to withhold law enforcement material that "could reasonably be expected to interfere with enforcement proceedings." Section 552(b)(7)(A). This exemption is a temporal restriction and only applies when law enforcement proceedings are expected, pending, or preventative. Thus, as the Supreme Court determined in *NLRB v. Robbins Tire & Rubber Co.*, it does not "endlessly protect material simply because it was in an investigatory file." Exemption 7(B) permits an agency to withhold "records or information compiled for law enforcement purposes [that] would deprive a person of a right to a fair trial or an impartial adjudication." Section 552(b)(7)(B) While this exemption is rarely invoked, at least one court, the D.C. Circuit Court of Appeals, has determined that Exemption 7(B) does not apply to material simply because it would affect a defendant's reputation or privacy, unless the material would also impact the fairness of the defendant's trial. *Chiquita Brands Int'l Inc. v. SEC.* Exemption 7(C) permits an agency to withhold information that "could reasonably be expected to constitute an unwarranted invasion of personal privacy." Section 552(b)(7)(C). This exemption protects the release of the private information of those involved in law enforcement investigations and prosecutions, whether suspects, witnesses, or investigators, as they have an interest in not being unfairly stigmatized or associated with illicit activity.

Exemption 7(D) protects information compiled during a criminal investigation or national security intelligence investigation that could reveal a confidential source of information provided by a source. Section 552(b)(7)(D). Exemption 7(E) permits agencies to withhold information that "would disclose techniques and procedures for law enforcement investigations or prosecutions, or would disclose guidelines for law enforcement investigations or prosecutions if such disclosure could reasonably be expected to risk circumvention of the law." Section 552(b)(7)(E). For the purposes of Exemption 7(E), courts have distinguished between its two clauses by interpreting "techniques and procedures" as "how" law enforcement investigations are conducted, while "guidelines" are "whether" investigations occur. Finally, Exemption 7(F) protects "records or information compiled for law enforcement purposes [that] could reasonably be expected to endanger the life or physical safety of any individual." Section 552(b)(7)(F). Courts have determined that the protection afforded by Exemption 7(F) is very broad and includes not only the names of federal and state law enforcement officers, but also non-law enforcement federal employees, third parties connected with a law enforcement proceeding and informants, and even the description of contraband. So long as the government can prove there is a reasonable expectation that someone's life or safety will be endangered, courts will generally uphold the government's invocation of Exemption 7(F).

REVIEW QUESTIONS

1. What events precipitated the Alien and Sedition Acts of 1789 and what did the Sedition Act prohibit? Did the Supreme Court ever issue a ruling specifically addressing the constitutionality of the Sedition Act of 1789?

2. What does a public official need to prove to win a defamation lawsuit? Is this a difficult standard to meet? Why or why not?

3. What events precipitated the Espionage and Sedition Acts of 1917 and what did the Acts prohibit?

4. What standard of judicial review did the Supreme Court first use to analyze the Espionage and Sedition Acts of 1917?

5. What was Justice Holmes's famous metaphor describing the value of free speech?

6. What standard of review did the Supreme Court announce in *Brandenburg v. Ohio*? Is it more or less protective of speech than the standard of review it replaced?

7. What is a prior restraint on speech? Can the government place a prior restraint on the media and prohibit it from releasing information that threatens national security?

8. What is symbolic speech? Can the government punish conduct that is intended to express an idea?

9. Why is burning the United States flag protected by the First Amendment?

10. What speech was prohibited by the Patriot Act's "material support" law? Did the prohibition violate the First Amendment? Why or why not?

11. What is FOIA's three-part system? How does each part of the system function to facilitate government transparency and protect sensitive information?

CRITICAL THINKING QUESTIONS

1. Do you agree with the Supreme Court's interpretation of the First Amendment regarding seditious libel? How might this interpretation of the First Amendment negatively affect public discourse and those considering entering politics? Are those negative effects worth the benefits?

2. Do you find Justice Holmes's famous "marketplace of ideas" metaphor persuasive? Some critics of the marketplace metaphor suggest that the marketplace of ideas can become distorted by, and thus manipulated to favor, those with more money or resources. Do you agree or disagree? Why or why not?

3. Consider the judicial standard announced in *Brandenburg v. Ohio*. Can you create a scenario in which someone's speech meets the standard and is thus punishable?

4. In *NY Times v. United States*, various Justices wrote concurring opinions that described the burden the government would need to meet to impose a prior restraint on the media in national security cases. Which Justice's burden was the most persuasive and why?

5. Do you agree with the Supreme Court's decision in *Texas v. Johnson*? Why or why not?

6. Do you agree with the Supreme Court's decision in *Holder v. Humanitarian Law Project*? Why do you think the Court came to a different decision in *Holder v. Humanitarian Law Project* when compared with other national security cases in this chapter?

7. Does FOIA strike the right balance between government transparency and government secrecy? Are there any Exemptions in the statute that you disagree with? If so, why?

CHAPTER 9

International Law in the United States and United States Law Internationally

The United Nations Headquarters, New York City

Learning Objectives

1. Be able to summarize the types of international law, including how they are formed.

2. Understand the effect on United States domestic law of treaties, executive agreements, and customary international law.

3. Be able to explain how and when the United States Constitution and United States statutes apply to persons and activities outside the United States.

9.1. INTRODUCTION

In previous chapters in this book we have been primarily concerned with how domestic United States law—especially the United States Constitution—affects United States national security. But another significant source of law affects United States national security: international law. The relevance of international law to United States law and United States government actions is subject to continuing debate. Whether actions within the United States—particularly those with national security consequences—can, or should, be controlled by anything other than United States law is a question with which politicians and judges wrestle. Supreme Court Justices continue to wrangle over the extent to which their opinions should be informed by international law generally. And in the specific context of national security, the extent to which international law should limit the nation's ability to preserve its national security is even more acute. Additionally, because numerous national security activities conducted by the United States government occur outside United States territory, the extent to which United States law governs or limits government actors when they are outside the United States is a critical question. While this is not an international law text, and this chapter is not an exhaustive presentation of international law, a basic understanding of international law and the **extraterritorial** application of United States domestic law is necessary to understand fully the legality of the various national security activities in which the United States government engages.

9.2. INTERNATIONAL LAW

As will be explained in this chapter, international law is generally formed in two ways: 1) by specific agreement—in the form of a **treaty** or **executive agreement**—among two or more states or 2) by custom. Each of these sources of international law is legitimate and can be "binding," though the effect of each on United States domestic law is not the same and their enforceability is often unclear.

9.2.1. Treaties

Under international law, a treaty is a written agreement between one or more states (nations) or international organizations. The agreement need not be titled "treaty" to be one; other common names for treaties include "convention" or "agreement." For instance, the most significant international agreement in existence today—the Charter of the United Nations—does not include "treaty" in its title, but is nevertheless a treaty.

9.2.1.1. Treaty Formation Process

Nations interested in participating in a treaty engage in negotiations that often take place over an extended time period. Nations are represented at such negotiations by persons with authority to negotiate on behalf of their nation, but final approval is usually required by some other governmental entity or figure. So, after the negotiating parties have reached agreement on language they believe will be acceptable, the treaty is "concluded by signature." At this point, international law requires that nations not defeat the "object and purpose" of the treaty through their actions. In other words, the nations that have signed, but not yet ratified, the treaty are not permitted to take actions that would make ratification impossible or meaningless. After conclusion by signature, each representative takes the treaty language back to their nation to go through whatever ratification and implementing processes are required by the domestic law of that nation.

A **bilateral treaty** (treaty between only to nations) goes into effect once both parties have ratified the treaty. When a **multilateral treaty** (treaty between three or more nations) goes into effect depends on the terms of the treaty. It might occur upon ratification by two or more parties, upon ratification by a specified number of parties, or at a specified date thereafter. Most treaties also specify mechanisms by which a state can withdraw from the treaty, though the absence of such language does not mean states cannot withdraw.

9.2.1.2. Treaty Conditions

Each nation participating in a treaty may, after concluding treaty negotiations, later insist on certain additional conditions. In the United States, these conditions could be asserted by the Senate or the President, though the latter is less likely because the Executive Branch leads treaty negotiations for the United States in the first place. There are several types of conditions placed on treaties:

1. **Amendments.** Amendments attempt to change the treaty language itself. These are the least common type of conditions because they essentially require the participating nations to renegotiate the treaty.

2. **Reservations.** Reservations are common today. A reservation is a condition that purports to change the substantive rights or obligations of nations, without actually changing treaty language. In essence, a reservation is one nation saying "this part of the treaty does not apply to us." If the treaty is bilateral, the other nation must agree to the reservation. If it is multilateral, reservations are permitted unless they are prohibited by the treaty or incompatible with the object and purpose of the treaty. Of course, whether a reservation is incompatible with

the object and purpose of a treaty is often controversial and difficult to determine. When a state attempts to assert a reservation in a multilateral treaty, the other states have several options. First, they can affirmatively accept the reservation. Second, they can do nothing, in which case acceptance is presumed after 12 months. Third, they can object to the reservation, but not oppose entry into force, the legal effect of which is that the element subject to the reservation does not apply, but the rest of the treaty does. Finally, they can object to the reservation and oppose the treaty's entry into force, the effect of which is that there is not a treaty between those nations. Considering that a multilateral treaty might have many different reservations by numerous participating states, there can be a number of distinct arrangements, relationships, and legal obligations within one treaty. In an attempt to protect against the degradation of treaty obligations and the effectiveness of treaties, a number of recent treaties have included language prohibiting reservations. One practical effect of this, however, is that sometimes nations who would have become parties to the treaty with a reservation, choose not to become a party at all. For example, the United States did not become a party to the "Rome Statute" treaty that created the International Criminal Court because the treaty explicitly prohibits reservations, and the United States was unwilling to be party to the statute without reservations.

3. **Understandings.** Understandings are a state's expression of what they believe the treaty language means. Understandings generally are not considered to have a legal effect, and thus are less likely to cause political friction or cause another state to reject the treaty. If a party to the treaty believes another party's understanding is actually a reservation, that state can treat it as a reservation.

4. **Declarations.** Declarations are official statements by nations regarding a matter contained in the treaty. Sometimes declarations are required in the treaty, in which case the declaration has legal effect. For example, a treaty may state that for a nation to join a human rights treaty it must formally declare its commitment to human rights. Confusingly, the term declaration has also been used interchangeably with understanding, meaning the state's interpretation of treaty language.

5. **Provisos.** Provisos are conditions internal to a particular nation that are not intended to have legal effect on the other parties to the agreement. For example, the Senate may include provisos when communicating its concerns about a particular treaty to the President.

9.2.1.3. Implementing Treaties

Though it may seem a treaty would have domestic legal effect as soon as it is ratified, that is often not the case. Nations treat treaties differently after they are ratified. Under some legal systems, ratification alone automatically makes the treaty effective domestically. But most nations require some subsequent domestic implementation, usually in the form of a statute. And in some nations, like the United States, whether a treaty has immediate effect varies based on the terms of the treaty. This issue is sometimes referred to as whether a treaty is "self-executing" or "non-self-executing." Self-executing treaties can be immediately and directly applied by courts, whereas non-self-executing treaties require some subsequent legislation before they are binding. For example, if a treaty says "No State Party shall expel, return or extradite a person to another State where there are substantial grounds for believing that he would be in danger of being subjected to **torture**," that language is self-executing because nothing further is required to "do" what the treaty says; extraditing someone to a place where the state had reason to believe they would be tortured would violate the treaty directly. By contrast, if a treaty were to require that each member state "adopt the necessary measures to implement its obligations under this Convention," that language would indicate the treaty is non-self-executing, because the nation is required to do something further to implement the treaty. The self-executing nature of a treaty is largely a concern regarding its *domestic* effect, though international law scholars have begun discussing the importance of whether a treaty is self-executing as a matter of international law.

Non-Self-Executing Treaties: Building the House

To understand the concept of non-self-executing treaties, it may help to think of an analogy: contracts. When a nation agrees to a treaty, it is committing to doing (or not doing) something. But the agreement to do something is often not the same as actually doing it. For instance, when a builder and a buyer enter a contract for a new house to be constructed, the contract detailing that a house will be built for an agreed upon price does not, itself, build the house. The parties must still do what they agreed to do: the builder must build the house and the buyer must pay the money. Building the house and paying the money are "executing" the contract. Similarly, if in a treaty a nation agrees to reduce carbon emissions from cars built in its country, the treaty itself does not reduce carbon emissions. Rather, after to agreeing to such a treaty, the nation must pass legislation requiring its automobile manufacturers to reduce their automobiles' emissions. That is a non-self-executing treaty; the subsequent implementing legislation executes the treaty.

9.2.2. Executive Agreements

Like treaties, executive agreements are pacts between the heads of government of two or more nations. Unlike treaties, executive agreements may not have undergone the participating nations' formal ratification processes. Sometimes international compacts are considered "executive agreements" only as a temporary status while ratification processes unfold, while other times there is no intent for the executive agreement to eventually become a treaty. Nevertheless, executive agreements are legally binding under international law when the parties intend for them to be. But not all executive agreements are intended to be *legally binding*; rather, they often reflect only political commitments, which are not legally binding under international law.

Easy Come, Easy Go: The "Iran Nuclear Deal"

The tenuous nature and legal significance of executive agreements was demonstrated by an agreement entered into between President Barack Obama and the nation of Iran regarding Iran's development of nuclear technologies. Under the agreement, the United States and numerous other nations agreed to lift economic sanctions in exchange for Iranian cessation of nuclear weapons development. During negotiation of the agreement that was ultimately reached in 2015, a large group of United States Senators who opposed the deal wrote a letter to Iran, observing that the agreement was "nothing more than an executive agreement between President Obama and Ayatollah Khamenei" that could be terminated by the next President "with the stroke of a pen." This is precisely what occurred when President Donald Trump, who had lambasted the Iran Nuclear Deal as "the worst deal ever negotiated," unilaterally withdrew the United States from the agreement in May 2018.

9.2.3. Customary International Law

Customary international law can be quite unusual to students used to thinking of law in the form of **positive law**, which is created by some form of government and usually written down. Customary international law is formed by practice and belief, not by the agreement and creation of formal, specific, written rules. Two key factors are required to form customary international law: 1) a sufficient number of states must generally behave consistently with the custom; and 2) states must do so because they accept that they have a legal obligation to do so, a concept sometimes referred to by the Latin phrase "***opinio juris***." So, customary international law is made by practice and belief, and only found or identified by courts or other bodies seeking to ascertain what a customary international law is. As states' practices and beliefs change, so too can customary international law.

As you might imagine, establishing—or proving the existence of—customary international law is difficult. In a world with hundreds of nations, demonstrating that a "sufficient" number of states behave consistently with a norm or principle is itself difficult, and demonstrating that they do so out of a sense of legal obligation even more so. Additionally, when law is created by practice, rather than codified, changing practices mean constantly evolving law. Further complicating the matter is that sometimes treaties are used as evidence of a customary international law. For example, once a sufficient number of states have signed a treaty and behave in accordance with it, that demonstrates both requirements for the formation of customary international law: state practice and legal obligation.

Once customary international law exists, it is binding on all nations, not just those who have demonstrated a willingness to be bound by it. However, a nation can escape being bound by customary international law by becoming a "persistent objector." For example, prohibition of the death penalty has become customary international law, but the United States has been a persistent objector through official statements, meaning that particular aspect of customary international law is *not* binding on the United States.

The Latin phrase ***jus cogens***, which means "compelling law," is used to describe a small subset of customary international law: laws that are binding on all nations whether or not a nation objects. Thus, *jus cogens* is an exception to the principle that nations can avoid customary international law by objecting to it. These principles—sometimes called "peremptory norms"—are considered so fundamental to the international order they are considered to be "universally accepted," even if that is not precisely the case. If the details of customary international law are difficult to prove, *jus cogens* is even more difficult. Only a few principles have risen to the level of *jus cogens*. These include the illegality of piracy, slavery, and genocide.

9.3. INTERNATIONAL LAW IN THE UNITED STATES

From early in the nation's history, the fact that international law would have some effect on United States domestic law was clear. In 1787 in Federalist 3, John Jay said "it is of high importance to the peace of America that she observe the laws of nations." Jay later reiterated the importance of international law when, as Chief Justice of the Supreme Court of the United States, while charging a grand jury he said "the laws of the United States admit of being classed under three heads of descriptions: 1st All treaties made under the authority of the United States; 2d The laws of nations; and 3rdly, the constitution, and statutes of the

United States." In what may be the most emphatic statement by the Supreme Court on the relevance of international law to domestic law, in 1900, in *The Paquete Habana* case, the Supreme Court said:

> international law is part of our law, and must be ascertained and administered by the courts of justice of appropriate jurisdiction, as often as questions of right depending upon it are duly presented for their determination. For this purpose, where there is no treaty and no controlling executive or legislative act or judicial decision, resort must be had to the customs and usages of civilized nations, and, as evidence of these, to the works of jurists and commentators who by years of labor, research, and experience have made themselves peculiarly well acquainted with the subjects of which they treat.

This strong assertion that when domestic law does not provide the answer to a legal question, judges should look to international law for an answer, has since been somewhat curtailed. In fact, in modern cases, the Supreme Court and important lower courts of appeals have attempted to curtail international law's influence on domestic law, leaving the extent to which international law affects domestic law in some flux. For example, in *Sosa v. Alvarez-Machain*, the Supreme Court determined that the Alien Tort Statute only creates causes of action under international law as it was understood in 1789. And *Medellin v. Texas*, the Court asserted that judgments of the **International Court of Justice** are not enforceable as domestic law unless Congress actually implements them.

9.3.1. Domestic Effect of Treaties

9.3.1.1. The Supremacy Clause and the Relationship Between Treaties and Other Domestic Law

The Supremacy Clause of the United States Constitution declares that:

> This Constitution, and the Laws of the United States which shall be made in Pursuance thereof; and all Treaties made, or which shall be made, under the Authority of the United States, shall be the supreme Law of the Land and the Judges in every State shall be bound thereby, any Thing in the Constitution or Laws of any State to the Contrary notwithstanding.

Thus, the effect of treaties in the United States seems clear: they enjoy the same place in the legal hierarchy as federal statutes, including being superior to state law. The Supreme Court confirmed this status, and its supreme role in interpreting treaties, early in the new Republic's existence. *Hunter v. Martin's Lessee.* Whether treaties enjoy real supremacy in practice today has been questioned.

While the Supremacy Clause establishes that international agreements in the form of treaties hold the same status as federal statutes, it also raises some significant questions. What is the relationship between treaties and the Constitution? What types of international agreements constitute a "treaty," and thus enjoy the status of being equal to domestic statutes? And what happens when a treaty and other "Laws of the United States" seem to conflict? The text of the Constitution does not directly answer these questions.

Surprisingly, the Supreme Court did not clearly establish the supremacy of the Constitution to treaties until the 1950s, and even then, did so only in a plurality opinion. In the famous case of *Reid v. Covert*, the Supreme Court addressed the relationship between international agreements and the Constitution. *Covert* involved two cases where civilian spouses of United States servicemembers living outside the United States were accused of murdering their servicemember husbands and were tried by court-martial rather than in civilian court. (See additional details in text box: The "Murdering Wives Cases" and Military Jurisdiction Over Civilians.) The two women challenged their court-martial convictions as violating several provisions of the Constitution, including three provisions that guarantee the right to trial by jury: Article III, the Fifth Amendment, and the Sixth Amendment. The government defended the courts-martial as being authorized by Status of Forces Agreements between the United States and the nations in which the murders occurred. The Supreme Court ultimately concluded that "No agreement with a foreign nation can confer power on the Congress, or on any other branch of Government, which is free from the restraints of the Constitution." The Court continued, holding that treaties and laws enacted pursuant to them, including executive agreements, must comply with the Constitution. In reaching this conclusion, the Court reasoned that government is a product of the Constitution, so it cannot obtain power to act outside the Constitution by means of an agreement with a foreign nation. Further, though the explicit text of the Supremacy Clause does not say that constitutional provisions trump treaties, if constitutional provisions do not trump treaties, then treaties could amend the Constitution, a result likely not intended by the **Framers** when they included the burdensome Article V amendment procedures. Finally, it would not make sense for treaties to be exempt from the Constitution when treaties are subordinate to subsequent statutes that are subject to the Constitution under the **last in time rule** (also known as "*lex posterior*"), which establishes that when two laws on the same level conflict, the more recent law trumps.

The "Murdering Wives Cases" and Military Jurisdiction Over Civilians

Reid v. Covert and *Kinsella v. Krueger* involved courts-martial prosecutions and convictions of civilian women accused of murdering their active duty military servicemember husbands. The cases are significant for three reasons. First, military lawyers know the case for the Supreme Court's ultimate holding that civilian dependents may not tried by court-martial because the Fifth Amendment's exception to the jury trial requirement ("except in cases arising in the land and naval forces") cannot trump a civilian's right to a jury trial established in the Fifth and Sixth Amendments. Second, for those interested in international law, the cases are known as the first in which the Supreme Court ruled that the Constitution supersedes treaties. Third, lawyers in general may know the cases as one of the few—and perhaps only—times the Supreme Court has reversed itself in the same case after publishing written opinions and without a controlling change in the composition of the court. The cases are collectively known as *Reid v. Covert*, with the ultimate decision by the Supreme Court often referred to as "*Reid II*." According to legend, the cases were known as "the murdering wives cases" in the halls and chambers of the Supreme Court. In addition to the legal significance, the two cases involve facts that are both sad and salacious.

Clarice Covert's husband was an active duty Air Force non-commissioned officer, stationed in England at the time she killed him. The Coverts had a strained marriage, including financial difficulty caused by Sergeant Covert's gambling debts, bad checks, and other financial misadventures. Mrs. Covert also apparently struggled with mental illness. On March 9, 1953, Mrs. Covert asked a military doctor to hospitalize her, but she was instead prescribed more medication, including Phenobarbital. The next night, while her husband slept, she used a hand axe to bludgeon him to death, after which she took a number of pills and lied down in bed next to his corpse. The next afternoon she dropped her two young boys at a nursery, then went to an appointment with her psychiatrist, where she confessed to the murder, saying "I killed Eddie last night."

Dorothy Krueger Smith was married to United States Army Colonel Aubrey Smith. Like the Coverts, the Smiths had a troubled marriage. Mrs. Smith suffered from mental health issues, and drug and alcohol addiction. Colonel Smith was alleged to be a gambler, partyer, and womanizer. The couple lived in Tokyo, Japan, for Colonel Smith's assignment to United States Far East Command. After multiple hospitalizations for mental health difficulties, Mrs. Smith killed Colonel Smith in their home near Tokyo. While her husband slept, she stabbed him in the side with an eight-inch knife. After hearing Colonel Smith's call for help, their housekeeper summoned a neighbor who later said that when he arrived, Colonel Smith was lying in a pool of blood while Mrs. Smith was lying on her bed attempting to light a cigarette. Apparently very intoxicated and incoherent, the neighbor said Mrs. Smith exclaimed "too bad I did not get him in the heart."

Both women were tried by court-martial, convicted, and sentenced to life in prison at a federal civilian facility for women. When their cases initially reached the Supreme Court, the Court upheld the military's exercise of **jurisdiction** over the women. In a 5–4 decision, the Court held that the Constitution does not require trial by an Article III court when the crimes are committed in a foreign country and when Congress had established a court for the purpose. Curiously, Justice Frankfurter issued a "reservation" instead of a dissent, which the wives' lawyer, famed appellate attorney Frederick Bernays Wiener, understood to be an invitation to petition for rehearing. After the rehearing, Justices Frankfurter and Harlan changed their votes and the Court reversed the wives' convictions. However, though sufficient Justices joined in the judgment to reverse the convictions, only three Justices joined Justice Black's opinion, meaning the case's important pronouncements were articulated in a plurality opinion with limited precedential value. After the Supreme Court's ruling in *Reid II*, the women were released from prison and no retrial was attempted. They slipped from public view and both died in the 1990s.

The problem of what to do with civilian dependents of United States military members when they commit serious crimes overseas was addressed decades later with the passage of the Military Extraterritorial Jurisdiction Act of 2000 (MEJA). MEJA allows for federal civilian court jurisdiction over felony-level crimes committed by persons "employed by or accompanying the Armed Forces" outside the United States. MEJA has had mixed success, with relatively few successful prosecutions since its enactment. Interestingly, MEJA was used to try yet another woman accused of murdering her active duty Air Force husband by stabbing him in 2003.

In addition to MEJA, Congress amended UCMJ Article 2(a)(10) to confer court-martial jurisdiction over civilians during time of declared war or "contingency operation." Importantly, this jurisdiction is limited to civilians who are "serving with or accompanying an armed force" and "in the field." In *United States v. Ali*, one of the first courts-martial of a civilian under the new Article 2(a)(10), the Court of Appeals for the Armed Forces determined that the requirements "ensure that the exercise of jurisdiction over civilians is 'restricted' to the 'narrowest jurisdiction deemed absolutely essential to maintaining discipline among troops in active service,' " and accordingly is constitutional. The Supreme Court declined to hear an appeal, suggesting military court-martial jurisdiction over civilians in such limited circumstances may be appropriate.

In practice, the Supreme Court has interpreted treaties as being on par with domestic federal statutes. When examining an international agreement and seemingly conflicting federal statutes, courts first apply the "*Charming Betsy*" principle, named after the Supreme Court case in which the principle was announced. In 1804, in *Murray v. The Schooner Charming Betsy*, the Supreme Court declared that "an Act of Congress ought never to be construed to violate the law of nations if any other possible construction remains. . . ." The Restatement (Third) of Foreign Relations Law echoes the *Charming Betsy* principle: "Where fairly possible, a United States statute is to be construed so as not to conflict with international law or with an international agreement of the United States."

As noted above, when a conflict between a statute and a treaty is unavoidable, courts apply the "**last in time rule**." Under this interpretive rule, when two laws of equal supremacy conflict, the later trumps. Thus, treaties can alter prior statutes and statutes can alter prior treaties. As one court put it, "The Constitution gives a treaty no superiority over an act of Congress. . .which may be repealed or modified by an act of a later date." *Committee of United States Citizens Living in Nicaragua v. Reagan* (D.C. Cir. 1988). Importantly, though a statute that violates a treaty may trump the treaty for purposes of domestic law, the treaty still has force and effect under international law.

9.3.1.2. Treaty Formation Process in the United States

For an international agreement to have the significant effect of a treaty under domestic United States law, the constitutionally mandated process must be followed and completed. Under Article II, Section 2, of the United States Constitution, the President has the authority, with advice and consent of two thirds of the Senate, to make treaties. The implication of this constitutional text is that negotiation of treaties is the responsibility of the Executive. Typically, the United States State Department takes the lead, though treaty negotiation delegations sometimes include members from affected federal agencies. Additionally, Congress is often involved in treaty negotiations. State Department regulations require that it keeps Congressional leaders advised regarding the status of negotiations. Also, Congresspeople and their staffs may be part of the negotiating delegation, though they must not stray from Executive's positions regarding the treaty. Ultimately, if nations agree, the President signs the treaty. Note, however, that until the United States officially ratifies a treaty following the constitutionally mandated requirements, the agreement is not yet in effect under United States law as a treaty.

Once treaty negotiations are concluded by signature, the ratification process begins. To obtain the Senate's advice and consent, the President sends the agreement to the Senate, requesting its "advice and consent." This request is usually accompanied by the Secretary of State's detailed analysis and recommendations. The Senate Foreign Relations Committee first addresses the treaty before the entire Senate may consider it. Upon consideration, the Senate may approve the treaty by a two-thirds majority, or disapprove. If the Senate approves, it may also add conditions in the form of amendments, reservations, understandings, declarations, and provisos. The Senate sends the agreement back to the President. Once he signs and conveys an instrument of ratification to the treaty partner or partners, the treaty is "ratified." If the Senate returns the treaty to the President with conditions with which he agrees, he can sign it and complete the ratification process. If he does not agree with the conditions, he can send the agreement back to the Senate requesting the conditions be changed, or return to the treaty partners, requesting changes to treaty. Once the United States is a party to the treaty, it is bound by international law to comply with its terms.

9.3.1.3. Interpreting Treaties

When determining the domestic meaning of a treaty, there is some uncertainty regarding whose interpretation should prevail. Of course, courts in the Judicial Branch are routinely tasked with interpreting the meaning of law, including treaties. But when they do so, on whose understanding of the treaty should they rely? When interpreting statutes, courts often consider what was intended by Congress when it created the law. But this begs the question of who creates treaties. The Executive Branch is responsible for creating and negotiating the treaty to begin with, so should its understanding of the words it negotiated be given great weight? In this instance, the roles are reversed, with the Executive "creating" the treaty and the Legislative consenting to it. Those suggesting there is a presidential treaty interpretation power have observed that the President is constitutionally obligated to "take Care that the Laws be faithfully executed," so presidential interpretation of law is constitutionally permissible. If the President's interpretation of a treaty is given significance, how much? That is, should the President's view be definitive or merely "important"?

On the other hand, the Senate approves the text of a treaty, not the President's interpretation, suggesting that only the explicit language of the treaty matters. Moreover, if the President's interpretation has the effect of expanding his power, should that be given deference? For example, President Reagan "reinterpreted" the Anti-Ballistic Missile Treaty with the Soviet Union. The new interpretation permitted the United States to create its Strategic Defense Initiative system for shooting down incoming missiles, even though the treaty appeared to bar it. The Executive Branch claimed the new interpretation was based on a "secret negotiating record" with the Soviets that had not been shared with the Senate when obtaining advice and consent. In response to this perceived abuse, the Senate Foreign Relations Committee passed a bill out of committee stating "the meaning of a treaty is to be determined in light of what the Senate understands the treaty to mean when it gives its advice and consent." Of course, this view risks overvaluing the Senate's interpretation and undervaluing the President's. Additionally, it is not clear how a definitive interpretation of the Senate, a body with 100 members with unique minds and interpretations, could be determined. The Senate bill never became law.

Whatever the merits of the academic debate regarding whose interpretation of a treaty should prevail, courts routinely give substantial deference to the interpretations of the Executive Branch. Though the Supreme Court has never declared that the Executive Branch's interpretation always trumps others, the Court has repeatedly noted that it is "well settled that the United States' interpretation of a treaty 'is entitled to great weight.' " *Medellin v. Texas*, quoting *Sumitomo Shoji America, Inc. v. Avagliano.*

9.3.1.4. Self-Executing and Non-Self-Executing Treaties

A well-respected treatise, Restatement (Third) of Foreign Relations Law, indicates a United States treaty is non-self-executing: "(a) if the agreement manifests an intention that it shall not become effective as domestic law without the enactment of implementing legislation, (b) if the Senate in giving consent to a treaty, or Congress by resolution, requires implementing legislation, or (c) if implementing legislation is constitutionally required." If those descriptions leave you confused regarding whether a treaty is self-executing or non-self-executing, you are in good company. There is little authoritative consensus regarding how to determine which is which.

Despite the uncertainty, the difference between self-executing and non-self-executing treaties is important. In 2008 in *Medellin v. Texas*, the Supreme Court noted "This Court has long recognized the distinction between treaties that automatically have effect as domestic law, and those that—while they constitute international law commitments—do not by themselves function as binding federal law." According to the Court, "self-executing" treaties have "automatic domestic effect upon ratification," whereas non-self-executing treaties do not, by themselves, give rise to domestically enforceable, binding federal law. Instead, they require subsequent implementing legislation passed by Congress. Since only self-executing treaties are enforceable as part of the law of the land and a non-self-executing treaty only gets domestic effect "upon implementing legislation passed by Congress," determining whether a treaty is self-executing has significant domestic legal consequences.

United States federal courts have articulated a presumption that treaties are non-self-executing, though the judiciary has provided little clarity regarding how to predict whether a particular treaty will be viewed as self-executing. A variety of factors may be considered, including whether the treaty: explicitly says it is or is not self-executing or articulates what is required to implement the treaty; attempts to do something that the United States Constitution says requires a statute; or creates a private right of action. For our purposes, it is most important to understand that self-executing treaties are judicially enforceable, and non-self-executing treaties are not, until they are executed by subsequent implementation. Importantly, because self-executing treaties are enforceable as part of domestic law, while non-executed, non-self-executing treaties are not, the latter do not constrain national security actors under domestic law.

Though the concept has now taken root in other nations, the distinction between self-executing and non-self-executing treaties originated with the United States, stemming largely from the Supremacy Clause's provision that makes treaties part of the law of the land. In most countries without a similar provision, treaties can only become part of the law of the land once the treaty is somehow implemented by the government, rendering the distinction between self-executing and non-self-executing treaties irrelevant for domestic law purposes.

9.3.1.5. Terminating Treaties

Somewhat surprisingly, the United States Constitution does not explicitly say how treaties can be terminated or by who. Because treaties are part of "the law of the land," the authority to terminate a treaty carries with it the power to cancel elements of domestic law. Several possibilities were suggested in a case called *Goldwater v. Carter*, in which the Court of Appeals for the D.C. Circuit heard Senator Barry Goldwater's challenge to President Jimmy Carter's unilateral (without Senate involvement) termination of a mutual defense treaty with Taiwan. Senator Goldwater argued treaties can only be terminated when the same parties that approved the treaty terminate it: the President and two thirds of the Senate. But that is not how the Supreme Court has handled other situations where the President gets advice and consent of the Senate. For instance, the President's appointment power requires Senate approval to confirm cabinet officials, but the Supreme Court has upheld the President's authority to terminate such officials unilaterally. Additionally, imposing this supermajority requirement to terminate treaties could have the practical effect of locking the United States into treaties more than other nations are locked in, to the United States' disadvantage.

The prevailing view of the D.C. Circuit judges in *Goldwater* was that the President may terminate treaties unilaterally. This makes some practical sense when considering that the primary purpose of a treaty is not to create domestic law, but is instead an instrument of foreign policy that needs to be flexible and rapidly alterable. As the government lawyers argued in *Goldwater*, the President has terminated treaties unilaterally many times.

One dissenting judge in the *Goldwater* case argued that because a treaty becomes part of United States law, it should only be terminated in the same method other parts of United States law is terminated: the entire Congress. And in fact, under the "last in time" rule, Congress can effectively neutralize the domestic effect of a treaty by subsequently enacting a law that completely contradicts the treaty, suggesting the whole Congress should have a role in terminating treaties, too. But, as the majority in *Goldwater* responded:

> The fact that the Constitution, statutes and treaties are all listed in the Supremacy Clause as being superior to any form of state law does not mean that making and unmaking of treaties can be analogized to the making and unmaking of domestic statutes any more than it can be analogized to the making or unmaking of a constitutional amendment.

Moreover, if the President and Senate can make or amend a treaty without participation by the House of Representatives, why should the House have a role in terminating treaties?

Though the *Goldwater* case provides helpful articulation of some of the possible views of a treaty termination power, it does not stand as precedent. After the opinion described here, Senator Goldwater appealed to the United States Supreme Court, which vacated the D.C. Circuit's opinion, holding that the case was non-justiciable because it posed a political question and was not ripe for **judicial review**. Accordingly, the important question of whether anything more than a presidential decision to terminate is required may never be subject to judicial decision.

9.3.2. Domestic Effect of Executive Agreements

An executive agreement is an international agreement that in some way does not meet the treaty requirements of the United States Constitution. In the United States, this usually means the agreement has not followed the process of obtaining advice and consent of the Senate or completed the ratification process. Though not explicitly mentioned in the Constitution, executive agreements have received Supreme Court approval. See, e.g., *American Ins. Ass'n v. Garamendi* (2003) ("the President has authority to make 'executive agreements' with other countries, requiring no ratification by the Senate . . . this power having been exercised since the early years of the Republic"). While these agreements might fit the international law definition of a treaty, they have a different status under United States law. Executive agreements have been used throughout United States history, with the total number of executive agreements outpacing the number of treaties by nearly 20 to one. And in recent years, Senate approval of treaties has slowed to a trickle while the President's creation and use of executive agreements has grown swiftly. In one study, the Congressional Research Service noted that in the first 50 years following the ratification of the Constitution, the United States entered into 60 treaties and 27 executive agreements, while during the 50-year period between 1939 and 1989, the 702 treaties the United States ratified were dwarfed by 11,698 executive agreements.

There are three principle types of executive agreements, with each type drawing its authority from somewhere different:

1. ***Congressional-executive agreements*** are international agreements where Congress either delegates to the President the authority to enter into an agreement or formally enacts into law an executive agreement into which the President has already entered. An example might be a trade agreement between the United States and one or more other nations that Congress authorizes in some way. The North American Free Trade Agreement was one such executive agreement.

2. ***Agreements pursuant to treaty*** are sub-agreements that draw their authority from a treaty. These agreements are necessary to implement or further clarify the treaty provisions. This type of agreement was implicitly approved by the Supreme Court in the case *Wilson v. Girard* in 1957, when it upheld the terms of a status of forces agreement with Japan under which the United States turned over to Japanese authorities a United States servicemember accused of murdering a Japanese woman.

3. ***Sole executive agreements*** are those in which Congress does not participate at all, either by authorizing the executive to enter into an agreement or by giving advice and consent on a treaty under which additional agreements are necessary.

Executive agreements are not treaties, but they may bind the parties as a matter of international law. The effect of executive agreements on domestic United States law, and especially the effect of sole executive agreements, is less clear. In one case, the United States Supreme Court declared that "international compacts and agreements . . . have a similar dignity" to formally ratified treaties. *United States v. Pink*. And in application, courts seem to accord congressional-executive agreements and agreements pursuant to treaty as having comparable domestic effect to federal statutes. Thus, later congressional-executive agreements and executive agreements pursuant to treaty could trump prior inconsistent statutes. This makes some sense, as the participation of Congress in making such agreements is consistent with the last-in-time rule and the necessary right of Congress and the President to alter prior law.

This rationale does not have the same weight with sole executive agreements, however. If sole executive agreements trump prior law in which Congress participated (whether the whole Congress participated in enacting a federal statute or only the Senate participated by giving advice and consent for a treaty), that gives the President the authority to unilaterally amend United States law. The Supreme Court has never clearly opined on whether sole executive agreements trump prior inconsistent federal law, though it has accepted sole executive agreements as having domestic legal significance. Recall that in *Dames & Moore v. Regan*, the Court upheld the President's ability to terminate claims in order to secure hostages through an executive agreement with Iran in which Congress played no role. And in a more recent case, the Supreme Court held that a sole executive agreement preempted state law, observing that "valid executive agreements are fit to preempt state law, just as treaties are." *American Ins. Ass'n v. Garamendi*. However, the Supreme Court has yet to clearly establish what is required for validity, or which, if any, sole executive agreements can trump inconsistent federal statutes.

9.3.3. Domestic Effect of Customary International Law

Though the *Paquete Habana* holding that "international law is part of our law" has not been overruled, there is significant modern judicial skepticism regarding the extent to which customary international law constitutes binding law domestically. While some scholars have asserted customary international law is part of federal law to the extent that treaties are, others have argued that considering customary international law part of federal domestic law contravenes democratic principles, as it allows the practice of other nations, rather than the American people, to determine law. The Supreme Court has not resolved the matter. For example, in *Sosa v. Alvarez-Machain*, the Supreme Court affirmed the idea that "the domestic law of the United States recognizes the law of nations," and rejected Justice Scalia's attempt to limit customary international law claims altogether, but simultaneously limited the extent to which customary international law could be imported into United States law through the Alien Tort Statute. And as noted above, in *Medellin*, the Supreme Court clearly established that non-self-executing treaties do not have domestic legal effect, suggesting customary international law would similarly be without legal effect until implemented by domestic legislation.

Much of the debate regarding the effect of customary international law centers around the extent to which federal "**common law**" exists after the Supreme Court's 1938 ruling in *Erie R.R. Co. v. Tompkins* that there is no "general federal common law." This debate is presented in *Al-Bihani v. Obama*, where various judges of the D.C. Circuit Court of Appeals debated whether customary international law is incorporated as part of United States domestic law. Ultimately, that court's majority determined the international law of war was *not* incorporated into domestic law for the purpose of creating a cause of action for Al-Bihani to challenge his detention as violating the international law of war. Despite the significant "incorporationist vs. non-incorporationist" debate argued by the D.C. Circuit judges, the Supreme Court declined to take up the case. Notably, the most vigorous non-incorporationist view was presented by then-judge, now-Justice, Brett Kavanaugh.

Concern about the incorporation of customary international law into United States domestic law has not been solely limited to the judiciary. In 2003, a bill was introduced into the House of Representatives stating that "[t]he Supreme Court should base its decisions on the Constitution and the Laws of the United States, and not on the law of any foreign country or any international law." While this bill was not enacted, and there are significant questions regarding its constitutionality if it had been, it demonstrates the serious objections some have regarding the relationship between international law and domestic law. The bill also raises one more important point: the discussion of the effect of the incorporation of customary international law here has been about customary international law as a binding rule of decision—in other words, as *law*. But customary international law may have another use for the judiciary: as a source of interpretation. Courts regularly refer to customary international law to help *interpret* the meaning of domestic law, and even that practice is controversial.

9.4. UNITED STATES LAW INTERNATIONALLY

9.4.1. Extraterritorial Constitution?

One might assume that whether the United States Constitution applies to United States government actions outside the United States is a simple question with a simple, binary answer. Surely, you might hope, there is a clear answer to this question. Alas, there is not!

The Constitution itself does not explicitly say whether it applies outside the borders of the United States. The Supreme Court has addressed the extraterritorial application of some parts of the Constitution, but has done so in a surprisingly piecemeal and unpredictable way. In *Reid v. Covert*, the Court not only addressed the question of whether international agreements can override the Constitution, but also addressed the extent to which the Constitution "applies" outside the borders of the United States. Surprisingly, a majority of the Supreme Court could not agree whether the Constitution applied to United States prosecutions of

United States citizens when those prosecutions occurred outside the United States.

Two ways of thinking about the extraterritorial application of the Constitution emerge from the plurality and concurring opinions in *Reid*, in which the Court held the constitutional guarantees to a trial by jury found in Article III, and the Fifth and Sixth Amendments did apply in that case: a formalist, bright-line approach, and a functional, pragmatic approach.

Consistent with his relatively "black and white" constitutional methodology, Justice Black articulated the formalist approach:

> While it has been suggested that only those constitutional rights which are 'fundamental' protect Americans abroad, we can find no warrant, in logic or otherwise, for picking and choosing among the remarkable collection of "Thou shalt nots" which were explicitly fastened on all departments and agencies of the Federal Government by the Constitution and its Amendments.

Thus, for the formalists, the Constitution should apply to United States government actions everywhere, at least when United States citizens are the subjects of the action.

In his concurrence, Justice Harlan articulated the more pragmatic, functionalist approach, asserting that:

> The proposition is, of course, not that the Constitution "does not apply" overseas, but that there are provisions in the Constitution which do not necessarily apply in all circumstances in every foreign place. In other words, it seems to me that the basic teaching of [precedent] is that there is no rigid and abstract rule that Congress, as a condition precedent to exercising power over Americans overseas, must exercise it subject to all the guarantees of the Constitution, no matter what the conditions and considerations are that would make adherence to a specific guarantee altogether impracticable and anomalous.

Thus, for functionalists, the answer to the question of whether the United States Constitution applies overseas is "it depends."

This formalist vs. functionalist debate has appeared in subsequent Supreme Court opinions. In 1990, in *United States v. Verdugo-Urquidez*, the majority applied a formalist approach, while in a concurrence, Justice Kennedy reasserted Justice Harlan's view when he wrote "there is no rigid and abstract rule that Congress, as a condition precedent to exercising power over Americans overseas, must exercise it subject to all the guarantees of the Constitution." But the functionalist approach seems to have won out, at least for now. In 2008, in *Boumediene v. United States*, a case regarding the applicability of the right to **habeas corpus** to challenge detention outside the United States, which we will discuss in greater detail in Chapter 13, a majority of the Supreme Court held that the common thread uniting the Court's precedent was "the idea that questions of extraterritoriality turn on objective factors and practical concerns, not formalism." Thus, with regard to whether the right to habeas corpus applies outside the United States, the Court rejected a bright line rule, but instead articulated a three part test under which courts must examine: 1) the citizenship and status of the detainee and the adequacy of the process through which that status determination was made; 2) the nature of the sites where the apprehension and detention took place; and 3) the practical obstacles inherent in resolving the prisoner's entitlement to habeas corpus.

While geography—whether a government action occurs within or without the territorial borders of the United States—appears to not by itself be dispositive in determining the application of a particular constitutional provision, one key factor in both the formalist and functionalist approaches seems to be the nature and extent of one's connection to the United States. As noted above, the citizenship and status of a detainee was the first factor identified in *Boumediene*. In other cases related to the extraterritorial reach of the Constitution, citizenship or connection to the United States has been significant. For instance, in *Verdugo-Urquidez*, the question of Fourth Amendment applicability turned on whether the target of the search or seizure had "sufficient contacts" with the United States, a theme we will see repeated in discussion of intelligence activities. Though there is a significant lack of clarity, to this point it seems a fair summary of precedent to say that outside the United States, constitutional protections likely will be available to United States citizens or persons with substantial connection to the United States and that for all others, pragmatic and political concerns will dictate whether constitutional protections apply.

9.4.2. Extraterritoriality of United States Statutes

Whether a United States *statute* applies extraterritorially is somewhat clearer than whether a particular constitutional provision applies. Under international law, the primary basis of jurisdiction is the "subjective territorial principle," which asserts that states have jurisdiction over conduct that, wholly or in substantial part, takes place within their territory. In addition, international law permits states to enact legislation related to conduct that takes place outside its geographic territory in circumstances described by five principles: 1) the objective territorial principle; 2) the protective principle; 3) the nationality principle; 4) the passive personality principle; and 5) the universality principle. Under the objective territorial principle, a state has jurisdiction to prescribe law regarding "conduct outside its territory that has or is intended to have substantial effect within its territory." Under the protective principle, a state can prescribe law with respect to "conduct outside its territory by persons not its nationals that is directed against the security of the state or against a limited class of other state interests." Under the nationality principle, a state may prescribe law regarding "the activities, interest, status, or relations of its nationals outside as well as within its territory." Under the passive personality principle, a "state may apply law—particularly criminal law—to an act committed outside its territory by a person not its national where the victim of the act was its national." Finally, under the universality principle, a "state has jurisdiction to define and prescribe punishment for certain offenses recognized by the community of nations as of universal concern, such as piracy, slave trade, attacks on or hijacking of aircraft, genocide, war crimes, and perhaps certain acts of terrorism." Restatement (Third) of International Law.

Domestic judicial opinions have generally followed these principles in determining whether Congress has authority to enact statutes with extraterritorial application. However, having authority to create such statutes does not mean that Congress always intends to do so. In determining whether Congress has intended a statute to have extraterritorial application, the Supreme Court has established a *presumption* that statutes do not apply outside the United States. In two relatively recent cases—*Morrison v. National Australia Bank* and *Kiobel v. Royal Dutch Petroleum*—the Court asserted that "[w]hen a statute gives no clear indication of an extraterritorial application, it has none." The "clear indication" can be explicit language or context, but the presumption means that courts will not go out of their way to find that a statute applies extraterritorially. The Supreme Court said it established this presumption to "ensure that the Judiciary does not erroneously adopt an interpretation of United States law that carries foreign policy consequences not clearly intended by the political branches." *Kiobel v. Royal Dutch Petroleum.* In other words, because of the significant effect court decisions applying statutes extraterritorially could have on international relations, courts will only do so when it is clear Congress and the Executive want laws to apply extraterritorially. So, if Congress wants a law to apply extraterritorially, it must be clear about its intent.

REVIEW QUESTIONS

1. Summarize the types of international law, including how they are formed.

2. Courts give significant deference to whose interpretation of the meaning of a treaty?

3. What is the difference between a self-executing and non-self-executing treaty?

4. Describe the difference between the formalist and functionalist approaches to determining whether the United States Constitution applies extraterritorially.

CRITICAL THINKING QUESTIONS

1. Are there any principles other than the illegality of piracy, slavery, and genocide, that are so important and so universal they should be considered "*jus cogens*?"

2. If the President unilaterally terminates treaties and Congress acquiesces by not objecting, does that create a customary presidential authority to terminate unilaterally?

3. What advantages and disadvantages do you see for the formalist and functionalist approaches to the question of whether the United States Constitution applies overseas?

4. What are the advantages and disadvantages of extending the protection of the Constitution only to United States citizens?

5. What explains: a) the significant increase in the overall number of international agreements in which the United States has entered; and b) the dramatic increase in the number executive agreements relative to the number of treaties? Is the use of widespread use of executive agreements appropriate?

6. When, if ever, is it appropriate for customary international law to be incorporated into United States domestic law? To be used as an interpretive tool?

7. If you were a Supreme Court Justice, what standard would you create and apply when determining whether sole executive agreements can override inconsistent statutes? Should they ever be permitted to do so?

CHAPTER 10

International Law and the Use of Military Force

M1A1 Abrams tanks pass through "Hands of Victory" in Baghdad, following the 2003 invasion of Iraq by the United States and partner nations. Photo by John L. Houghton, Jr., United States Air Force

Learning Objectives

1. Understand the primary purpose of the UN Charter and how the UN Charter attempts to limit uses of military force.

2. Understand how customary international law addresses certain use of force issues, including explanation of the terms "use of force" and "armed attack," when self-defense is authorized, and the principle of non-intervention.

3. Understand how international law affects use of military forces in humanitarian and peace operations.

4. Apply your understanding of international law to analyze the legality of military uses of force in specific instances where nations have used force.

10.1. INTRODUCTION

War has plagued humankind throughout recorded history and war's catastrophic consequences have led many nations and thinkers to seek ways to avoid war altogether. For millennia, philosophers, including those in the western and eastern traditions, have grappled with limiting the justifications for war. Similarly, theologians from major faith traditions, including Hinduism, Judaism, Christianity, and Islam articulated various theories of "just war" that were premised on religious principles for limiting the justifications for war. Jurists and political thinkers like Hugo Grotius and Alberico Gentili translated the concept of just war into international law rules for war. The body of international law addressing the right of states to use military force is known as ***jus ad bellum***.

As nation states became more bellicose in the eighteenth and nineteenth centuries, the excesses and horrors of their conflicts led them—often the same nation states who had engaged in war themselves—to begin attempts to limit war through international law. The 1899 and 1907 Hague Conventions required a **declaration of war** before conflict could lawfully begin. After World War I and its estimated 40 million casualties, the League of Nations was formed. The League of Nations, never joined by the United States despite its primary champion being the United States President Woodrow Wilson, did not formally outlaw war, but instead required states to attempt to settle disputes peacefully. Not long after the League was established, the Paris Peace Pact of 1928—also known as the Kellogg-Briand Pact—was negotiated between the United States and other nations including France, Germany, Great Britain, Italy, and Japan, and was ultimately joined by over 60 nations. The Peace Pact outlawed war, but provided no enforcement mechanism. Many scholars and politicians have derided the Peace Pact as hopeless idealism, especially in light of the wars of aggression that followed soon thereafter, initiated by several original signatories to the Peace Pact. Japan invaded Manchuria in 1931 and China in 1937, and attacked the United States in 1941; Italy invaded Ethiopia in 1935; and Germany invaded Poland in 1939 and Denmark, Norway, Belgium, the Netherlands, Luxembourg, and France in 1940, the same year it attacked Great Britain. Despite its complete failure to prevent war, some have argued the Peace Pact represented an important fundamental shift in thinking about the best way to limit war: by renouncing it altogether, rather than focusing on justifications for it. Notably, the Peace Pact included no exceptions to the requirement that all disputes between nations be sought through "pacific means."

10.2. THE UN CHARTER

After the numerous invasions mentioned in the previous paragraph and the resulting Second World War, with its estimated 60 million deaths, nations attempted a new approach to avoiding war. The Charter of the United Nations (UN Charter or Charter) carried forward the Peace Pact's approach of outlawing war. Though the UN has many roles and is influential in world affairs outside the prevention of military conflict, peace is its primary purpose. The Preamble begins by establishing the goal "to save succeeding generations from the scourge of war, which twice in our lifetime has brought untold sorrow to mankind" and the first provision in the operative portion of the **treaty** states the UN's purpose is to "maintain international peace and security."

The UN Charter outlawed **international armed conflict**. Article 2, Paragraph 4, demands that "[a]ll Members shall refrain in their international relations from the threat or use of force against the territorial integrity or political independence of any state, or in any other manner inconsistent with the Purposes of the United Nations." Unlike the Paris Peace Pact, the UN Charter included an enforcement mechanism in the form of establishing the **United Nations Security Council (UNSC)** responsible for "the maintenance of international peace and security." Also unlike the Paris Peace Pact, the Charter recognized two exceptions to the prohibition against the use of force: 1) use of force approved by the UNSC to respond to a threat to the peace, breach of the peace, or an act of aggression; and 2) individual or **collective self-defense**.

10.2.1. The Text of the UN Charter

Here are some excerpts of the text of the UN Charter most relevant to national security issues.

Preamble

WE THE PEOPLES OF THE UNITED NATIONS DETERMINED

to save succeeding generations from the scourge of war, which twice in our lifetime has brought untold sorrow to mankind, and

to reaffirm faith in fundamental human rights, in the dignity and worth of the human person, in the equal rights of men and women and of nations large and small, and to establish conditions under which justice and respect for the obligations arising from treaties and other sources of international law can be maintained, and

to promote social progress and better standards of life in larger freedom,

AND FOR THESE ENDS

to practice tolerance and live together in peace with one another as good neighbours, and

to unite our strength to maintain international peace and security, and

to ensure, by the acceptance of principles and the institution of methods, that armed force shall not be used, save in the common interest, and

to employ international machinery for the promotion of the economic and social advancement of all peoples,

HAVE RESOLVED TO COMBINE OUR EFFORTS TO ACCOMPLISH THESE AIMS

. . .

Article 1

The Purposes of the United Nations are:

To maintain international peace and security, and to that end: to take effective collective measures for the prevention and removal of threats to the peace, and for the suppression of acts of aggression or other breaches of the peace, and to bring about by peaceful means, and in conformity with the principles of justice and international law, adjustment or settlement of international disputes or situations which might lead to a breach of the peace;

To develop friendly relations among nations based on respect for the principle of equal rights and self-determination of peoples, and to take other appropriate measures to strengthen universal peace;

To achieve international co-operation in solving international problems of an economic, social, cultural, or humanitarian character, and in promoting and encouraging respect for human rights and for fundamental freedoms for all without distinction as to race, sex, language, or religion; and

To be a centre for harmonizing the actions of nations in the attainment of these common ends.

Article 2

The Organization and its Members, in pursuit of the Purposes stated in Article 1, shall act in accordance with the following Principles.

The Organization is based on the principle of the sovereign equality of all its Members.

All Members, in order to ensure to all of them the rights and benefits resulting from membership, shall fulfill in good faith the obligations assumed by them in accordance with the present Charter.

All Members shall settle their international disputes by peaceful means in such a manner that international peace and security, and justice, are not endangered.

All Members shall refrain in their international relations from the threat or use of force against the territorial integrity or political independence of any state, or in any other manner inconsistent with the Purposes of the United Nations.

All Members shall give the United Nations every assistance in any action it takes in accordance with the present Charter, and shall refrain from giving assistance to any state against which the United Nations is taking preventive or enforcement action.

The Organization shall ensure that states which are not Members of the United Nations act in accordance with these Principles so far as may be necessary for the maintenance of international peace and security.

Nothing contained in the present Charter shall authorize the United Nations to intervene in matters which are essentially within the domestic jurisdiction of any state or shall require the Members to submit such matters to settlement under the present Charter; but this principle shall not prejudice the application of enforcement measures under Chapter VII.

. . .

Article 24

In order to ensure prompt and effective action by the United Nations, its Members confer on the Security Council primary responsibility for the maintenance of international peace and security, and agree that in carrying out its duties under this responsibility the Security Council acts on their behalf.

. . .

Article 25

The Members of the United Nations agree to accept and carry out the decisions of the Security Council in accordance with the present Charter.

. . .

Article 39

The Security Council shall determine the existence of any threat to the peace, breach of the peace, or act of aggression and shall make recommendations, or decide what measures shall be taken in accordance with Articles 41 and 42, to maintain or restore international peace and security.

Article 40

In order to prevent an aggravation of the situation, the Security Council may, before making the recommendations or deciding upon the measures provided for in Article 39, call upon the parties concerned to comply with such provisional measures as it deems necessary or desirable. Such provisional measures shall be without prejudice to the rights, claims, or position of the parties concerned. The Security Council shall duly take account of failure to comply with such provisional measures.

Article 41

The Security Council may decide what measures not involving the use of armed force are to be employed to give effect to its decisions, and it may call upon the Members of the United Nations to apply such measures. These may include complete or partial interruption of economic relations and of rail, sea, air, postal, telegraphic, radio, and other means of communication, and the severance of diplomatic relations.

Article 42

Should the Security Council consider that measures provided for in Article 41 would be inadequate or have proved to be inadequate, it may take such action by air, sea, or land forces as may be necessary to maintain or restore international peace and security. Such action may include demonstrations, blockade, and other operations by air, sea, or land forces of Members of the United Nations.

Article 43

1. All Members of the United Nations, in order to contribute to the maintenance of international peace and security, undertake to make available to the Security Council, on its call and in accordance with a special agreement or agreements, armed forces, assistance, and facilities, including rights of passage, necessary for the purpose of maintaining international peace and security.

2. Such agreement or agreements shall govern the numbers and types of forces, their degree of readiness and general location, and the nature of the facilities and assistance to be provided.

3. The agreement or agreements shall be negotiated as soon as possible on the initiative of the Security Council. They shall be concluded between the Security Council and Members or between the Security Council and groups of Members and shall be subject to ratification by the signatory states in accordance with their respective constitutional processes.

. . .

Article 45

In order to enable the United Nations to take urgent military measures, Members shall hold immediately available national air-force contingents for combined international enforcement action. The strength and degree of readiness of these contingents and plans for their combined action shall be determined within the limits laid down in the special agreement or agreements referred to in Article 43, by the Security Council with the assistance of the Military Staff Committee.

. . .

Article 47

1. There shall be established a Military Staff Committee to advise and assist the Security Council on all questions relating to the Security Council's military requirements for the maintenance of international peace and security, the employment and command of forces placed at its disposal, the regulation of armaments, and possible disarmament.

2. The Military Staff Committee shall consist of the Chiefs of Staff of the permanent members of the Security Council or their representatives. Any Member of the United Nations not permanently represented on the Committee shall be invited by the Committee to be associated with it when the efficient discharge of the Committee's responsibilities requires the participation of that Member in its work.

3. The Military Staff Committee shall be responsible under the Security Council for the strategic direction of any armed forces placed at the disposal of the Security Council. Questions relating to the command of such forces shall be worked out subsequently.

4. The Military Staff Committee, with the authorization of the Security Council and after consultation with appropriate regional agencies, may establish regional sub-committees.

Article 48

1. The action required to carry out the decisions of the Security Council for the maintenance of international peace and security shall be taken by all the Members of the United Nations or by some of them, as the Security Council may determine.

2. Such decisions shall be carried out by the Members of the United Nations directly and through their action in the appropriate international agencies of which they are members.

Article 49

The Members of the United Nations shall join in affording mutual assistance in carrying out the measures decided upon by the Security Council.

. . .

Article 51

Nothing in the present Charter shall impair the inherent right of individual or collective self-defence if an armed attack occurs against a Member of the United Nations, until the Security Council has taken measures necessary to maintain international peace and security. Measures taken by Members in the exercise of this right of self-defence shall be immediately reported to the Security Council and shall not in any way affect the authority and responsibility of the Security Council under the present Charter to take at any time such action as it deems necessary in order to maintain or restore international peace and security.

. . .

Article 52

1. Nothing in the present Charter precludes the existence of regional arrangements or agencies for dealing with such matters relating to the maintenance of international peace and security as are appropriate for regional action provided that such arrangements or agencies and their activities are consistent with the Purposes and Principles of the United Nations.

2. The Members of the United Nations entering into such arrangements or constituting such agencies shall make every effort to achieve pacific settlement of local disputes through such regional arrangements or by such regional agencies before referring them to the Security Council.

. . .

Article 53

1. The Security Council shall, where appropriate, utilize such regional arrangements or agencies for enforcement action under its authority. But no enforcement action shall be taken under regional arrangements or by regional agencies without the authorization of the Security Council, with the exception of measures against any enemy state, as defined in paragraph 2 of this Article, provided for pursuant to Article 107 or in regional arrangements directed against renewal of aggressive policy on the part of any such state, until such time as the Organization may, on request of the Governments concerned, be charged with the responsibility for preventing further aggression by such a state.
2. The term enemy state as used in paragraph 1 of this Article applies to any state which during the Second World War has been an enemy of any signatory of the present Charter.

. . .

Article 107

Nothing in the present Charter shall invalidate or preclude action, in relation to any state which during the Second World War has been an enemy of any signatory to the present Charter, taken or authorized as a result of that war by the Governments having responsibility for such action.

. . .

10.2.2. UNSC-Authorized Use of Force

Article 24 gives to the United Nations Security Council "primary responsibility for the maintenance of international peace and security." The makeup of the UNSC has had a significant impact on peace, conflict, and the legality of uses of force. The UNSC is comprised of 15 member nations, five of which are permanent (China, France, Russia, the United Kingdom, and the United States). The other ten members are elected for two-year terms by the UN General Assembly. Though UNSC decisions are made by majority vote, the permanent members each hold a veto power that is absolute.

A use of force authorized by the UNSC does not violate Article 2.4's prohibition. Thus, the UNSC, and especially its five permanent members, are able to determine the legality or illegality of many uses of force. Under Article 39, the UNSC has the authority to determine the existence of a threat to the peace, breach of the peace, or act of aggression. Then, under Article 41, the UNSC can authorize measures "not involving the use of armed force" that should be employed to address the situation. Or, under Article 42, the UNSC can authorize the use of military force, which includes "such action by air, sea, or land forces as may be necessary to maintain or restore international peace and security." On a few occasions, the UNSC has determined a breach of peace or threat to the breach of peace existed. Through 1990, the UNSC had only authorized military force due to aggression by one State against another in two instances: the Korean War in 1950 and Iraq's invasion of Kuwait in 1990. The UNSC has taken an increasingly active role in authorizing use of military force, authorizing "all necessary means" or "all necessary measures" by multinational forces to address breaches of peace in Somalia, Haiti, Rwanda, Eastern Zaire, Albania, Bosnia and Herzegovina, East Timor, Bunia in the Democratic Republic of Congo, and Liberia. The Security Council has also authorized naval blockades to enforce its sanctions imposed under Article 41. Additionally, the UNSC has on occasion authorized something less than "all necessary means" by authorizing **peacekeeping** forces.

Armed forces acting pursuant to UNSC authorization might be organized in two ways. First, member states may retain control of their armed forces and use them pursuant to an Article 42 authorization to use military force. When members use their own armed forces to enforce UNSC decisions, they retain command and control of the forces and member participation is purely voluntary. Alternatively, under Article 43, nations could contribute military forces to the UNSC, and the UNSC itself would have command and control. In some conceptions of this arrangement, this would have provided the UNSC with a "standing army" to use at it deemed necessary. In practice, no Article 43 agreement between a member and the UNSC has ever been reached, meaning the UNSC has never had armed forces to control directly. So, all UNSC authorizations for the use of force have required member states to participate directly; the UNSC has never directly engaged in the use of military force.

One instance of member states gaining approval for the use of military force occurred after Saddam Hussein's Iraqi forces invaded Kuwait in 1990. After passing a series of resolutions that unsuccessfully attempted to force Iraq to withdraw its forces from Kuwait, the UNSC adopted Resolution 678:

> The Security Council . . . [a]uthorizes Member States co-operating with the Government of Kuwait, unless Iraq on or before 15 January 1991 fully implements [previous UNSC resolutions to leave Kuwait] to use all necessary means to uphold and implement [UNSC Resolution 660, which had demanded Iraq withdraw from Kuwait, and all subsequent

relevant resolutions] and to restore international peace and security in the area.

This was the explicit authorization necessary for over 30 nations to participate in the coalition military action to push Iraqi forces out of Kuwait.

10.2.3. UN Charter-Permitted Self-Defense

The second exception in the UN Charter to Article 2.4's prohibition on the use of force is Article 51, which permits nations to defend themselves or another state "if an **armed attack** occurs against a Member of the United Nations, until the Security Council has taken measures necessary to maintain international peace and security." This is an attempted codification of the **customary international law** right to use self-defense. Note however, that this right to self-defense only arises "if an armed attack occurs." This has led to significant debate among nations and scholars regarding the Charter's intent. Some suggest that under the Charter, the purpose of which is to maintain international peace and security, the right to self-defense arises only once the armed attack has actually begun. Others see this interpretation as too limiting, especially in light to Article 51's reference to the "inherent right" of self-defense, which some argue refers to a custom that includes a right to self-defense that is broader than simply the right to respond to armed attacks after they are initiated. This debate will be discussed more below in the context of customary international law.

"Armed attack" is not defined by the Charter, but whatever the term means, it clearly establishes a higher threshold for when a nation may engage in self-defense than the threshold required for the UNSC to authorize the use of force. Recall that under Article 39, the UNSC may authorize the use of force when it determines there exists "any threat to the peace, breach of the peace, or act of aggression," a standard that permits the UNSC to authorize the use of military force in a wide range of situations that do not involve an actual armed attack.

Note that Article 51 confirms the right to self-defense "until the Security Council has taken measures necessary to maintain international peace and security." Some argue this was meant to limit self-defense only until the Security Council has acted, meaning that once the UNSC has acted, a nation's right to self-defense terminates, and that if the UNSC does not act, perhaps because one or more permanent members veto such action, the right of self-defense is indefinite. Others maintain that Article 51 simply restates the inherent right of individual and collective self-defense and that this right survives until the nation—and potentially also the Security Council—has *successfully* repelled the armed attack.

Article 51 includes not only the right of an individual nation to defend itself, but the right to *collective* self-defense, meaning the right of nations to defend other nations against an armed attack. The circumstances under which other nations that have not been attacked may join in the military use of force to defend the attacked nation against the offensive attacker(s) are not detailed in the Charter, but have been addressed in customary international law, discussed below.

10.2.4. United States Participation in the UN

As we discussed in the prior chapter, treaties are the "supreme law of the land." The UN Charter is a treaty, raising questions regarding what the President's authority or obligation may be to act in accordance with the UN. Article 2.5 of the UN Charter requires all members to "give the United Nations every assistance in any action it takes in accordance with the present Charter," and Article 25 requires that "Members of the United Nations agree to accept and carry out the decisions of the Security Council." So, is the President obliged or empowered to "execute" the terms of the Charter under his responsibility and authority to "take care that the laws be faithfully executed"? As we noted in the prior chapter, courts in the United States have determined that a treaty must be self-executing to have domestic legal effect without subsequent implementing legislation. Courts in the United States have generally held that the UN Charter is non-self-executing, so without further implementation, it does not by itself grant authority or impose obligation on the President.

Concerned that the new Charter might arguably provide the President authority to make war without congressional approval, in the same year the United States ratified the UN Charter, Congress enacted the "United Nations Participation Act," which President Truman signed into law. The UNPA conceptually allows the President to provide military forces to UNSC under an Article 43 agreement, but such "special agreements" require congressional approval. The UNPA also prohibits President from providing military assistance to the Security Council outside of Article 43 agreements or separate authorization. Thus, under the UNPA, the President may not use UNSC authorization as a basis for using military force absent congressional approval at some point in the process.

10.3. CUSTOMARY INTERNATIONAL LAW

As we discussed in the previous chapter, international law is formed in two ways: through international agreements, such as treaties and **executive agreements**, and through custom. The relationship between customary international law and the UN Charter is contentious and confusing. Though the UN Charter codified many customary international law principles, much international law regarding the use of force predates the UN Charter and remains customary international law apart from the UN Charter. Additionally, after the UN Charter came into existence, international legal understanding of the law regarding the use of force has continued to evolve. Thus, even if the two bodies of law (customary international law and the Charter) were identical at the precise moment the Charter came into effect, customary international law continues to change in response to judicial opinions and the behavior of states. Under the concept of *lex posterior* (**last in time rule**), these new understandings can help interpret the meaning of the UN Charter and may be customary international law in their own right.

A significant area of concern regarding the relationship between the UN Charter and customary international law is the extent to which customary international law authorizes uses of force beyond what the UN Charter explicitly allows. By its own terms, the UN Charter purports to be the only lawful basis for the use of force. And yet, the Charter, established in 1945, does not fully reflect the modern understanding of the use of force by of some states and does not address issues regularly faced by states acting in an increasingly connected global environment. There are numerous areas where customary international law addresses uses of force by nations. Here we will focus on a few.

10.3.1. Defining Terms

One significant way in which customary international law provides additional substance to the UN Charter is in clarifying the meaning of terms the UN Charter uses but does not define or explain. A failure to define terms—even critical terms—is not unusual in treaties. Parties to large, multilateral treaties, often agree upon very general language so that differences regarding specific issues do not prevent agreement from being reached at all. Whatever the reason, the Charter does not define two critical terms: "use of force" and "armed attack."

10.3.1.1. Use of Force

Given that one of the primary purposes of the United Nations Charter is to prohibit the use of force and limit the human suffering that comes from uses of force, it may strike some as odd that "use of force" is not defined in the treaty. There was some discussion during the UN Charter drafting conference regarding what should or should not be considered a use of force, including whether "force" included all forms of pressure. For example, some member states asked whether economic pressure aimed at the territorial integrity or political independence of another state constitutes a "use of force." This question was eventually answered in the negative during the UN General Assembly's Declaration on Friendly Relations in 1970, over 20 years after the UN Charter was completed. Ultimately, the UN Charter failed to define the term "use of force."

Customary international law has similarly failed to produce a clear threshold for what does and does not constitute a "use of force." Some actions are clearly uses of force, such as an invasion by an infantry division. The world community has generally accepted that economic and political pressure are not uses of force. But many actions lying between those ends of the spectrum are not so clear. In determining whether a particular act constitutes a "use of force," some considerations include the military character of the action, the directness of the link between the act and its effects, including the severity, immediacy, and measurability of those effects, and the act's "invasiveness."

In a case addressing Nicaragua's claims that the United States violated international law with illegal uses of force, the **International Court of Justice (ICJ)** opined on whether several alleged actions of the United States in support of the Contras against the Sandinista government of Nicaragua constituted "uses of force." The United States was not alleged to have engaged in direct military action against Nicaragua, but rather in covert acts, mostly committed by the United States Central Intelligence Agency. Actions the ICJ determined constituted uses of force included laying mines in harbors and ports, certain low-level sabotage attacks on Nicaraguan ports, oil installations, and a naval base carried out by small teams of civilians. The ICJ also concluded that arming and training Contra military forces was a "use of force" by the United States. On the other hand, providing funds to the Contras was determined not to be a use of force.

10.3.1.2. Armed Attack

Another important term that is surprisingly undefined in the UN Charter is the phrase "armed attack." The significance of this term is that under Article 51, a nation has the right to self-defense "if an armed attack occurs." This right to self-defense will be discussed more below, but understanding what an armed attack includes is clearly important. First, it is critical to understand that "armed attack" is not the same as "use of force." As understood in international law, a use of force might not rise to the level of "armed attack," which requires something more than merely a use of force.

In the *Nicaragua* case, the ICJ determined that customary international law had settled what constitutes an "armed attack": "There appears now to be general agreement on the nature of the acts which can be treated as constituting armed attacks." The ICJ ruled that "armed attacks" certainly include military action by regular armed forces across an international border, but can also include action by armed groups, mercenaries, and irregular forces sent by a state if the "scale and effects of the operation would have been classified as an armed attack rather than a mere frontier incident had it been carried out by regular armed forces." Note, however, that this circular definition is rather unhelpful in determining what level of force is required to constitute an armed attack. Importantly, the ICJ held that merely providing weapons or logistical support to rebels in another state would not constitute an "armed attack," though it would constitute a use of force, indicating that not all uses of force rise to the level of armed attacks.

10.3.2. Self-Defense

The right to self-defense codified in Article 51 of the UN Charter is limited to situations when "an armed attack occurs." But nations have asserted lawful self-defense might arise in other situations. Nations and jurists have articulated a variety of theories of self-defense they believe are supported by international law. Whether those situations constitute additional customary international law-based exceptions to the prohibition on the use of military force is unclear. One step removed from the well-accepted "actual attack" standard is the theory of **anticipatory self-defense**, and one step further removed is the theory of **preemptive self-defense**.

10.3.2.1. Anticipatory Self-Defense

If an actual armed attack must begin before self-defense is authorized, nations may not engage in uses of force to prevent armed attacks from being launched. Some nations have argued this constrains states too much. For instance, the United States has asserted that Article 51's use of the word "inherent" when describing the right to self-defense incorporates broader situations than only when a nation has been subject to an actual armed attack. The most widely accepted circumstance where self-defense might be justified without the triggering event of an armed attack is "anticipatory self-defense." Under the theory of anticipatory self-defense states have the right to "anticipate" that an attack is imminent or in the process of being mounted and use force in self-defense to prevent or limit the effects of the anticipated attack. One of the earliest articulations of this right came in 1842. British troops had crossed into the United States from Canada to seize and destroy a ship—the *Caroline*—that the British suspected of being used to launch low-level attacks into Canada. The British claimed self-defense. But United

States Secretary of State Daniel Webster argued that anticipatory self-defense should be limited to situations that "show a **necessity** of self-defence, instant, overwhelming, leaving no choice of means, and no moment for deliberations." Webster argued that Britain's actions had not been self-defense, but rather an illegal offensive attack. Webster's articulation of the customary international law of anticipatory self-defense is still used today.

The notion of "no moment for deliberations" suggests an imminence of offensive attack necessary to justify anticipatory self-defense. Most nations and scholars agree that the defending state need not wait until an attack is completed to defend itself. For example, when a state determines that enemy planes are on the way to drop bombs, under the theory of anticipatory self-defense, the attacked nation need not wait until the bombs actually begin falling to defend itself. Rather, the attacked nation can use force to defend itself once the attack is in process, such as when credible evidence exists that the bomber aircraft are being fueled for an attack. Of course, determining precisely when an attack is "imminent" or "underway" is difficult, and nations suspecting they are about to be attacked may be unlikely to wait for some clear legal triggering event.

Because one nation's assertion that it used anticipatory self-defense against an imminent attack can be difficult to verify, some scholars object to the theory, and argue that Article 51 intentionally excludes anticipatory self-defense. That is, Article 51's requirement that an armed attack actually occur for the right to self-defense to arise ensures a collective, multi-national, objectively verifiable assessment that the nation claiming self-defense was actually attacked. By contrast, anticipatory self-defense allows a unilateral determination by the nation claiming self-defense, often based on intelligence evidence that the nation does not wish to share. Thus, states may be tempted to use "self-defense" as a pretext for offensive uses of force, which of course runs contrary to the overall approach of the UN to reducing war: states cannot unilaterally use force, but rather must have approval, with collective international approval preferred.

In modern times, the United States has argued that anticipatory self-defense justifies using military force before an anticipated attack when the defensive action is taken during the "last window of opportunity," before an offensive attack becomes operational. The length of that "last window," however, is controversial. In fact, the United States has used this theory to justify **drone** strikes against terrorist groups, arguing that the length of time terrorist attacks can be in the execution phase before they become known justifies earlier "defensive" action. Additionally, the potentially *ongoing* nature of terror attacks by a particular group raises the question of imminence. When a terrorist organization vows, or is believed to plan, to engage in repeated attacks, all strikes against the group may "anticipate" future attacks.

Multiple United States Presidents have justified such anticipatory actions against suspected terrorists. For example, in reporting missile strikes against Al Qaeda sites in Afghanistan and Sudan in 1998, President Clinton asserted "[t]hese strikes were a necessary and proportionate response to the imminent threat of further terrorist attacks against United States personnel and facilities. These strikes were intended to prevent and deter additional attacks by a clearly identified terrorist threat." Similarly, in its 2013 United States Policy Standards and Procedures for the Use of Force in Counterterrorism Operations Outside the United States and Areas of Active Hostilities, the Obama Administration confirmed "the United States will use lethal force . . . against a target that poses a continuing, imminent threat to United States persons," acknowledging that in the United States' view, an ongoing threat is sufficient to justify "anticipatory attacks."

There is general agreement that defensive use of force is justified once an attack has gotten underway. But this modern extension of the anticipatory self-defense doctrine to threats that are ongoing, but perhaps not imminent in the sense of an attack that is "underway," has not yet achieved universal acceptance. Indeed, the United States' current understanding seems to contradict Secretary Webster's early pronouncement of the limits of anticipatory self-defense.

10.3.2.2. Preemptive Self-Defense

Even more controversial than anticipatory self-defense is the assertion by a few states of the right of *preemptive* self-defense. Preemptive self-defense justifies actions in response to a mere perceived *threat* before an attack is imminent or even possible. Israel claimed this justification in 1981 after it attacked a nuclear facility in Iraq. Arguing it was acting in self-defense, Israel claimed the atomic reactor it destroyed would have eventually enabled Iraq to manufacture nuclear weapons, which Iraq might have used against Israel.

Not long after the 9/11 terror attacks, the United States also adopted the theory of preemptive self-defense. In the 2002 National Security Strategy of the United States of America, the United States asserted:

> For centuries, international law recognized that nations need not suffer an attack before they can lawfully take action to defend themselves against forces that present an imminent danger of attack. Legal scholars and international jurists often conditioned the legitimacy of preemption

> on the existence of an imminent threat—most often a visible mobilization of armies, navies, and air forces preparing to attack.
>
> We must adapt the concept of imminent threat to the capabilities and objectives of today's adversaries. Rogue states and terrorists do not seek to attack us using conventional means. They know such attacks would fail. Instead, they rely on acts of terror and, potentially, the use of weapons of mass destruction—weapons that can be easily concealed, delivered covertly, and used without warning.
>
> The targets of these attacks are our military forces and our civilian population, in direct violation of one of the principal norms of the law of warfare. . . .
>
> The United States has long maintained the option of preemptive actions to counter a sufficient threat to our national security. The greater the threat, the greater is the risk of inaction—and the more compelling the case for taking anticipatory action to defend ourselves, even if uncertainty remains as to the time and place of the enemy's attack. To forestall or prevent such hostile acts by our adversaries, the United States will, if necessary, act preemptively.

Known as the key feature of the so-called "Bush Doctrine," the unilateralism and notion of preemption articulated in the National Security Strategy in 2002 was central to the Bush Administration's decision to invade Iraq in 2003, in large part premised on the belief that Iraqi President Saddam Hussein possessed weapons of mass destruction he *might* use against the United States or its allies.

Summarizing the concern many states and scholars perceive regarding accepting anticipatory and preemptive self-defense, two scholars articulated the practical legal problem with these forms of self-defense:

> The claim to preemptive self-defense is a claim to entitlement to use unilaterally, without prior international authorization, high levels of violence to arrest an incipient development that is not yet operational or directly threatening, but that, if permitted to mature, could be seen by the potential preemptor as susceptible to neutralization only at a higher and possibly unacceptable cost to itself. . . . As one moves from an actual armed attack as the requisite threshold of reactive self-defense, to the palpable and imminent threat of attack, which is the threshold of anticipatory self-defense, and from there to the conjectural and contingent threat of the mere possibility of an attack at some future time, which is the threshold of preemptive self-defense, the self-assigned

> interpretive latitude of the unilateralist becomes wider, yet the nature and quantum of evidence that can satisfy the burden of proof resting on the unilateralist becomes less and less defined and is often, by the very nature of the exercise, extrapolative and speculative.

Michael Reisman & Andrea Armstrong, *The Past and Future of the Claim of Preemptive Self-Defense,* American Journal of International Law, 2006.

The controversial nature of preemptive self-defense, along with the relatively few nations who have supported it so far, suggest it is not yet customary international law. Nevertheless, national political leaders' attraction to the concept of preemptive self-defense is perhaps understandable in an era of weapons of mass destruction, when waiting for an armed attack to occur in the reactive sense that Article 51's language suggests would pose an existential threat to the nation and its leaders' political existence. For instance, if a "rogue state" hostile to the United States possesses a nuclear weapon capable of being delivered to the United States and declares its intention to use the weapon, an attack against that capability by the United States would likely be considered "preemptive," and possibly illegal under international law, yet supported by many within the United States.

10.3.2.3. Necessity and Proportionality

In addition to identifying circumstances sufficient to trigger the defensive use of military force, customary international law limits acceptable actions in self-defense by imposing the dual self-defense principles of **necessity** and **proportionality**. Necessity means that the use of force in self-defense must be actually necessary for achieving self-defense. In other words, the use of force in self-defense is necessary because anything less would be ineffective under the circumstances. This implicitly means that the amount of force used in defense must be comparable to the amount of force used in the attack. This somewhat restrictive principle is to prevent minor provocations from serving as justifications for major "defensive" retaliation and resulting protracted conflict. The principle of proportionality relates in a way to necessity, as proportionality requires that the defensive use of force is proportionate to the offensive use of force in the attack; force beyond that which is proportional is excessive and not justified self-defense. A hyperbolic example demonstrating this principle is that an attack by a small unit of infantry soldiers could not be "defended against" with a nuclear strike annihilating a city. Note: the terms "necessity" and "proportionality" in the *jus ad bellum* self-defense context have different meaning than they do in the **law of armed conflict** (***jus in bello***) context, which we are not addressing here.

10.3.2.4. Reprisal

While states maintain an inherent right of self-defense, punitive acts of retaliation, also known as reprisals, are prohibited. The primary difference between self-defense and reprisal rests on the motivation of the state actor. If the state is simply retaliating or punishing the attacker, it is an unlawful reprisal; if the state is protecting itself, it is lawful self-defense. The distinction is, of course, difficult to prove. The distinction between self-defense and reprisal also has a temporal aspect, as the longer the claimed defensive use of force occurs after the triggering offensive use of force, the likelier it seems to be an act of reprisal rather than self-defense. Reprisals clearly are not an authorized use of force under the UN Charter, though actual state practice of engaging in reprisal suggests their prohibition in customary international law is uncertain.

10.3.2.5. Collective Self-Defense Under Customary International Law

Collective self-defense—the ability of one or more nations to use military force to defend another—is an uncontroversial right enshrined in the UN Charter. In the *Nicaragua* case, the ICJ observed that the inherent right of collective self-defense also exists as a norm of customary international law independently of Article 51, meaning UNSC approval is not required for states to engage in collective self-defense. While the existence of the right of collective self-defense is uncontroverted, the circumstances giving rise to justified collective self-defense are subject to some disagreement. For example, in the *Nicaragua* case, the ICJ opined that for collective self-defense to be applicable, there must be an armed attack and the attacked country must declare it is the victim of an armed attack. In that case, the United States had argued that some of its activities against Nicaragua were justified because it was engaged in collective self-defense of El Salvador. But the ICJ determined that the only action Nicaragua took against El Salvador was to provide arms there, an action that fell short an "armed attack." The ICJ's skepticism also stemmed from the fact that El Salvador's public declaration that it was a victim of an armed attack by Nicaragua, and its public request for United States assistance, came months *after* the United States' activities in Nicaragua that the United States claimed were justified by self-defense. Further, neither the United States nor El Salvador reported the Nicaraguan activities to the UNSC under Article 51.

Collective self-defense most often arises in the context of allies defending each other pursuant to mutual defense treaties. For instance, one of the justifications the United States provided for its use of military force in Vietnam was the United States' purported obligation under the **Southeast Asia Treaty Organization (SEATO)**, which had been created to prevent further communist expansion in Southeast Asia. The **North Atlantic Treaty Organization (NATO)** is another treaty created primarily for the purpose of collective self-defense.

One collective self-defense issue that is not as well settled is the notion of the collective self-defense of non-states. The United States has argued several of its uses of military force were justified by collective self-defense of non-state actors. For example, both the Obama and Trump administrations have invoked collective self-defense of the African Union Mission in Somalia (AMISOM) to justify strikes against an Al-Shabaab terror camp in Somalia. The United States has not only used the notion of collective self-defense to justify defense of state-supported forces like AMISOM, but has asserted that "collective self-defense in this context means extension of United States unit self-defense to foreign or irregular partner forces or persons." Senator Tim Kaine, *Letter to the Secretary of Defense*, October 2, 2018. The Trump Administration invoked the collective self-defense of Syrian Democratic Forces (SDF) in June 2017 to justify the downing of a Syrian regime jet, and again in February 2018 to justify strikes against Syrian pro-regime forces, despite the fact that no *state* was threatened by Syrian regime forces.

10.3.2.6. Consent

Somewhat related to the idea of collective self-defense is the notion of **consent** as a basis for using military force in another nation. Though the UN Charter does not address consent explicitly, it prohibits "the threat or use of force *against* the territorial integrity or political independence of any state." Thus, a use of force by one nation in another nation may not violate the Charter or customary international law when that use of force is invited or allowed by the nation in which it occurs. Usually, the state in which the force occurs allows the use of force for self-defense purposes. For example, today some nations permit the United States to use military force against terrorist groups in their country. Because of the "host nation's" consent, this use of force is not against the territorial integrity or political independence of a state, and thus does not violate the UN Charter.

10.3.2.7. Protection and Rescue of Nationals

When a nation's citizens or representatives are imperiled in another nation, what uses of military force are permitted under international law to rescue those citizens? The UN Charter does not answer this question explicitly. Certainly, if the citizens are imperiled as part of an "armed attack" by a foreign state, self-defense of those citizens would be justified under Article 51. This right appears to extend to self-defense against armed attacks on nationals by non-state actors as well. State A may invade the territorial sovereignty of State B to protect State A's nationals if State B, where State A's nationals are located, is unable or unwilling to protect the nationals. When a host state is unable or unwilling to prevent a nonstate actor from engaging in attacks in its own state, states have claimed authority to rescue their nationals as an act of self-defense, even without the host state's consent. In 2016, the United States announced this as official United States policy. President Barack Obama, *Report on the Legal and Policy Frameworks Guiding the United States' Use of Military Force and Related National Security Operations*.

In a case arising after several dozen United States diplomatic staff were taken hostage in Iran in 1979, the ICJ opined that the hostage-taking constituted an armed attack. However, in the same case, the ICJ declined to rule on the legality of a failed rescue attempt in Iran by the United States military, and in fact expressed frustration with the rescue attempt as being "calculated to undermine respect for the judicial process in international relations." Another modern example of rescue of nationals as self-defense was when Israel raided Uganda to rescue Israeli passengers from a hijacked Air France plane.

10.3.3. Non-Intervention

Another customary international law limitation on the use of force is the principle of **non-intervention**, which demands that states not interfere with another state's choice of political, economic, social, or cultural system, or its formulation of foreign policy. This principle is based on the notion of state sovereignty. The *Nicaragua* case again presents a modern example of the application of this customary international law. The ICJ determined that activities that violate the law of non-intervention include acts like financial support, training, supply of weapons, and intelligence and logistic support to factions in the country whose purpose is to overthrow the government. The court further opined that a state suffering an illegal intervention may not use force to respond to the intervention unless the intervention includes activities rising to the level of an "armed attack." The court also held that customary international law does not permit collective self-defense actions against *intervention* that does not rise to the level of an armed attack, so only the state suffering an intervention may respond to an interventionist state's use of force that is short of an armed attack. Importantly, under the principle of non-intervention, states may not participate in civil wars in another sovereign state without that sovereign government's consent.

10.4. HUMANITARIAN AND PEACE OPERATIONS

Not all intervention in foreign nations is prohibited. Today, military forces are often utilized in situations where armed conflict is not intended, including intervening in humanitarian crises and in various peace operations.

10.4.1. Humanitarian Intervention

When a humanitarian disaster is imminent or ongoing, states sometimes use military force to relieve the humanitarian suffering. **Humanitarian intervention** can be defined as "the threat or use of force by a state, group of states, or international organization primarily for the purpose of protecting the nationals of the target state from widespread deprivations of internationally recognized human rights." Sean Murphy, HUMANITARIAN INTERVENTION: THE UNITED NATIONS IN AN EVOLVING WORLD ORDER (1996). While these humanitarian crises can be caused by the government or breakdown of government, such as in Libya in 2011 or in Syria beginning in 2011, they can also be in response to natural disasters, such as when the United States military intervened in Haiti after a massive earthquake in 2010.

Humanitarian intervention as an exception to UN Charter Article 2.4 is a relatively new concept, and one that is not stated in the UN Charter itself. As an "emerging norm of customary international law," its status as a legal justification for the use of force is not yet certain. Even newer and more controversial is the idea that some humanitarian crises provide not just an *authorization* for intervention by foreign states, but an *obligation* to protect another nation's citizens from avoidable catastrophe, such as mass murder or starvation. This obligation has been termed the "**responsibility to protect**" **(R2P)**. The 2001 International Commission on Intervention and State Sovereignty report on the Responsibility to Protect concluded that sovereign states have a responsibility to protect their own citizens from avoidable catastrophe, and when they are unwilling or unable to do so, that responsibility becomes the collective responsibility of the "broader community of states." The report has been embraced by many nations, as has general acceptance of the obligation of the world community to come to the aid of humans who are suffering because their government cannot or will not help them. However, the extent to which the R2P theory justifies the use of military force to protect other nations' citizens has not yet crystallized in international law.

10.4.2. Peace Operations

"Peace operations" are another form of intervention where armed conflict is not intended, but the use of military troops suggests the risk of armed conflict is greater. Generally, "**peacekeeping**" refers to the use of military force and forces to support the implementation of a ceasefire or peace agreement or otherwise maintain peace when a state lacks the capacity to do so itself. Typically, while some hostilities can be expected, the risk of armed conflict during peacekeeping is usually low. By contrast, "**peacemaking**" is another type of peace operation that addresses conflicts in progress and usually involves both diplomacy and military force to restore tranquility and bring hostile parties to a negotiated agreement. Thus, peacemaking usually precedes peacekeeping.

The UNSC has authorized dozens of peace operations. Forces acting under UN auspices are known colloquially as "blue hats" because of the distinctive blue helmets they often wear. Authority for these non-combat peace operations is not as explicit in the UN Charter as one might expect. Article 34 of the Charter says the "Security Council may investigate any dispute, or any situation which might lead to international friction or give rise to a dispute, in order to determine whether the continuance of the dispute or situation is likely to endanger the maintenance of international peace and security." But, that does not itself suggest the authority to deploy military forces for peacekeeping. And as noted above, Articles 39 and 42 also provide authority for the Security Council to determine the existence of breaches or threats to the peace and "decide what measures shall be taken," including "such action by air, sea, or land forces as may be necessary to maintain or restore international peace and security." Notably, this refers to *international* peace, not solely intra-national peace and security, suggesting the UNSC may need some other justification for activities taking place and affecting only one state. The second UN Secretary General suggested peacekeeping was a "Chapter Six and a Half" activity, between the peaceful dispute resolution mechanisms authorized in Chapter VI of the Charter and the traditional military force authorized in Chapter VII. In any event, sending military forces into areas where peace needs to be "made" or "kept" inevitably involves risk that further conflict will occur, but the intention usually is that UNSC involvement rather than unilateral action is a potential way to reduce the chance of unauthorized uses of force.

10.5. CASE STUDIES

What follow are several "case studies" presenting some basic facts of various United States uses of force over the past several decades. As you walk through each timeline, ask yourself what international legal authority existed—or did not exist—for *each* use of force by the various actors. That is, consider the legality of each actor's use of force based on the facts that existed at each moment in time. For brevity, many details have been omitted; consider conducting some research where you have questions regarding details that might impact your legal analysis.

10.5.1. Korean Police Action, 1950

Background: After the Soviet Union and United States liberated Korea from Japan at the end of World War II, they divided Korea along the 38th parallel (latitude line), with the Soviet Union administering the northern half and the United States administering the southern half. Eventually, the north developed into a communist state and the south into a capitalist one, with each claiming sovereignty over the whole of Korea.

- 25 June 1950—Korean People's Army (KPA, the North Korean military) invaded South Korea with nearly 90,000 infantry and artillery troops. North Korea claimed this was in response to a South Korean attack and that it was looking to apprehend and execute the President of South Korea, Syngman Rhee. South Korean troops defended against the assault
- 25 June—Later the same day, the UNSC issued a resolution (UNSCR 82) calling on North Korea to stop aggression and asking member states to "render every assistance to the UN in execution of this resolution."
- 25 June—United States President Truman ordered the United States military to evacuate American citizens in Korea.
- 26 June—President Truman ordered United States troops to support the South Korean military.
- 27 June—United States Air Force began combat against North Korean People's Air Force.
- 27 June—The UNSC adopted second resolution (UNSCR 83) in which it "recommends" members "furnish such assistance to the Republic of Korea as may be necessary to repel the armed attack and to restore international peace and security in the area."
- 1 July—United States ground forces arrived in South Korea and began active combat operations against the KPA.

Consider: What was the international legal authority for each nation's military actions on each day identified above? What counterarguments are there that such legal authority did not exist?

10.5.2. Libya, 1986

Background: Under dictator Colonel Moammar Qaddafi, Libya supported various terrorist organizations hostile to the United States.

- 5 April 1986—A terrorist group linked to Libya bombed a nightclub in West Berlin, Germany, in an attack that was clearly aimed at American servicemembers. Three people died, including two United States soldiers, and 229 were injured.
- 15 April—The United States launched air strikes against Libya. Eighteen USAF F-111 fighter-bombers dropped about 60 tons of munitions on an airfield in Tripoli, on a training center at a naval academy alleged to be used to train terrorists in underwater sabotage, and on a military barracks believed to be the "command and control headquarters for Libyan terrorism." United States Navy aircraft also attacked radar and anti-aircraft sites. The United States claimed this attack was in self-defense against Libya's state-sponsored terrorism. Addressing the American people while some United States aircraft were still in the air, President Reagan said "Self-defense is not only our right, it is our duty. It is the purpose behind the mission. . .a mission fully consistent with Article 51 of the U.N. Charter."
- 15 April—During the air attack by the United States, a Libyan missile shot down one F-111, killing two United States Air Force officers.

Consider: What was the international legal authority for each nation's military actions on each day identified above? Is there more than one basis for claiming legal authority? What are the counterarguments that such legal authority did not exist?

10.5.3. The Persian Gulf War, 1990

Background: Iraqi President Saddam Hussein believed neighbor state Kuwait was involved in an anti-Iraqi **conspiracy** among middle eastern countries and complained about Kuwait's oil policy, including alleged slant-drilling by Kuwait into an oil field under Iraq. Iraq alleged that various Arab League policies were costing it $1 billion per year. Iraq demanded Kuwait pay $10 billion to cover lost revenues from the oil field, but Kuwait offered only $500 million. Instead of continuing negotiations, Iraq invaded Kuwait.

- 2 August 1990—120,000 Iraqi troops invaded Kuwait, beginning an occupation that would last seven months.
- 2 August—The UNSC passed UNSCR 660, condemning the invasion and demanding Iraq's immediate and unconditional withdrawal.
- 6 August—The UNSC passed UNSCR 661, imposing economic sanctions on Iraq. UNSCR 665 then authorized a naval blockade of Iraq to enforce sanctions.
- 7 August—United States troop buildup began in Saudi Arabia. "Operation Desert Shield" involved the buildup of coalition forces and protection of Saudi Arabia from Iraqi invasion
- 29 November—UNSCR 678 imposed a 15 January 1991 deadline for Iraq to withdraw from Kuwait and authorized member states to "use all necessary means to uphold and implement resolution 660 and all subsequent resolutions" to restore international peace and security in the area if Iraq did not withdraw.
- Late December—Iraq proposed to withdraw from Kuwait if all foreign troops left the region, if an agreement was reached regarding the Palestinian problem, and if weapons of mass destruction were banned from the region, including Israel and Iraq. The United States declined.
- 8 January 1991—United States President George H.W. Bush asked Congress to pass a resolution supporting UNSCR 678, arguing unity between branches of the United States Government would have a deterrent effect on Iraq.
- 9 January—President Bush declared that he did not need a congressional resolution, claiming "I have the authority to fully implement the United Nations resolutions."
- 14 January—Congress passed an **authorization for the use of military force (AUMF)** authorizing the President to "use United States Armed Forces pursuant to UNSCR 678."
- 16 January—Coalition forces led by the United States began airstrikes against Iraqi forces in Kuwait and Iraq. By this date, the

"coalition" of nations allied against Iraq numbered 34 countries and nearly one million troops.

- 17 January—Iraq began launching SCUD missiles against military and civilian targets in Israel and Saudi Arabia. SCUD missile attacks would occur for weeks.
- 29 January—Iraqi forces invaded a lightly defended city in Saudi Arabia, but were driven back two days later by the Saudi National Guard, and Qatari and United States forces.
- 15 February—Coalition forces launch ground combat operations into Kuwait and Iraq. After liberating Kuwait, coalition forces push into Iraq, but stop their northern push before reaching the capital, Baghdad.
- 28 February—United States President Bush declares a ceasefire.

Consider: What was the international legal authority for use of force on each day identified above? Is there more than one basis for claiming legal authority? What are the counterarguments that such legal authority did not exist?

10.5.4. United States Invasion of Iraq, 2003

Background: As part of the cease fire between Iraq and the UN, in April 1991, the UNSC issued UNSCR 687, under which, among other things, Iraq was required to destroy all chemical and biological weapons, longer-range missiles, and development facilities. The last paragraph of UNSCR 687 stated that the UNSC "[d]ecides. . .to take such further steps as may be required for the implementation of the present resolution and to secure peace and security in the area." In 2002, the administration of President George W. Bush determined there was a link between Iraq and Al Qaeda, which had launched the terror attacks on the United States on September 11, 2001. It further determined, based on intelligence that would later turn out to be faulty, that Iraq possessed weapons of mass destruction that violated the terms of UNSCR 687 from 11 years earlier. On November 8, 2002, the UNSC issued UNSCR 1441, noting Iraq had breached multiple UNSCRs, including 678, repeating warnings to Iraq about serious consequences for continued violations of its obligations under the UNSCRs, and pledging to reconvene immediately following any report of future breaches to consider the situation and the need for full compliance. In 2003, the United States tried, but failed, to obtain a second UNSCR specifically authorizing the use of military force. Based on the theory of preemptive self-defense, President Bush ordered an invasion of Iraq. In March 2003, a coalition of approximately 300,000 troops from the United States, Britain, Australia, and Poland invaded Iraq. The commander leading the invasion, United States General Tommy Franks, stated the invasion had eight objectives:

> First, ending the regime of Saddam Hussein. Second, to identify, isolate, and eliminate Iraq's weapons of mass destruction. Third, to search for, to capture, and to drive out terrorists from that country. Fourth, to collect such intelligence as we can relate to terrorist networks. Fifth, to collect such intelligence as we can relate to the global network of illicit weapons of mass destruction. Sixth, to end sanctions and to immediately deliver humanitarian support to the displaced and to many needy Iraqi citizens. Seventh, to secure Iraq's oil fields and resources, which belong to the Iraqi people. And last, to help the Iraqi people create conditions for a transition to a representative self-government.

Consider: What was the international legal authority for the United States' invasion in March 2003? Is there more than one basis for claiming legal authority? What are the counterarguments that such legal authority did not exist?

10.5.5. United States Bombing in Syria, 2017 and 2018

Background: During a protracted civil war in Syria, the government regime of President Bashar al-Assad repeatedly used prohibited chemical weapons against Syrian civilians. In response, the United States attacked Syrian government targets in April 2017 and again in April 2018. Before the latter strikes, United States President Donald Trump said "We can't let atrocities like we all witnessed, and you can see that and it's horrible, we can't let that happen in our world. Especially when we're able to, because of the power of the United States, because of the power of our country, we're able to stop it." No UNSC authorization existed for the airstrikes. Repeated attempts by members of the UNSC to issue resolutions to eliminate Assad's ability to use chemical weapons were vetoed by Russia, a permanent member of the UNSC with close ties to Assad. After the US-led airstrikes, Russia attempted to get the UNSC to issue a resolution condemning the airstrikes, but its proposed resolution received only three votes of the 15 members of the UNSC.

Consider: What was the international legal authority for the United States airstrikes in April 2017 and again in April 2018? Is there more than one basis for claiming legal authority? What are the counterarguments that such legal authority did not exist?

REVIEW QUESTIONS

1. What are the two exceptions to the prohibition on the use of force in the UN Charter?

2. What do the terms "use of force" and "armed attack" mean, and how do they relate to each other?

3. Summarize the differences between the circumstances authorizing self-defense under Article 51, by the theory of anticipatory self-defense, and by the theory of preemptive self-defense.

4. When may military forces be lawfully used in humanitarian and peace operations?

CRITICAL THINKING QUESTIONS

1. What does the UN Charter's primary purpose suggest regarding how ambiguities in the UN Charter language should be interpreted?

2. Why does the UN Charter give greater latitude to use armed force to the UNSC than it does to nations acting in self-defense? Do you agree with the different standards?

3. Does Congress have the constitutional authority to limit the President in the way it did in the UNPA?

4. Why do you suppose there is no authoritative definition of "use of force" in international law?

5. An "armed attack" will always be a "use of force," but not every use of force is an armed attack. Why would "armed attack"—the threshold for self-defense under Article 51—be higher than the standard for determining whether an illegal "use of force" has occurred?

6. In the *Nicaragua* case, the ICJ held that providing weapons to the Contras constituted a use of force by the United States, but that providing money to the Contras, which ostensibly could be used to purchase weapons, did *not* constitute a use of force? Does that make sense?

7. Consider the following hypothetical situation: A terrorist group declares it wants to kill Americans "wherever they can be found." After two restaurant bombings where Americans congregate, the United States launches a strike against a known training camp for that group, claiming self-defense. Would that be anticipatory or preemptive self-defense?

CHAPTER 11

Cyber War

Cadets at the United States Air Force Academy train for cyber warfare at an exercise sponsored by the National Security Agency

"*The potential for the next Pearl Harbor could very well be a cyber attack.*" Leon Panetta, Director of the Central Intelligence Agency, *Testimony Before the House of Representatives Permanent Select Committee on Intelligence*, February 10, 2011.

Learning Objectives

1. Understand the law of armed conflict as it relates to cyber operations.

2. Distinguish between cyber operations that constitute a use of force and those that do not.

3. Understand when and how nations can legally respond to an adversary's cyber operation.

4. Understand the legal limitations on how cyber operations are conducted once combatant nations have initiated hostilities.

11.1. INTRODUCTION

The idea that legal norms should govern warfare is not a modern phenomenon. Some of the earliest references to rules governing war can be found in the Twenty-fifth Century BCE where the Sumerians and Egyptians recognized self-imposed restrictions that limited their freedom to begin an armed conflict. Other pre-modern civilizations such as the Hittites, Greeks, and Romans also imposed rules upon themselves before resorting to armed combat. As long ago as the Seventh Century BCE, the Babylonians recognized rules that governed the treatment of prisoners and civilians during war. Similarly, Sun Tzu's *The Art of War*, the Hebrew Bible, and the Koran all regulate, to some degree, the responsibilities of combatants after a victory over their enemies. However, the Sumerians, Egyptians, Greeks, and Romans, could never have imagined computers, the internet, or waging war in cyberspace.

The attempt to identify the first time cyberspace was used to engage in hostile, war-like acts has caused some debate among experts. Many point to an event in Estonia in 2007 where numerous Estonian government websites were defaced and shut down, halting various government services. These attacks, which mostly originated from actors in Russia, occurred at the same time the Estonian government decided to remove Soviet-era monuments celebrating the Soviet Union's victory in World War II. While experts believe the Russian government was likely involved, it never took responsibility for the aggressive activity. Other experts believe the Stuxnet virus that crippled Iranian nuclear enrichment facilities in late 2009 constituted the first cyber attack. Stuxnet was **malware**, or a computer worm, that attacked the software controlling Iranian nuclear centrifuges. Once the software was infected with the Stuxnet virus, it stopped functioning in the proper way and caused many of the centrifuges to ultimately break down. While no nation took responsibility for the attack, most experts believe the United States and Israeli governments developed and launched the virus. Whether either of these events constituted the first cyber attack, or cyber "act of war," it is indisputable that aggressive **cyber operations**—the offensive employment of cyber capabilities to achieve objectives through cyberspace—by both governments and non-governmental actors are the newest frontier in armed conflict.

Unlike many of the internationally accepted laws governing the use of traditional military force discussed in previous chapters, there continues to be a debate about the legal principles that govern the use of force in cyberspace. Some nations and experts have suggested new treaties are needed to address the specific and unique issues presented by cyber operations and the prospect of cyber warfare. Other nations and experts suggest that even though no **treaty** exists, the traditional concepts of ***jus ad bellum*** and ***jus in bello*** apply to all newly developed weapons, including cyber weapons. Even among nations and experts that agree the existing norms govern hostilities in cyberspace, there is disagreement about how broadly or narrowly to interpret those norms when it comes to cyberspace. In 2003, **the North Atlantic Treaty Organization's (NATO's)** Cooperative Cyber Defense Center of Excellence published an extensive analysis of how the United Nations Charter and **customary international law** can be applied to hostilities in cyberspace. This analysis, the *Tallinn Manual*, serves as the basis for the discussion of the law governing cyber operations in this chapter. While the *Tallinn Manual* is not the only authority on this topic, it provides a benchmark for understanding the questions raised by the battlefield that is cyberspace.

11.2. CYBER OPERATIONS AND THE USE OF FORCE

The United Nations Charter and customary international law prohibit nations from resorting to war, except when certain preconditions are met. This concept is known as *jus ad bellum*. Customary international law identifies a list of factors, discussed in Chapter 10, that nations must consult and weigh before concluding that a decision to go to war is both just and legal. These factors apply whether the war is waged traditionally or in cyberspace. Article 2 of the United Nations Charter, however, has a relatively absolute view of when nations may resort to armed conflict. It states "[a]ll members shall refrain in their international relations from the threat or the use of force against the territorial integrity or political independence of any state . . . ." Therefore, to determine whether a cyber operation is prohibited under the United Nations Charter, one must first define what "force" means in cyberspace. Experts agree that when cyberspace is used to engage in hostilities that result in physical injuries or damage to physical objects, those cyber operations are considered "force" even though the damage is not caused by traditional, kinetic weapons like missiles and bombs. However, cyber attacks are not always targeted at causing damage in the physical world. Sometimes cyber attacks are targeted at causing damage in cyberspace. Nevertheless, these attacks still can be just as harmful as attacks that result in physical damage. Because the possible harms inflicted in cyberspace are varied and countless, it is difficult to create a definition of "force" that will capture every imaginable situation. As a result, the following factors are used to determine whether a cyber operation constitutes a use of force.

Severity

The severity of the damage caused by the cyber operation must be considered when determining whether it meets the definition of force. Cyber operations that result in nothing more than simple inconveniences or annoyances do not constitute a use of force. However, as cyber operations become more than inconveniences and begin to affect a country's critical national interests, the more likely they will be considered a use of force. In addition, the more widespread, the longer lasting, and the more extreme the effects, the more likely the attack will meet the definition of a use of force.

Immediacy

Cyber operations can have consequences that manifest themselves very quickly or over long periods of time. Harmful effects from cyber operations that manifest themselves slowly over time provide countries opportunities to seek peaceful resolutions to the dispute that caused the cyber aggression. In addition, a cyber attack that takes time to develop is often more easily and effectively repelled by the target country. However, a cyber operation that has immediate effects leaves no room for diplomacy and is more difficult to defend against. Therefore, the more immediate the effects, the more likely the cyber operation is a use of force.

Directness

While the immediacy factor discussed above focuses on the amount of time between when a cyber operation begins and when its effects materialize, the "directness" factor focuses on whether a cyber operation is the actual source of harm. In other words, a question of cause and effect; how close a cyber operation is related to an ultimate, identified consequence of the operation. The more attenuated, or farther removed, a cyber operation is from a harm, the less likely it constitutes a use of force. On the other hand, if there is a close link and direct relationship between a cyber operation and its consequences, it is more likely to be considered a use of force.

Invasiveness

The invasiveness factor requires an analysis of the target of a cyber operation. As you can imagine, the level of security, secrecy, and sensitivity of the various targets of a cyber operation will range from very low to very high. For example, there is a significant difference between the electronic files on a computer at your local library when compared to the electronic files on a computer in the Pentagon. Likewise, there is a difference between a website for a musician and a cyber system that controls a nation's power grid. The more sensitive and crucial to a nation's interests, the more likely a cyber operation will be considered a use of force. In addition, the more focused a cyber operation is on a specific nation, the more likely it is to be a use of force. That is to say, if a cyber operation's consequences are indiscriminate and it affects cyber systems throughout the world, it is less likely to constitute a use of force.

Measurability of Effects

In traditional warfare, a nation could observe and measure the effects of kinetic weapons. For example, a nation could count the number of buildings destroyed in a bombing raid. In a cyber attack, however, measuring the level of destruction associated with an attack can prove to be more difficult. As a result, the more a nation can detect and measure the objective effects of a cyber operation, the more likely it will be to constitute a use of force. Instead of counting the number of buildings destroyed, like the example above, nations would try to measure the quantity of files corrupted on a server or the number of websites disabled. As those numbers increase, so does the likelihood the cyber operation that caused those effects will be considered a use of force.

Military Character

The more a cyber operation has the characteristics of a military operation, the more likely it will constitute a use of force. When the nations of the world drafted the United Nations Charter prohibiting the use of force, they were particularly focused on regulating the use of military force. As a result, to determine whether a cyber operation constitutes a use of force one must consider the source and target of the operations. Cyber operations that are carried out by militaries or other armed forces, or are directed at military targets, will more likely be characterized as uses of force.

State Involvement

One of the many difficulties presented by cyberwarfare is identifying the degree of a nation's involvement with a particular cyber operation. On the one hand, a nation may retain complete command and control over a cyber operation. On the other hand, a nation may have no involvement in a cyber operation. One can imagine that between these two extremes lies a range of possibilities for a nation to be more or less involved in a cyber operation. The more marginal and attenuated a nation's involvement, the less likely a cyber operation will be considered a use of force by that nation.

Actions That Do Not Constitute the Use of Force

Some cyber operations that one might consider hostile or adversarial are not considered uses of force. For example, cyber espionage is the clandestine collection and transmission of information through the use of cyber capabilities. Most nations outlaw cyber espionage under their domestic law and reserve the right to arrest and jail spies. However, while cyber espionage is undoubtedly a hostile act, it does not typically constitute a use of force under international law. Similarly, while a nation may use its cyber capabilities to distribute adversarial propaganda in another nation, this alone does not constitute a use of force.

11.3. ATTRIBUTION

Even if a cyber operation constitutes a use of force, it is often difficult to determine who is responsible for the attack. Cyber operations can be conducted by a variety of actors including militaries, clandestine intelligence services, terrorists, and other non-state actors. This poses a problem in ascribing responsibility to a specific nation for a cyber attack. Certainly, if a nation's military, domestic security services, or intelligence agencies are directly and identifiably responsible for a cyber attack, that nation is legally responsible under the **law of armed conflict**. In addition, if a nation has empowered a private entity, such as a company, to act on the nation's behalf, the nation will be legally responsible for a cyber attack initiated by the company. However, for many cyber operations, identifying their origin and assigning responsibility can be difficult, particularly when the perpetrators are non-state actors.

Imagine a situation where a United States citizen carries out a terrorist attack against another nation. Simply because the terrorist is a United States citizen does not mean the United States is responsible for the attack. The conclusion is no different in cyberspace. If an individual or group independently engages in cyber operations, those actions will not be attributed to the nation of which they are citizens. Similarly, a nation will not necessarily be responsible for a cyber operation simply because the operation originated within that nation's cyber infrastructure. However, if an individual or group engages in cyber attacks based on instructions from a nation, or under a nation's direction or control, the cyber operations may be attributable to that nation. In these situations, the nation assumes the legal responsibility for the cyber operation.

For cyber operations to be attributed to a nation based on its instructions to an individual or group, the individual or group need not be a government employee or a government organization. Private, non-state actors that assist a nation can also have their cyber operations attributed to the nation they assist. As a result, if a nation enters into a contract with a company or requests the help of volunteers to engage in cyber operations, the actions of those private entities are attributable to the requesting nation. Similarly, when a nation exercises the authority to begin, manage, and end a cyber operation conducted by a non-state actor, the nation is considered to be in effective control of the operation. However, if a nation's interaction with a non-state actor is limited to incidentally providing funding or training, this alone will not be enough to attribute the non-state actor's cyber operations to the nation.

11.4. THE RIGHT TO RESPOND TO A CYBER OPERATION

The United Nations Charter distinguishes between two basic uses of force in international relations: 1) a minor use of force that, while still an act of aggression, only has a negligible impact on the target nation and 2) a significant use of force that has risen to the level of an **armed attack**. It is important to differentiate between these two concepts as international law authorizes different kinds of responses based on whether an aggressive act reaches the "armed attack" threshold. Understanding and identifying the difference can be difficult because all armed attacks are acts of aggression, but not all acts of aggression are armed attacks. Classifying an aggressor's actions becomes all the more important in the digital age as cyber operations enable nations to engage in an infinite amount of aggressive activities that can range from annoying, to disruptive, to catastrophic.

Consider, for example, the 2014 cyber hack of the Sony Pictures film studio. As part of an alleged effort to pressure Sony Pictures into abandoning its plan to release a movie that poked fun at the North Korean leader, Kim Jong-Un, a hacker group erased a significant amount of Sony's digital data. The group also stole and published unreleased scripts and movies, as well as confidential information about Sony employees including Social Security numbers and emails. Although there was a debate about who was responsible for the hack, the United States government ultimately attributed it to the North Korean government. Regardless of the origins, the hack was certainly a disruptive, aggressive act targeting Sony's cyber infrastructure and data. However, was it the sort of aggressive act that should trigger a war? Most people would not equate the Sony Pictures hack with, for example, a North Korean military aircraft dropping a bomb on the Sony Pictures building and killing hundreds of people. These questions of degree are the sorts of questions raised by cyber operations. The answers to these questions dictate how the victim of a cyber operation may respond under the law of armed conflict.

11.4.1. The Armed Attack Threshold

Article 51 of the United Nations Charter recognizes that nations have an inherent right to self-defense and they may exercise that right if they are the victim of an armed attack. This right was recognized in the United Nations Charter long before the digital era and initially presupposed the use of kinetic weapons. While cyber operations do not employ weapons in the traditional sense, like bombs and guns, experts unanimously agree that cyber operations can nonetheless have a sufficiently destructive effect to be considered an armed attack. In other words, what is important is not how an attack is carried out, but the scale and effects of the attack. In fact, the **International Court of Justice** has determined that an aggressive act is an armed attack only when the scale and effects are grave. Put differently, the scope and results of the aggressive act must be severe. For example, cyber operations that result in an annoying denial of service of non-essential services will likely not rise to this level. However, a cyber operation that results in the death and destruction of a significant number of people and property will constitute an armed attack.

Cyber operations, however, may not always take the form of one, spectacular and catastrophic aggressive action. Instead, less significant cyber operations can, over time, build up to cause substantial damage. In these cases, so long as multiple cyber operations originate from the same nation and, taken together, the collective scale and effects are grave, the group of operations will be considered an armed attack. Moreover, a minor cyber operation may cause minimal cyber-related damage to an operating system, but have catastrophic effects on people's lives. For example, consider a cyber operation targeting a hydroelectric dam in order to inhibit electricity production. If the operation causes the dam to fail and flood a nearby town, causing death and destruction, those effects may be considered part of the operation if the dam's failure was a reasonably foreseeable result of targeting the operating system. In that case, the cyber operation may be considered an armed attack.

11.4.2. Self-Defense

As was discussed above, determining whether an aggressive cyber operation is an armed attack is important. If a cyber operation does not rise to the level of an armed attack, then an injured nation may respond with countermeasures, discussed below. However, if a cyber operation meets the armed attack threshold, then the injured nation may engage in self-defense. Legally permissible self-defense measures must comply with the **necessity** and **proportionality** principles of *jus ad bellum*. First, an injured nation's cyber operation used in self-defense must be necessary. That is to say, a cyber use of force must be needed to stop the cyber operation of an aggressor state's imminent or ongoing armed attack. If an alternative cyber action, that does not constitute a use of force, is available to stop an attack, then a use of force would be illegal. For example, if a nation can rely on computer firewalls to repel an aggressor nation's cyber armed attack, then an active, more forceful cyber operation is legally impermissible. If firewalls cannot stop the cyber attack, but the injured nation can stop the aggressor nation with less cyber force than would meet the armed attack threshold, it must do so. In other words, the victim nation is required to use no more force than what is necessary to stop the attack.

Once an injured nation determines whether force is necessary, it must comply with the proportionality principle. The proportionality principle requires the amount of force—its intensity, reach, and duration—be proportional to the military objective. An injured nation may legally respond with cyber operations that last as long, are as intense, and are as broadly impactful on the aggressor nation as is necessary to stop an imminent armed attack or defeat an ongoing armed attack. The proportionality principle does not limit the type of attack a nation may resort to in self-defense. If an aggressor nation uses a traditional method of armed attack like missiles or bombs, the injured nation can respond with cyber operations. Likewise, if an aggressor nation uses cyber operations to initiate an armed attack, the injured nation can use traditional military force in response.

11.4.3. Countermeasures

Cyber operations can occur during peacetime or during an armed conflict. The state of relations between two nations will dictate what options are legally available to a nation that is the target of a cyber operation by another nation. If a nation, during peacetime, has engaged in a cyber operation that constitutes a low-intensity, yet unlawful use of force, international law authorizes the targeted nation to engage in countermeasures. Thus, if two nations are not at war, yet one nation engages in a minor, but still harmful cyber operation, the injured nation may respond. However, the injured nation's response is limited by international law. First, the injured nation must notify the aggressor nation that it holds the aggressor responsible for an unlawful action. The injured nation must also notify the aggressor nation that it intends to take countermeasures. Finally, the injured nation must offer to negotiate. These notifications are particularly important regarding a suspected aggressor nation's use of cyber operations because of the ease with which a cyber attack can be successfully masqueraded and appear to originate from a nation that is not in fact responsible for the aggression. If notification of the intent to engage in countermeasures does not result in bringing an end to the unlawful cyber operation, the injured nation may resort to its own use of force.

The injured nation, however, may not retaliate with force that would meet the definition of an armed attack. Instead, the injured nation is limited to using force that incentivizes or causes the aggressor nation to cease the cyber operation and resume its compliance with international law. The goals of any countermeasure should be moderation and an effort to resolve the dispute. Additionally, because countermeasures are intended to return nations to the **status quo** that existed prior to the aggressive cyber operation, countermeasures should be temporary and reversible. As a result, an acceptable countermeasure might include a cyber operation by an injured state that locks the data of an aggressor state until the aggressor ceases its harmful actions. Once the harmful actions cease, the injured state can unlock the data. However, if the injured nation erased the data as part of a countermeasure, that cyber operation may exceed the acceptable amount of force of a countermeasure.

Remember, the law of armed conflict applies only to nations. Accordingly, this discussion of countermeasures has referred specifically to nations and their use of cyber operations because countermeasures can only be directed at state actors, not non-state actors. If a non-state actor residing in one nation engages in a cyber operation aimed at another nation, and the two nations are not engaged in armed conflict, the injured nation cannot direct countermeasures against the non-state actor. Of course, the nation where the non-state actor resides is responsible for using its law enforcement authority to ensure its territory is not used to launch cyber operations. However, a nation will only be responsible for a non-state actor's cyber operation in certain circumstances, discussed above in the Attribution section. Countermeasures can only be directed at non-state actors whose actions are attributable to an aggressor nation.

11.5. *JUS IN BELLO*

Once a nation has determined that a cyber operation is a legally justifiable use of force, it is further limited by *jus in bello. Jus in bello* legal principles govern the *way* in which, or how, nations may use force against each other once hostilities have begun. These principles govern both traditional and cyber uses of force regardless of whether hostilities between the nations were initiated legally. If an aggressor nation illegally initiates an armed conflict, the attacked nation, though legally justified to respond, must nevertheless abide by *jus in bello* principles regarding the way it conducts its responsive attacks. *Jus in bello* includes five governing legal principles: **distinction**, military necessity, proportionality, unnecessary suffering, and perfidy. Belligerent nations must abide by each of these principles in order for a use of force to be considered legal.

Distinction

The International Court of Justice has recognized the concept of "distinction" as one of the most fundamental legal principles when considering whether a particular use of force is legal. Under the concept of distinction, uses of force are only legally legitimate when directed against an enemy's military forces. The corollary to this principle is that it is illegal to target civilian populations and civilian infrastructure. At times, nations can easily comply with the distinction principle by ensuring they only target and use force against an enemy's uniformed troops and military hardware, such as tanks. For example, a bombing run that targets an enemy's military fighter jets would be legal under the distinction principle. If, instead of using bombs to destroy the enemy's fighter jets, a nation's military used malware to infect and disable the computer systems of those same fighter jets, that would likewise be legal under the distinction principle. The key is that parties to a military conflict are only directing their operations toward the destruction of military targets. The nature of military targets, however, can vary. The two basic types of military targets are military personnel and military objects, and each has unique considerations for the purposes of a distinction analysis.

It is clear that the members of an enemy's armed forces are legitimate targets for the purposes of a distinction analysis. While members of a nation's armed forces are always legitimate targets, an enemy's civilian population is never a legitimate target. However, civilians often support or even operate a military's cyber missions. In fact, in some countries, civilians often have more experience and expertise in the cyber realm when compared with their nation's military. Under these circumstances, civilians can shift from being illegal targets and become legal targets if and when they are directly participating in hostilities.

For example, imagine a software engineer that works for a private corporation by day. After leaving her day job, she arrives at her second job at a military base where she has been hired to conduct offensive military cyber operations for a few hours at night. Under these circumstances, she is not a legal target during the day, but is a legal target while she works at night. Sometimes, however, the military will not directly employ a cyber operator and will instead hire a private firm to conduct cyber operations on its behalf. In that situation, the contractors are considered to have been incorporated into the military, by virtue of the contract. As a result, while the employees of the private firm are not employed directly with the military, they lose their civilian status as their employer is serving a cyber combat function for the military. The focus here is on the direct, as opposed to unwitting or passive, participation in cyber operations. If a civilian's computer is hacked and used as a means to launch a cyber operation, that person is not a legal target. Likewise, if a hacker posts a malware program on a website that is publicly available to anyone, and a military discovers the malware and uses it in an offensive cyber operation, the hacker is not a legal target.

For the purposes of distinction, it is only legal to target an object when its total or partial destruction—based on the nature, location, or purpose of the object—would provide an obvious military advantage. Within the context of cyber operations, military objects can take many forms. For example, by their very nature, the destruction of military computers, military cyber infrastructure, military surveillance equipment, military communications equipment, and military reconnaissance equipment would provide a distinct military advantage; thus each of these would be legitimate targets. A target can also be legal based on its tactical geographic location. As a result, if the main transportation route for an enemy's military includes a computer controlled drawbridge spanning a river, it would be legal to conduct a cyber operation attacking the computer's operating system which results in the malfunctioning of the drawbridge. Cyber software and hardware intended for military use are also legitimate targets. Therefore, it is legal to target a manufacturing plant that builds computers for the military.

Targeting an enemy's cyber infrastructure poses unique problems for the purposes of distinction because cyber infrastructure can support both civilian and military objectives. As a result, the targets must be considered on a case-by-cases basis. For example, while it would be illegal to target the cyber infrastructure behind a civilian blog that accused the enemy of war crimes, it would be legal to target that same infrastructure if the blog passed coded messages to troops in the field. At times, however, cyber infrastructure and cyber networks are used equally for both civilian and military purposes. Under international law, objects cannot be both civilian and military; they must be one or the other. If, for example, a cyber network is used for both military and civilian communication, then it is a military object. As a result, it can be legally targeted, however, the other *jus in bello* principles discussed below must be considered.

Implicit in the concept of choosing only military targets for attack is the idea that indiscriminate attacks are impermissible. A cyber operation is illegal if it cannot be directed at a specific military object or members of the armed forces. Likewise, if a cyber operation cannot be limited in its effects such that civilian and military objects are destroyed without distinction, this is also an illegal attack. Absolute precision is not required. Instead, what is forbidden is cyber operations that employ means and methods that are equivalent to a scatter shot. For example, consider a cyber operation that utilizes malware and introduces it into an enemy's military cyber infrastructure. If the military cyber infrastructure is connected to the nation's larger cyber infrastructure, and the malware is incapable of distinguishing between military and civilian cyber infrastructure, this would likely constitute an illegal indiscriminate attack. On the other hand, changing the facts in the example above, imagine that the military's cyber infrastructure was known to be walled off and disconnected from the civilian infrastructure. If a military member mistakenly transferred the malware to the civilian infrastructure through an infected flash drive, this would likely not constitute an indiscriminate attack.

Military Necessity

If one's legal analysis of the use of force during a military conflict only considered the distinction principle, one might conclude that *any* military target may be lawfully destroyed. However, differentiating between military and civilian targets is legally insufficient for the purposes of *jus in bello.* Once a target is determined to be military in nature, one must then identify the military purpose for destroying the target. If destroying or otherwise neutralizing the target does not provide a definite military advantage, then it may not legally be the object of an attack. In determining whether the destruction or neutralization of a target provides a military advantage, one must consider the target's nature, location, purpose, or use at the time of the proposed attack. While it may seem counterintuitive to suggest that combatants may not destroy each other's military targets during a military conflict, the purpose of the military necessity principle is to ensure that combatants use no more force than is necessary to secure a military victory. Put simply, military targets may not be destroyed for the sake of destruction alone. The military necessity principle applies no less in the context of cyber operations than in the physical world.

Imagine a low-intensity military conflict between two nations, A and B, fighting over a piece of territory along their shared border. Cyber operations that target the enemy's military command and control cyber infrastructure along the border would meet the military necessity principle. Likewise, grounding the enemy's fighter jets stationed along the shared border by inserting malware into their navigation systems would also meet the military necessity principle. Now imagine the following situation, based on the hypothetical above. A military lawyer who graduated from nation A's military academy met her ex-husband while studying as an exchange student in nation B. She is stationed on the opposite side of the country from where the conflict is occurring and is responsible for writing wills for her fellow military servicemembers. Her ex-husband is now a cyber operator for nation B's military. If he inserts malware into nation A's military cyber infrastructure to corrupt files containing his ex-wife's college records to retaliate against her for ending their marriage, that cyber operation is unlikely to meet the military necessity principle. The retributive destruction of his ex-wife's college records is unlikely to provide a military advantage in the border dispute and hasten a military victory.

Proportionality

When there is an ongoing armed conflict, civilian collateral damage is often a newsworthy event. Belligerent nations are often criticized for the collateral damage their conflicts inflict on civilian populations and objects. The level of criticism may lead one to believe that any civilian deaths or destruction of civilian property is prohibited as a violation of the laws of armed conflict and *jus in bello*. This, however, is not true. Instead, the law of armed conflict recognizes that civilian deaths and destruction is a terrible, though at times unavoidable, consequence of armed conflict. The *jus in bello* proportionality principle attempts to deal with this humanitarian concern.

Unfortunately, the term "proportionality" is a bit misleading. Intuitively, one may think that it regulates the *amount* of force a nation is legally permitted to use in response to an attack. For example, one may think that proportionality prohibits a nation from dropping a two-ton bomb on a single enemy soldier armed with only a pistol. This is not the case. Instead, after identifying a lawful target through distinction and military necessity analyses, and before initiating the attack, the proportionality principle requires **belligerents** to consider the collateral damage that will be inflicted on civilians. Civilian loss of life, objects, and resources need not be zero for the attack to be lawful. Instead, the impact on civilians may not be excessive in relation to the concrete and direct military advantage to be gained by the attack. In other words, a significant, or major, civilian loss of life, objects, and resources would not be legally permissible if the military target provides an insignificant, or minor, military advantage. There is no mathematical equation that accompanies the proportionality analysis. Instead, the analysis and decision must be conducted based on the information available at the time the attack is being considered, and the ultimate conclusion must be reasonable in light of the then available information.

The proportionality principle must, of course, be met if the cyber operation will have impacts in the physical world and is likely to result in a loss of civilian life or physical objects. Consider, for example, a cyber operation that inserts malware into a country's air traffic control system used for both military and civilian aircraft. If the malware disables the air traffic control's radar, this failure may result in military and civilian aircraft accidents, and thus the loss of civilian lives and objects. In that case, the loss of civilian lives and aircraft may not be excessive in comparison to the concrete and direct military advantage. The proportionality principle, however, is not limited solely to physical civilian losses. The proportionality principle must also be met if a cyber operation's impact is a loss to civilian cyber infrastructure and cyber networks. As with any proportionality analysis, the significance of the loss to civilian cyber infrastructure functionality cannot be excessive in comparison to the direct and concrete military advantage. An attack on a communications network shared by both the military and civilian sectors that results in a complete loss of civilian electronic communication capabilities would likely require a proportionality analysis. However, cyber operations that merely result in inconvenience and annoyances to the civilian population do not likely meet the threshold of collateral damage. Imagine a cyber operation that directs malware at an enemy's military cyber infrastructure in an effort to deny internet service to the military—undoubtedly a legal target under distinction and military necessity analyses. If the malware is likely to escape into the civilian cyber infrastructure and have the effect of shutting down all the civilian entertainment websites, this is not collateral damage for the purposes of a proportionality analysis.

Cyber operations will not always be segregated from more traditional, kinetic military operations. In fact, a nation's military might find that the most effective use of force to neutralize a target consists of a two pronged attack; both cyber and traditional. In those circumstances, the cyber operation portion of the attack cannot be considered in isolation for the purposes of a proportionality analysis. Instead, in conducting a proportionality analysis the impact on civilians must be considered in light of the entire attack, including both the cyber and kinetic operation.

Unnecessary Suffering

While the proportionality principle discussed above focuses on the loss of civilian lives and infrastructure, the unnecessary suffering principle is focused on the suffering of enemy combatants. While a legitimate goal of an armed conflict is to kill the enemy, it is an illegitimate and unlawful goal to cause unnecessary suffering to those same combatants. Undoubtedly, many combatants engaged in armed conflict will suffer because of their participation in the conflict. However, in an effort to ensure wars are conducted as humanly as possible, it is a violation of the law of armed conflict to inflict suffering on an enemy when the suffering does not provide a military advantage. When the suffering becomes excessive or nonessential to the military objective, then the suffering is unnecessary. This most often arises within the context of legal and illegal weapons. For example, a traditional bullet manufactured from lead and other metals can kill an enemy combatant as effectively as a glass bullet. Where the lead bullet may kill an enemy combatant instantly, a glass bullet may shatter upon entering the body and may be less likely to kill on impact. Instead, the glass bullet can cause significant damage to internal organs causing a combatant to bleed to death slowly and excruciatingly. Additionally, glass bullet fragments are difficult to find in the body, so a glass bullet that does not kill the enemy is more likely to cause continuing injury and suffering than a lead bullet that does not kill. The military advantage is gained by killing the enemy soldier, not in causing her suffering.

Unnecessary suffering is perhaps a less likely issue to arise in the *jus in bellum* analysis of a cyber operation. An unnecessary suffering analysis considers the way in which a particular weapon, or the use of a weapon, needlessly increases suffering. Because the means and methods of conducting cyber operations are fundamentally reducible to moving electrons, it is difficult to imagine, with today's technology, many ways that cyber operations could cause unnecessary suffering. One could conceive of a cyber operation that interfered with an enemy combatant's brain implant. If the cyber operation could instantly kill the combatant by causing the implant to malfunction, that would be a permissible use of force. However, if the same cyber operation delays his death and, in the meantime, intentionally causes the combatant's brain to perceive he was in excruciating pain before killing him, that would violate the unnecessary suffering principle.

Perfidy

The perfidy principle prohibits deception and a betrayal of trust. It may be counterintuitive to expect enemy forces to be able to trust each other and legally require combatants to live up to that trust. Certainly, in many cases, it is unreasonable to expect that enemy forces would not try to deceive each other. For example, a counterintelligence operation that suggests an attack will occur on a specific day, at a specific location, in an attempt to misdirect enemy forces and reinforcements is entirely permissible under the perfidy principle. The perfidy principle, however, prohibits a different type of deception. Perfidy prohibits a combatant from taking advantage of the laws of armed conflict to trick an enemy into believing, to its detriment, it is afforded protection. Consider the well-known example of "raising the white flag." Raising a white flag is a symbol, throughout the world, that those who raised the flag are offering to surrender or offering a truce. If an opposition force attacked a combatant that had discarded his weapon and waived a white flag, that would be a violation of international law for killing a surrendering enemy. The perfidy principle prohibits that same, surrendering combatant from relying on his enemy's compliance with the laws of armed conflict to lure the unwitting enemy into a trap or ambush. In that example, the "surrendering" combatant has violated the perfidy principle.

The perfidy principle is violated when four elements are met: 1) there is an act that invited the confidence of the adversary; 2) the act was done with the intent to betray the confidence of the adversary; 3) there is a specific protection provided for under the law of armed conflict that attaches to, or is associated with, the act; and 4) the deceived adversary is killed or injured. The information needed to assess the first, second, and fourth elements are found in the specific facts and circumstances surrounding the alleged violation of perfidy. However, the third element requires some knowledge of the various protections provided by the law of armed conflict. While a discussion of all of those protections are beyond the scope of this chapter, the examples below will help illustrate the perfidy principle within the context of cyber operations.

The law of armed conflict recognizes that a combatant's medical personnel are not lawful targets. For example, it is a violation of the law of armed conflict to target a vehicle on the battlefield that displays the Red Cross, Red Crescent, or Red Star of David symbol. It would be a violation of the perfidy principle to paint the Red Cross, Red Crescent, or Red Star of David symbol on a vehicle and use the vehicle to launch a surprise attack on an enemy's outpost. In the cyber context, imagine a combatant that disguises an email by using the Red Cross, Red Crescent, or Red Star of David symbol. It would likely be a violation of the perfidy principle to use the email to communicate with the enemy's commanders about humanitarian medical aid and surreptitiously insert malware into the enemy's cyber infrastructure through the counterfeit email, if the malware results in the injury or death of enemy combatants.

Remember the fourth element of the perfidy principle identified above. The key, particularly in the cyber context, is that the death or injury must be the **proximate cause** of the deceptive act. The deceptive act must directly result in the injury or death, with no other intervening acts or events causing the death. Consider again the Red Cross, Red Crescent, or Red Star of David email example above. Imagine the malware caused the enemy's military cyber network to fail. Further imagine that as a result of the network failure, a military member is released from work early and is hit by a drunk driver on her way home. That military member's death would not be a proximate cause of the deceptive act.

REVIEW QUESTIONS

1. Why is defining "force" important for the purposes of cyber operations?

2. What factors must be considered to determine if a cyber operation constitutes a use of force?

3. What is the importance of the concept of attribution in the context of cyber operations?

4. Can you distinguish between a minor use of force and an armed attack? Why is the distinction important? Is it more difficult to make this distinction in the context of cyber operations?

5. What are the legal principles that limit a nation's right to self-defense?

6. What are countermeasures, when are they legally permissible, and what are their legal limitations?

7. What is *jus in bello*? What factors must be considered to comply with *jus in bello* and how do they apply in the context of a cyber operation?

CRITICAL THINKING QUESTIONS

1. Do you think cyber operations should comply with the laws of armed conflict? What if no physical damage or injuries result from a cyber operation? Does that matter?

2. Why does the military character of a cyber operation, or state involvement, matter for the purposes of defining force in the context of a cyber operation? Should these factors matter? How does considering these factors affect the analysis of a cyber operation by non-state actors?

3. Can you imagine a cyber operation that reaches the armed attack threshold but does not directly cause death or the destruction of physical resources?

4. Throughout this chapter, various concepts rely on the distinction between cyber operations that are mere annoyances and those with more serious effects. Do you agree those distinctions should matter legally? If a nation conducts any sort of hostile cyber operation against another nation, should that constitute an act of war?

5. Imagine a situation where an aggressor nation targets the cyber infrastructure of a civilian business in another nation, like a bank or financial institution, and deletes all of its data such that it cannot be recovered. This sort of cyber operation would undoubtedly have a significant, detrimental impact on the business and its customers. Is this any different from an aggressor nation dropping a bomb and completely

destroying the civilian business' building such that it is rendered useless? Is the analysis of the cyber attack different from the kinetic attack?

CHAPTER 12

Interrogating Terror Suspects

Drawing of an Inquisition torture chamber, by Bernard Picard, 1716

Learning Objectives

1. Know the international law that prohibits torture.

2. Know the United States domestic laws limiting torture and other coercive interrogation techniques.

3. Be able to apply domestic and international law to specific interrogation techniques used by the United States after 9/11.

12.1. INTRODUCTION

One might think the statement "**torture** is illegal" is an uncontroversial and simple assertion with which everyone would agree. And yet, that statement is not so simple. While there is general agreement that torture is wrong and illegal, there is widespread disagreement regarding what actions constitute torture and whether there are any exceptions that justify torture.

Investigators use a wide range of techniques to extract information from suspects or persons believed to have information relevant to criminal or national security investigations. One end of the spectrum of these methods involves simple, voluntary questioning. At the other end lies torture. Along the spectrum are techniques that are increasingly coercive, and thus increasingly controversial, both regarding their legal and moral acceptability, and regarding their practical effectiveness. Determining when an investigative method is illegal is more complex than one might think, and that complexity is the subject of this chapter.

The extent of United States activities in interrogating terror suspects has been especially controversial since the 9/11 terror attacks. As will be discussed in the last section of this chapter, during the administration of President George W. Bush, agents of the United States attempted to extract information from terrorist suspects through a variety of means, including some so-called "**enhanced interrogation techniques**" **(EITs)** that many consider to be torture. Congress's response to these perceived abuses quelled some of the controversy, but it was reignited in 2015 when then-candidate, and later President, Donald Trump campaigned suggesting he favored authorizing some previously prohibited interrogation tactics. "Would I approve waterboarding? You bet your ass I'd approve it. In a heartbeat. And I would approve more than that. . . It works. Only a stupid person would say it doesn't work," he proclaimed.

Torture has sometimes been used simply to inflict pain for retribution or masochistic purposes. For example, many of the abuses uncovered during the disgraceful Abu Ghraib prison scandal, in which United States military personnel abused detainees at a prison in Iraq, were of this type: pain for pain's sake. The illegality of such behavior is unquestioned and is not the primary focus of this chapter. Rather, this chapter explores interrogation activities intended to produce information, and the limits on such practices imposed by international and domestic United States law, focusing on the practice of some interrogation techniques that may constitute torture.

12.2. INTERNATIONAL LAW

12.2.1. *Jus Cogens* Prohibition of Torture

The international ban on torture is widely considered to be ***jus cogens***—a universal international norm that cannot be set aside by a state's objection. (See Chapter 9 for more discussion of *jus cogens*.) United States federal courts have recognized the universality of the prohibition on torture in a variety of cases. For example, see *Nuru v. Gonzales* (9th Cir. 2005); *Siderman de Blake v. Republic of Argentina* (9th Cir. 1992); and *Filartiga v. Peña-Irala* (2d Cir. 1980). This elevation to *jus cogens* is the product of numerous international laws and a recognition that the domestic law of nearly every state in the world prohibits torture.

The most significant international law regarding torture is the Convention Against Torture, discussed in detail in the next section, but that **treaty** was preceded by other important international law norms. In 1948, the Universal Declaration on Human Rights (UDHR) was adopted by the United Nations. The UDHR declares that "no one shall be subjected to torture or to cruel, inhuman or degrading treatment or punishment." The UDHR has been invoked by nations since its adoption and is thought by many scholars to be part of binding **customary international law**, though courts in numerous countries have concluded it is non-self-executing and therefore "does not of its own force impose obligations as a matter of international law." *Sosa v. Alvarez-Machain*, United States Supreme Court.

The post-World War II Geneva Conventions also clearly banned torture in "Common Article 3," a provision that appears in all four Geneva Conventions, and applies "in the case of armed conflict not of an international character occurring in the territory of one of the [parties]." Parties to the Geneva Conventions are prohibited from engaging in "violence to life and person, in particular murder of all kinds, mutilation, cruel treatment and torture" and "outrages upon personal dignity, in particular humiliating and degrading treatment." Article 75 of Geneva Conventional Additional Protocol I also forbids "torture of all kinds, whether physical or mental" and "outrages upon personal dignity, in particular humiliating and degrading treatment. . . any form of indecent assault . . . and threats to commit any of the foregoing acts." Notably, the United States is not a party to Additional Protocol I, though the United States has formally acknowledged it is customary international law.

The UDHR's prohibition on torture was echoed in the International Covenant on Civil and Political Rights (ICCPR), adopted in 1966. The ICCPR prohibits torture and cruel, inhumane, and degrading treatment. Like the UDHR, the ICCPR has been deemed by numerous courts in the United States and around the world to be non-self-executing. However, because this treaty has ultimately been ratified by 172 parties, its provisions are evidence of customary international law banning torture.

Though the prohibition on torture is considered *jus cogens*, what conduct qualifies as "torture" is the subject of modern debate and disagreement. A prime example is whether the enhanced interrogation techniques used by the United States Central Intelligence Agency (CIA) and others after 9/11 constitute "torture," or something less. Also controversial is whether there are any exceptions to the prohibition on torture, for instance, when pressing a suspect to reveal information regarding a "ticking time bomb."

12.2.2. Convention Against Torture (CAT)

In 1984, the United Nations General Assembly unanimously adopted the most significant international law banning torture: the Convention Against Torture and Other Cruel, Inhuman or Degrading Treatment or Punishment ("Convention Against Torture" or "CAT"). As of this writing, 169 states are party to the Convention Against Torture, including the United States. The CAT is arguably the codification of the *jus cogens* customary international law norm against torture.

12.2.2.1. CAT Definition of Torture

Though the numerous international laws discussed in the previous section explicitly prohibit torture, there has been some significant concern that none *defined* torture. The Convention Against Torture attempted a definition:

> [A]ny act by which severe pain or suffering, whether physical or mental, is intentionally inflicted on a person for such purposes as obtaining from him or a third person information or a confession, punishing him for an act he or a third person has committed or is suspected of having committed, or intimidating or coercing him or a third person, or for any reason based on discrimination of any kind, when such pain or suffering is inflicted by or at the instigation of or with the consent or acquiescence of a public official or other person acting in an official capacity. It does not include pain or suffering arising only from, inherent in or incidental to lawful sanctions.

When the United States Senate gave its advice and consent of the Convention Against Torture for ratification, it did so with some "understandings" that narrowed the definition of torture somewhat regarding intentionally inflicting mental pain. Under United States criminal law, specific intent crimes differ from general intent crimes in that specific intent crimes require the offender to actually intend their actions and the harm they cause. Accordingly, the Senate declared that "in order to constitute torture, an act must be specifically intended to inflict severe physical or mental pain or suffering." In this case, the torturer must specifically intend severe physical or mental pain/suffering—it cannot be an accidental byproduct of a lesser intent. Moreover, the Senate stated the mental harm must be *prolonged*, an understanding of the prohibition of torture that would appear in the United States' implementing legislation, discussed later in this chapter.

12.2.2.2. CAT: Cruel, Inhuman, or Degrading Treatment

In addition to the CAT Article 5 requirement that states must prevent acts of torture, Article 16 of the CAT requires that states "undertake to prevent other acts of cruel, inhuman, or degrading treatment." However, unlike with the CAT's discussion of torture, the CAT does not define those terms and does not require states to criminalize cruel, inhuman, and degrading treatment, recognizing the significant international disagreement over what constitutes that type of treatment and whether it should be criminalized.

In fact, the United States' ratification of the CAT contained a reservation saying "the United States considers itself bound by the obligation under Article 16 to prevent 'cruel, inhuman, or degrading treatment or punishment,' only insofar as [that] means the cruel, unusual and inhumane treatment or punishment prohibited by the Fifth, Eighth, and/or Fourteenth Amendments to the Constitution of the United States." This reservation means that cruel, inhuman, or degrading punishment only includes government conduct that would rise to the level of violating the Constitution, as interpreted by the United States.

Additionally, there is disagreement regarding whether the CAT's ban on "cruel, inhuman, and degrading treatment" applies outside the territory of the party to the CAT. At one point, the United States suggested it did not accept that the CAT applied to United States government activities conducted outside of the jurisdictional territory of the United States. Then, in 2014, the Acting Legal Adviser to the State Dept clarified the United States position by formally stating to the Committee Against Torture (an organization created by the CAT):

> [W]here the text of the Convention provides that obligations apply to a State Party in 'any territory under its jurisdiction,' such obligations, including the obligations in Articles 2 and 16 to prevent torture and cruel, inhuman or degrading treatment or punishment, extend to certain areas beyond the sovereign territory of the State Party, and more specifically to all places that the State Party controls as a governmental authority.

She also stated that the detention facility at Guantanamo and United States-registered ships and aircraft are included in places the "United States controls" for the purpose of assessing **extraterritorial** application.

12.2.2.3. CAT Application to Armed Conflict Outside the United States

Another murky area regarding the CAT is whether it applies to military operations during an armed conflict. Generally, **international humanitarian law (IHL)**—also known as the **law of armed conflict (LOAC)**—applies to armed conflict. What is less clear is whether during an armed conflict **international human rights law (HRL)** also applies to military activities. Specifically, must detention and interrogation operations that take place in the context of an armed conflict also comply with human rights law? Torture is prohibited both by the CAT and under IHL, so this is not a question of whether the military is permitted to engage in torture, but rather, which body of law, including that law's procedural rights and reporting requirements, applies. At one point during the administration of President George W. Bush, the United States formally announced the position that military operations are governed only by international humanitarian law, while many other states argued that military operations are governed by both IHL and HRL. Eventually, during the same 2014 report to the Committee Against Torture discussed in the previous section, the United States agreed that the prohibitions of torture and cruel, inhuman, or degrading treatment or punishment "remain applicable in times of armed conflict and are reinforced by complementary prohibitions in the law of armed conflict."

12.3. DOMESTIC LAW

12.3.1. Constitutional Limits

Though the United States reservation to the CAT limited the definition of what constitutes "cruel, inhuman, or degrading" treatment to whatever would violate the Fifth, Eighth, or Fourteenth Amendment, the extent of those constitutional protections is uncertain. And there is little case law regarding coercive interrogation methods outside of traditional criminal investigations to guide government actors in their understanding of what the Constitution prohibits.

12.3.1.1. Fifth Amendment

Under Supreme Court precedent, the Fifth Amendment prohibits coerced self-incrimination in the context of a criminal case. In *Miranda v. Arizona*, the Supreme Court held the Fifth Amendment requires that all **custodial interrogation**s must be preceded by a rights advisement, unless an exception applies. But the Supreme Court has only held that this procedural protection is violated if an unwarned statement is *introduced at trial.* That is, the due process violation occurs when the statement is admitted, not necessarily when the statement is coerced. *Chavez v. Martinez.*

Surprisingly less clear is whether the Fifth Amendment prohibits coercion when compulsive questioning occurs *without* subsequent use of the confession in a criminal case. Under a theory of constitutional rights known as substantive due process, the Due Process Clauses of the Fifth and Fourteenth Amendments have been interpreted as providing protection against some infringements on certain fundamental rights by the government. These include the "fundamental right" to marry, to use contraception, and to procreation. In *Chavez v. Martinez* in 2003, the Supreme Court considered whether coercive questioning outside of compelling self-incrimination in a criminal case violates a due process right. A majority the Justices could not agree whether obtaining an involuntary confession through "compulsive questioning" constituted its own violation of the Fifth Amendment. The Justices' complex web of opinions suggested that if investigatory behavior "shocks the conscience," it violates the substantive component of the Due Process Clause. This leaves the Fifth Amendment analysis of coercive behavior murky, relying on assessment of whether a particular interrogation method "shocks the conscience."

12.3.1.2. Quarles *and the Public Safety Exception*

A key exception to the *Miranda* requirement that law enforcement must provide a rights advisement prior to engaging in custodial interrogations is the "public safety exception," first announced by the Supreme Court in *New York v. Quarles*. Under the public safety exception, a *Miranda* rights advisement need not precede a custodial interrogation when law enforcement personnel "ask questions reasonably prompted by a concern for the public safety." The classic example of this is a police officer asking a suspect "what's the deactivation code for the ticking bomb?" However, although *Quarles* created a public safety exception to the rights advisement requirement, it did not create an exception to the general prohibition of law enforcement coercing confessions.

12.3.1.3. Eighth Amendment

The Eighth Amendment to the United States Constitution prohibits "cruel and unusual punishment." It is the last word of that phrase—punishment—that makes the Eighth Amendment largely irrelevant to coercive interrogation techniques. This is because in *Ingraham v. Wright*, the United States Supreme Court held that the Eighth Amendment applies only to punishment that follows a conviction: "The State does not acquire the power to punish with which the Eighth Amendment is concerned until after it has secured a formal adjudication of guilty in accordance with due process of law." This means that poor treatment of detainees prior to trial cannot, by definition, be "cruel and unusual *punishment*." This seems to make little sense, given the **Framers'** hatred of torture as an instrument of government tyranny. However, the Eighth Amendment remedy has been provided by courts only in post-conviction punishment settings that are largely inapplicable to terrorism-related interrogations.

12.3.1.4. Extraterritorial Application of Constitutional Rights

As discussed in greater detail in Chapter 9, the extraterritorial application of constitutional protections is unclear. The Supreme Court has not established a consistent, formal test for determining which elements of the Bill of Rights apply to interrogations of non-United States persons that take place outside the United States. However, suggesting an answer, the second most influential national security court—the Court of Appeals for the D.C. Circuit—has held that the Fifth Amendment does not apply to claims of torture of aliens by United States government agents that occurs outside the United States. *Christopher v. Harbury*, reversed by the Supreme Court on other grounds. In that case, the plaintiff alleged her alien husband was tortured on behalf of the CIA in Guatemala. The D.C. Circuit, citing Supreme Court cases like *Johnson v. Eisentrager* and *Verdugo-Urquidez*, which were not about harsh interrogation practices, held the Fifth Amendment does not apply to interrogations outside the United States

12.3.2. Statutes

In contrast to the relative lack of clarity regarding constitutional limitations on interrogation practices, several United States federal statutes impose fairly clear restrictions on government interrogators' actions.

12.3.2.1. Anti-Torture Act

Article 2 of the CAT requires each party to "take effective legislative, administrative, judicial or other measures to prevent acts of torture in any territory under its **jurisdiction**," meaning the treaty is non-self-executing. In 1994, Congress enacted the Anti-Torture Act, also known as The Torture Act, to implement the CAT. Under the Torture Act, torture is defined as "an act committed by a person acting under the color of law specifically intended to inflict severe physical or mental pain or suffering (other than pain or suffering incidental to lawful sanctions) upon another person within his custody or physical control." Severe "mental pain or suffering" is defined as:

> (1) the intentional infliction or threatened infliction of severe physical pain or suffering;
>
> (2) the administration or application, or threatened administration or application of mind altering substances or other procedures calculated to disrupt profoundly the senses or the personality;
>
> (3) the threat of imminent death; or
>
> (4) the threat that another person will imminently be subjected to death, severe physical pain or suffering, or the administration or application of mind altering substances or other procedures calculated to disrupt profoundly the senses or personality.

Thus, the Torture Act generally follows the CAT, including the United States' ratification reservations and understandings adding a specific intent element and adding the "prolonged mental harm" requirement for a victim's mental pain or suffering to be considered torture. Importantly, the Torture Act only prohibits torture committed *outside* the United States, and exerts jurisdiction over offenders who are United States nationals and non-United States nationals who happen to be in the United States.

12.3.2.2. War Crimes Act

Enacted in 1996, the War Crimes Act (WCA) criminalizes war crimes committed inside or outside the United States when "the person committing such war crime or the victim of such war crime is a member of the Armed Forces of the United States or a national of the United States. "War crime" was originally defined as any violation of the Geneva Conventions. However, as part of the Military Commissions Act of 2006, the WCA was amended to criminalize only conduct defined as "grave breaches" of the Geneva Conventions, including grave breaches of Common Article 3. While generally easy to apply, whether the fight against terrorist organizations rises to the level of an armed conflict such that Common Article 3 applies has not always been clear. In *Hamdan v. Rumsfeld*, the Supreme Court opined that Common Article 3 applies to the conflict against Al Qaeda in the context of Hamdan's right to trial by a "regularly constituted court," leading many to believe all of Common Article 3, including its prohibition of "cruel treatment and torture" and "outrages upon personal dignity, in particular humiliating and degrading treatment," applies to the conflict with Al Qaeda, thus implicating the War Crimes Act. Whether counterterrorism operations against other, less well-organized, terror organizations would also be considered an "armed conflict not of international character" such that Common Article 3 applies is an unresolved question.

12.3.2.3. Detainee Treatment Act

Perhaps the most significant legislation after 9/11 involving the interrogation of terror suspects was the Detainee Treatment Act of 2005 (DTA). The DTA was enacted as a response to perceived interrogation abuses by the United States. As the Abu Ghraib scandal and interrogation practices at Guantanamo Bay and elsewhere became public, Senator John McCain, himself a survivor of torture by the North Vietnamese during the Vietnam conflict, led the legislative charge to reign in the United States' interrogation practices.

The DTA's language focuses on potential victims, rather than their abusers: "No individual in the custody or under the physical control of the United States Government, regardless of nationality or physical location, shall be subject to cruel, inhuman, or degrading treatment." Notably, there are no criminal sanctions for violations of the DTA.

The DTA does not separately define torture and it uses the same definition of cruel, inhuman, or degrading treatment as in the Anti-Torture Act, referencing the Constitution and reflecting the United States understandings and reservations to the CAT: "The term 'cruel, inhuman, or degrading treatment or punishment' means the cruel, unusual, and inhumane treatment or punishment prohibited by the Fifth, Eighth, and Fourteenth Amendments to the Constitution of the US, as defined in the United States Reservations, Declarations, and Understandings to the UN Convention Against Torture."

The DTA requires military interrogations to be performed according to the United States Army Field Manual for Human Intelligence Collector Operations (**Army Field Manual**). The Army Field Manual contains specific guidance regarding what an interrogator may and may not do, suggesting that the DTA is practically more helpful than broad definitions of torture in other statutes. Of course, such specificity is also helpful to those preparing to resist interrogations by the United States Also, by referencing the Army Field Manual, Congress placed in the Executive Branch's hands the ability to specify how detainees may be interrogated.

12.3.2.4. Military Commissions Act of 2006

In addition to creating **military tribunals** and unsuccessfully attempting to eliminate **habeas corpus** rights for terrorist suspects, the Military Commission Act of 2006 modified the War Crimes Act to criminalize only "grave breaches" of Common Article 3, rather than all violations of Common Article 3, as had previously been the case. Such "grave breaches" include only the following: "torture; cruel or inhuman treatment; performing biological experiments; murder, mutilating or maiming; intentionally causing serious bodily injury; rape; sexual assault or abuse; and hostage-taking." Not included in this list of criminalized acts are "[o]utrages upon personal dignity, in particular, humiliating and degrading treatment" and "[t]he passing of sentences and the carrying out of executions without previous judgment pronounced by a regularly constituted court affording all the judicial guarantees which are recognized as indispensable by civilized peoples."

Under the MCA of 2006, "torture" is defined as "an act specifically intended to inflict severe physical or mental pain or suffering." "Cruel or inhuman treatment" is defined as "an act intended to inflict severe or serious physical or mental pain or suffering." "Severe physical pain or suffering" means "bodily injury that involves (i) a substantial risk of death; (ii) extreme physical pain; iii) a burn or physical disfigurement of a serious nature (other than cuts, abrasions, or bruises); or (iv) significant loss or impairment of the function of a bodily member, organ, or mental faculty." These definitions are sufficiently limited that they do not criminalize the enhanced interrogation techniques that had become known to the public and precipitated the DTA of 2005. The MCA of 2006 states that "The definitions in this subsection are intended only to define the grave breaches of common Article 3 and not the full scope of United States obligations under that Article." Thus, Congress acknowledged the United States' responsibility to comply with all the prohibitions contained in Common Article 3, even though Congress did not regard itself as obliged to hold individuals *criminally accountable* for violating the prohibitions.

12.3.2.5. Uniform Code of Military Justice

The Uniform Code of Military Justice (UCMJ) is another federal statute that restricts interrogative techniques, though its application is somewhat narrower than other statutes, because the UCMJ governs only military members and persons "accompanying the force" in military operations. The UCMJ gives courts-martial jurisdiction over offenses against the laws of war, thus incorporating those bodies of law. Additionally, the UCMJ prohibits cruelty or maltreatment toward any person subject to one's orders and "disorders and neglects" to the prejudice of good order and discipline.

As was demonstrated in the aftermath of the abuses of detainees by United States servicemembers at Abu Ghraib, the UCMJ's broader and more malleable crimes such as "maltreatment" or "disorder" impose a different legal standard on servicemembers than on other government actors, such as CIA officers. The "**torture memos**" (see Section 12.4.2.2 below) that permitted CIA officers to use enhanced interrogation techniques did not exculpate servicemembers from maltreatment, even though CIA officers had introduced harsh tactics at military prisons like Guantanamo.

12.4. COERCIVE INTERROGATIONS BY THE UNITED STATES AFTER 9/11

Though torture seems clearly prohibited by both international and domestic law, what is less clear is what specific acts "torture" includes. This murkiness is highlighted by the debate over "enhanced interrogation techniques" used by the CIA during its interrogation program following the 9/11 terror attacks in 2001.

12.4.1. The CIA Interrogation Program

In the aftermath of the horrific 9/11 terrorist attacks, the United States government engaged in a broad range of activities to attempt to prevent a similar attack from occurring again. These activities included massive military force in Afghanistan, Iraq, and elsewhere, and interrogations of persons suspected of terrorism. Encouraged by political leaders to do whatever it could to prevent another attack, the CIA embarked on an ambitious intelligence gathering effort that included, in the words of the Senate Committee that later investigated the matter, "a program of indefinite secret detention and the use of brutal interrogation techniques in violation of United States law, treaty obligations, and our values." See *Report of the Senate Select Committee on Intelligence Committee Study of the Central Intelligence Agency's Detention and Interrogation Program* (Senate Report).

Determining whether interrogation techniques violate domestic or international law requires a factual understanding of what specific interrogation techniques involve. An internal CIA Inspector General investigation produced in 2004 identified ten enhanced interrogation techniques described by the CIA and for which the CIA obtained approval from the Department of Justice:

1. The **attention grasp** consists of grasping the detainee with both hands, with one hand on each side of the collar opening, in a controlled and quick motion. In the same motion as the grasp, the detainee is drawn toward the interrogator.

2. During the **walling technique**, the detainee is pulled forward and then quickly and firmly pushed into a flexible false wall so that his shoulder blades hit the wall. His head and neck are supported with a rolled towel to prevent whiplash.

3. The **facial hold** is used to hold the detainee's head immobile. The interrogator places an open palm on either side of the detainee's face and the Interrogator's fingertips are kept well away from the detainee's eyes.

4. With the **facial or insult slap**, the fingers are slightly spread apart. The interrogator's hand makes contact with the area between the tip of the detainee's chin and the bottom of the corresponding earlobe.

5. In **cramped confinement**, the detainee is placed in a confined space, typically a small or large box, which is usually dark. Confinement in the smaller space lasts no more than two hours and in the larger space it can last up to 18 hours.

6. **Insects** placed in a confinement box involve placing a harmless insect in the box with the detainee.

7. During **wall standing**, the detainee may stand about 4 to 5 feet from a wall with his feet spread approximately to his shoulder width. His arms are stretched out in front of him and his fingers rest on the wall to support all of his body weight. The detainee is not allowed to reposition his hands or feet.

8. The application of **stress positions** may include having the detainee sit on tile floor with his legs extended straight out in front of him with his anus raised above his head or kneeling on the floor while leaning back at a 45 degree angle.

9. **Sleep deprivation** will not exceed 11 days at a time.

10. The application of the **waterboard technique** involves binding the detainee to a bench with his feet elevated above his head. The detainee's head is immobilized and an interrogator places a cloth over the detainee's mouth and nose while pouring water onto the cloth in a controlled manner. Airflow is restricted for 20 to 40 seconds and the technique produces the sensation of drowning and suffocation.

According to the Senate Report, a few additional techniques were used by CIA operatives during interrogations of terrorist suspects after 9/11, including:

1. The **abdominal slap**, in which the interrogator slapped the detainee's abdomen with the back of his hand. The purpose was to cause the detainee to feel fear and despair, to punish certain behavior and humiliate or insult the detainee, according to a description in government documents, obtained by the American Civil Liberties Union in 2009.

2. **Dietary manipulation** involved switching a detainee's diet back and forth from solid foods to liquid.

3. **Finger press** (no further information)

4. **Nudity** (self explanatory)

5. **Water dousing** involved stripping a detainee naked, shackling him in the standing position for up to 72 hours, and dousing the detainee repeatedly with cold water.

6. **Sensory dislocation** included shaving detainee's head, exposing him to loud noise in a white room with white lights, keeping him "unclothed and subjected to uncomfortably cool temperatures," and shackling him "hand and foot with arms outstretched over his head, with his feet firmly on the floor and not allowed to support his weight with his arms.

7. **Light deprivation**, which apparently involved extended periods of time during which the detainee was kept in total darkness.

12.4.2. Legal Support for Harsh Interrogation

As noted above, the CIA sought legal approval for various enhanced interrogation techniques. Indeed, lawyers were intimately involved in the CIA's interrogation program, issuing numerous legal opinions regarding the legality of interrogation methods. In what were originally referred to as the "Torture Memos" (the term has been applied to more documents since), attorneys from the Office of Legal Counsel (OLC) at the United States Department of Justice authored three memoranda dated August 1, 2002, outlining their opinions regarding the legality of various interrogation techniques to be used on Al Qaeda operatives.

Torture Memo #1. Purportedly in response to President George W. Bush's request for a legal opinion regarding the CAT and the Torture Act, Jay Bybee, then an Assistant United States Attorney General and chief of the Office of Legal Counsel, addressed a memorandum to Counsel to the President Alberto Gonzalez titled "Standards for Conduct for Interrogation under 18 U.S.C. §§ 2340–2340A." In it, Mr. Bybee concludes that prohibited torture only includes extreme acts under the Convention Against Torture: "serious physical injury, such as organ failure, impairment of bodily function, or even death" are required to meet the CAT's requirement of "severe pain," and prohibited prolonged mental harm is harm that must last for "months or even years." In addition, Mr. Bybee concluded that "cruel, inhuman, or degrading" treatment is not torture according to the torture statute, and thus the Torture Act did not criminalize such actions. Finally, Mr. Bybee asserted that "prosecution under Section 2340A may be barred because enforcement of the statute would represent an unconstitutional infringement of the President's authority to conduct war," and that "under the current circumstances, **necessity** or self-defense may justify interrogation methods that might violate Section 2340A." Accordingly, Mr. Bybee concluded the CIA's proposed EITs did not violate the CAT or Torture Act.

Torture Memo #2. On the same date as the memorandum to Mr. Gonzalez, Mr. Bybee also addressed a memorandum to the acting General Counsel of the CIA, John Rizzo, applying the Torture Act to the specific interrogation of suspect Abu Zubaydah. The memorandum described in detail the proposed techniques, including attention grasp, walling, facial hold, insult slap, cramped confinement (large and small and with and without an insect), wall standing, stress positions, sleep deprivation, and waterboarding. Mr. Bybee concluded that none of the techniques constituted torture.

Torture Memo #3. John Yoo, then Deputy Assistant Attorney General in the Office of Legal Counsel, wrote a separate memorandum to Mr. Gonzalez, supplementing Mr. Bybee's memorandum. Mr. Yoo addressed Mr. Gonzalez' concerns about whether interrogation methods used on Al Qaeda suspects would violate the Convention Against Torture and whether such actions could be the basis of prosecution in the International Criminal Court. Mr. Yoo concluded that the interrogation techniques would not violate the Convention Against Torture because of the United States reservations when ratifying the CAT. Specifically, the

United States' differing understanding of what constitutes "severe pain or suffering," how prolonged mental harm must be to constitute "severe mental pain or suffering," and the United States' requirement of "specific intent" to torture meant the CIA's enhanced interrogation techniques would not violate the CAT *as ratified by the United States*. Mr. Yoo also opined that neither members of Al Qaeda nor the Taliban were prisoners of war under the Geneva Conventions, and thus the enhanced interrogation techniques would not violate the Geneva Conventions. This interpretation was disputed by lawyers at the State Department and by President Bush's Secretary of State, Colin Powell.

Though not one of the three original torture memos, Mr. Yoo later wrote another memorandum to the General Counsel of the Department of Defense addressing the extraterritorial jurisdiction of the Torture Act. In his March 14, 2003, memorandum, Mr. Yoo concluded that "federal laws against torture, assault and maiming would not apply to the overseas interrogation of terror suspects." In 2008, Senate investigations would find that this memorandum was used by the DOD to "justify harsh interrogation practices on terror suspects at Guantánamo Bay" and Abu Ghraib.

In 2004, new OLC chief Jack Goldsmith withdrew the torture memos, concluding they were legally incorrect. Believing that his withdrawal of the memos caused some in the Bush Administration to no longer trust his legal advice, Mr. Goldsmith resigned shortly after withdrawing the memos. In a series of memoranda issued and withdrawn over the subsequent years, the OLC's legal advice regarding what constituted torture expanded and contracted. Just before the end of President George W. Bush's second term, OLC chief Steven Bradbury repudiated all OLC opinions on the subject of interrogation and executive power issued between 2001 and 2003 and opined that those opinions "should not be treated as authoritative for any purpose." Two days after taking office in January 2009, President Barack Obama issued an **Executive Order** rescinding all previous OLC opinions regarding "detention or the interrogation of detained individuals."

While some have argued that lawyers who wrote legal opinions authorizing EITs should themselves—along with the interrogators—face criminal prosecution, in April 2009, President Obama publicly announced his administration would not prosecute the authors of the memoranda or the CIA and DOD personnel who implemented enhanced interrogation techniques believing they were legal. Less than one year after issuing his two torture memos, Mr. Bybee was appointed by President George W. Bush to a lifetime federal judgeship on the Ninth Circuit Court of Appeals. After Mr. Yoo left government, he became a tenured professor at the University of California Berkeley Law School.

12.4.3. Senate Select Committee Investigation

Over several years, the abuses at Abu Ghraib prison and details regarding the CIA's interrogation program and techniques led to public outcry and, ultimately, a massive investigation of the CIA program by the Senate Select Committee on Intelligence. The vast Senate Report, an abridged and redacted portion of which was released publicly, included 20 findings regarding the CIA's coercive interrogation program. Here are the verbatim findings, along with selected summary explanations the Committee offered in the publicly released portion of the report:

> **1. The CIA's use of its enhanced interrogation techniques was not an effective means of acquiring intelligence or gaining cooperation from detainees.**
>
> The Committee finds, based on a review of CIA interrogation records, that the use of the CIA's enhanced interrogation techniques was not an effective means of obtaining accurate information or gaining detainee cooperation. For example, according to CIA records, seven of the 39 CIA detainees known to have been subjected to the CIA's enhanced interrogation techniques produced no intelligence while in CIA custody. CIA detainees who were subjected to the CIA's enhanced interrogation techniques were usually subjected to the techniques immediately after being rendered to CIA custody.
>
> Other detainees provided significant accurate intelligence prior to, or without having been subjected to these techniques.
>
> While being subjected to the CIA's enhanced interrogation techniques and afterwards, multiple CIA detainees fabricated information, resulting in faulty intelligence. Detainees provided fabricated information on critical intelligence issues, including the terrorist threats which the CIA identified as its highest priorities.
>
> **2. The CIA's justification for the use of its enhanced interrogation techniques rested on inaccurate claims of their effectiveness.**

3. The interrogations of CIA detainees were brutal and far worse than the CIA represented to policymakers and others.

Beginning with the CIA's first detainee, Abu Zubaydah, and continuing with numerous others, the CIA applied its enhanced interrogation techniques with significant repetition for days or weeks at a time. Interrogation techniques such as slaps and "wallings" (slamming detainees against a wall) were used in combination, frequently concurrent with sleep deprivation and nudity. Records do not support CIA representations that the CIA initially used an "an open, nonthreatening approach," or that interrogations began with the "least coercive technique possible" and escalated to more coercive techniques only as necessary. The waterboarding technique was physically harmful, inducing convulsions and vomiting. Abu Zubaydah, for example, became "completely unresponsive, with bubbles rising through his open, full mouth." Internal CIA records describe the waterboarding of Khalid Shaykh Mohammad as evolving into a "series of near drownings." Sleep deprivation involved keeping detainees awake for up to 180 hours, usually standing or in stress positions, at times with their hands shackled above their heads. At least five detainees experienced disturbing hallucinations during prolonged sleep deprivation and, in at least two of those cases, the CIA nonetheless continued the sleep deprivation. Contrary to CIA representations to the Department of Justice, the CIA instructed personnel that the interrogation of Abu Zubaydah would take "precedence" over his medical care, resulting in the deterioration of a bullet wound Abu Zubaydah incurred during his capture. In at least two other cases, the CIA used its enhanced interrogation techniques despite warnings from CIA medical personnel that the techniques could exacerbate physical injuries. CIA medical personnel treated at least one detainee for swelling in order to allow the continued use of standing sleep deprivation.

At least five CIA detainees were subjected to "rectal rehydration" or rectal feeding without documented medical necessity. The CIA placed detainees in ice water "baths." The CIA led several detainees to believe they would never be allowed to leave CIA custody alive, suggesting to one detainee that he would only leave in a coffin-shaped box. One interrogator told another detainee that he would never go to court, because "we can never let the world know what I have done to you." CIA officers also threatened at least three detainees with harm to their families—to include threats to harm the children of a detainee, threats to sexually abuse the mother of a detainee, and a threat to "cut [a detainee's] mother's throat."

4. The conditions of confinement for CIA detainees were harsher than the CIA had represented to policymakers and others.

5. The CIA repeatedly provided inaccurate information to the Department of Justice (DOJ), impeding a proper legal analysis of the CIA's Detention and Interrogation Program.

From 2002 to 2007, the Office of Legal Counsel (OLC) within the Department of Justice relied on CIA representations regarding: (1) the conditions of confinement for detainees, (2) the application of the CIA's enhanced interrogation techniques, (3) the physical effects of the techniques on detainees, and (4) the effectiveness of the techniques. Those representations were inaccurate in material respects.

The Department of Justice did not conduct independent analysis or verification of the information it received from the CIA. The department warned, however, that if the facts provided by the CIA were to change, its legal conclusions might not apply. When the CIA determined that information it had provided to the Department of Justice was incorrect, the CIA rarely informed the department.

Prior to the initiation of the CIA's Detention and Interrogation Program and throughout the life of the program, the legal justifications for the CIA's enhanced interrogation techniques relied on the CIA's claim that the techniques were necessary to save lives. In late 2001 and early 2002, senior attorneys at the CIA Office of General Counsel first examined the legal implications of using coercive interrogation techniques. CIA attorneys stated that "a novel application of the necessity defense" could be used "to avoid prosecution of United States officials who tortured to obtain information that saved many lives."

Having reviewed information provided by the CIA, the OLC included the "necessity defense" in its August 1, 2002, memorandum to the White House counsel on Standards of Conduct for Interrogation. The OLC determined that "under the current circumstances, necessity or self defense may justify interrogation methods that might violate" the criminal prohibition against torture.

On the same day, a second OLC opinion approved, for the first time, the use of 10 specific coercive interrogation techniques against Abu

Zubaydah—subsequently referred to as the CIA's "enhanced interrogation techniques." The OLC relied on inaccurate CIA representations about Abu Zubaydah's status in al-Qa'ida and the interrogation team's "certainty" that Abu Zubaydah was withholding information about planned terrorist attacks. The CIA's representations to the OLC about the techniques were also inconsistent with how the techniques would later be applied.

In March 2005, the CIA submitted to the Department of Justice various examples of the "effectiveness" of the CIA's enhanced interrogation techniques that were inaccurate. OLC memoranda signed on May 30, 2005, and July 20, 2007, relied on these representations, determining that the techniques were legal in part because they produced "specific, actionable intelligence" and "substantial quantities of otherwise unavailable intelligence" that saved lives.

6. The CIA has actively avoided or impeded congressional oversight of the program.

7. The CIA impeded effective White House oversight and decision-making.

8. The CIA's operation and management of the program complicated, and in some cases impeded, the national security missions of other Executive Branch agencies.

9. The CIA impeded oversight by the CIA's Office of Inspector General.

10. The CIA coordinated the release of classified information to the media, including inaccurate information concerning the effectiveness of the CIA's enhanced interrogation techniques.

11. The CIA was unprepared as it began operating its Detention and Interrogation Program more than six months after being granted detention authorities.

On September 17, 2001, the President signed a covert action Memorandum of Notification (MON) granting the CIA unprecedented counterterrorism authorities, including the authority to covertly capture and detain individuals "posing a continuing, serious threat of violence or death to United States persons and interests or planning terrorist activities." The MON made no reference to interrogations or coercive interrogation techniques. The CIA was not prepared to take custody of its first detainee. In the fall of 2001, the CIA explored the possibility of establishing clandestine detention facilities in several countries. The CIA's review identified risks associated with clandestine detention that led it to conclude that United States military bases were the best option for the CIA to detain individuals under the MON authorities. In late March 2002, the imminent capture of Abu Zubaydah prompted the CIA to again consider various detention options. In part to avoid declaring Abu Zubaydah to the International Committee of the Red Cross, which would be required if he were detained at a United States military base, the CIA decided to seek authorization to clandestinely detain Abu Zubaydah at a facility in Country [Redacted]—a country that had not previously been considered as a potential host for a CIA detention site. A senior CIA officer indicated that the CIA "will have to acknowledge certain gaps in our planning/preparations," but stated that this plan would be presented to the president. At a **Presidential Daily Briefing** session that day, the president approved CIA's proposal to detain Abu Zubaydah in Country [Redacted].

The CIA lacked a plan for the eventual disposition of its detainees. After taking custody of Abu Zubaydah, CIA officers concluded that he "should remain incommunicado for the remainder of his life," which "may preclude [Abu Zubaydah] from being turned over to another country."

The CIA did not review its past experience with coercive interrogations, or its previous statement to Congress that "inhumane physical or psychological techniques are counterproductive because they do not produce intelligence and will probably result in false answers." The CIA also did not contact other elements of the United States Government with interrogation expertise. In July 2002, on the basis of consultations with contract psychologists, and with very limited internal deliberation, the CIA requested approval from the Department of Justice to use a set of coercive interrogation techniques. The techniques were adapted from the training of United States military personnel at the United States Air Force Survival, Evasion, Resistance and Escape (SERE) school, which was designed to prepare United States military personnel for the conditions and treatment to which they might be subjected if taken prisoner by countries that do not adhere to the Geneva Conventions.

As it began detention and interrogation operations, the CIA deployed personnel who lacked relevant training and experience. The CIA began interrogation training more than seven months after taking custody of Abu Zubaydah, and more than three months after the CIA began using its "enhanced interrogation techniques." CIA Director George Tenet issued formal guidelines for interrogations and conditions of confinement at detention sites in January 2003, by which time 40 of the 119 known detainees had been detained by the CIA.

12. The CIA's management and operation of its Detention and Interrogation Program was deeply flawed throughout the program's duration, particularly so in 2002 and early 2003.

13. Two contract psychologists devised the CIA's enhanced interrogation techniques and played a central role in the operation, assessments, and management of the CIA's Detention and Interrogation Program. By 2005, the CIA had overwhelmingly outsourced operations related to the program.

The CIA contracted with two psychologists to develop, operate, and assess its interrogation operations. The psychologists' prior experience was at the United States Air Force Survival, Evasion, Resistance and Escape (SERE) school. Neither psychologist had any experience as an interrogator, nor did either have specialized knowledge of al-Qa'ida, a background in counterterrorism, or any relevant cultural or linguistic expertise. On the CIA's behalf, the contract psychologists developed theories of interrogation based on "learned helplessness," and developed the list of enhanced interrogation techniques that was approved for use against Abu Zubaydah and subsequent CIA detainees. The psychologists personally conducted interrogations of some of the CIA's most significant detainees using these techniques. They also evaluated whether detainees' psychological state allowed for the continued use of the CIA's enhanced interrogation techniques, including some detainees whom they were themselves interrogating or had interrogated. The psychologists carried out inherently governmental functions, such as acting as liaison between the CIA and **foreign intelligence** services, assessing the effectiveness of the interrogation program, and participating in the interrogation of detainees in held in foreign government custody.

. . .

14. CIA detainees were subjected to coercive interrogation techniques that had not been approved by the Department of Justice or had not been authorized by CIA Headquarters.

Prior to mid-2004, the CIA routinely subjected detainees to nudity and dietary manipulation. The CIA also used abdominal slaps and cold water dousing on several detainees during that period. None of these techniques had been approved by the Department of Justice. At least 17 detainees were subjected to CIA enhanced interrogation techniques without authorization from CIA Headquarters. Additionally, multiple detainees were subjected to techniques that were applied in ways that diverged from the specific authorization, or were subjected to enhanced interrogation techniques by interrogators who had not been authorized to use them. Although these incidents were recorded in CIA cables and, in at least some cases were identified at the time by supervisors at CIA Headquarters as being inappropriate, corrective action was rarely taken against the interrogators involved.

15. The CIA did not conduct a comprehensive or accurate accounting of the number of individuals it detained, and held individuals who did not meet the legal standard for detention. The CIA's claims about the number of detainees held and subjected to its enhanced interrogation techniques were inaccurate.

16. The CIA failed to adequately evaluate the effectiveness of its enhanced interrogation techniques.

17. The CIA rarely reprimanded or held personnel accountable for serious or significant violations, inappropriate activities, and systematic and individual management failures.

18. The CIA marginalized and ignored numerous internal critiques, criticisms, and objections concerning the operation and management of the CIA's Detention and Interrogation Program.

19. The CIA's Detention and Interrogation Program was inherently unsustainable and had effectively ended by 2006 due to unauthorized press disclosures, reduced cooperation from other nations, and legal and oversight concerns.

The CIA required secrecy and cooperation from other nations in order to operate clandestine detention facilities, and both had eroded significantly before President Bush publicly disclosed the program on September 6, 2006. From the beginning of the program, the CIA faced significant challenges in finding nations willing to host CIA clandestine detention sites. These challenges became increasingly difficult over time. With the exception of Country [X] the CIA was forced to relocate detainees out of every country in which it established a detention facility because of pressure from the host government or public revelations about the program.

Beginning in early 2005, the CIA sought unsuccessfully to convince the United States Department of Defense to allow the transfer of numerous CIA detainees to United States military custody. By 2006, the CIA admitted in its own talking points for CIA Director Porter Goss that, absent an Administration decision on an "endgame" for detainees, the CIA was "stymied" and "the program could collapse of its own weight."

Lack of access to adequate medical care for detainees in countries hosting the CIA's detention facilities caused recurring problems. The refusal of one host country to admit a severely ill detainee into a local hospital due to security concerns contributed to the closing of the CIA's detention facility in that country. The United States Department of Defense also declined to provide medical care to detainees upon CIA request.

In mid-2003, a statement by the President for the United Nations International Day in Support of Victims of Torture and a public statement by the White House that prisoners in United States custody are treated "humanely" caused the CIA to question whether there was continued policy support for the program and seek reauthorization from the White House. In mid-2004, the CIA temporarily suspended the use of its enhanced interrogation techniques after the CIA inspector general recommended that the CIA seek an updated legal opinion from the Office of Legal Counsel. In early 2004, the United States Supreme Court decision to grant certiorari in the case of Rasul v. Bush prompted the CIA to move detainees out of a CIA detention facility at Guantanamo Bay, Cuba.

In late 2005 and in 2006, the Detainee Treatment Act and then the United States Supreme Court decision in Hamdan v. Rumsfeld caused the CIA to again temporarily suspend the use of its enhanced interrogation techniques.

> By 2006, press disclosures, the unwillingness of other countries to host existing or new detention sites, and legal and oversight concerns had largely ended the CIA's ability to operate clandestine detention facilities.
>
> After detaining at least 113 individuals through 2004, the CIA brought only six additional detainees into its custody: four in 2005, one in 2006, and one in 2007. By March 2006, the program was operating in only one country. The CIA last used its enhanced interrogation techniques on November 8, 2007. The CIA did not hold any detainees after April 2008.
>
> **20. The CIA's Detention and Interrogation Program damaged the United States' standing in the world, and resulted in other significant monetary and non-monetary costs.**

12.4.4. Modern Approved Interrogation Techniques

As noted above, the DTA of 2005 limits interrogators of persons in United States custody to employing only those interrogation techniques listed in the Army Field Manual for Human Intelligence Collector Operations, FM 2-22.3 (Army Field Manual). As of this writing, here are the techniques approved by the Army Field Manual. Brief descriptions of the interrogation techniques are provided here, but more detail regarding how these techniques are used is included in the Army Field Manual.

> **Direct approach.** Almost all [Human Intelligence (HUMINT)] collection begins with the direct approach. The exception to this is during elicitation operations that by their very nature are indirect. In using the direct approach, the HUMINT collector asks direct questions. The initial questions may be administrative or nonpertinent but the HUMINT collector quickly begins asking pertinent questions. The HUMINT collector will continue to use direct questions as long as the source is answering the questions in a truthful manner. When the source refuses to answer, avoids answering, or falsely answers a pertinent question, the HUMINT collector will begin an alternate approach strategy. The fact that the source is answering questions does not preclude the HUMINT collector from providing an incentive to reward the source and continue his cooperation as long as that incentive does not slow down the collection. For example, a HUMINT collector might offer the source coffee or cigarettes to reward his cooperation.
>
> **Incentive approach.** The incentive approach is trading something that the source wants for information. The thing that you give up may be a

material reward, an emotional reward, or the removal of a real or perceived negative stimulus. The exchange of the incentive may be blatant or subtle. On one extreme, the exchange may be a formal cash payment for information during some contact operations while on the other extreme it may be as subtle as offering the source a cigarette. Even when the direct approach is successful, the HUMINT collector may use incentives to enhance rapport and to reward the source for cooperation and truthfulness. The HUMINT collector must be extremely careful in selecting the options offered to a detainee source. He cannot deny the detainee anything that he is entitled to by law.

Emotional approaches. Emotional approaches are centered on how the source views himself and his interrelationships with others. Through source observation and initial questioning, the HUMINT collector can often identify dominant emotions that motivate the [detainee]. The motivating emotion may be greed, love, hate, revenge, or others. The emotion may be directed inward (feelings of pride or helplessness) or outward (love of family). The HUMINT collector employs verbal and emotional ruses in applying pressure to the source's dominant emotions. He then links the satisfaction of these emotions to the source's cooperation. Often, the presentation of like experiences and presenting the source with an opportunity to express his emotions is sufficient to result in cooperation. However, sometimes the source must be presented with a specific action or tangible manifestation of support.

Emotional love. Love in its many forms (friendship, comradeship, patriotism, love of family) is a dominant emotion for most people. The HUMINT collector focuses on the anxiety felt by the source about the circumstances in which he finds himself, his isolation from those he loves, and his feelings of helplessness. The HUMINT collector directs the love the source feels toward the appropriate object: family, homeland, or comrades. If the HUMINT collector can show the source what the source himself can do to alter or improve his situation or the situation of the object of his emotion, the approach has a chance of success.

Emotional hate. The emotional hate approach focuses on any genuine hate, or possibly a desire for revenge, the source may feel. The HUMINT collector must clearly identify the object of the source's hate and, if necessary, build on those feelings so the emotion overrides the source's rational side. The source may have negative feelings about his country's regime, immediate superiors, officers in general, or fellow soldiers. The emotional hate approach may be used in any [military source operation (MSO)] where the source's state of mind indicates that the approach may be effective.

Emotional fear-up. Fear is another dominant emotion that can be exploited by the HUMINT collector. In the fear-up approach, the HUMINT collector identifies a preexisting fear or creates a fear within the source. He then links the elimination or reduction of the fear to cooperation on the part of the source. The HUMINT collector must be extremely careful that he does not threaten or coerce a source. Conveying a threat may be a violation of the UCMJ. The HUMINT collector should also be extremely careful that he does not create so much fear that the source becomes unresponsive. The HUMINT collector should never act as if he is out of control or set himself up as the object or focal point of the source's fear. If the HUMINT collector acts in this manner, it is extremely difficult to then act as the outlet for the fear. Supervisors should consider the experience level of their subordinates before approving their use of this approach.

Emotional fear-down. A fearful subject is reassured "through verbal and physical actions" to calm him and cause him to view the interrogator as a "protector."

Emotional-pride and ego-up. The emotional-pride and ego-up approach may be used in any MSO. It exploits a source's low self-esteem. Many HUMINT sources including [Enemy Prisoners of War (EPWs)] and other detainees, retained persons, civilian internees, or refugees may suffer from low self-esteem and feelings of helplessness due to their immediate circumstances. Others, such as individuals or members of social or ethnic groups that have been discriminated against or low-ranking members of organizations (including the military), may also show low self-worth. In this technique, the source is flattered into providing certain information in order to gain credit and build his ego. The HUMINT collector must take care to use a flattering somewhat in-awe tone of voice, and speak highly of the source throughout this approach while remaining believable. This should produce positive feelings on the source's part as he receives desired recognition. The source will eventually reveal pertinent information to solicit more favorable comments from the HUMINT collector.

Emotional-pride and ego-down. The emotional-pride and ego-down approach is based on attacking the source's ego or self-image. The source, in defending his ego, reveals information to justify or rationalize his actions. This information may be valuable in answering collection requirements or may give the HUMINT collector insight into the viability of other approaches. This approach is effective with sources who have displayed weakness or feelings of inferiority. A real or imaginary deficiency voiced about the source, loyalty to his organization, or any other feature can provide a basis for this technique.

Emotional-futility. The questioner uses factual information to try to convince the source that resistance is futile. This approach generally must be combined with another, such as the emotional love approach, to be effective.

We know all. In the "we know all" approach technique, the HUMINT collector subtly convinces the source that his questioning of the source is perfunctory because any information that the source has is already known. This approach may be employed in conjunction with the "file and dossier" technique or by itself. If used alone, the HUMINT collector must first become thoroughly familiar with available data concerning the source and the current situation. To begin the collection effort, the HUMINT collector asks questions based on this known data.

File and dossier. The file and dossier approach is a variation of the "we know all" approach. The HUMINT collector prepares a dossier containing all available information concerning the source or his organization. The information is carefully arranged within a file to give the illusion that it contains more data than actually there. The file may be padded with extra paper if necessary. Index tabs with titles such as education, employment, criminal record, military service, and others are particularly effective. It is also effective if the HUMINT collector is reviewing the dossier when the source enters the room and the source is able to read his name on the dossier and sees the numerous topics and supposed extent of the files.

Establish your identity. The subject is told that he has been "identified as an infamous individual wanted by higher authorities on serious charges." In a sincere effort to correct this mistake, against the interrogator's persistent denials, he may provide leads for further development.

Repetition. The repetition approach is used to induce cooperation from a hostile source. In one variation of this approach, the HUMINT collector listens carefully to a source's answer to a question, and then repeats the question and answer several times. He does this with each succeeding question until the source becomes so thoroughly bored with the procedure, he answers questions fully and candidly to satisfy the HUMINT collector and gain relief from the monotony of this method. The repetition technique must be judiciously used, as it will generally be ineffective when employed against introverted sources or those having great self-control. It may also provide an opportunity for a source to regain his composure and delay the collection effort. In this approach, the use of more than one HUMINT collector or a tape recorder has proven effective.

Rapid fire. The rapid-fire approach is based upon the principles that everyone likes to be heard when he speaks and it is confusing to be interrupted in mid-sentence with an unrelated question. This approach may be used by one, two, or more HUMINT collectors to question the source. In employing this technique, the HUMINT collectors ask a series of questions in such a manner that the source does not have time to answer a question completely before the next one is asked. This confuses the source, and he will tend to contradict himself as he has little time to formulate his answers. The HUMINT collectors then confront the source with the inconsistencies causing further contradictions. In many instances, the source will begin to talk freely in an attempt to explain himself and deny the HUMINT collector's claims of inconsistencies. In this attempt, the source is likely to reveal more than he intends, thus creating additional leads for further exploitation. This approach may be orchestrated with the emotional pride and ego-down or fear-up approaches. Besides extensive preparation, this approach requires experienced and competent HUMINT collectors, with comprehensive case knowledge and fluency in the source's language.

Silent. The silent approach may be successful when used against either a nervous or confident source. When employing this technique, the HUMINT collector says nothing to the source, but looks him squarely in the eye, preferably with a slight smile on his face. It is important not to look away from the source but force him to break eye contact first. The source may become nervous, begin to shift in his chair, cross and re-cross his legs, and look away. He may ask questions, but the HUMINT collector should not answer until he is ready to break the silence. The source may blurt out questions such as, "Come on now, what do you want with me?" When the HUMINT collector is ready to break silence, he may do so with questions

Change of scenery. The change of scenery approach may be used in any type of MSO to remove the source from an intimidating atmosphere such as an "interrogation" room type of setting and to place him in a setting where he feels more comfortable speaking.

Bringing a source into a formal setting to conduct an interrogation or debriefing has psychological implications. On the positive side, it places the HUMINT collector in a superior position since he is operating on his "home turf" and has set the conditions for the meeting. It allows the HUMINT collector control over the immediate environment including the positioning of the participants, to establish the desired atmosphere for the approach.

Mutt and Jeff. The goal of this technique is to make the source identify with one of the interrogators and thereby establish rapport and cooperation. This technique involves a psychological ploy that takes advantage of the natural uncertainty and guilt that a source has as a result of being detained and questioned. Use of this technique requires two experienced HUMINT collectors who are convincing actors. The two HUMINT collectors will display opposing personalities and attitudes toward the source. For example, the first HUMINT collector is very formal and displays an unsympathetic attitude toward the source. He may, for instance, be very strict and order the source to follow all military courtesies during questioning. Although he conveys an unfeeling attitude, the HUMINT collector is careful not to threaten or coerce the source. Conveying a threat of violence is a violation of the UCMJ.

False Flag. The goal of this technique is to convince the detainee that individuals from a country other than the United States are interrogating him, and trick the detainee into cooperating with United States forces. For example, using an interrogator who speaks with a particular accent, making the detainee believe that he is actually talking to representatives from a different country, such as a country that is friendly to the detainee's country or organization. The False Flag approach may be effectively orchestrated with the Fear-Down approach and the Pride and Ego-Up.

Separation. [*Authors' Note: Separation is a restricted technique, the procedures and safeguards for which are detailed at great length in a separate appendix in the Army Field Manual.*] As part of the Army's efforts to gain actionable intelligence in the war on terrorism, HUMINT collectors may be authorized, in accordance with this appendix, to employ the separation interrogation technique, by exception, to meet unique and critical operational requirements. The purpose of separation is to deny the detainee the opportunity to communicate with other detainees in order to keep him from learning counter-resistance techniques or gathering new information to support a cover story; decreasing the detainee's resistance to interrogation. . . . Separation will only be used during the interrogation of specific unlawful enemy combatants for whom proper approvals have been granted in accordance with this appendix. However, separation may not be employed on detainees covered by Geneva Convention Relative to the Treatment of Prisoners of War (GPW), primarily enemy prisoners of war (EPWs). The separation technique will be used only at [Combat Commander] COCOM-approved locations. Separation may be employed in combination with authorized interrogation approaches—

- On specific unlawful enemy combatants.
- To help overcome resistance and gain actionable intelligence.
- To safeguard United States and coalition forces.
- To protect United States interests.

[*The two forms of separation are:*]

Physical separation. Prevent the detainee from communicating with other detainees (which might increase the detainee's resistance to interrogation) and foster a feeling of futility.

Field expedient separation. Prolong the shock of capture. Prevent the detainee from communicating with other detainees (which might increase the detainee's resistance to interrogation) and foster a feeling of futility.

REVIEW QUESTIONS

1. What international law prohibits torture and cruel, inhuman, or degrading treatment?

2. How does the law distinguish between torture and cruel, inhuman, or degrading treatment?

3. Briefly describe the constitutional limits on interrogation.

4. What are the key United States statutes restricting how United States government officials may act when conducting interrogations?

CRITICAL THINKING QUESTIONS

1. Reading the CAT's definition of torture by itself, is it clear what type of coercive investigatory techniques are, or are not, prohibited? If unclear, how could the CAT's definition be improved?

2. Why do you think the Senate included the reservation regarding cruel, inhuman, and degrading treatment when consenting to the CAT?

3. In acknowledging that the CAT's prohibition on cruel, inhuman, or degrading treatment (CIDT) applies in territory the United States controls, the United States representative also stated that the detention facility at Guantanamo and United States-registered ships and aircraft are included in "territory the United States controls." What places where CIDT might occur might *not* be included in that definition?

4. Examine the EITs used by the CIA during its interrogations and assess their legality under international and domestic law identified in this chapter. Which do you believe are torture? Cruel, inhuman, or degrading treatment? What other questions does your analysis raise?

5. Put yourself in the shoes of a CIA interrogator soon after the 9/11 attacks, during which nearly 3,000 Americans were killed. You believe a known terrorist in your custody has information regarding planned future attacks that will kill many more Americans. You have attempted to use the various techniques in the Army Field Manual to gather information, but the suspect has not provided any actionable intelligence. What would you do next? To what extent would *law* impact your decision?

6. As noted in the explanation of Senate Report finding #19, and as demonstrated in the Torture Memos, law and lawyers played a role in the CIA's analysis of whether and how to use enhanced interrogation techniques. How would you describe the role law and lawyers played? What does that say about the larger role law and lawyers play in controlling national security activities?

7. Do any of the techniques currently approved in the Army Field Manual constitute torture or cruel, inhuman, or degrading treatment?

CHAPTER 13

Detaining Terror Suspects

Camp Delta at Guantanamo, Cuba, where many terrorist suspects have been detained since 9/11

Learning Objectives

1. Understand under what circumstances the military may detain non-combatants and combatants, based on the Constitution, statute, and precedent.

2. Know the types of civilian preventive detention and their limitations for counter-terrorism purposes.

3. Understand why Blackstone referred to the writ of habeas corpus as "the great writ" and why United States courts have carefully protected the right.

4. Understand the right to the writ of habeas corpus and how it applies to challenges to government detention in the national security context.

5. Understand why the government's ability to detain is an important national security issue.

13.1. INTRODUCTION

One of the clearest examples of the tension between national security and individual liberty is demonstrated by the government's power to detain. The **Framers** viewed this power as a fundamental danger to liberty and a pathway to tyranny. The Constitution's Suspension Clause, discussed in Section 13.4. below, and the Fifth Amendment's Due Process Clause were attempts by the Framers to protect against the kind of arbitrary detention in which the Crown had engaged in England.

In the United States, detention usually occurs in the context of criminal acts. Criminal suspects may be detained before trial, subject to judicial oversight, or may be imprisoned after a conviction as part of a sentence. And yet, sometimes detention of persons with intent to do harm to the United States or its citizens may be necessary without criminal action. This has primarily occurred in the context of war, when persons hostile to the United States, whether acting as a member of an enemy military, as part of a large-scale criminal organization like the terrorist group Al Qaeda, or acting independently, have threatened harm to the United States and the United States has sought to detain such individuals. Courts have been wary of the government's power to detain, and accordingly have limited that power in a variety of ways. Key to determining of the extent of the government's authority to detain have been: 1) the status of the person as a combatant or non-combatant; 2) status of the person as a citizen or non-citizen; 3) the activities in which the person is thought to have been engaged or planning; 4) the location of the individual's capture and detention; 5) whether the ordinary civilian judicial system is available; and 6) whether sufficient judicial oversight has been afforded to avoid concerns of unilateral overreach by the Executive.

13.2. MILITARY DETENTION

13.2.1. Military Detention of Non-Combatants

Detention of non-combatants who are perceived to be a security threat is not a new phenomenon in the United States, and has been repeatedly upheld in a variety of circumstances.

13.2.1.1. Alien Enemy Act

As early as 1798, Congress expressed concern about the presence of "alien enemies" who might pose a risk to national security. At the request of President John Adams, Congress passed the **Alien Enemy Act** (one of the "Alien and Sedition Acts"). The Act stated that:

> whenever there shall be a declared war between the United States and any foreign nation or government, or any invasion or predatory incursion shall be perpetrated, attempted, or threatened against the territory of the United States, by any foreign nation or government, and the President of the United States shall make public proclamation of the event, all natives, citizens, denizens, or subjects of the hostile nation or government, being males of the age of fourteen years and upwards, who shall be within the United States, and not actually naturalized, shall be liable to be apprehended, restrained, secured and removed, as alien enemies.

Thus, the President had the authority to detain any non-citizen male age 14 and older. The Alien Enemy Act, and the notion that otherwise protected liberty might be suspended to preserve national security, has survived to this day. Calls to detain perceived national enemies have been voiced during most American wars, including the War of 1812, the Civil War, World War I, World War II, and in the wake of the terror attacks of September 11, 2001.

13.2.1.2. Ex Parte Milligan

Ex Parte Milligan involved a Confederate sympathizer during the Civil War named Lambdin Milligan. Milligan, an Indiana resident, United States citizen, and attorney, had been arrested in Indiana for an alleged plot to attack a Union armory and then use the weapons obtained at the armory to free Confederate prisoners from a Union prison. Milligan was not in any way associated with the Confederate Army or acting at the direction of the Confederacy—he was merely sympathetic to the Confederate cause. At the time of his arrest and conviction, the civilian courts were still functioning in Indiana, but he was brought before a military tribunal where he was charged with violation of the laws of war, found guilty, and sentenced to be hanged. He challenged his detention, conviction, and sentence in a case that reached the United States Supreme Court.

As discussed elsewhere in this text, the *Milligan* case was an important test of the President's authority to enforce national security, even against those not directly participating in the conflict. The Supreme Court in *Milligan* addressed two issues: 1) whether Milligan had the right to seek review of his detention through the principle of ***habeas corpus***; and 2) whether the President had authority to detain non-combatants as part of a war effort. As discussed below, the Supreme Court ultimately determined: 1) Milligan had the right to use the habeas corpus process to challenge his detention; and 2) that the President did *not* have the unilateral or inherent authority to try Milligan before a **military commission** under the circumstances, because he was a United States citizen and the civilian courts were open and functioning, and outside the war zone. Though the Supreme Court ultimately split on whether Congress could have granted the President such authority, it had not, and so the Court concluded Milligan's detention, conviction, and arrest were without authority.

13.2.1.3. Korematsu v. United States *and* Ex Parte Endo

The Supreme Court again visited the question of the President's authority to detain United States citizens not engaged in combat during the notorious case of *Korematsu v. United States*. Roughly 10 weeks after Japan attacked the United States in Pearl Harbor, Hawaii, President Franklin D. Roosevelt signed **Executive Order** 9066, which authorized the Secretary of War and subordinate armed forces to remove people of Japanese ancestry from areas designated by the military as exclusion zones. Subsequently, General John DeWitt of the United States Army issued a Civilian Exclusion Order requiring all persons of Japanese descent to leave an area of the West Coast. The Alien Enemy Act was still in force during World War II, and was ultimately used to apprehend, restrain, detain, and remove thousands of German, Italian, and Japanese persons during the conflict. But, the Alien Enemy Act was insufficient and the Executive Order was necessary because the Alien Enemy Act applies to non-citizens and the government wished to control the location not only of non-citizens, but of United States citizens of Japanese descent. In fact, two thirds of the more than 120,000 persons relocated from the West Coast of the United States were United States citizens. Most of these individuals were subsequently detained in internment camps throughout the western and midwestern United States. One such citizen, Fred Korematsu, decided not to comply with the Civilian Exclusion Order. After he was arrested, Korematsu appealed to the Supreme Court.

The government's justification for the exclusion of United States citizens was military necessity. A majority of the Supreme Court deferred to this judgment and the assertion made by the military that a danger of sabotage and espionage existed. Specifically, the Supreme Court noted "we cannot reject as unfounded the judgment of the military authorities and of Congress that there were disloyal members of that population, whose number and strength could not be precisely and quickly ascertained." Ultimately, the majority determined that the prevention of espionage and sabotage was a proper exercise of the Legislative and Executive Branches' war powers, especially when the branches were acting together. Justice Frankfurter issued a concurring opinion suggesting the government's action was constitutional because of the total war in which the United States was involved, while acknowledging the action might have been unlawful in peacetime.

Two important dissents highlight some of the contentious issues raised by the *Korematsu* case, including the racially discriminatory basis for the military order. Justice Frank Murphy argued that though deference to the military is important, there must be limits to military discretion, "especially where martial law has not been declared." Murphy's suspicion was well-placed. We now know there was significant influence on General DeWitt's decision to issue the order that had nothing to do with military necessity, including California businesses looking to eliminate competition. The United States Department of Justice's and Solicitor General's subsequent involvement in suppressing knowledge of possible falsehoods in the "Final Report of General DeWitt" also undercuts the military necessity claim. Solicitor General Charles Fahy hid from the Supreme Court a wartime report that concluded very few persons of Japanese descent posed a risk and almost all who did were already in custody when President Roosevelt's Executive Order was enforced. Justice Murphy saw the exclusion of persons of Japanese ancestry as falling "into the ugly abyss of racism" and ironically resembling "the abhorrent and despicable treatment of minority groups by the dictatorial tyrannies which this nation is now pledged to destroy."

In another dissent, Justice Jackson argued that Korematsu's arrest was based not on Congress's statute or the President's Executive Order, but rather upon General DeWitt's order alone. He further expressed concern that the Supreme Court should not have decided the case at all, because a judicial order, as opposed to a military order, would never expire and thus a Supreme Court opinion upholding the exclusion order would essentially *constitutionalize* the order, when that was unnecessary. Jackson's view suggests that the military's "extra-constitutional" behavior may be acceptable within the proper military sphere: "When an area is so beset that it must be put under military control at all, the paramount consideration is that its measures be successful rather than legal." Justice Jackson is essentially conceding that the order and Korematsu's arrest were unconstitutional, but believed that the Court should not sanction what was unconstitutional. Instead, the Court should stay out of the matter and let the political process deal with the unconstitutional behavior. "Once a judicial opinion rationalizes such an order to show that it conforms with the Constitution, or rather rationalizes the Constitution to show that the Constitution sanctions such an order, the Court for all time has validated the principle of racial discrimination in criminal procedure and of transplanting American citizens."

The *Korematsu* decision has never been formally overturned by the Supreme Court, though in 2018, a majority of the Court in *Trump v. Hawaii* finally stated that *Korematsu* had been wrongly decided. Korematsu's conviction was overturned in 1983 when a federal district court judge agreed the original conviction was so tainted by prosecutorial misconduct it should be void.

Technically, *Korematsu* was not a "detention" case, as it related to whether Korematsu's conviction for disobeying the exclusion order was lawful, not whether his subsequent detention was lawful. However, in *Korematsu* the Court upheld the same order that served as the basis for the military detention of tens of thousands of United States citizens. In the case of *Ex Parte Endo*, decided on the same day as *Korematsu*, the Supreme Court took a more skeptical view of the government's detention authority. There, a United States citizen of Japanese ancestry named Mitsuye Endo challenged her continued detention in an internment camp. The government could not show Ms. Endo was a threat to the nation's security. Whereas in *Korematsu* the Court had placed significance on the cooperation between Congress and the President in authorizing the exclusion zones, in *Endo*, the Court demanded that if Congress wanted to authorize the President to detain loyal United States citizens, that statute must include a "clear statement" that that was its intent. Because the statute authorizing the exclusion of Japanese-Americans from the West Coast had not included a clear statement that it was authorizing the President to detain loyal Americans, the Court held that military detention exceeded the President's authority.

13.2.1.4. Al-Marri v. Puciarelli

The President's authority to rely on national security as a basis to detain persons who are not participating in traditional armed conflict remains an issue. Since 9/11, the federal judiciary has decided several cases where apparent non-combatants have been detained by the military. In *Al-Marri v. Puciarelli*, the Fourth Circuit Court of Appeals faced the following facts: Ali Saleh Kahlah al-Marri was detained pursuant to a presidential declaration that he was an "enemy combatant." Al-Marri was Qatari citizen, but lawful United States resident, originally arrested in the United States as a material witness in a terrorism investigation and later charged with credit card fraud. Al-Marri was then transferred to the United States Naval Brig in Charleston, South Carolina. The government claimed Al-Marri trained with Al Qaeda in the mid-1990s, years before the 9/11 attacks, and was ordered to the United States as an Al Qaeda "sleeper agent." But, the government did not assert Al-Marri was associated with any armed force at war with the United

States, that he escaped from the battlefield, or that he was even living in Afghanistan at the time of the military conflict with Al Qaeda.

The issue facing the court in the case was whether there was authority for the military to detain Al-Marri as an enemy combatant. A majority of judges concluded that though the international law of war might give the President authority to detain enemy combatants, they did not need to decide the law of war issue because the **Authorization for the Use of Military Force (AUMF)** granted power to the President to detain enemy combatants. Recall that the AUMF stated:

> the President is authorized to use all necessary and appropriate force against those nations, organizations, or persons he determines planned, authorized, committed, or aided the terrorist attacks that occurred on September 11, 2001, or harbored such organizations or persons, in order to prevent any future acts of international terrorism against the United States by such nations, organizations or persons.

In ruling against Al-Marri, the court opined "Al Marri would have us rule that when Congress authorized the President to deal militarily with those responsible for the 9/11 attacks upon our country, it did not intend to authorize the President to deal militarily with AQ operatives identically situated to the 9/11 hijackers." The court concluded that Al Qaeda was the specific group Congress was targeting in the AUMF and that nothing in the AUMF suggested the military response must be limited to foreign lands. The court found unpersuasive the argument that because Al Qaeda was not a "nation state" for purposes of the laws of war that its members could not be detained. In essence, Congress had declared Al Qaeda an enemy in authorizing the use of military force in the AUMF. Therefore, for United States purposes, Al Qaeda was the enemy, and persons associated with Al Qaeda could be detained.

In a dissenting opinion, Judge Motz asserted that though the question of detention would ordinarily be controlled by the law of war, there is no category of "enemy combatant" under the international law of war. Thus, Judge Motz argued, the court should look to solely domestic law, which generally emphasizes *Milligan*'s holding that the Constitution does not permit the government to subject civilians within the United States to military detention: "civilians within this country may not be subjected to military control and deprived of constitutional rights." Even if this is an accurate statement of *Milligan*'s holding, it does not answer the question of whether someone can be both a "civilian" and an "enemy combatant" for purposes of detention, and if so, whether *Milligan* applies.

The *Al-Marri* case appeared to be headed to a Supreme Court resolution after the Court granted certiorari, but after the Fourth Circuit's opinion, the government transferred Al-Marri to civilian custody and charged him with civilian criminal activity, mooting the question of whether military detention was authorized.

13.2.1.5. Hedges v. Obama

The 2012 National Defense Authorization Act included a provision that stated non-United States persons who "substantially supported" Al Qaeda, the Taliban, or associated forces could be detained. In *Hedges v. Obama*, the plaintiffs were a group of individuals (investigative journalists, human rights advocates, lawyers) who expressed concern that they might be detained in military custody based on the 2012 NDAA because their activities might be considered "support." The case posed a significant substantive legal question regarding the breadth, scope, ambiguity, and potential **chilling effects** on free speech, of the phrase "substantial support." However, the Second Circuit did not address that substantive issue, instead deciding the case on procedural grounds. It ruled that for non-United States persons to have standing to sue under the NDAA, the NDAA alone had to make it more likely that such persons would be subjected to detention authority than under the pre-existing AUMF. In other words, the NDAA alone had to cause the "injury" of which the plaintiffs complained in order for them to have standing to challenge the NDAA. The court found that the NDAA was merely an endorsement of the view previously expressed by federal courts that the President's authority under the AUMF included the authority to detain those responsible for 9/11, as well as those who were part of or substantially supported Al Qaeda, the Taliban, or associated forces. So, the NDAA did not provide any more authority to the President than the AUMF had, and could not inflict an injury sufficient to provide standing. Further, for United States persons, which many of the plaintiffs were, the NDAA could not cause any injury because its own language explicitly prevented the NDAA's detention authority from applying to United States persons.

13.2.2. Military Detention of Belligerents

13.2.2.1. Ex Parte Quirin

Recall that in *Milligan*, the Supreme Court held that a United States citizen in the United States, but outside the war zone, could not be tried by a military commission while the civilian courts were still functioning. In the *Quirin* case during World War II, the Supreme Court determined that a United States citizen caught outside the war zone *could* be detained and tried by military commission while the civilian courts were still functioning. In that case, eight German nationals, including two dual-United States-German citizens (Herbert Haupt and Ernest Burger), came to the United States to engage in sabotage. The Germans arrived by U-boat (German submarine) on two Atlantic beaches under cover of darkness in 1942. After arriving in uniform, the Germans changed into civilian clothes and began preparations to sabotage manufacturing plants, freight rails, and other key infrastructure. One of the saboteurs, however, reconsidered and alerted the Federal Bureau of Investigation of their plans. No actual attacks were executed. The eight were caught and President Franklin D. Roosevelt ordered they be tried by a **military tribunal**. These tribunals were established to try nationals of enemy states and those who, under those states' direction, committed acts of sabotage, espionage, or "violations of the law of war."

The military commission conducted a trial. After the defense rested its case, but before the tribunal issued its decision, the defense appealed to the Supreme Court, arguing the military tribunal was illegally constituted. Citing *Milligan*, the saboteurs' lead defense counsel argued that the beaches where the eight had come ashore could not be considered "zones of military operation" as there was no combat there, and that because the civil courts were still functioning, they were the appropriate venue for charges against the eight to be heard. The Supreme Court unanimously denied the appeal, holding "The military commission was lawfully constituted . . . petitioners are held in lawful custody for trial before the military commission and have not shown cause for being discharged by **writ of habeas corpus**." The members of the tribunal then deliberated, finding all eight men guilty and recommending six of the eight be executed, which President Roosevelt then ordered. Less than one week after the military tribunal announced its verdict, and several months before the Supreme Court issued its full written opinion in the case, the six were executed by electric chair in Washington, D.C.

In deciding the case, the Supreme Court declined to rule on the President's constitutional authority under Article II, instead finding authority for the detention and military commission under the Articles of War. The Court found the saboteurs to be enemy combatants by their own admission and held that they had clearly violated the laws of war. The Court further held that Congress legally used the international laws of war and Article 15 of the United States Articles of War to authorize the President to convene military commissions. Importantly, the Court did not base its holding on the fact that detaining enemy combatants is incident to the conduct of war, but rather on specific statutory authority.

Though the defense counsel for the German saboteurs cited *Milligan* for the proposition that the military tribunal was inappropriate, there were several key differences between the cases. First, Milligan was a United States citizen, while at least six of the eight Germans were not. That said, the Supreme Court did find that the military tribunal could try the dual citizen. Second, the Civil War was an undeclared war, while WWII was a declared war against a declared and identifiable enemy, an enemy for which the German saboteurs admitted they were working. Third, Milligan was a civilian, not a **belligerent** Confederate soldier, whereas the Germans in *Quirin* were uniformed (until they took them off) soldiers of an enemy state.

One reading of *Quirin* is that it creates a "declared enemy exception" to the open court rule of *Milligan*, suggesting that *Milligan* is the rule and *Quirin* the exception. A different interpretation of the cases reverses their significance, making *Quirin* the rule and *Milligan* the exception; this reading is supported by the fact that the Court in *Quirin*—the later case—says that *Milligan* should be confined to its facts. Nevertheless, the Supreme Court has overruled neither *Milligan* nor *Quirin*. Under *Milligan*, the military cannot detain United States citizens who are not associated with the military arm of the enemy government, as long as civilian courts are open and functioning. Under *Quirin*, the military can, with statutory authority, detain and try enemy combatants in the United States outside the war zone during war, even if they are United States citizens.

Sabotaging the Sabotage: *Ex Parte Quirin*

The *Quirin* case involved a strange but true story of Germany's attempt to infiltrate and sabotage the continental United States during World War II. Germany's military intelligence unit—the Abwehr—decided to attack the United States' military production and transportation lines. Code named "Operation Pastorius," the plan sought to attack production facilities like aluminum plants and raw materials processing factories for aluminum, necessary for manufacturing aircraft. Additionally, waterways and rail lines would be targeted throughout the northeast and Midwest. The grand plan was to land saboteurs on United States beaches by German U-boat (submarine) every six weeks. The Germans had a ready supply of saboteurs who could blend in in the United States, as thousands of Germans who had lived for a long time in the United States and could speak English well had returned to Germany in the early days of the war.

After several months of training in Germany, two four-man teams boarded submarines bound for the United States' east coast. In June 1942, one team of saboteurs led by George Dasch arrived on the coast of Long Island, their submarine scraping the ocean floor as it neared the beach. The men wore German military uniforms, presumably so that if they were captured immediately upon their arrival they would be entitled to prisoner of war status. After rowing to shore, they changed into civilian clothes. Almost immediately, one of the men—a dual United States and

German citizen named Ernest Burger—began to sabotage the sabotage mission, placing obvious German items in the sand where they were sure to be discovered. The men were discovered by a Coast Guardsman patrolling the beach. He returned to his station to sound an invasion alarm and a search party returned to the beach at dawn and found many items the saboteurs had left, some of which were buried and some deliberately left visible by Burger. Though they escaped capture on the beach, Dasch and Burger ultimately decided to turn themselves in to the Federal Bureau of Investigation (FBI). Dasch ultimately traveled to Washington, where he revealed the plan to the FBI, which apprehended the other three members of Dasch's team. Not long thereafter, the four members of the team that had landed in Jacksonville, Florida, around the same time were also caught. All eight Germans were in custody without having attempted one act of sabotage.

Less than a week after the men were captured, President Roosevelt established a military commission to try "all enemies who have entered upon the territory of the United States as part of an invasion or predatory incursion." Two days later, on July 4, 1942, a military tribunal convened in the main Department of Justice building. After a trial that lasted nearly three weeks, and included Dasch and Burger testifying against their fellow saboteurs, the saboteurs' military defense counsel, Colonel Kenneth Royall, challenged the lawfulness of the military tribunal by demanding a writ of habeas corpus. Ultimately, the Supreme Court met in special session on July 29, 1942, and on July 31 issued its unanimous opinion that the military commission was lawful because the men were belligerents who were not entitled to prisoner of war status. On August 3rd, the seven members of the military commission found all eight men guilty and recommended they be executed. The commission noted the assistance Dasch and Burger had provided in the apprehension of the teams and by testifying for the prosecution during the trial, and recommended their death sentences be commuted to life in prison. President Roosevelt agreed with the military commission's recommendations, and on August 8, the six were executed by electric chair. The Supreme Court issued its written opinion on October 29, 1942, months after the men had been executed. Though the opinion was unanimous, Supreme Court Justices later revealed significant disagreements regarding whether the Court should have reviewed the case at all, some arguing that addressing the rights of enemy belligerents during a war involved national security and political issues outside the judiciary's purview. Ultimately, Chief Justice Stone, worried about the Court's reputation, was able to secure unanimity among the Justices.

13.2.2.2. Hamdi v. Rumsfeld

The United States Supreme Court addressed both *Milligan* and *Quirin* in a post-9/11 case involving military detention of a United States citizen alleged to be an enemy combatant. Yaser Hamdi was a United States citizen by virtue of his birth in Louisiana. Hamdi was captured in Afghanistan by the Northern Alliance, an Afghan group that fought against the Taliban. During the United States invasion of Afghanistan in 2001, the Northern Alliance transferred Hamdi to the United States military, which initially detained him at Guantanamo, but upon learning he was a United States citizen, transferred him to the Naval Brig in

Charleston, South Carolina. The Bush administration claimed that Hamdi was an "enemy combatant" because he was caught with the Taliban.

The Supreme Court agreed to hear Hamdi's challenge to his detention. Ultimately, no single opinion received a majority of votes, though six Justices agreed that the Executive Branch does not have the power to hold a United States citizen indefinitely without providing some due process and **judicial review**. Justice O'Connor's plurality opinion addressed several key questions, but declined to say whether the President had Article II authority to order the military detention of a United States citizen under the circumstances. Instead, the plurality found there was sufficient statutory authority from the 2001 AUMF. The Court acknowledged that the AUMF did not reference "detention," but noted that it did give the President power to use "all necessary and appropriate" force. The Court held that detention is included in "all necessary and appropriate" force, given that the purpose of detention is to prevent captured individuals from "returning to the field of battle and taking up arms once again," and that purpose is applicable regardless of the citizenship of the combatant who has associated himself with an enemy military.

A dissenting opinion concluded the AUMF did not establish Congressional authorization for the detention of enemy combatants. Dissenting Justices argued that the Non-Detention Act (NDA), which prohibited detention of United States citizens by the United States except pursuant to an act of Congress, was specifically adopted to avoid "another *Korematsu*." Thus, the dissent opined, a "clear statement of authorization to detain" from Congress is required to satisfy the NDA. The dissenters asserted that the AUMF, which did not mention detention, was not a sufficiently clear statement. The dissenters also noted that the Court's rationale allows the President to "have it both ways": the Commander in Chief could feasibly use the AUMF to detain United States citizens incident to the law of war, but then hold them in conditions that violate the law of war (e.g., incommunicado, and without a status determination). The dissenters further noted that 38 days after passing the AUMF, the same Congress passed the **USA PATRIOT Act**, which authorized initial detention of alien terrorists for no more than seven days absent criminal charges or deportation. The dissenters complained: "It is very difficult to believe that the same Congress that carefully circumscribed executive power over alien terrorists on home soil would not have meant to require the government to justify clearly its detention of an American citizen held on home soil incommunicado."

Some have wondered why the Court did not side with Hamdi, based on precedent set in *Milligan*. Several differences are important: Milligan was not a prisoner of war, was arrested at home in the United States, and was not associated with the Army of the Confederacy. In other words, while Milligan may have been a criminal, he was not an enemy combatant. A significant question during the modern era of international terrorism is whether this distinction remains relevant. By contrast, a dissenting opinion signed by Justices Scalia and Stephens found no basis for continued detention of Hamdi. In their view, because Hamdi was a citizen, historic precedent—especially *Milligan*—mandated the government had only two options to detain Hamdi: 1) Congress must suspend the right to habeas corpus; or 2) Hamdi must be tried under normal criminal law.

The *Hamdi* Court citied *Quirin* for the proposition that "capture, detention, and trial of unlawful combatants" are "important incidents of war," and for the idea that "[t]here is no bar to this nation's holding one of its own citizens as an enemy combatant." The *Hamdi* plurality noted that *Quirin* was a unanimous opinion that post-dated *Milligan*, and that if *Milligan* once could have been viewed as standing for the proposition that the military does not have the authority to try an American citizen accused of spying against his country during wartime, "*Quirin* makes undeniably clear that that is not the law today." Despite the Hamdi plurality's reliance on *Quirin*, Hamdi's case was not precisely the same as *Quirin*; Hamdi challenged his categorization as an enemy combatant, which makes the case different than *Quirin*, where Haupt did not argue his classification as an enemy combatant against the United States.

Adding up the votes from several plurality opinions issued in one case can be confusing, but the mesh of opinions can be distilled to a few key points. First, the idea that United States citizens can be detained by the military under certain circumstances garnered five votes, a majority. Six Justices agreed United States citizens must be accorded due process when determining whether they are an enemy combatant. But only four Justices agreed that the 2001 AUMF authorized the detention of Hamdi under the circumstances.

After *Hamdi*, extended detention of United States persons requires statutory authority and individualized assessments of the factual basis for detention (due process). However, *Hamdi* left open some important questions. May the military detain a United States citizen who has never been on the battlefield? What about a United States citizen who is caught in the United States? What about legal aliens captured in the United States, to whom the Non-Detention Act does not apply? What about legal aliens who were never on the battlefield? In the years after *Hamdi* was decided, several federal Courts of Appeals would try to answer some of these questions.

13.2.2.3. Rumsfeld v. Padilla

In May 2002, the FBI arrested Jose Padilla when his flight from Pakistan landed in Chicago. A United States citizen, Padilla had trained in Afghanistan with Al Qaeda and moved as an armed member of the group, in addition to serving as an armed guard on a Taliban outpost. Because the Taliban controlled the government of Afghanistan at the time, Padilla's actions made him not only a member of a terrorist organization, but an affiliate of an enemy state as well. Law enforcement believed that he intended to execute a "**dirty bomb**" attack in the United States. When he arrived in Chicago, he was arrested by FBI agents on a material witness **warrant**, though his status was later changed to "enemy combatant."

Padilla's lawyer challenged his detention. In late 2002, the District Court for Southern New York held that the President of the United States, as Commander in Chief, had the authority to designate an American citizen captured on United States soil as an enemy combatant and detain him for the duration of the conflict with Al Qaeda. The Second Circuit Court of Appeals subsequently reversed, holding that "The President lacked inherent constitutional authority as Commander-in-Chief to detain American citizens on American soil outside a zone of combat." Additionally, the court held the AUMF did not provide authorization for detention incident to war because the AUMF authorized only detention of enemies "arrayed against us in the field of battle," which was not Padilla's situation when he was detained. The court also noted that the Non-Detention Act requires a clear statement for detention of United States citizens captured on United States soil. Finally, the court relied on the case of *Youngstown Sheet & Tube Co. v. Sawyer*, where the United States Supreme Court ruled that President Truman could not use his position and power as Commander-in-Chief, created under Article II, Section 2 of the United States Constitution, to seize the nation's steel mills on the eve of a nation-wide steelworkers' strike (we discuss this in more detail in Chapter 2). The court determined that under the Constitution, extraordinary government power to curb civil rights and liberties during crises, such as times of war, lies with Congress and not the President. For instance, Article I, Section 9, Clause 2, of the United States Constitution grants Congress, and not the President, the power to suspend the right of habeas corpus during a period of rebellion or invasion.

The government appealed the Second Circuit ruling to the Supreme Court of the United States, which remanded because it found the Second Circuit did not have **jurisdiction** over Padilla's case. The Supreme Court ruled that the Second Circuit did not have jurisdiction because Padilla was no longer detained in New

York, within the jurisdiction of the Second Circuit, but was now detained in the Naval Brig in Charleston, South Carolina.

After Padilla challenged his detention in the District of South Carolina, his case was eventually decided by the Fourth Circuit Court of Appeals in 2005. Between the Second Circuit and Fourth Circuit decisions in *Padilla*, the Supreme Court had decided the *Hamdi* case, which significantly damaged Padilla's claim that the President could not militarily detain United States citizens who had been captured "off the battlefield." Relying on factual similarities between *Padilla* and *Hamdi*, the Fourth Circuit determined that the AUMF authorized his detention because although he was captured in the United States, he had previously been traveling with Al Qaeda and the Taliban during military operations. The Fourth Circuit found that *Hamdi* had made no distinction between enemy combatants captured on the battlefield and those captured in the United States after they fled the battlefield.

Padilla appealed the Fourth Circuit ruling to the Supreme Court of the United States. On the eve of the Supreme Court decision regarding whether to grant certiorari to hear the case, President Bush ordered him to be removed from military custody and returned to civilian custody, rendering his challenge to his military detention, including his appeal to the Supreme Court, moot. This maneuver infuriated the Fourth Circuit, which responded:

> The government has left the impression that it may have come to the belief that the principle in reliance upon which it has detained Padilla for this time, that the President possesses the authority to detain enemy combatants who enter into this country for the purpose of attacking America and its citizens from within can, in the end, yield to expediency with little or no cost to its conduct of the war against terror—an impression we would have thought the government likewise could ill afford to leave extant. And these impressions have been left, we fear, at what may ultimately prove to be substantial cost to the government's credibility before the courts. . . .

Ultimately, Padilla was convicted in civilian federal court and ultimately sentenced to 21 years in prison.

13.2.2.4. Al-Bihani v. Obama

Another detention question arose in *Al-Bihani v. Obama*. Ghalem Nassar Al-Bihani, a Yemeni citizen, had been captured in Afghanistan while he was with the Taliban. Al-Bihani claimed he was merely a cook for the Taliban, and because he was not a combatant and had committed no direct hostile act, he should not be subject to detention under the international law of war. The United States government did not refute that Bihani was a cook, but noted that he was armed and that his activities as part of the Taliban authorized his indefinite detention.

A panel of judges of the District of Columbia Circuit Court of Appeals, including future Supreme Court Justice Brett Kavanaugh, heard Bihani's case. In its opinion published in 2010, the court boldly claimed "In this decision we aim to narrow the legal uncertainty that clouds military detention." The court found that all of Bihani's arguments against his detention relied heavily on the premise that the war powers granted by the AUMF and other domestic statutes were limited by the international law of war. The court rejected this assertion, noting "This premise is mistaken." The court found there was no indication in the AUMF, the Detainee Treatment Act of 2005, or the 2006 or 2009 Military Commissions Acts, that "Congress intended the international laws of war to act as extra-textual limiting principles for the President's war powers under the AUMF." Further casting doubt on the relevance of international law to determining domestic detention cases, the court observed "The international laws of war as a whole have not been implemented domestically by Congress and are therefore not a source of authority for United States courts."

Recalling that in *Hamdi*, the Supreme Court had seemingly relied in part on the general law of war to determine the scope of the AUMF's "necessary and proper" clause, in *Bihani*, the Circuit Court of Appeals for the District of Columbia (D.C. Circuit) responded that "While the international laws of war are helpful to courts when identifying the general set of war powers to which the AUMF speaks, their lack of controlling legal force and firm definition render their use both inapposite and inadvisable when courts seek to determine the limits of the President's war powers." This view seems inconsistent with the Supreme Court of the United States' explicit reference to the law of war in *Hamdi* and arguably contradicts what the Supreme Court had articulated in the *Quirin* case: "from the very beginning of its history this Court has recognized and applied the law of war as including that part of the law of nations which prescribes, for the conducts of war, the status, rights and duties of enemy nations as well as of enemy individuals." Nevertheless, when Bihani appealed the D.C. Circuit ruling to the Supreme Court, the Court declined to hear the case.

The *Bihani* case seems to stand for the proposition that the international law of war does not limit domestic authority regarding detention. Additionally, the case signaled a new reality in terms of the relative importance of federal courts, in which the D.C. Circuit is the primary player in determining legality of detention in other military activities in counter-terrorism. As noted national security law scholar Professor Robert Chesney has noted:

> The habeas courts have become, for better or worse, the central United States government institution engaged in the critical—and ultimately unavoidable—task of tailoring the laws governing military activity to suit the increasingly important scenario in which states classify clandestine non-state actors as strategic threats requiring a military response.

In other words, federal courts have, perhaps reluctantly and by congressional default, taken the lead in crafting new principles for asymmetric warfare.

13.2.2.5. Feinstein Amendment, 2012 NDAA

Apparently attempting to clarify the President's authority to use the military to detain, the 2012 National Defense Authorization Act included a provision that stated the government could militarily detain "a person who was a part of or substantially supported al-Qaeda, the Taliban, or associated forces that are engaged in hostilities against the United States or its coalition partners, including any person who has committed a belligerent act or has directly supported such hostilities in aid of such enemy forces." Senator Diane Feinstein successfully added an amendment that added the following language: "Nothing in this section shall be construed to affect existing law or authorities relating to the detention of United States citizens, lawful resident aliens of the US, or any other persons who are captured or arrested in the US." While some members of Congress thought that adding the Feinstein Amendment was prohibiting detention of United States citizens, a careful reading of the amendment makes clear that the Feinstein Amendment only codified the **status quo** as of the end of 2011.

Detention at Guantanamo

Following the terror attacks of September 11, 2001, President George W. Bush announced the United States' engagement in a "global war on terror," and prosecuted hostilities against terror groups pursuant to the 2001 AUMF. In that pursuit, in January 2002, the United States opened the now infamous detention camp in Guantánamo Bay, Cuba, often referred to simply as Guantanamo or "Gitmo." Because the facility, used to detain and interrogate suspected terrorists and Al Qaeda affiliates pretrial, was not located on United States soil, President Bush and Pentagon officials asserted that United States legal protections for detention did not apply to individuals held there. United States officials further claimed that, because Al Qaeda members were not "lawful combatants" by nature of the methods they employed to conduct warfare, the protections of the Geneva Conventions and international law did not apply.

Over the years since its establishment, Guantanamo has been investigated by numerous organizations including the International Committee of the Red Cross (ICRC), the United States Naval Criminal Investigation Service, and the United States Senate for alleged abuse, maltreatment, and **torture** of detainees. The question of jurisdiction has resulted in a storied legal history, beginning the month following its opening, when detainees first sought a review of the legality of their detention through habeas corpus challenges. In *Rasul v. Bush*, the Supreme Court found that detainees had a statutory right to habeas corpus. Congress responded with the Detainee Treatment Act, which granted detainees the privilege of review of their status by a military tribunal.

In the ensuing legal battle, the Supreme Court held in *Boumediene v. Bush* that legislative attempts to provide a military substitute for the right to habeas corpus were inadequate, and that detainees at Guantanamo retained the right to petition for review in federal courts per the Constitution. The Court further held in *Hamdan v. Rumsfeld* that, because the United States has ratified the relevant portion (Article 3) of the Geneva Conventions protocols, detainees are considered prisoners of war in a United States-controlled territory and guaranteed protections pursuant to that article.

In 2009, President Barack Obama announced his administration's intention to fully close operations at the Guantanamo Bay detention camp. However, President Obama's Executive Order to close the facility met with strong congressional opposition. Congress then blocked funding for any federal government activities that would close the camp, effectively using is "power of the purse" to achieve its preferred national security policy of continuing to detain terror suspects at the military prison. In 2015, the administration announced intentions once again to close Guantanamo. This plan, never fully disclosed, failed to materialize before President Donald Trump's inauguration in 2017. In January 2018, President Trump signed an Executive Order to keep Guantanamo open indefinitely. As of May 2018, Guantanamo holds 40 detainees. The camp remains a landmark phenomenon in the history of detention in a national security context.

Detention Disaster: Abu Ghraib

The collapse of the Hussein regime in 2003 left the Iraqi Abu Ghraib prison facility in total disrepair. Seizing the opportunity, American military officials renovated and repurposed the prison as a detention facility for terrorists, their affiliates, and individuals deemed a threat to United States military personnel in the region.

Without providing any corrections instruction, the Army activated reserve Brigadier General Janice Karpinski to take command of the facility. The guards, all United States troops, many of whom were themselves Reserve or Guard soldiers, also received little to no training in the handling and guarding of prisoners. Only a handful had any background in prison work at all. As a result, the facility suffered from very little administrative oversight, and even less procedure or corrections experience.

By October 2003, reports of prisoner abuse had surfaced, leading Lieutenant General Ricardo Sanchez, the commander of United States military forces in Iraq at the time, to direct an investigation into Abu Ghraib. Major General Antonio Taguba's investigation revealed widespread human rights violations, as well as violations of international law regarding detention. His report confirmed rape of male and female prisoners, sexual assault with various objects, torture, posing prisoners naked in human pyramids, urinating and defecating on prisoners, and physical beatings and abuse, including pouring acid on detainees and tying ropes to their genitals and dragging them across the floor. Some of the raped female prisoners were impregnated and later killed by their families in "honor killings."

In addition to wanton and sadistic criminal abuse, United States investigators found that hundreds of civilian detainees held at Abu Ghraib posed no threat to military personnel, and yet had been held there for months. These detainees' appeals and requests for procedural protections had failed to make it past the prison's walls, even while many were compelled to perform humiliating acts while held in austere conditions. In addition to abuse of detainees by some United States military personnel, the CIA performed harsh interrogations at the facility.

The story became public with publication of photographs of the abuse by CBS News and an article published in *The New Yorker*, which lambasted Army leadership and condemned the abuses at the facility. In the years since, the Army has released most of General Taguba's report.

General Karpinski was relieved of command and admonished. An Army colonel was also relieved of command. An Army lieutenant colonel was court-martialed, but acquitted of all charges related to prisoner maltreatment. Eleven junior enlisted personnel were convicted by court-martial. Many of the facts surrounding Abu Ghraib remain shrouded in mystery, and the relative lack of accountability for all but the most junior military personnel at the facility continues to anger many. Beyond the moral condemnation, the scandal caused significant damage to the United States' reputation internationally, and became a recruiting tool for terrorist organizations seeking to harm the United States.

13.3. CIVILIAN PREVENTIVE DETENTION

Another way in which the government of the United States might detain someone is through **preventive detention**, which is detention not because someone has been charged with or convicted of a crime, but rather detention for the purpose of preventing something from happening. The idea of "preventive detention" may seem to violate some basic fundamental premises of liberty enshrined in multiple places in the United States Constitution. For example, the Fourth Amendment requires that law enforcement has **probable cause** that a crime has been committed before making an arrest. Likewise, the Due Process Clauses of the Fifth and Fourteenth Amendments require government to provide due process when depriving someone of their liberty. The Supreme Court has observed that "government detention violates [the Due Process] Clause unless the detention is ordered in a criminal proceeding with adequate procedural protections, . . . or, in certain special and 'narrow' non-punitive circumstances, where a special justification, such as harm-threatening mental illness, outweighs the 'individual's constitutionally protected interest in avoiding physical restraint.' " *Zadvydas v. Davis*. In *Zadvydas*, the Court seemed to be inviting Congress to create a terrorism-related basis for preventive detention when it noted that it was not deciding whether "terrorism or other special circumstances where special arguments might be made for forms of preventive detention and for heightened deference to the judgements of the political branches with respect to matters of national security." In fact, the Supreme Court has never opined on whether terrorism or other national security threats constitute such a special circumstance, though it has upheld civil detention of persons not convicted of a crime in several circumstances, most of which do not involve the criminal process at all. These situations include:

1. Pre-trial detention of criminal arrestees who are flight risks or dangerous;
2. Non-citizens facing deportation;
3. Civil commitment of the mentally ill;
4. Civil commitment of violent sexual offenders after they complete their criminal sentence; and
5. Temporary **quarantine** of the infectious.

Limitations on detention by the government are imposed not only by the Constitution, but have been imposed by statute as well. For instance, the Non-Detention Act states that "No citizen shall be imprisoned or otherwise detained by the United States except pursuant to an Act of Congress."

13.3.1. Immigration Detention

Despite the apparent lack of authority for civil preventive detention explicitly related to terrorism, immigration detention enacted in the USA PATRIOT Act provides one possible basis for detention, albeit a limited one. Under the PATRIOT Act, Section 412, an alien may be detained for seven days when suspected of terrorism-related activities or "is engaged in any other activity that endangers the national security of the United States." Importantly, a detainee "whose removal is unlikely in the reasonably foreseeable future, may be detained for additional periods of up to six months only if the release of the alien will threaten the national security of the United States or the safety of the community or any person." Thus, Section 412 empowers the government to arrest non-citizen terrorism suspects based on little or no evidence, and hold them for seven days before releasing them, charging them, formally initiating immigration proceedings, or, possibly continuing that detention for additional periods of six months at a time. The government can use this authority, intended to prevent terrorist activity and escape of terrorist suspects, to aid in its effort to bring criminal charges against those suspects. However, this authority has its limitations. First, it applies only to "out of status" aliens, meaning the authority cannot be used to detain those lawfully in the United States. Secondly, the ultimate "remedy" under this authority is deportation, but United States policy does not typically involve returning suspected terrorists to their countries of origin. This solution also poses political and legal issues raised by the perception of indefinite unauthorized detention on United States soil. Finally, many alien terror suspects come from particular ethnic and religious backgrounds, and using PATRIOT Act authority to detain so many individuals of this profile has raised accusations of institutional discrimination against the United States.

The relatively limited opportunities for detention under the above limitations has incentivized the federal government to "get creative," leading the Executive Branch to engage in forms of "preventive detention" using two mechanisms: pretextual arrest and material witness detention.

13.3.2. Pretextual Arrest and Detention

Pretextual arrests occur when persons are arrested for relatively minor crimes, such as credit card or identify fraud, petty larceny, smuggling contraband, etc. These are called pretextual arrests not because the evidence of the crime does not exist, but rather because the minor crimes are not the real reason the government is interested in detaining the suspects. Rather, the government arrests these individuals for minor crimes because it suspects them of terrorism-related activity, but lacks sufficient evidence to charge, arrest, and detain for that basis. Pretextual arrests have been judicially challenged, but courts do not normally explore the underlying reasons for an arrest so long as there is sufficient evidence that the individual committed the minor crime in question. The United States Supreme Court vindicated this practice in *Whren v. United States* when it held that, as long as objective probable cause exists for the stated basis of the arrest, an arresting officer's subjective intent for executing it is not subject to judicial review.

Though judicially upheld, pretextual arrests in terrorist cases have a practical challenge: the minor crimes involved usually entitle the detainee to quick bail or bond hearings, after which most judges are likely to release the detainee rather than continue detention until trial for a minor crime. Thus, this method of preventing terrorism suspects from engaging in terrorist activities or escaping while the government continues gathering evidence often lasts mere days.

13.3.3. Material Witness Detention

Under the federal material witness statute, the first version of which became law in 1789, a witness can be detained by the government to ensure their availability to testify at a criminal proceeding if the government can meet the following requirements:

1) produce a sworn affidavit showing that the witness's testimony is material in a subsequent criminal proceeding;
2) show that it is impractical to obtain the testimony by subpoena (e.g., presumably because the witness may flee); and
3) obtain a judicial order for the arrest of the witness.

Using this provision to detain terrorism suspects has its own limitations. First, the statute also says that no material witness may be detained if testimony can be adequately secured by deposition and if further detention is not necessary to prevent a failure of justice. Thus, in many cases a witness may be able to secure his release by agreeing to be deposed, meaning he "has the keys to his own cell door." Second, the statute requires a neutral magistrate to issue a judicial order to arrest, which means a judge must agree that the supposed material witness should be detained for someone else's trial. This may be difficult for the government to show, especially when the detention is pretextual and the government's primary purpose is actually not to obtain the testimony of the detained witness. Additionally, the procedures for demonstrating someone should be detained as a material witness are poorly suited for national security matters, because the detained witness is entitled to an open court hearing, access to an attorney, and may make evidentiary demands on the government that the government would rather not satisfy.

***Ashcroft v al-Kidd*, US, 2011**

The FBI arrested Abdulla Al-Kidd, a United States citizen, using a material witness warrant as he was about to fly to Saudi Arabia. The FBI claimed it wanted Al-Kidd to testify against a terrorism suspect named Sami Omar Al-Hussayen. Al-Kidd was detained for 16 days, then released under supervision for an additional 15 months. Al-Kidd was arrested one year before the trial in which he was supposed to be a witness, though ultimately he never testified at any trial. Additionally, he had been interviewed by, and cooperated with, the FBI and he alleged there were few signs that he was a flight risk. After Al-Kidd was not called to testify at the trial, he sued the United States, alleging the FBI misused the material witness statute. Specifically, he argued that even if probable cause is not necessary for a material witness detention, the Fourth Amendment requires reasonableness in order to deprive someone of liberty, and reasonableness does not exist where an arrest was not actually for the purpose of procuring his testimony.

The Supreme Court rejected al-Kidd's lawsuit, citing its earlier decision in *Whren* for the proposition that the only issue in such a situation is whether "the circumstances, viewed objectively, justify the challenged action," and the actual subjective intent motivating the relevant officials is irrelevant. Because individualized suspicion that al-Kidd might testify and might flee supported the issuance of the material witness arrest warrant, and al-Kidd did not assert that his arrest would have been unconstitutional absent the alleged pretextual use of the warrant, the Court held there was no Fourth Amendment violation.

13.4. THE "GREAT WRIT": THE WRIT OF HABEAS CORPUS

Understanding the right to the **writ of habeas corpus** is essential to understanding detention law, primarily because habeas is a significant way to challenge *any* type of detention. Habeas corpus is a Latin phrase that means "have the body," and a **writ** is a formal written order; thus, a writ of habeas corpus is an order declaring the legality of a person's detention. It refers to the power of a court to order a custodian (jailor, prison warden, or other person responsible for the detention) to bring the detainee into the court so the judge can inquire into the legality of the detention, and includes the authority to order the prisoner to be released if the judge determines that the detention is unlawful. Generally, in the United States, the request for habeas corpus can be filed at any time by someone who is detained. Importantly, detainees can challenge their detention outside of a criminal process. In other words, it provides an opportunity to be released without convincing a court that one is "not guilty" or that their conviction should be overturned.

13.4.1. The Three Bases for the Writ of Habeas Corpus

13.4.1.1. The Common Law Basis for Habeas Corpus

The right of habeas corpus was originally a **common law** right, meaning it was a right created by judges without a statutory basis. The right predates the United States Constitution. Historians believe judges created this right to increase judicial power over the other branches of the government of England, including Parliament and the Crown. Protection of individual rights that the right to habeas corpus offers was a byproduct of this push by the judiciary to provide a check on Parliament. What originated as a check on parliamentary power incidentally produced the protection of an individual liberty. In English practice, the right only addressed pretrial detentions, but American practice has gone far beyond, providing judicial authority to review any detention by the government at any point.

William Blackstone, the English legal philosopher whose writings significantly influenced the Framers of the United States Constitution, called the writ of habeas corpus "the great writ." He argued that imprisonment was a more dangerous form of government tyranny than even murder:

> Of great importance to the public is the preservation of this personal Liberty: for if once it were left in the power of any, the highest, magistrate to imprison arbitrarily whomever here or his officers thought proper. . . there would soon be in end of all other rights and immunities. . . . To bereave a man of life, or by violence to confiscate his estate, without accusation or trial, would be so gross and notorious and act of despotism, as must at once convey the alarm of tyranny throughout the whole Kingdom. But confinement of the person, by secretly hurrying him to gaol, where his sufferings are unknown or forgotten; is a less public, a less striking, and therefore more dangerous engine of arbitrary government. . . .

Thus, according to Blackstone, imprisonment is more pernicious than execution because it is often hidden from public view.

13.4.1.2. The Constitutional Basis for Habeas Corpus

Ordinarily, common law can be superseded by statute. That is, if judges create law through their decisions, subsequent legislative action can modify or eliminate the common law altogether. For example, if over time judges create and recognize a particular defense to a crime, a legislature that agrees with that common law provision can enshrine it in law by codifying it in a statute. Similarly, a legislature that disagrees with the common law can pass a statute eliminating the common law, or modify it to suit the legislature's preferences. In fact, the British Parliament had done just that to the right to the writ of habeas corpus several times, most notably withdrawing the right to the writ from Americans during the Revolutionary War.

In the United States, the right to obtain a writ of habeas corpus is enshrined in the Constitution. Perhaps because of the Framers' recent experience with parliamentary suspensions of habeas corpus, they addressed this right in the original text of the Constitution, albeit in a confusing way. Article I, Section 9, Clause 2 (the "Suspension Clause") says: "The Privilege of the Writ of Habeas Corpus shall not be suspended, unless when in Cases of Rebellion or Invasion the public Safety may require it." Note that this language does not expressly grant a "right" to habeas corpus. Rather, it implicitly does so by stating the privilege can only be suspended in certain circumstances. The implication is that if the government can take something away only in limited circumstances, there must be a right to it in the first place.

The question of whether the Suspension Clause implies a substantive constitutional grant of the right to the writ of habeas corpus was addressed early in the nation's history, though it remains debated today. In 1830, in the case of *Ex Parte Bollman*, Chief Justice John Marshall noted the Constitution did not provide the right itself, and suggested Congress had been required to authorize the writ:

> "[a]cting under the immediate influence of [the Habeas Corpus Clause], [Congress] must have felt, with peculiar force, the obligation of providing efficient means by which this great constitutional privilege should receive life and activity; for if the means be not in existence, the privilege itself would be lost, although no law for its suspension should be enacted."

Under one interpretation of Chief Justice Marshal's words, until Congress provided the "means" to the right by enacting a statute, as it did in the Judiciary Act of 1789 (discussed below), the right did not exist. This view suggests the common law right to the writ of habeas corpus did not survive the ratification of the United States Constitution. That is not the view of modern courts, which have repeatedly asserted that the constitutional right to habeas corpus is the right "at least as it existed in 1789" under common law. *INS v. St. Cyr.* Under that view, the Suspension Clause implicitly recognized and cemented the common law right as one that could not be taken away.

In addition to the question of whether the Suspension Clause implies a constitutional right to the writ of habeas corpus, the language of the Suspension Clause raises numerous other questions that will be addressed below, including: 1) who can suspend the right; 2) how is it properly suspended; 3) what is the effect of a suspension; and 4) to whom and where does the right to habeas apply (or, more specifically, to whom and where does the Suspension Clause apply)? Despite the less than clear language of the Suspension Clause, the importance of the right to the **Founders** is made clear by this simple fact: it is one of only two individual rights addressed in the original Constitution (the Bill of Rights later added many more).

13.4.1.3. The Statutory Basis for Habeas Corpus

First enacted in the Judiciary Act of 1789, the federal *statutory* right to the writ of habeas corpus has existed throughout the nation's history, and has generally tended to expand in scope rather than contract. Under the current statute (28 USC 2241), the writ of habeas corpus extends to a prisoner who is:

> (1) in custody under or by color of the authority of the United States or is committed for trial before some court thereof; or
>
> (2) in custody for an act done or omitted in pursuance of an Act of Congress, or an order, process, judgment or decree of a court or judge of the United States; or
>
> (3) in custody in violation of the Constitution or laws or treaties of the United States; or
>
> (4) being a citizen of a foreign state and domiciled therein is in custody for an act done or omitted under any alleged right, title, authority, privilege, protection, or exemption claimed under the commission, order or sanction of any foreign state, or under color thereof, the validity and effect of which depend upon the law of nations; or
>
> (5) necessary to be brought into court to testify or for trial.

For purposes of national security law, it is important to note that detention in violation of treaties serves as a basis for requesting the writ of habeas corpus under the statute. The statute also provides for the process through which a writ must be requested. First, the detainee must file an application (request) for the writ. As currently interpreted by the Supreme Court, the court in which the detainee must file the request for a writ of habeas corpus is the court with jurisdiction over the *custodian* (for example, the warden, jailer, or other authority figure responsible for the detainee's detention), not necessarily the court with jurisdiction over the detainee. The judge considering the application can either award a writ of habeas corpus or order the custodian to show cause why the writ should not be granted. In practice, courts almost never issue the writ without first issuing a show cause order to the custodian, giving the opportunity for a substantive discussion of the merits of the detainee's allegation of unlawful detention before the writ is actually issued. Once the writ or show-cause order is received by the custodian, he must submit a "return" certifying the basis for detention within three days (20 days, if the custodian can show good cause for additional time). A hearing is set for no more than five days later, at which the "body" of the detainee must be produced—in other words, the detainee must be present—unless the case involves only questions of law, not fact. The court then determines whether the detention is lawful and issues an appropriate decision and order. This can include ordering the custodian to release the detainee or a modification of the detainee's conditions of detention.

13.4.2. Suspension of the Writ of Habeas Corpus

13.4.2.1. Who Has the Power to Suspend?

The Suspension Clause leaves several important questions unanswered, one of the most important of which is: who can suspend the right to habeas corpus? This question arises from the Clause's use of passive voice, meaning that it does not identify the subject.

Those asserting the power to suspend is a congressional right note that the Suspension Clause appears in Article I, which is primarily about the Legislative Branch. Moreover, Article I, Section 9, focuses on limitations to Congress's powers, suggesting that the suspension power resides with Congress. On the other hand, some argue that in the emergency situations that allow for the suspension of this right, Congress cannot realistically convene. Thus, the power to suspend must lie with the President, who requires no vote or assembly of a legislature. Indeed, the Suspension Clause is one of few places in which the Constitution addresses emergency situations, and calls to mind the Supreme Court's conclusion in *The Prize Cases* (see Chapter 2) that, in some instances, an emergency may grant special authority to the President that he would not otherwise have. Proponents of a presidential power to suspend also note there are other limitations in Article I, Section 9, that seem to apply to the President rather than Congress (for example, withdrawals from Treasury).

In a Civil War era case titled *Ex Parte Merryman*, Supreme Court Chief Justice Roger Taney, sitting as a circuit judge, found the President does not have the authority to suspend habeas corpus unilaterally. However, because the Chief Justice was not sitting in his Supreme Court capacity, his opinion is not binding precedent.

The "Not So Great Writ?": *Ex Parte Merryman*

Ex Parte Merryman is an odd case involving multiple Executive Branch decisions to disregard the federal judiciary. In April 1861, in response to President Lincoln's request for states to provide militia troops to the federal government, troops from northern states traveled to Washington. When these troops passed through Baltimore, Maryland, mobs attacked some of the troop transports. Concerned that Maryland might attempt to cut off Washington, D.C., from the north, President Lincoln delegated limited authority to the Army to suspend habeas corpus in Maryland.

> Specifically, he told General Winfield Scott (commanding general of the Army) that if there was any resistance along the "military line" from Annapolis to Washington, Scott or "the officer in command" was authorized to suspend habeas corpus if necessary.
>
> A member of Maryland's militia, Lieutenant John Merryman, participated in the destruction of some railroad bridges and was arrested and detained by the Union Army. Because a federal district judge's writ of habeas corpus had been defied by the commander of Fort McHenry in an earlier case, those representing Merryman asked Chief Justice Taney, author of the notorious Dred Scott opinion that had preserved slavery in 1857, to issue a writ of habeas corpus to have Merryman released. Chief Justice Taney ordered General George Cadwalader (who was overseeing Fort McHenry) to bring Merryman to Taney's chambers, but, citing authority from President Lincoln, Cadwalader refused. Justice Taney then ordered a United States Marshal, a member of the Executive Branch, to seize Cadwalader. However, the Union Army denied the Marshal entry into Fort McHenry to serve the order.
>
> In *Ex Parte Merryman*, Chief Justice Taney issued an opinion that the President did not have the authority to suspend habeas corpus, noting that in England, only Parliament, and not the Crown, had had authority to do so. The implication of Taney's opinion was that Lincoln's suspension of habeas corpus was invalid. Curiously, Taney did not explicitly order the Executive Branch to release Lieutenant Merryman, and President Lincoln did not release Lieutenant Merryman. Lincoln defended this decision in an address to Congress when it reconvened in July 1861, in which he famously asked "Are all the laws but one to go unexecuted, and the Government itself go to pieces lest that one be violated?"

As in other areas discussed in this book, it is natural to ask whether the power to suspend the writ of habeas corpus can be delegated. In other words, if Congress has the authority to suspend the writ of habeas corpus, can it be delegated to the president? That was one of several questions at issue in a famous national security law case titled *Ex Parte Milligan*. We have already explored *Ex Parte Milligan* in the Military Detention section of this chapter for the precedent it set in military commissions, but the case is important in the area of habeas corpus law as well. In 1863, Congress had authorized President Lincoln to suspend habeas corpus when, in his judgment, public safety required it. Lincoln used this privilege almost immediately. The Congressional authorization for the suspension contained several limitations, including a requirement that the government provide a list of all detainees to federal courts on a periodic basis. The suspension authorization also included a provision that if 20 days passed after a person's arrest, and a grand jury of the district had either not met or adjourned without **indicting** the accused, the right to habeas corpus had to be reinstated. *Ex Parte Milligan* involved a Confederate sympathizer named Lambdin Milligan who had been arrested, tried by military commission, and sentenced to death in Indiana for an alleged plot to attack a Union armory and then free Confederate prisoners from a Union prison. However, because the civilian grand jury had not indicted him within the designated timeframe, he challenged his detention and capital sentence in federal court asserting his right to habeas corpus.

The first habeas corpus issue the Supreme Court addressed was whether Milligan had the right to the writ of habeas corpus at all. The Supreme Court held that he did, noting that the President did not have the authority to change the nature of the suspension limitations imposed by Congress. In Milligan's circumstances, the authority for the suspension of the writ had passed because the 20-day period had elapsed, and the grand jury had not indicted him.

The Court then turned to the more relevant question to our current discussion: who has the power to suspend habeas corpus? Although the Court did not conclusively or explicitly answer this question, it found that when Congress has delegated authority to suspend the writ of habeas corpus, the President is obligated to follow the conditions of that delegation. By conceding that Congress may place limitations on the suspension, the Court's ruling seems to imply that this power must have been Congress's to delegate in the first place. This idea recalls the case of *Little v. Barreme*, discussed in Chapter 3, where the Supreme Court enforced the literal terms of Congress's authorization to seize ships going *to* French ports, but not *from* French ports. Here, too, the Supreme Court required that the President comply with limitations on suspension authority granted to him by Congress.

Though the Supreme Court has never expressly opined on the question, it is not difficult to imagine good reasons why the President might need to suspend habeas corpus until Congress can act. Such situations call to mind emergencies of the type discussed in *The Prize Cases*, where the Court upheld President Lincoln's use of military force while waiting for Congress to convene.

In conclusion, though the Supreme Court of the United States has never explicitly held that only Congress may suspend the right to obtain a writ of habeas corpus (absent emergency circumstances), its rulings have suggested that, and scholars generally agree.

13.4.2.2. How Is Habeas Suspended?

The Supreme Court's repeated jurisprudence makes it clear the Court disfavors suspending habeas corpus. One of the manifestations of this disfavor is the high bar it has established regarding *how* to suspend habeas corpus. In addition to the question of *who* can suspend (which is also a "how" question), the government actor suspending habeas corpus must do so with precision. For example, in *INS v. St. Cyr*, an alien living in the United States was being deported because of a felony drug conviction. He challenged his detention and deportation through a habeas corpus proceeding. The government argued that Mr. St. Cyr had no right to habeas because the Antiterrorism and Effective Death Penalty Act and the Illegal Immigration Reform and Immigrant Responsibility Act had both stripped the federal district courts of habeas corpus jurisdiction over deportable aliens. Based on the principle of **constitutional avoidance**, which is that, if possible, courts should interpret statutes avoiding constitutional conflict and interpretation, the Supreme Court held those statutes had not stripped federal courts of habeas jurisdiction. The Court said that none of the statutes expressed a "clear and unambiguous statement of Congress's intent to bar habeas corpus petitions," even though one of the provisions came under the title "Elimination of Custody Review By Habeas Corpus." In his dissent, Justice Scalia sardonically referred to the Supreme Court's conclusions that such a provision did not strip federal courts of habeas corpus as a "superclear" requirement.

Justice Scalia's concern seems justified based on the Supreme Court's repeated findings that Congress had not lawfully removed habeas corpus jurisdiction, even when it had apparently intended to. For example, the Detainee Treatment Act of 2005 (DTA) purported to remove habeas corpus jurisdiction over detainees at Guantánamo Bay and elsewhere, but in *Hamdan v. Rumsfeld*, the Court found the DTA was ambiguous about whether it applied to cases pending at the time the DTA was enacted. The Court thus held that it did not strip habeas jurisdiction for pending cases, which was *all* of them related to the detainees at Guantanamo Bay. Later, in the *Boumediene* case (discussed below), the Court ruled that the Military Commissions Act of 2006 was not a valid suspension of the right of habeas corpus, despite the following language:

> No court, justice, or judge shall have jurisdiction to hear or consider an application for a writ of habeas corpus filed by or on behalf of an alien detained by the United States who has been determined to buy the United States to have been properly detained as an enemy combatant or is awaiting such determination.

The last time the Supreme Court upheld a suspension of the right to habeas corpus was in 1871, so it is not entirely clear what specific language is required for suspending the rights to the writ of habeas corpus. However, it does seem clear that the Supreme Court will look for any opportunity to find that Congress has not suspended the writ if one is available.

13.4.2.3. What Effect of Suspension?

There is little precedent regarding what happens if habeas corpus is properly suspended. This is in part because Congress has not effectively suspended habeas corpus since 1871, and because, if habeas corpus is properly suspended, there is little avenue for courts to review cases and issue opinions. One question raised by precedent and scholarship is whether suspension of habeas corpus affirmatively *authorizes* detention or just functionally *allows* it by taking away the detainee's right to challenge the detention. In other words, does suspending the right to the writ of habeas corpus authorize the government to detain when it otherwise would not have had lawful authority to detain?

The prevailing view on this question is that the right to habeas corpus is simply a right to access a court, not an authorization of detention. In *Milligan*, the Court said, "suspension of the writ does not authorize the arrest of anyone, but simply denies to one arrested the privilege of this writ in order to obtain his liberty." More recently, the Court has made it clear that using the 2001 AUMF as detention authority does not necessarily waive the detainee's right to habeas corpus. *Hamdi v. Rumsfeld.* Implicitly, this means Congress may authorize the detention of United States citizens within the United States without suspending habeas corpus. In other words, the question of whether the government detained an individual under valid authority is separate from the question of whether that authority, statutory or otherwise, explicitly provides the right to habeas corpus. Thus, it is important not to confuse the right to petition for a writ of habeas corpus with the right to be *released* (or not be detained). Rather, a habeas corpus hearing is the proper place to challenge the authority under which the government has detained an individual. The right to habeas corpus is merely an opportunity to challenge the lawfulness of an individual's detention; it is far from a guarantee that a court will find that detention unlawful and order the release of the detainee.

13.4.3. The Personal and Territorial Scope of the Right to Habeas Corpus

United States citizens enjoy the right to the writ of habeas corpus to challenge their detention regardless of where they are being detained. However, it is far less clear where the right to the writ of habeas corpus applies for non-United States citizens. Whether non-United States citizens receive the right to habeas corpus hinges, in part, on whether they seek protection on a statutory or constitutional basis.

13.4.3.1. Statutory Habeas

When the right to the writ of habeas corpus is claimed based on United States statute, the terms of the statute control the extent of the writ. The current habeas corpus statute contains no limitation on the location of the prisoner. In *Rasul v. Bush*, the Supreme Court found the statute required that the court considering the detainee's request for a writ of habeas corpus have jurisdiction over the detainee's custodian. In *Rasul*, the custodian was the Secretary of Defense, who was in the United States, so the court had jurisdiction over the habeas corpus petition, even though Rasul was not detained in the United States.

13.4.3.2. Constitutional Habeas

By contrast, the **extraterritorial** application of the *constitutional* habeas corpus right has been far less clear. Indeed, the United States Supreme Court has issued seemingly contradictory opinions over time.

***Johnson v. Eisentrager*, 1950**

In *Johnson v. Eisentrager*, German soldiers still fighting against the United States in China after Germany had surrendered were captured and convicted by military tribunal. They were subsequently imprisoned by the United States military in an area of post-war Germany for which the United States was responsible. Lawyers for the German detainees brought a habeas corpus action in United States federal court.

Ultimately, the Supreme Court found that the detainees were not entitled to habeas corpus for several reasons. First, they were aliens who lacked connections to the United States. The Court noted that aliens might have the right to habeas corpus, but that such a right was not absolute. For example, aliens with some substantial connections with the United States would normally have some protections, but the Court concluded that any rights extended should be limited during a time of war because aliens are not necessarily loyal to the United States. Importantly, the Court noted that it would be unusual for the Constitution to have extraterritorial application, meaning the *constitutional* right to habeas corpus does not exist where the United States government is not sovereign. Additionally, the Court noted certain practical impediments to allowing habeas corpus jurisdiction for aliens outside the United States. For example, typically the evidence of the lawfulness (or not) of the detention is located outside the United States. This presents a logistical problem for bringing evidence and witnesses to a United States courtroom, and carries possible negative effects on national security, including degrading the commander's ability to focus on the military mission, and diverting resources and military personnel to address habeas corpus cases. Finally, the Court also expressed concern that allowing habeas corpus to aliens detained outside the United States could ultimately lead to a flood of litigation in United States federal courts.

***Boumediene v. Bush*, 2008**

After the 9/11 terrorist attacks, the Bush Administration needed to identify a suitable location for detaining terrorist suspects, especially those detained in and around Afghanistan. Given the seemingly clear precedent of *Eisentrager* that the right to the writ of habeas corpus did not apply to aliens detained outside the sovereign territory of the United States, the Bush Administration concluded that it could detain the terror suspects at the United States naval base at Guantánamo, Bay, Cuba, without fear that the detainees would have the right to the writ of habeas corpus.

In a case that ultimately reached the United States Supreme Court, some of the detainees at Guantánamo challenged their detention and asserted their right to the writ of habeas corpus. Because the Military Commissions Act of 2006 had stripped *statutory* habeas corpus jurisdiction from federal courts for "an alien detained by the United States who has been determined by the United States to have been properly detained as an enemy combatant or is awaiting such determination," the Supreme Court had to address whether the Constitution's Suspension Clause applied extraterritorially (in other words, whether there was a *constitutional* right to habeas corpus that applied). The detainees were all aliens who had been designated as enemy combatants by the United States. None of them were citizens of a nation that the United States was currently at war with, and each had denied being a part of Al Qaeda and the Taliban. In arguing that the right to the writ of habeas corpus did not extend to detainees at Guantanamo, the government noted that though the United States had a lease of land for the Guantánamo base that gave it significant control, it did not have formal legal sovereignty over the land, which remained with Cuba, and thus the *Eisentrager* precedent controlled.

The Supreme Court rejected what it described as the "formalist" approach that the extraterritorial application of the right to the writ of habeas corpus depended solely upon legal sovereignty. Instead, the Court determined that whether a particular constitutional provision applies extraterritorially depends upon "particular circumstances, the practical necessity, and the possible alternatives Congress had." The Supreme Court interpreted *Eisentrager* as having been in large part based on practical considerations, concluding that courts should use a *functional* approach to determining extraterritorial application of constitutional rights, when it said "questions of extraterritoriality turn on objective factors and practical concerns, not formalism." The Court then outlined factors it found applicable when determining the reach of the Suspension Clause that had been discussed in *Eisentrager*:

1. The citizenship and status of the detainee in the adequacy of the process through which that status determination was made;

2. The nature of the sites where apprehension and then detention took place; and

3. The practical obstacles inherent in resolving the prisoner's entitlement to the writ.

Applying these factors to the detention of the terror suspects at Guantánamo Bay, the Court determined that they *did* have the right to the writ of habeas corpus. Regarding the citizenship of the detainees, the Court noted that they were all aliens with no or minimal connections to the United States. Regarding status, unlike the *Eisentrager* detainees who had acknowledged they were fighting for Germany, the detainees in *Boumediene* disputed their connection with enemies of the United States. Regarding the location of apprehension, the Court noted that the detainees were captured outside the United States, and some were captured on the battlefield by United States military forces. Regarding the nature of the location of the detention, the Court observed that the Guantanamo base was in United States territory, subject to a 100 year lease, secure from attack, and under the absolute control of the United States, thus attempting to distinguish the facts of the *Boumediene* from those of *Eisentrager*. Finally, regarding the practical obstacles inherent in resolving the prisoner's entitlement to the writ of habeas corpus, the Court noted that though there would be expenses incurred in convening a hearing for the detainees at Guantánamo, all hearings involve some cost. Additionally, the Court suggested it was sensitive to the issues of diverting time and focus of military personnel to habeas corpus petitions, but determined that that factor alone is not dispositive of whether the detainee should have the right to the writ of habeas corpus. The Court also suggested that the practical obstacles of a habeas corpus at Guantánamo would be less than if the detainees were detained in the theater of war.

Having already noted the constitutional importance of the privilege of habeas corpus, the majority in *Boumediene* expressed concern that denying habeas corpus to the Guantánamo detainees would upset the constitutional balance of powers, because it would allow Congress and the President to decide when and where the Constitution applies.

You Be the Judge: Habeas Corpus for Detainees?

The Supreme Court's opinion in the *Boumediene* case means that future questions of whether the constitutional rights to the writ of habeas corpus applies to aliens outside the United States be decided on a case-by-case basis. Each of the three factors courts should consider in determining whether the right to the writ of habeas corpus applies extraterritorially present a continuum of possible facts. For example, the continuum of the citizenship factor runs from United States citizens overseas (reminder: United States citizens are automatically entitled to the writ and access to the courts close) to aliens with substantial connections to the United States to aliens with no or minimal connections in the United States.

You are a federal judge who has received a habeas petition from three detainees under the following circumstances:

> The detainees are all aliens with no connections to the United States. One was taken into custody in Pakistan by Pakistani military forces, one in Thailand by Thai police, and one on the battlefield in Afghanistan by United States military forces. The detainees are being held by the United States at a prison on a United States Air Base in Afghanistan during active hostilities between the United States and the Taliban and Al Qaeda. The lease agreement for the base in Afghanistan "consigns all facilities and land located at Bagram airbase to the United States and coalition forces," but the base is in sovereign Afghan territory. The base is subject to occasional attacks by individual "suicide bomber" terrorists and by rockets and mortars that are occasionally fired into the base.

Apply the three *Boumediene* factors to these facts and compare them to the facts in *Boumediene* and *Eisentrager* to determine whether the right to the writ of habeas corpus should apply to these detainees.

13.4.4. Substitutes for Habeas Corpus

The Supreme Court has suggested that when the right to the writ of habeas corpus has not been properly suspended, the Suspension Clause requires, at minimum, an adequate substitute for the writ. Thus, unless the writ has been suspended under conditions consistent with the Constitution, if the government takes away the jurisdiction of federal courts to entertain habeas corpus petitions in certain types of cases or for certain types of detainees, it should provide a substitute method for judicial review of government detention. The idea is that whether a particular process is *called* "habeas corpus" or called something else, if it provides sufficient opportunity for judicial review of government detention, it can fulfill the purpose of the Suspension Clause.

In the *Boumediene* case, the government argued that two procedures provided adequate substitute for the right to habeas corpus: 1) the Combatant Status Review Tribunal (CSRT) process; and 2) appeals to the Court of Appeals for the

D.C. Circuit, which had been provided by Congress under the Detainee Treatment Act of 2005. The Supreme Court rejected both procedures as being inadequate substitutes for habeas corpus.

Under the CSRT process, the military held limited hearings during which evidence of the detainee's status as an enemy combatant was presented. The *Boumediene* Court determined the CSRTs to be an insufficient substitute for habeas corpus because the purpose of habeas corpus is that the review "comes from the outside." With CSRTs, the military was reviewing its own actions, rather than review by an authority outside of the Executive Branch.

The Supreme Court also found the appeal process inadequate. Under the DTA, the Court of Appeals' role in reviewing detainee cases was limited to determining whether the CSRT followed the Department of Defense "standards and procedures" and assessing whether those standards and procedures were lawful. Importantly to the Supreme Court, the Court of Appeals was not permitted to make findings of fact or consider evidence outside the CSRT record. So, the Court of Appeals could not review, add to, or correct factual determinations made by the CSRT, and the detainee had no opportunity to present relevant exculpatory evidence to the Court of Appeals. These limitations, in conjunction with the detainee's limited rights to present evidence at the CSRT hearing, led the Supreme Court to determine that this appeal procedure was an insufficient substitute for habeas corpus rights.

Thus, in *Boumediene*, the Supreme Court concluded that there are some fundamental elements of habeas corpus review that were not present in the procedures available to the Guantanamo detainees, but that should be present in an adequate substitute for habeas corpus: 1) the ability of the detainee to obtain and present evidence; and 2) review of executive action by an Article III federal judge (as opposed to a judge in the Executive Branch) that was not "unduly circumscribed" in their power. The Supreme Court did not purport to identify all of the elements of an adequate substitute, nor did it detail what the inferior federal courts were required to look for regarding Guantánamo detainees. This led to significant uncertainty regarding whether Congress could ever provide an "adequate substitute" for the right to the writ of habeas corpus.

13.4.5. Post-*Boumediene* Habeas Practice

Following *Boumediene*, habeas corpus petitions from detainees at Guantanamo are all handled the same way, ostensibly in order to provide consistency and clarity in decisions related to detention. The detainee submits a petition to the federal district court for the District of Columbia only; consideration of petitions by other federal district courts is not permitted. These trial judges may consider written evidence from the government and the detainee and may also consider the detainee's testimony, provided through a real-time, two-way, secured video conference from Guantanamo. After the trial judge's decision, the losing party may appeal to the D.C. Circuit Court of Appeals, and then to the United States Supreme Court.

As of 2020, the Supreme Court had not entertained any more habeas corpus cases from Guantanamo since the *Boumediene* decision in 2008, leaving the D.C. Circuit Court of Appeals as the de facto final court for habeas cases. Relying on the Supreme Court's *Hamdi* ruling that detention is generally a power possessed by a party in an armed conflict to prevent the captured from returning to battle, the D.C. Circuit has created a functional test for determining whether a detainee has sufficient ties to the conflict to be detained. The functional test employs a "totality of the circumstances" approach, where the court determines whether the detainee is sufficiently tied to Al Qaeda or the Taliban through things like attending Al Qaeda or Taliban training camps, staying at Al Qaeda "guesthouses," living with known fighters near battle lines, and possessing military weapons. Responding to concerns that individuals might be detained based only on circumstantial evidence or inference, the D.C. Circuit responded that if the subject "looks like a duck. . .walks like a duck, and. . . quacks like a duck," it is a duck. *Hussain v. Obama.*

Indefinite Detention in the "Forever War"

As of 2020, the United States was continuing to detain terrorism suspects it had first apprehended in the months following the September 11, 2001, terror attacks, at Guantanamo Bay, without charge or trial. In *Hamdi*, Justice O'Connor looked to the international law of war principle that enemies may be detained for the duration of a conflict to prevent their return to the battlefield, and ultimately determined the 2001 AUMF justified the President's authority to detain. But what should happen in a war of such long duration and without a clear end? When nation states war with each other, some act usually demarcates the end of the war, or at least the end of hostilities. In fact, international law regarding the detention of enemies developed with such conflicts in mind. But when the "enemy" is an evolving and amorphous group of persons engaged in terrorism, can the war ever be conclusively terminated? What factors would signify an end to the armed conflict against Al Qaeda and the Taliban such that the justification for detention during armed conflict—the right of the captor to prevent the captured from returning to the battlefield—would terminate? Withdrawal of ground forces from Afghanistan? A truce with the Taliban? A peace **treaty**? The dissolution of Al Qaeda? The international law justification for detention in the **non-international armed conflict** with Al Qaeda requires armed conflict of a sufficient intensity and duration waged against an "armed group." As of 2020, the United States still engages in military action against Al Qaeda members, especially through the use of **drone** strikes, though Al Qaeda's organization and influence seems to be waning.

The open-ended nature of the 2001 AUMF authorizing the President to use all "necessary and appropriate force," combined with the enduring nature of a terror threat, pose important questions regarding detention in conflicts that appear to lack any defined end. The Fourth Geneva Convention suggests that detention of ongoing security threats is permissible, so long as the detainee's current dangerousness is periodically reviewed by the detaining power. Since 2013, the United States has conducted continued dangerousness reviews of detainees called "Periodic Review Boards." Some detainees have been released following periodic review. Is that a sufficient fix to the problem of indefinite detention to a war that lasts "forever?"

REVIEW QUESTIONS

1. Based on the Constitution, statute, and precedent, under what circumstances may the military detain combatants?

2. What are the types of civilian preventive detention and what are the advantages and disadvantages of each for counter-terrorism purposes?

3. Why did Blackstone refer to the writ of habeas corpus as "the great writ" and why have courts in the United States so carefully protected it?

4. When can the writ of habeas corpus be suspended, and by who?

5. What justification did the government offer for not providing habeas corpus in Guantánamo? Why did the Court say the government was wrong?

6. How has the *Boumediene* case affected the right to habeas corpus for detained terror suspects?

CRITICAL THINKING QUESTIONS

1. Do you agree with Justice Frankfurter's suggestion in *Korematsu* that what might be otherwise unlawful or unconstitutional during peace might be lawful and constitutional during wartime?

2. Thinking about *Korematsu*, if the government has the constitutional authority to draft people to serve in the military and ultimately die, or to seize entire industries in order to wage a war, why does it not have the authority to exclude people from certain areas or intern them in specific places?

3. In *Korematsu*, did the Supreme Court abdicate its role by failing to examine the military's assertions that the exclusion order was motivated by military necessity rather than racial prejudice and economic opportunism?

4. In both *Milligan* and *Korematsu*, the Supreme Court assessed detention of non-combatant United States citizens away from combat. How do you explain the Supreme Court's differing decisions in *Milligan* and *Korematsu*?

5. How does the "military necessity" rationale for limiting United States citizens' rights in wartime in the *Hamdi* case differ from that rationale in the *Korematsu* case?

6. Was it "militarily necessary" to detain Hamdi without trial in this case? What if there were thousands of detainees in Hamdi's situation? Should a court's deference to military necessity decline as the length of detention grows?

7. Are the facts in the *Hamdi* case more like the facts in *Milligan* or *Quirin*? Are the facts of the *Padilla* case more like the facts in *Milligan* or *Quirin*?

8. Why do you think the Bush administration moved Padilla to civilian custody just before the Supreme Court decided whether to hear his appeal of the Fourth Circuit ruling?

9. Should the government be able to change the classification of a detainee from enemy combatant to material witness/domestic criminal, and vice-versa? What implications could this practice have for a detainee's ability to be rendered proper due process?

10. To what extent should the international law of war limit or dictate domestic law regarding detention? Was it proper for the D.C. Circuit to ignore international law in its holding in *Al-Bihani*?

11. What features should a "terrorist preventive detention" statute contain in order to meet constitutional due process requirements? Draft such a statute.

12. Do you agree with the Supreme Court in *Whren* that courts need not examine an arresting officer's subjective intent regarding the "real" reason for the arrest?

13. Are pretextual arrests and material witness arrests a loophole, or a legitimate means to their end? Do they support the intent of the *due process* protections of the Constitution? Are they consistent with liberty? Or are they a prime example of sacrificing liberty for the sake of security?

14. Suppose you are a government investigator with some imprecise and uncertain evidence that an individual is involved in a plot to engage in a terrorist act. You do not know when the act will occur and you do not have sufficient evidence to establish probable cause to arrest and charge the individual with a crime. What detention options do you have to preserve national security while also preserving the values of liberty enshrined in the Constitution?

15. There is presently no "terrorism detention" statute. Would it be a good idea to enact a statute authorizing detention of suspected terrorists? Draft the language of such a statute.

16. Can you imagine circumstances in which the President legitimately might need the authority to suspend habeas corpus without involving Congress?

17. If you were advising Congress on how to effectively suspend the writ of habeas corpus, what language would you suggest for such a statute?

18. Should the right to habeas corpus apply to non-United States citizens at all?

CHAPTER 14

Rendering Terror Suspects

Aircraft N313P, the plane operated by "Premier Executive Transport Services" for the United States Central Intelligence Agency to engage in extraordinary rendition of "high value detainees" and others, including Khaled el-Masri, whose extraordinary rendition is detailed in this chapter

Learning Objectives

1. Understand the difference between "ordinary rendition" and "extraordinary rendition."

2. Be able to identify different types of laws that might be violated by extraordinary rendition operations.

3. Understand how the United States Supreme Court's jurisprudence has potentially contributed to extraordinary rendition by the United States government.

14.1. TYPES OF RENDITION

"**Rendition**" is a legal term describing the transfer of a person from one **jurisdiction** to another. In the United States, this term has often been used to describe the transfer of a person accused of a crime from one state to another. In fact, the United States Constitution, Article IV, Section 2, Clause 2, specifically requires rendition in certain circumstances. In the context of modern counterterrorism operations, however, rendition usually refers to the international transfer of a terrorist suspect from one nation state to another. This is usually accomplished through ordinary extradition treaties and processes, under which both governments agree to transfer the person involved.

Rendition has been approved by the United States Supreme Court, even when the subject of the rendition is a United States citizen. In *Munaf v. Green*, a United States citizen detained by the United States military in Iraq for terrorism offenses he committed after the United States invasion in 2003 asked a federal court to block his transfer from United States custody to the custody of Iraq, which intended to prosecute him for those offenses. His request reached the United States Supreme Court, which ruled that federal courts did have **habeas corpus** jurisdiction to hear his challenge, but the Court ruled against him on the merits of his request to block rendition. The Court opined that a federal court did not have the authority to prevent the United States from transferring a terror suspect to the custody of another government for prosecution because "habeas corpus does not require the United States to shelter such fugitives from the criminal justice system of the sovereign with authority to prosecute them." The Court concluded that a United States citizen traveling abroad who commits a crime in a foreign country has the same rights as a national of that country. Though Munaf argued he risked being tortured by Iraqi authorities, the Supreme Court was convinced the United States government had fulfilled its duty to investigate whether the Justice Ministry of Iraq would **torture** Munaf. Chief Justice Roberts agreed that had the facts been different—for instance, if the United States government believed there was a risk of torture and transferred the detainee anyway—there might be a role for United States federal courts in blocking such transfers. Munaf's presence in Iraq was due to his voluntary travel there. Because he was already in Iraq, his transfer was based on the sovereignty of the nation in which he was voluntarily present when he committed the alleged offenses, and so his transfer to Iraqi custody was a type of rendition not requiring a **treaty** or statute to effectuate.

In counterterrorism operations, another type of rendition has arisen: **extraordinary rendition**. Extraordinary rendition—sometimes called extrajudicial rendition—is the transfer of a person from one country to another *without* legal process. Extraordinary rendition includes the subjects of the two previous chapters: interrogation and detention. Extraordinary rendition typically involves one nation abducting a suspect present in a second nation, and transporting that person to a third nation, where detention and interrogation occur. Sometimes the nation abducting the suspect conducts the detention and interrogation itself, while in other cases the abducting nation turns the person over to a third nation to detain and interrogate, sometimes with the tacit understanding that the third nation may engage in detention or interrogation practices considered illegal in the abducting nation or under international law. On occasion the country in which the suspect is initially abducted is complicit or participates in the abduction, turning the person over to the abducting nation.

Extraordinary rendition can potentially violate the domestic law of the abducting nation, the law of the nation in which the person is abducted, the law of the nation where the person is ultimately detained and interrogated, and international law. For example, governments engaging in extraordinary rendition often operate under national legal systems prohibiting abduction, false imprisonment, and torture. Similarly, the countries where the abduction originally occurs typically criminalize abduction. And often the laws of the country where the detention and interrogation ultimately take place prohibit false imprisonment and torture.

In the previous chapter we discussed detention of terrorism suspects in situations where the government claims it is acting in accordance with applicable domestic and international law. By contrast, the purpose of extraordinary rendition is usually to *circumvent* one or more system of laws or, at a minimum, to prevent public knowledge of the detainee's whereabouts. Rather than claim these renditions are consistent with applicable law, governments often tend to deny they are occurring, making corroboration of some claims of illegal activity difficult or impossible.

In the wake of the 9/11 attacks, the United States Central Intelligence Agency (CIA) launched an extraordinary rendition program to detain and interrogate suspected terrorists. After the CIA abducted detainees from countries outside the United States, the program involved two variants. In some situations, the CIA would conduct its own detention and interrogation operations at so-called "**black sites**," which were secret detention facilities located outside the United States. These interrogations sometimes involved "**enhanced interrogation techniques**," discussed in Chapter 12. In the other variant, the CIA delivered the detainee to the custody of another country for interrogation. In the words of one United States government official, "We don't kick the [expletive] out of them. We send them to other countries so they can kick the [expletive] out of them." Another former CIA official was more specific: "If you want a serious interrogation, you send a prisoner to Jordan. If you want them to be tortured, you send them to Syria. If you want someone to disappear—never to see them again—you send them to Egypt." Typically, the CIA conducted its own detention and interrogation of the highest value suspects, sending only so-called "second tier" suspects to other governments.

14.2. UNITED STATES DOMESTIC LAW REGARDING EXTRAORDINARY RENDITION

14.2.1. Constitutional Law

Some plaintiffs seeking compensation for allegedly having been subject to extraordinary rendition at the hands of the United States CIA have asserted that extraordinary renditions are deprivations of liberty without legal process, and therefore violate the Due Process Clause of the Fifth Amendment to the United States Constitution. Ostensibly, kidnapping and detention by United States officials constitutes a "deprivation of liberty." While it is clear that United States citizens enjoy the protections of the Fifth Amendment when being subjected to United States government action, the more common question in the context of extraordinary rendition is whether *non-citizens* outside the United States are protected by the Fifth Amendment. As noted elsewhere in this text, the Supreme Court has not issued clear guidance. The *Boumediene* case, in which the Supreme Court found that non-citizens can have a right to habeas corpus outside the United States suggested a functionalist approach to answering questions of **extraterritoriality**, but that case is not precisely on point regarding the question of whether the *Fifth Amendment* right to due process is to be treated the same.

14.2.2. Statutory Provisions Related to Extraordinary Rendition

United States domestic law prohibits abduction. But state and federal criminal prohibitions generally do not apply to actions taken by United States government agents outside the United States, which is where abduction, transport, and detention and interrogation generally occur in extraordinary renditions. Nevertheless, some United States laws prohibit some elements of the extraordinary rendition program allegedly engaged in by the United States CIA. For instance, the Torture Act and the Detainee Treatment Act, enacted in response to the discovery of post-9/11 CIA abuses, prohibit torture and certain other interrogation practices in which the United States CIA was alleged to have engaged. Additionally, the United States has implemented elements of international treaties in domestic law, including the principle that persons should not be sent or returned to nations where their torture or maltreatment is likely.

14.2.3. Executive Authorizations

Several United States presidents have explicitly authorized extraordinary rendition programs. Presidents Ronald Reagan, George H.W. Bush, and Bill Clinton are known to have authorized extraordinary rendition to the United States for the purpose of criminal prosecution. In President Reagan's since-declassified order, such renditions were to occur only from countries where extradition to the United States was not authorized or available. President Clinton additionally authorized rendition to foreign governments. After 9/11, President George W. Bush reportedly issued a directive authorizing the CIA to conduct extraordinary renditions for the purpose of detention and interrogation, even where there was no expectation of criminal prosecution. In 2009, President Barack Obama curtailed somewhat the extraordinary rendition program by issuing an **Executive Order** that directed the CIA to close any "black sites" it was operating. Notably, the Executive Order did not fully end the practice of extraordinary rendition, but instead established a task force to evaluate the practice. Though the task force's report was not made public, the Obama administration later adopted the policy that the United States would not transfer any individual to a foreign country if it is "more likely than not" that the person would be tortured in that country. President Obama left office without publicly ending the practice of extraordinary rendition, and in fact appeared to adopt President George W. Bush's ultimate practice of sending terrorist suspects to foreign countries for detention and interrogation. Similarly, as of this writing, President Obama's successor, Donald Trump, had not publicly ended extraordinary rendition.

14.2.4. United States Judicial Treatment of Extraordinary Rendition

Extraordinary rendition has a long history in the United States and has received some support from a surprising source: the United States Supreme Court. As early as 1886, the Supreme Court permitted criminal prosecution of a suspect who had been brought to the United States for prosecution after being forcibly and illegally abducted in Lima, Peru. In the case of *Ker v. Illinois*, the Supreme Court held that the fact that the abductor did not utilize an existing extradition treaty between the United States and Peru did not give rise to a due process defense to criminal prosecution. The Court further held that the only action that could give rise to such a defense would be violation of the terms of such a treaty. The Supreme Court reiterated this point half a century later in *Frisbie v. Collins* when it noted "[t]his Court has never departed from the rule announced in [*Ker*] that the power of a court to try a person for crime is not impaired by the fact that he had been brought within the court's jurisdiction by reason of a 'forcible abduction.' " The idea that abducted criminal defendants could be tried in United States courts so long as the terms of an extradition treaty were not violated became known as the *Ker-Frisbie* doctrine.

In 1992, in a case captioned *United States v. Alvarez-Machain*, the Supreme Court applied the *Ker-Frisbie* doctrine to an abduction of Mexican doctor Humberto Alvarez-Machain by agents of the United States Drug Enforcement Agency (DEA). Doctor Alvarez-Machain was suspected of having participated in the torture and murder of a DEA agent. During the extraordinary rendition, DEA agents kidnapped the doctor from his medical office in Guadalajara, Mexico, and flew him to El Paso, Texas, where he was arrested by different DEA agents. Though there was an extradition treaty between Mexico and the United States, the Supreme Court interpreted the treaty to not prohibit extraordinary rendition, essentially finding that because the treaty did not explicitly prohibit extraordinary rendition, engaging in rendition did not violate the treaty. Though the Supreme Court acknowledged that the abduction of the doctor might be considered "shocking," and that it might violate general international law principles, it found that, absent a violation of the extradition treaty, the defendant doctor's forcible abduction did not prohibit his trial in a court in the United States. The Supreme Court thus accepted that the United States government could forcibly abduct a citizen from another country in violation of that country's law, and possibly international law, and such action would not preclude the United States from prosecuting the abducted person in United States court. The dissent noted that the majority opinion failed to differentiate the conduct of private citizens in the prior cases like *Ker* from the actions of agents of the Executive Branch of the United States government in this case.

Even though the Supreme Court has apparently concluded that *how* a criminal defendant is brought into court does not affect the court's jurisdiction over him, that does not mean the Court has expressly approved of extraordinary rendition. Hoping to seek compensation and a declaration of wrongdoing involved in extraordinary rendition operations, some plaintiffs have attempted to sue the United States, its agents, and even non-government contractors involved in extraordinary rendition operations. As discussed in Chapter 4, these lawsuits have typically failed because courts have found the cases involve non-justiciable "state secrets." For example, in *Mohamed v. Jeppesen Dataplan, Inc.*, the plaintiff alleged various theories of liability under the Alien Tort Statute, claiming that Jeppesen, a private contractor providing flight logistics services, had assisted the CIA in its extraordinary rendition program. Before Jeppesen even answered the complaint, the United States moved to intervene and dismiss the plaintiff's lawsuit, arguing that allowing the case to proceed would jeopardize state secrets. The Ninth Circuit Court of Appeals agreed, asserting it had "independently and critically confirmed that . . . disclosure could be expected to cause significant harm to national security." The court noted "there is precious little Jeppesen could say about its relevant conduct and knowledge without revealing information about how the United States government does or does not conduct covert operations."

The *El-Masri* case based on allegations detailed in Section 14.4.1 of this chapter similarly ended when the Fourth Circuit Court of Appeals held that permitting the case to proceed would jeopardize state secrets. The United States Supreme Court denied certiorari in both the *Jeppesen* and *El-Masri* cases, allowing the Circuit Court rulings to stand. Thus, though the United States federal judiciary did not expressly *approve* extraordinary rendition, its rulings allowed the United States government and related contractors to avoid legal liability for such activities.

14.3. FOREIGN AND INTERNATIONAL LAW REGARDING EXTRAORDINARY RENDITION

14.3.1. Foreign Laws

Whether extraordinary rendition violates a foreign country's law is a fact- and country-specific question. For instance, most nations have laws prohibiting abduction, but when the government of a nation in which the abduction occurs authorizes or participates in the abduction, that might, under the law of some nations, serve as a defense to criminal liability for the abduction. In other nations, like the United States, the government cannot authorize extrajudicial abduction of persons in its jurisdiction, even if the government **consents** or participates. Additionally, many nations have laws prohibiting torture or unlawful detention. So, participants in extraordinary rendition can be subject to criminal prosecution, if evidence is available and there is political will to do so. In fact, this occurred in the Abu Omar case discussed in Section 14.4.2.

14.3.2. International Law

Extraordinary rendition ostensibly violates several provisions of international law. Article Three of the U.N. Convention against Torture and Other Cruel, Inhuman or Degrading Treatment or Punishment (UNCAT), to which the United States and over 150 other nations are party, requires that no state "shall expel, return ("refouler") or extradite a person to another State where there are substantial grounds for believing that he would be in danger of being subjected to torture." This prohibition has been interpreted to include a right to "effective, independent, and impartial review" of the decision to transfer an individual to another country. *Committee Against Torture in case of Ahmed Agiza*. Similarly, the International Covenant on Civil and Political Rights (ICCPR), to which the United States is also a party, and the European Convention on Human Rights (ECHR) prohibit transfer of an individual to another county in the face of a real risk of torture or cruel, inhuman, or degrading treatment. As with the UNCAT, these treaty obligations have been interpreted to include opportunity for "effective, independent review" of a decision to expel or transfer a person to a country where there is an arguable risk of torture prior to the person's transfer. *U.N. Human Rights Committee in the case of Muhammed al-Zery.*

Extraordinary rendition can violate international law even when there is no risk of maltreatment in the country to which the person is ultimately transferred. Article Nine of the ICCPR also states that "[e]veryone has the right to liberty and security of person. No one shall be subjected to arbitrary arrest or detention. No one shall be deprived of his liberty except on such grounds and in accordance with such procedure as are established by law." Additionally, the International Convention for the Protection of All Persons from Enforced Disappearances prohibits "enforced disappearance," which are defined as

> [t]he arrest, detention, abduction or any other form of deprivation of liberty by agents of the state or by persons or groups of persons acting with the authorization, support or acquiescence of the state, followed by a refusal to acknowledge the deprivation of liberty or by concealment of the fate or whereabouts of the disappeared person, which place such a person outside the protection of the law.

Multiple treaty bodies have interpreted this to be an absolute prohibition of taking of hostages, abductions or unacknowledged detention, and no circumstances, including states of war or public emergency, can justify such actions. Importantly, these provisions have been interpreted to be norms of **customary international law,** applicable to all nations.

Some political leaders have contended the United States' extraordinary rendition program was part of a "war on terror," and thus different rules should apply to anti-terror operations because of their warlike nature. However, the Geneva Convention Relative to the Treatment of Prisoners of War and the Geneva Convention Relative to the Protection of Civilian Persons in Time of War both require the detaining party to provide significant rights to detainees. These rights include humane treatment, proper living conditions, communication with family, and other rights that were allegedly not provided by the CIA or partner nations when they engaged in extended detention operations after extraordinary rendition.

Several international treaty bodies have condemned the United States' post-9/11 extraordinary rendition program as violating international law. For example, the UN Working Group on Arbitrary Detention ruled that the CIA's detention of at least 26 individuals were secret, and therefore arbitrary and illegal under Article Nine of the ICCPR. In 2006, the U.N. Committee Against Torture demanded the United States "cease the rendition of suspects," concluding that "detaining persons in such conditions constitutes, *per se*, a violation of the [UNCAT]." Similarly, the U.N. Human Rights Committee urged the United States to "immediately cease its practice of secret detention and close all secret detention facilities" and "take all necessary measures to ensure that individuals, including those it detains outside its own territory, are not returned to another country by way of, *inter alia*, their transfer, rendition, extradition, expulsion or refoulement if there are substantial reasons for believing that they would be in danger of being subjected to torture or cruel, inhuman or degrading treatment or punishment."

14.4. CASE STUDIES

14.4.1. Case Study: Khaled El-Masri

According to a lawsuit filed by Khaled El-Masri against the United States, Mr. El-Masri was the subject of an extraordinary rendition by the United States CIA. Mr. El-Masri was born in Kuwait, but settled in Ulm, Germany, and became a German citizen in 1995. The following allegations come directly from the largely unconfirmed complaint his lawyers filed on his behalf during the lawsuit:

* * * * *

> In December 2003, Mr. El-Masri visited Macedonia for a vacation. Shortly after he arrived, Macedonian law enforcement officials confiscated Mr. El-Masri's passport and detained him for several hours.

He was then transferred by armed plainclothes officers to a hotel in Skopje, Macedonia.

Mr. El-Masri was detained in the hotel for 23 days, guarded at all hours by rotating shifts of armed Macedonian officers. The curtains were closed day and night, and Mr. El-Masri was not permitted to leave the room. His requests to see a lawyer, translator, or German consular official, and to contact his wife, were denied. When he once moved toward the door and stated that he intended to leave, three captors pointed pistols at his head and threatened to shoot him.

Mr. El-Masri was interrogated repeatedly by Macedonian agents throughout the course of his detention in Skopje. He was questioned about what he did in Ulm, the persons with whom he associated there, and the persons who attended his mosque. Mr. El-Masri's interrogators pressed him continuously about a meeting he allegedly had in Jalalabad, Afghanistan with an Egyptian man, and about possible Norwegian contacts. Mr. El-Masri responded that he had never been to Jalalabad and knew no one from Norway. On the seventh day of his confinement, a man who appeared to be in charge of the interrogators proposed to Mr. El-Masri that if he confessed his involvement with Al Qaeda, he would be returned to Germany. Mr. El-Masri refused. On the thirteenth day of his confinement, Mr. El-Masri commenced a hunger strike to protest his continued unlawful detention, and he did not eat again during the remaining ten days of detention in Macedonia. On January 23, 2004, seven or eight Macedonian men dressed in civilian clothes whom Mr. El-Masri had not seen before entered the hotel room. The men then handcuffed and blindfolded him and placed him in a car.

After driving approximately one hour, the car came to a halt, and Mr. El-Masri could hear the sound of airplanes. He was removed from the vehicle, still handcuffed and blindfolded, and was led to a building. Inside, he was told that he would be medically examined. Instead, he was beaten severely with fists and what felt like a thick stick. His clothes were sliced from his body, leaving him in his underwear. He was told to remove his underwear and he refused. He was beaten again, and his underwear was forcibly removed. He heard the sound of pictures being taken. He was thrown to the floor. His hands were pulled back and a boot was placed on his back. He then felt a firm object being forced into his anus.

Mr. El-Masri was pulled from the floor and dragged to a corner of the room. His blindfold was removed. A flash went off and temporarily blinded him. When he recovered his sight, he saw seven or eight men dressed in black and wearing black ski masks. Mr. El-Masri believed the men were American members of a CIA "black renditions team." One of the men placed El-Masri in a diaper. He was then dressed in a dark blue short-sleeved track suit, and placed in a belt with chains that attached to his wrists and ankles. The men put earmuffs and eye pads on him, blindfolded him, and hooded him.

Mr. El-Masri was walked to an airplane. Once inside, he was thrown to the floor face down and his legs and arms were spread-eagled and secured to the sides of the plane. He felt an injection in his shoulder, after which he became lightheaded. He felt a second injection that rendered him nearly unconscious. Mr. El-Masri was dimly aware of the plane landing and taking off again. When the plane landed for the second time, he was unchained and taken off the plane. It was warmer outside than it had been in Macedonia, and Mr. El-Masri realized that he had not been returned to Germany. He believed he might be in Guantánamo, or possibly Iraq. He learned later that he was in Afghanistan.

Mr. El-Masri was removed from the plane and shoved into the back of a waiting vehicle. After the car drove for about ten minutes, Mr. El-Masri was dragged from the vehicle, pushed into a building, thrown to the floor, and kicked and beaten on the head and the small of his back. He was left in a small, dirty, concrete cell. When he adjusted his eyes to the light, he saw that the walls were covered in crude Arabic, Urdu, and Farsi writing. The cell did not contain a bed. It was cold, but Mr. El-Masri had been provided only one dirty, military-style blanket and some old, torn clothes bundled into a thin pillow. Mr. El-Masri believed he had been transferred to a CIA-run prison facility known as the "Salt Pit," which was an abandoned brick factory north of the Kabul business district that was used by the CIA for detention of some high-level terror suspects.

That night, Mr. El-Masri was removed from his cell and transferred to an interrogation room. There were six or eight men dressed in the same black clothing and ski masks as the men in the Macedonian airport, as well as a masked doctor who spoke American-accented English, and a translator who spoke Arabic with a Palestinian accent. Mr. El-Masri was stripped naked, photographed, and medically examined by one of the masked men. Blood and urine samples were taken. Mr. El-Masri complained to the man who seemed to be a doctor about the unhygienic water and poor conditions in his cell. The man responded that the Afghans were responsible for the conditions of his confinement. Then Mr. El-Masri was returned to his single-person cell, where he would be detained for more than four months, with no reading or writing materials, and without once being permitted outside to breathe fresh air.

On his second night in the Salt Pit, Mr. El-Masri was woken by masked men and once again brought to the interrogation room. Again, six or eight masked, black-clad men were in the room. Mr. El-Masri was interrogated by a masked man who spoke Arabic with a South Lebanese accent. The man asked him if he knew why he had been detained; Mr. El-Masri said he did not. The man then stated that Mr. El-Masri was in a country with no laws, and that no one knew where he was, and asked whether Mr. El-Masri understood what that meant.

Mr. El-Masri was interrogated on three or four occasions, each time by the same man, and each time at night. His interrogations were accompanied by threats, insults, pushing, and shoving. Two men who participated in the interrogations identified themselves as Americans. Mr. El-Masri repeatedly demanded that he be permitted to meet with a representative of the German government, but these requests were ignored.

In March 2004, Mr. El-Masri and several other inmates with whom he communicated through cell walls commenced a hunger strike to protest their continued confinement without charges. After 27 days without food, Mr. El-Masri was given an audience with two unmasked Americans, one of whom was the prison director and the second an even higher official whom other inmates referred to as "the Boss." The Afghan prison director was also present, along with the translator with the Palestinian accent. Mr. El-Masri insisted that the Americans either release him, bring him before a court, allow him access to a German official, or watch him starve to death. The American prison director replied that he could not release Mr. El-Masri without permission from Washington, but stated that Mr. El-Masri should not be detained in the prison. Mr. El-Masri was returned to his cell, where he continued his hunger strike.

Mr. El-Masri's health deteriorated on a daily basis. He received no medical treatment during his confinement, despite repeated requests. Mr. El-Masri believed CIA officials at the "Salt Pit" realized early on during his detention they had detained the wrong person. In March 2004, Mr. El-Masri's passport was examined by CIA officials in Langley, Virginia and determined to be valid.

On the thirty-seventh day of his hunger strike, hooded men entered Mr. El-Masri's cell, dragged him from his bed, and bound his hands and feet. They dragged him into the interrogation room, sat him on a chair, and tied him to it. A feeding tube was then forced through his nose to his stomach and a liquid was poured through it. After this procedure, Mr. El-Masri was given some canned food as well as some books to read. Mr. El-Masri was weighed. Since the time of his seizure in December of 2003, Mr. El-Masri had lost more than sixty pounds. Following his force-feeding, Mr. El-Masri became extremely ill and suffered severe pain. An American doctor visited Mr. El-Masri's cell in the middle of the night and administered medication, but Mr. El-Masri remained bedridden for several days.

In early May 2004, the prison director brought Mr. El-Masri to the interrogation room, where he met an American who identified himself as a psychologist, accompanied by a female interpreter with a Syrian accent. The psychologist told Mr. El-Masri that he had traveled from Washington, D.C., to check on him and ask him some questions. At the conclusion of the conversation, the man promised that Mr. El-Masri would be released from the facility very soon.

Soon thereafter, Mr. El-Masri was visited by a German speaker who identified himself only as "Sam." Sam was accompanied by the American prison director and an American translator. Mr. El-Masri asked Sam whether he was a representative of the German government, and whether the German government knew that Mr. El-Masri was being held in Afghanistan. Sam declined to answer. Mr. El-Masri asked Sam whether his wife knew where he was; Sam replied that she did not. Sam then proceeded to ask Mr. El-Masri many of the same questions he had previously been asked regarding his alleged associations with extremists in Ulm, Germany.

On May 27, 2004, the American doctor visited Mr. El-Masri's cell. He instructed Mr. El-Masri not to eat or drink anything, as the next day he would be transported back to Germany, and during the transit, he would not be permitted to use the bathroom. The next morning, the doctor and the American prison director arrived in his cell. Mr. El-Masri was blindfolded and cuffed, led out of his cell, and driven for about ten minutes. He was then locked in what seemed to be a shipping container until he heard the sound of an aircraft arriving. Mr. El-Masri was released from the shipping container, and his belongings were returned to him. He was told to change back into the clothes he had originally worn in Macedonia, and was given two new t-shirts. He was then driven to the waiting plane, blindfolded and ear-muffed, and led onto the plane, where he was chained to his seat.

The man named Sam accompanied Mr. El-Masri on the plane. Mr. El-Masri also heard the muffled voices of two or three Americans. Shortly after take-off, Mr. El-Masri asked Sam if he could have the earmuffs removed; Sam obliged, after consulting with the Americans. Sam informed Mr. El-Masri that Germany had a new President. He said that the plane would land in a European country other than Germany, because the Americans did not want to leave clear traces of their involvement in Mr. El-Masri's ordeal, but that Mr. El-Masri would eventually continue on to Germany. Mr. El-Masri feared that he would not be returned home, but rather taken to another country and executed.

When the plane landed, Mr. El-Masri, still blindfolded, was taken off the plane and placed in the back seat of a vehicle. He was not told where he was. He was driven in the vehicle up and down mountains, on paved and unpaved roads, for more than six hours. When the car stopped, Mr. El-Masri was taken from the car, and his blindfold was removed. His captors gave him his belongings and passport, removed his handcuffs, and directed him to walk down the path without turning back. It was dark, and the road was deserted. Mr. El-Masri believed he would be shot in the back and left to die. Mr. El-Masri rounded a corner and came across three armed men. They immediately asked for his passport. They saw that his German passport had no visa in it, and asked him why he was in Albania without legal permission. Mr. El-Masri replied that he had no idea where he was. He was told that he was near the Albanian borders with Macedonia and Serbia. The men led Mr. El-Masri to a small building with an Albanian flag, and he was presented to a superior officer. The officer observed Mr. El-Masri's long hair and long beard and told him he looked like a terrorist. Mr. El-Masri asked to be taken to the German embassy, but the man told him he would be taken to the airport instead.

Mr. El-Masri was driven to the airport in Tirana, Albania. He boarded a plane that landed at Frankfurt International Airport at 8:40am. Mr. El-Masri was by then about forty pounds lighter than when he had left Germany, his hair was long and unkempt, and he had not shaved since his arrival in Macedonia. From Frankfurt he traveled to Ulm, and from there to his home outside the city. His house was empty and had been so for some time. He was told that his family had relocated to Lebanon when he failed to return from his holiday in Macedonia.

In June 2004, the Office of the Prosecuting Magistrate in Munich, Germany, opened an investigation into Mr. El-Masri's allegations that he had been unlawfully abducted, detained, and interrogated in Macedonia and Afghanistan. German officials corroborated Mr. El-Masri's account that he had traveled to Macedonia and had been detained shortly after entering that country. To evaluate Mr. El-Masri's account of his detention in Afghanistan, German authorities conducted scientific tests, including radioactive isotope analysis of Mr. El-Masri's hair. Those tests were consistent with Mr. El-Masri's account that he had spent time in a South Asian country and had been deprived of food for an extended period.

Mr. El-Masri was deeply traumatized by his treatment during his seizure and detention. He was repeatedly beaten and threatened; had an object forced into his anus; was denied access to counsel, consular officials, or his family; was roughly interrogated on numerous occasions; and was secretly detained in squalid conditions for nearly half a year without charge or explanation. He suffered physical injuries, pain and suffering, and severe mental anguish, as well as loss of income and livelihood.

* * * * *

According to a CIA Inspector General Report regarding the El-Masri extraordinary rendition, during his detention, Mr. El-Masri was "openly tearful and speechless" and suffering from "feelings of helplessness, hopeless . . . [and] wishing he was dead." The Report concluded:

> [T]here was an insufficient basis to render and detain al-Masri and the [CIA's] prolonged detention of al-Masri was unjustified. His rendition and long detention resulted from a series of breakdowns in tradecraft, process, management, and oversight. [A CIA office] and [redacted]

> failed to take responsible steps to verify al-Masri's identity. [Another CIA office] exaggerated the nature of the data it possessed linking al-Masri to terrorism. After the decision had been made to repatriate al-Masri, implementation was marked by two months of delay due to "bureaucratic infighting" and "bureaucratic differences."

The CIA Inspector General referred the case to the Department of Justice, but DOJ declined to prosecute anyone.

14.4.2. Case Study: Extraordinary Rendition of Abu Omar

According to allegations in an Italian court, in February 2003, agents of the CIA abducted an Imam named Hassan Mustafa Osama Nasr, also known as Abu Omar. Omar was abducted on the street in Milan, Italy, as he was walking to a mosque, then driven in a van to a United States Air Force base in northern Italy. From there, Omar was flown first to a United States Air Force base in Germany, then to Cairo, Egypt, where he was transferred to the custody of the Egyptian State Security Investigations Service, the security and intelligence service of Egypt's Ministry of Interior. Omar claims he was tortured by beating, electric shock, and rape, though his own lawyer at one point said there were "no signs of torture." In 2007, Omar was released after an Egyptian court ruled that his imprisonment was "unfounded."

In 2005, an Italian judge issued arrest **warrants** for 22 people alleged to be agents or operatives of the CIA. The judge determined the abduction violated Italian sovereignty and international law. Though initially alleged to be a United States operation, Italian prosecutors subsequently also charged high-ranking Italian intelligence officers for their involvement in the abduction. Ultimately, 26 Americans and nine Italians were **indicted**. In 2009, an Italian judge convicted 22 CIA agents, a colonel in the United States Air Force, and two Italian secret agents, *in absentia* (without them being present for court), in what is believed to be the first criminal convictions in the world of persons involved in the CIA's post-9/11 extraordinary rendition program.

REVIEW QUESTIONS

1. What is the difference between "rendition" and "extraordinary rendition?"
2. Which nation's laws might be broken during extraordinary rendition?
3. How has the Supreme Court's jurisprudence contributed to extraordinary rendition by the United States government?

CRITICAL THINKING QUESTIONS

1. Extraordinary rendition usually involves illegal activity, at least in one of the affected jurisdictions. Even if an activity is not illegal under United States law, should the United States government intentionally engage in illegal activity, even to protect national security? What effect does acting illegally have on the United States' claim to promoting the rule of law?

2. In situations where the United States suspects a person of participating in terrorist activity and no other government is willing to detain or interrogate the suspect, what are the United States' reasonable alternatives to extraordinary rendition? Does your analysis change if the United States reasonably believes the suspect has information that may help prevent a future terrorist attack?

3. Often, the country from which a person is disappeared in an extraordinary rendition does not complain publicly about the abduction. What might be the political causes of this failure to assert a violation of sovereignty, and what should be the legal effect? One report indicated that 54 countries participated in CIA secret detention and extraordinary rendition operations in some way. How does this affect your answer?

4. Both case studies in this chapter relate to allegations by persons abducted during CIA extraordinary rendition operations who were later determined to be innocent of any connection with terrorism. However, United States extraordinary rendition operations also involved persons who were not innocent. Does that matter?

5. Which sources of law detailed in Sections 14.2 and 14.3 in this chapter were potentially violated by each government participating in the extraordinary renditions recounted in Section 14.4?

CHAPTER 15

Prosecuting Terror Suspects

The twelve military officers who comprised the military commission of Lambdin Milligan, whose conviction was later overturned by the Supreme Court

"We think [the military commissions system] guarantees that we'll have the kind of treatment of these individuals that we believe they deserve."

-Vice President Dick Cheney, referring to trial of suspected terrorists

Learning Objectives

1. Know the history of the Supreme Court's analysis of the circumstances when military commissions are appropriate.

2. Understand the key elements of, and difficulties encountered with, the military commission system for trying terrorist suspects since 9/11.

3. Understand the key elements of, and difficulties encountered with, using federal civilian criminal courts for trying terrorist suspects since 9/11.

4. Evaluate the key differences between federal criminal court and military commissions in prosecuting terrorist suspects.

5. Assess alternatives to the current two systems for prosecuting terrorist suspects.

15.1. INTRODUCTION

Under current law, there are four potential fora in which to prosecute terrorists apprehended by the United States for their alleged crimes: 1) trial in federal civilian court; 2) trial by **military commission**; 3) trial by court-martial; and 4) trial by an international tribunal.

In the wake of the 9/11 terror attacks, successive presidential administrations have chosen only the first two of these options. Why trials by court-martial or international tribunal have been rejected involves some speculation. Trial by court-martial under the Uniform Code of Military Justice may have been perceived to be too advantageous to accuseds or too similar to trial in civilian court to justify. And trial by international tribunal—whether a standing international tribunal like the International Criminal Court (ICC), or an **ad hoc** tribunal such as the International Criminal Tribunal for the former Yugoslavia and International Criminal Tribunal for Rwanda—seems to have never been seriously considered. This may be due to the Bush Administration's rejection of the ICC generally. Perhaps it was due to the fear of the loss of United States control over the process and outcome that delivering suspected terrorists to an international tribunal might entail. This chapter addresses the two forms of prosecution that *have* been used since 9/11: trial by military commission and trial in federal civilian courts.

15.2. TRIAL BY MILITARY COMMISSION

A **military commission** is a tribunal ordered into existence by a military commander to prosecute people for alleged crimes related to military conflict or violation of **martial law**. Military commissions are usually ad hoc tribunals, established for specific situations, rather than standing courts that perpetually exist. Historically, these circumstances have been to try enemies for law of war violations or to administer a criminal justice system when the military commission is substituting for civilian courts in occupied territories or war zones. In short, military commissions are extraordinary tribunals for extraordinary times.

Though the intent to produce evidence and determine guilt are similar to civilian criminal trials, military commissions vary significantly from civilian trials, in ways that raise significant tensions between individual rights and security. In most military commissions, military officers perform the traditional roles of "judge and jury," including deciding what evidence they will consider and whether the accused is guilty of the charged offenses. But these military officers are neither judges nor juries in the traditional sense. Traditionally, unlike judges, officers serving on military commissions are not legally trained and maintain no separation and independence such as that provided by the lifetime appointment of Article III federal judges. However, military commissions often have legal advisors, and the post-9/11 military commissions have military judges. Additionally, the officers are appointed by a commander and are neither "peers" of the accused, nor a neutral and randomly identified cross-section of society. Indeed, when a military commission tries enemies for law of war violations, commission members are part of the very organization fighting against the accused. Military commissions generally use rules of procedure created specifically for that military commission. Several constitutional concerns regarding individual rights are raised with military commissions, including especially the right to a grand jury before trial for a felony-level offense and the right to a jury trial.

Military commissions have been used throughout United States history. General George Washington used military commissions to try suspected enemy spies, including Major John Andre, whose spying related to Benedict Arnold's treason. Likewise, during the War of 1812, military commissions were used to try and convict spies. During the Mexican-American War, military commissions were used in large numbers. Similarly, numerous military commissions took place during the Civil War, including a number of Confederate officers and soldiers found in and behind Union lines in disguise, who were tried and convicted by military commission for being spies. Thousands of military commissions during the Civil War tried suspects for violations of the laws of war. One Civil War military commission led to one of the most significant Supreme Court cases regarding national security: *Ex parte Milligan*. Military commissions were used during and after World War II. And in the post-9/11 era, military commissions have again been resurrected as an instrument of national security.

15.2.1. Authority to Establish and Jurisdiction

Because military commissions pose such extraordinary risks to individual freedoms, including their significant departures from expected civilian criminal process protections, courts have carefully limited the circumstances under which they may operate. Though various presidents have claimed authority to establish military commissions unilaterally, courts have clearly preferred military commissions be created through cooperation of Congress and the President.

While there have been relatively few cases addressing military commissions, the Supreme Court has carefully controlled the extent of military commissions' **jurisdiction**. Four such decisions establishing some boundaries for military commissions are *Ex parte Milligan*, *Ex parte Quirin*, *Duncan v. Kahanamoku*, and *Hamdan v. Rumsfeld*, discussed below.

15.2.1.1. Ex Parte Milligan*, 1866*

Ex parte Milligan was the first significant Supreme Court decision regarding military commissions. We first encountered *Milligan* in Chapter 13, in the context of the United States military's ability to detain. But *Milligan* is primarily a case about the President's authority to institute military commissions. Lambdin Milligan was an Indiana resident who was arrested for planning to raid a federal arsenal in Indiana. Mr. Milligan was not a member of the Confederate Army or acting at its direction, though he was sympathetic to the Confederate cause. The armory Milligan attempted to attack was nowhere near any military conflict, and the civilian courts in Indiana were still functioning. Milligan was imprisoned by the military and then brought before a **military tribunal** where he was charged with "violation of the laws of war," including **conspiracy** against the government and inciting insurrection. He was convicted and sentenced to be hanged. As usual, the military commission that convicted Milligan lacked the rights usually afforded to an accused in civilian criminal trials for serious offenses, including the right to be **indicted** by a grand jury and tried by a jury with a presiding judge.

The Supreme Court agreed with Milligan's claim that the military commission was unlawful. The Court observed that Congress had not authorized military commissions to try civilian citizens who were not combatants in the military conflict and where the civilian courts were open and functioning outside the theater of war. The majority also suggested that Congress could not have authorized a military commission under such circumstances, though concurring Justices believed Congress could have authorized a tribunal, but simply had not.

The Court found that the "laws of war" for which Milligan was tried were irrelevant in the case, because

> they can never be applied to citizens in states which have upheld the authority of the government, and where the courts are open and their process unobstructed. . . . [N]o usage of war could sanction a military trial there for any offense whatever of a citizen in civil life, in nowise connected with the military service.

The Court's unwillingness to allow military tribunals to substitute for available civilian courts rests in large part on the persistent concern that military commissions are anathema to liberty:

> When peace prevails . . . there is no difficulty of preserving the safeguards of liberty . . . but if society is disturbed by civil commotion—if the passions of men are aroused and the restraints of law weakened, if not disregarded—these safeguards need, and should receive, the watchful care of those intrusted with the guardianship of the Constitution and laws. . . . [Martial law] . . . destroys every guarantee of the Constitution, and effectually renders the "military independent of and superior to the civil power"—the attempt to do which by the King of Great Britain was deemed by our fathers such an offense, that they assigned it to the world as one of the causes which impelled them to declare their independence.

15.2.1.2. Ex Parte Quirin*, 1942*

Recall from Chapter 13 that *Ex parte Quirin* also involved an after-the-fact assessment of whether a trial by military commission was lawful. In *Quirin*, eight German nationals, at least one of whom—Herbert Haupt—was also a United States citizen, came to United States to sabotage the industrial war effort. President Franklin D. Roosevelt issued an order establishing a military commission to try any nationals of enemy states, or those who act under their direction, for sabotage, espionage, or "violations of the law of war." A military commission conducted a trial in a facility in Washington, D.C., not far from the fully functioning federal civilian courts, and sentenced the eight saboteurs to death. When the military commissions were challenged, the Supreme Court affirmed the convictions 24 hours after oral argument, and six of eight saboteurs were executed within one week of the Supreme Court's decision.

Months later, the Supreme Court issued its written opinion in the case, in which it found the military commissions lawful. The Court declined to rule on the President's claim to have unilateral authority to institute military commissions under Article II of the United States Constitution, instead finding statutory authority under the Articles of War. Specifically, the Court determined Congress had incorporated the law of war in the then-existing Articles of War and authorized the President to order military commissions to try violations of the law of war. Article 15 of the Articles of War said that provisions in the Articles of War establishing courts-martial should not be construed as "depriving military commissions . . . or other military tribunals of concurrent jurisdiction in respect of offenders or offenses that by statute or by the law of war may be triable by such military commissions. . . ." Though that language does not affirmatively authorize military commissions, but rather clarifies that the existence of courts-martial does not implicitly de-authorize military commissions, the Court was persuaded that the military commission in *Quirin* was the product of cooperation between Congress and the President, and therefore lawful. Article 15 of the Articles of War would later become Article 21 of the Uniform Code of Military Justice, enacted in 1950 and still in effect today, and a basis for modern presidents to assert their right to institute military commissions. Like Article 15 had, Article 21 says "provisions of this chapter conferring jurisdiction upon courts-martial do not deprive military commissions, provost courts, or other military tribunals of concurrent jurisdiction with respect to offenders or offenses that by statute or by the law of war may be tried by military commissions, provost courts, or other military tribunals."

As to Congress's power to authorize military commissions in the first instance, the *Quirin* court was persuaded that several provisions of Article I of the United States Constitution provide Congress's power. Specifically, Article I authorized Congress to "provide for the common Defence," "make Rules for the Government and Regulation of the land and naval Forces," "declare War . . . and make Rules concerning Captures on Land and Water," "define and punish . . . Offences against the Law of Nations," and to make "all Laws which shall be necessary and proper for carrying into Execution the foregoing Powers."

Understanding how *Milligan* and *Quirin* relate to each other is important. In *Milligan*, the Supreme Court held that a United States citizen in the United States and not in a war zone could not be tried by a military commission while the civilian courts were still open and functioning. In *Quirin*, the Court held that a United States citizen (Haupt) in the United States and not in a war zone *could* be tried by a military commission despite the fact that the civilian courts were still open and functioning. How can this be?

One suggested difference between the cases is that the Civil War was an undeclared war, while WWII was a declared war against an identifiable enemy. So, if a constitutionally authorized war is a predicate for the President to enforce the law of war by military commission, clearly the President had the authority to do so in *Quirin*. But, the *Milligan* decision and other cases decided by the Supreme Court at that time, such as *The Prize Cases*, did not seem to rest on the fact that the Civil War was not a traditionally declared war.

Another difference seems to be more significant: Milligan's status as a civilian and the *Quirin* defendants' admitted status as **belligerents**. Indeed, the *Quirin* defendants were uniformed soldiers of an enemy state. Under *Milligan*, the military cannot try a United States citizen not associated with the military arm of the enemy government as long as civilian courts are open and functioning, but under *Quirin*, the military can, with appropriate authority, detain and try enemy combatants during war. It is the *Quirin* defendants'—including United States citizen Haupt's—status as admitted enemy belligerents that changes the result. Importantly, the Court in *Quirin* did not articulate a standard for when a citizen will be considered a belligerent or sufficiently associated with the enemy to be susceptible to trial by military commission, but that is likely because it was obvious in *Quirin* and the citizen did not challenge his belligerency.

Some have wondered whether *Quirin* created an exception to *Milligan*, or vice versa. One reading of *Quirin* is that it creates a declared enemy exception to the "open court rule" of *Milligan*. On the other hand, the Court in *Quirin* said that *Milligan* should be confined to its facts, suggesting it is *Milligan*, rather than *Quirin*, that should be read narrowly. In any event, both *Milligan* and *Quirin* remain valid precedent today.

15.2.1.3. Duncan v. Kahanamoku, *1946*

During World War II, Hawaii, which was not yet a state, was administered under the Hawaiian Organic Act (Organic Act), which Congress enacted to establish rules for governing the Territory of Hawaii. On December 7, 1941, after the Japanese attack on Pearl Harbor, the Territorial Governor of Hawaii, relying on Section 67 of the Organic Act, placed the entire Territory of Hawaii under martial law. In Section 67, Congress authorized the Territorial Governor to institute martial law "in case of rebellion or invasion, or imminent danger thereof, when the public safety requires it." The Governor's proclamation authorized the Commanding General "during . . . the emergency and until danger of invasion is removed, to exercise all the powers normally exercised" by the Governor and by "the judicial officers and employees of the Territory." Accordingly, the Commanding General proclaimed himself "Military Governor," and on December 8, 1941, established military tribunals to replace civil and criminal courts. These tribunals were forbidden to summon jurors and witnesses and to try cases.

Lloyd Duncan was a civilian shipfitter employed at the Navy Yard at Honolulu. On February 24th, 1944, he engaged in a brawl with two armed Marine sentries at the yard and was arrested by military police. By this time, over two years after the Pearl Harbor attack, military rule in Hawaii had eased some. Schools, bars, and movie theaters had reopened. Civilian courts had been authorized to "exercise their normal functions," including conducting criminal trials. An exception to the courts' resumed jurisdiction, however, was that only military tribunals were permitted to try "Criminal Prosecutions for violations of military orders," which still covered a wide range of day-to-day civilian conduct. Duncan was charged with violating one of these orders, which prohibited assault on military or naval personnel with intent to resist or hinder them in the discharge of their duty. Assault was also a crime under the civilian law of the Territory of Hawaii. Nevertheless, Duncan was tried and convicted by a military tribunal, rather than a Territorial Court, and sentenced to six months' imprisonment.

Duncan appealed, arguing the military did not have authority to try him under the Organic Act or under the Constitution. The United States Supreme Court ultimately held that the Organic Act did not "give the armed forces power to supplant all civilian laws and to substitute military for judicial trials under the conditions that existed in Hawaii at the time [Duncan was] tried." In reaching this conclusion, the Court was careful to identify what it was *not* deciding, implicitly identifying the circumstances under which it believed martial law and military commissions might be lawful:

> Our question does not involve the well established power of the military to exercise jurisdiction over members of the armed forces, those directly connected with such forces, or enemy belligerents, prisoners of war, or others charged with violating the laws of war. We are not concerned with the recognized power of the military to try civilians in tribunals established as a part of a temporary military government over occupied enemy territory or territory regained from an enemy where civilian government cannot and does not function. For Hawaii, since annexation, has been held by and loyal to the United States. Nor need we here consider the power of the military simply to arrest and detain civilians interfering with a necessary military function at a time of turbulence and danger from insurrection or war. And finally, there was no specialized effort of the military, here, to enforce orders which related only to military functions, such as, for illustration, curfew rules or blackouts. For these petitioners were tried before tribunals set up under a military program which took over all government and superseded all civil laws and courts.

Though it was interpreting whether the Organic Act provided the military with the authority it exercised over Duncan, the Supreme Court found it necessary to examine the history of martial law in the United States in order to determine what Congress meant by the term "martial law" in the Organic Act. As articulated by the Court, the question was:

> Have the principles and practices developed during the birth and growth of our political institutions been such as to persuade us that Congress intended that loyal civilians in loyal territory should have their daily conduct governed by military orders substituted for criminal laws, and that such civilians should be tried and punished by military tribunals?

After reviewing United States history and precedent, including *Milligan* and *Quirin*, the Court concluded:

> We believe that, when Congress passed the Hawaiian Organic Act and authorized the establishment of "martial law," it had in mind and did not wish to exceed the boundaries between military and civilian power in which our people have always believed, which responsible military and executive officers had heeded, and which had become part of our political philosophy and institutions prior to the time Congress passed the Organic Act. The phrase "martial law," as employed in that Act, therefore, while intended to authorize the military to act vigorously for the maintenance of an orderly civil government and for the defense of the island against actual or threatened rebellion or invasion, was not intended to authorize the supplanting of courts by military tribunals.

Importantly, this was not a determination about the constitutionality of martial law generally, but rather what the term "martial law" meant, absent clear indication in the statute. Nevertheless, in *Duncan*, the Supreme Court reiterated its disfavor of military tribunals of civilian citizens when the courts are functioning.

Not all the Justices agreed, however. Justice Frankfurter believed the Supreme Court was inappropriately inserting its judgment for that of the wartime military commander in a location that had been physically attacked and might have been attacked again:

> The actual presence of battle in a community creates a substantially different condition from that which exists in other parts of a nation at war. That conditions of war and the means of meeting its emergencies were within the contemplation of the Constitution of the United States is shown by the broad authority vested in the President of the United States as Chief Executive and as Commander in Chief of the Army and Navy, and in the war powers of the Congress and the Chief Executive to preserve the safety of the nation in time of war.
>
> . . .

> In order to recognize the full strength of our Constitution, both in time of peace and in time of war, it is necessary to protect the authority of our legislative and executive officials, as well as that of our courts, in the performance of their respective obligations to help to "establish Justice, insure domestic Tranquility, provide for the common defence, promote the general Welfare, and secure the Blessings of Liberty to ourselves and our Posterity."

15.2.1.4. **Hamdan v. Rumsfeld***, 2006*

Following the 9/11 terror attacks, the Bush Administration sought to determine how to try suspected terrorists. In an important legal opinion, the Office of Legal Counsel asserted the President had the authority to institute military commissions, based on the President's inherent authority under Article II, and based on the idea from *Quirin* that Article 21 of the UCMJ, which preserves but does not create military commissions, was sufficient authority. The OLC opinion included an interesting assertion that Congress's power regarding military commissions was, in essence, "one-way." The memorandum noted that Congress has power to declare war, raise and support armies, and make rules for the government and regulation of the land and naval forces, and therefore has the authority to authorize the President to order military commissions. But, the OLC asserted, Congress does not have the authority to "interfere with the President's authority as commander in Chief." In other words, the memorandum suggested the Constitution gives Congress the authority to allow military commissions, but not to disallow or limit them. The memorandum also makes one of the strongest arguments for a presidential authority to order military commissions, noting that "[o]ne of the necessary incidents of authority over the conduct of military operations in war is the power to punish enemy belligerents for violations of the laws of war." In other words, if the President has the authority to order the killing of enemy belligerents, he must have the authority to try enemy belligerents for war crimes.

After the OLC opinion, President Bush issued an **Executive Order** creating military commissions to try terror suspects. The tribunals were the first military commissions run by the United States military since World War II, and seem to have largely copied the *Quirin* tribunals from that era. One such military commission was instituted against Salim Ahmed Hamdan. Hamdan challenged the lawfulness of his military commission, and in 2006, the Supreme Court agreed it was unlawful. The government argued Congressional authorization for the military commission came from Article 21 of the UCMJ. But, the Court held that

Article 36 of the UCMJ required that rules and regulations for military commissions be "uniform insofar as practicable" to courts-martial and the Court determined the commissions the President ordered violated that requirement. The Court reserved judgment regarding whether the President has authority to order military commissions on his own, but implicitly insisted that when Congress has authorized military commissions with limitations, such limitations must be followed. Of course, this calls to mind the Court's similar admonition in *Little v. Barreme*, discussed in Chapter 3. Moreover, because the President's order establishing the military commissions conflicted with Congress's will as expressed in Article 36 of the UCMJ, the order was in Justice Jackson's *Youngstown* "category three," meaning the Court would accord little deference to the President. The Court struck down the military order as exceeding his constitutional authority.

15.3. MILITARY COMMISSIONS ACT

Congress responded swiftly to the *Hamdan* decision by enacting the Military Commissions Act of 2006 (MCA of 2006). The express purpose of the Act was "to authorize trial by military commission for violations of the law of war, and for other purposes." The MCA of 2006 included numerous provisions discussed throughout this text, including an attempt to strip federal courts of **habeas corpus** jurisdiction. Important for our purposes here, the MCA of 2006 created specific procedures the commissions would follow and identified crimes the commissions could try. After President Obama took office in 2009, his administration announced it would be attempting some changes to the military commissions procedure. In response, Congress enacted the Military Commissions Act of 2009 (MCA of 2009). Here we will discuss and refer to the Military Commissions Act (MCA) as it currently exists, including the 2009 amendments.

15.3.1. Jurisdiction

The MCA gives military commissions jurisdiction over "alien unprivileged enemy belligerents," defined as "an individual (other than a privileged belligerent) who has engaged in hostilities against the United States or its coalition partners; or has purposefully and materially supported hostilities against the United States or its coalition partners. . . ." A "privileged belligerent" means an individual who is entitled to prisoner of war status under one of the eight categories set forth in Geneva Convention on Prisoners of War, and generally does not include terrorist suspects.

The MCA gives military commissions jurisdiction to try any offense explicitly made punishable by the MCA or punishable under the law of war, so long as the offense occurred "in the context of and associated with hostilities" against the United States or its coalition partners. Military commissions are expressly authorized to determine their own jurisdiction.

15.3.2. Offenses Under the MCA

The MCA specifically identified a number of offenses for which an accused could be tried by military commission. These offenses include: murder of protected persons; attacking civilians, civilian objects, or protected property; pillaging; denying quarter; taking hostages; employing poison or similar weapons; using protected persons or property as shields; **torture**, cruel or inhuman treatment; intentionally causing serious bodily injury; mutilating or maiming; murder in violation of the law of war; destruction of property in violation of the law of war; using treachery or perfidy; improperly using a flag of truce or distinctive emblem; intentionally mistreating a dead body; rape; sexual assault or abuse; hijacking or hazarding a vessel or aircraft; terrorism; providing **material support** for terrorism; wrongfully aiding the enemy; spying; contempt; perjury; and obstruction of justice. The MCA also makes punishable conspiracy, attempts, and solicitation to commit the above-listed crimes.

15.3.2.1. Material Support and the **Ex Post Facto** *Prohibition*

One offense that has formed a substantial number of the total charges in post-9/11 military commission prosecutions, and also raised significant legal issues, is "material support for terrorism." Under international and domestic law, defendants have the right to fair warning that conduct is considered criminal before they commit the act. This rule is enshrined in the United States Constitution's Ex Post Facto Clause, which requires that states warn people in advance that certain acts are prohibited. The **Framers** included the Ex Post Facto Clause because of perceived abuses by Britain when it used ***ex post facto*** (after the fact) laws to rule North American colonies. The issue with *ex post facto* laws in the context of the MCA is that the MCA encompasses not only specific, identified offenses, but also the catch-all "law of war." Moreover, *ex post facto* protections are considered venue-specific, meaning that the accused must have been warned that a military commission would be able to prosecute him for an offense before he committed it. Because the MCA authorized prosecution by military commission for offenses that occurred before the MCA of 2006 was enacted, some argued that prosecution for those offenses is prohibited by *ex post facto* rules. The issue then becomes whether those offenses could reasonably be understood to have been prohibited under the law and triable by military commission before the MCA of 2006.

Material support for terrorism is not considered a crime under the international law of war. As the D.C. Circuit Court of Appeals noted in *Hamdan v. United States* (*Hamdan II*), no **treaty** or prior decision by an international tribunal supports the existence of a "material support" claim under international law. Additionally, before the MCA of 2006, no United States military commission has recognized the crime of material support. Accordingly, because such charges were not part of the "law of war" in effect as of September 11, 2001, material support charges for conduct occurring before military commissions first considered material support a crime violate the Ex Post Facto Clause. See *Hamdan II.*

15.3.2.2. Conspiracy

Another controversial crime that has formed a significant percentage of charges against terrorists is conspiracy. Conspiracy refers to an agreement among two or more persons to commit a criminal act. When a conspiracy results in a completed criminal act, conspiracy is generally not considered its own separate criminal offense, but rather is a theory of liability under which to charge the completed criminal act. By contrast, ***inchoate conspiracy*** refers to an agreement to commit a crime when the crime itself is never completed. International tribunals have generally not recognized inchoate conspiracy as a crime. But under domestic United States law, such an unfulfilled agreement is a crime. United States military tribunals have convicted accuseds of conspiracy, including those involved in the assassination of President Lincoln, and inchoate conspiracy, such as the *Quirin* saboteurs who did not conclude the attacks they conspired to finish. The question for some conspiracy cases became whether Congress has the authority to establish military commissions to try enemy combatants for the offense of "conspiracy to commit war crimes" that were not ultimately committed when inchoate conspiracy is not an offense under the international law of war. In a fractured *en banc* opinion, the D.C. Circuit Court of Appeals ruled that the "law of war" referred to by the MCA refers not only to the international law of war, but also to United States precedent like the Lincoln assassination tribunal and *Quirin* case, where military commissions convicted accuseds of conspiracy. Thus, reasoned the court, an accused terrorist had notice of possible trial by military commission when he committed the conspiracy, and the MCA did not violate Ex Post Facto Clause. *Al Bahlul v. United States.*

15.3.3. Procedure and Review of Military Commissions

Military commissions feature some processes and substantive rights that are similar to the federal criminal court system and courts-martial under the UCMJ. For example, under the MCA, the accused is entitled to a presumption of innocence, and the proof required for conviction is "legal and competent evidence beyond reasonable doubt." However, some aspects of military commissions depart significantly from civilian courts and military courts-martial.

Right Against Self-Incrimination

Regarding the constitutional right to not incriminate oneself, in the federal civilian criminal court system, statements made by a defendant under duress, or made during a **custodial interrogation** prior to a *Miranda* warning, are inadmissible. Under UCMJ, Article 31, an accused must be advised of their right to remain silent prior to *any* questioning, custodial or otherwise. By contrast, under the MCA, the Secretary of Defense is authorized to permit admission of coerced or compelled confessions, so long as they are not the product of torture or cruel, inhuman, or degrading treatment. Statements of the accused remain inadmissible unless the military judge finds that the totality of the circumstances renders the statement reliable and possessing sufficient probative value, *and* that the statement was either: 1) made incident to military operations, where the interests of justice would best be served by admission of the statement into evidence; or 2) voluntarily given, taking into consideration all relevant circumstances, including military and intelligence operations during hostilities, the accused's age, education level, military training, and the change in place or identity of interrogator between that statement and any prior questioning of the accused. Thus, unwarned confessions during custodial interrogations may be admitted so long as they are deemed "voluntary" and arguably involuntary confessions may be admitted if they were made incident to military operations and admitting them serves "the interests of justice." Coerced statements during capture as part of a military operation are potentially admissible. Like in federal criminal trials or military courts-martial, in a military commission trial itself, the accused has the right to not testify.

Right Against Unreasonable Searches and Seizures

Freedom from unreasonable searches and seizures enjoyed by civilians in federal criminal court and military personnel in courts-martial is also different in military commissions. Under the original MCA of 2006, evidence was permitted if judged to have probative value to a reasonable person, unless it was obtained under circumstances that would render it unreliable. However, there was no requirement for a **warrant** or search authorization, as are generally required in federal criminal court and courts-martial requirement. After the MCA of 2009 amendment, evidence seized outside the United States may not be excluded from trial by military commission on the grounds that the evidence was not seized pursuant to a search warrant or other authorization.

Defense Counsel

In the federal criminal court system and under the UCMJ, defendants are permitted to retain counsel at their own expense. Additionally, in the federal system, defense lawyers are appointed for defendants who cannot afford them. In courts-martial, all accuseds are provided a military defense counsel at no cost, regardless of ability to pay. Similarly, under the MCA, the accused has a right to a free military defense counsel who herself cannot be subject to adverse personnel actions because of "the zeal with which such officer, in acting as counsel, represented any accused before a military commission . . . ." Additionally, the accused may be represented by a civilian attorney, subject to some restrictions, including that the attorney is a United States citizen and has a secret security clearance, or higher security clearance if a particular case requires it. Despite these rights to counsel, defense counsel have complained they lack adequate resources to advocate for their clients and have insufficient access to witnesses. Additionally, the accused has the right to be present at all sessions of the military commission except deliberation or voting, unless the military judge determines that the accused persists in disruptive or dangerous conduct.

Presentment of Charges

As under the UCMJ, the accused has a right to have the charges against them presented to them in writing. However, in a significant departure from court-martial and civilian practice, no pre-trial inquiry such as an Article 32 investigation or grand jury indictment is required. Additionally, there is no right to a speedy trial, as has been demonstrated by the many years some detainees have waited for the beginning of their military commissions.

Juries

In federal criminal court, potential jurors are randomly selected to be part of the jury pools from which jurors are drawn. On the other hand, as is true with courts-martial under the UCMJ, under the MCA, the United States military convening authority hand-picks both the judge and the commission members (equivalent of jurors). Further, the MCA requires that the military commissions be made up of a military judge and at least five members (12, if the death penalty is sought), and a conviction requires concurrence of at least two-thirds of the commission members. This follows what was true of general courts-martial, until the UCMJ was revised, effective January 2019, to require eight members and three-fourths concurrence for convictions in general courts-martial. Federal criminal juries must generally be comprised of 12 jurors and a verdict must be unanimous.

Classified or Sensitive Information

The MCA of 2006 allowed the Secretary of Defense to create rules that would redact classified information or provide unclassified summaries of evidence to the defendant. However, after the MCA of 2009, the general approach to disclosure under the Classified Information Procedures Act (CIPA) applies. As is discussed in greater detail later in this chapter, under CIPA, the government may, with court approval, provide unclassified summaries or substitutes for classified information, so long as "the defendant [has] substantially the same ability to make his defense." Additionally, under CIPA, a defendant is required to give pretrial notice of any intended use of classified information and the government may petition the court to determine its admissibility before trial.

Appeal

Under the MCA, convicted persons have the right to appeal a final decision of a military commission to the **United States Court of Military Commission Review (USCMCR)**. The USCMCR is composed of military judges or persons with comparable qualifications for civilian judges. The USCMCR may "affirm only such findings of guilty and the sentence or such part or amount of the sentence, as the USCMCR finds correct in law and fact and determines, on the basis of the entire record, should be approved." After appeals to the USCMCR are exhausted, the accused may appeal a final decision to the United States Court of Appeals for the District of Columbia Circuit. Unlike the USCMCR, the D.C. Circuit may take action regarding matters of law, including the sufficiency of the evidence to support the verdict. The D.C. Circuit's decisions may be reviewed by the Supreme Court. Additionally, the MCA of 2009 removed the MCA of 2006's prohibition of any other review by civilian courts, such as the right to habeas corpus or to collateral review.

15.4. PROSECUTION IN FEDERAL CIVILIAN CRIMINAL COURTS

Those who object to military commissions of terror suspects have pointed to the availability of a viable alternative to such tribunals: federal civilian criminal courts. And the data support the argument that these courts are effective in prosecuting terrorists. In the first two decades after September 11, 2001, federal prosecutors achieved hundreds of terrorism-related convictions in federal criminal court, with a conviction rate of over 80%, compared to only a handful of convictions by military commissions.

15.4.1. Federal Crimes Related to Terrorism

Federal law criminalizes a host of terrorism-related activities. Regarding acts of international terrorism, 18 U.S.C. Sections 2332, 2332a, and 2332b, collectively prohibit terrorist killing and physical violence, including using weapons of mass destruction, against Americans outside and inside the United States. 18 U.S.C. 2332 and 2339 also criminalize acts of terrorism in a host of other contexts, such as: bombing public places; using missile systems designed to destroy aircraft; harboring; concealing; financing; and providing material support to terrorists; or receiving military-type training from foreign terrorist organizations. In addition to specific terrorism statutes, federal criminal law includes many other prohibitions that relate to common terrorist activities, including prohibitions against: fraud; theft; drug trafficking; false statements; immigration violations; national security matters from weapons security to assassination attempts to espionage and treason; racketeering; and violent crimes. The most commonly charged offenses since 9/11 historically have been general criminal conspiracy, and material support for terrorists and foreign terrorist organizations.

15.4.2. Common Issues with Prosecuting Terrorism Cases in Federal Criminal Court

Prosecution of terrorist suspects in federal civilian court raises several legal concerns, some of which military commissions were originally intended to avoid. These include use of, and access to, classified evidence, the defendant's right to a speedy trial, and the right against self-incrimination. Each of these concerns has been addressed in some way by courts or Congress.

15.4.2.1. Federal Courts and Classified Evidence

One of the most difficult aspects of trying terrorism cases in federal criminal court rather than by military commission is the need to protect classified information from disclosure. Constitutional and statutory rules provide defendants with certain rights to discovery of information in the prosecution's possession before the trial that the government sometimes does not wish to disclose. At trial, prosecutors may want to use classified information to prove guilt beyond a reasonable doubt, without revealing that information to the defense, the jury, or the public. Similarly, defendants may want to use classified information to demonstrate their innocence or refute or call into question the prosecution's evidence, but the government seeks to prevent the disclosure. Attempts to accommodate these competing interests have met with mixed results.

Pre-Trial Discovery

During the pretrial discovery phase of litigation, federal criminal defendants have a constitutional right to access all exculpatory information in the possession of the prosecution (*Brady v. Maryland*), a statutory right to all statements made by the prosecution's witnesses (Jencks Act), and procedural right to access one's own prior statements (Fed. Rule of Criminal Procedure 16(a)(1)(A)–(B)).

In the federal criminal case against Zacharias Moussaoui, the "20th 9/11 attacker," the defendant raised this issue. He requested access to a terrorist named Ramzi bin al-Shibh, who was in federal custody and who Moussaoui believed could provide exculpatory evidence. But the government contended that giving Moussaoui access to al-Shibh would compromise national security. The federal district court held that Moussaoui's Sixth Amendment right to compulsory process was not outweighed by claims that the government's intelligence-gathering efforts would be undermined, and ordered that Moussaoui be given access to, and permission to present to the jury, summaries of statements bin Al-Shibh made to the government.

Courts have generally held that when a government agency is sufficiently closely aligned with the prosecution, its information is subject to the prosecution's discovery obligations. Concern over these discovery obligations was a key contributing factor in the *de facto* wall erected between the intelligence and law enforcement communities, a separation that some have contended was the primary reason the United States government was unable to assemble separately collected pieces of information to thwart the 9/11 attacks. Intelligence officials know that information shared with law enforcement will be considered in the "possession of the prosecution," and thus must be turned over to the defense to avoid prosecution, so they prefer not to share their intelligence with law enforcement.

The Silent Witness Rule

The silent witness rule (SWR) was suggested by government prosecutors as a way to accommodate the trial participants' need to see evidence and the public's right to open trials, while not divulging sensitive information. One federal court described the SWR procedure this way:

> Under such a rule, the witness would not disclose the information from the classified document in open court. Instead, the witness would have

> a copy of the classified document before him. The court, counsel and the jury would also have copies of the classified document. The witness would refer to specific places in the document in response to questioning. The jury would then refer to the particular part of the document as the witness answered. By this method, the classified information would not be made public at trial but the defense would be able to present that classified information to the jury. *United States v. Zettl.*

Typically, under the SWR, trial participants refer to classified names, statements, places, and documents through code words printed on a "key card." The trial participants, including judge, lawyers, defendant, and jury, each have access to the key card, so they can know what is being referenced, while the public in attendance do not. In one case, the government attempted to also prevent the defendant, though not his lawyers, from accessing the key, but that was determined to violate the defendant's Sixth Amendment confrontation right. The appeals court chastised the trial judge, declaring "[w]e do not balance a criminal defendant's right to see the evidence which will be used to convict him against the government's interest in protecting that evidence from public disclosure," suggesting the defendant's right to see the evidence being used against him may be absolute. *United States v. Ahmed Abu Ali.*

The SWR has rarely been used, but was approved and used in an espionage prosecution involving state secrets. *United States v. Rosen.* There, the trial judge found that the SWR was permissible, but because it effectively "closes the trial" to the public when being used, the judge ruled that

> it is appropriate to approve use of the [SWR] only when . . . the government establishes (i) an overriding reason for closing the trial, (ii) that the closure is no broader than necessary to protect that interest, (iii) that no reasonable alternatives exist to closure, and (iv) that the use of the [silent witness rule] provides defendants with substantially the same ability to make their defense as full public disclosure of the evidence, presented without the use of codes.

The judge determined that the limited use of the SWR in that case adequately accommodated the defendant's constitutional right to confrontation and a public trial, as well as the public's right to a public trial.

Classified Information Procedures Act (CIPA)

Sometimes the defendant claims he must disclose classified information in order to defend against charges. Prior to enactment of the Classified Information Procedures Act (CIPA), government prosecutors encountered a problem, known euphemistically as "**graymail**," where prosecutors were faced with either allowing the defense to disclose the national security information during trial or drop the charges. Often, these decisions had to be made by prosecutors without knowing whether the defense would actually disclose classified evidence or whether judges would even find the evidence admissible. Under the procedures established in CIPA, the admissibility of sensitive information is determined in advance of trial, allowing the government to know the information cost of a prosecution before proceeding with it.

CIPA requires defendants to provide pretrial notice of any intended use of classified information. Defendants have challenged the statute as requiring them to "tip their hand" before trial, when trials without classified information would have no such disadvantage. Courts have generally rejected these challenges, noting that other defenses—such as alibi and insanity defenses—also require pretrial notice and that the "Confrontation Clause does not guarantee the right to undiminished surprise with respect to cross-examination of prosecutorial witnesses."

CIPA also provides a mechanism by which, during the discovery and pretrial phases of a prosecution, the government can seek court approval to not provide certain information or to offer unclassified summaries or substitutes of classified information to the defense, as long as the summary or substitute provides "the defendant with substantially the same ability to make his defense as would disclosure of the specific classified information." Prosecutors have successfully availed themselves of this procedure in terrorism cases. During the discovery phase of a prosecution of four defendants for providing material support to terrorists through fundraising for Anwar al-Awlaki and Al Qaeda, the government requested the court permit it to not disclose certain information to the defendants. Because the court found the information was not "relevant and helpful" to the defense, it granted the government's motion. *United States v. Mohammad.* Another federal court similarly has held in multiple cases that CIPA gives discretion to district courts to permit the government to withhold "classified information that might otherwise have been discoverable," as long as this information is neither "helpful [n]or material to the defense."

In providing a mechanism for prosecutors to learn whether certain classified information will be discoverable by the defense or admissible at trial, CIPA imposes upon trial courts a duty to guard against the unauthorized "disclosure of any classified material disclosed by the United States to any defendant in any criminal case." Ultimately, the court must determine whether the information is discoverable and whether it involves a state secret such that there is a reasonable danger that compulsion of the evidence will expose matters that, in the interest of national security, should not be divulged. If so, the court must then determine if the information is useful to counter the government's case or to bolster a defense. If it is, the government's interest in national security must "give way to the defendant's right to present a meaningful defense." If not, the government may withhold the evidence. Thus, the prosecution knows before trial what the cost of its prosecution might be in terms of forced disclosure of sensitive information.

Each instance of CIPA-based non-disclosure requires a fact-specific inquiry. In some instances, while determining the discoverability or admissibility of specific evidence, courts might permit defense counsel, but not the defendant, to see classified evidence. This raises the concern that the defendant's constitutional rights to counsel, to testify, and to confrontation might be violated. One court addressing those concerns in the context of a terrorism prosecution found that the district court's decision to exclude the defendants was justified because the risk of a "disastrous security breach" outweighed an absolute line of communication between a defendant and his attorneys, did not prejudice the defendants' ability to present a complete defense, and did not involve the defendant's right to confront witnesses. Note that this non-disclosure to the defense is different than the issue raised when evidence was disclosed to the *jury*, but not the defendant, at trial. As noted above, that violates the defendant's Sixth Amendment rights.

15.4.2.2. Federal Courts and the Right Against Self-Incrimination

In *Miranda v. Arizona*, the United States Supreme Court held that a defendant's Fifth Amendment right to not be "compelled in any criminal case to be a witness against himself" requires law enforcement to provide a rights advisement before questioning suspects during custodial interrogation. Under the corresponding exclusionary rule, unwarned confessions are inadmissible at trial.

A problem arises when the suspect is believed to possess information that may be critical to stopping an ongoing or future crime. In *New York v. Quarles*, the United States Supreme Court recognized an exception to the *Miranda* requirement in cases where interrogations are driven by concern for public safety, rather than ordinary law enforcement and criminal punishment. In *Quarles*, a rape victim told police that her attacker (Quarles) had entered a nearby store. When the police arrested Quarles inside the store, they saw an empty gun holster. One of the officers asked Quarles where the gun was, and his answer led officers to the weapon. Because Quarles was in custody at the time of the question, and law enforcement did not provide a warning regarding the right to remain silent, Quarles' self-incriminating admission that he knew where the gun was, and the gun itself, would ordinarily be inadmissible at trial under *Miranda*. But in *Quarles*, the Supreme Court held that when custodial interrogation is "reasonably prompted by a concern for the public safety," rather than investigation demonstrating the suspect's culpability, *Miranda*'s warning requirement does not apply. The Court held that the motivation of the officer asking Quarles for the location of the gun was to ensure immediate safety for the officers and public, thus no *Miranda* warning was necessary.

In the context of terrorism investigations and prosecutions, the Quarles public safety exception provides a powerful response to those who argue that if *Miranda*-based rights advisements are given, important terrorism prevention investigations will be hampered, or that, if rights advisements are not given, prosecutions in federal criminal courts will be hindered. The *Quarles* exception provides a compelling incentive to law enforcement to not warn suspects before engaging in custodial interrogation of terrorists, because terror-related questioning frequently involves public safety. In fact, in 2010, the FBI issued a policy that instructed: "agents should ask any and all questions that are reasonably prompted by an immediate concern for the safety of the public or the arresting agents without advising the arrestee of his *Miranda* rights." Then, after "all applicable public safety questions have been exhausted, agents should advise the arrestee of his *Miranda* rights and seek a waiver of those rights before any further interrogation occurs. . . ."

Federal courts have extended the *Quarles* exception to terrorism cases. In *United States v. Khalil*, after Khalil was injured during a raid of his apartment by law enforcement, he was taken to the hospital. There, officers asked him "about the construction and stability of the bombs" they had discovered in his apartment and "whether he had intended to kill himself in detonating the bombs." At trial, Khalil challenged admission of his response to the question about his intent to kill himself, arguing that that question was unrelated to public safety. The Second Circuit disagreed, "given that [the defendant's] vision as to whether or not he would survive his attempt to detonate the bomb had the potential for shedding light on the bomb's stability." In a more recent case, another federal court held that unwarned interrogation by the FBI of an airplane passenger who had attempted to explode an airplane by igniting explosives in his underwear fell within the *Quarles* public safety exception due to agents' justified concern that there could be additional, imminent attacks on airplanes throughout the world.

Under *Quarles*, the government gets to preserve public safety by asking the questions it wishes to ask *and* gets to use the result of those questions at a later criminal trial, without the pesky requirement to advise of *Miranda* rights. Accordingly, the *Quarles* public safety exception has been advanced by some as strong evidence that federal courts—not only military commissions—are capable of accommodating the government's interests in terrorism prosecutions and promoting security. On *Quarles*, some civil liberties advocates find themselves stuck: the *Quarles* public safety exception arguably allows law enforcement to infringe on the right against self-incrimination enshrined in the Fifth Amendment, which civil libertarians oppose, but *Quarles* also accommodates security concerns in a way that favors federal criminal courts for terrorism cases, which many civil libertarians favor over military commissions.

The Underwear Bomber

On December 25, 2009, Omar Farouk Abdulmutallab attempted to ignite explosives concealed in his underwear as his plane approached Detroit, Michigan, from Amsterdam. He succeeded in catching his trouser leg and the wall of the plane on fire, but the device did not detonate as intended. He told a flight attendant that he had an "explosive device" in his pocket. Upon the plane's arrival in Detroit, Abdulmutallab was taken to the hospital for treatment of his burns. FBI Special Agent Timothy Waters, who had been told that Abdulmutallab had admitted to the flight attendant that he had detonated an explosive device hidden in his underwear and that he was acting on behalf of Al Qaeda, questioned Abdulmutallab for 50 minutes before advising him of his *Miranda* rights. Among the questions Agent Waters asked were:

> Where he traveled, when he had traveled, how, and with whom; the details of the explosive device; the details regarding the bomb-maker, including where Defendant had received the bomb; his intentions in attacking Flight 253; who else might be planning an attack; whether he associated with, lived with, or attended the same mosque with others who had a similar mindset as Defendant about jihad, martyrdom, support for al-Qaeda, and a desire to attack the United States by using a similar explosive device on a plane and what these individuals looked like.

Before trial, Abdulmutallab argued his statements to Agent Waters should be suppressed because he had not been advised of his *Miranda* rights. The Federal District Judge disagreed, finding the questioning to be within the *Quarles* exception to *Miranda*. The court believed that, based on Abdulmutallab's "self-proclaimed association with al-Qaeda and knowing the group's past history of large, coordinated plots and attacks, the agents logically feared that there could be additional, imminent aircraft attacks in the United States and elsewhere in the world. . . ."

Ultimately, Abdulmutallab pleaded guilty to eight charges, including the attempted use of a weapon of mass destruction and the attempted murder of 289 people on the plane. The judge sentenced him to four consecutive life sentences plus 50 years in prison. Like many convicted of terrorism, Abdulmutallab is incarcerated at the "supermax" United States Penitentiary in Florence, Colorado.

15.4.2.3. Federal Courts and the Right to Speedy Trial

The Sixth Amendment to the United States Constitution guarantees that "[i]n all criminal prosecutions, the accused shall enjoy the right to a speedy . . .trial." What constitutes "speedy" is a difficult question the United States Supreme Court has called "amorphous," "slippery," and "necessarily relative." *Vermont v. Brillon.* To determine whether a defendant's claim that his speedy trial right has been violated, the Supreme Court has established a balancing test considering four factors:

(1) the length of the delay;

(2) the reasons for the delay;

(3) whether the defendant asserted his right in the run-up to the trial; and

(4) whether the defendant was prejudiced by the failure to bring the case to trial more quickly. *Barker v. Wingo.*

In an instructive case involving a terrorism prosecution and speedy trial, *United States v. Ghailani*, the Second Circuit Court of Appeals determined that a nearly six-year delay between apprehension by the CIA and trial did not violate the defendant's constitutional right to a speedy trial. Ahmed Khalfan Ghailani participated in the terrorist bombings of United States embassies in Africa in 1998. He was indicted (charged by a federal grand jury) in 1998, though he was not present in the United States or in custody at the time. Ghailani was ultimately apprehended by the CIA in 2004 and held at a secret "**black site**" detention facility outside the United States for roughly two years while the CIA questioned him to obtain intelligence. In 2006, Ghailani was transferred to DOD custody at Guantanamo Bay. In 2007, a Combatant Status Review Tribunal determined Ghailani was properly held as an enemy combatant. In 2008, Ghailani was charged by a military commission and arraigned. Approximately six months later in March 2009, when Ghailani asserted his right to a speedy trial in a *habeas corpus* petition, the government announced it would try him in federal criminal court, instead of by military commission. In October 2010, his trial began, and he was convicted approximately one month later. He then challenged his conviction based on a Sixth Amendment right to a speedy trial.

In analyzing the time between his arrest and trial, the court divided the delay into two phases: the period during which Ghailani was held by the CIA from July

2004 to September 2006, and the period from September 2006 through June 2009, during which Ghailani was held at Guantanamo Bay. Regarding the CIA detention, the court observed that:

> although a delay intended unfairly to interfere with the defense or purely to harass the defendant would count quite heavily in favor of a violation of the Speedy Trial Clause, the Speedy Trial Clause prohibits only trial delays that, on balance, are unreasonable in light of the public and private interests at stake in the particular case.

The Second Circuit noted that "the Supreme Court has stated in no uncertain terms that '[i]t is obvious and unarguable that no governmental interest is more compelling than the security of the Nation.' " *United States v. Ghailani*, quoting *Haig v. Agee.*

By contrast, the *Ghailani* court was not persuaded that the length and reasons for the delay during Ghailani's detention by DOD at Guantanamo were justified as necessary for national security. Instead, the court analyzed those three years as being in preparation for a military commission. The court determined that the government's original strategy to try Ghailani before a military commission was "long, and largely a product of the government's own choices," and accordingly determined that under the *Barker* analysis, these factors weighed against the government and in favor of Ghailani's Speedy Trial Clause claim. Nevertheless, the court determined that the government was "not acting with the intent to cause prejudicial delay but was acting under the good faith belief that Ghailani would be tried by military commission" until President Obama took office in January 2009 and suspended the military commissions (a decision his administration later reversed). Additionally, the court determined that the delay did not prejudice Ghailani's defense at trial. Accordingly, the court rejected Ghailani's speedy trial challenge.

In *United States v. Padilla*, another federal court also assessed whether lengthy military detention violates a defendant's Speedy Trial Clause rights during a subsequent federal criminal prosecution. Jose Padilla had originally been arrested and held as a material witness in May 2002. In June 2002, Padilla was transferred to military detention as an "enemy combatant." In November 2005, he was charged in federal court with conspiracy to commit murder, kidnap, and maim people overseas, but he was not transferred from military detention to civilian custody until January 2006. Padilla was ultimately tried in federal civilian court in May 2007, five years after he had originally been arrested on a material witness warrant. In an unpublished opinion, the district court judge rejected Padilla's claim that his military detention triggered his rights under the Speedy Trial Clause. The

Ghailani and *Padilla* cases thus suggest that constitutional speedy trial rights are generally not a bar to prosecution of terrorism suspects, even those detained by the federal government for lengthy periods of time.

In addition to the broad right to a speedy trial established by the Sixth Amendment, a federal statute—the Speedy Trial Act of 1974—establishes specific time limits for various stages of pretrial procedure after a defendant is charged in the federal system. These time periods are short enough that they might present serious problems with some terrorism cases in which the suspect is detained for long periods before trial. However, the Speedy Trial Act "clock" only begins once the defendant is charged with an "offense," a term the Act defines to exclude "an offense triable by court-martial, military commission, provost court, or other military tribunal." Thus, the Speedy Trial Act clock does not start based only a defendant's military detention, or even a defendant being charged by military commission. Instead, only a federal criminal charge starts the clock. Accordingly, defendants can be detained for many years in military custody before being transferred to the federal criminal system without triggering the Speedy Trial Act.

15.5. FEDERAL CRIMINAL COURT VS. MILITARY COMMISSIONS

Since the Bush Administration's announcements of military commissions early in the months following the 9/11 attacks, the question of whether terror suspects should be tried by military commission or in federal criminal court has been a hotly contested political debate. After replacing President Bush, the Obama Administration clearly favored federal criminal trials to military commissions. In 2009, the Obama Administration announced that Guantanamo would be closed and that 9/11 mastermind Khalid Sheikh Mohammed (KSM) and his 9/11 co-conspirators would be tried in federal court. In 2011, the Obama Administration backed away from that plan, announcing KSM would be tried by a military commission that, as of 2020, had still not yet occurred.

15.5.1. The Case for Federal Criminal Court Prosecutions of Terror Suspects

Those who favor trial in federal court and disfavor military commissions argue that the insufficient legal protections for accuseds in military commissions are inconsistent with American legal and constitutional rights. They also argue that the federal courts are superior because of the novel and untested nature of military tribunals, the failure of military commissions to prosecute many cases in the nearly two decades since they were instituted compared to the hundreds of convictions achieved in federal criminal court, and the fact that career federal prosecutors and judges are more competent than participants in an ad hoc and evolving system. Moreover, they contend several of the perceived advantages of military commissions, such as the ability to better protect sensitive information, have not come to fruition. For instance, in the pre-trial hearings for KSM's military commission, significant delay and disagreement focused on declassification of certain evidence desired by the defense, just as might be the case in a trial in federal criminal court.

The military commission of Abd Al Rahim Al Nashiri, who is accused of orchestrating the bombing of the U.S.S. Cole in 2000, has been a fiasco many claim is representative of the entire military commissions process. Capital charges against him were announced in 2009, then after that first military commission disbanded, DOD convened a second commission in 2011. Extensive pretrial motions and appeals delayed the commission trial for years. In 2017, the military commission judge held in contempt and had confined to quarters the chief defense counsel for all military commissions—a general officer in the United States Marine Corps—because he allowed Nashiri's defense attorneys to leave the case after they determined they could no longer represent Al Nashiri because the CIA was surreptitiously recording their conversations with their clients. In 2018, the convening authority for all military commissions and the legal adviser to the convening authority were fired, allegedly due to their ineffectiveness as director and chief of staff of the Office of Military Commissions. Not long thereafter, the judge put the proceedings in indefinite abeyance, claiming there were too many unanswered questions to continue, and protesting "We're going to continue to spin our wheels and go nowhere until somebody who owns the process looks in and does something. . . . We need action. We need somebody to look at this process. We need somebody to give us direction." In 2019, when the case made its *fourth pre-trial* appearance before the D.C. Circuit Court of Appeals (the second level appeals court after the CMCR), the D.C. Circuit vacated four years' worth of orders by the military commission judge assigned to the case because the judge had applied for a job with the Department of Justice and not disclosed it to the parties, creating a "disqualifying appearance of partiality." In its ruling, the D.C. Circuit noted "criminal justice is a shared responsibility. Yet in this case, save for Al-Nashiri's defense counsel, all elements of the military commission system—from the prosecution team to the Justice Department to the CMCR to the judge himself—failed to live up to that responsibility."

Between 2002 and 2019, military commissions produced *eight* convictions, six of which were obtained by plea bargain, and only *one* of which had survived a post-conviction appeal. By contrast, in the same period, terrorism prosecutions in federal criminal court had yielded over 600 convictions.

15.5.2. The Case for Military Commissions

Those who favor military commissions refer to the greater likelihood that a defendant might be acquitted in federal court due to perceived higher legal protections defendants receive there. These protections include enhanced procedural rights under the Fifth and Sixth Amendments, like greater due process, right against self-incrimination, right to remain silent, access to evidence and speedy trial. In addition to perceived legal advantages to the prosecution, those who favor military commissions often note that providing public federal criminal trials gives the defendants a national stage from which to voice their ideology, imperil safety during trial and any subsequent imprisonment, risk disclosure of classified information, treat terrorists like common criminals rather than war criminals, and provide constitutional rights that Americans—but not suspected terrorists—should enjoy. Supporters of military commissions observe that the Obama Administration's embarrassing decision that KSM would be tried by military commission after all reflects the political difficulty of trying notorious terrorists in federal courts.

The *Ghailani* case, mentioned in the above discussion of speedy trial, has been hailed by supporters of federal criminal prosecution as demonstrating that such prosecutions can afford constitutional rights *and* be successful. But supporters of military commissions point out that evidentiary rulings by the federal judge at trial resulted in Ghailani nearly being acquitted. He was convicted of just *one* out of 285 charges, whereas a military commission judge's evidentiary determinations might not have been so constrained. Key evidentiary differences between military commissions and federal criminal trials under current rules include the fact that the following may be admissible in military commissions, but not in federal court: evidence obtained without a warrant; statements made by suspects without rights advisements; and hearsay evidence, so long as the witness is unavailable and if the evidence is "material, probative, reliable, and the interests of justice will be served by its admission."

15.5.3. The Case for a Third Way: National Security Courts

Some scholars, judges, and politicians have proposed creating a new national security court. Many varieties of national security court have been suggested. One proposal suggests combining favored elements of the federal criminal courts and military commissions. It would be an Article III court, established by Congress, that could have concurrent jurisdiction with military commissions to try alien enemy combatants and possibly to handle habeas and other terror-related appeals currently handled by federal courts, along with the intelligence issues currently handled by the Foreign Intelligence Surveillance Court. Judges would be traditional federal judges with lifetime tenure, appointed and confirmed in the usual Article III process. Prosecution and defense lawyers would have security clearances and be drawn from lawyers at the DOJ and from the DOD. Juries could be made up of military officers or other permanent personnel with security clearances. Under one such proposal, rules of evidence could be relaxed, appeal rights limited, and the right of public access restricted. Under this approach, national security courts could operate like military commissions, but with Article III judges.

National security courts could offer several advantages. They would allow for a highly specialized bench and bar to address cases efficiently, and if properly resourced, could ease the strain on "normal" federal courts that terror-related cases often involve. National security courts might be able to address some of the evidentiary problems and concern about protection of classified information. Additionally, a clearly demarcated national security court procedure could prevent the "seepage" of some terror-related relaxation of rules such as CIPA and the SWR into other types of criminal cases, where such relaxation is unnecessary and inappropriate.

On the other hand, a "hybrid" national security court, when newly created, might suffer from some of the same issues that have plagued military commissions, as every new procedure and rule is appealed and tested. The advantages of federal criminal courts and their well-established procedure would possibly be lost. Further, if national security courts are Article III courts, it seems the usual constitutional protections of defendants' rights would remain an issue that a separately named court would not solve. That is, if a defendant's constitutional rights are the problem, a national security court is not the solution. Finally, some argue that national security courts are simply unnecessary. There are too few cases to merit creating another judicial system, and the hundreds of cases that have led to convictions of terrorist defendants in federal court demonstrate that the current system is up to the task.

15.5.4. The Case for No Cases

Finally, the difficulties in both the federal criminal courts and military commissions outlined above lead some to argue that the United States ought not try terrorism suspects at all. Those vigorously advocating the United States abandon trials of high-profile terror suspects ask whether trying such suspects is prudent or necessary. Former Assistant Attorney General for the Office of Legal Counsel at DOJ, and preeminent national security law scholar, Jack Goldsmith, and well-known national security scholar and journalist Benjamin Wittes, have repeatedly argued against prosecuting high-profile terrorists, including Ghailani and KSM. They contend that military detention under the **authorization for the use of military force (AUMF)** and the law of war is lawful regardless of the outcome of a prosecution, and that military detention is sufficient to remove these individuals from the public, thus maximizing public security. Further, military detention without trial circumvents concerns about revealing sensitive information, dodges the politically difficult headaches of choosing a proper forum, and escapes the dilemma of what to do if a suspect is prosecuted and acquitted, as nearly happened with Ghailani.

Those who reject the notion of relying on indefinite detention rather than prosecution argue that without trial, detention lacks the legitimacy that imprisonment following conviction provides, noting that indefinite detention without trial is inconsistent with American values of justice and liberty. Further, detention does not offer the ultimate—and for some Americans, the only acceptable—punishment for mass murder: the death penalty. Finally, detention does not offer the cathartic opportunity for public judgment of guilt that conviction provides.

The question of whether terror suspects should be tried at all once again raises the larger question of whether counter-terrorism is law enforcement or armed conflict, and whether terrorists are criminals or warrior combatants. The federal criminal system capably handles criminals, while military detention may suitably manage detention of combatants. But if terrorists are simultaneously criminals and combatants, the appropriate system for prosecution—or whether prosecution is necessary at all—is less clear.

REVIEW QUESTIONS

1. Explain the common objections to military commissions for prosecution of terrorist suspects.

2. Explain the common objections to federal criminal courts for prosecution of terrorist suspects.

3. Explain how the public safety exception to the *Miranda* requirement affects interrogation of terrorist suspects and the ability to use their statements in federal court.

4. Describe the options available for dealing with classified evidence in federal criminal court.

5. How have federal courts addressed speedy trial issues in terrorism trials?

CRITICAL THINKING QUESTIONS

1. What does the history of military commissions in the United States, and the Supreme Court's opinions about them, suggest about the appropriateness of using military commissions to try modern terrorism suspects?

2. What does the *Abdulmutallab* ("underwear bomber") case suggest about how the Fifth Amendment and *Miranda* affect prosecutions for terrorism in federal criminal court? When is questioning of terrorism suspects *not* motivated by public safety and preventing further terror attacks?

3. Which forum best accommodates the legal and political issues surrounding trials of terrorism suspects? Federal courts? Military commissions? Something else? Why?

4. Do you agree with Professor Goldsmith that the United States ought to abandon trials of high-profile terrorist suspects in favor of indefinite detention? Why or why not?

CHAPTER 16

Killing Terror Suspects

An armed USAF MQ-9 Reaper unmanned aerial vehicle (drone) on a mission over Afghanistan. (United States Air Force Photo/Lt. Col. Leslie Pratt)

Learning Objectives

1. Understand the international law implications of targeted killing in an armed conflict versus targeted killing in a law enforcement context.

2. Evaluate targeted killing in light of international humanitarian law.

3. Know the various sources of authority for, and constraints imposed on, targeted killing under United States domestic law.

4. Analyze specific instances of targeted killing in light of international and domestic law.

16.1. INTRODUCTION

Targeted killing refers to "lethal force . . . intentionally and deliberately used, with a degree of pre-meditation, against an individual or individuals specifically identified in advance by the perpetrator." Philip Alston, *Report of the Special Rapporteur On Extrajudicial, Summary or Arbitrary Executions, Addendum: Study on Targeted Killings Study on Targeted Killings*, May 28, 2010. In a targeted killing, the specific goal of the operation is to use lethal force. In the context of anti-terrorism operations, "targeted killing" involves a state actor's killing of a terrorist. Since 9/11, the most common method of targeted killing has been by using a **remotely piloted aircraft (RPA)**, also known as an **unmanned aerial vehicle (UAV)** or, more colloquially, a "**drone**." RPAs can fire precision-guided missiles at targets that have been identified through a variety of means of intelligence gathering. The use of RPAs is not the only method of targeted killing; more traditional uses of lethal force like snipers and small squad assault teams, as used in the raid that killed Osama bin Laden, can also accomplish targeted killings. However, because RPAs have been by far the most common weapons system employed for targeted killing in the twenty-first century, our discussion here will primarily focus on that method. That said, while it can be easy to get too focused the technology employed in a targeted killing, most of the legal issues remain roughly the same regardless of the killing method employed.

Targeted killing presents a model example of the dichotomy between legal paradigms that is posed by the global attempt to counter terrorism. As noted elsewhere in this text, whether a particular use of force is properly considered armed conflict or law enforcement dictates answers to significant legal questions. The existence of an armed conflict results in far more permissive use of lethal force than in the absence of an armed conflict. In this chapter, we explore the various legal questions posed by targeted killing within each paradigm, beginning with the default presumption that a particular use of force does not occur within an armed conflict unless the circumstances for armed conflict exist.

Before analyzing targeted killing, it is important to understand the difference between two terms that sound similar, but in the context of law, are quite different. **International human rights law (IHRL)** refers to international laws and norms that establish basic civil, political, economic, social, and cultural rights that all human beings should enjoy and that all states are obliged to protect. By contrast, **international humanitarian law (IHL)**, also known as the **law of armed conflict (LOAC)**, refers to a set of rules that, for humanitarian reasons, attempts to limit the adverse effects of armed conflict. International humanitarian law applies only when there is an armed conflict. There exists significant disagreement regarding whether one legal paradigm *replaces* the other in a situation, or whether they can coexist. For example, the United States' view has been that when an armed conflict exists, only IHL applies, and it replaces IHRL. The predominant European view, and the view taken by the U.N. Special Rapporteur on Extrajudicial, Summary or Arbitrary Executions, is that HRL always applies, and co-exists with IHL in the context of armed conflict. Though the two sets of laws are presented separately in this chapter, consider whether IHL and IHRL should—or even can—coexist.

16.2. TARGETED KILLING AND INTERNATIONAL HUMAN RIGHTS LAW

The legality of a targeted killing that occurs outside the context of armed conflict is governed by ordinary peacetime international human rights law. IHRL is made up of a collection of treaties and **customary international law**, including the International Covenant on Civil and Political Rights (ICCPR), to which the United States and most other nations are parties. Article 6 of the ICCPR asserts: "Every human being has the inherent right to life. This right shall be protected by law. No one shall be arbitrarily deprived of his life." This individual right to life is also found in many other treaties regarding human rights law, including the Universal Declaration of Human Rights, Convention for the Protection of Human Rights and Fundamental Freedoms, African Charter on Human and People's Rights, American Convention on Human Rights, and European Convention for the Protection of Human Rights and Fundamental Freedoms. The right to life has also been held to be a rule of customary international law, binding on all States regardless of whether they are **treaty** signatories.

Under IHRL, state killing of human beings is legal only in three circumstances: 1) pursuant to a "final judgment rendered by a competent court," if imposed only on adults and only "for the most serious crimes"; 2) in the context of armed conflict; and 3) in an extrajudicial context when the killing is "proportionate and necessary." Under IHRL, "proportionate" means that the killing is required to protect human life and "necessary" means there is no other means of protecting human life, such as capture or non-lethal incapacitation. Thus, when a targeted killing is not the death penalty and is not in the context of an armed conflict, it must be for the purpose of protecting life and there must be no alternative.

Some suggest that under human rights law, a targeted killing can never be legal, because it can never be legal for the sole objective of an operation to be to kill the target. Others have argued there may be exceptional circumstances in which the target is imminently carrying out a deadly attack and there is no means of preventing the loss of life other than to kill the target, such as when capturing the target is infeasible. Overall, however, under IHRL, targeted killing will most often be unlawful.

There have been very few judicial opinions analyzing state extrajudicial killing based on IHRL, but one such opinion suggested there could be circumstances where an extrajudicial killing might be justified. In *McCann v. United Kingdom*, Special Air Service (SAS) members of the United Kingdom government clandestinely tracked three members of the Provisional Irish Republican Army (PIRA). The SAS members followed the PIRA members into Gibraltar. Believing the PIRA members were about to detonate a car bomb after they parked a car and walked away from it in a crowded area, the SAS shot and killed all three PIRA members. Investigation later revealed the car did not contain any explosive devices, though one of the PIRA members had in his possession keys to another car, which contained keys to a third car that did contain hundreds of pounds of explosives.

In assessing the lawfulness of the SAS actions, the European Court of Human Rights determined that international law (specifically, the European Convention on Human Rights) required that the use of lethal force be "absolutely necessary." In applying that standard, the majority found there were other options the SAS could have taken to prevent the potential loss of life, such as arresting the suspects at the border before they reached the crowded area in Gibraltar, or assessing the accuracy of their intelligence. Additionally, the European Court found that the United Kingdom's decision to use combat teams rather than law enforcement personnel was inappropriate and contributed to the United Kingdom's breach of the suspects' right to life. The case was closely decided, and the dissenters argued the soldiers made reasonable judgments based on the information available to them at the time, especially considering the large number of civilians the shooters believed were in danger.

The *McCann* majority's discussion of the identities of the shooters presents an interesting issue related to the differences between IHRL and IHL, but also the identities of the persons involved in the targeted killing. The majority opined that use of combat teams rather than law enforcement was inappropriate. Law enforcement personnel are trained to use lethal force as a last resort, while combat personnel are generally trained to use lethal force as a first resort. The United Nations Basic Principles on the Use of Force and Firearms by Law Enforcement Officials states that "intentional lethal use of firearms may only be made when strictly unavoidable in order to protect life." That document also demands that law enforcement officers must identify themselves, give clear warning of their intent to use firearms, and provide sufficient time for the warnings to be observed before using lethal force. The only exception is when following this procedure puts the law enforcement officers at risk or would create risk to other persons. By contrast, combat troops are not trained—or required by law in armed conflict—to provide warning when they are about to use lethal force.

The "absolutely necessary" standard the court applied in McCann also raises questions regarding whether targeted killings are "necessary" in some places, but not others. For example, in *McCann*, the court determined the UK could have acted earlier, preventing the later need for the use of force. While this may be true in Western Europe, it is not always the case when attempting to stop terrorists in other places, such as the location of many United States drone strikes, like Yemen and Pakistan. Some argue that the geographic remoteness or the incapability or unwillingness of local authorities makes non-lethal capture impossible and creates the "absolutely necessary" condition required for an extrajudicial targeted killing.

16.3. TARGETED KILLING IN ARMED CONFLICT

16.3.1. Existence of an Armed Conflict

The international humanitarian law that applies during an armed conflict is much more permissive than IHRL regarding use of lethal force. If targeted killing occurs within an armed conflict, it will more likely be legal than under IHRL's near prohibition of extrajudicial killing. There are two types of armed conflict under international law.

Because the applicability of IHL rests upon whether a conflict is an "armed conflict," it is important to understand what constitutes an armed conflict. The Geneva Conventions avoided defining "armed conflict," perhaps deliberately. One international court—the International Criminal Tribunal for the former Yugoslavia (ICTY)—has been particularly influential in defining the term. The ICTY has held that "an armed conflict exists whenever there is a resort to armed force between States or protracted armed violence between Governmental authorities and organized armed groups or between such groups within a State." In a different case, the ICTY explained that the test for whether an armed conflict exists contains two prongs: "(i) the intensity of the conflict and (ii) the organization of the parties to the conflict." Stated differently, there must be "protracted armed violence" and identifiable "parties" to the conflict. "[M]ere act[s] of banditry or . . . unorganized and short-lived insurrection[s]" are excluded from the definition.

The intensity prong of the test for determining whether an armed conflict exists requires that some threshold level of violence—marked by intensity or duration—exists. The ICTY has identified factors in determining whether the intensity prong has been met:

> the number, duration and intensity of individual confrontations; the type of weapons and other military equipment used; the number and calibre of munitions fired; the number of persons and type of forces partaking in the fighting; the number of casualties; the extent of material destruction; and the number of civilians fleeing combat zones.

Additionally, while no court has given a clear definition regarding the minimum length of time necessary to meet the duration threshold for armed conflict, another tribunal—the International Criminal Tribunal for Rwanda—has suggested that armed violence lasting a few months might be of sufficient duration to be considered "protracted."

The "organization of the parties" prong of the test for determining whether an armed conflict exists requires that the non-State armed group must be identifiable, so that States are able to distinguish between lawful targets and "civilians." The ICTY suggested a number of indicators of a group's status as a "party":

> the existence of a command structure and disciplinary rules and mechanisms within the group; the existence of a headquarters; the fact that the group controls a certain territory; the ability of the group to gain access to weapons, other military equipment, recruits and military training; its ability to plan, coordinate and carry out military operations, including troop movements and logistics; its ability to define a unified military strategy and use military tactics; and its ability to speak with one voice and negotiate and conclude agreements such as cease-fire or peace accords.

Thus, the existence of an armed conflict is a case-by-case, fact-specific question. In each instance of a targeted killing, whether an armed conflict exists must be determined in order to know whether IHL applies. For instance, while there is little legitimate disagreement about whether the United States' conflict with Al Qaeda in Afghanistan constituted an "armed conflict" in the early years following the 9/11 attacks by Al Qaeda, there is less agreement whether its targeted killing of terror suspects in Al Qaeda splinter groups in other countries in 2020 are part of the same armed conflict, or any armed conflict at all.

International armed conflicts (IACs) are armed conflicts between two or more states, and are governed by the 1949 Geneva Conventions and the 1977 First Additional Protocol to the Geneva Conventions. **Non-international armed conflicts (NIACs)** are armed conflicts between a state and an organized armed group that is not a state, and are governed by Common Article 3 of the Geneva Conventions. Thus, distinguishing between IACs and NIACs affects which body of law applies.

The prevailing view is that an armed conflict between a state and a non-state armed group need not occur in the territory of the state involved in the conflict for the conflict to be considered a NIAC. That is, a conflict between a state and an armed group within its borders can be a NIAC, as can a conflict between a state and an armed group occurring in another state. For instance, the United States' armed conflict against Al Qaeda in Afghanistan constituted a NIAC, as did the Afghan government's conflict against Al Qaeda in Afghanistan. This prevailing view was adopted by the United States Supreme Court in *Hamdan v. Rumsfeld*, when considering whether Geneva Conventions Common Article 3 applied to the conflict with Al Qaeda. The Court agreed that "an important purpose of the provision was to furnish minimal protection to rebels involved in one kind of 'conflict not of an international character', i.e., a civil war." The Court opined that under a plain interpretation of Common Article 3, any armed conflict that is not a conflict "between nations" is a "conflict not of international character."

16.3.2. IHL Issues and Targeted Killing

Though this text intentionally does not present a comprehensive orientation to international humanitarian law, understanding the legality—or illegality—of targeted killing requires some familiarity. IHL—also known as ***jus in bello*** and the law of armed conflict—concerns itself primarily with rules for how warfare should be conducted, with the ultimate purpose of reducing the suffering associated with armed conflict. Importantly, IHL does not begin with the presumption that extrajudicial killing is illegal. Quite to the contrary, IHL recognizes that the existence of an armed conflict might include significant legal killing. However, failure to "play by the rules" of IHL is often referred to as a "war crime." Three principles of IHL are implicated by targeted killing activities: distinction, **necessity**, and **proportionality**.

16.3.2.1. Distinction

One of the fundamental principles if IHL is **distinction**, which requires combatants to distinguish between legitimate targets of armed force—combatants and military objectives—and protected, illegitimate targets. In traditional international armed conflict, distinction is an easy principle to understand. Members of the armed forces of each state party are "combatants" who have the right to use lethal force when fighting, the right to be treated as prisoners of war when captured, and are lawful targets of the enemy forces' attacks, except in limited circumstances where they are considered "out of combat," such as when shipwrecked or injured to a degree that they cannot participate in hostilities. Everyone who is not a combatant is a civilian, and is not the legitimate target of attack "unless and for such time as they take a direct part in hostilities." In a non-international armed conflict, distinction can be more difficult to apply. Often, states are not willing to accept that non-state armed forces enjoy the privileges associated with the status of "combatant" though they wish these persons to be considered combatants for the purpose of being lawfully targeted. Additionally, members of non-state armed groups often do not wear distinctive uniforms or distinguish themselves from the civilian population, making distinction difficult.

The disagreement regarding whether non-state armed forces should be treated as combatants has significant consequences for the legality of targeted killings. Combatants are generally lawful targets, while civilians are never lawful targets, except "for such time as they directly participate in hostilities." Under the most restrictive understanding of that exception, lethal force can only be used against civilian members of armed groups who are not considered "combatants" at the precise moment they are engaged in hostilities. Under the somewhat broader view adopted by the International Committee of the Red Cross, individuals in an "organized armed group" are those persons who take on a "continuous combat function" for the non-state party to the conflict. ICRC Clarification Process on The Notion Of Direct Participation In Hostilities Under International Humanitarian Law (2009) ("ICRC Position"). Under this view, a member of an armed group may be targeted with lethal force at any time, so long as he has assumed a continuous combat function" to conduct hostilities on behalf of the non-State party to the conflict. Under the ICRC's view,

> individuals whose continuous function involves the preparation, execution, or command of acts or operations amounting to direct participation in hostilities are assuming a continuous combat function. An individual recruited, trained and equipped by such a group to continuously and directly participate in hostilities on its behalf can be

> considered to assume a continuous combat function even before he or she first carries out a hostile act.

To this list, the UN Special Rapporteur on the Promotion And Protection Of Human Rights And Fundamental Freedoms While Countering Terrorism has added "individuals who have directly participated in hostilities on repeated occasions in support of an organized armed group in circumstances indicating that their conduct reflects a continuous combat role rather than a spontaneous or sporadic or temporary role assumed for the duration of a particular operation." Excluded from the list of persons having a continuous combat function are those who would not be considered a part of the armed forces if they were associated with a state party, such as purely political leaders with no military function, propagandists supporting the organization, and individuals who provide support for the war effort but who do not actually participate in the fighting. The ICRC position occupies a middle ground, with some organizations like Amnesty International arguing it allows state parties too much leeway to target persons they believe should be classified as civilians, and some states arguing the ICRC's position does not accurately reflect the realities of modern warfare and is too restrictive. For now, the ICRC's position seems to be the predominant view.

Even if a person is not deemed a combatant, and is therefore a civilian, under Geneva Convention Additional Protocol 1, civilians may be targeted "for such time as they directly participate in hostilities." Unfortunately, there is no clearly defined understanding of what constitutes "direct participation" other than the obvious examples of committing violence against others. Courts have taken an exemplar approach to suggesting the meaning of "direct participation in hostilities." For instance, the ICTY stated:

> Examples of active or direct participation in hostilities includes: bearing using or taking up arms, taking part in military or hostile acts, activities, conduct or operations, armed fighting or combat, participating in attacks against enemy personnel, property or equipment, transmitting military information for the immediate use of a belligerent, transporting weapons in proximity to combat operations, and serving as guards, intelligence agents, lookouts or observers on behalf of military forces.

By contrast, the ICTY suggested:

> Examples of indirect participation in hostilities include: participating in the activities in support of the war or military effort of one of the parties of the conflict, selling goods to one of the parties of the conflict, expressing sympathy for the cause of one of the parties to the conflict,

> failing to act to prevent an incursion by the parties to the conflict, gathering and transmitting military information, transporting arms and munitions, and providing supplies, and providing specialist advice regarding the selection of military personnel, their training or the correct maintenance of the weapons.

In attempting to provide some definition of "directly participating in hostilities," the ICRC has suggested a test with three elements, all three of which must exist for an act to be considered "direct participation in hostilities":

> (i) there must be a threshold of harm likely to result from the act, either by impacting military operations or harming civilians;
>
> (ii) there must be a relationship of direct causation between the act and the expected harm; and
>
> (iii) there must be a belligerent nexus between the act and the hostilities conducted between the parties to an armed conflict, meaning that it must be specifically designed to support the military operations of one party to the detriment of another.

The temporal element imposed by Additional Protocol I—"*for such time as* they directly participate in hostilities"—has also been subject to considerable disagreement, and is important when determining the legality of targeted killing. Under the ICRC view, a person who has joined an insurgency group or terrorist organization and commits to continuous participation in hostilities has forfeited his rights as a civilian, while ordinary civilians only lose their protection for the duration of *each specific act* amounting to direct participation in hostilities. As in other areas, the ICRC view occupies a middle ground. Some argue that all civilians, whether or not they have joined an armed group and committed to continuous participation in hostilities, can only be targeted during the duration of the specific act that constitutes direct participation in hostilities. On the other end of the spectrum, the United States has rejected what it views as a "revolving door of protection," because repeated participation in hostilities, interspersed with claims of protected civilian status, would endanger protections for civilians who do not participate at all. The United States has asserted the position that:

> Common Article 3 does not alter the fundamental law of war principle concerning a belligerent party's right in an armed conflict to target individuals who are part of an enemy's armed forces or eliminate a nation's authority to take legitimate action in national self-defense. The language of Common Article 3 "makes clear that members of such armed forces [of both the state and non-state parties to the conflict] . . .

> are considered as 'taking no active part in the hostilities' only once they have disengaged from their fighting function ('have laid down their arms') or are placed hors de combat; mere suspension of combat is insufficient.

DOJ White Paper, *Lawfulness of a Lethal Operation Directed Against a United States Citizen Who Is a Senior Operational Leader of Al-Qa'ida or An Associated Force*, Draft, November 8, 2011.

In summary, under IHL, the principle of distinction requires parties to armed conflict to attack only legitimate targets. Lawful targets include combatant members of armed groups in armed conflict, or civilians while directly participating in hostilities. All others are *not* lawful targets. There is significant disagreement regarding whether each person targeted by the United States during its counterterrorism targeted killing operations have been lawful targets under this understanding.

16.3.2.2. Necessity

Under the IHL principle of necessity, only actions that are necessary to achieving a legitimate military objective are permitted. Additional Protocol I describes valid military objectives as "those objects which by their nature, location, purpose or use make an effective contribution to military action and whose total or partial destruction, capture or neutralization, in the circumstances ruling at the time, offers a definite military advantage." This principle is thus an attempt to permit necessary military advancement toward concluding the war while attempting to limit the amount of unnecessary death, destruction, and suffering along the way. Some argue that the principle of necessity means that a combatant may not kill an enemy if capturing the enemy is equally viable and will accomplish the same strategic military benefit. In the context of targeted killing, this would mean that every targeted killing would need to be preceded by an analysis of whether capture or other non-lethal method of "eliminating" the target is possible. However, the prevailing view is that military forces do not need to evaluate the possibility of capturing the enemy when deciding whether to employ lethal force because the principle of necessity does not require armed forces to assume additional risk in order to capture rather than kill an enemy. Indeed, war would look very different if the law required attempted capture in all cases. In any event, the principle of necessity requires that killing the target must actually produce a definite military advantage. Some have objected that the United States government's targeted killing program sometimes violates the principle of necessity, because the targets are of questionable military value, an assertion the United States government refutes.

16.3.2.3. Proportionality

The IHL principle of **proportionality** prohibits attacks that may be expected to cause incidental loss of civilian life, injury to civilians, or damage to civilian objects, that would be "excessive" in relation to the concrete and direct military advantage anticipated. Thus, with each attack, the attacking force must consider anticipated collateral damage to civilians in the form of injury and destruction of objects, the expected military advantage that a successful attack will likely bring, and to then weigh the two. So long as the expected collateral damage is not "excessive" when weighed against the military advantage, it is proportional.

Proportionality has been one of the primary battlegrounds for debate regarding the legality of targeted killing by drone strike. Many arguments center around whether the mechanism of a drone strike inherently leads to skewed proportionality assessments by military operators. Some argue the distance the RPA pilot is from the target makes it more likely the pilot will undervalue collateral damage, while others argue the extended and intimate way in which RPA pilots are able to see their targets before and after strikes, an intimacy that has led to incidents of PTSD in operators, causes pilots to properly value civilian life. Others debated whether drone strikes increase or decrease the likelihood of civilian collateral damage, with some arguing drone strikes kill more civilians because data show that more civilians than combatants are killed in an average strike, while others counter that, because of their precision, drone strikes produce fewer civilian casualties than attacks by manned aircraft. Law professor and former DOD policy lawyer Rosa Brooks articulated a middle ground during testimony before Congress:

> [T]here does not appear to be anything inherent in drones as a weapon that tends to inflict more civilian harm than other kinds of weapons. . . . [C]ritics often assert that United States drone strikes are morally wrong because they kill innocent civilians. This is undoubtedly true and tragic—but it is not really an argument against drone strikes as such. War kills innocent civilians, period. But the best available evidence suggests that United States drone strikes kill civilians at no higher a rate, and almost certainly at a lower rate, than most other common means of warfare.

The Constitutional and Counterterrorism Implications of Targeted Killings, Hearing Before the Senate Judiciary Subcommittee on the Constitution, Civil Rights, and Human

Rights, 113th Cong. (2013). Similarly, the U.N. Special Rapporteur on the Promotion and Protection Of Human Rights and Fundamental Freedoms While Countering Terrorism concluded "If used in strict compliance with the principles of international humanitarian law, remotely piloted aircraft are capable of reducing the risk of civilian casualties in armed conflict by significantly improving the situational awareness of military commanders." *Interim Report to The General Assembly on The Use of Remotely Piloted Aircraft In Counter-Terrorism Operations*, 2013.

16.3.2.4. Responsibility for War Crimes?

Some have wondered whether the legality of targeted killing may vary based on *who* conducts the operation. Specifically, if there is an armed conflict, may government agents who are not members of the armed forces lawfully participate? The U.N. Special Rapporteur on Extrajudicial, Summary or Arbitrary Executions, Philp Alston, opined:

> Under IHL, civilians, including intelligence agents, are not prohibited from participating in hostilities. Rather, the consequence of participation is two-fold. First, because they are "directly participating in hostilities" by conducting targeted killings, intelligence personnel may themselves be targeted and killed. Second, intelligence personnel do not have immunity from prosecution under domestic law for their conduct. They are thus unlike State armed forces which would generally be immune from prosecution for the same conduct (assuming they complied with IHL requirements). Thus, CIA personnel could be prosecuted for murder under the domestic law of any country in which they conduct targeted drone killings, and could also be prosecuted for violations of applicable United States law.
>
> It is important to note that if a targeted killing violates IHL (by, for example, targeting civilians who were not "directly participating in hostilities"), then regardless of who conducts it—intelligence personnel or State armed forces—the author, as well as those who authorized it, can be prosecuted for war crimes.

16.3.3. Targeted Killing and *Jus Ad Bellum*

Targeted killing, which usually involves one state killing someone who is present in another state, raises issues not only of *jus in bello*, but also ***jus ad bellum***, which is discussed in detail in Chapter 10. We suggest reading or reviewing the *jus ad bellum* discussion in that chapter before considering its application to targeted killing here, as the following presumes a general understanding of *jus ad bellum* principles. Without completely revisiting that discussion, we will identify some key concerns regarding the legal justification of self-defense in the context of targeted killing.

Launching a drone strike from an aircraft loitering in the air space over another state, or landing a small assault force in another state, necessarily implicates violation of sovereignty and the U.N. Charter and customary international law prohibitions on use of military force against another state.

Since 9/11, a primary justification for using force in the form of targeted killing has been the **consent** of the states in which the targeted killing occurs. U.N. Charter Article 2(4)'s prohibition on using military force against other states is not violated when the state in which the targeted killing occurs consents. Though confidential agreements between states are not available to evaluate, publicly available information suggests that most United States drone strikes have occurred in states where the host government has consented to the United States' activity.

Where no consent exists, some other legal justification for targeted killing must. Self-defense is the primary remaining justification. Article 51 of the U.N. Charter preserves every state's "inherent right of individual or **collective self-defense** if an **armed attack** occurs." Customary international law may support a broader understanding of the triggering event for self-defense, including the theories of **anticipatory self-defense**, where states have the right to "anticipate" that an attack is imminent or in the process of being mounted and use force in self-defense to prevent or limit the effects of the anticipated attack before they occur, and **preemptive self-defense**, where a state may take defensive action to thwart a possible future threat. Indeed, United States officials have claimed "the inherent right to national self-defense recognized in international law (see, e.g., U.N. Charter art. 51)," continuing "It was on these bases that the United States responded to the attacks of September 11, 2001, and '[t]hese domestic and international legal authorities continue to this day.' " DOJ White Paper, quoting Harold Hongju Koh, Legal Adviser, United States Department of State.

United States officials have also argued for a flexible understanding of "imminence" in the context of counterterrorism, suggesting that

> the absence of specific evidence of where an attack will take place or of the precise nature of an attack does not preclude a conclusion that an armed attack is imminent for purposes of the exercise of the right of self-defense, provided that there is a reasonable and objective basis for concluding that an armed attack is imminent.

Brian Egan, Legal Adviser, United States Department of State, *International Law, Legal Diplomacy, and the Counter-ISIL Campaign*. United States officials have pushed the self-defense justification even further, arguing "it is not necessary as a matter of international law to reassess whether an armed attack is imminent prior to every subsequent action taken against that group, provided that hostilities have not ended." *Id.*

The inherent right of self-defense is available against non-state actors, not just states, as long as the non-state actor engages in, or threatens, an "armed attack." Second, although not all terrorist attacks rise to the level of "armed attack," a terrorist attack can suffice, if it is of sufficient intensity (scale and effect). Additionally, repeated smaller attacks can be accumulated to constitute an armed attack. Thus, the terrorist attacks against the United States on 9/11 were sufficient to constitute an "armed attack" by Al Qaeda, permitting use of military force in self-defense. However, the duration of that justification is limited by the idea that self-defense must actually be defending against attack. Actions taken 20 years after 9/11 are not properly considered a defense against that attack. But terrorist attacks continue against United States forces and persons around the world, returning to the question of whether such smaller attacks are of sufficient intensity to constitute an armed attack for purposes of Article 51. And the context of the 9/11 attacks suggests terror attacks may vary between "smaller" attacks and a massive attack like 9/11, with states concerned about preventing both. Additionally, theories of anticipatory self-defense and preemptive self-defense may be asserted by some states employing targeted killing in an effort to thwart imminent or prevent future attacks. The international criticisms of those theories of self-defense, and questions they pose, apply to targeted killing.

16.4. TARGETED KILLING UNDER UNITED STATES DOMESTIC LAW

16.4.1. Legal Authorization

As with other uses of force discussed in this text, the President must have domestic legal authority to order Executive Branch agents to engage in targeted killing. Presidents may claim constitutional authority for targeted killing based on the host of theories of presidential authority discussed in Chapter 2. For targeted killings in the context of counterterrorism efforts, the President's defensive powers as Commander in Chief and executive authority to repel attack and defend the nation are most applicable. A broad customary power to advance United States interests internationally may also be claimed. Some have argued that though those broad powers may authorize *some* of the targeted killings in which the United States has engaged, they do not authorize all such targeted killings, as not all have a clear nexus to an imminent threat to the nation.

The President may also claim statutory authority for targeted killing under an **Authorization for the Use of Military Force (AUMF)**. For example, after the 9/11 attacks in 2001, Congress authorized the President to:

> use all necessary and appropriate force against those nations, organizations, or persons he determines planned, authorized, committed, or aided the terrorist attacks that occurred on September 11, 2001, or harbored such organizations or persons, in order to prevent any future acts of international terrorism against the United States by such nations, organizations or persons.

Targeted killings of persons in the organizations described in the 2001 AUMF, including Al Qaeda, the Taliban, and "associated forces," are thus explicitly authorized by Congress. The General Counsel of the DOD explained that DOD interpreted "associated force" to mean a force that is "(1) an organized, armed group that has entered the fight alongside al Qaeda and (2) is a cobelligerent with al Qaeda in hostilities against the United States or its coalition partners." On the other hand, the statutory authorization for targeted killing of persons not included in the AUMF is less clear. The 2002 AUMF authorizing the war against Iraq has also been claimed as authority for uses of force against ISIL, a terrorist group that was operating primarily in Syria and Iraq, though the claim that the 2002 AUMF authorizes activities to *protect* Iraq from ISIL has been widely criticized.

Congress has also given the President authority under the **Covert Action Statute** for covert operations against terrorists presenting an imminent threat. Unlike the AUMF, the CAS is not limited to specific terrorist groups associated with the 9/11 attacks. Here too, the extent of authorization is uncertain. The CIA General Counsel once opined to Congress that the CAS does not authorize the President to authorize a covert action that would violate the Constitution or statute of the United States, but that it did authorize violation of some forms of international law. Interestingly, after the raid by United States Navy Seal Teams that killed Osama bin Laden in 2011, CIA Director Leon Panetta, claimed the raid had been "a title 50 operation," referring to the section of the United States Code that authorizes intelligence actions and includes the Covert Action Statute. Reference to a raid conducted by military operatives as being an intelligence operation is an example of the significant overlap between military and intelligence activities in counterterrorism efforts, and also suggests the CAS may have been the primary authorization for the raid that took place on Pakistani soil.

16.4.2. Legal Constraints

16.4.2.1. Constitutional and Statutory Constraints

The Constitution and various federal laws not only provide authorization for some targeted killings, they also impose constraints. For example, the broad discussion of legal authority for using force discussed in Chapters 1–5 of this text applies to targeted killing, too.

Some scholars and lawyers have suggested the United States government's targeted killing program violates the Fifth Amendment's due process guarantee. In cases like *Goss v. Lopez* and *Mathews v. Eldridge*, the Supreme Court has opined that the right to due process of law demands that before the government deprive someone of their life, liberty, or property, the government must, at a minimum, give notice and provide an opportunity to be heard. Some have argued targeted killing violates this requirement, as targets are not provided "notice" or an opportunity to claim their innocence before they are killed. Additional due process arguments include the idea that allowing the Executive Branch alone to determine whether to kill violates the Due Process Clause's mandate a neutral decision-maker should be involved, and that the Executive Branch's process for deciding whether to target an individual should be subject to some **judicial review**.

Questions of due process were central to a lawsuit challenging the legality of targeted killing of United States citizens. Anwar Al-Aulaqi, a United States citizen, was suspected by the United States of terrorism-related activities. Suspecting his son might be on a list of persons identified for targeted killing, Al-Aulaqi's father filed suit in 2010, asking a federal court to enjoin the United States government from killing his son. Al-Aulaqi argued that a targeted killing would violate his son's Fourth and Fifth Amendment rights. The district court dismissed the suit when it determined that the case involved non-justiciable political questions, including whether Al-Aulaqi posed a sufficient threat, whether means short of lethal force could be employed while protecting national security, and broad strategic considerations that would require a court to "assess the merits of the President's . . . decision to launch an attack on a foreign target." *Al-Aulaqi v. Obama.* In September 2011, a United States drone strike killed Anwar Al-Aulaqi, a fact the United States admitted in May 2013. Subsequently, the Center for Constitutional Rights and the American Civil Liberties Union (ACLU) filed a lawsuit claiming damages for the United States' targeted killing of Al-Aulaqi and others. A different district court judge dismissed this second case, not on the basis of the political question doctrine, but instead ruling that no viable claim existed. *Al-Aulaqi v. Panetta.*

A draft of a 2010 Department of Justice White Paper (DOJ White Paper) addressing the legality of targeting Al-Aulaqi was made public pursuant to a Freedom of Information Act lawsuit brought by the New York Times and the American Civil Liberties Union. The DOJ White Paper provides great insight into the government's legal theories regarding why the Fourth Amendment's prohibition on unreasonable searches and seizures and the Fifth Amendment's Due Process Clause did not protect Al-Aulaqi from being targeted.

The Fourth Amendment of the United States Constitution prohibits unreasonable searches and seizures. While typically a government "seizure" of a person involves arrest or detention, it can also include their killing. Regarding the Fourth Amendment, the DOJ White Paper applied the test from *Tennessee v. Garner*, which "balances the nature and quality of the intrusion on the individual's Fourth Amendment interest against the importance of the governmental interests alleged to justify the intrusion." The DOJ concluded that

> at least in circumstances where the targeted person is an operational leader of an enemy force and an informed, high-level government official has determined that he poses an imminent threat of violent attack against the United States, and those conducting the operation would carry out the operation only if capture were infeasible, the use of lethal force would not violate the Fourth Amendment . . . [because] the intrusion on any Fourth Amendment interests would be outweighed by the importance of the government interest that justify the intrusion . . .—the interest in protecting the lives of Americans.

Overall, the DOJ acknowledged that Fourth and Fifth Amendment rights applied to United States citizens outside the United States, but asserted that United States citizenship does not "give that person constitutional immunity from attack." Citing *Hamdi* and *Mathews v. Eldridge*, the DOJ said that a balancing test was appropriate, but that United States citizens outside the United States could be targeted with lethal force in the following circumstances:

> (1) where an informed, high-level official of the United States government has determined that the targeted individual poses an imminent threat of violent attack against the United States;
>
> (2) where a capture operation would be infeasible-and where those conducting the operation continue to monitor whether capture becomes feasible; and
>
> (3) where such an operation would be conducted consistent with applicable law of war principles.

> In these circumstances, the "realities" of the conflict and the weight of the government's interest in protecting its citizens from an imminent attack are such that the Constitution would not require the government to provide further process to such a United States citizen before using lethal force.

Statutory authorities also impose limitations. For example, the 2001 AUMF's authorization only applies to certain groups of people. And the CAS also includes procedural and reporting rules with which the President must comply for targeted killing relying on that statutory authority to be lawful.

16.4.2.2. Executive Self-Constraint?

Perhaps the most obvious law limiting targeted killing is **Executive Order** 12,333, which prohibits assassination. Numerous scholars have argued targeted killing violates E.O. 12,333. Other scholars and government representatives have argued that so long as targeted killing operations are consistent with the law of war, they do not constitute "assassinations," so E.O. 12,333 does not apply. Perhaps more important than the debate over whether a targeted killing is an assassination is the form this law takes. Executive Orders are issued by the President and can arguably be withdrawn or rescinded, whether in whole or as it relates to specific operations. Because executive orders are published in the **Federal Register**, there is some debate regarding what form a withdrawal or rescission must take, but at least some scholars believe E.O. 12,333 could be construed as only banning assassinations, that they are undertaken without presidential approval. Regardless of the debates regarding the legal effect of E.O. 12,333, it seems that as a statement of presidential policy, subsequent presidents are likely not to view it as ultimately controlling what they may order.

16.4.3. The United States Approach to Targeted Killing

Targeted killing program details are mostly classified and difficult to ascertain. However, the Obama Administration released some details late in his presidency. In 2016, the Administration released a redacted version of its classified Presidential Policy Guidance (PPG): "Procedures for Approving Direct Action Against Terrorist Targets Located Outside the United States and Areas of Active Hostilities the PPG." The PPG outlined the policies and procedures the United States used for targeted killing of terrorists.

The PPG articulated a preference for capturing, rather than killing, terrorist suspects, and details legal standards for such captures. The PPG also details a substantial multi-level, interagency approval process ending in White House-level approval for targeted killing. Some have argued this elaborate approval process satisfies due process concerns, while others have objected that because the entire process occurs within the Executive Branch, it is insufficient, no matter how thorough.

Substantively, the PPG establishes two basic requirements for lethal action: the individual must be "lawfully targeted under existing authorities" and the individual's activities must pose "a continuing, imminent threat to United States persons." Assuming those requirements are met, the PPG establishes conditions that must be met before lethal action may be taken:

a) near certainty that the lawful terrorist target is present;

b) near certainty that noncombatants will not be injured or killed;

c) REDACTED;

d) assessment that capture is not feasible at the time of the operation;

e) assessment that the relevant governmental authorities in the country where action is contemplated cannot or will not effectively address the threat to United States persons; and

f) an assessment that no other reasonable alternatives to lethal action exist to effectively address the threat to United States persons.

Some of these standards exceed those required under international humanitarian law applicable during armed conflict. For instance, IHL does not require "near certainty" that noncombatants will not be injured or killed. This is in part due to the applicability of the PPG. The PPG says that it applies to targeting operations *outside* "areas of active hostilities," meaning drone operations in countries like Afghanistan and Syria are likely not governed by the PPG.

The PPG emphasizes that "international legal principles, including respect for sovereignty and the law of armed conflict, impose "[i]mportant constraints on the ability of the United States to act unilaterally—and the way in which the United States can use force." Even if a target is lawful, in each case a separate policy determination must be made regarding whether the proposed target *should* be targeted for **direct action**.

In addition to the PPG, in July 2016 the Obama administration issued and made public Executive Order 13,732, *United States Policy on Pre- and Post-Strike Measures to Address Civilian Casualties in United States Operations Involving the Use of Force*. The E.O. addressed efforts to limit civilian casualties in United States military operations. Unlike the PPG discussed above, the E.O. applies to areas inside and outside active hostilities. While accepting that civilian casualties are an unavoidable consequence of the use of force, the E.O. asserts the United States' commitment to law of armed conflict principles: "As a Nation, we are steadfastly committed to complying with our obligations under the law of armed conflict, including those that address the protection of civilians, such as the fundamental principles of necessity, humanity, distinction, and proportionality."

A RAND Corporation study concluded that the net effect of the Obama administration's targeted killing policies was to describe in the PPG the operational restraint that the United States voluntarily chooses to apply as a matter of policy in areas outside of active hostilities, while its interpretation of international law retains the flexibility to define broadly where armed conflict exists, "when it may wish to apply warfighting principles." Lynn E. Davis, Michael McNerney, and Michael D. Greenberg, *Clarifying the Rules for Targeted Killing: An Analytical Framework for Policies Involving Long-Range Armed Drones*, RAND Corp., 2016. Former Legal Advisor for the Department of State Harold Koh evaluated the blended effect as a "combined law-of-war approach with law-enforcement methods to bring all available tools to bear against Al Qaeda." Though this understanding may accurately describe the United States' approach, it does not resolve the complex legal issues associated with actions that might simultaneously be analyzed as law enforcement and armed conflict.

Targeted Killing of General Qassem Soleimani

The extent to which the Trump Administration has modified or rescinded Obama Administration-era policies regarding targeted killing, including civilian casualties, has not been publicized and is not fully known as of this writing. However, the legal explanation for one targeted killing may somewhat elucidate the Trump Administration's approach.

On January 2, 2020, the United States military conducted an air strike in Iraq targeting Qassem Soleimani, a major general in the Islamic Revolutionary Guard Corps of Iran, and the commander of an expeditionary Revolutionary Guard unit called the Qods Force. The United States Air Force used an MQ-9 Reaper drone, which launched several missiles at a convoy of vehicles as it departed Baghdad International Airport. General Soleimani was killed in the attack, along with nine others.

The Qods Force was established in 1990 and had been designated a terrorist organization by the United States several other countries. According to the United States government, the Qods Force has become Iranian leaders' favored all-purpose expeditionary mission force "to conduct operations outside Iran, provide support for Islamic militants, and collect intelligence against Iran's enemies." The United States government also has asserted that "Iran-supported . . . Shia militias remain the primary threat to United States personnel" in Iraq and that using Iranian-provided weapons, Qods Force-backed militias are estimated to have killed more than 600 United States personnel serving in Iraq between 2003 and 2011. The United States believed Soleimani was the "lead architect behind Iran's campaign of terrorism, assassinations, arms-smuggling, and violence throughout the Middle East, including against United States personnel in Iraq." United States Secretary of State Mike Pompeo stated "There is no terrorist except Usama bin Laden who has more American blood on his hands than . . . Qassem Soleimani." United States government officials claimed that in the months leading up to the January 2020 strike on Soleimani, Iran-backed groups, including the Qods Force, engaged in a series of escalating attacks on United States interests and personnel.

In a March 2020 speech to a group of law students, Paul C. Ney, then General Counsel of the United States DOD (DOD GC), defended the targeted killing as justified self-defense under Article 51 of the U.N. Charter. Asserting that the United States had been subject to an escalating series of armed attacks by Iran and Iran-supported militias in the Middle East, including in Iraq, the United States believed use of force was necessary and justified. Moreover, the United States asserted that "an imminent attack is not a necessary condition for resort to force in self-defense in this circumstance because armed attacks by Iran already had occurred and were expected to occur again." Importantly, the United States argued that "although Article 51 refers explicitly to self-defense only in response to an actual armed attack, the United States maintains that international law also includes the right to use force where an armed attack is imminent."

Regarding domestic authorization, the DOD GC asserted that the President's order of the targeted killing was justified under his constitutional authority as Chief Executive and Commander in Chief. Responding to the argument that Congress should have been involved in attacking another sovereign nation's military leader, the General Counsel asserted that the use of force did not rise to the level of requiring advanced congressional approval because it was not a "substantial military engagement" and "the President decided based upon available intelligence that the targeted operation would be unlikely to escalate into a full-scale war." The DOD GC also claimed legal justification under the 2002 AUMF, which had authorized the President "to use the Armed Forces of the United States as he determines to be necessary and appropriate in order to . . . defend the national security of the United States against the continuing threat posed by Iraq." Addressing the objection that General Soleimani, an Iranian military member, was not a "threat posed by Iraq," the DOD GC argued:

> the United States has relied consistently upon the 2002 AUMF to authorize the use of force for the purpose of establishing a stable, democratic Iraq and addressing terrorist threats emanating from Iraq under the George W. Bush, Obama, and Trump Administrations. Such uses of force need not only address threats from the Iraqi Government apparatus but may also address threats to the United States posed by militias, terrorist groups, or other armed groups in Iraq. For example, the Obama Administration invoked the 2002 AUMF (along with the 2001 AUMF) as domestic legal authority for conducting military operations against ISIS in Iraq and also operations in Syria to address threats emanating from Iraq.

Following the air strike, the House and Senate of the United States Congress passed a **joint resolution** directing President Trump to terminate the use of United States armed forces for hostilities against Iran unless explicitly authorized by a congressional **declaration of war** or a specific **authorization for the use of military force** against Iran. President Trump vetoed the measure, and the Senate failed to override the veto.

REVIEW QUESTIONS

1. How does the legality of targeted killing in an armed conflict differ from its legality in the law enforcement context?

2. What are the possible sources of authority for targeted killing under United States domestic law. What domestic law constrains targeted killing?

CRITICAL THINKING QUESTIONS

1. Applying the "absolutely necessary" standard imposed by the European Court in the *McCann* case, are targeted killings ever "absolutely necessary?" If so, under what circumstances?

2. What reasonable alternatives exist to targeted killing of terror suspects? In answering this question, assume facts most favorable to the government claiming it needs to engage in targeted killing—the intelligence regarding a particular target clearly demonstrates the target's ongoing leadership of, preparation for, and participation in terror strikes aimed at killing large numbers of civilians.

3. In this chapter we have considered the legal implications of all forms of targeted killing broadly. Now, consider what specific additional legal issues are raised by specific methods of targeted killing. For example, what legal issues are different when the targeted killing occurs by drone strike rather than a small assault team that raids a suspected terrorist compound?

4. Would a United States strike against a small terrorist organization's leader be justified as self-defense when the organization has never attacked the United States or its people, but has publicly declared a desire to do so?

5. Do you agree with the DOJ White Paper regarding why the Fourth and Fifth Amendment did not protect United States citizen Anwar Al-Aulaqi from being subject to a targeted killing?

6. Is it appropriate for the United States government's targeted killing program to combine "a law-of-war approach with law-enforcement methods to bring all available tools?" What are the advantages and disadvantages of viewing counterterrorism activities and the laws governing them in this way?

7. Did the targeted killing of General Soleimani comply with international law? Did President Trump have domestic legal authority to order the strike? Did the strike

violate any United States domestic law constraints? After Congress's joint resolution directing the President to terminate use of military force against Iran, would *another* targeted killing of an Iranian general be constitutional?

8. Evaluate the legality under international law and domestic United States law of one or more of the following targeted killings: the May 2016 killing of Mullah Akhtar Mansour; the December 2015 killing of Abdirahman Sandhere; the February 2016 strikes on a jihadist safe haven in Pakistan that killed some suspected militants of the Haqqani Network; and/or the February 2010 attack by helicopter gunship and drone on a suspected Taliban vehicle convoy that killed at least 15 civilians.

CHAPTER 17

Organization and Authority of the Intelligence Community

The constellation of agencies involved in the Intelligence Community

Learning Objectives

1. Understand the inception, evolution, and legal authority of the United States Intelligence Community.

2. Understand the intelligence cycle and the sources and methods of intelligence gathering.

3. Identify the organizational members of the United States Intelligence Community and describe their various missions and intelligence gathering expertise.

4. Identify and describe the committees, offices, and agencies responsible for oversight of the United States Intelligence Community.

17.1. INTRODUCTION

The Intelligence Reform and Terrorism Prevention Act of 2004 defines "intelligence" as information gathered, either domestically or outside the United States, that involves: 1) threats to the United States, its people, property, or other interests; 2) the development, proliferation, or use of weapons of mass destruction; or 3) any other matter bearing on national security. The United States uses intelligence to make national security decisions and to understand the consequences of those decisions. The United States Intelligence Community, often referred to as the "IC," is a group of seventeen federal government agencies within the Executive Branch that collect intelligence to both protect national security and conduct foreign relations. The Director of National Intelligence coordinates the intelligence activities among these various agencies and is the principal intelligence advisor to the President of the United States. While it may seem the United States has always had a unified, directed approach to collecting intelligence, it has taken over 200 years of experience for an organized and cooperative modern Intelligence Community to develop.

17.2. THE HISTORY AND DEVELOPMENT OF INTELLIGENCE GATHERING AUTHORITY IN THE UNITED STATES

17.2.1. Intelligence Gathering from the Revolution to the Civil War

Collecting intelligence to protect national security has been part of the American experience since the country was founded. In 1775, a year before the Declaration of Independence, the Continental Congress created the Committee of Secret Correspondence. The Committee operated in Europe and collected **foreign intelligence**, engaged in clandestine operations, and disseminated propaganda in support of America's independence from Britain. General George Washington, during the Revolutionary War, was known for appreciating the usefulness of intelligence in winning the War of Independence. In 1777, the same year the Continental Congress approved a permanent Continental Army to fight the British, General Washington wrote a letter to Elias Dayton who was setting up a spy ring for Washington in New York. In his letter, Washington wrote:

> "The necessity of procuring good intelligence is apparent and need not be further urged-All that remains for me to add is, that you keep the whole matter as secret as possible. For upon Secrecy, success depends in most Enterprises of the kind, & for want of it, they are generally defeated, however, well planned. . . ." George Washington, *From George Washington to Colonel Elias Dayton*, July 26, 1777.

As further evidence of Washington's appreciation for intelligence gathering, during his first State of the Union address, Washington requested Congress fund intelligence operations. In response, Congress created the Contingent Fund of Foreign Intercourse, or the Secret Service Fund, which primarily funded covert intelligence operations in Europe. However, the Fund was not a formal organization or agency. Instead, it simply funded various operations with little public oversight or transparency. The Civil War, however, ushered in an era of a more formalized approach to intelligence gathering.

The Culper Ring

One of the earliest organized American intelligence efforts, the Culper Ring, began as a small New England operation in 1778. Major Benjamin Tallmadge, alias John Bolton, headed the operation at Washington's direction. Tallmadge, in turn, appointed Abraham Woodhull and Robert Townsend as leaders under the aliases of Samuel Culper, Sr. and Samuel Culper, Jr., respectively.

The Culper Ring provided critical intelligence from its 1778 inception until 1783, when British forces left New York. Its operatives provided detailed information to the Continental Army about the British occupation, including battle readiness assessments, detailed fleet reports, and updates on loyalist activity. Arguably the most well-known attribute of the Ring was its use of cryptography. The members and leaders of the Culper Ring developed a complex code for communicating their reports, allowing operatives to preserve the secrecy of their messages in the event of intercept or capture. Operatives transmitted their messages in a myriad of ways, including concealing papers inside coat buttons, **dead drops**, and even publishing coded reports in newspapers.

As a testament to the Culper Ring's unprecedented success, its existence remained completely unrevealed to the general public until 1929 when letters to Samuel Culper, Jr. were associated with Robert Townsend through handwriting examination. Washington himself did not know the true identity of the Culper operatives. As a result of the thoroughness of its operatives, the full extent of the Culper Ring's contribution to the American war effort remains a mystery.

Though neither the North nor the South had a permanent intelligence service, in 1863, the Union general in Command of the Army of the Potomac created the Bureau of Military Intelligence (BMI), which existed until the end of the Civil War. The BMI collected intelligence from various sources including prisoners of war, spies in the Confederate military, and documents collected from dead Confederate soldiers. The Confederate States had their own secret services including a Signal Corps that conducted both military and civilian espionage. However, most historians suggest the first permanent American intelligence agencies were not established until the late Nineteenth Century, after the end of the Civil War.

In 1865, very soon after the end of the Civil War, the federal government established the Secret Service. Initially, it was charged with investigating rampant counterfeiting, but within a few years its responsibilities included investigating the Ku Klux Klan, bootleggers, and smugglers. Founded in 1882 and 1885, respectively, the United States Navy's Office of Naval Intelligence (ONI) and the United States Army's Military Intelligence Division were created to collect military intelligence. Unlike previous military intelligence operations, however, these organizations were intended to conduct intelligence gathering in both peacetime and in war. Naval and Army officers were stationed in various European countries to collect publicly available information. However, with the beginning of the Spanish-American war in 1898, these military officers also began engaging in covert espionage.

17.2.2. Intelligence Gathering During the World Wars and the National Security Act

At the beginning of the Twentieth Century, the United States was investing significantly less in foreign intelligence collection. Instead, it turned its attention to domestic intelligence. In addition to the Secret Service's domestic operations, the Department of Justice (DOJ) created the Bureau of Investigation—the precursor to the Federal Bureau of Investigation (FBI). This new agency not only collected domestic law enforcement-related intelligence, it also operated on the United States border with Mexico to thwart smuggling and uncover violations of United States neutrality commitments with the Mexican Revolution. The Department of State was also collecting foreign intelligence as World War I began in Europe, but it was not until the United States declared war on Germany in April 1917 that it dramatically increased its foreign intelligence capabilities. In May 1917, only a month after the United States declared war, the United States Army created a Military Intelligence Section (MIS). The MIS was responsible for, among other things, collecting foreign intelligence, counterespionage, and signals intelligence. MIS, along with the Navy's ONI and their civilian counterparts, worked to disrupt various German attempts at espionage, sabotage, and psychological warfare within the United States.

In the years between World War I and World War II, the United States intelligence agencies had little time to rest. The need to monitor and counteract German and Japanese attempts at espionage and sabotage required vigilance. While MIS was disbanded at the end of World War I, the Department of State and the United States Army still saw a need to collect intelligence and, more specifically, decipher encrypted communications. As a result, the Department of State and the United States Army created a new joint venture called the Cypher Bureau, or Black Chamber. This new organization was the first peacetime intelligence organization devoted to cryptanalysis, or deciphering coded communication. What the United States lacked, however, was a cohesive, national, centralized intelligence policy and intelligence organization.

In light of this lack of a coordinated approach to intelligence gathering, and with World War II seeming unavoidable, President Franklin D. Roosevelt created the Office of the Coordinator of Information (OCI). President Roosevelt intended for the OCI to coordinate the various intelligence-gathering agencies throughout the federal government. However, after the intelligence community's failure to anticipate the Japanese attack on Pearl Harbor, President Roosevelt split the OCI into two new agencies: the Office of Strategic Services (OSS) and the Office of War Information (OWI). Now that the United States would be entering World War II, the OSS was charged with coordinating intelligence, espionage, and covert propaganda efforts and reporting to the Joint Chiefs of Staff. The OWI was charged with creating war propaganda, directly attributable to the United States, for both domestic and foreign consumption. While the OWI and the OSS were disbanded after the War ended, some of their duties were taken over by the State Department and the military. However, the nation continued to need a coordinated approach to gathering intelligence.

After World War II, there were calls to completely reorganize the military and intelligence agencies. President Harry Truman realized that the government needed an agency to coordinate post-war intelligence activities while Congress debated the proposed reorganizations. As a result, he created the Central Intelligence Group (CIG) and the Director of Central Intelligence (DCI) to manage the organization. President Truman's intent was that the CIG would continue the foreign intelligence gathering the OSS had conducted during the War. The CIG, however, was not an independent agency conducting its own intelligence operations. Instead, it was an interdepartmental agency that relied on the efforts of the various intelligence organizations throughout the federal government. Within six months of President Truman creating the CIG, the first DCI resigned. Its new director worked quickly to acquire his own staff, acquire the agency's own intelligence gathering capabilities, and prove itself to be a valuable, independent intelligence agency.

Two years after the end of World War II, the continued calls to reorganize the military and intelligence agencies culminated in the 1947 National Security Act—still the most consequential legislation dealing with the intelligence community to this day. This historic law created the United States Air Force, ensured the Marine Corps's independence within the United States Navy, and brought all of the branches of the United States Military together under the Department of Defense (DOD)—originally named the National Military Establishment. In addition, the National Security Act created the National Security Council (NSC) to coordinate national security policy and advise the President. Importantly, for the intelligence community, the National Security Act transformed the CIG into the Central Intelligence Agency (CIA) with the DCI at the helm of the new organization. The CIA would report to the NSC, and the CIA would be the only national agency whose sole mission was the collection of national security intelligence. However, while the DCI and CIA would help coordinate intelligence efforts across the government, they would not control the government's various intelligence capabilities. Instead, the other federal agencies, both civilian and military, would retain control over their independent intelligence gathering capabilities. Moreover, Congress intentionally prohibited the CIA from engaging in domestic law enforcement-related intelligence. Instead, the FBI would retain those responsibilities.

17.2.3. Intelligence and the Cold War

The Cold War with the Soviet Union, beginning in the 1950s, resulted in a dramatic increase in the United States' intelligence efforts. President Truman used a secret memorandum to create the National Security Agency (NSA) and placed it within the DOD. President Truman created the NSA to centralize signals intelligence gathering into a single organization that would coordinate with both civilian and military agencies, including the FBI, CIA, and Department of State. Meanwhile, the CIA's authority and reach increased to include training counter-revolutionary forces in communist countries and working with the United States Air Force to gather intelligence on Soviet defense capabilities. Because a significant amount of intelligence gathered about the Soviet Union was collected through reconnaissance, the National Reconnaissance Office (NRO) was established in the early 1960s to coordinate these efforts. Around this time, the

DOD established the Defense Intelligence Agency (DIA) to consolidate intelligence gathered by the various agencies throughout the United States military. All the while, on the domestic front, the FBI was the main organization responsible for conducting domestic counterintelligence activities against suspected communists within the United States.

The FBI and Dr. Martin Luther King

In 1955, Reverend Dr. Martin Luther King, Jr. rose to the spotlight as a staunch advocate for desegregation and a uniting force for the Civil Rights movement. In the same year, Congress and President John F. Kennedy tasked FBI Director J. Edgar Hoover with investigating "radicals" and "subversives." Hoover used this mandate to justify the monitoring of numerous figures in the Civil Rights movement, including Dr. King.

The nature of the FBI's interest in King was reportedly twofold: not only was the Civil Rights movement—of which King had become a figurehead—considered radical in its own right, but some within the FBI suspected communist influence over King as well. In its monitoring, the FBI tapped phone lines, bugged hotel rooms, and inserted agents around King. Director Hoover even met with King at one point after a public back-and-forth, taking the opportunity to advise him of some of the FBI's concerns, and to assure him that the FBI had no intention of undermining the movement. Notably, the FBI's actions included dispatching an undercover protective detail for King on a 1965 flight, based on suspicion of an impending assassination. Nevertheless, the FBI's efforts at collecting intelligence on the revered civil rights leader have sparked debate over the proper limits and potential pitfalls of domestic intelligence gathering.

By the 1970s, the United States intelligence community was disorganized, contained redundancies, and had, in some situations, run amok. For example, the CIA, along with the NSA, was spying on Americans and was implicated in the assassinations of foreign leaders. The FBI was investigating and attempting to thwart the Civil Rights and antiwar movements. As the public learned of these activities, Congress impaneled various Committees to investigate the intelligence community and recommend changes. Congress created its own oversight committees—the United States Senate Select Committee on Intelligence and the House's Permanent Select Committee on Intelligence—and passed the Intelligence Oversight Act in 1980. The Intelligence Oversight Act required the intelligence community to keep the Congressional oversight committees informed of its intelligence activities. Presidents Gerald Ford and Jimmy Carter reasserted the DCI's authority to lead the CIA and manage the intelligence community's efforts, including budgetary issues. However, the DCI still lacked the authority and capability to truly control the United States government's entire intelligence community.

With President Ronald Reagan's election in 1980, the intelligence community received renewed attention, including an increase in authority and funding. President Reagan appointed William Casey, with whom he had a close personal relationship, to be the DCI. President Reagan also elevated the DCI position to a Cabinet-level position; a sign of the DCI's influence and respect within the Reagan Administration. President Reagan also issued one of the most consequential **Executive Orders** ever signed by a president—Executive Order 12333. While Executive Order 12333, which is in part still in effect today, continued some of the Presidential policies that had previously governed the intelligence community, it also increased some of its powers. For example, Executive Order 12333 permitted the CIA to covertly collect intelligence within the United States so long as the target of its investigation was not the domestic activities of United States citizens or companies. It also authorized the CIA to conduct clandestine activities within the United States, as directed by the President, so long as the activities were not intended to influence United States politics or public opinion. Executive Order 12333 also permitted the FBI to collect foreign intelligence, and assist other agencies with collecting foreign intelligence, within the United States. Executive Order 12333 authorized not only the collection of **metadata** resulting from electronic communication between United States citizens within the United States, but also the content of electronic communication, so long as it was collected incidentally. Twenty years later, this authority would become part of the public debate about the NSA and accusations that it spied on United States citizens after the 9/11 terrorist attacks.

In the 1990s, Congress attempted to more efficiently organize, modernize, and centralize the intelligence community. For example, it passed the Intelligence Organization Act of 1992, which, among other things, identified three roles for the DCI: 1) head the nation's intelligence community; 2) act as the primary intelligence adviser to the president; and 3) lead the CIA. The Intelligence Organization Act also authorized the DCI to propose, and to some extent control, the intelligence community's budget. In addition, the Intelligence Organization Act mandated that the DCI would play a role, in coordination with the Secretary of Defense, in choosing the heads of the DIA, NSA, and NRO. The DCI was also authorized to set intelligence community policy and consolidate redundancies. At the same time, the intelligence needs of the nation began to change. With the dissolution of the Soviet Union, the rise of the Internet, and increased globalization, the United States intelligence community lacked the integration and agility needed, and was arguably unprepared, for the threat from international terrorism.

17.2.4. The 9/11 Terrorist Attacks and a Change in the Intelligence Community

On September 11, 2001, terrorists attacked the United States. Within a year, the National Commission on Terrorist Attacks Upon the United States (9/11 Commission) was created to investigate the circumstances surrounding the attack and propose recommendations to avert further attacks. A significant portion of the 9/11 Commission's investigation and recommendations centered on the United States intelligence community. The Commission found that in the summer of 2001, the intelligence community had various indications that Al Qaeda was planning an imminent strike and failed to take advantage of several opportunities to foil the attack. The 9/11 Commission suggested the problem was that the various pieces of intelligence that could have thwarted the plot were dispersed among the individual intelligence agencies. The 9/11 Commission observed that there was no single department responsible for synthesizing the diverse sets of data collected throughout the intelligence community. After the 9/11 Commission's report was published, Congress acted to pass, and President George W. Bush signed, the Intelligence Reform and Terrorism Prevention Act of 2004 (IRTPA). The IRTPA proved to be the most significant overhaul of the United States intelligence community since the 1947 National Security Act.

Perhaps most importantly, the IRTPA reorganized the intelligence community in an effort to facilitate a more coordinated national effort. To that end, the IRTPA eliminated the DCI and created a Director of National Intelligence (DNI) position within the United States government. The DNI, who is appointed by the President and approved by the Senate, is the head of the Intelligence Community. Pursuant to the IRTPA, the DNI is responsible for managing and ensuring the implementation of a coordinated national approach to intelligence gathering. The DNI is the principal intelligence advisor to the President, the National Security Council, and the Homeland Security Council, and is responsible for ensuring they, along with Congress and military leaders, receive the most current and useful intelligence. The DNI develops the Intelligence Community's budget, sets policies, and facilitates collaboration and sharing of information across the Intelligence Community. In eliminating the DCI and creating the DNI, the IRTPA also established a new Director of Central Intelligence (D/CIA) position. The D/CIA's sole responsibility, unlike the former DCI, is to lead the CIA and report to the DNI. A more thorough discussion of the Intelligence Community, its responsibilities and authorities, and its organizational structure can be found below in section 17.4.

17.3. THE INTELLIGENCE CRAFT

The collection of intelligence is a cycle that begins and ends with elected officials and policymakers, or what the intelligence community sometimes refers to as its "customers"—those who consume and make policy decisions based on intelligence. The National Security Act of 1947, and its amending statutes, identifies the intelligence community's customers as: 1) the President of the United States; 2) the National Security Council; 3) the heads of departments and agencies of the Executive Branch; 4) the Chairman of the Joint Chiefs of Staff and senior military commanders; and 5) Congress. There are five steps in the intelligence gathering cycle: direction, collection, processing, analysis, and dissemination.

Direction, the first step in the process, is when a customer tasks the intelligence community with an intelligence goal that will assist the customer with formulating policy and decision-making. Once the intelligence community receives direction, it assesses what it already knows about the issue and what it needs to find out. Next is collection. The intelligence community creates a collection plan by identifying the sources and methods most suitable to collect the necessary intelligence. Intelligence can be gathered from various sources. For example, it can be gathered overtly from open source, publicly available materials, such as newspapers and television. Intelligence can also be gathered covertly, or secretly. Finally, the intelligence community can gather intelligence from other domestic and foreign intelligence agencies. The third step is processing. When intelligence is collected, it often consists of raw, unfiltered information and data. This information and data must be translated—perhaps from a foreign language—evaluated for its reliability, and assessed for its relevance and usefulness. Fourth, the information must be analyzed. Intelligence officers synthesize and contextualize the processed information so conclusions or predictions can be made and the customer's questions or requests can be answered. Often the analysis stage results in the production of an intelligence report. These reports include narratives, maps, videos, and other material. The final step is dissemination. The intelligence is delivered to the customer that requested it so it can be used to inform the customer's decision-making. At times, when the intelligence is delivered to the customer, it results in a new direction and the cycle begins again. Moreover, there are some institutionalized directions, for example in the context of terrorisms, where intelligence agencies are constantly collecting intelligence on a particular topic and need not wait for a specific request from a customer.

Agencies within the intelligence community have a variety of sources and methods of gathering intelligence. Generally, those sources and methods fall into one of the following categories: human intelligence, open-source intelligence, signals intelligence, image intelligence, measurement and signature intelligence, and geospatial intelligence. The intelligence community rarely relies on a single source or method alone. Instead, the various intelligence sources and methods, and the data they provide, are combined to offer the most thorough and useful intelligence to the intelligence communities' customers. In fact, a single agency within the intelligence community might use multiple intelligence-gathering sources and methods to accomplish its mission. The primary sources and methods intelligence agencies use are discussed below.

Human Intelligence

Human intelligence (HUMINT) is the original and oldest method of collecting intelligence. It consists of information collected from human sources through personal interaction and contact. HUMINT is most often as simple as a voluntary submission of information to those seeking the intelligence. For example, HUMINT might take the form of a briefing voluntarily provided by a foreign military at the request of an intelligence agency. However, though less common, HUMINT also includes more dramatic intelligence gathering techniques such as spies conducting espionage or interrogations of prisoners.

Open-Source Intelligence

Open-source intelligence (OSINT) is publicly available information. OSINT is gathered through accessing news media, the Internet, radio, television, books, or public performances. It also consists of the information found in publicly available government, academic, and commercial or business reports.

Signals Intelligence

Signals intelligence (SIGINT) is intelligence gathered by intercepting signals. These signals can be communication between people (COMINT) or non-communicative information (ELINT). COMINT includes not only the substance of the information communicated between people, but also their identity and location, the time and duration of the communication, and nature of the signals used to communicate. ELINT is gathered by using sensors to collect non-communicative emissions in order to understand the implications and capabilities of the source emitting the signal. For example, collecting ELINT on a radar system enables the intelligence community to identify its location, capabilities, and the role it plays in the larger system of which it is a part.

Imagery Intelligence

Imagery intelligence (IMINT) consists primarily of pictures and other visual representations of objects taken through the use of photography, radar, or other technology that can produce an image. The images are typically captured through the use of satellites or an aircraft using aerial photography.

Measurement and Signature Intelligence

Measurement and signature intelligence (MASINT) is the use of sensing instruments to collect and analyze the distinctive data—like chemical, biological, or acoustic traits—emitted from an object. The data is used to identify and describe the features and characteristics of the object for the purposes of measuring, identifying, and classifying it. For example, MASINT might consist of collecting and analyzing the radioactivity levels in soil after a nuclear weapons test.

Geospatial Intelligence

Geospatial intelligence (GEOINT) is intelligence gathered by analyzing the natural features of the earth, human made objects, and human activities in relation to their geographical location. The data collected to do the analysis typically consists of photographs and other aerial imagery. For example, geospatial intelligence may be gathered by using a satellite to observe the movement of troops and supplies from one location to another in an attempt to predict an enemy force's intent to attack.

17.4. THE INTELLIGENCE COMMUNITY'S ORGANIZATION AND AGENCIES

The United States Intelligence Community is comprised of seventeen Executive Branch agencies, both civilian and military. The agencies have complex and intertwined relationships, with sometimes different and sometimes overlapping missions and capabilities. As a result, there are various ways to organize the agencies. Some agencies are housed within larger federal government organizations and some are independent, stand-alone organizations. For example, the Department of Defense (DOD) has multiple, separate organizations within the department that are responsible for collecting intelligence, while the Central Intelligence Agency (CIA) is an independent agency that reports directly to the Director of National Intelligence (DNI). Moreover, while some of the agencies are "housed" within a larger department, they are considered "hybrid" organizations whose staff include agents from other intelligence agencies. For example, while the National Reconnaissance Office (NRO) is an intelligence agency within the DOD, it is not staffed only by military members. The NRO also includes civilian agents from the CIA and DOD. Because the Intelligence Reform and Terrorism Prevention Act of 2004 (IRTPA) legally empowers the Office of the Director of National Intelligence (ODNI) to chart a unified approach to United States intelligence gathering, its organizational structure—Program Managers, Departmental Components, Service Components—is used below to group the various intelligence agencies. (See Table 17.1.) Each of the seventeen member organizations plays a unique and specific intelligence-related function within the larger Intelligence Community, and in some circumstances, within its own organization.

17.4.1. The Office of the Director of National Intelligence

The ODNI was created by the IRTPA. Congress's goal was to create an Executive Branch agency that would coordinate and improve information sharing among the Intelligence Community agencies. To that end, the ODNI coordinates the intelligence-related relationships among the other sixteen member organizations of the Intelligence Community. It ensures that intelligence collection and analysis, including counterintelligence, is a unified and integrated national effort. Importantly, the ODNI is also responsible for formulating a budget for the Intelligence Community and setting priorities. The DNI leads the ODNI and is the principal advisor to the President and National Security Advisor, for intelligence related issues. In addition, the ODNI is responsible for managing and directing the **National Intelligence Program**.

There are four main departments within the ODNI, each responsible for coordinating national intelligence efforts within their defined purview. The National Intelligence Council (NIC) is responsible for intelligence estimates and long-term strategy for the Intelligence Community. The NIC produces the National Intelligence Estimate—the DNI's official assessment of intelligence regarding national security. The National Counterterrorism Center (NCTC) is responsible for coordinating counterterrorism intelligence analysis and strategic planning. The National Counterproliferation Center (NCPC) is responsible for intelligence efforts focused on countering the proliferation of weapons of mass destruction. The National Counterintelligence Executive (NCIX) is responsible for coordinating the United States' counterintelligence policy, strategy, and programs.

17.4.2. Program Managers

The Program Managers are the six intelligence agencies responsible for advising and assisting the ODNI in identifying requirements, developing budgets, managing finances, and evaluating the Intelligence Community's performance. More specifically, the heads of these agencies, along with the DNI's Associate Director and deputies, work together to advise the DNI on the needs, policies, and effectiveness of the Intelligence Community. Below you will find a list and description of each Program Manager.

Central Intelligence Agency

The CIA is an independent civilian agency responsible for collecting, analyzing, and evaluating primarily foreign intelligence. The CIA also conducts counterintelligence operations and **covert actions**. The CIA is not a law enforcement agency and is prohibited, by the National Security Act, from engaging in law enforcement activities. The CIA is separated into five offices. The Directorate of Operations is responsible for the CIA's own clandestine operations primarily focused on collecting HUMINT. It is also responsible for coordinating clandestine operations throughout the Intelligence Community. The Directorate of Analysis is responsible for assessing and analyzing raw intelligence and providing that analysis to intelligence consumers. For example, the Directorate of Analysis contributes a significant amount of information to the **Presidential Daily Briefing** and is responsible for producing the **World Intelligence Review**. The Directorate of Science & Technology is staffed by engineers, scientists, and computer programmers. Its goal is to provide technological support to CIA operatives, such as electronic surveillance, satellite reconnaissance, and secure communications. It also assists in analyzing technical and electronic data to support the CIA's mission. The Directorate of Support handles the day-to-day logistical operations of the agency, such as its human resources management and procurement. In addition, it supports the operational needs of the CIA's intelligence agents in the field, such as providing medical attention or building and operating CIA facilities. The Directorate of Digital Innovation is focused on developing the CIA's digital and cyber capabilities.

Defense Intelligence Agency

The Defense Intelligence Agency (DIA) is an agency within the DOD. It is focused on collecting and analyzing foreign military intelligence, including the military capabilities of non-state actors, in support of national defense, military planning, and operations. It collects **all-source intelligence**, both overt and clandestine, and also engages in counterintelligence. The DIA also assists in coordinating intelligence capabilities across the military services. The DIA is not housed within a specific branch of the military; therefore, its director, the Director of the Defense Intelligence Agency, reports directly to the Secretary of Defense.

The Director of the Defense Intelligence Agency is the highest-ranking intelligence officer in the military.

The DIA is divided into four Directorates. The Directorate for Operations is responsible for gathering HUMINT and coordinating military diplomatic relationships with foreign countries and militaries. The Directorate for Analysis analyzes the agency's intelligence gathered on foreign military capabilities and defense issues. It informs policy makers' decisions regarding military issues such as weapons procurement and development, as well as military planning. The Directorate for Science & Technology is responsible for the DIA's technology-related intelligence capabilities and the Directorate for Mission Services provides administrative and personnel support to the DIA.

National Geospatial Intelligence Agency

The National Geospatial Intelligence Agency (NGA) is an agency within the DOD. Its primary mission is to provide imagery, geospatial, and targeting intelligence primarily for combat support purposes. The NGA also assists in intelligence gathering for non-military matters such as natural disasters, humanitarian relief, and major public events. The NGA is the primary agency within the Intelligence Community for GEOINT.

National Reconnaissance Office

The National Reconnaissance Office (NRO) is an agency within the DOD. It designs, builds, and operates the Nation's reconnaissance satellites. It conducts independent research and development of satellite technology and works with the private sector to build and maintain its technology. NRO satellites provide SIGINT and GEOINT to the CIA and its sister agencies within the DOD to help plan military operations, facilitate, and monitor communication, or track international terrorists. NRO satellites not only support national security intelligence gathering, but also civil society needs. For example, NRO satellites track crop production, monitor the environment, and facilitate mobile phone communication.

National Security Agency

The **National Security Agency (NSA)** is an agency within the DOD. It is at the forefront of the Intelligence Community's communications and information technology. It is the Intelligence Community's premier **cryptologic** organization. The NSA is responsible for coordinating, directing, and performing **information assurance** and producing foreign SIGINT. The NSA supports military and civilian policymakers as well as United States counterterrorism and counterintelligence efforts. The Central Security Service (CSS) is a part of the NSA and is the military's primary, unified agency responsible for cryptology. The CSS coordinates the cryptology efforts of the various branches of the United States Armed Forces and ensures the military is effectively integrated into the SIGINT and information assurance missions of the NSA. The Director of the NSA also serves as the Chief of CSS and reports to the Secretary of Defense and DNI.

Federal Bureau of Investigation—National Security Branch

The Federal Bureau of Investigation (FBI) is the Department of Justice's principal investigative agency and the principal federal law enforcement agency. It is also responsible for both national security and intelligence gathering. The FBI's National Security Branch oversees the FBI's national security programs by combining its various national security-related missions and resources into a single agency within the FBI. It has five divisions. The Counterterrorism Division (CTD) focuses on both domestic and international terrorism. The Counterintelligence Division (CD) investigates and prevents foreign intelligence activities within the United States and espionage activities in the United States and overseas. The Weapons of Mass Destruction Directorate (WMDD) prevents individuals and groups from acquiring WMD capabilities and technologies for use against the United States. The National Security Branch also houses the Terrorists Screening Center (TSC) and the High Value Detainee Interrogation Group (HIG). The TSC consolidates and coordinates the United States' terrorist screening efforts, including maintaining the government's list of known or suspected terrorists—the Terrorist Watchlist—and the HIG coordinates the Intelligence Community's interrogation resources to collect intelligence from key terror suspects.

17.4.3. Departmental Components

Departmental components are offices and agencies within the Intelligence Community that are embedded within federal departments, other than the DOD. These components focus primarily on serving their parent department's intelligence needs. Below you will find a list and description of the five federal departments that house agencies or offices that are part of the Intelligence Community.

Department of Homeland Security

The Department of Homeland Security (DHS) is responsible for leading the United States' national security efforts related to customs, border, and immigration enforcement, emergency response to natural and man-made disasters, terrorism, and cyber threats. There are two agencies within the DHS that are part of the Intelligence Community. DHS's own Office of Intelligence and Analysis (I&A) collects and analyzes intelligence for the various mission elements within the DHS. It is the only member of the Intelligence Community legally responsible for providing intelligence to, and collecting intelligence from, state, local, tribal, and territorial governments, as well as the private sector. The Under Secretary for I&A (U/SIA) is the I&A's Director and also serves as DHS Chief Intelligence Officer. The U/SIA is responsible to both the Secretary of Homeland Security and the DNI.

The United States Coast Guard is the only branch of the United States Armed Forces within DHS. It is the principal federal agency responsible for maintaining the maritime safety and security of the nation's ports, inland waterways, and coastal waters. Its various responsibilities require it to maintain military, regulatory, law enforcement, and humanitarian capabilities. Its intelligence branch, Coast Guard Intelligence, has five units. The Coast Guard Investigative Service investigates crimes; the Coast Guard Cryptologic Group collects and analyzes SIGINT; the Coast Guard Counterintelligence Service conducts counterintelligence; and the Coast Guard Cyber Program works to identify and defend against cyber threats.

The Department of State

The Department of State is the principal agency for United States foreign policy and diplomacy. For example, it is responsible for advising the President on foreign affairs, negotiating agreements, such as treaties, with foreign countries, and representing the United States at the United Nations. The Department of State Bureau of Intelligence and Research provides intelligence analysis to State Department ambassadors, negotiators, and foreign service officers to further the United States' diplomatic and foreign policy goals. It does not collect any of its own intelligence. Instead, it analyzes all-source intelligence collected throughout the Intelligence Community. It routinely provides analysis included in the Presidential Daily Briefing and is the Intelligence Community's principal agency focused on foreign public opinion research and analysis.

The Department of Justice

The Department of Justice (DOJ) is primarily responsible for administering justice and enforcing federal laws. It enforces and prosecutes violations of both criminal and civil laws, including tax laws, civil rights laws, environmental and business regulatory laws. The DOJ's Drug Enforcement Administration (DEA) is responsible for enforcing the United States' narcotics laws and regulations. The DEA's Office of National Security Intelligence (ONSI) collects and analyzes intelligence about drug organizations and their members involved in growing, manufacturing, or distributing narcotics. Its goal is to provide useful intelligence that will lead to the seizure of illicit drugs as well as arrests and prosecution. It also provides policy makers with intelligence pertaining to trends in consumption and distribution of illicit drugs.

The Department of Energy

The Department of Energy (DOE) is responsible for the United States' energy policy. It is responsible for the Nation's energy production and distribution system. It also coordinates the United States' nuclear security and policy, including ensuring the integrity and safety of the nation's nuclear weapons, advancing nuclear nonproliferation, and promoting international nuclear safety. The DOE's Office of Intelligence and Counterintelligence is responsible for all DOE intelligence and counterintelligence efforts, and focuses on assessing nuclear terrorism and counterproliferation. It is also charged with evaluating foreign energy and technology threats, and providing the Intelligence Community with energy-related information and technical expertise.

The Department of the Treasury

The Department of the Treasury (USDT) is responsible for promoting the United States' economic prosperity and financial security through, among other things, encouraging sustainable economic growth and fostering improved governance in financial institutions. The USDT oversees the production of money as well as the collecting and borrowing of revenues for the United States government. More specifically, with regard to national security, it implements United States economic sanctions and combats national security threats to the United States' financial systems. The USDT's Office of Terrorism and Financial Intelligence (TFI) provides all-source intelligence to the USDT and the Intelligence Community regarding domestic, international, and terrorist threats to the United States' financial systems. For example, the TFI develops and implements the United States' strategy to enforce the National Money Laundering Act aimed at eliminating the funding of criminal organizations. The TFI is also responsible for developing and implementing policies to eliminate financing for terrorist organizations

17.4.4. Service Components

The United States military retains its own intelligence personnel. While those intelligence officers primarily support the branch of the military service to which they are assigned, they are also part of the larger Intelligence Community. Each branch of the military has its own preeminent intelligence organization, along with several minor intelligence organizations focused on specialty matters. Each branch's primary intelligence unit is discussed below.

United States Army

The United States Army's mission is to fight and win the United States' land-based combat operations. The United States Army Military Intelligence Corps (G-2) is the Army's operational intelligence force. It establishes, conducts, and coordinates imagery, signals, human, measurement, and signature intelligence, as well as counterintelligence and security countermeasures for the United States Army. It provides intelligence related linguist support, acquisitions and logistics support, and communications support for the United States Army.

United States Navy

The United States Navy's mission is to maintain, train and equip combat-ready seaborne forces capable of winning wars, deterring aggression, and maintaining freedom of the seas. The United States Navy's Office of Naval Intelligence (ONI) collects, analyzes, and produces maritime-related intelligence to thwart seaborne threats to the United States such as foreign naval weapons, threats to civil maritime usage, and narcotics and smuggling operations. The ONI is divided into four "centers of excellence." The Farragut Technical Analysis Center is responsible for intelligence related to foreign naval capabilities. The Kennedy Irregular Warfare Center is responsible for intelligence tailored specifically to support the United States Navy and DOD in **irregular warfare** missions. The Hopper Information Services Center provides information technology and services for the ONI. Finally, the Nimitz Operational Intelligence Center integrates the various intelligence capabilities of the ONI to provide analysis to decision makers regarding maritime policy.

United States Marines Corps

The United States Marine Corps is a semi-autonomous component of the United States Navy responsible for expeditionary and amphibious combat in support of naval operations. The Marine Corps Intelligence Department relies primarily on HUMINT, GEOINT and SIGINT to provide tactical and operational intelligence and counterintelligence to the Marine Corps. It is responsible for the United States Marine Corps's intelligence related policy, planning, programming, budgets, and staffing. Unlike other military branches, a majority of intelligence officers serve in the operating forces. The Department is divided into two units: the Marine Corps Intelligence Activity (MCIA) is responsible for developing and analyzing intelligence and the Marine Cryptologic

Support Battalion, which is primarily responsible for the Marine Corps's SIGINT and cyber information assurance.

United States Air Force

The United States Air Force is responsible for the United States' combat operations in air, space, and cyberspace. The United States Air Force's Twenty-fifth Air Force (25 AF or Air Force Intelligence) collects and analyzes intelligence, surveillance, and reconnaissance from various sources including airborne, space, and cyberspace sensors. Its operational units are responsible for cryptologic activities, electronic warfare, and reconnaissance. The 25 AF's Air Force Technical Applications Center (AFTAC) is the Nation's premiere organization responsible for monitoring compliance with nuclear treaties and nuclear proliferation via seismic, hydroacoustic, and satellite detection systems. The United States Space Force is the nation's newest branch of the military and falls within the Department of the Air Force. While its scope of responsibilities is likely to increase, its first intelligence-related mission has been to assume those functions that had been performed by Air Force Space Command elements within the National Reconnaissance Office.

17.5. OVERSIGHT OF THE INTELLIGENCE COMMUNITY

The Intelligence Community has been the subject of controversy and allegations of abuse of power at various times throughout the history of the United States. As a result, beginning primarily in the late 1970s, the government has sought to exert oversight over the Intelligence Community to ensure its activities are conducted legally. Oversight is accomplished by various groups both outside and within the Intelligence Community. Oversight functions can generally be categorized as residing either within the Executive or the Legislative Branch. The major oversight entities are discussed below.

17.5.1. Executive Branch Oversight of the Intelligence Community

President of the United States

Executive Branch oversight of the Intelligence Community ultimately resides with the President. The President retains executive authority to appoint the directors of various intelligence agencies and members of the various boards specifically responsible for oversight. More specifically, the President has the authority, through Executive Orders, to appoint special commissions to investigate Intelligence Community related issues. For example, Executive Order 12333 lays out the principles that govern the Intelligence Community regarding collection, retention and dissemination of intelligence and establishes the authority of the Attorney General and DNI—both appointed by the President—to direct the Nation's intelligence efforts. Additionally, Congress has vested the President with the exclusive authority to authorize certain intelligence activities. For example, in an effort to rein in abuses and exert authority over the CIA's covert and clandestine operations, the Intelligence Authorization Act requires all of the CIA's covert actions be approved by the President.

National Security Council

The National Security Council (NSC), created by the National Security Act, is responsible for advising the President on domestic, foreign, and military national security policies. It also takes the lead on coordinating national security policies among federal government agencies. The members of the NSC, designated in the National Security Act, are the President, the Vice President, the Secretary of State, the Secretary of Defense, the Secretary of Energy, and the Secretary of the Treasury. The President is authorized to appoint additional members to the NSC. In the past, those members have included senior government officials like the DNI, the Director of National Drug Control Policy, and the Chairman of the Joint Chiefs of Staff. Pursuant to Executive Order 12333, the NSC is the preeminent Presidential advisory body for intelligence-related policy and oversight. This oversight includes making recommendations regarding whether the President should approve the CIA's proposed covert actions.

President's Intelligence Advisory Board

Pursuant to Executive Order 13462, the President's Intelligence Advisory Board (PIAB) is responsible for providing the President with objective advice on the Intelligence Community's effectiveness and whether it is meeting the nation's intelligence needs. The PIAB is typically comprised of no more than 16 legal, military, industry, and national security experts outside of government who are appointed by the President. Because the PIAB is an oversight board created and authorized by an Executive Order, its influence, effectiveness, and staffing are dependent upon the President and the role the President envisions for the PIAB.

Intelligence Oversight Board

The Intelligence Oversight Board (IOB), also authorized by Executive Order 13462, is a committee within the PIAB. It is comprised of no more than five members of the PIAB appointed by the President. The IOB is responsible for more directly and granularly overseeing the Intelligence Community's compliance with the laws of the United States, including Executive Orders and Presidential Directives. Within its oversight power, the IOB has the authority to refer issues directly to the President or the Attorney General.

Privacy and Civil Liberties Oversight Board

The Privacy and Civil Liberties Oversight Board (PCLOB) is an independent agency responsible for oversight and advice created by the Implementing Recommendations of the 9/11 Commission Act. It is authorized to review the Intelligence Community's intelligence-related efforts to protect the nation from terrorism and ensure American citizens' privacy and civil liberties are protected. The PCLOB is also empowered to review existing and proposed legislation, regulations, and policies to advise the President and federal agencies on considering and ensuring the protection of Americans' privacy and civil liberties. The PCLOB is composed of five members, four part-time members and a full-time chairperson, appointed by the President and confirmed by the Senate.

Office of Management and Budget

The Office of Management and Budget (OMB), created by the Budget and Accounting Act of 1921, is a unit within the President's Executive Office. The OMB oversees the implementation of the President's vision across the Executive Branch. It assists in developing and executing the budget, managing, and overseeing the various federal agencies, implementing federal regulations and regulation policy, reviewing and coordinating legislation with Congress, and implementing the President's Executive Orders and Memoranda.

Office of Inspector General

An Office of Inspector General (OIG) is a division of an agency responsible for preventing and investigating claims of illegal activities, waste of resources, and mismanagement. Within the Intelligence Community, each Program Manager, Departmental Component, and Military Service has its own Office of Inspector General. For example, the CIA, the Department of State, and the United States Navy each have an OIG. In addition, the ODNI has its own Office of the Inspector General of the Intelligence Community (IC IG). The Intelligence Authorization Act of Fiscal Year 2010 created the IC IG and charged it with conducting audits of the Intelligence Community, as well as investigating and inspecting risks and deficiencies that cut across the Intelligence Community.

17.5.2. Legislative Branch Oversight of the Intelligence Community

The National Security Act requires the Intelligence Community to keep congressional intelligence committees "fully and currently" informed regarding the Nation's intelligence activities. Following the Watergate scandal in the early 1970s, congressional investigations revealed various and widespread abuses of power by the Intelligence Community that had occurred throughout the Twentieth Century. In response to these revelations, Congress created the Senate Select Committee on Intelligence (SSCI) and the House Permanent Select Committee on Intelligence (HPSCI). Certainly, there are other Congressional committees that can exert oversight and funding influence over the Intelligence Community, such as the House and Senate Armed Services Committees, Judiciary Committees, Homeland Security Committees, and Appropriations Committees. However, the SSCI and HPSCI are the primary congressional committees that coordinate with, and receive reports from, the Intelligence Community, and propose legislative changes to intelligence-related laws.

Senate Select Committee on Intelligence

The Senate Select Committee on Intelligence (SSCI) is charged with studying and overseeing Intelligence Community activities on behalf of the Senate and reporting its findings to the Senate. It is the primary Senate Committee responsible for receiving activity reports from the Intelligence Community regarding covert action and other significant activities, as well as proposing intelligence-related legislation. It has exclusive jurisdiction over legislation related to the CIA, the DNI, and the National Foreign Intelligence Program, and shares jurisdiction over the other Intelligence Community agencies with other Senate Committees. Pursuant to Senate rules, the SSCI is composed of eight senators from the majority party and seven senators from the minority. Senate Committees typically reflect the proportional ratio of majority and minority party representation in the Senate. However, the SSCI is structured to reflect the nonpartisan nature of intelligence and to encourage bipartisanship. While all Senators have access to classified information, members of the SSCI have special, higher level clearance and access to highly classified information about intelligence sources and methods, programs, and budgets.

House Permanent Select Committee on Intelligence

The House Permanent Select Committee on Intelligence (HPSCI) is the House of Representatives's Committee responsible for oversight of the Intelligence Community. Like the SSCI, the HPSCI is the principal House

Committee responsible for oversight and legislation, but shares the responsibility with other committees. Unlike the SSCI, the HPSCI is the only House Committee with exclusive oversight over military intelligence. The HPSCI and SSCI play very similar roles regarding the Intelligence Community's reporting requirements and Congressional legislative initiatives. A notable and significant difference between the Committees lies in the makeup of the HPSCI. Unlike the SSCI, the HPSCI's membership is proportional; the numerical make up of majority and minority party members in the House of Representatives is reflected in the membership of the HPSCI.

REVIEW QUESTIONS

1. What was President Roosevelt's first attempt at creating a national, unified approach to intelligence gathering and why was the organization divided into two separate agencies?

2. What post-World War II law was the most consequential reorganization of the intelligence community and United States military? How did it reorganize the intelligence community?

3. How was the Intelligence Community reorganized after the 9/11 terrorist attacks?

4. Who are the Intelligence Community's five, statutorily identified customers and what are the five steps of the intelligence-gathering process?

5. Identify and describe the various missions of the Program Managers, Departmental Components, and Service Components of the Intelligence Community.

6. What agencies and committees are responsible for oversight of the Intelligence Community?

CRITICAL THINKING QUESTIONS

1. Consider the major changes and reorganizations of the intelligence community throughout the history of the United States. Why did these major changes and reorganizations occur after a significant national event? Would it be better to make major changes to the intelligence community before a crisis? Why might that be difficult?

2. Are there too many agencies involved in gathering intelligence? Would it be more efficient and effective to combine intelligence-gathering missions into a handful of agencies? Would that enable easier oversight? Are there benefits to having seventeen different intelligence agencies?

3. Why should Congress be involved in oversight of the Intelligence Community? Is the oversight provided by the Executive Branch and its various boards and agencies enough?

4. What is the greatest national security threat to the United States and what are the three most important methods of gathering intelligence to thwart the threat?

Table 17.1.

Structure of the United States Intelligence Community

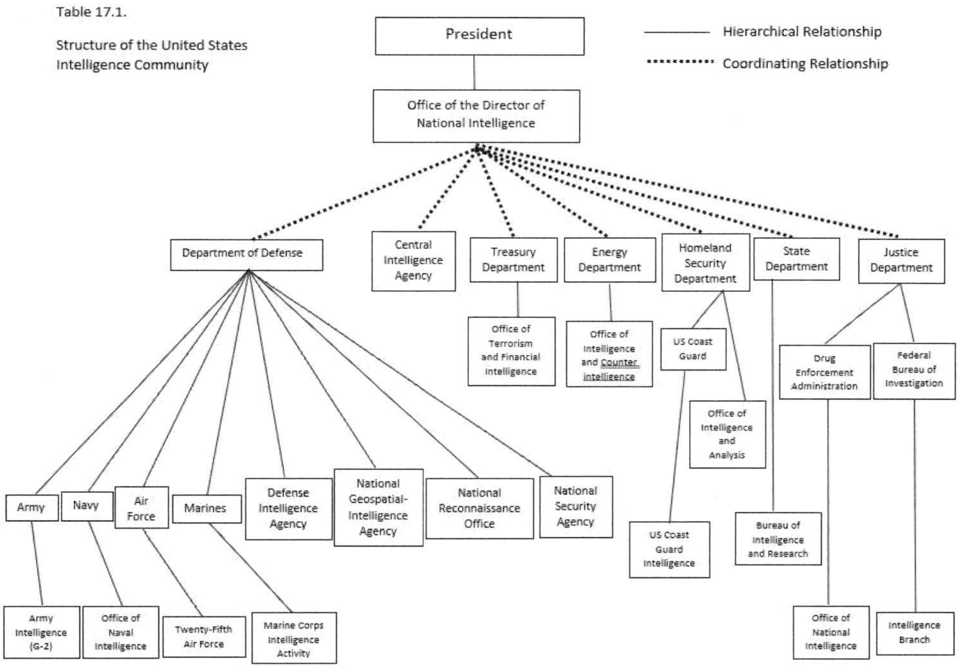

CHAPTER 18

Covert Action

Members of a United States Joint Special Operations Team

Learning Objectives

1. Understand how and why the legal authorization for covert action developed over time in the United States.

2. Understand the National Security Act's process for Presidential authorization of a covert action.

3. Identify the basic types of covert action.

4. Identify the principal United States agencies responsible for carrying out covert action.

18.1. INTRODUCTION

Many of the government's most effective efforts in furtherance of national security are commonplace activities conducted in full view of the public. However, the government also relies on secret, often classified, activities to further its national security aims. Covert actions are an important and unique subset of these activities. While often conducted by members of the intelligence community, covert actions are not primarily focused on gathering intelligence. Instead, the National Security Act (NSA) defines a covert action as "[a]n activity or activities of the United States Government to influence political, economic, or military conditions abroad, where it is intended that the role of the United States Government will not be apparent or acknowledged publicly." With a covert action, the United States' role in the operation is meant to be concealed, not necessarily the activity itself. In fact, certain covert activities, like propaganda, are not intended to remain concealed. It is this definition that sets covert action apart from clandestine operations, which are focused on gathering intelligence and intended to go unnoticed.

Imagine a spy trying to collect intelligence by eavesdropping on a telephone call. The spy would want her actions to go unnoticed and remain secret. Covert actions, however, are tools leaders and policy makers use to affirmatively exert influence and encourage political, economic, or military change. Here, you can imagine a foreign government using an operative to disseminate propaganda to influence an election. In this example, the action itself is less secret; the secret is the operative's connection to the sponsor of the activity. These activities can be extraordinarily effective at accomplishing foreign policy goals and protecting national security. Nevertheless, in democratic countries committed to the rule of law, covert activities also pose important questions concerning oversight and transparency. As you read about the United States' history and laws governing covert action, consider whether the nation has struck the right balance between accountability and using covert action to further national security.

18.2. THE HISTORY OF UNITED STATES COVERT ACTION AND ITS LEGAL AUTHORIZATION

18.2.1. Covert Action from the Founding Era to the Civil War

Perhaps one of the earliest, most famous Americans to engage in covert action was Benjamin Franklin in his efforts on behalf of the American Revolution. For example, in 1777, two years after the Revolution began, Franklin used propaganda and subterfuge to undermine Prussian mercenaries fighting on behalf of British forces. He forged a letter from a Prussian Prince to the mercenaries' commander questioning the truthfulness of the British government's casualty figures. The letter also discussed British war crimes and suggested the British would pay more money for a dead mercenary than a wounded one. Many historians credit the letter with causing numerous desertions among Prussian troops. Franklin is also credited with coordinating with **privateers** to impersonate official British maritime vessels to obstruct and attack the British Navy in Europe.

After winning the Revolutionary War, the United States continued to support and engage in covert action. For example, during his first State of the Union Address in 1790, President George Washington requested that Congress create a "secret service fund" for covert and clandestine operations. That same year, Congress heeded the President's request and created the Contingent Fund of Foreign Intercourse. While Congress initially allocated $40,000 for the Fund, over the course of only three years, the Fund was increased to $1,000,000. Congress required very little oversight of the President's use of the money in the Fund. The President had the authority to conceal the purposes for which he used the money and the names of those who received it. The President was only required to account for and certify the amount of money he spent on operations financed by the Fund. In the early 1800s, Thomas Jefferson used resources from this Fund to finance the United States' covert attempt to overthrow a foreign government in North Africa. President James Madison also used the Fund to pay for propaganda and paramilitary forces to encourage American settlers to declare independence from Spain and drive Spain from Florida. The **Founders**, however, were not the only Americans to rely on covert action. Covert action continued into the Civil War. Both the Union and Confederacy used propaganda to influence their allies and enemies in Europe. At home, the Confederacy effectively used propaganda to encourage Indiana, Illinois, and Ohio to leave the Union and saboteurs to set fires in New York City.

18.2.2. Covert Action and the World Wars

In the late Nineteenth and early Twentieth Century, after the Civil War, the United States was more often the victim than the initiator of covert operations. For example, the British circulated propaganda urging the American public and President Woodrow Wilson to support the British war effort in World War I. At the same time, Germany disseminated propaganda and engaged in industrial sabotage in the United States. Initially though, as a neutral party, the United States was more focused on counterintelligence operations than its own offensive covert action. Once the United States entered World War I, its lack of covert capabilities was evident. It was limited to using existing operatives, with little experience in covert action, to engage in propaganda operations. The propaganda was most often aimed at encouraging German soldiers to surrender or reducing pro-German sentiment in neutral European countries. The United States also used propaganda to subvert the Bolsheviks in Russia after the fall of the Tsar. As the need for a more planned approach to propaganda became evident, President Wilson issued **Executive Order** 2594 establishing the Committee on Public Information (CPI). Initially the CPI was focused on domestic propaganda to encourage support for the war effort. Later in the war, the CPI's responsibilities included producing propaganda for foreign consumption. Though disbanded after World War I, the CPI was the first, official attempt at an organized United States propaganda effort.

Between World Wars I and II, the United States covert action capabilities diminished. However, as World War II began to take shape, the country again began to think seriously about the need for an agency responsible for covert operations. Initially, President Franklin D. Roosevelt created the Office of the Coordinator of Information (OCI) and charged it with coordinating United States intelligence and propaganda policy. The OCI, however, existed for less than a year. After World War II began, upon order of the President, it was divided into the Office of War Information (OWI) and the Office of Strategic Services (OSS). The OWI was responsible for propaganda directly attributable to the United States government, like the radio station *Voice of America*, which began broadcasting in 1942 to combat Nazi propaganda. The OSS was responsible for intelligence activities and covert action, and reported to the Joint Chiefs of Staff. Throughout World War II, the OSS covertly worked with resistance groups, maintained its own paramilitary special forces unit, delivered personnel and material behind enemy lines, produced propaganda, and waged psychological warfare against the enemy.

Operation Fortitude South

Perhaps the most elaborate and successful covert operation by the United States and its allies during World War II took place as the Allies prepared for D-Day—the day the Allies invaded France and liberated Western Europe from Nazi Germany. Operation Fortitude South was a ploy, through misinformation and propaganda, to convince the Germans that the Allies would invade France near its northern border with Belgium instead of the real location, Normandy, which lay 180 miles south. The Allies went so far as to create a fake invasion force, the First United States Army Group, which consisted of inflatable tanks and wooden airplanes to trick German reconnaissance. Operation Fortitude South was so successful that, for two months after D-Day, the Germans continued to withhold sending crucially needed units to repel the Allies in Normandy, because they were still expecting the fake First United States Army Group's invasion of northern France.

18.2.3. The Cold War and the Nation's Increased Reliance on Covert Action

After the end of World War II, President Harry Truman issued Executive Order 9621, which terminated the OSS. The OSS's capabilities were subsumed by the Department of State (DOS) and the precursor to the Department of Defense (DOD), the Department of War. The DOS acquired the analytical capabilities of the OSS, while the Department of War acquired the espionage and covert operation capabilities. However, those activities were significantly curtailed after World War II while the nation demobilized. It was not until the Cold War against the Soviet Union began to materialize that the United States' modern covert capabilities fully matured into an internationally relevant tool to accomplish the Nation's policy goals.

Realizing the benefit of having a single government agency responsible for coordinating and collecting intelligence and engaging in clandestine operations, President Truman created the Central Intelligence Group (CIG) in 1946 and the National Intelligence Authority to oversee the CIG. However, the CIG existed for only one year. In 1947, Congress passed the National Security Act (NSA). At the time, the NSA was the most significant overhaul and reorganization of the intelligence community and military. Among many other things, the NSA created the National Security Council (NSC), which in practice replaced the National Intelligence Authority. The NSA charged the NSC with acting as the principal forum for providing advice and coordinating national security policy for the President, including clandestine intelligence gathering and covert operations. The NSA also created a new independent organization, the Central Intelligence Agency (CIA), to replace the CIG and take the lead on the nation's intelligence gathering. The NSA specifically authorized the CIA to collect and analyze intelligence and "perform such other functions and duties related to intelligence affecting the national security." While the NSA was ambiguous as to what these "other functions" were, President Truman had no doubt that they included covert action.

Within a year of signing the NSA, President Truman issued two secret Presidential directives, NSC-4A and NSC10/2. These directives authorized the CIA to engage in covert psychological warfare and other operations such as "economic warfare; preventive **direct action**, including sabotage, anti-sabotage, demolition and evacuative measures; subversion against hostile states, including assistance to underground resistance movements, guerrillas and refugee liberation groups, and support of indigenous anti-communist elements in threatened countries of the free world." The CIA quickly got to work. For example, in response to concerns about an Italian government friendly to the Soviet Union, the CIA attempted to influence the 1948 Italian election through funding opposition candidates and producing propaganda. That same year, the CIA coordinated covert operations with British intelligence agencies in an attempt to foment a civil war in Albania. It became clear that the CIA's Cold War covert operations would focus primarily on fighting the spread of communism through undermining or overthrowing communist governments and defeating communist insurgents. Its covert operations were authorized by Presidential orders and shielded through statutory law. In 1949, Congress passed the Central Intelligence Agency Act (CIAA). The CIAA permitted the CIA to use confidential fiscal and administrative procedures and exempted the CIA from many of the usual statutory limitations on spending money. Under the CIAA, the CIA's budget was undisclosed, thus ensuring the secrecy of its covert operations.

Challenging Secret Budgets in the Courts

Twenty years after Congress passed the CIAA, a United States citizen named William B. Richardson filed a lawsuit challenging the Act. Richardson argued that the CIAA violated the "statements and account clause" in Article I, Section 9 of the Constitution. The clause requires "a regular Statement and Account of the Receipts and Expenditures of all public Money [to] be published from time to time." Richardson argued that because the CIAA permitted the CIA's budget and funding to remain confidential, the CIAA violated the Constitution. In *United States v. Richardson*, the Supreme Court held that Richardson lacked **standing** and thus could not file a lawsuit to challenge the constitutionality of the CIA's secret budget. In other words, the Court determined that because Richardson could not prove he suffered an identifiable harm with sufficient connection to the CIAA and the CIA's secret budget, he could not file a lawsuit challenging it. The Court reasoned that Richardson's lawsuit, in reality, was simply a general grievance and being upset about how one's taxes are spent is not a distinguishable, personal harm that confers the right to file a lawsuit.

Throughout the mid-Twentieth Century, the CIA remained the United States' preeminent agency for covert action. It supported the United States' efforts in the Korean War and, in response to concerns about governments friendly to the Soviet Union, it used covert tactics to incite coups in countries around the globe including Iran, Guatemala, Syria, Indonesia, and Chile. In 1961, in one of the CIA's most well-known covert operations, it trained and equipped a guerilla army of Cuban exiles in Guatemala to invade Cuba and overthrow Fidel Castro's government. The Cuban government discovered the CIA's plan and, after a disastrous attempt at an invasion, the Cuban military killed or captured over 1,000 guerillas. Nevertheless, from the 1940s through the early 1970s, the CIA was subjected to very little oversight. That would change, however, with President Richard Nixon and the Watergate scandal.

In 1972, as President Nixon was running for reelection, burglars associated with his campaign broke into the office of the Democratic National Committee located in the Watergate Hotel. After his repeated attempts to cover up the scandal and his connection with the burglars was revealed, President Nixon resigned. In addition to the Watergate scandal, the *New York Times* published an article in 1974 describing years worth of CIA covert action ranging from assassination attempts to subversion of foreign governments. In response, the United States Senate formed the United States Senate Select Committee to Study Governmental Operations with Respect to Intelligence Activities. This special Committee became known as the Church Committee, named after the Chair of the Committee, Senator Frank Church from Idaho. The Church Committee's 16-month investigation revealed over 30 years worth of numerous and serious abuses of power by the United States' intelligence agencies, including the CIA, Federal Bureau of Investigation (FBI), and **National Security Agency (NSA)**. At the same time, the Senate Armed Services Committee was investigating covert military operations conducted throughout Southeast Asia during the Vietnam War. These investigations, and the information they revealed, led to various laws regulating the intelligence community's activities.

For the purposes of United States covert action, the most significant regulation appeared in the Foreign Assistance Act of 1974. Known as the Hughes-Ryan Amendment, the law exerted Congress's "power of the purse" and provided it oversight over United States covert action. It prohibited funding for CIA covert action unless two requirements were met. First, the President was required to determine that each covert action was important to the national security of the

United States. Second, the President was required to submit a report detailing each operation to eight different Congressional Committees, including the Senate's Committee on Foreign Relations and the House of Representatives's Committee on Foreign Affairs. Exempted from the reporting requirement, however, was the President's use of military force and thus covert military operations.

Less than a year after passage of the Hughes-Ryan Amendment, the Senate Foreign Relations Committee investigated the CIA's report that it was engaging in covert actions in Angola. The Committee was particularly unhappy that the CIA was providing weapons to an Angolan political faction that aligned itself with South Africa's apartheid government. Congress then passed, and President Gerald Ford signed, an amendment to a defense appropriation bill that prohibited the expenditure of CIA and DOD funds for covert operations in Angola. This became the first time Congress defunded, thereby ending, a covert action. The Intelligence Oversight Act of 1980 amended the Hughes-Ryan Act by limiting to two the number of Committees to which covert action reports must be submitted—the House Permanent Select Committee on Intelligence (HPSCI) and the Senate Select Committee on Intelligence (SSCI). The Act also provided detailed requirements for the reports submitted to Congress. However, there would not be a significant Congressional update to the laws governing covert action until President Ronald Reagan's Iran-Contra Affair in the mid-1980s.

18.2.4. The Iran-Contra Affair: A Turning Point in the Laws Governing Covert Action

During the 1980 Presidential election campaign, candidate Ronald Reagan's agenda was staunchly anti-communist. He promised to assist anti-communist forces throughout the world. After his election, President Reagan highlighted the Nicaraguan Contras as one of the anti-communist forces worthy of the United States' support. The Contras were a group of right-wing insurgents fighting the socialist Nicaraguan government. The CIA provided covert assistance to the Contras in the early days of President Reagan's first term. While the Contras were anti-communist, they funded their insurgency with money made through cocaine trafficking. As a result, Congress, which was controlled by the Democratic Party after the midterm elections of 1982, passed the Boland Amendment. The Boland Amendment, attached to the Defense Appropriations Act of 1983, prohibited the United States from funding operations, including covert activities, intended to overthrow the Nicaraguan government. There were concerns by some in Congress that despite the Boland Amendment, the CIA continued to conduct covert operations in Nicaragua and failed to keep Congressional oversight

Committees informed of their activities. Congress was so concerned about the CIA's continued work in Nicaragua that in 1984 it passed, and President Reagan signed, a law referred to as "Boland II." This new law specifically prohibited the CIA, DOD, or any United States agency from supporting the Contras directly or indirectly.

At the same time, an Iranian terrorist organization had captured seven Americans in Lebanon. In an attempt to free the hostages, the Reagan Administration secretly agreed to sell missiles to Iran, which constituted a violation of the United States' trade embargo with Iran. The United States then used the money from the missile sales to support the Contras in Nicaragua. After a Lebanese newspaper published a story recounting the arms deal, President Reagan initially denied it occurred. Ultimately, Lieutenant Colonel Oliver North, a member of the National Security Council staff, admitted that he funneled the money to the Contras. Lieutenant Colonel North suggested the National Security Advisor, Admiral John Poindexter, knew about the arrangement and he believed the President knew as well.

President Reagan commissioned the Tower Commission, led by Senator John Tower from Texas, and charged it with investigating what became known as the Iran-Contra affair. The Commission found that the CIA failed to keep Congress and the President fully informed of the weapons sales to Iran and the funding to the Contras. At the same time the Tower Commission was investigating the Iran-Contra affair, the Senate and House of Representatives each formed special committees to investigate the scandal. The committees held joint hearings and issued a joint report in which they found staff members from the National Security Council solicited funds from other countries and private individuals to support the Contras after Congress cut off their aid. The report also found that National Security Council staff sold weapons to Iran and used the proceeds to fund the Contras. Various people were **indicted** for lying to Congress during its investigation, including the CIA's clandestine services chief.

In reaction to the Iran-Contra affair, and the resulting revelations, Congress's oversight committees attempted to pass laws requiring the President to inform Congress within 48 hours of any covert action. President George H. W. Bush, however, vetoed the legislation. After continuing negotiations, Congress passed and President Bush signed the Intelligence Authorization Act of 1991 (IAA), which amended the National Security Act (NSA). The IAA, though modified slightly since being signed into law, has remained virtually unchanged and is the definitive law governing covert action. Most importantly, for the first time in the

United States' history, the IAA's amendments to the NSA provided a legal definition for the term "covert action" and an oversight role for Congress.

18.3. COVERT ACTION, THE NSA, AND CONGRESSIONAL OVERSIGHT

The United States' covert action capabilities reside in the Executive Branch of the government. However, the NSA, and its IAA amendment, provide for a unique Congressional oversight regime. The specific oversight Congress has over covert actions, however, is only applicable if the activity meets the legal definition of "covert action." As discussed above, the NSA defines "covert action" as United States activity intended to influence foreign political, economic, or military conditions where the United States intends its role in the activity to not be apparent or acknowledged publicly. The NSA specifically excludes the following from the definition of covert action: traditional intelligence activities, traditional military and diplomatic activities, traditional law enforcement activities, and traditional activities in support of United States agencies' overt operations. However, since the 9/11 terrorist attacks and the proliferation of non-state hostile forces, the military's **special operations** forces have taken on an increased role in what one might consider covert action. As a result, it is increasingly difficult to distinguish covert action from traditional military activities.

For example, the military often engages in missions it labels "Operational Preparation of the Environment" (OPE). OPE missions are activities to prepare a future battlefield or military theater for follow-on military operations. The military also engages in "Sensitive Military Operations." These are offensive and self-defense military operations outside a declared theater of active armed conflict, often to capture or kill a **High Value Target** or support an allied armed force. While these operations are often clandestine and sometimes covert, because they are conducted by the military, they have customarily been considered as meeting the NSA's military exclusion definition for covert action. As a result, the covert action definition and oversight procedures are most commonly applied to the CIA's covert activities.

A Recommendation to Consolidate Paramilitary Operations Under One Agency

Following the 9/11 terrorist attacks, Congress created the National Commission on Terrorist Attacks Upon the United States (9/11 Commission). The 9/11 Commission was an independent, bipartisan Commission created to review and assess the circumstances surrounding the 9/11 terrorist attacks and the United States' response. The 9/11 Commission was also charged with providing recommendations to guard against future attacks. Recommendation 32 of the 9/11

Commission's *Final Report of the National Commission on Terrorist Attacks Upon the United States* (9/11 Commission Report) suggested that "the lead responsibility for directing and executing paramilitary operations, whether clandestine or covert, should shift to the Defense Department. There it should be consolidated with the capabilities for training, direction, and execution of such operations already being developed in the Special Operations Command." The 9/11 Commission Report identified, as a concern, the CIA's lack of investment in developing its in-house paramilitary capabilities. The 9/11 Commission Report also suggested that the United States did not have the resources to build dual capabilities, in both the CIA and the military, to carry out secret military operations. As a result, it recommended that the DOD be the only agency with legal authority to carry out paramilitary operations. A year after the 9/11 Report was published, both the CIA and the DOD rejected the 9/11 Commission's recommendation and the Bush Administration reportedly agreed. To date, both the CIA and the DOD retain the authority to conduct paramilitary operations.

The NSA's oversight procedures envision a cooperative relationship between the President and Congress. The NSA requires the President to authorize all covert actions before they occur, and come to specific findings, or conclusions, about the need for each operation. Once the President makes a finding that a covert action is necessary, he must submit a report to Congress. Below is a more specific list of the requirements the NSA places on the President regarding covert actions:

- The President must authorize any United States activity that meets the definition of a covert action, not only those activities conducted by the CIA.
- Before authorizing a covert action, the President must determine the operation supports an identifiable foreign policy objective and it must be important to national security.
- The finding must also identify all United States agencies and third parties, such as foreign governments, involved in funding or participating in the covert action.
- The finding may not authorize any covert action intended to influence United States politics, public opinion, policies, or media.
- The finding may not violate the Constitution or other laws of the United States.
- The President must reduce his finding to writing before the covert action occurs or, in the case of an emergency, within 48 hours after the President makes the finding.

- The President must report his finding to the Senate Select Committee on Intelligence and the House Permanent Select Committee on Intelligence prior to the covert action, or in a timely fashion after making the finding.
- If the President does not report the finding prior to the operation, the President must explain why prior notice was not provided to Congress.
- If the President decides there are extraordinary circumstances that require him to limit access to a finding, the President may limit notification of the finding to select members of Congress often referred to as the "Gang of Eight." The Gang of Eight includes the chairs and ranking minority members of the House of Representatives and Senate intelligence committees, the Speaker of the House of Representatives, the minority leader of the House of Representatives, and the majority and minority leaders of the Senate.
- If the President provides his findings to the Gang of Eight alone, the President must fully inform the Senate Select Committee on Intelligence and the House Permanent Select Committee on Intelligence in a timely fashion. The President must also inform the Committees why he did not provide prior notice of the relevant finding.
- After 180 days, the President must either provide all members of the intelligence committees with access to the findings or explain why access must remain limited.
- If there is a significant change in a covert action that has already been reported to Congressional oversight committees, the Committees must be informed of the change.
- The Director of National Intelligence is required to keep Congress's intelligence oversight committees fully and currently informed about all covert action.

As you can see above, Congressional oversight over covert action is somewhat limited. For example, Congress does not have the legal authority, under the NSA, to stop a covert action because it determines the President was wrong in finding that a particular covert action supports an identifiable foreign policy objective. However, Congress has some powerful tools it can use to influence the President's use of covert action. Under the Constitution, Congress retains the authority to declare war. Congress also has statutory powers to limit the President's use of armed force under the War Powers Act and Authorizations for Use of Military Force. In addition, Congress has the authority to pass new legislation and appropriate funds in ways that can limit the President. Perhaps one of its most powerful tools, however, lies within the political process itself. Covert actions can be controversial. In addition, they have the potential to be risky and dangerous for many of those involved in the operations. As a result, because the potential for political fallout is significant, political expediency may be enough to motivate a President to coordinate with Congress and keep it fully informed.

18.4. THE 9/11 TERRORIST ATTACKS AND THE FUTURE OF COVERT ACTION

The 9/11 terrorist attacks on the United States, Congress's 2002 Authorization to Use Military Force, and the War on Terror presented new questions regarding covert action. The lines have blurred between traditional military activities, **unconventional warfare**, and covert action traditionally conducted by agencies such as the CIA. Whether it is CIA **Black Sites** for interrogating terrorist suspects, **extraordinary renditions**, or the use of Special Operations Forces to conduct covert wars against terrorist groups, these blurred lines have posed a challenge to distinguishing United States covert action from other activities.

Within a week of the 9/11 terrorist attacks, President George W. Bush signed a secret Memorandum of Notification authorizing the CIA to "undertake operations designed to capture and detain persons who pose a continuing, serious threat of violence or death to United States persons and interests or who are planning terrorist activities." George W. Bush, *Memorandum of Notification for Members of the Security Council*, September 17, 2001. A month after the attacks, Congress passed an Authorization for the Use of Military Force authorizing President Bush to use force against those he determined were connected with the 9/11 terrorist attacks. That same month, the United States began to prepare for Operation Enduring Freedom, also known as the War on Terror. A significant part of Operation Enduring Freedom was the United States invasion of Afghanistan in 2001.

Before the war began, and throughout the conflict, the United States used covert CIA agents and special operations soldiers to lay the groundwork for the invasion, to capture and kill suspected terrorists and Taliban leaders, and to support the conventional warfare waged by the United States and its allies. In addition to engaging in paramilitary operations and supporting allied Afghan forces, the CIA and military also began using **unmanned aerial vehicles (UAV)**, or **drones**, to conduct attacks on **High Value Targets**. This tactic would be exported to other parts of the world as an integral part of the United States' War on Terrorism.

After the United States' invasion of Afghanistan, and the invasion of Iraq that followed in 2003, the United States War on Terrorism became a global effort. As part of the United States' anti-terrorism activities and its ongoing military operations, the CIA and United States military would come to rely on covert action in a significant way. Both the CIA and the military reportedly conducted drone strikes in Yemen, Pakistan, and Somalia; trained and equipped allied forces in Africa and the Middle East; and captured or killed High Value Targets. While military prisons were erected in Iraq and Afghanistan to house detainees captured by United States soldiers, secret prisons to house High Value Terrorist suspects, were established by the CIA throughout the world. These Black Sites became indefinite detention centers where the CIA engaged in **enhanced interrogation technique**, which critics labeled **torture**. As some of these covert actions were made public by the media, President Bush's Administration was forced to defend the practices, some of which were ended and some of which were increased with the election of President Barack Obama in 2008. Chapters 13 and 14 provide a more thorough discussion of the United States' efforts to render and detain terror suspects.

After his election, President Obama issued orders to close the CIA's Black Sites and cease the CIA's use of enhanced interrogation techniques. President Obama also authorized a significant increase in the use of targeted killings in Yemen, Pakistan, and Somalia, through drone strikes. However, President Obama also issued orders that greatly curtailed the covert use of drones by the CIA, and shifted the majority of those operations to the military. In 2009, while he drew down the number of United States forces in Iraq, President Obama also increased the number of United States conventional soldiers in Afghanistan. This increase in conventional soldiers came with an increase in covert paramilitary operations and direct action by the CIA and special forces soldiers. However, the increase in covert action was not limited to Afghanistan. Within a few years, covert action also increased in Yemen. President Donald Trump continued many of the same policies of using unmanned drones and special operations forces. As the United States continues its fight against insurgents, extremists, and terrorists throughout the world, it seems clear that covert action will be an integral part of United States foreign policy.

18.5. TYPES OF COVERT ACTION

Covert actions cannot easily be divided into distinct categories. Often, covert actions overlap to include a variety of methods and goals. Additionally, covert actions vary widely in the level of violence typically associated with the activity. The more violent the activity, the more difficult it is to maintain plausible deniability and the more likely the activity will ultimately be attributable to the source. Below is a list of the most common covert actions and a description of their methods and goals.

Covert Propaganda

Propaganda is perhaps one of the oldest covert activities used to undermine an adversary. It consists of using media, social organizations, and other outlets to disseminate information in an effort to produce a specific political, social, military, or economic outcome. The information can support friendly forces, undermine opposition forces, or sow confusion and discontent through rumors and innuendo. Propaganda can be either covert or overt. Covert propaganda, often referred to as black propaganda, disguises the originator of the information. Overt propaganda, often referred to as white propaganda, is attributable to the originator of the information. Black propaganda is one of the least violent means of covert activity.

Covert Political Operations

Covert political activity is a direct intervention in the political affairs and conditions of a target government. The typical goal of covert political activity is to support allied governments and organizations or undermine adversaries. Covert political operations are often conducted using propaganda, either positive or negative. Hostile covert political operations may focus on disrupting the political organizations and activities of adversaries. On the other hand, a covert operation may focus on providing economic support, grassroots organizing, and public relations assistance to friendly political organizations. Additionally, covert political operations can focus on exploiting the political leaders of the target government or organization in an effort to persuade them to make decisions in their official capacity. While a covert political operation could entail low-level violence through, for example, inciting physical confrontations at a political rally, it is typically a less violent means of covert activity.

Covert Economic Operations

Covert economic operations are intended to disrupt an adversary's economy. Scarcity of resources and low standards of living are immediately evident to the general population and can cause unrest and social turmoil. As a result, covert economic operations can be even more disruptive to an adversary than covert political operations. Covert economic operations can include, for example, intentionally disrupting the production capabilities or technological advancements of an adversary. Used in concert, economic operations can reinforce propaganda and political operations. Because of the chance for significant harm to a population's resources and supplies, covert economic operations are more likely than propaganda or political operations to cause violence or physical suffering.

Coup

A coup is the overthrow of an adversary's leader or government. This can be accomplished indirectly through encouraging and supporting surrogates, whether indigenous or otherwise. A coup can also be accomplished through direct involvement by the originator's agents. Often, a coup is preceded by covert propaganda, political activity, or economic operations to facilitate the coup. Coups often involve the takeover of government buildings, imprisonment, or assassination of a leader. These actions can result in the use of violence to accomplish the coup or defend against it. As a result, coups, when compared with other covert operations, are much more likely to result in the use of violence.

Paramilitary Operations

Paramilitary operations are activities involving the use of armed force against an adversary by non-military personnel. Paramilitary forces use military force to accomplish military objectives and achieve political aims. While the personnel executing a paramilitary operation are trained, equipped, and organized like traditional military forces, they are not officially part of the originating government's military. Often, paramilitary forces are relied upon to avoid using official military force, which could constitute an act of war. The personnel conducting the operation often consist of indigenous forces, expatriates, or mercenaries. The originator of a paramilitary operation typically relies on its own civilian agents to train, support, or help choose objectives for an armed attack. Occasionally, an originator's military members may also be used in a support capacity. However, these military members must be careful because if they engage in combat, they may be unlawful combatants and not entitled to the rights guaranteed to lawful Prisoners of War under the Geneva Conventions.

18.6. UNITED STATES AGENCIES ENGAGED IN COVERT ACTION

Most of the United States' covert actions are carried out by the CIA. However, members of the United States military's Special Forces units also take part in covert operations. Below is a list of the principal United States agencies and military units most often involved in covert operations.

Central Intelligence Agency

The CIA is the primary organization responsible for United States covert action. While a significant amount of the CIA's responsibilities revolve around intelligence operations, the Special Activities Division (SAD) is responsible for CIA covert operations. The SAD is further divided into two branches, the Political Operations Group (SAD/POG) and the Special Operations Group (SAD/SOG). The SAD/POG is charged with coordinating and implementing covert political operations, including the use of covert propaganda and covert economic operations. The SAD/SOG is primarily responsible for covert paramilitary operations and military threat assessments of hostile nations and organizations. The SAD/SOG is divided into three branches: 1) the Ground Branch, which is responsible for land based operations; 2) the Maritime Branch, which is responsible for maritime and amphibious operations; and 3) the Air Branch, which is responsible for aerial operations.

United States Military

The United States Special Operations Command (SOCOM) is the principal military command unit of the DOD's various special operations forces. It is responsible for coordinating special operation budgets, procurements, policies, strategies, and tactics for the United States Armed Forces. The Joint Special Operations Command (JSOC) is a subunit within SOCOM, which is responsible for conducting joint special operations missions. JSOC is also responsible for ensuring the various branches standardize their equipment and communications to ensure seamless joint special operations activities among the various special operations units. Each of the units described below participates in **special operations** and direct action for the United States military.

The United States Army's 1st Special Forces Operational Detachment-Delta (Delta Force) is the most elite covert operations unit in the Army. Its primary mission is anti-terrorism operations. While Delta Force members are trained for various missions including hostage rescue, surgical strikes, and combat support, it is primarily focused on capturing or killing High Value Targets. The Army's 1st Special Forces Command (Airborne or Green Berets) is the Army's primary unconventional warfare unit. Green Berets provide training, logistics, and support for allied guerrilla forces. They also conduct counterinsurgency operations against adversarial insurgency groups.

The United States Navy's Naval Special Warfare Development Group (NSWDG or SEAL Team Six) is the Navy's premier covert operations unit. It is the Navy's counterpart to the Army's Delta Force. Like Delta Force, SEAL Team Six's primary mission is anti-terrorism and neutralizing High Value Targets. SEAL Team Six, however, specializes in maritime-related operations. Like Delta Force, SEAL Team Six is also capable of various missions like training, hostage rescue, and combat support.

The United States Marines' Marine Raider Regiment is a comparatively new addition to the military's covert operations units. The Marine Raider Regiment participates in a variety of activities including anti-terrorism missions, counter-insurgency support for foreign allies, and support for United States allied insurgency movements in enemy territory.

The United States Air Force's 24th Special Tactics Squadron provides air and ground support for the United States military's covert operations units. It establishes and operates airfields for the insertion or extraction of special operations units; provides targeting and air traffic control for aerial assaults; and supplies meteorological information for special operations missions. The 24th Special Tactics Squadron also specializes in rescue operations and providing battlefield medical attention.

REVIEW QUESTIONS

1. What sort of covert action did the Founders use during the Revolutionary War and in the early years of the United States? What role, if any, did Congress play in authorizing or providing oversight?

2. What organizations were established to engage in covert action during World War I and how were they established?

3. How did President Truman organize and direct the United States' approach to using covert action? Did Congress play a role?

4. Describe the events and revelations that caused Congress to exert some oversight authority over covert action in the 1970s. What legislation did Congress enact in response to these events?

5. Why did the Iran-Contra Affair motivate Congress to pass legislation taking on more oversight over covert operations?

6. Describe the process in the National Security Act by which the President must inform Congress about a covert action. How does the National Security Act define covert action? What sort of operations are excluded?

7. Describe the four basic types of covert action.

8. Identify the principal United States agencies responsible for covert operations and their various expertise.

CRITICAL THINKING QUESTIONS

1. For much of the United States' history, covert action was authorized by Presidential decree or Executive Order. Is that the proper way for the United States to engage in covert action? What efficiencies does it provide? What problems might arise?

2. Is the NSA's oversight process too permissive or too onerous for the President? Should the NSA require Congress to play more of a role or less of a role overseeing covert action? How would you change the NSA to reflect your answers to these questions?

3. In this chapter you learned about four basic types of covert action. Should the degree of Congressional oversight increase or decrease depending on the type of covert action ordered by the Executive Branch? What would be the advantages and disadvantages of such a system?

4. Would there be a benefit to limiting the legal authority to conduct covert operations to one agency within the United States government? Would that result in more effective Congressional oversight and more accountability? Would there be any disadvantages?

5. Consider the international law discussed in Chapters 12, 13, and 14. Might the United States' covert actions be legal under domestic law, but illegal under international law? If so, how can that be reconciled with the United States' commitment to the rule of law?

CHAPTER 19

Homeland Security

President George W. Bush signs the Homeland Security Appropriations Act

Americans have a "traditional and strong resistance . . . to any military intrusion into civilian affairs [that] has deep roots in our history. . . ." United States Supreme Court, Laird v. Tatum.

Learning Objectives

1. Appreciate the differences between the ways in which the United States responded to national crises before the mid-Twentieth Century and today.

2. Understand the Stafford Act, Presidential declarations, and the Federal Emergency Management Agency's role in responding to disasters.

3. Understand the President's authority under the National Emergencies Act and Congress's oversight responsibility.

4. Appreciate the Department of Homeland Security and its operational components.

5. Understand the United States military's role in domestic security, its powers, and its constraints.

6. Using the example of a biological outbreak, appreciate some of the legal issues that arise during the government's response to a homeland security threat.

19.1. INTRODUCTION

Most political scientists and philosophers believe sovereign governments possess inherent emergency powers—the authority to suspend laws and traditional limits on government to respond to a crisis. The United States Constitution, however, does not expressly provide the President, or any other branch of the United States government, with expansive emergency powers. In fact, one of the only references to emergency powers appears in the Constitution's Suspension Clause which allows the government to suspend the "privilege of the **writ of habeas corpus** . . . in cases of rebellion or invasion the public safety may require it." Still, some scholars suggest the Constitution implicitly provides the United States government with emergency powers throughout the document, such as Congress's authority to "provide for the common Defense and general Welfare." Whether the Constitution implicitly or explicitly contemplates the existence of emergency powers, Presidents throughout history have relied on the concept to justify various actions taken during what they considered emergencies that threatened the nation's security. Emergencies, however, are not limited to events that threaten the nation's existence. Emergencies can be more localized events, like a natural disaster, that threaten the life and property of citizens located in a specific state or region of the country. In those circumstances, it may also be beneficial for the United States government, and local governments, to suspend the typical limits on government power to prepare for and respond to a crisis. As a result, homeland security is an expansive idea. It implicates numerous laws the United States government relies on to increase security, reduce the nation's vulnerabilities, and prevent and respond to man-made and natural disasters. These laws were primarily developed in the Twentieth and Twenty-first Century. However, the United States government, particularly Presidents, has a long history of invoking emergency powers to respond to a crisis.

19.2. THE HISTORICAL DEVELOPMENT OF EMERGENCY RESPONSE AUTHORITIES

For its first 200 years, the United States government relied on piecemeal declarations of emergency powers to handle crises as they arose. Congress would pass legislation providing the President with extraordinary powers, or a President would invoke extraordinary powers, to deal with emergencies on a case-by-case basis. As early as George Washington's presidency, Congress enacted the Calling Forth Act. The law authorized President Washington to "call forth" the militias in Pennsylvania, Virginia, Maryland, and New Jersey to enforce federal tax law and suppress what would become known as the Whiskey Rebellion. However, the authorization to use these state militias was only temporary; the Calling Forth Act authorized President Washington to use the militias for no more than three years. While Congress reauthorized the President's use of the militias after the three-year limit, the reauthorization was again limited in time and President Washington strictly adhered to the specific restrictions and defined authorizations in the law.

After the Calling Forth Act, Congress continued to pass laws authorizing emergency powers so the President could act in times of national crisis. However, the most expansive and bold invocation of emergency power in the first 100 years of the nation's history did not arise out of a law passed by Congress. Instead, it arose from President Abraham Lincoln's prosecution of the Civil War. Soon after his inauguration, with Congress in recess, President Lincoln invoked the dissolution of the nation to justify emergency action that was not authorized by Congress and arguably beyond his Executive Branch authority. Although Congress retains the Constitutional authority to declare war, raise an army, and appropriate funds, President Lincoln issued a blockade of secessionist Southern ports, significantly increased the number of soldiers and sailors in the Army and Navy, increased the number of Naval vessels, and spent approximately $2,000,000 of unappropriated funds. Even those who supported the Union derided his moves as despotism. Nevertheless, all of his emergency actions were either later authorized by Congress or went unchallenged in court.

After the Civil War, and throughout the rest of the Nineteenth Century, Presidents continued to rely on congressionally authorized emergency powers to suppress those who challenged the United States government's policies and authority. For example, Presidents Rutherford B. Hayes and Grover Cleveland claimed they had the power, under the Insurrection Act, to order federal troops to break labor strikes. President Ulysses S. Grant relied on the Enforcement Act, also known as the Ku Klux Klan Act, to suspend habeas corpus and dismantle the Ku Klux Klan in the South. However, it was not until the Great Depression, the Cold War, and Congress's attempt to reign in the Executive Branch that the modern concept of emergency powers began to take shape and lead to the enactment of most laws that govern today.

In 1929, the Great Depression began to grip the nation. Banks were going bankrupt and the unemployment rate skyrocketed. In early 1933, the nation's banking system began to falter, spelling disaster for the country's economy. On March 6, 1933, only thirty-six hours after his inauguration, President Franklin D. Roosevelt declared that economic conditions had "created a national emergency." Relying on the Trading With the Enemy Act, President Roosevelt issued Proclamation 2039, also known as the 1933 Bank Holiday. The Proclamation instituted a weeklong moratorium on all bank transactions throughout the country to stave off a collapse of the banking sector. President Roosevelt also issued national emergency Proclamations 2352 and 2487, in 1939 and 1941 receptively. Proclamation 2352 declared a national emergency in response to the outbreak of World War II in Europe and a need to strengthen peacetime national defenses. Proclamation 2487 declared an "unlimited national emergency" in response to the growing threat posed by the Axis powers and the need to prepare United States Military and civilian defenses to repel an attack.

After the end of World War II, the United States turned its attention to the expansion of communism throughout the world. Communist revolutions in Europe, Africa, and Asia, coupled with the threat of communists operating in the United States, led to a Presidential national emergency declaration and one of the major pieces of legislation that controls emergency management law to this day. In November 1950, after five months of United States military forces aiding South Korea in its military conflict with North Korean forces, hundreds of thousands of Chinese forces entered the battle. In response, President Harry S. Truman issued Proclamation 2914 and announced "the existence of a national emergency" due to the threat of "communist imperialism." The declared national emergency ultimately allowed the Administration to institute wage and price controls to aid the war effort in Korea. President Truman also relied on Proclamation 2914 when he attempted to nationalize the country's steel industry to prevent a labor strike. The President's attempts to nationalize the steel industry, however, were thwarted by the Supreme Court in its historic *Youngstown Sheet & Tube Co. v. Sawyer* case. In *Youngstown*, the Court determined the President had acted without constitutional or congressional authority and thus did not have the power to seize and operate the steel mills. Nevertheless, President Truman's declaration of a national emergency resulted in the most significant increase in Executive Branch power since World War II.

During this same time, the United States was coping with the possibility of nuclear war with the Soviet Union. Hitherto, the United States government had a piece-meal approach to dealing with emergencies and catastrophes. Congress would pass laws and allocate funding to handle disasters as they arose. Alternatively, **Executive Orders**, like those discussed above, created specific programs to support the civil defense on an **ad hoc** basis. With no single law in place to deal with the likely catastrophe and resulting emergencies that would follow a nuclear attack, Congress passed the Civil Defense Act of 1950. The Civil Defense Act was the United States' first legislation to deal with homeland security and emergency management in a proactive way. Congress intended the Civil Defense Act to be a framework for local, state, and federal authorities to coordinate the emergency responses necessary to provide for the civil defense following an enemy attack. To that end, the Civil Defense Act created the Federal Civil Defense Administration (FCDA), which was responsible for coordinating the federal and states' preparation for, and response to, an attack. In the event of an attack, the Civil Defense Act empowered the FCDA's Administrator to manage the distribution of resources to provide health and welfare services to the affected populations. However, the Civil Defense Act envisioned state and local governments as primarily responsible for providing those services, with the federal government offering support and coordination. This division of labor would become a fundamental feature of future homeland security preparation and response legislation.

While the Civil Defense Act was the new national plan for how to prepare for and respond to enemy attacks, the federal government still lacked a cohesive approach to respond to other sorts of disasters. For example, the Civil Defense Act did not create the infrastructure for a federal response to natural disasters like floods, tornadoes, and hurricanes. As a result, the same year Congress enacted the Civil Defense Act, it passed the Disaster Relief Act of 1950. With the passage of the Disaster Relief Act, state and local governments would no longer have to wait until Congress passed legislation to allocate funds in response to a specific disaster. In a significant move, with separation of powers implications, Congress transferred much of its authority to the President. Pursuant to the Disaster Relief Act, the President had the authority to declare a disaster and coordinate the response by federal agencies. While Congress ultimately amended and renamed the Disaster Relief Act, the legal framework for the federal government's response to disasters remains intact today—Congress allocates funding for responding to national disasters and the Executive Branch declares disasters and coordinates the response.

19.3. THE STAFFORD ACT

Various United States statutes address specific homeland security issues ranging from bioterrorism to regulating the aviation industry. Yet there is perhaps no other law more often relied upon by the government and homeland security professionals than the Robert T. Stafford Disaster Relief and Emergency Assistance Act (Stafford Act). As a result, understanding the Stafford Act, when it can be invoked, and what resources it authorizes is key to understanding United States homeland security law. The Stafford Act relies primarily on a "bottom-up" approach to preparedness and response. In keeping with the United States' commitment to **federalism**, state and local governments are principally responsible for managing and providing assistance to their citizens in times of emergency. Realizing, however, that significant catastrophic events can overwhelm state and local authorities, the Stafford Act empowers the President to direct federal resources to support local efforts. Additionally, the Stafford Act provides the Executive Branch the legal authority to establish a nationwide system for preparing, organizing, and standardizing response efforts. Through the Stafford Act, the United States can more efficiently and effectively coordinate a comprehensive approach to incident management.

19.3.1. Presidential Declarations

The Stafford Act, and its available resources, can be invoked for two reasons: an "emergency" exists or "major disaster" has occurred. Each of these terms has its own specific legal definition, which is described in detail below. As a general matter, however, an emergency is declared in anticipation of, or prior to, a catastrophic event. On the other hand, a major disaster is often declared after a catastrophic event has occurred. Ultimately, it is the President's responsibility to assess the facts and circumstances of a situation and issue an "emergency declaration" or a "major disaster declaration." As you will see, these separate declarations summon different resources, roles, and responsibilities on behalf of the federal government.

Emergency Declarations

The President may issue an emergency declaration under two circumstances. First, the President may issue an emergency declaration in response to a request by the Governor of a state or a Native American tribal chief executive. Under this option for declaring an emergency, a state or tribe will conduct a Preliminary Damage Assessment (PDA), which evaluates the damage that was caused, or will be caused, and the resources needed to respond to a catastrophic event. The

Governor or tribal chief executive must then provide a formal request to the President describing the catastrophic event that threatens the state or tribe and explain why the threat is so overwhelming the state or tribe will be incapable of handling it on its own. The request must also describe the state's or tribe's emergency plans, the actions it has taken, and the resources it has employed to prepare for the emergency. Finally, the request must describe the federal resources that have already been accessed and the additional resources needed. These requests can be made in anticipation of any type of catastrophic event or within 30 days of an event occurring. If the President determines federal assistance is needed to help prevent or reduce the impact of a catastrophic event, save lives, protect public health and safety, or protect property, he may issue an emergency declaration. The President can also issue an emergency declaration unilaterally, without receiving a request from a state or tribe, if he determines an emergency exists and the federal government has the primary responsibility to respond to the situation. These emergency declarations are often associated with catastrophes that affect federal government property, such as the terrorist attack on the Murrah Federal Building in 1995.

Whether requested by a state or tribe, or declared by a President unilaterally, an emergency declaration facilitates the release of resources to the affected state or tribe and may not exceed $5,000,000. When compared with a major disaster declaration, as you will see below, the resources made available during an emergency declaration can only be used for limited reasons: debris removal and emergency protective measures. Debris removal includes clearing things like trees, mud, sand, gravel and building wreckage deposited on public lands. Emergency protective measures include assistance like sandbagging, shoring up damaged structures, and providing emergency shelters and medical care. If the costs associated with responding to the emergency exceed $5,000,000, the President must issue a report to Congress. The report must explain why continued emergency assistance was required.

Major Disaster Declaration

While emergency declarations are often requested and granted in anticipation of a catastrophic event, a major disaster declaration is more often made after an event has occurred. Additionally, a disaster declaration brings with it more resources and an expanded role for federal agencies in assisting in recovery from a catastrophe. Like an emergency declaration, the decision to declare a major disaster resides solely with the President and follows a similar process. First, a state or tribe completes a PDA and executes its emergency response plans. If the state or tribe is incapable of satisfactorily responding to the catastrophe, the

Governor or tribal chief executive may request the President declare a major disaster. In the request, the Governor or tribal chief executive must detail the catastrophic event, estimate its damage, describe the local resources that have been or will be allocated to respond to the event, and explain why federal assistance is needed. Although the President may issue emergency declarations for any type of catastrophic event, a major disaster declaration may only be issued in response to a natural catastrophe, fire, flood, or explosion, regardless of the cause.

A major disaster declaration provides a wide array of assistance from the federal government. In addition to the resources available under an emergency declaration—debris removal and emergency protective measures—resources for permanent repair work also become available. States and tribes can use the resources to repair roads and bridges, water control facilities, water treatment facilities, public buildings, and public recreational infrastructure.

19.3.2. The Federal Emergency Management Agency

Since President Jimmy Carter created the Federal Emergency Management Agency (FEMA) through an Executive Order in 1979, the acronym has become synonymous with the federal government's disaster response and relief efforts. In an attempt to centralize federal disaster preparation, mitigation, response, and recovery responsibilities, President Carter transferred those duties from various federal agencies, such as the Department of Defense and Housing and Urban Development, into the new agency. Less than ten years later, the Stafford Act both clearly defined FEMA's role in the federal government's response to disasters and became the primary statutory authority under which FEMA operates. While FEMA initially operated as an independent agency, after the 9/11 terrorist attacks, it became one of the federal agencies to make up the newly created Department of Homeland Security.

The Stafford Act recognizes FEMA as the primary federal agency responsible for preparing and implementing a comprehensive emergency management system for the United States. While FEMA is most often associated with preparing for and responding to natural disasters, its statutory authority also extends to other emergencies such as acts of terrorism and other man-made disasters. In recognition of the "bottom up" approach to emergency response, FEMA is also statutorily mandated to coordinate with state and local governments to fund, train, and assist with preparedness efforts. To more effectively coordinate these responsibilities among state and local governments, FEMA is organized into 10 Regional Offices, with each office responsible for a distinct area of the country. In addition to its Regional Offices, FEMA's headquarters at the National

Response Coordination Center provides larger scale, nation-wide coordination efforts. Additionally, FEMA's National Integration Center formulates FEMA's national policies and best practices for disaster preparedness and response. Two of the most important of these policies are the National Incident Management System (NIMS) and the National Response Framework (NRF).

The NIMS is the federal government's premier strategic plan of action for managing disasters. It provides guidance to the various levels of government, private industry, and non-governmental organizations to work together to avert or reduce the loss of life and property during a catastrophic event. The NIMS is broken up into five components: preparedness strategies; communications and information management; resource allocation management; command and control structures; and a plan for management and maintenance of the NIMS itself. Each of the five components provide flexible guidance to coordinate the distinct, but interrelated, steps of responding to a catastrophic event. While the NIMS provides a template for preparing for, managing, and recovering from an event, the NRF—a companion to the NIMS—provides the structure and mechanisms for national-level policy for incident management. The NRF begins with the basic premise of federalism and assumes catastrophic events should, to the extent possible, be handled at the lowest level. Additionally, it differs from the NIMS as the NRF focuses on immediate response and recovery instead of all the various phases of incident management. The intent behind the NRF is that it be scalable and flexible, with a focus on best practices for prevention, protection, mitigation, and recovery before, during, and after a disaster. Both the NIMS and NRF seek to ensure an integrated, focused, organized process to align disaster management efforts.

19.4. THE NATIONAL EMERGENCIES ACT

The United States Constitution is conspicuously silent regarding the declaration of a national emergency or whether the government may assume extraordinary powers during such time. Other countries' constitutions specifically describe how a state of emergency may be declared and provide the head of state with emergency powers. For example, Article 16 of the French Constitution allows the French President to assume "extraordinary powers" in certain circumstances. Because the United States Constitution does not provide a process or allow for the suspension of any of its provisions, except for the Suspension Clause in Article I, declaring a national emergency has been undertaken in two ways over the course of United States history. First, relying on an argument they possess inherent executive authority, Presidents have declared national emergencies through presidential proclamations. Second, Congress has passed legislation recognizing and providing for the response to national emergencies. Because of the patchwork approach to national emergency declarations and Congress's concern that Presidents were expanding their power by invoking national emergencies, Congress passed the National Emergencies Act (NEA) in 1976. The goals of the NEA were two-fold. The NEA ended all presidentially declared states of emergency that existed at the time the NEA was enacted, one of which dated back as far as 1933. Additionally, the NEA provided something that had been lacking—a process for declaring, overseeing, and ending national emergencies.

With the first goal of the NEA being accomplished simply by enacting the statute, the longer-term effects of the NEA have been the statutory procedures that control a national emergency declaration. If a President determines there is a need to declare a national emergency she must do four things:

1. The President must formally declare the national emergency, transmit notification of the proclamation to Congress, and publish the declaration in the **Federal Register**. This ensures a transparent process that specifically identifies the emergency and identifies when the state of emergency officially begins.

2. The President must identify which statutory emergency authorities she intends to invoke in response to the emergency. This ensures a President does not simply rely on general, ill defined, or unlimited emergency authority. Presidents have over 100 statutory defined emergency powers they may rely on when declaring a national emergency. Most often, Presidents have both declared a national emergency and identified the authorities they intend to invoke in the same proclamation.

3. The President, and federal agencies, must retain and transmit to Congress a record of each order, rule, and regulation promulgated to carry out the response to the national emergency.

4. The President must, every six months, transmit to Congress an accounting of the costs associated with responding to the declared national emergency.

Once a President properly declares a national emergency, Congressional oversight begins. Through the notifications discussed above, Congress has the ability to monitor a President's use of her emergency powers and the costs associated with responding to the emergency. The NEA mandates that both the

House of Representatives and the Senate shall meet every six months after the declaration of a national emergency. The purposes of this statutorily mandated meeting is to consider whether Congress should terminate the state of emergency. While this has never happened, it is one of the three ways a national emergency may be terminated. Initially, the NEA required a **concurrent resolution**, approved by both the House of Representatives and the Senate, to terminate a national emergency. However, in 1985, the NEA was amended to require a **joint resolution** of Congress. As a result, even if Congress votes to end a national emergency, a President can veto the resolution. Congress then could allow the veto to stand, thus allowing the national emergency to continue. Alternatively, Congress could attempt to override the President's veto with a two-thirds vote in both the House of Representatives and the Senate. A national emergency can also be terminated if the President declares it to be over. Otherwise, a national emergency ends automatically after one year, unless the President renews it by way of a proclamation published in the Federal Register.

Legislative Vetoes

In 1985, Congress voted to amend the NEA and limit its own ability to end a presidentially declared national emergency. It changed the NEA from requiring a concurrent resolution to a joint resolution. While the decision to reduce its own power over the President's authority might seem counterintuitive, Congress was essentially forced to do so. Two years earlier, in 1983, the Supreme Court determined that "legislative vetoes" of Executive Branch decisions were unconstitutional if they did not follow the constitutionally prescribed process.

In *INS v. Chadha*, the Immigration and Naturalization Service began deportation proceedings against Jagdish Rai Chadha, a foreign exchange student who overstayed his student visa. On Chadha's request, the INS agreed to suspend his deportation due to the "extreme hardship" he would face if he was deported. After the INS transmitted a report of its decision to Congress, the House of Representatives exercised its then-existing statutory right to veto the INS decision. Chadha challenged the constitutionality of the statute that permitted the Houses of Representatives to veto the INS's decision. The Supreme Court determined that, based on the Constitution's separation of powers principles, single-house legislative vetoes of the Executive Branch's actions were unconstitutional. For this reason, Congress was forced to amend the NEA and change the process for terminating a state of emergency.

The NEA does not define the term "national emergency." As a result, the definition has been the subject of litigation in the courts. At the time of this writing, the Supreme Court has not issued a ruling on the question. Not only does the NEA lack a definition of a national emergency, it does not contain a list of powers and authorities a President may invoke during a state of emergency.

Instead, those powers and authorities are found in a group of, at times, unrelated statutes that regulate some sort of conduct and then provide for an exception to the regulation during times of a declared national emergency. As was mentioned above, over 100 statutes provide Presidents with extraordinary powers during a national emergency. These statutes range the gamut from allowing a President to suspend the laws that govern the disposal of garbage at sea, to temporarily appointing officers in the military, to prohibiting the export of any agricultural commodity. At the time of this writing, over 30 national emergencies were in effect, with some having lasted for decades.

President Trump's Barrier Along the United States Border with Mexico

On February 15, 2019, President Donald J. Trump issued his *Presidential Proclamation on Declaring a National Emergency Concerning the Southern Border of the United States*. In the proclamation, President Trump declared a national emergency along the United States border with Mexico. A national emergency existed, the President proclaimed, because of threats to "border security," a "humanitarian crisis," "large-scale unlawful migration" and "criminals, gang members, and illicit narcotics . . ." entering through the border. The President invoked his authority under the Military Construction Codification Act to divert funding from military construction projects to the construction of a barrier along the border. In response to President Trump's proclamation, a number of states and organizations filed lawsuits challenging the proclamation.

The states and organizations argued that no national emergency existed and that the President had exceeded his authority. Among other things, they argued that the President had requested funding from Congress for the barrier and said that if his Administration did not get a "fair deal from Congress" he would "use the powers afforded" him to build it. Additionally, during the press conference announcing his national emergency proclamation, President Trump stated "I could do the wall over a longer period of time. I didn't need to do this. But I'd rather do it much faster." His statements, the states and organizations argued, proved that President Trump issued his proclamation because he could not secure the funds from Congress, not because an actual national emergency existed. The Trump Administration responded by arguing that the official description of the declared national emergency was found in his proclamation, not in his unscripted comments. Moreover, the Administration argued, the NEA empowers the President alone to determine whether a national emergency exists and he complied with the process outlined in the NEA. Thus, the Administration posited, the President legally invoked the statutory authority provided to him by various statutes. To date, the Supreme Court has not issued a ruling resolving the dispute. If the Court considers the challenges to the President's authority, it may finally define what constitutes a "national emergency."

19.5. THE UNITED STATES DEPARTMENT OF HOMELAND SECURITY

After the 9/11 terrorist attacks, Congress passed the Homeland Security Act of 2002 (HSA) creating the Department of Homeland Security (DHS). The HSA represented a massive shift in the way the federal government is organized and responds to national crises. It served as the foundation for the federal government to reorganize and consolidate incident management functions, assets, and personnel in a single department. Most importantly, the HSA established the DHS, and consolidated the missions, assets, and personnel of numerous federal departments and agencies. The missions of DHS include reducing the vulnerability of the United States to the threats it faces, preventing terrorist attacks within the United States, and responding to natural and man-made disasters. Understanding DHS and its operational components is key to understanding how the United States enforces its homeland security laws.

Reflecting the importance of homeland security, the Secretary of Homeland Security is a Cabinet-level, Senate approved government official appointed by the President. He oversees one of the largest federal agencies measured both by the size of its budget and its workforce. The DHS, which he leads, is responsible for preventing, mitigating, and responding to a range of security threats to the United States including terrorism, cybersecurity, aviation security, border security, port security, and maritime security. The DHS is also responsible for enforcing immigration laws, protecting national leaders, protecting infrastructure, protecting against chemical, biological and nuclear threats, and responding to disasters. Each agency and directorate within DHS has a discrete responsibility within the United States homeland security apparatus and the leader of each agency and directorate reports to the Secretary of Homeland Security. Below is a list of operational and support components of DHS along with their responsibilities and role within the larger DHS organization.

Science and Technology Directorate

The Science and Technology Directorate is responsible for providing the DHS and its agencies with the advice, development, and acquisition of new scientific and technological capabilities. Its experts work internally, with industry, and with academic institutions to develop solutions in support of DHS and its agencies' specific needs. Its projects are organized into six focus areas: borders and maritime security; chemical and biological defense; critical infrastructure and resilience; cybersecurity; explosives; and first responders. The Science and Technology Directorate has assisted in the development of a range of technologies from passenger screening devices for airport security to heartbeat detector devices for first responders searching for survivors after a disaster.

Office of Intelligence and Analysis

The Office of Intelligence and Analysis collects, manages, analyzes, and shares intelligence with the various DHS agencies and directorates. It not only provides intelligence to other federal agencies, it is also statutorily responsible for sharing intelligence with state, local, and tribal officials in an effort to identify and mitigate threats throughout the United States. The Office of Intelligence and Analysis has five Mission Centers: the Counterintelligence Mission Center; the Counterterrorism Mission Center; the Cyber Mission Center; the Economic Security Mission Center; and the Transnational Organized Crime Mission Center. Each Mission Center is responsible for collecting and analyzing intelligence relevant to one of DHS's major security responsibilities. In addition to being a directorate within DHS, it is also a member of the United States Intelligence Community. As a result, DHS's Office of Intelligence and Analysis is not only responsible for reporting to the Secretary of Homeland Security, but also the Director of National Intelligence.

Cybersecurity and Infrastructure Security Agency

The Cybersecurity and Infrastructure Security Agency is responsible for monitoring and mitigating threats to the United States cyber and physical **infrastructure** as well as building resiliency into the various systems. The Agency's Cybersecurity Division takes the lead within the federal government for protecting the ".gov" network and works with the private sector to protect the ".com" network. Its Infrastructure Security Division works with state and local governments to identify and reduce risks to critical physical infrastructure that supports the nation's security, health and safety, and economic activity. The Agency's Emergency Communications Division evaluates and supports communication services and infrastructure used by emergency responders. Finally, its National Risk Management Center coordinates among the private sector and government agencies to identify, analyze, and manage risks to the nation's critical infrastructure.

Countering Weapons of Mass Destruction Office

The Countering Weapons of Mass Destruction Office is a support agency within DHS that works with operational agencies to prevent weapons of mass destruction attacks against the United States. In particular, its goal is to enable and coordinate federal and local agencies' detection and response to chemical, biological, and nuclear weapons threats. The Office also manages DHS's

BioWatch Program. In an effort to provide early warning of a bioterrorist attack, the BioWatch Program coordinates air monitoring, analysis, notification procedures, and risk assessment for over 30 municipalities across the United States.

United States Citizenship and Immigration Services

The United States Citizenship and Immigration Services is responsible for administering the immigration-related processes and services of the Immigration and Nationality Act. When an immigrant is seeking to become a United States citizen through one of the various **naturalization** programs, the United States Citizenship and Immigration Services is responsible for adjudicating those requests. The agency also administers the Permanent Resident Card program, or Green Card, which permits immigrants to live and work permanently in the United States. The agency's third major function is to manage and adjudicate the United States' asylum and refugee programs.

United States Coast Guard

The United States Coast Guard is the only branch of the military not housed within the Department of Defense. It is responsible for the maritime safety and security of United States ports, waterways, and coasts. It engages in law enforcement operations, such as disrupting drug smuggling and illegal immigration, as well as assisting with maritime navigation, search and rescue, and maritime environmental protection. While the United States Coast Guard's primary assets are water based, such as boats and cutters, it also operates a small cadre of fixed and rotary wing aircrafts. In addition, the United States Coast Guard is responsible for managing various land-based assets such as lighthouses and the stations from which it launches its missions.

United States Customs and Border Protection

United States Customs and Border Protection is the federal government's law enforcement agency dedicated to managing the safety and security of United States borders and ports of entry. Its officers are stationed at airports, land borders, and seaports to enforce the United States' trade laws and screen visitors and citizens entering the country. The Office of Field Operations is the primary agency within the United States Customs and Border Protection and it is responsible for managing and inspecting cargo and people entering and exiting the United States. As a result, it enforces the United States' import and export laws, immigration laws, and agriculture inspections. Air and Marine Operations officers use aircraft and marine vessels to prevent unlawful people and cargo from entering United States borders, while the United States Border Patrol is responsible for guarding United States borders between ports of entry.

Federal Emergency Management Agency

The Federal Emergency Management Agency (FEMA) coordinates disaster preparedness, mitigation, and response in the United States. FEMA's national office in Washington D.C. houses the National Response Coordination Center (NRCC), which coordinates the federal response to catastrophic natural and man-made disasters in the United States. Once activated, the NRCC liaises with one or more of FEMA's 10 Regional Offices throughout the country. Each Regional Office is responsible for working with state, local, and tribal officials to assist in their preparation for, or response to, disasters. In addition to helping state, local, and tribal governments coordinate their resources and responses, FEMA maintains its own teams it can activate and dispatch to a disaster area. Its Mobile Emergency Response Support team assists with telecommunications, power generation, and logistics, while its Urban Search and Rescue Task Force assists with locating, extricating, and stabilizing trapped victims. FEMA also collaborates with the Department of Health and Human Services to utilize and direct its medical, pharmaceutical, and nursing teams in response to a disaster. FEMA also has a robust training program through which it trains first responders, private sector industries, and private citizens in emergency preparedness and response.

Federal Law Enforcement Training Centers

The Federal Law Enforcement Training Centers (FLETC) provide training primarily for law enforcement officers and agents. The FLETC not only trains law enforcement officers in the Homeland Security Department, but also works with law enforcement across the federal government including the military, the Intelligence Community, the Postal Service, the Department of the Treasury, the Department of Transportation, and many others. The FLETC also provides training for some international, state, local, and private law enforcement agencies. The training includes a variety of skills needed to perform the duties of a law enforcement officer including vehicle operation, interviewing suspects, firearm handling, and leadership.

United States Immigration and Customs Enforcement

United States Immigration and Customs Enforcement (ICE) is responsible for enforcing United States immigration and customs laws. Not to be confused with United States Customs and Border Protection, the majority of ICE's personnel and assets operate within the interior of the United States' borders. There are two primary operational divisions in ICE: Homeland Security

Investigations (HSI) and Enforcement and Removal Operations (ERO). HSI enforces a variety of federal laws that govern transnational crimes including commercial fraud, cybercrimes, human trafficking, cross-border criminal syndicates. HSI is further subdivided into specialty focus areas of operation including domestic field operations, international operations, terrorism, and intelligence. ERO is the immigration enforcement division within ICE. It locates, detains, and institutes removal proceedings for unlawful aliens. Like HSI, ICE divides its operational efforts into various focus areas including enforcement, custody, removal, and health services for suspects in ICE custody.

United States Secret Service

The United States Secret Service has two, seemingly disconnected, responsibilities. It was established by Congress in 1865 for the purpose of investigating, seizing, and preventing the counterfeiting of United States money. It still pursues that mission. However, it has expanded its finance-related investigations and enforcement operations to combat financial cybercrimes and threats to the United States' financial infrastructure. The United States Secret Service is probably most well known for its mission to protect the United States' highest elected officials, a responsibility it assumed in the early 1900s after the assassination of President William McKinley. In addition to protecting current and former Presidents, Vice Presidents, and their minor children, the United States Secret Service is responsible for protecting visiting heads of state as well as presidential and vice presidential candidates and their spouses. It is also responsible for security operations at significant national events that may be the target of criminals or terrorists.

Transportation Security Administration

The Transportation Security Administration (TSA) was created, along with DHS, after the 9/11 terrorist attacks. Its mission is to protect the United States transportation systems. Its primary responsibility is to ensure the safety of air travel through screening passengers and luggage as well as in-flight security provided by the Federal Air Marshal Service. TSA also provides security oversight for freight railroad, passenger rail, mass transit, maritime travel, and pipelines. Its three operational security offices are focused on domestic aviation, international coordination, and surface operations. Though not part of the United States Intelligence Community, TSA also has a division focused on collecting and analyzing intelligence to ensure the safety and security of United States transportation.

19.6. THE UNITED STATES MILITARY'S DOMESTIC SECURITY ROLE

Though the United States military has participated in massive overseas war efforts costing millions of lives and trillions of dollars, significant combat has not occurred in the United States since the Civil War, over 150 years ago. While skirmishes and isolated attacks have occasionally visited the territory of the United States, such as the Japanese attack on Pearl Harbor, the use of the military to actively defend the nation on its soil has been limited. This is not to say that the military has not had a large role in keeping Americans safe. Indeed, throughout most of the Cold War, thousands of United States military personnel were on alert defending against possible attack. Nevertheless, the American people have not witnessed military personnel engaged in homeland defense. On the other hand, some military personnel have been visibly prominent in assisting with homeland security.

As the Supreme Court has noted, Americans harbor a "traditional and strong resistance . . . to any military intrusion into civilian affairs [that] has deep roots in our history. . . ." *Laird v. Tatum*. The Constitution reflects this resistance. Article I, Section 8, restricts Congress to funding the military for a maximum of two years at a time, a limitation applicable to no other element of the national government. Additionally, Article II places control of the military in the hands of a civilian elected official who must answer to the American people. The Third Amendment's prohibition on quartering troops in civilian homes further reflects a distrust of too much military presence in civilian life. Military involvement in domestic security thus walks a delicate balance between using a resource the nation needs and one the nation fears.

The United States military consists of six services in several departments. The United States Department of Defense includes within it the Department of the Army, the Department of the Navy, which includes the Navy and Marine Corps, and the Department of the Air Force, which now includes both the United States Air Force and the United States Space Force. Additionally, the United States Coast Guard, which is ordinarily assigned to the Department of Homeland Security, is a uniformed military service that is controlled by the Secretary of Defense during times of war.

The United States military consists of three components: active federal forces, reserve federal forces, and the National Guard and corresponding Air National Guard, which serves as the militia of each state. A curious incident of the United States' federal system is that the National Guard's default status is state control, with the governor as Commander in Chief. Importantly, National Guard activities can occur in several distinct statuses. "State Active Duty" includes activities where the National Guard has been activated by a governor for some period of time. While in State Active Duty status, all activities are controlled by the governor as Commander in Chief and are funded by the state. "Title 32" status refers to Title 32 of the United States Code, which permits some National Guard activities to be funded by the federal government while the forces remain under state control. Finally, "Title 10" status occurs when National Guard units are "federalized" by the President for federal service, during which time the President is the Commander in Chief and the federal government funds the activities. While their uniforms do not change based on their status, National Guardsmen's status can significantly impact the activities in which they are legally permitted to engage.

19.6.1. Posse Comitatus Act

A "posse comitatus" is a group of citizens who are given temporary authority to enforce the law, something similar to "deputizing" a citizen temporarily for a particular purpose that is commonly seen in old Western movies. Though such posses are infrequent today, they were once more common. After the Civil War, federal military forces were used extensively for law enforcement functions throughout the South, including monitoring polling stations. Perceived overreach and abuses by the federal military led to the Posse Comitatus Act of 1878 (PCA).

The PCA is a significant limitation on what the federal military may do domestically. As currently written, the PCA states:

> Whoever, except in cases and under circumstances expressly authorized by the Constitution or Act of Congress, willfully uses any part of the Army or the Air Force as a posse comitatus or otherwise to execute the laws shall be fined under this title or imprisoned not more than two years, or both.

Though the PCA explicitly identifies only the Army and Air Force, DOD regulations extend the prohibition to the Navy and Marine Corps, as well. The prohibition does *not* extend to the United States Coast Guard, which includes law enforcement as one of its core functions. Importantly, the PCA applies only to the federal military, and does not apply to National Guard services so long as the National Guard remains under control of the governor, either in a State Active Duty or Title 32 status. However, when federalized, and acting with the President as Commander in Chief, the PCA applies to National Guard activities.

What does "posse comitatus or otherwise to execute the laws" mean? In other words, what is prohibited by the PCA? The PCA itself does not say, leaving us to rely on court opinions to define the extent of the PCA's prohibition. No Supreme Court opinion exists regarding the meaning of "posse comitatus or otherwise to execute the laws," but several lower federal court opinions shed some light. One such opinion suggests that prohibited law enforcement is activity that is "regulatory, proscriptive, or compulsory." *Bissonette v. Haig*. In that case, the court found that setting up roadblocks around a town, establishing armed patrols that effectively created an armed perimeter, and seizure of persons amounted to prohibited law enforcement. Another court found that the PCA prohibits "direct, active" use of the military in law enforcement. *United States v. Red Feather*. In another case, the court determined that the PCA is violated when activities of the Army or Air Force "pervaded the activities" of civil law enforcement. *United States v. Jaramillo*. However, when the military activity's "primary purpose" is military in nature, and has only an incidental effect on civil law enforcement, it is not prohibited. *Applewhite v. United States Air Force*.

The PCA is a criminal statute, meaning violators can be prosecuted. Beyond that, its legal effect is unclear. Violation of the PCA might, in egregious circumstances, lead to exclusion of evidence obtained by military forces acting as a posse comitatus. On the other hand, a violation likely does not create a tort cause of action, though it could perhaps create a cause of action for violating constitutional rights.

19.6.2. Exceptions to the Posse Comitatus Act

The text of the PCA explicitly creates exceptions "in cases and under circumstances expressly authorized by the Constitution or Act of Congress." There are arguments available for several constitutional exceptions to the PCA, including:

- Article I, Section 8's authorization for Congress to "provide for calling forth the Militia to execute the Laws of the Union"
- Article II's Take Care Clause
- Article IV, Section 4, which states: "The United States shall guarantee to every State in this Union a Republican Form of Government, and shall protect each of them against invasion; and on Application of the Legislature, or of the Executive (when the Legislature cannot be convened) against domestic Violence."

There are several statutory exceptions to the PCA, the most important of which is the Insurrection Act. The Insurrection Act was initially enacted as the Militia Act in 1792, and gave the President authority to use the federal military to suppress rebellion. Subsequently, the Supreme Court determined that using the Insurrection Act is within the President's discretion and not subject to **judicial review**. *Martin v. Mott.*

There are a number of provisions in the Insurrection Act that constitute exceptions to the PCA. These fall into two main categories: 1) providing military support to state authorities; and 2) using the military to enforce federal law. The former is addressed in Section 251 of the Insurrection Act, which states:

> Whenever there is an insurrection in any State against its government, the President may, upon the request of its legislature or of its governor if the legislature cannot be convened, call into Federal service such of the militia of the other States, in the number requested by that State, and use such of the armed forces, as he considers necessary to suppress the insurrection.

Note that this provision requires the State to request assistance.

The second situation is addressed by Section 252, which states:

> Whenever the President considers that unlawful obstructions, combinations, or assemblages, or rebellion against the authority of the United States, make it impracticable to enforce the laws of the United States in any State by the ordinary course of judicial proceedings, he may call into Federal service such of the militia of any State, and use such of the armed forces, as he considers necessary to enforce those laws or to suppress the rebellion.

The second situation is also authorized by Section 253, which states:

> The President, by using the militia or the armed forces, or both, or by any other means, shall take such measures as he considers necessary to suppress, in a State, any insurrection, domestic violence, unlawful combination, or conspiracy, if it—
>
> (1) so hinders the execution of the laws of that State, and of the United States within the State, that any part or class of its people is deprived of a right, privilege, immunity, or protection named in the Constitution and secured by law, and the constituted authorities of that State are unable, fail, or refuse to protect that right, privilege, or immunity, or to give that protection; or

> (2) opposes or obstructs the execution of the laws of the United States or impedes the course of justice under those laws.

Note that under both Sections 252 and 253, the President makes the determination unilaterally; an invitation by the state is not required.

After Hurricane Katrina in 2005, which included complaints that the federal government should have taken a more active role in responding to the disaster and maintaining order in Louisiana, Congress temporarily amended Section 253 to allow the President to employ the armed forces to:

> restore public order and enforce the laws of the United States when, as a result of a natural disaster, epidemic, or other serious public health emergency, terrorist attack or incident, or other condition in any State or possession of the United States, the President determines that:
>
> > 1) domestic violence has occurred to such an extent that the constituted authorities of the State or possession are incapable of maintaining public order; and
> >
> > 2) such violence results in a condition that so hinders the execution of the laws of a State or possession. . . that any part or class of its people is deprived of a right, privilege, immunity or protection named in the Constitution and secured by law. . . .

Congress repealed this provision a year later.

The Stafford Act also arguably serves as an exception to the PCA under certain circumstances, as it allows the President to direct the DOD to provide emergency assistance "essential for the preservation of life and property" for up to ten days. While not a direct authorization of law enforcement activities, it is reasonable to conclude that if emergency assistance necessarily includes law enforcement functions, the Stafford Act serves as a statutory exception to the PCA for 10 days.

19.7. THE MILITARY'S ROLE IN HOMELAND SECURITY

Among other things discussed earlier in this chapter, the Homeland Security Act made the Department of Homeland Security the lead agency for homeland security, and FEMA the lead agency for "the Nation's efforts to prepare for, protect against, respond to, recover from, and mitigate against the risk of natural disasters, acts of terrorism, and other man-made disasters, including catastrophic incidents." The DOD has primary responsibility for homeland defense, but is subordinate to DHS in homeland security matters, raising the question of the difference between homeland defense and homeland security. The DOD defines those terms this way:

> **homeland defense**. The protection of United States sovereignty, territory, domestic population, and critical infrastructure against external threats and aggression or other threats as directed by the President.
>
> **homeland security**. A concerted national effort to prevent terrorist attacks within the United States; reduce America's vulnerability to terrorism, major disasters, and other emergencies; and minimize the damage and recover from attacks, major disasters, and other emergencies that occur. Joint Chiefs of Staff, *Joint Publication 3–27, Homeland Defense*, April 10, 2018.

Further, the DOD elaborates on the scope of the "homeland," defining it as "the physical region that includes the continental United States (CONUS), Alaska, Hawaii, United States territories, and surrounding territorial waters and airspace." In describing the way in which the homeland is protected, the DOD states:

> The United States Government (USG) employs all instruments of national power to continuously detect, deter, prevent, and defeat threats to the homeland. This national imperative translates operationally into homeland security (HS), defense support of civil authorities (DSCA), and homeland defense (HD). The Department of Defense (DOD) is the lead federal agency (LFA) for defending against traditional external threats or aggression (e.g., nation-state conventional forces or weapons of mass destruction [WMD] attack) and against external asymmetric threats that are outside of the scope of HS operations. The Department of Homeland Security (DHS) is the LFA for HS, and the United States Coast Guard (USCG) is the LFA for maritime homeland security (MHS). By law, DOD is responsible for two missions in the homeland: DSCA and HD. Joint Chiefs of Staff, *Joint Publication 3–27, Homeland Defense*, April 10, 2018.

Whether in a homeland defense role or providing military support to civil authorities, when federal troops are used to address domestic issues, the military chain of command remains in effect for those troops. Typically, these forces will be assigned to a Joint Task Force under the operational command of NORTHCOM, the unified combatant command in the DOD responsible for homeland defense and for military activities involving homeland security. The commander of NORTHCOM is directly controlled by the Secretary of Defense and the President.

As noted earlier, when state National Guard troops are used in their state status for homeland defense or homeland security, the governor is in command. Using the National Guard for some defense support to civil authorities provides increased flexibility. First, National Guard troops can—and often do—participate in law enforcement activities because the PCA does not apply while they are in state status. Additionally, while the federal military does not receive training in law enforcement (except for the law enforcement parts of the federal military services, like Military Police and Security Forces) and disaster relief, National Guard troops receive law enforcement and disaster relief training. Law enforcement and disaster relief involve skills and capabilities quite different from combat operations. Bluntly put, the skills necessary to calm an angry crowd of people are quite different from those required to eliminate an enemy infantry division.

19.7.1. Immediate Response Authority

Another way in which the military might engage in homeland security issues is the temporary ability to assist civil authorities. Federal military commanders, heads of DOD Components, and responsible DOD civilian officials are given "Immediate Response Authority" by a DOD Directive. Joint Chiefs of Staff, *Joint Publication 3–28, Defense Support of Civil Authorities*, October 29, 2018. In response to a request for assistance, DOD officials may provide an immediate response by temporarily employing resources under their control to support a civil authority. However, such response can only occur under imminently serious conditions and if time does not permit approval from higher authority, and must be for the purpose of saving lives, preventing human suffering, or mitigating great property damage within the United States, its territories, or the District of Columbia. Notably, Immediate Response Authority is explicitly *not* an exception to the PCA, as it does not permit actions that would subject civilians to the use of military power that is regulatory, prescriptive, proscriptive, or compulsory. Commanders' immediate response authority does not ordinarily extend beyond 72 hours.

19.7.2. Martial Law

Under **martial law**, the military commander, governor, or President who imposed martial law controls some specific geographic territory. At its core, martial law means that the military replaces ordinary civil law, as administered by the Executive and Judicial Branches in the affected area. The concept of martial law is anathema to many Americans who favor individual liberty and democratic institutions that are subsumed during periods of martial law.

Though fairly limited, martial law has been imposed in the United States on several occasions. For instance, General Andrew Jackson briefly imposed martial law on New Orleans while fighting against the British in the War of 1812. In the Civil War, as new Confederate territory became controlled by the Union Army, the Union Army imposed martial law. This imposition extended beyond the end of hostilities in the Civil War. The Civil War also marks the last time a United States President declared martial law. A few other instances of martial law in the United States demonstrate how limited the scope of its use has been, and how military officers have generally been hesitant to use this authority. Around the time of World War I, United States Army General Leonard Wood twice declared martial law, once in Omaha, Nebraska, to quell a race riot and again in Gary, Indiana, to manage a steel strike. Both declarations were limited to the specific cities. In addition to the Gary, Indiana strike, martial law has been ordered in a few other strike-related situations. Additionally, the Governor of Hawaii declared martial law, apparently with President Roosevelt's approval, after Japan's attack on Pearl Harbor. This declaration led to one of the few opinions the Supreme Court has issued regarding the reach of martial law, *Duncan v. Kahanamoku*, discussed below. Federal martial law has not been declared since World War II, including in the aftermath of the 9/11 terrorist attacks or the COVID-19 Coronavirus pandemic.

Widely misunderstood, in large part because there is so little legal guidance, martial law is the "option of last resort" for maintaining order under government control. Generally, the possibility of martial law is often mentioned when considering public crises, yet little law exists to authorize or limit it. The Constitution does not mention martial law, suggesting imposition of martial law, though perhaps necessary, might be unconstitutional or extra-constitutional. No federal statute authorizes or describes martial law. However, the Insurrection Act does provide the President with authority to use the military in circumstances that might be similar to a martial law setting, and some scholars have suggested it actually authorizes (implicitly) martial law. And as of this writing, there are no publicly known federal regulations regarding martial law.

Supreme Court opinions regarding martial law are few, and though they do not prohibit martial law, they clearly disfavor and restrict it. Ironically, the most important case establishing the Court's support for martial law is *Ex parte Milligan*, a case in which the Court explicitly found that martial law did not, and could not, exist under the circumstances presented by the facts of the case. In deciding that the **military commission** that tried Milligan had no **jurisdiction** to do so, the Court observed that martial law did not exist in Indiana at the time of Milligan's alleged crimes, arrest, detention, and trial. Though the Supreme Court agreed that the case did not pose "a question of the power to proclaim martial law," it nevertheless proceeded to discuss the circumstances that might authorize martial law. The Court opined that "[m]artial law cannot arise from a threatened invasion. The necessity must be actual and present; the invasion real, such as effectually closes the courts and deposes the civil administration." The Court continued:

> there are occasions when martial rule can be properly applied. If, in foreign invasion or civil war, the courts are actually closed, and it is impossible to administer criminal justice according to law, then, on the theatre of active military operations, where war really prevails, there is a necessity to furnish a substitute for the civil authority, thus overthrown, to preserve the safety of the army and society; and as no power is left but the military, it is allowed to govern by martial rule until the laws can have their free course.

The Court felt the need to reiterate its earlier point again, asserting "[m]artial rule can never exist where the courts are open, and in the proper and unobstructed exercise of their jurisdiction. It is also confined to the locality of actual war."

In 1909, in *Moyer v. Peabody*, the Supreme Court upheld Colorado Governor James Peabody's declaration of martial law in one county, opining that "the governor's declaration that a state of insurrection existed is conclusive of that fact . . . . When it comes to a decision by the head of the state upon a matter involving its life, the ordinary rights of individuals must yield to what he deems the necessities of the moment." The Court withdrew this deference in 1932, when, in *Sterling v. Constantin*, a unanimous Court struck down Texas Governor Ross Sterling's declaration of martial law for the purpose of blocking oil and gas production to prevent falling prices due to a glut. The Court opined that if it upheld the martial law declaration, "the fiat of a state Governor, and not the Constitution of the United States, would be the supreme law of the land . . . Under our system of government, such a conclusion is obviously untenable." The Court did not articulate a standard, in either *Moyer* or *Constantin*, for when martial law is permitted.

During World War II, the Supreme Court again took a wary view of martial law in *Duncan v. Kahanamoku*. In that case, Congress had passed the Organic Act authorizing the Territorial Governor of Hawaii, in case of "rebellion or invasion, or imminent danger thereof . . . to suspend the privilege of the writ of habeas corpus" or "place the Territory . . . under martial law." After the Pearl Harbor attack, the Governor declared martial law pursuant to the Organic Act. Subsequently, two civilians (including Kahanamoku) were tried, convicted, and imprisoned by **military tribunals** for crimes against military members. In finding the military tribunals unlawful—in part because the civilian courts in Hawaii were functioning—the Court determined that when Congress authorized the establishment of martial law, "it had in mind, and did not wish to exceed, the boundaries between military and civilian power in which our people have always believed, which responsible military and executive officers had heeded, and which had become part of our political philosophy and institutions." Further, the Court held that "[t]he phrase 'martial law,' as employed in that Act, while intended to authorize the military to act vigorously for the maintenance of an orderly civil government and for the defense of the islands against actual or threatened rebellion or invasion, was not intended to authorize the supplanting of courts by military tribunals." In reaching this conclusion, the Court expressed its significant reservations about martial law, observing that "[o]ur system of government is the antithesis of total military rule, and its founders are not likely to have contemplated complete military dominance within the limits of a territory made a part of this country and not recently taken from an enemy."

19.8. HOMELAND SECURITY IN ACTION

The United States faces an assortment of threats to homeland security. Preparing for and responding to natural disasters like hurricanes and forest fires, as well as catastrophic man-made incidents like terrorist attacks, are constantly on the minds of those whose job it is to protect the health and safety of Americans. Unfortunately, it is impossible to chart a response to every possible threat to homeland security in a single chapter of a national security law textbook. However, using the example of a biological outbreak, below you will find an exploration of some of the legal issues that might arise during one of the many challenges to United States homeland security.

Biological threats are of particular concern to the national security of the United States and global security as of the time of this writing, during the COVID19 global pandemic. Whether deliberately injected into the human species by enemy adversaries or naturally occurring, biological threats present unique challenges. Biological threats pose significant risks of economic harms, massive social upheaval, continuity of government concerns, and overall national security threats. Additionally, an effective government response to biological threats often necessitates imposing significant restrictions on the liberty of large swaths of the population, again raising the continuing concern about the trade-offs between individual liberty and collective security.

The two most significant government powers used to address biological threats that impose restrictions on liberty are 1) the physical restrictions of **quarantine** and **isolation** and 2) the imposition of vaccination programs on people, regardless of their consent. The government's authority for such activities has been the subject of much discussion in the wake of COVID19, but these questions are not new.

Public health measures in emergency situations involve balancing the rights of individuals with the state's police power to protect the needs of public health, safety, and general welfare. "Quarantine" typically refers to the "separation and restriction of movement of persons who, while not yet ill, have been exposed to an infectious agent and therefore may become infectious." In contrast, "isolation" refers to the "separation of persons who have a specific infectious illness from those who are healthy and the restriction of their movement to stop the spread of that illness." Thus, healthy people are quarantined, while sick people are isolated. CDC, *Fact Sheet on Isolation and Quarantine*, January 20, 2004

19.8.1. State Authority

The government's authority to quarantine relies on the general state police power preserved in the Tenth Amendment of the Constitution. The Supreme Court has confirmed this authority several times. In 1824, in *Gibbons v. Ogden*, the Court noted that a state's authority to quarantine derived from the fact that quarantine affects public health. Again in 1902, in *Compagnie Francaise de Navigation a Vapeur v. Louisiana Bd of Health*, the Court upheld a quarantine in New Orleans during a yellow fever outbreak.

The government's authority to impose compulsory vaccinations similarly relies on state police powers to protect public health. In 1905 in *Jacobson v. Massachusetts*, the Court upheld a mandatory vaccination program in Massachusetts during a smallpox outbreak. Since 1905, states have used the broad authority suggested by the Court in *Jacobson* in a wide range of contexts, including the state of Texas asserting it had the constitutional right to ban abortions during the COVID19 crisis.

At the state level, authority for various public health powers usually comes from the state constitution or legislative enactments. Historically, there was significant state-to-state variability regarding a variety of public health enforcement matters, including who could issue quarantine orders, isolation orders, vaccination orders, and other public health-related matters. Additionally, what circumstances allow such orders, and the acceptable conditions and duration of such orders, has varied by state. In 2001, the Model State Emergency Health Powers Act (MSEHPA) was promulgated and has since been adopted by a majority of states. The MSEHPA addressed many of the state-to-state inconsistencies and provided very broad power to state governments. For instance, under the MSEHPA a governor is authorized to suspend *any* statutes or regulations in a public health emergency and the governor has plenary control over property, health care facilities, and transportation. The MSEHPA suggests "conditions and principles" to be considered when issuing orders that affect individual liberty. However, groups advocating for greater individual liberty, including the ACLU, have objected to the MSEHPA on the grounds that it grants power to restrict individual liberties that is far too broad.

19.8.2. Federal Authority

Surprisingly to some, the federal government of the United States does not have a constitutional "general police power." Rather, as a **limited government**, the federal government has only those powers specifically provided to it by the People in the Constitution. Thus, all federal government activity must have a constitutional source. Federal quarantine and isolation authority derives from the Commerce Clause of the Constitution, which states that Congress shall have the power "[t]o regulate Commerce with foreign Nations, and among the several states." This suggests that any authority or regulation regarding public health must relate to interstate or international commerce in some way.

The Public Health Service Act (PHS Act) grants the Secretary of Health and Human Services (Secretary) the authority to make and enforce regulations necessary "to prevent the introduction, transmission, or spread of communicable diseases from foreign countries into the States or possessions, or from one State or possession into any other State or possession." This means that the federal government's ability to quarantine is more limited than the states'. As evidence of this, the Center for Disease Control and Prevention (CDC)—part of the Department of Health and Human Services (HHS)—which is primarily responsible for the medical understanding and response to biological threats, acknowledges a deference to state authority:

> In general, HHS defers to the state and local health authorities in their primary use of their own separate quarantine powers. Based upon long experience and collaborative working relationships with our state and local partners, CDC continues to anticipate the need to use this federal

authority to quarantine an exposed person only in rare situations, such as events at ports of entry or in similar time-sensitive settings. CDC, *Questions and Answers on Legal Authorities for Isolation and Quarantine*, January 20, 2004.

The Interstate Quarantine Regulations govern when the CDC may impose quarantine:

> Whenever the Director of the Centers for Disease Control and Prevention determines that the measures taken by health authorities of any State or possession (including political subdivisions thereof) are insufficient to prevent the spread of any of the communicable diseases from such State or possession to any other State or possession, he/she may take such measures to prevent such spread of the diseases as he/she deems reasonably necessary. . . . 42 CFR Section 70.2.

These include authorization for detention, isolation, quarantine, or conditional release of individuals, for the purpose of preventing the introduction, transmission, and spread of the communicable diseases listed in the Public Health Service Act or an Executive Order. Of significance during the COVID19 crisis, in 2014, President Barack Obama issued Executive Order 13674 and added the following to the list of communicable diseases:

> Severe acute respiratory syndromes, which are diseases that are associated with fever and signs and symptoms of pneumonia or other respiratory illness, are capable of being transmitted from person to person, and that either are causing, or have the potential to cause, a pandemic, or, upon infection, are highly likely to cause mortality or serious morbidity if not properly controlled. This subsection does not apply to influenza.

19.8.3. Conflicts Between Federal and State Authority

Within one state, public health authority is usually clear. However, a state's authority to enforce quarantine or isolation measures that affect people from out of state or interstate is far less clear. These issues were implicated by various governors' actions in response to the spread of COVID19. For example, the Governor of Florida imposed checkpoints on major highways leading into the state and law enforcement personnel informed travelers from certain places that they were required to self-quarantine for 14 days. Similarly, the Governor of Rhode Island temporarily required state police to stop cars crossing its border bearing New York license plates and used the National Guard to conduct house-to-house searches of travelers from New York, demanding they self-quarantine for 14 days. These activities implicate the well-settled constitutional right to interstate travel established in Supreme Court cases such as *Crandall v. Nevada* and *Kent v. Dulles.*

While no governor as of this writing was refusing to allow admittance to persons from other states, that too might have raised constitutional concerns. However, one Supreme Court case suggests a governor might have such authority to restrict interstate travel in the context of public health emergencies. In *Compagnie Francaise*, the Court rejected a shipping company's challenge to a Louisiana state law excluding healthy persons from a geographic area infested with a disease, whether they came from inside or outside the state. The Court found the law did not violate the federal government's prerogatives under the Commerce Clause, despite having an effect on interstate commerce. In a later case, the Court reiterated "it is 'well settled' that states may impose quarantines to prevent the spread of disease even though quarantines 'affect interstate commerce.' " *Oregon-Washington R. & Navigation Co. v. United States.*

Under the Supremacy Clause of the Constitution, when federal public health actions conflict with those of a state, the federal authorities should trump, but only if the federal government has some constitutional basis of authority. The Commerce Clause allows federal regulation of "those activities having a substantial relation to interstate commerce." *United States v. Lopez.* The Supreme Court has also found that Congress may not regulate noneconomic activities within a state solely because they have an effect on interstate commerce. *United States v. Morrison.* The constitutional question, therefore, is whether a federal quarantine, isolation, or other public health order within one state, and affecting only one state, sufficiently relates to interstate commerce to permit federal control. This question seems less relevant in the context of a nationwide or global pandemic, such as that experienced by the world in 2020.

REVIEW QUESTIONS

1. What are two examples of Presidents acting on their own, without congressional approval, to declare and respond to a national emergency?

2. What historical events motivated Congress to pass the Civil Defense Act? What was Congress's goal in passing the Civil Defense Act?

3. How does the Stafford Act reflect the United States' commitment to federalism?

4. What is the difference between an emergency declaration and a major disaster declaration in the Stafford Act? Can the President ever declare an emergency or major disaster on his own, without the request from a Governor or tribal chief executive?

5. What are the four things a President must do to legally declare a national emergency under the National Emergencies Act?

6. How would you define what is prohibited by the Posse Comitatus Act? What are the exceptions to the Posse Comitatus Act?

7. What is "Immediate Response Authority"? Why is it not an exception to the Posse Comitatus Act?

8. How would you define martial law? Is it ever constitutionally permissible? Under what circumstances?

9. What are the differences between the states' powers and the federal government's powers during a pandemic? Why are their powers different?

CRITICAL THINKING QUESTIONS

1. Why would the Framers of the Constitution omit a provision dealing with national emergencies? Should the Constitution list certain conditions that must exist before the government may declare a national emergency and invoke special powers? What would they be?

2. Consider the Stafford Act and the process by which a President declares an emergency or major disaster. What are the checks on a President's decision to declare or refuse to declare an emergency or major disaster? Does a President have too much latitude? What would stop a President from making those decisions based purely on political favoritism or other arguably illegitimate reasons?

3. The National Emergencies Act allows the President to suspend the enforcement of various laws when he proclaims a national emergency. Are there any extraordinary powers that should not be available to the government during a national emergency?

4. You have been tasked with writing a statutory definition of "national emergency" to be inserted into the National Emergencies Act. What is the benefit of drafting a broad definition? What is the benefit of drafting a narrow definition? Now write your definition.

5. Some critics of the Department of Homeland Security (DHS) have alleged it is too big and its mandate is too broad. For example, the Secretary of Homeland Security is ultimately responsible for the United States' response to hurricanes, screening passengers at airports, and rooting out counterfeiters. Are there any agencies within

DHS that do not belong? Are there any that seem to do duplicative work? If you had the power to reorganize DHS, would you? Why and how?

6. What are the pros and cons of extending the President's authority like Congress did temporarily when it amended the Insurrection Act after Hurricane Katrina?

7. The limitations of the Posse Comitatus Act raise the question of whether the United States military's participation in the "war on terror" constitutes war or civil law enforcement. Recall the *Padilla* case, discussed in Chapter 13, where the military detained a terrorist suspect for years following his arrest by civilian authorities, only to later turn him back over to civil authorities for criminal trial. Was such activity "law enforcement?"

8. Considering the purpose(s) underlying the Posse Comitatus Act, is the presence of camouflaged troops patrolling the streets, airports, etc., less troubling to Americans because the troops are part of the National Guard rather than the federal military? Except for the possibility of a small patch that identifies the unit, the National Guard uniforms are the same as their federal military counterparts. Does the public appreciate the difference?

9. During a pandemic, should the government have the authority to quarantine people without their consent? Should states have the power to limit travel from other states? What are the pros and cons of allowing state or federal governments to make those decisions?

Glossary

acquiescence—the idea that when Congress knows of an executive decision or action and does nothing about it or acts in a way that suggests it does not object, such congressional action or inaction confers implied authority on the Executive

ad hoc—when necessary, or when needed; created for a particular purpose; not ongoing or regular

Alien Enemy Act—1798 statute giving the President the authority to detain non-citizen males who were citizens of enemy nations

all-source intelligence—analysis of information from every available source, usually combining open source information, like news articles and social media activity, and classified information, such as surveillance reports

anticipatory self-defense—defensive action under circumstances of an imminent, but not yet completed attack; under the theory of anticipatory self-defense, states have the right to "anticipate" that an attack is imminent or in the process of being mounted and use force in self-defense to prevent or limit the effects of the anticipated attack

appropriations power—Congress's formal allocation of money to specific government activities; under Article I, Section 9, Clause 7 of the United States Constitution Congress alone has the power to appropriate money from the Treasury; also known as the "power of the purse," Congress's appropriations power is one of its most important ways to influence national security policy

armed attack—term used by the U.N. Charter to indicate when a nation may use self-defense; relatively undefined in international law, it includes military action by regular armed forces across an international border, but can also include action by armed groups, mercenaries, irregular forces sent by a state if the "scale and effects of the operation would have been classified as an armed attack rather than a mere frontier incident had it been carried out by regular armed forces"

Army Field Manual—United States Army regulation detailing how interrogations may be conducted

authorization for the use of military force (AUMF)—an act of Congress passed by both houses specifically authorizing the President to engage in military hostilities

belligerent—a hostile person belonging to a recognized enemy state, and thus an enemy subject to the laws of war; distinct from a foreign citizen not engaged in hostilities who is not subject to the laws of war

bilateral treaty—treaty between only two states (nations)

black site—secret detention facility outside the United States where the CIA engaged in detention and interrogation of abducted detainees

chilling effect—in the context of free speech, the effect of government threatening consequences, either explicitly or implicitly, for individuals saying certain things, thus discouraging those messages

collective self-defense—the right of nations to defend others, not just themselves, against an armed attack

common law—body of law made through judicial opinions over time; can usually be altered or eliminated by acts of the legislature

concurrent resolution—a resolution adopted by both the House of Representatives and the Senate that lacks legal authority and is not approved by the President

conscription—compulsory military service ("the draft")

consent—a Fourth Amendment doctrine that permits a law enforcement officer to conduct a search if the target of the search gives the officer permission voluntarily; in the context of *jus ad bellum*, agreement by one state to a use of force by another state

conspiracy—an agreement among two or more persons to commit a criminal act

constitutional avoidance—a common law rule that, where possible, courts should resolve cases based on non-constitutional bases, rather than raising and answering constitutional questions

Covert Action Statute—federal law that authorizes the President to engage in "covert actions," which are defined as "activities of the United States Government to influence political, economic, or military conditions abroad, where it is intended that the role of the United States Government will not be apparent or acknowledged publicly"

cryptologic—having to do with cryptography, which is the study, production, and solving of codes

custodial interrogation—questioning by police when a suspect's freedom of movement is restrained

customary international law—observances, traditions, and principles that have evolved over time to become legally binding obligations among nations

cyber operations—the offensive use of cyber capabilities to achieve objectives through cyberspace

dead drop—an exchange of intelligence information in which a transmitting operative "drops" the item at a decided location, to be retrieved later by the receiving operative, in order to avoid meeting

declaration of war—legal proclamation by Congress that asserts a state of war exists with another nation or nations and that authorizes the President to engage in military hostilities

delegation of authority—when one government body grants its power to another; in the national security context, this most often refers to Congress granting power to the President

dicta—extraneous language in a judicial opinion that is not necessary to the holding in the case, and thus is not binding precedent for future cases

direct action—special operation, offense strikes that are short and limited in size and intended to capture or destroy a target

dirty bomb—a bomb that combines conventional explosives with radioactive material, usually intended to inflict more widespread damage than a mere localized explosion; though they use radiation to cause injury, dirty bombs should not be confused with nuclear weapons, which are exponentially more powerful and destructive

distinction—principle of customary international law that requires combatants to distinguish between legitimate targets of armed force—combatants and military objectives—and protected, illegitimate targets

domino theory—the idea that the spread of communism to one country in Asia would lead to many nations adopting communism

drone—in the context of counter-terror operations, a flying aircraft without a human pilot on board; also known as a remotely piloted aircraft (RPA) or unmanned aerial vehicle (UAV); in the context of targeted killings, these vehicles are known for their ability to loiter undetected over a target for many hours and can be armed with air-to-ground missiles capable of killing humans

Electronic Communications Privacy Act—the law that governs the government's use of electronic surveillance of domestic crime and domestic threats to national security

emergency statute—law in which Congress grants specific authority to, or imposes specific limitations on, the President if she declares the existence of a national emergency

enhanced interrogation techniques (EITs)—term used by the United States government during the George W. Bush administration to describe harsh questioning tactics used by some government agents; many criticized the term as a euphemism for torture

ex parte—an uncommon situation in which a court is asked to make a decision and only one party, or one side of the dispute, is represented and permitted to make an argument in support of its position

ex post facto—Latin phrase meaning "after the fact"; in United States law, refers to the constitutional prohibition of criminalizing behavior after it has occurred

executive agreement—an international agreement that in some way does not meet the treaty requirements of the United States Constitution

Executive Order—a document (order) issued by the President of the United States, unilaterally directing the Executive Branch to perform or refrain from performing a certain action

exigent circumstances—an exception to the Fourth Amendment's warrant requirement that allows a law enforcement officer who has probable cause to conduct a search for evidence of criminal activity may do so without a warrant due to the likelihood the evidence will be lost or destroyed imminently

explicit powers—powers that are explicitly granted in the text of the Constitution

extraordinary rendition—the transfer of a person from one country to another without legal process

extraterritorial—outside the borders or legal territory of a nation

Federal Register—the United States government's official publication and repository for public notices including proposed rules and regulations, finalized rules and regulations, notices of government meetings, and presidential proclamations and orders

federalism—a political system comprised of separate states or regional governments where the separate political entities retain parity with a central government

Federalist Papers—a series of 85 essays written by James Madison, Alexander Hamilton, and John Jay, attempting to convince the American public to ratify the newly drafted Constitution; published in 1787 and 1788

foreign intelligence—information that can help the United States government protect against sabotage, international terrorism, or spying and hostile acts of a foreign power and its agents

Foreign Intelligence Surveillance Act (FISA)—the law that governs the United States government's collection of information about foreign powers, agents of foreign powers, and terrorist suspects

Founders—the individuals credited with architecting the American Revolution and the new government of the United States; this term is broader than "Framers," which generally includes only those persons who helped create the Constitution

Framers—the individuals responsible for creating the Constitution, whether through debating it or writing it; this term is somewhat narrower than Founders, which includes other key figures to the creation of the new nation who were not directly involved in drafting the Constitution, such as Thomas Jefferson

general warrants—an effectively limitless warrant issued by a judge or other official providing a law enforcement officer broad authority to search for an unspecified person or thing

Geneva Accord—international agreement in 1954 to divide Vietnam between north and south, with the north being controlled by the Viet Minh, and the south being governed by the "State of Vietnam."

graymail—situation where criminal defendants threaten to disclose classified or sensitive information in the course of defending themselves at trial in order to coerce prosecutors into dropping charges

Gulf of Tonkin Resolution—act of Congress that provided the President with congressional authority to take military action in Vietnam

habeas corpus—Latin term meaning "have the body" that refers to the power of a court to order a jailor or custodian to bring the detainee or prisoner into the court so the judge can inquire into the legality of the detention

High Value Targets—a person or resource that an enemy commander needs to complete his mission successfully and the loss of which would undermine the enemy commander capabilities; in counter-terrorism operations, the term often used to refer to terror suspects with seniority in their organization

humanitarian intervention—the threat or use of force primarily for the purpose of protecting the nationals in another state from widespread deprivations of human rights

imperfect war—term used by international law theorists to describe a military conflict that is something less than a perfect war, because it does not involve formal declaration of war and does not entirely "interrupt the peace" of the nations involved; also called informal war or low intensity conflict

inchoate conspiracy—an agreement between two or more people to commit a crime when the crime itself is never completed; generally not recognized as a crime under international law, but is a crime under domestic United States law

indict—to lay charge against a person; an indictment requires the prosecution to present enough evidence to prove that a trial could reasonably result in conviction; a criminal defendant must be indicted before being charged and tried

information assurance—the management of information and data managing risks related to the use, processing, storage, and transmission of information or data and the systems and processes used for those purposes

inherent powers—authority that is neither explicitly nor implicitly provided for in the text of the Constitution, but which exists solely by virtue of the nature of the office

injunction—a legal remedy, often achieved through a judicial order, that compels a person to do something or prohibits a person from doing something

international armed conflict (IACs)—an armed conflict between two or more states, governed by the 1949 Geneva Conventions and the 1977 First Additional Protocol to the Geneva Conventions

International Court of Justice (ICJ)—also known as the "World Court," this court is one of the principal organs of the U.N.; its jurisdiction relies on the consent of the parties, which can only be states

international human rights law (IHRL)—the set of international laws and norms that establish basic civil, political, economic, social, and cultural rights that all human beings should enjoy and that all states are obliged to protect

international humanitarian law (IHL)—also known as the law of armed conflict (LOAC), IHL refers to a set of rules that, for humanitarian reasons, attempt to limit the adverse effects of armed conflict; international humanitarian law thus applies only when there is an armed conflict

irregular warfare—military conflict between an established state and a non-state group, such as a conflict between a terrorist groups and the government of the country in which it operates

isolation—in the context of epidemic or pandemic, the separation of infected individuals from those who are not infected

joint resolution—a piece of legislation passed by both the House of Representatives and the Senate and sent to the President for his signature with the intent that it become a law

judicial review—the power of a court to declare acts of the other branches of government unconstitutional or unlawful, and therefore void

jurisdiction—the authority of a court to hear and render judgment in a particular case against a particular defendant or defendants; must be conferred by the Constitution or statute (not inherent)

jus ad bellum—the body of international law addressing the right of states to use military force

jus cogens—customary international laws that are binding on all nations, whether or not a nation objects to it

jus in bello—law governing the way warfare is conducted; see international humanitarian law

justiciability—whether a case can or should be decided by a court, either under limitations imposed by the Constitution or by prudence; the limits on a court's ability to render a decision in a case

last in time rule—rule of legal interpretation that says when two laws of equal supremacy conflict, the later law trumps; sometimes referred to by the Latin phrase "*lex posterior*"

law of armed conflict (LOAC)—see international humanitarian law

libel—a published statement that is both false and harms a person's reputation

limited government—the theory that government has only those powers expressly given to it, rather than government having all power except that which is withheld from it

mail cover—an investigative technique whereby law enforcement officers collect and record the observable information about a letter or package sent through the mail without opening the item

malware—computer software that has been intentionally designed to perform some sort of hostile action such as damaging a victim's computer system or gaining unauthorized access

martial law—imposition of military control over civil functions, where military authority replaces or preempts civil government, usually including military exercise of legislative, executive, and judicial authority

material support—in the context of terrorism, providing assistance to terrorists or terrorist organizations in the form of property, service, currency or monetary instruments, financial services, lodging, training, expert advice or assistance, safehouses, false documentation or identification, communications equipment, facilities, weapons, lethal substances, explosives, personnel, and transportation; does *not* include provision of medicine or religious materials

metadata—in the context of electronic data and surveillance, metadata is the information that describes things like who, where, when, and for how long a surveillance target communicated with another person

military commission—a tribunal ordered into existence by a military commander to prosecute people for alleged crimes related to military conflict or violation of martial law; also referred to as a military tribunal

military tribunal—see military commission

minimization procedures—the measures the government uses to reduce the likelihood it collects information unrelated to foreign intelligence

multilateral treaty—treaty between three or more states (nations)

National Intelligence Program—all of the Intelligence Community's funding, programs, projects and activities

National Security Agency (NSA)—the United States intelligence agency whose primary responsibility is collecting signals intelligence from foreign powers and international terrorists

national security letter (NSL)—an administrative subpoena, or order, issued by the government as part of a national security investigation that requires the disclosure of information in the recipient's possession

naturalization—the legal process by which a non-citizen becomes a United States citizen as established in the Immigration and Nationality Act

necessity—in the context of self-defense, the requirement that the use of force in self-defense is actually necessary for achieving the aims of self-defense; in the context of IHL, the principle that only actions that are necessary to achieving a legitimate military objective are permitted

nondelegation doctrine—rule established by the Supreme Court that does not permit Congress to delegate its core legislative responsibility to the Executive Branch

non-international armed conflict (NIAC)—an armed conflict between a state and an organized armed group that is not a state, and is governed by Common Article 3 of the Geneva Conventions

non-intervention—customary international law principle that prohibits states from interfering with another sovereign state's choice of political, economic, social, or cultural system, or its formulation of foreign policy

North Atlantic Treaty Organization (NATO)—alliance of nations for the purpose of collective self-defense by Western nations, originally against the Soviet Union

nullification—a legal theory that suggests states may invalidate a federal law if they find it to be a violation of the Constitution

opinio juris—belief by states that they are legally obligated to behave in a certain way

peacekeeping—the use of military force and forces to support the implementation of a ceasefire or peace agreement or otherwise maintain peace when a state lacks the capacity to do so itself

peacemaking—the use of diplomacy and military force and forces to end hostilities and restore tranquility

pen register—a device that can identify the dialing or routing information transmitted from wire or electronic communication, including telephones and internet platforms

perfect war—term used by international law theorists to describe a type of total war, involving entire nations opposing each other, complying with the formalities of nations at war, and affecting the entire populace of each nation; distinguished from imperfect war

plain view—an exception to the Fourth Amendment's warrant requirement that allows law enforcement to seize evidence of criminal activity that is in plain sight, so long as the officer has a legal right to be in the place he views the evidence

political question doctrine—idea that the judicial system is not the appropriate venue for resolving disputes that should be resolved through the political system

positive law—law that is actually created and written down; opposite of natural law, which exists without human or government involvement

preemptive self-defense—defensive action due to the possibility of a future threat

Presidential Daily Briefing—a classified report presented to the President of the United States and other key administration officials each day, detailing the most current intelligence on national security issues

preventive detention—detention not because someone has been charged with or convicted of a crime, but rather detention for the purpose of preventing something from happening

prior restraint—a censorship or prohibition of speech before it is published

privateers—privately owned maritime vessels that received a special commission to engage in armed conflict on behalf of a government during a war

privilege—a rule that allows the holder of some types of communications to refuse to disclose the communication or allow it to be admitted into evidence; a successful assertion of the privilege means the evidence will not be included in the case

probable cause—a Fourth Amendment warrant requirement that places a burden on the government to prove, through the presentation of facts to a judge, that there is a fair probability that evidence of a crime will be found in a place the government would like to search

proportionality—in the IHL (LOAC) context, the principle that prohibits attacks that may be expected to cause incidental loss of civilian life, injury to civilians, or damage to civilian objects, that would be excessive in relation to the concrete and direct military advantage anticipated; in the self-defense context, the principle that requires that the use of force in defense is proportionate to the force used in the attack; not to be confused with the term proportionality as used in the law of armed conflict, which requires that collateral civilian damage arising from military operations must not be excessive in relation to the direct and concrete military advantage anticipated from such operations

proximate cause—an event that is sufficiently related to a harm or injury that it can reasonably be deemed to have caused the harm or injury

public interest advocate—a lawyer appointed by the Foreign Intelligence Surveillance Court who represents civil liberty and privacy concerns when the court decides there is a novel issue presented by the government's request for surveillance authorization

quarantine—the separation of individuals who have been exposed to an infection but are not yet ill from others who have not been exposed to the transmissible infection

ratcheting effect—effect of a law, policy, or action that tends to move only in one direction, as in an ever-expanding power that for structural reasons never lessens

reasonable expectation of privacy—a Supreme Court interpretation of the Fourth Amendment used to define and identify the places and things the government cannot search without a warrant

reckless disregard—a state of mind in which a person commits an action without an specific intent to cause harm but nevertheless ignores the reasonably foreseeable dangerous consequences of the action

remotely piloted aircraft (RPA)—a flying aircraft without a human pilot on board; also known as a UAV or drone; in the context of targeted killings, these vehicles are known for their ability to loiter undetected over a target for many hours and can be armed with air-to-ground missiles capable of killing humans

rendition—the transfer of a person from one jurisdiction to another

responsibility to protect (R2P)—theory of international law that when states are unwilling or unable to protect their citizens from avoidable catastrophe, responsibility for those citizens becomes a collective responsibility of the "broader community of states," justifying intervention

ripeness—the requirement that a case present a current dispute that is ready for adjudication, not one that is contingent on future events

rule of construction—consistently applied rule for interpreting legal documents that may include inconsistencies or ambiguities

seditious libel—a criminal offense which prohibits a spoken statement or publication that criticizes the government or undermines its authority

Southeast Asia Treaty Organization (SEATO)—treaty created in 1954 to prevent communist expansion in Southeast Asia

special operations—operations that are often secret, high-risk, and time sensitive and conducted in hostile or politically sensitive locations, using unique and unconventional tactics and equipment

specific selection term—a term the government provides to the Foreign Intelligence Surveillance Court that precisely identifies a person, account, address, or personal device in an effort to limit, as much as possible, the scope of things sought in the government's request for surveillance authorization

standby statutes—laws in which Congress delegates to the President the authority to take certain actions when she determines a national emergency exists

standing—the ability of a particular plaintiff to bring a case based on an injury that is redressable (fixable) by that court, meaning that the parties fall under the court's jurisdiction, and usually requires the individual to be personally affected by whatever they are challenging in court

state secrets privilege—an evidentiary privilege that allows information considered to be a state secret to be excluded from civil litigation

status quo—the current state of affairs, situation, or set of circumstances

status quo *ante*—the state of affairs that existed before an event occurred

subversive speech—speech intended to undermine or overthrow the government

targeted killing—force intentionally and deliberately used against an individual specifically identified in advance the goal of which is death of the target

textualist—Justice or judge whose interpretive methodology focuses on only what is explicitly stated in the text of the document being interpreted (for example, the Constitution)

third-party doctrine—the legal principle, in the Supreme Court's Fourth Amendment case law, that if one voluntarily hands over information to another person, one can no longer have a reasonable expectation of privacy in that information and the government need not obtain a warrant to collect it from the third party

torture—a term of widely varying definitions; defined by the Detainee Treatment Act as an "act committed by a person acting under the color of law specifically intended to inflict severe physical or mental pain or suffering (other than pain or suffering incidental to lawful sanctions) upon another person within his custody or physical control"

Torture Memos—a group of memoranda in which highly placed legal counsel at the United States Department of Justice and Department of Defense opined that the CIA's and DOD's "enhanced interrogation techniques" and operations were lawful

***Totten* bar**—judicially created rule that courts must dismiss cases when the core subject matter of the litigation is itself a state secret

trap and trace device—devices that record the incoming electronic markers that identify the source of wire or electronic communication and can thus detect and record, for example, the phone number or email address that is calling or sending messages to a surveillance target

treaty—a written agreement between one or more states (nations) or international organizations

unconventional warfare—military and paramilitary covert or clandestine operations often in coordination with local or proxy forces

United States Court of Military Commission Review (USCMCR)—first intermediate appeals court with jurisdiction over military commissions under the Military Commissions Act

unmanned aerial vehicle (UAV)—see remotely piloted aircraft (RPA)

USA PATRIOT Act—sometimes also referred to as the PATRIOT Act, or Patriot Act, this bill was passed immediately following the 9/11 terrorist attacks, and legalized many practices to enable the United States to prosecute the war on terror

warrant—formal, legal authorization from a judge to carry out some law enforcement activity like the search of a specified location or the arrest of a person

World Intelligence Review—a classified publication authored by the CIA detailing several intelligence analyses and provided to the United States military and senior policy officials

writ of habeas corpus—the right of an imprisoned individual to have a federal court review the constitutionality of their imprisonment or detention; the "writ" is the legal document issued by a judge to a custodian of a detainee to bring the detainee or prisoner into the court; "habeas corpus" means "have the body" and historically referred to the requirement that the actual prisoner be brought into the court for the judge to see

Index